A MYTH OF INNOCENCE

MARK AND CHRISTIAN ORIGINS

A MYTH
OF INNOCENCE

BURTON L. MACK

FORTRESS PRESS
PHILADELPHIA

COPYRIGHT © 1988 BY FORTRESS PRESS
First paperback edition 1991

Library of Congress Cataloging-in-Publication Data

Mack, Burton L.
   A myth of innocence.

   Bibliography: p.
   Includes index.
   1. Bible. N.T. Mark—Criticism, interpretation, etc. 2. Christianity—Origin. 3. Sociology, Christian —History—Early church, ca. 30–600. I. Title.
BS2585.2.M225 1988   226'.306   86–45906
ISBN 0–8006–2113–1 (cloth)
ISBN 0–8006–2549–8 (paper)

Printed in the United States of America   AF 1-2549

02   01   00   99   98   3   4   5   6   7   8   9   10   11   12

For Hal Taussig
whose critical agreements
have been my challenge
and
For Burt, Jr.,
whose penetrating critique
has been my delight

CONTENTS

FIGURES

PREFACE

Since Foucault published his *Archaeology of Knowledge,* New Testament scholars have thought of their work as digging. I have therefore tried to imagine my task as sifting through the layers of accumulated constructions upon a certain site. The image is attractive in some respects and disconcerting in others. An aura of archeology is gratifying mainly because it seems to bless the labor as worthwhile. But textual sites differ somewhat from tells, cemeteries, and village dumps. And in the case of the mass of traditions, texts, and commentaries that make up the mound for doing biblical archeology, the site is still inhabited. That complicates the digging. Worse still, the site has already been dug up so many times no stone has been left unturned. Diggers keep looking for the foundations even while the builders keep busy at the surface of the heap as if the foundations were there, solid, and known. Thus the layers of accretion are constantly being disturbed and rearranged, and hardly an artifact is found embedded in its proper stratum. Given this living tell of textual tradition, it is to our credit, I suppose, that we New Testament scholars have managed to reconstruct any outline at all of the earliest layers of the edifice called Christianity.

It is disconcerting nonetheless to see what happens when the metaphor is pressed too far. One catches sight of a very messy dig and of diggers in disagreement about what they are looking for. Not only is there confusion about what counts as an artifact, there is no clarity about what a firm foundation might be were one ever to be found. This, at any rate, has been my own uneasiness with the jumble of mystifying conclusions regularly drawn at the end of scholarly books and articles in quest of Christian origins. I fear, frankly, that we have been picking away at the wrong layer looking for stones that were never there.

It has usually been thought that the laying of the foundations, stone of stumbling and all, happened with the historical Jesus. That is how the gospels paint the picture and that is what scholars have somehow been content to imagine, though in other terms. Something unique and powerful, it is assumed, must have taken place then in order to account for the novelty of Christianity. Even if that dramatic moment cannot be located, described, or comprehended, so the logic seems to run, it must be posited in order to make sense of all the stories that came to be told about divine events at the beginning.

I found that odd, for the notion of an incomprehensible origin is clearly mystifying and mythological, and all critical scholars say that they know the gospels to be mythic. When the gap between what we know about myth-making, symbols, and social formation on the one hand, and the tedious rehearsal of apologies for not adequately grasping the mysterious originary moment on the other became unbearable, I decided to switch sites.

This book was written to show how the picture of Christian origins might change with a single shift in perspective on the social history documented by the early texts. What if one acknowledged that the gospel story was Christianity's charter document and regarded its formation as an essential moment in the "laying of the foundations"? Then the focus would not fall solely on the life of Jesus as the stratum within which all of the crucial, originary events are to be found. Instead it would be the later occasions for imagining Jesus that way which one should want to understand. Complex social histories of many diverse groups and movements would have intervened as all scholars know. Complicated textual histories would have to be traced and situated within these social histories in order to locate points of contact, conflict, and accommodation that may have determined the way in which a group construed its world. The gospels were put together two and three generations later than the time of Jesus out of very diverse traditions, lore, and even full-blown myths. If the social circumstances of that later time were regarded as the "foundational" stratum, and the composition of the gospel taken as the "originary" moment of significance for Christian origins, the fantastic events depicted in the gospel might actually begin to make sense. They would not make the kind of sense New Testament scholars have hoped to find at the beginnings of Christianity. But they might make very good sense of the kind myths make in general. Supposing that the gospels were myths of origin for social formations in need of a charter, the scholar's quest would have to be to understand the moment when the gospel was designed. Foucault's archeology refers, after all, not to a quest for extraordinary events of generation prior to social formation, but to critical moments of social interest within a given discourse.

I considered that we already knew much about the occasion for the composition of the first gospel, and that it would be a rather easy task to put the pieces back together that had been taken apart when the "secondary" layer of "interpretation" was dismantled in the quest for the "original" site. Alas. I found the foundational pieces strewn here and there or buried in the piles of tailings left over from that exhausting effort. Sifting through the debris, however, I did find a real stone of stumbling and several other building blocks as well. I have tried to resituate them in order to reconstruct the outline of the social situations that gave rise to the gospels. I cannot be sure I have found all the stones, nor that every text and its occasion fit together perfectly. But the patterns of early Christian movements that emerge appear to be very reasonable reconstructions, and the occasion for the composition of the gospel seems to have been located within that larger picture quite precisely.

To imagine the pieces falling into place was easier than to write a book about it. The size of the book is due to the fact that many texts not Markan and several movements not Mark's own had to be placed in the new arrangement in order to make sure of the larger design. The result is an essay many of my colleagues may find strange and uncomfortable. I have not had the leisure to recite all of the history of the pertinent scholarly discoveries at a given locus, for instance, nor the space to represent the arguments normally expected when making exegetical judgments of my own. Still, New Testament scholars will know that I constantly had them in mind while the book was being written. They will understand the reasons why the book had to be an essay, not a monograph. They will also understand the ruse of my writing, not for them, but for any interested reader. I do hope there are such, naturally, and that my colleagues find it possible to join them in the reading. I would like to think of my readers, both colleagues and after-hours thinkers at large, as delighting once again in the curiosity all of us have on occasion about the way in which Jesus became the Christ.

I am deeply grateful to those who have given the manuscript a critical reading and shared with me their judgments. They include Ron Cameron, Elizabeth Castelli, Wendell Dietrich, Bob Funk, Bob Hamerton-Kelly, Merrill Miller, Jonathan Z. Smith, Hal Taussig, Ann Taves, and students at Brown University and the School of Theology at Claremont. I am grateful as well to those institutions that set me free to write this book. The School of Theology at Claremont graciously agreed to a research leave for the year 1984–85, and the Association of Theological Schools generously provided an Issues Research Grant for that period. A visiting professorship at Brown University in the fall of 1986 provided the appropriate setting for thinking through the final revisions.

Wayland Manor
Providence, R. I.
November 1986

CHRISTIAN ORIGINS
AND THE IMAGINATION

> Neither the historian nor the theologian
> should try to answer these questions.
>
> Helmut Koester
> *Introduction to the New Testament* 2.84

CHRISTIAN ORIGINS
AND THE IMAGINATION

1. THE QUEST FOR CHRISTIAN ORIGINS

The goal of New Testament scholarship has been to give an account of the origins of Christianity. For more than two hundred years an amazingly rigorous and critical discourse has pursued this goal, probing the texts produced by early Christians in order to get behind them. Some event, it is thought, or moment, or impulse, needs to be discovered as the source for the novelty Christianity introduced into the world. In spite of this concentrated effort, however, there is no agreement about what that mysterious moment was or had to have been. One might think that the failure to reach an agreement on such a fundamental objective would eventually call attention to itself and force a reconceptualization of the discipline. That has never happened and the quest continues unabated.

To the historian who has no theological proclivity, such persistence in the quest for a singular genesis of Christianity is curious. The very notion of an origin within history is strange if taken to the extreme as is the case in New Testament studies. It is doubly strange because, though the notion of a radically new beginning is pervasive throughout this scholarly discourse, it has never been taken up for examination by those who posit it as the goal of their intellectual pursuits. Silence on this subject is odd, especially so because the discipline of biblical studies is known for its care about methods and the precision with which it seeks to define them and their objectives. If one asks further how it could be that such a careful discipline could sustain a problematic assumption as its stated objective, the peculiar nature of this scholarship is compounded once again. That is because everyone seems to know that the objective is ultimately beyond reach. The origins of Christianity are known to lie on the other side of limits set by the nature of the texts at the scholar's disposal and the nature of the history that can be reconstructed from them. Thus the methods of historical literary criticism, the hallmark of this discipline, are tacitly acknowledged to be inadequate from the start. It is as if the scholar's texts and tools are known only to

3

scratch the surface of the social histories stemming from Jesus; they cannot account for their generation. To do that, it is assumed, one must introduce yet another kind of reflection, either about the texts in hand, in which case the reflection will be called hermeneutics, or about the history learned, in which case the reflection will be called theology. That which counts does not lie on the surface of things, but beneath it, or beyond it, or prior to it.

The reason for this unusual situation—a scholarship in quest of an objective known to be unreachable by scholarly tools and methods—is not difficult to understand. It stems from basic assumptions about Christianity that underlie the discipline, motivate its energies, and influence the way in which texts are taken up for investigation. The fundamental persuasion is that Christianity appeared unexpectedly in human history, that it was (is) at core a brand new vision of human existence, and that, since this is so, only a startling moment could account for its emergence. The code word serving as sign for the novelty that appeared is the term unique (meaning singular, incomparable, without analogue). For the originary event the word is transformation (rupture, breakthrough, inversion, reversal, eschatological). For the cognitive effect of this moment the language of paradox is preferred (irony, parable, enigma, the irrational). It is this startling moment that seems to have mesmerized the discipline and determined the applications of its critical methods. All of the enormous labor devoted to the preparation of texts, the honing of linguistic instruments, and the devisement of methods has been organized just in order to approach as closely as possible that moment of mystery even if, in the last analysis, some leap of the imagination will be required to posit its presence.

Where to locate the mystery has been the unacknowledged question guiding the twists and turns of the scholarship. There has been a general agreement that it was the appearance of Jesus that made all the difference, but efforts to be more definite have invariably run into horrendous complications. That is because the image of Jesus presented by early Christian texts is so complex that decisions cannot be made as to the exact reason for his influence without distorting other features of the picture. The options run from superior personhood (whether because of character or charisma), through startling activity (whether as a manifestation of uncommon compassion or a display of miraculous power), and the marvelous words (whether as announcement, pronouncement, or invitation to enlightenment), to his remarkable death, unexpected resurrection, and overpowering appearances to his followers as the new society was formed. At one time or another each of these manifestations of the unusual has been championed as the moment that made the critical difference. None has held the field for long, though, without revision. Shifts in perspective and changes in method mark the junctures of a very restless search for some way to determine which factors were the more or most significant. At each juncture something more was learned about the early histories, of course, but new knowledge about the histories has not settled the question of origination.[1]

The hardest lesson has always been that the texts in hand are "late," the product of many moments of memory and imagination that occurred between the time of Jesus and the time of their writing. This fact, underscored in any first lecture on the critical study of the New Testament, has frequently been stated as the problem and challenge of the discipline. Jesus was active in the late twenties of the first century C.E. The earliest evidence of his influence comes from the fifties, the Pauline correspondence with communities of believers in Asia Minor, Greece and Rome. Even then, however, there are no reminiscences of Jesus' activity, but only fragments from a Christ cult that had formed around myths and rites in memory of his death and resurrection. The first surviving document to contain reminiscences of Jesus and his activity in Galilee comes from the early seventies, the Gospel of Mark, a full forty years removed from Jesus' time. The document known as the Source (Q) for Jesus' sayings, though thought to contain some authentic words of Jesus, presents a problem of even greater magnitude. It must first be reconstructed by comparing the ways in which Matthew and Luke employed it in the writing of their gospels during the last decades of the century. Because the data available to historians for reconstructing the life of Jesus comes from documents removed in time by one, two, or even three generations of social history, New Testament scholarship can be described as an archeology of early traditions about Jesus and the Christ: the attempt to work back from later texts to earlier memories closer to the source. Early traditions and events have always been associated with the originary, late compositions always regarded as developments of earlier traditions.

The archeological efforts of two hundred years of scholarship can be thematized by tracing two main tracks along which the quest for Christian origins has traveled. The one has been the quest for the historical Jesus, working back through the gospel accounts to retrieve some picture of the man as he appeared in Galilee. The other has been the quest for the earliest christology, working back through layers of mythic interpretations to determine the first identification made. Each of these quests has been pursued somewhat in isolation from the other, not only because the literary corpora

---

1. *History of scholarship.* The standard handbook on the history of New Testament scholarship is Werner G. Kümmel, *The New Testament.* Kümmel charts the shifts in critical approaches to a fairly small set of issues that have guided scholarly interests from the beginning. The book follows the German tradition primarily and breaks off about the time of the Second World War, but it can be used nevertheless to make observations about the discipline wherever pursued and the nature of the questions it has entertained. To cover the period since the war, Scholars Press has promised a series of volumes on The Bible and Its Modern Interpreters.

seem to divide that way, with the gospels providing the Jesus materials and the letters the earliest christological formulations, but also for strategic reasons. Those who have concentrated upon the figure of the historical Jesus have always hoped to discover something about him that could account for his crucifixion and the beliefs of early Christians in his continuing influence among them. Those who have worked back toward the first visions, experiences, or interpretations of his death and/or resurrection have always hoped to find some connection between those startling claims and the kind of person Jesus may have been. The strategy has been to close the gap, if possible, on those events that must have taken place between the appearance of the man Jesus and the first formation of the Christian community after his death. Most of the methods designed for reading New Testament texts, therefore, have aimed explicitly at sorting out the earliest traditions in order to gain some access to those crucial events suspicioned to have inaugurated the Christian time.[2]

The quests have produced a huge amount of learning, but they have not pinned down the inaugural event. Undaunted, New Testament scholars have pressed ahead, taking sides on this or that preference and working out ever more sophisticated ways of imagining how it all must have begun. Currently, those who emphasize the effectiveness of Jesus' way with words on the imagination are using the languages of presence, immediacy, "nakedness," and even silence in order to name the critical moment of transformation. Others, also concerned to pinpoint the significant moment

---

2. *Quest for the historical Jesus.* The classical study of the lives of Jesus that were written during the nineteenth century is Albert Schweitzer's *The Quest of the Historical Jesus.* Underlying the quest were assumptions about myth and history that were severely criticized in the first two decades of the twentieth century. James M. Robinson, in *A New Quest of the Historical Jesus,* discusses the reasons for this critique, especially from the point of view of Rudolf Bultmann and his students, a proposal for a renewed attempt along existentialist lines. Anglo-American scholars did not react dramatically to the trauma in Germany created by the end of the nineteenth-century quest, nor did they swing easily to existentialist methods to interpret the mythic language found embedded in New Testament texts. For a recent statement that reflects more the Anglo-American tradition, though sobered somewhat by the continental discussion, see Howard C. Kee, *Jesus in History.* The difficulty scholars have had in agreeing upon a reconstruction of the historical Jesus has given rise to a burgeoning literature on the fringes of the discipline. Novelistic works have taken advantage of scholarly uncertainties to romanticize the history; others have begun to appear that express extreme skepticism about the possibility of knowing anything at all about the historical Jesus. An example of the later genre is the book by G. A. Wells, *The Historical Evidence for Jesus.* Scholars with theological interests have scarcely taken note of this literature.

Quest for the earliest christology. Summarizing half a century of scholarship, major studies appeared in the sixties: Reginald H. Fuller, *The Foundations of New Testament Christology;* Werner Kramer, *Christ, Lord, Son of God;* Ferdinand Hahn, *The Titles of Jesus in Christology.* Many scholars have thought to find the bridge between the two quests in the description of the Son of Man attributed to Jesus in the synoptic tradition of the gospels. One of the more sophisticated attempts of this type is that of Willi Marxsen, *The Beginnings of Christology.*

in the life of the historical Jesus, rather than in the events of his death and resurrection, have begun to confess openly that the miracle stories told about him have to be given their due. The term most often used in this regard to indicate that about Jesus which instigated change is charismatic power. Those who think that Jesus' death made the difference, the way he died and how it affected his followers, are not talking openly at the moment. Not too long ago, however, scholars commonly used the term Christ event. Preference for a theology of the cross is still strong enough among New Testament scholars in the German Lutheran tradition to influence the way in which both texts and history continue to be read.

All scholars seem to agree, however, on the importance of the resurrection. Three terms are frequently used, each encoded by custom within the discourse of the discipline, to refer euphemistically to the resurrection of Jesus from the dead: Easter, appearance, and spirit. The casual reader may not notice how often recourse is made to these terms in the language of New Testament scholarship, thinking perhaps that their occurrence is to be attributed to the idiosyncrasy of an occasional confessional writer. After reading seriously into the field and at length, however, the repetition of these terms creates a crescendo that becomes quite shrill. These coded signs, usually capitalized, do not enlighten because they mark the point beyond which the scholar chooses not to proceed with investigation, indeed, the point beyond which reasoned argument must cease. They serve as ciphers to hold the space for the unimaginable miracle that must have happened prior to any and all interpretation. They have become an all too convenient rhetorical device for evoking the myth of Christian origins without having to explain it.[3]

---

3. *The resurrection.* Appeal to "the resurrection" is the most mystifying of all the ciphers used to protect the myth of Christian origins from critical investigation. The notion is used regularly to distinguish "pre-Easter" from "post-Easter" performances of Jesus' sayings, for instance, as if the resurrection were a datable piece of evidence. By allowing the mystery of Easter and the appearances to mark the point from which the Spirit effected the new age of Christian experience and mission, everything else can be examined rigorously without threatening the notion of originary uniqueness. A statement recently made by Helmut Koester, a New Testament scholar highly regarded for his critical acumen, can serve as an example of this strange compartmentalization: "The content and effect of the appearances were decisive. . . . It is presupposed, of course, that the Jesus of Nazareth who died on the cross is now alive. But this is not a fact of any significance for Jesus and his fate. Nor is the statement that he now lives identical with a clear and unanimous explanation of the significance of Jesus' mission. . . . The resurrection and the appearances of Jesus are best explained as a catalyst which prompted reactions that resulted in the missionary activity and founding of the churches, but also in the crystallization of the tradition about Jesus and his ministry. But most of all, the resurrection changed sorrow and grief, or even hate and rejection, into joy, creativity, and faith. Though the resurrection revealed nothing new, it nonetheless made everything new for the first Christian believers. . . . They were radically different . . . from other Jews in Jerusalem because of their enthusiastic consciousness of the possession of the spirit; this was the spirit of God which was to be poured out at the end of times, which brought the gift of tongues and of prophecy, worked miracles, and

The reader who dares to enter this discourse from the humanities, or from the social sciences, cannot avoid coming to a certain conclusion. The events that center the massive amounts of scholarly learning are exactly those that haunt the average Christian imagination as well. They are exactly those suggested by the Christian gospel, the gospel that sets them forth as inaugural and foundational for Christian history and faith. The Christian gospel, it is well known, claims that the same events serve, at one and the same time, to grant the church its charter and to offer to the individual Christian transformation or renewal. They are those events at the beginning where, according to Christian teaching, God entered into human history. The private contemplation of these events draws the imagination of the believer, not only to the symbols of personal salvation, but to the originary chapter of the history of the church. Social and personal interests intersect there, as well as mythic schemes for joining history and heaven. Insofar as Christianity actually is peculiar as a religion, and thus the scholarly hunch on target, it is certainly due to just this notion of an event within history that interrupted the normal course of human social activity and created a new kind of time and society. For the church, it should be noted, the events all go together—Jesus, his teachings and activities, the supper, cross, and resurrection. These, it should then be emphasized, are just those moments thought by scholars to be candidates for the point of Christian origins. They are taken from the gospel, actually, the gospel that Mark wrote, others enlarged, and the church eventually claimed for its charter. So the suspicion cannot be avoided that the scholarly quest for the origins of Christianity has, in effect, been driven by the Christian imagination. Though the gospel story has been critically analyzed at the level of its textual history, at another level, the level of the scholarly imagination of Christian origins, the claims of the gospel have been accepted as self-evident.

What if the notion of a single, miraculous point of origin was acknowledged for what it was, not a category of critical scholarship at all, but an article of faith derived from Christian mythology? Then the quest would have to be turned around. Not the mythic events at the beginning, but the social and intellectual occasions of their being imagined would be the thing to understand. To ask when, where, and why early followers of Jesus dared

---

granted assurance to the members of the community that they belonged to God's elect people" (*Introduction to the New Testament* 2:84–87). If the historian hardly knows what to make of such a statement, its purpose, apparently, has been achieved. A point of origin has been established that is fundamentally inaccessible to further probing or clarification. It guarantees the uniqueness of early Christianity by locating its novelty beyond data and debate. Koester's scenario simply reproduces the Lukan myth of Christian origins written around the turn of the first century or later. Koester agrees to the later dating of Luke-Acts, *Introduction to the New Testament* 2:310.

to think such audacious thoughts, that would be to learn something. The task would be to account for the formation of the gospel itself in the context of a later social history, not to use it as a guide to conjure up chimeras at the beginning. Instead of assuming eruptions of inexplicable energy penetrating the human scene from without, giving shape to certain vehicles of influence ("traditions," "trajectories," "messages," "syntagmatic structures") that could bear the aura of mystique and spiritual empowerment, then stream out in all directions from a common source, commissioning, transforming, spreading, and pressing to fill the whole world with a novel presence, one would look for historical circumstances, intellectual resources, and social motivations for early Christians to have imagined such a cosmic drama. What if the historical origins of the Jesus movements were not all that dramatic? What if the formation of the gospel were regarded as the origin of the Christian notion of dramatic origins? Then the "later" texts would be just as interesting as the earlier ones, perhaps even more interesting because of their greater degree of fantasy. To understand the original purpose of the belated gospel would be to understand the social function of the Christian claim to pure origination, unique vision, and novel social order. The fantasy of an order of things without precursor might actually be capable of explanation. If so, Christian and scholarly obsession with the notion, whether in full or partial mythic dress, might be explained as well. It might even be possible to say something about the persistence of such a fantasy in modern times, a fantasy that, apparently, modernity has not been able to challenge.

2. CHRISTIAN ORIGINS AND THE GOSPEL OF MARK

As Mark told the story, Jesus appeared in Galilee announcing that the kingdom of God was drawing near. He cast out demons in the synagogues of Galilee, confronted scribes and Pharisees with a new authority, marched to Jerusalem to cleanse the temple, was condemned by the chief priests there, and executed by the Roman procurator as the king of the Jews. The historian has to be suspicious. The story was written forty years after the events, in the shadow of the Jewish War and the destruction of the temple. According to Mark the crucifixion of Jesus and the destruction of the temple were related events, related because Jesus had predicted the end of the temple, and also because God's hand was evident in both events. Thus Mark's story is about a conflict that God and his Son Jesus had with Judaism, a conflict of apocalyptic proportions. The kingdom Jesus announced was introduced in unmitigated violence and would be consummated in a display of sheer divine power. In the meantime Christians

looked back upon a crucified king, out upon a landscape of social devasta-
tion, and ahead to an hour of brilliant and final vindication for their embattled cause.

The history of Jesus retrievable by critical scholarship cannot have gone
that way. Critical scholars have not been able to discern any geopolitical
drama on such a grand scale among the fragments of tradition most
plausibly authentic for the time of Jesus. Jesus appeared telling parables, for
instance, teasing the Galilean imagination, confronting persons, not institutions, with the challenge to look at things again, and differently. There
was social critique implicit in all he said and did, to be sure. But to imagine
a better world is one thing, to organize for a political cause another. And to
march against the temple in Jerusalem yet another still. Scholars have not
been able to establish any necessary connection at all between what is
known about Jesus' activity in Galilee and what must have happened in
Jerusalem. Designs on the powers invested in the institutions and offices of
Jerusalem do not follow from the nature of Jesus' social critique in Galilee.[4]

---

4. *The crucifixion.* There is no scholarly consensus on why Jesus was crucified. The
proposed solutions have run from Jesus' activity as a "Zealot," his "messianic" claims to be
the rightful king of the Jews, and less politically intended actions taken in and against the
temple, to inadvertent threats against civil order created by the crowds he attracted and
their unruly ways, the practice of magic, and speaking in parables. Few accept any longer
Mark's story that the Pharisees were so angered by Jesus' teaching and Sabbath behavior
that they plotted to have him killed, of course, but the assumption persists here and there
that it was "the religious leaders" who found Jesus intolerable. The problem has always
been to relate Jesus as the preacher or teacher in Galilee with some reconstruction of civil
disturbance in Jerusalem.

In his book *Jesus and the Zealots,* S. G. F. Brandon argued the Zealot hypothesis.
Martin Hengel refutes this hypothesis in *Was Jesus a Revolutionist?* albeit from a Christian
apologetic point of view. See also Hengel's *Victory Over Violence.* In a recent set of studies,
particularly in "Popular Messianic Movements," Richard Horsley has shown that the very
notion of Zealots as a typical phenomenon rests upon a mistaken reading of Josephus. The
contenders, whom Josephus called Zealots, were actually leaders of guerrilla bands, better
called *sicarii,* and best limited to the period immediately prior to the Jewish War in the
sixties. The most forthright attempt to solve the problem comprehensively is E. P. Sanders,
Jesus and Judaism. Sanders' view is that Jesus fully expected an apocalyptic event in which
the Jerusalem temple would be destroyed and in which he would be installed as king to
"restore" the kingdom of Israel. Sanders regards Jesus' "cleansing" of the temple portrayed
in Mark 11:15–18 as historical, an act borne of apocalyptic vision, not political program, an
act arising from a claim well enough understood both by his disciples and the Jewish
establishment to have triggered the histories unleashed. Jesus threatened the Jews, according
to Sanders, not the Romans, and the Jews arranged to have him killed. Jesus' disciples
accepted his vision, and they accordingly produced the church, continuing the belief that
Jesus was the Messiah-king of an otherworldly kingdom yet to appear.

All scholarly reconstructions include critical "evidence" taken from the passion narrative
of the Gospel of Mark. It should be emphasized that, apart from Mark's passion narrative,
there is no indication that Jesus or his early followers looked for the destruction of the
temple. Neither is there any indication before Mark, either in the pre-Markan memories of
Jesus or in the Pauline documentation of the Christ cult, that Jesus' death was understood
by his followers to be the result of a "messianic" conflict with the Jerusalem establishment.
Sanders struggles with this problem throughout the book, but resolves it by interpreting

Neither does the scholarly reconstruction of the early movements in the name of Jesus support Mark's story and contention. The variety of movements that took their rise from Jesus tells against the view that he held any specific intentions about particular social programs. The energy and excitement in some of the movements are obvious, and that does indicate some social dimension to the effect Jesus had upon people. But none of the materials coming from the early movements directs that excitement toward political programs with designs against the temple. There is no evidence even of hostility against the temple either as an institution or as an ideal. Such an idea would, in fact, have been regarded as absurd by Jews and Christians alike before the destruction of the temple by the Romans. The conflict that early Jesus and Christ movements had with Judaism was directed rather toward the synagogue, an institution of the diaspora. There is quite a difference between the issue underlying such a conflict and that imagined between Jesus and the temple as Mark conceived it.

The conflict with the synagogue in Mark's experience had been heated. It had come to a head shortly before Mark's time, and gone badly for the followers of Jesus. The pre-Markan materials of memory from this time are full of hostility, indeed. But, and this is the important point, none of the material bearing the scars of those battles suggests that any connection had been made in the minds of the followers of Jesus between that conflict and the crucifixion of Jesus in Jerusalem. This means that Mark's story is most probably Mark's fiction. The forty years from Jesus to Mark's Gospel must be taken into account, and not just at the level of the history of ideas or the "development" of "traditions" heavy with implicit significance flowing from a directional impulse given to the trajectory by Jesus. No. Social history must also be in view as well as the creativity of authors such as Mark who recast the past in keeping with later needs to rationalize a social experiment in trouble.

By degrees scholars have been moving slowly toward the view that the gospel was indeed Mark's creation, a narrative that brought together two distinctively different types of written material representative of two major types of early sectarian formation. One stream was that of movements in Palestine and southern Syria that cultivated the memory of Jesus as a founder-teacher. The other was that of congregations in northern Syria, Asia Minor and Greece wherein the death and resurrection of the Christ were regarded as the founding events. Neither of these movements had produced a gospel before Mark, nor would they have done so independently

---

Jesus' message as thoroughly apocalyptic, thus claiming historical plausibility for a great deal of the gospel accounts. His work can be viewed as the Anglo-American counterpart, eighty years later, to Schweitzer's "thoroughgoing apocalypticism" of Jesus in *The Quest of the Historical Jesus*.

of one another. That is because each had remembered Jesus (Christ) differently, so differently in fact, that Mark's combination of their disparate memory traditions has to be seen as a very daring and experimental moment. Mark stood, apparently, at the intersection of these two streams of social history at a very auspicious and troubling time, drew some conclusions about what to think and do under the circumstances, then made his proposal by writing the story he did. The gospel must have recast both types of memory traditions in fairly drastic ways. If one wants to understand the origins of the Christian gospel of origins, one must study the way in which Mark fabricated his story, and determine why he wrote it the way he did.[5]

The plan for the present study is simply to position Mark within the social and textual histories of the several early Jesus movements, determine the changes he introduced in the writing of the gospel, and then assess his accomplishment and its legacy. The goal will be to trace out the circumstances and reflections that led to the formation of such a dramatic myth of origins.

The first part of the study will provide a sketch of the first forty years of the early Jesus and Christ movements. Several points will be made, beginning with an emphasis upon the differences that can be noted among the several movements. It will be seen that each movement differed from the others not only in respect to its memory of Jesus, but in regard to the ways in which it distinguished itself over against some form of Judaism. Since marking boundaries belongs to the process of social identification, it is important to know how each movement defined not only its past, but itself in relation to other groups. The groups over against which early Jesus movements defined themselves were, moreover, various. To understand the differences among the various Jesus movements, each must be distinguished not only in relation to other Jesus movements, but in relation to that particular configuration of Judaism with which it begged to differ.

Judaism has been very difficult for Christian mentality to grasp. Stereotypes of monolithic proportions are often set forth as the "Jewish background" against which early Christianity lodged its critique and from which it sought its departure as a new cultural formation. But "Jewish" has been defined frequently in self-serving, theological terms, not by means of

---

5. *The Gospel of Mark.* There is a phenomenal bibliography of studies on the Gospel of Mark. Its historical importance as the earliest gospel has caught scholarly attention by degrees, increasing dramatically in recent time as form critical approaches to the Jesus traditions modulated into redaction criticism of the gospels and, finally, literary critical approaches to narrative and composition. This scholarship cannot be discussed fully within the constraints of the present study. Parts 2–4 of this book will present positions on major works, theses, and particular contributions to the investigation of Mark. See the *Bibliography for the Gospel of Mark* by Hugh M. Humphrey. A history of the interpretation of Mark is available by Seán P. Kealy, *Mark's Gospel.*

inquisitive historical description. It is true that the older idea about a "normative" Palestinian Judaism (read "Rabbinic") in distinction from a Hellenistic Judaism in the diaspora (read "unorthodox") is now discredited, mainly because the very strong influence of Hellenistic thought and practice has been documented for Palestine as well as for the diaspora. But the resulting conception of a pervasive Hellenistic cast to all Judaisms of the period is not necessarily an advance. One monolithic notion may merely have been substituted for another, and pluriform must still be seen as the rule. Mark, of course, lumps all forms of Judaism together. The prevailing scholarly distinction between the "mission to the Jews" versus the "mission to the Gentiles" also lumps things all together. Since this will not do, a sketch of pluriform Judaism will have to be given at the beginning of the study in order to reconceive the social terrain upon which the early Jesus movements made their way.

It is important to keep in mind that the first forty years of early Christianity were also the last forty years of Second Temple Judaism. It is important to know also that the temple's fate had long been sealed by conflicts on and within the borders of Judaism. Jesus was not the only critical voice to sound during this time. And Judaism was not devoid of other exciting movements of reform during the forty years when the Jesus movements intertwined and clashed with them in the battle for the right to carry the legacy of Israel into the future. They all drew upon the glorious heritage of Israel, though the selection of authorities and social markers differed. It is important to set the stage for the study by emphasizing this, for the unbelievable concentration of authority upon the figure of Jesus that accrued during this early period is related directly to the quest for legitimation in the face of such competition. It will become clear that a movement's view of Jesus as its founder can be correlated with positions taken by the group in the process of distinguishing itself from that form of Judaism experienced as its competitor, as well as from other movements stemming from Jesus.

Another correlation also will be possible. It will be seen that the notion of novelty occurred in the process of social self-definition. Mark was not the first one to think of Jesus as a founder of a new movement, or to reflect upon the death of the Christ as a transforming event. Each of the several movements stemming from Jesus had worked out a rationalization for its distinctiveness in which Jesus played a founder's role by inaugurating just those features of the new social unit that set it apart. But newness and difference are contrasting terms, and it makes some difference what the old and the other are against which novelty is judged. There was no agreement about matters such as these among the diverse Jesus movements. Each defined its novelty in relation to other Jewish institutions and reform movements. None before Mark needed to read the history of the forty years as an apocalyptic catastrophe in order to justify the existence of the new society of Israel in Jesus' name and imagine its divine originality.

Mark's conception of Jesus and Judaism must be worked out as his own peculiar construction in distinction from the several other early views held by various Jesus and Christ movements. From the historian's point of view, it will be clear, Mark's theory of Jesus' authority and the end of Second Temple Judaism might be regarded only as a little pretention hardly worth a modern smile but for its legacy. Since Mark's view became the canonical theory, however, the fiction deserves a thorough analysis. It cannot be analyzed, much less seen as the fiction it was, though, without some knowledge of the pluriform nature both of Judaism and of early Christianity during those fateful forty years. Thus the need for the statements in part 1 of the book.

The major studies in parts 2 and 3 of the book take up the question of the materials Mark used to compose the gospel. These materials can be treated as building blocks—parables, pronouncement stories, miracle stories, and passion narratives. But they can also be studied as remnants of pre-Markan traditions, traditions that may have developed in different movements, each with its own particular configuration of Jesus and peculiar social history. Each type of narrative material deserves, at any rate, its own analysis. In each case the scholarship will be reviewed, paying attention to the scholarly quests for pre-Markan traditions and the desire to trace things back to Jesus at the beginning. In discussion with this scholarship, however, the direction of the quest will be reversed, focusing attention rather upon the stages determined for the traditions and asking what each might reveal of the social circumstances addressed. Finally, Mark's employment of the stories will be analyzed in order to see how he fit them into his own narrative designs. In order to follow the argument, the reader will want to have a copy of the Gospel of Mark in hand and a picture of its storyline in mind. An outline is given in Appendix IV to enable an overview of the composition and facilitate the location of textual units under discussion within the structure of the whole.

In part 4 an attempt will be made to assess the function of the gospel Mark wrote by paying attention to its overall structures. Though composed of small units of narrative material, the story does hang together, develops several narrative themes throughout, and has a discernible if complicated plot. How and why Mark put it together in just the way he did is the question to be asked. Only after that question has been answered will some remarks be made about the legacy of Mark's literary achievement, a legacy of almost two thousand years' duration, a legacy for the most part unrecognized by those influenced by it as the story of modern scholarship, Christian mission, and Western imperialism demonstrates.

3. THE QUEST FOR THE ORIGINS OF THE GOSPEL

The approach to be taken to texts and social history will not be unfamiliar to New Testament scholars, except perhaps in the emphasis to be placed upon social experience as the occasion for imaginative activity and literary production. In the course of the quest for the historical Jesus many methods have been devised in order to locate the social-historical setting for a particular text. Scholars know how important it is to do this as part of the process by which the transmission history of a text can be traced. It is true that scholarly interest has lodged primarily in the identification of authentic kernels of "tradition" that might be thought to have originated with Jesus, rather than in the layers of "interpretation" that may have accrued in the transmission of a story or saying. Nevertheless, the methods used to retrieve the original kernels are the same as those used to remove "later embellishments." These methods (called "criticisms" by New Testament scholars) have been highly refined by repeated application, and scholars have repeatedly pored over every small narrative unit in the gospel tradition in order to determine its place in the "stages" that run from Jesus to Mark and beyond. These stages have been identified by paying attention both to authorial traits and to reflections of specific kinds of "community concerns" embedded in the language of these small units. In the course of bracketing indications of community concern that may have introduced changes into sayings and stories about Jesus, a large number of social circumstances have been identified that must have pertained during certain phases of early social history in different movements among the followers of Jesus. Thus there is a wealth of information available about authors, texts, textual traditions, social histories, community conflicts, and mythmaking for the times between Jesus and the composition of the Gospel of Mark. This information can be used to great advantage in the present study. Most of it will not be new to New Testament scholars, though the way in which it will be organized may be, as well as the conclusions that will be drawn from the new arrangements.

The rearrangement of this material information is made possible by a single shift in perspective on texts taken up to be analyzed. Instead of discounting the accretions of interpretation in the attempt to retrieve an authentic reminiscence of the historical Jesus, texts will be read in relation to their social settings in order to determine why it was that Jesus was reimagined in just the ways he was. The quest for the historical Jesus is not therefore to be given up, for a plausible reconstruction can help highlight the changes that occur in the later portrayals. Neither is all innovation necessarily to be denied the founder of the new movements that claimed origination from him. The caution introduced by the shift in emphasis is, rather, not to assume that every innovation attributed to Jesus by his followers from later times describes the situation of Jesus accurately. The picture of Jesus presented by the Gospel of Mark, for instance, is the product of two generations of vigorous social activity and energetic, imaginative labor. That means a gradual construction emerging out of many, many incidents at the level of social experience and out of the need of those who shared those experiences to forge and hold a common understanding of them. The shift in perspective is required as soon as it is realized that the creative replication of the memory of Jesus took place in the interest of articulating not only how it was at the beginning, but how it was or should be at the several junctures of social history through which a memory tradition traveled.

The normal procedure when dealing with the Jesus tradition has been to regard subsequent fictions as hermeneutical variations of some original pronouncement or action of Jesus. The interpretation is usually understood to have been aimed at an application of the significance of the first event to the new situation in which it was spoken, thus accounting for changes that may have occurred. In the case of the sayings of Jesus, scholars now use the term "generative matrix" to describe Jesus' first utterances in relation to which all subsequent replications are called "performancial variations." This guarantees that the "development" of the social history follows the directionality of the hermeneutical impulse, namely, from Jesus to the new situations addressed. Seldom has the reciprocal and thus reverse function of reinterpretation been investigated seriously. What if the social circumstances were regarded as the generative matrix for a recasting of the memory tradition? What if novelties that enter the memory tradition were to be viewed as creating as well as interpreting the imagined origins of the movements? What if the really interesting question were given its due, why and how his early followers came to create the aura of divine originality for Jesus in the first place? What if the several diverse pictures of Jesus contained in the New Testament were less hermeneutical with regard to the historical Jesus and more the creation of myths of origin for movements in need of rationalization? To test such a suspicion would be to pay more attention to the social histories subsequent to the time of Jesus than has normally been the custom in this scholarship.[6]

---

6. *The criticisms.* Biblical scholarship is known for its employment of "historical-literary" criticism. Surprisingly, however, theories of history and literature have not been produced directly from within the discipline, but borrowed from other fields. During the nineteenth century, prevailing notions of history (e.g., "report") and literature (e.g., "biography") were accepted while the troubling issues of myth, miracles, and legend in the gospels were confronted. During the first two decades of the twentieth century scholars learned that the gospels were not biographies and that they sustained a very problematic relation to history. This insight caused a shift of scholarly attention specifically to questions

Two recent trends in New Testament studies make it possible to proceed with such an undertaking. During the past fifteen years many American scholars learned to read New Testament texts as literary critics read literary

---

about literary form and function. Three types of "criticism" have been used, each influenced by extra-biblical theories of literature. Each criticism has been applied to the study of gospel materials in the interest of retrieving the earliest or most basic form of the "tradition," as well as to gain insight into the function of the primary articulations. The three types are (1) "form criticism," influenced by formalist theories of literature, (2) "aesthetic object criticism," derived from the so-called New Criticism, and (3) "structuralist exegesis," drawing upon structuralism. A history of the application of critical theory to New Testament texts has not been written, but descriptive introductions to the three approaches are available.

Introductions to the form critical tradition can be found in the Fortress Guides to Biblical Scholarship: Edgar V. McKnight, *What Is Form Criticism?;* Norman Perrin, *What Is Redaction Criticism?;* Edgar Krentz, *The Historical-Critical Method;* and William A. Beardslee, *Literary Criticism of the New Testament.* Contact with New Criticism was made in the sixties by Amos Wilder, Robert W. Funk, and J. Dominic Crossan as will be discussed in chaps. 2 and 6 of the present study. Introductions to aesthetic object criticism can be found in Robert C. Tannehill, *The Sword of His Mouth,* and Dan O. Via, *The Parables.* French scholars introduced America to structuralism at the Johns Hopkins symposium in 1966 on "The Languages of Criticism and the Sciences of Man." The proceedings of this symposium were published in 1970 by Richard Macksey and Eugenio Donato, *The Structuralist Controversy.* For a systematic presentation of structuralist criticism see Jonathan Culler's *Structuralist Poetics.* Frank Lentricchia discusses the challenge of structuralist thought to New Critical theory in *After the New Criticism.* The influence of structuralism on New Testament interpretation can be followed in the experimental journal *Semeia,* started in 1974 by R. Funk. Introductory statements for biblical scholars have been published by Daniel Patte, *What is Structural Exegesis?* and Robert M. Polzin, *Biblical Structuralism.*

The reference made earlier to the language of "presence," "immediacy," and "silence" in recent interpretations of Jesus' speech from a literary critical point of view had in mind such works as: J. D. Crossan, "Divine Immediacy and Human Immediacy"; James Breech, *The Silence of Jesus;* and W. Kelber, *The Oral and the Written Gospel.* As these works show, ways have been found to combine form critical, New Critical, and structuralist perspectives in the quest to identify the earliest form and function of the sayings of Jesus. Crossan, *In Fragments,* even uses the essentially ahistorical, structuralist notion of the "generative" rules underlying all actual "performances" of speech to describe the originary function of the "aphoristic core" prior to variant forms of the sayings of Jesus as preserved in the later textual traditions. According to structuralist theory, however, the rules that "generate" speech belong to a grammar shared by a culture. Language is viewed as a human construction, an arbitrary system of signs that can be used to mediate communication within a social unit. The notion of "presence" is, according to Derrida, the expression of a desire peculiar to metaphysical and theological views of language in Western Christian culture. From this point of view, the attribution of "presence" to the sayings of Jesus betrays the influence of traditional theological investment in sacred texts (and speech) as the source of special revelation. This appears to be true even though the experience of presence has been (1) equated with the (secular) romantic disposition inherent in the poetics of the New Criticism, (2) rationalized in terms of theory about metaphor and the imagination, and (3) discussed without reference to the canonical privilege held by the gospel materials. The position taken in the present study is one of suspicion with regard to the unique nature of Jesus' speech to create (divine) presence. A critical approach to the performance of speech contained in the New Testament needs to account for more than private moments of imaginative experience. Because social identity and formation are at stake at every turn, the social function of speech, language, and literature needs always to be under review.

texts. Much of the theory informing the criticisms used by New Testament scholars (New Criticism and structuralism) was uninterested in the historical placement of a text or its social function. One detects a change in attitude at this point, however, now that interest has focused upon what might be called the rhetorical functions of literary performance. Such matters as reader response, social context, and the intertextual, historical nature of human discourse are now being talked about as important considerations for understanding New Testament texts. This development can be viewed as a complement and corrective to older (form critical) methods for the determination of a text's "setting" in the life of a "community." By paying attention to the rhetoric of a particular text or text-type it is now possible to be more precise about the question of its social context.[7]

A second trend of significance for the present study is a growing interest in the sociology of early Christian groups. Work in this area provides a most welcome corrective to traditional preoccupations with the history of ideas and texts alone. How groups formed, defined their boundaries, elaborated activities, selected authorities, remembered experiences, forged social markers, created codes, and adjudicated conflict now are recognized as having had as much to do with the origins of Christianity as the thoughts that were thought and the literature produced. Looked at in this way, the picture of early Christianity is one of plural movements with diverse sociologies and rationales. In most cases, two or three stages in the life and thought of a movement can be discerned, each with its change in rhetoric and the introduction of new, imaginative mythologies. Less is known about social practice, organization, and the experience of history than one would

---

7. *Rhetorical criticism.* Rhetoric, the study of the logic of persuasion in the composition of speech and literature, has invaded scholarly discourse about biblical texts slowly and without great fanfare during the last fifteen or twenty years. It has come to serve as a corrective to the tendency among New Critics to mystify the poetic experience, for a rhetorical approach to literature raises questions about the way in which a composition communicates, that is, "intends" to be taken or "may" be heard. Rhetorical criticism is not clearly defined as a discipline with grounding in a particular theory of anthropology and language, but can appeal to the long tradition of rhetorical education in Western culture as well as to more recent studies of rhetoric by literary critics. Important works outside the field of New Testament criticism are those by Ch. Perelman and L. Olbrechts-Tyteca, *The New Rhetoric;* Kenneth Burke (several titles); and Wayne Booth (several titles). A. Wilder introduced the consideration of rhetoric as an approach to understanding the language of early Christians with his *Early Christian Rhetoric* in 1964. Since then many New Testament texts and genres have been analyzed with both modern and classical rhetorical theory in mind, including, e.g., *Galatians* by Hans-Dieter Betz; "Romans as an Ambassadorial Letter" by Robert Jewett, and the pronouncement stories of the gospels by Burton L. Mack and Vernon K. Robbins to be discussed in chap. 7. In a recent publication, *New Testament Interpretation,* George Kennedy has pointed out the pervasiveness of rhetorical techniques used in the composition of many types of early Christian literature. The demonstration of rhetorical knowledge and skill in the formation of early Christian speech by a scholar of classical rhetoric suggests that rhetoric may be one bridge from literary analyses of New Testament texts to questions about their social function.

like to know. But some things are known, and these can be used to establish a set of factors to control a comparative study. Those familiar with the Pauline congregations know about the significance of ethnic mix, the problem of multiple social roles and authorities, and competition with other groups, both Christian and Jewish, for the right to lay claim to the heritage of Israel and the memory of Jesus. A similar set of issues is reflected in the Jesus materials and traditions, though they have other nuances and are less well known. The goal must be to bring these social histories together with what is known of textual traditions and seek to understand each in the light of the other.[8]

For such an investigation it would be helpful to have a sociology of literature in hand, a fund of knowledge about the ways in which literature, whether oral or written, gets produced and how it then functions within the society or culture of production. Unfortunately, there is no agreement in the academy on a social theory of literature. There is, however, a burgeoning body of knowledge about the way in which symbol systems, myths, and rituals function in relation to social institutions and shared patterns of activity within groups. This knowledge is available in fields of study that focus on the anthropology of cultures from a human sciences perspective. In general, these recent approaches to the understanding of religious articulations see them as ordering activities involving the thoughtful observation, classification, and perfecting of systems of signs and practices fundamental to the operation of social units. Thus religious phenomena are intimately related to the construction and maintenance of social structures.

---

8. *Sociology of early Christianity.* The history of New Testament scholarship is dotted with works that show some interest in the social world of early Christianity. Examples include Shailer Mathews, *The Social Teaching of Jesus;* Carl Kautsky, *Der Ursprung des Christentums;* Shirley Jackson Case, *The Evolution of Early Christianity;* F. C. Grant, *The Economic Background of the Gospels;* Joachim Jeremias, *Jerusalem in the Time of Jesus;* and E. A. Judge, *The Social Pattern of the Christian Groups.* Social factors and forces have seldom been considered seriously by the majority of New Testament scholars, however, oriented as they have been to the history of ideas and the priority of language over practice. In the form critical tradition, for instance, "setting in life," though understood as a social-historical datum, was less the occasion within which ideas and speech forms were generated, and more the place where a particular form of tradition or *logos* functioned to engender religious experience. This circumstance of scholarship began to change in the late 1970s when a number of studies were published that sought to reconstruct the larger picture of early Christian social experience and group formation. In 1975 J. Z. Smith called for the "Social Description of Early Christianity." In the next few years major works appeared, including those of John Gager, *Kingdom and Community;* Abraham J. Malherbe, *Social Aspects of Early Christianity;* Gerd Theissen, *Sociology of Early Palestinian Christianity;* Bruce J. Malina, *The New Testament World;* Wayne Meeks, *The First Urban Christians;* and John Elliott, *A Home for the Homeless.* The momentum created by these efforts is still building. As the social history of early Christian movements comes into view, the question of the production and function of early Christian literature will have to be engaged both by social historians and by literary critics. The present study is an investigation of the relation between imaginative composition and social experience in early Christian circles.

Religious symbols function, however, at a certain distance from the actual
state of affairs experienced in the daily round. They articulate a displaced
system (imaginary, ideal, "sacred," marked off) as a counterpoint to the way
things usually go. The inevitable incongruence between the symbol system
and the daily round provides a space for discourse. It is the space within
which the negotiations fundamental to social intercourse take place—
reflection, critique, rationalization, compromise, play, humor, and so forth.
Early Christian views of Jesus can be studied from this perspective, and
early Christian literature can be viewed as evidence for the investments
early Christians made in their new social formations and their rationalizations. The New Testament does appear to be a literary residue of extremely
thoughtful and calculated reflection upon the grounds and purposes of new
social formations, and the many differing views of Jesus do appear to be the
result of various attempts to give an account of new social identities. If the
requirement of the study is to reconstruct social and literary histories that
created the climate for Mark's own composition, the trick must be to find a
way to locate particular texts at specific junctures of social formation in
order to be able to assess their mutual interrelations.[9]

The present study is neither strictly sociological, nor primarily literary
critical, but an attempt to combine both perspectives in order to redescribe a
certain set of entangled textual and social histories of importance for the
composition of the Gospel of Mark. It is not a sociology of early Jesus
movements, for no attempt will be made to describe fully the several groups
under discussion systematically according to any current theoretical model,
nor assess infrastructures according to any modern theory of functions. The

---

9. *Imagination, symbols, and cultural anthropology.* Recent studies in cultural anthropology have made it possible to theorize about the social function of myth, mythmaking,
and symbols. Because early Christian literature is marked by a highly imaginative
production of myths and symbols, insights from cultural anthropology can be used to
investigate the social settings of particular configurations and assess their importance for
social identifications. The present essay is an application of insights gained from a
comparative reading of constructive thinkers on the subjects of symbol, myth, and ritual in
social perspective. Émile Durkheim, Marcel Mauss, Claude Lévi-Strauss, Victor Turner,
Mary Douglas, Åke Hultkrantz, Walter Burkert, and Roy Rappaport have each contributed
forceful theoretical models of mythmaking and ritual as a means of making sense of social
activity. However, Jonathan Z. Smith's constructive theory of religion, more than any other,
informs the position taken in this book. According to Smith, myths, rituals, and symbols are
ways of thinking about, or making sense of, social practices and orientations to the world.
Symbol systems construct imaginative worlds that perfect and rationalize aspects of the
world of social experience, not to mystify, but to enable discourse and exchange to take
place by reference to a commonly shared set of signs, codes, and values. Ritual rehearsal is
not intended to overcome the incongruity that exists between the symbolic world and the
actual, more messy state of affairs that always pertains, but to replicate the occasions for
rethinking and remembering. For Smith, what has come to be called religion is actually a
social mode of thinking about social identity and activity. Smith's theory of ritual, together
with the author's comparison between Smith's works and those of Walter Burkert and René
Girard, has been published in *Violent Origins*, edited by Robert G. Hamerton-Kelly.

data in hand would not be sufficient for such an enterprise in any case. Nevertheless, the study is very much interested in the process of group formation and the social factors that may have been of significance for the imaginative constructions of a group. It is therefore a sociological study in the sense that texts will be construed consistently as reflections of and upon social experience.

The major studies will be devoted almost entirely to texts and thus will appear to be primarily literary critical discussions. This focus should not be misunderstood, as if the book were interested after all in the history of texts and ideas. Attention to the texts is quite necessary. For much of the social description desired by the social historian these texts are the only documentation in hand. They are also part of the complex social equation that is under review. They cannot be left out of account in any description of the social units within which they were produced even though their effectiveness or actual function among the many factors that gave shape to social discourse and practice may be difficult to determine. They are important for another reason as well, namely, because they are the legacy in hand, that articulation of early Christianity according to which the Christian church still reads its first chapter of history as foundational charter. The goal is to understand how these texts came to be. In order to do that they will be construed as imaginative constructions functional within a much larger set of factors at work in the social formation of early Christian groups. In keeping with their peculiar nature as evidence and legacy, however, the study will have to concentrate just upon them.

There is no single set of criticisms in place to control in tandem the necessary operations: first a reconstruction of early Christian societies from the texts they produced, then a literary-rhetorical analysis of those very same texts, and finally an assessment of whether their rhetorical potential may have been effective. Critical methods now being used in New Testament studies describe a very complicated, messy intertwining of perspectives and theories both of literature and of society. That fact, however, does not create an impossible situation. It merely introduces the necessity of being clear about one's own interests as textual-social relationships are investigated and theories sought to explain them.

The attempt will be made at every turn to position a text or a set of texts at some intersection of social and intellectual history. Viewed as a thoughtful composition at a particular juncture of human experience, a text becomes (temporarily) the center around which many other textual and social moments are organized. Every text (every story or saying) is both new and old. It is new because of context even if it appears to be "merely" a replication of an old, traditional saying. It is old even if it appears as a novel formulation in comparison to the way things have been said or seen before. No text is without multiple precursors because human discourse takes place within an intricate arrangement of overlapping systems of signs that allow for intercourse to focus and proceed without sealing off any of the many other relationships sustained and considerations possible in any given moment of social existence. To position a text at its approximate intersection of multiple textual and social articulations would be not only to understand it, for meaning is (1) a function of intertextual translation, but to discern its intention, for meaning is (2) a display of interest or desire.

Knowing that discourse occurs at a remove from both the accidental nature of human experience and the social structures that order practice, discrepancy between the way things were said to be and the way they actually went must always be kept in mind. In the case of the gospel traditions this factor of incongruency is exaggerated and compounded by the fact that social issues were reflected and addressed not by discourse directly related to the contemporary situations of concern, but by means of repeated reference to Jesus at the beginning. The intervening history was erased systematically at this level of "memory" by selecting just those features of concern from it that required inclusion in the authoritative activity of Jesus as founder. Thus the question of fasting as a ritual code of social identity was not worked out by appeal to any form of authority or argumentation other than the pronouncements of Jesus, even though such an issue could have arisen only at a much later time (Mark 2:18–22). Care needs therefore always to be taken when seeking to position a particular text for discussion. Because of the high rhetorical coefficient of early Christian discourse, and because of the extravagant idealization characteristic of early Christian mythology, the gospel texts, participating as they do in both of these traits of early Christian speaking, cannot be taken as mirror images of actual states of affair no matter what particular period of history is decided upon as context. And because of the penchant for projecting later conditions back upon the time of Jesus, as well as the lag that appears to be normal for the process of mythmaking, reflections of social experience in these texts cannot always be taken as sure indications of their placements in time. Nevertheless, precisely because something is known about the phenomena of discrepancy and lag at the level of the intellectual labor that supports social construction, it will be possible to identify a variety of discrete intersections where particular texts and specific social configurations kept company for a time. By tracing out a number of sequences and comparing several different combinations of Jesus myths and social experiments, a history of sectarian formation can be given for the time between Jesus and Mark. This history can be used, then, to control the investigation of Mark's particular achievement.[10]

---

10. *Mythmaking.* Theoretical foundations for the view on mythmaking taken in this study are given in the works of J. Z. Smith. The following essays can serve as introductions

The Gospel of Mark does present a special problem in regard to situation. Mark stood at an intersection of several movements and it is not immediately clear in which tradition he himself may have been at home. It is also the case that his creative use of prior materials sometimes makes it difficult to know which idea was his own, or which was taken from others. Thus the complex interweaving of the several strands of early traditions needs to be unraveled in order to determine the distinctive features of each. The study will therefore unfold by bits and pieces. Only toward the end will Mark's own designs upon his situation begin to surface. But in the process of unraveling the textual fabric, one can learn much about the origins of the Christian myth of origins.

A final word should be given about the style of discourse used in the study. The book is an essay, not a monograph. It addresses the entire history of the early period of Christianity and attempts to make sense of a privileged text by filling in the social space between the time of Jesus, the protagonist of the story, and the time when the story was written. Sense in this case means the kind of social sense produced by imaginative activity and myth-making. Thus the entire range of earliest Christian imagery will have to be touched upon. The study also attempts to make sense of over two hundred years of scholarship on this text and its social history. In the course of the essay many other New Testament texts will be touched upon as well as many of the enduring questions of New Testament scholarship. Positions will be taken on most issues in the interest of offering a consistent and coherent thesis without, however, always producing the customary exegetical argumentations and scholarly documentations at every turn. A few exegetical novelties will surface here and there that call for some discussion and support. But even these will not be belabored in the grand tradition of exhaustive commentary upon all aspects of the text that may pertain to the thesis. The broad sweep is necessary in order to make the point. That point is that the emergence of early Christianity and its literatures can be understood without recourse to assumptions or caveats with regard to miracles, resurrections, divine appearances, presences, or unusual charismatic phe-

---

to his thought: "Symbols and Social Change"; "A Pearl of Great Price and a Cargo of Yams"; and "The Bare Facts of Ritual." It is Smith who has emphasized the lack of fit between symbolic and social world, although the phenomenon is now widely recognized by cultural anthropologists. See, for example, Pierre Bourdieu, *Outline of a Theory of Practice.* Smith's contribution is to have made of the observation a dictum that, namely, the difference between what people do and what they say they do is the truly interesting object of scholarly investigation.

The notion of "intertextuality" underlying the present study draws upon a number of insights into the nature of language, discourse, and literature pervasive in recent French thought. Of critical importance are the works of Jacques Derrida and Michel Foucault. Special mention may be made of Derrida's *Of Grammatology* and *Dissemination,* as well as Foucault's *The Archaeology of Knowledge, The Order of Things,* and *Madness and Civilization.*

nomena. The reader is asked to grant the assumption of another kind of sense to it all, as readily as the assumption of the mysterious and unique has been granted to most other New Testament monographs. The point about making social sense is not the only aim of the essay, however. It is the structure and function of the gospel thus created that always is in view. The early Jesus movements did not bequeath the social origins of Christianity to the church. They bequeathed their myth of the historical Jesus as the account of a divine origination. This book is about the plotting of that myth of origins and its designs upon the social histories, both of those who first produced it, and of those who still accept its charter.

PART I

CHRISTIAN BEGINNINGS

> Under Tiberius nothing happened.
>
> Tacitus
> *History* 5.9

1

THE TEMPLE AND
THE LAND OF PALESTINE

1. THE TEMPLE AS SYMBOL AND
SOCIAL SYSTEM

During the Second Temple period Judea was a temple state on the model of ancient Near Eastern civilizations, except for one thing. A king was not in the picture during the period of its formation. Both a king and a priest belonged to the ancient pattern, however, the king holding power and representing the hierarchy of administration based upon it, the priest possessing status and representing the stratification of classes in the society. There was a penetrating logic to the social formation of the temple state as scholars have analyzed it. A binary code of checks and balances is probably the best way to understand the dynamic of the social structure represented by the priest-king pattern. The code was based upon a logic of two systems of differences that may be fundamental both to human societies in general and to the human capacity to think. Together the king and the priest built a city as the locus and symbol of civilization. The king's house had to be grand, for all things were his possession by virtue of the power vested in him. But the priest's house was grander still, for the priest symbolized status, not power, and status found its compensation in display. The priest's performance had to match the glories of all the human achievements upon which the city was founded.

The house built for the god symbolized the total investment of all those who had shared in a common aspiration and labor. Its grandeur was the pride of the ancient Near Eastern city and the civilization it sustained. The myths were about its construction, the histories about its fates, the festivals librettos for its song of praise. It not only symbolized the city, it was the city. There the records were kept, intellectual activity cultivated, and the skills requisite to the administration of the kingdom taught and refined. Were one to imagine a perfect city, a temple would stand at the center of the picture.[1]

---

1. *The temple as symbol and social system.* The dual system of classification fundamental to the ancient Near Eastern temple state is described in a brilliant study by J. Z. Smith, *To*

Ezekiel's vision in Babylon was about the new temple to be built in Jerusalem. When the Jews returned from Babylon, they first built an altar on the ruins of the old city, then the walls, and then the temple. Ezra brought the texts and ordered the priests. Reports from the end of the fourth century describe a flourishing city busy with priests offering marvelous displays at the temple. The picture one hundred years later is even more impressive. There were leading families with landed estates. There were commerce, culture, education, and the practice of the trades. Meetings of elders took care of city affairs and rendered justice. Ben Sira, a priestly scribe, had leisure for books, meditation, and writing. One of his poems, the Hymn in Praise of the Pious (Sirach 44–50), traces the glory of the temple and the high priest Simon back through the history of Israel's illustrious leaders to the beginning when the covenants were established by God. In Ben Sira's eyes, Simon's glory, appearing from the sanctuary on the high Day of Atonement, surrounded by priests in their festive attire, was the reflection of the creation's glory and a human society with its house in order and its act together. There were shouts, trumpets, and anthems.

Ben Sira's vision of Simon's glory was, of course, the fantasy of a deeply pious poet. He chose to erase all signs of the painful struggles Jews had experienced in the construction of the temple system, as well as of the precarious situation in which Simon's successor, the high priest Onias III, stood at the time the poem was written (ca. 180 B.C.E.). Left out of the picture were the foreign kings already in battle for control of Palestine and the fact that Judea had no royal office or army to withstand the political designs foreign powers had upon its land and people. Missing also were conflicts within, leading families and princes soon to depose Onias III and change the character of the high priest's office forever. It was, however, just this tenuous political situation that justified the glory Ben Sira saw in the Second Temple system. In spite of the lack of royal power, Jews had succeeded in constructing a theory of a fully self-governing nation state. They had done so by translating all royal functions except political imperialism into sacerdotal institutions. They did this under the very noses of the Persians, Alexander the Great, the Ptolemies and Seleucids. The rubric appealed to in their negotiations with these powers was the freedom to practice the ancestral "traditions." Ancient Near Eastern custom acknowledged local deities, rites, and ethnic practices. Tolerance with regard to local traditions was usually the rule of the conquerer as long as political subservience and the payment of taxes were granted. The Jews took what

---

Take Place. Smith draws upon the important study of Louis Dumont, *Homo Hierarchicus,* to describe two different myth and ritual systems focused upon Jerusalem—the Jewish and the Christian. For background to the social significance of the temple, see Menahem Haran, *Temples and Temple-Service in Ancient Israel.*

they had, the ancestral traditions and the privilege of practicing a local cult, and constructed from them a complex, self-sustaining society. One can only marvel at this accomplishment.[2]

Modern scholarship has viewed Second Temple Judaism as a "sacrificial system" with a mixture of religion and law that was unenlightened. This view fails completely to appreciate the fact that it was a working society, complete with laws, courts, industry, education, festivals, and the maintenance of cultural traditions. Only half of the ancient model for temple state construction could be exploited. Vassalage determined that all executive functions had to be justified as, or appear to be, sacerdotal functions. Priestly institutions had to serve civic functions and cultic codes became a kind of social metaphor for what, in reality, was a Jewish nation experimenting with law instead of autocracy as the principle of governance.

The way they did this can be summarized. The office of the high priest was expanded to include administrative and executive responsibilities for the temple state. Legislation and policy-making occurred in a council of priests and princes over which the high priest presided. Tithes and offerings were regulated and a system of taxation developed from them. Priestly scribes came to serve as administrators for a complex system of production and marketing. As the economy flourished, the temple treasury received the wealth and became an institution of banking and commerce. Granted privilege in a nation state governed by a temple system, priestly families rose to positions of leadership and power, vying with princes and their landed estates. An aristocracy emerged and with it, of course, the problems of equity, distribution of goods, and social welfare for the peasantry. Regulations were called for.

Using priestly codes, a system of governance was created that addressed many of the issues facing a fully active and productive society. Laws regulating the distribution of tithes made some provision for the poor. The administration of tithes and offerings, payable in produce, created a "department of agriculture." Foods were classified as to country of origin, modes of production, and care in preparation. Laws governing marriage and divorce considered personal and family rights, property and inheritance, as well as matters of ethnic identity (citizenship) and social status. Piety, social concern, national interest, and the cultivation of cultural heritage were all of one piece.

Fundamental to the sacrificial system was a yearly cycle of major festivals plus a weekly cycle of temple services. Rites marked the social and cultural

---

2. *The Second Temple state.* The survey of conditions in Judea from the end of the fourth century B.C.E. until the beginning of the second draws heavily upon Victor Tcherikover, *Hellenistic Civilization,* chaps. 1 and 3. For the importance of Ben Sira as evidence for scribal activity in the period just before the civil wars see B. Mack, *Wisdom and the Hebrew Epic.*

calendar, combining religious observance, commemoration of epic history, and social celebration. An essentially agrarian economy was integrated in this way with the crafts and trades by subsuming both in the larger social unit represented by the temple. Sabbath observance was prescribed. It was also a day of rest and religious celebration. In the villages there were assigned places ("stations"; *ma'amadoth*) for priestly blessings and scriptural readings coordinated with the temple services in Jerusalem. The great festivals were times of pilgrimage. The cultic requirement was that every Judean make pilgrimage three times per year. Thus, religious occasion and law were used to cultural and social advantage, for pilgrimage fostered social exchange as well as national loyalty.[3]

Creating a nation state by expanding a cultic system did not make the Jews more religious than other peoples. The view that, because Second Temple Judaism was based on a sacrificial system, Jews were preoccupied with the problem of sin and atonement is simply wrong. But the sacerdotal system did anchor social identity and what moderns call ethics in a cultural heritage that was deeply religious in its epic articulation. That heritage was in many respects as anachronistic as the temple institution, reaching back to mythic and archaic times, replete with cult etiologies, genealogies, credos, legal codes, and stories of divine intervention in a glorious history with a definite destiny. Epic fosters a particular kind of memory and a special sense of purpose. In the case of the Jews, that memory was inextricably interwoven with theological mandate to produce a civilization ordered by worship and governed by law.

One very important result of the Second Temple experiment was the transformation of the Hebrew epic into a charter document with legal functions. The process by which this happened is difficult to trace, but the books of Chronicles, Ezra, Nehemiah, and Sirach show that it had happened at least by the beginning of the third century B.C.E. Priestly codes (Leviticus) and genealogical records (Numbers) were written into the Mosaic legislation. Ben Sira refers to the "Book of the Covenant of the Most High God, the Law which Moses commanded us" (Sir 24:23). The ancient quest for a legal constitution that was not available to autocratic manipulation, a constitution that could be used to call even kings to order, had been solved in principle by linking law to sacred traditions. Thus the books of Moses came to serve not only as Israel's epic history of the primeval period, but as the account of divine instruction and legislation for what Israel was to be in the land. As the nation of priests understood it, the temple state was

---

3. *Social and administrative structure.* The description given is a summary of general knowledge available in histories of the period. See especially V. Tcherikover, *Hellenistic Civilization;* and Martin Hengel, *Judaism and Hellenism.* On the institution of the *ma'amadoth,* or "stations," see Sidney Hönig, "The Ancient City Square."

exactly what Israel was meant to be. Ben Sira's hymn marks the end of that first constructive phase of social experimentation in Judea.[4]

2. THE PRESSURES OF POLITICAL HISTORY

A heavy price would have to be paid for thinking so grandly of Jerusalem. It was positioned on the Syrian-Palestine corridor where armies marched in the cultural and political confrontation unleashed by Alexander's conquest (334–323 B.C.E.). Syria and Palestine would be the smithy where the metals of cultures and peoples East and West would be tested and forged into new configurations. Jews thought to withstand the flames and aggrandize Jerusalem even more. But in the end, city, temple, and land fell to the furnace.

The crucial event was the infamous decree of Antiochus IV Epiphanes in 167 B.C.E., that the books of the law be confiscated and burned, the sabbath outlawed, and the temple used for sacrifice to the Hellenistic-Syrian patron deity of Antioch. The decree did not suddenly appear without provocation. Jewish aristocracy had learned about international affairs under the Ptolemies, and Jewish intellectuals, for their part, had mastered a great deal of Greek language, literature, and thought. A party had formed, called the Hellenists by the Maccabean historians, who had regarded with favor the shift to Seleucid rule at the turn of the century. It was time, they thought, for Jerusalem to take its place among the great cities of the Hellenistic empires. On the surface of it, conversion was not difficult to imagine. Without a king or tyrant, governance in Jerusalem bore striking resemblance to the Greek *polis*. The council of elders could become the city's *boulē*, the aristocratic families of lineage the registered *demos*, and the temple school the patron for the gymnasium. But the situation was more complex than that.

Theoretically, the *polis* was based on the principles of citizenship, freedom, and autonomy. Founded in the Near East as a means of colonial conquest, however, the Hellenistic city actually served the interests of the tyrant king in Antioch. Only the registered citizenry had franchise in return for loyalty to the king; all others lost their voice in the political process. That meant that the entire system of scribal vocation, crafts, and agricultural production was in danger in Judea. When the high priest at Jerusalem, guardian until now of this system and its cultural heritage, moved to Hellenize the constitution, two systems of law clashed and the social structure of Judea was torn. Revolts occurred in the streets of Jerusalem.

---

4. *The Torah as epic and constitution.* Selections from a large literature on this topic include: James A. Sanders, *Torah and Canon;* Morton Smith, *Palestinian Parties;* Leo Landman, *Jewish Law in the Diaspora;* Meinrad Limbeck, *Die Ordnung des Heils;* and Joseph Blenkinsopp, *Wisdom and Law.*

Antiochus responded with his edict. And a guerrilla leader in the country-side, Judah Maccabee (the Hammer), organized an army to set things right. The banner under which they fought was "the traditions of the fathers," and "the law of God."[5]

The story of the next one hundred years is well known. With the support of a group called the hasidim (the "pious," that is, "conservatives") Judah Maccabee was able to rout several Syrian armies sent to quell the unrest and, in three years, rededicate the temple and reestablish the priestly courts (164 B.C.E.). But the social fabric was now in shreds. It was another twelve years before his brother, Jonathan, was recognized by the Syrians as high priest, and yet another ten before Simon, the third Maccabee brother, defeated the Syrian garrison on the akra in Jerusalem and became not only the high priest, but *strategos* and *ethnarch* of Judea as well. It was this political independence and power that allowed Simon to found the Has-monean dynasty, a line of high priests that ruled, eventually as kings, until the conquest of Pompey in 63 B.C.E. It was in the course of that one hundred years that Judea had its kings and experimented with power as a way to enforce the Mosaic law. It did not go well. The popular leaders moved into Hellenistic palaces, high priests took on the ways of tyrants, and armies of liberation turned to conquest. The ancient Near Eastern priest-Hellenistic king combination was questionable.

The dream of the Hasmoneans was, nonetheless, to reconstitute the kingdom of David and Solomon. But the lands were now populated with Idumeans, Samaritans, Galileans, and others. Many of these people had supported the Syrians in the attempt to squelch the Maccabees. Some were fiercely loyal to local shrines and traditions, the Samaritan temple on Mount Gerizim being only the most obvious example. All had worked out their compromises with Hellenization, and Greek cities ringed the borders of Galilee. None of these people would welcome Jerusalem over Antioch. But the plan was set in motion, nevertheless, each ruler adding territory until, under Alexander Jannaeus (103–76 B.C.E.), the Hasmonean kingdom stretched from Caesarea Philippi in the north to Raphia in the south. The kingdom had finally been regained, but not necessarily the loyalty of all the people. The conquest had been bloody, Mount Gerizim had been leveled, the Idumeans were forced to be circumcised. Nevertheless, following on the heels of the army, scribal magistrates set up shop, expanding the Judean system of Second Temple governance in the towns and cities. Temple taxes then were levied, administration of agriculture and commerce cared for, and pilgrimage encouraged both for reasons of loyalty to the temple state and for the collection of tithes. Jerusalem filled with pomp and circum-

---

5. *Antiochus IV Epiphanes.* The description of this event is based upon the convincing reconstruction of its circumstances by V. Tcherikover in *Hellenistic Civilization.*

stance, becoming the capital city of the realm, the scene of high intellectual and political drama. Some saw it as a time of greater glory, others were distressed.

It has been customary to think of the Hasmoneans as champions of Second Temple institutions in the face of Hellenistic threat. A more sobered view would be to notice that their times were troubled by internal dissent. No sooner had Simon announced the founding of the Hasmonean line of priests than another leading priest withdrew to the desert to found the community at Qumran. During the hundred years, other hasidim were often critical and finally drew the wrath of Alexander Jannaeus, who executed thousands. At the end, hasidim who may have been precursors of the Pharisees helped to unsettle Hyrcanus II and Aristobulus II (67–63 B.C.E.). The issues were over the priesthood, and the kingship, and the laws, and accommodation to Hellenistic ways. The essential weaknesses of the Hasmonean temple state were brought to light when Pompey appeared in Syria. Jerusalem was handed over, Syria-Palestine became a Roman province, and the high priesthood a Roman appointment. For many pious Judeans, this was the beginning of the end.

Under the Romans, the office of the high priest-king was divided. The kings appointed by the Romans would not be able to lay any claim at all to the grand epic traditions still vividly etched in the popular imagination. Herod the Great, an Idumean (37–4 B.C.E.), aggrandized the temple even as Jewish respect for his authority withered, then turned to hostility. After Herod, Palestine was carved up again into provinces ruled by tetrarchs (with Herod Antipas the tetrarch of Galilee from 4 B.C.E. to 39 C.E.), and in 6 C.E. Judea became a Roman procuratorship. The priests appointed by the Romans sought to keep the system going, but slowly lost their grip on the loyalties of the people who began to distinguish between the temple as symbol and the priests as the temple establishment. At the time of Jesus the high priest's council no longer presided over a temple state, but over a network of scribal stations concerned only with cultic matters. From the people's point of view, all authorities had been tarnished. Sects had formed in Judea, falling back on old ideals. Parties of legal interpretation had formed in Jerusalem, in effect experimenting with the substitution of cultic law for establishment power.[6]

As the period came to its end, the high priest and his council lost control. The people hated Roman rule. And a famine in the forties of the first century C.E. exacerbated matters. Banditry and rebellion ensued, with

---

6. *The Maccabees and the Hasmonean Dynasty.* Critical studies of this period include Elias Bickermann, *From Ezra to the Last of the Maccabees;* M. Stern, "The Hasmonean Revolt"; V. Tcherikover, *Hellenistic Civilization;* and Solomon Zeitlin, *The Rise and Fall of the Judean State.* There are many other histories available.

sicarii eventually focusing upon the temple as the place to take matters into their own hands. Factions formed, the wealthy were plundered, and the high priest driven out. Before the Romans solved the problem once again with their armies, Jerusalem was already a desolate citadel. The priest-kings were gone, the Jerusalem council gone, as was the sacrificial system, the temple tax, and the treasury. Only four things remained: the people, the priests, the diaspora synagogues, and the law of Moses. From them another social institution would have to be built.[7]

3. JEWISH GROUPS AND MOVEMENTS

The political history of Second Temple Judaism is the larger screen upon which the social situation at the time of Jesus should be projected. The sweep of four hundred years or so provides a way to imagine Judaism as a single configuration before going on to describe several distinguishable patterns of Jewish life and thought at the end of the era. It also explains some characteristics and concerns held in common by most of the Jewish movements, sects, and parties that describe the social landscape of early Christianity.

Of singular importance was the written epic that functioned as mythology and served as mandate for the Jewish sense of tradition, legal charter for institutional and social constructions, and sounding board for vociferous debate about what Jews should be doing. It is quite inadequate to limit Jewish preoccupation with the books of Moses to the modern category of "law." The books were invested with legal status because Jews had learned to derive the authority for their social formations from epic mythology, and "law" was the way to conceptualize social codes and constitutions during the Hellenistic period. All of the many social constructions that appeared in the shadow of the dying temple system appealed to the Torah as "law." Closely examined, however, each had also created a sophisticated hermeneutical logic in order to make the connections. One needs to keep in mind both the singular importance of the Torah, as well as its plurisignificance, in order to understand the varieties of Judaism during the first century, including the many Jesus movements that emerged.

A second characteristic common to most conceptions of Judaism during the period was an orientation to ritual. The importance of the temple system for the definition of Judaism is not easily exaggerated. The temple state provided the actual incarnation of Judaism for the entire history of the Second Temple era. It became a model for imagining a society centered theocratically, structured according to the codes of purity, and held together by a cycle of ritual occasions. For Jews living in Judea, the temple

---

7. *The Jewish War.* The primary document is Josephus, *Jewish War.*

system was simply and actually the form of their social existence. Outside of Judea, in the diaspora synagogues, social institutions other than the temple were more the daily experience. Some diaspora communities were related to the temple in Jerusalem only loosely in an institutional sense. But the temple continued to function for all Jews as the definition of Judaism. Because it was there, in Jerusalem, to manifest Judaism as a people, nation, religion, and tradent of hoary tradition, Jews living outside of Judea were in the "diaspora."

Only in the lands of Palestine other than Judea would there have been confusion about the importance of the Jerusalem temple for Jewish identity. That is because "Jewish" identity itself was a much more complex matter for these peoples. Most of them shared generally in the memories of Moses, David and Solomon without having to be reminded by the Jews of Judea. During the Hasmonean conquest, then, a Judean identity was superimposed upon local traditions. In the case of the Samaritans, that superimposition by force was simply not accepted. In Galilee there was a more passive response, but that should not be taken as a sign that the annexation was thought of as a homecoming. In Samaria, and perhaps also in Galilee, the books of Moses and the epic traditions of Israel may have provided a link to local traditions held to be of more importance even than the institution of the temple at Jerusalem. Nevertheless, the temple as institution and symbol was firmly in place because of the history, and would be the model used by many to reimagine a new society, even a society without benefit of cultic personnel.

A less clearly articulated common characteristic should also be mentioned. The passion for self-governance and social constructions based on law instead of autocracy courses through this history. Brought to bear upon the question of the authority to be invested in the highest office, the persistent bickering about the high priest and the kingly office begins to make sense. A certain social notion can be detected as the matrix from which the eternal debates arose. There really never was a concerted desire for a king. The Hasmoneans fell into kingship mainly because of circumstances. But kings there were, and they could not be easily excluded from either the archaic or the contemporary model for thinking about power and authority. If things really got confusing, as they did toward the end of the era for some, kings might appear in the scenarios they imagined necessary to set things right. But even then, the office of the priest was always preferred. It was the locus for the kind of authority Jews thought more appropriate for a society governed by (divine) law. It will become clear that the Pharisaic reform was fairly definite about this issue, though a few Pharisees got caught in popular messianic movements, as did a few of the early rabbis. It was, however, the priestly model, pared down to the status of teacher, that prevailed in this reform movement, the tradition that eventually put the pieces back together after the destruction. It is wrong, therefore, to think of Judaism in general as determined by messianism, the desire for a king. All sectarian movements were organized rather around offices and functions that derived from priesthood. It was Christianity that picked up the other option, deciding for a king instead of a priest.

Judaism of the time of Jesus was, nevertheless, not a culture in agreement about how to apply its authorities and construct alternative institutions. The landscape of Judaism within which Christianity carved out a niche was actually quite rugged. Early Christian literature does not paint an adequate picture. The tendency in the New Testament was to flatten things out and borrow from many streams as if from a common source. Pharisees, scribes, synagogues, prophets, messiahs, miracle workers, the temple, the priests, and the law all are merged together. If the argument was polemical, these figures stood for Judaism. If the argument was the claim Christians had upon them, these figures represented "Israel." But it is important to be more precise than that, to locate social roles and notions within specific movements and try to determine under what circumstance which Jesus movement took note of them. Many of these social identifiers, as well as many of the fantastic notions appropriated by early Christians, can be placed within particular Jewish movements. The more important of these deserve a brief description.[8]

---

8. *Pluriform Judaism under the Romans.* Older scholarship knew about the difference between "Palestinian" and "diaspora" Judaism, as well as about the three "philosophies" in Palestine, i.e., Sadducees, Pharisees, Essenes, and the new or "fourth philosophy," Zealots, as Josephus describes the situation. See the helpful survey by Jacob Neusner, *From Politics to Piety,* chap. 3. It has now become necessary to recognize that the social landscape was even more broken and diverse than that. Profiles can be gained from the works of M. Stone, *Scriptures, Sects, and Visions;* and George W. E. Nickelsburg, *Jewish Literature.*

The importance of the temple system as an imaginative model for conceptualizing and rethinking "Israel" is a judgment based upon its pervasive incidence in the literatures of the period irrespective of diverse social settings. The temple model dominates the thought of the Qumran sectarians, for instance, but also that of Philo of Alexandria. J. Neusner's many works on formative Judaism demonstrate that application of the ritual laws of purity during the time of the Second Temple provided the bridge to the later emergence of Rabbinic Judaism. In a fine statement, *Das pharisäische und talmudische Judentum,* Neusner shows that, though the temple model was common to such different movements as the Qumran sectarians and the Rabbis, divergent views of "history" and "world" resulted in contrastive "locations" of the temple that Israel was imagined to be.

The point made about "self-governance" is a judgment based upon the history of Jewish attitudes and activities in evidence throughout the entire Second Temple period, both in Palestine and in the diaspora. See the interesting study by S. Safrai, "Jewish Self-Government." In a similar way, other Jewish and early Christian groups found it possible to rationalize new social configurations by adjusting the symbol systems given with the temple state model. On the point about preferring "priestly" to royal figures and categories as Jews sought to rethink Israel, Freyne offers an insightful comment: "There was . . . a consistent critique of existing kingship both Hasmonean and Herodian throughout the first century B.C.E. in Palestine" (*Galilee,* 214). Freyne does not think that the idea of "the messianic king of David's line" was therefore rejected. The question this raises has to do with the

3.1 The Essene Community at Qumran

Before the discovery of the ruins at Qumran in the early 1950s it was difficult to imagine the seriousness with which pious priests could take the institutions of Second Temple Judaism. As the pieces fell into place, the picture of a fully organized sectarian community began to appear with attitudes quite the opposite of those that characterized the Hasmonean establishment. Positioned in the desert to bide their time, these priests had constructed a large compound of buildings, water works and facilities for agrarian production in order to reconstitute a pure kingdom of priests. The extent of the enterprise and the energies invested in its fantastic conceptualizations are truly astonishing.

The sect was strictly ordered and ranked with entrance and novitiate requirements carefully spelled out. The Levitical laws of purity were enforced, instruction in the rules of the community clear, and the calendar for the regulation of labor and liturgy precise. A teacher-priest was in command of a community that imagined itself on the model of the battle camp in the wilderness (Numbers). But in the villages of Judea, apparently, others could belong to the "order of the land," forming little camps of sectarians also waiting for the time. The temple dominated the imagination. The hope was to see it cleansed, again the center of a nation obedient to the theocratic ideals of Israel.

The story of this amazing movement, left untold by Josephus, can now be reconstructed. The consternation of purist priests, hasidim, at the Hellenistic reforms of Jason and Antiochus IV set the stage. Finding satisfaction neither from subsequent high priestly appointments designed to appease, nor from the Maccabees' successes that turned too quickly toward the enticements of power, a leading priest finally decided to withdraw. This happened most probably about the time of Simon's inauguration (140 B.C.E.) that signaled the end of hopes for an early remedy. Small beginnings are attested for the first phase of occupation. But during the reigns of John Hyrcanus and Alexander Jannaeus, peaking roughly around the turn of the century, a large commune was flourishing. An earthquake in 31 B.C.E. disrupted occupation of the site until after the death of Herod (4 B.C.E.). Destroyed by the Romans in the Jewish War, the legacy of two hundred years of social experimentation was lost.

The library, however, survived, hidden away hurriedly in nearby caves high on the cliffs overlooking the Dead Sea. From it a remarkable history of intellectual effort can be pieced together, documenting the rationale for the sect's activities. It is not surprising to find that the books of Moses had been

---

function of ideal figures imagined during this time. For a study in their function as rationalizations involving social judgments, see B. Mack, "Wisdom Makes a Difference."

read with utmost seriousness. They contained the divine constitution for the priestly theocracy as well as the epic paradigm for Israel's preparation to enter into the land. Having withdrawn to the desert, the priests of the new covenant were getting ready for a replay. The sectarian scrolls (Manual of Discipline, Damascus Document, and War Scroll) show how thoroughly the charter document had been read. They also show that the charter documents had been misread creatively by selecting materials from them that could reflect the sect's own view of itself. This idealization occurred in the process of justifying the sectarian claims to the charter, on the one hand, while bringing severe criticism to bear upon the Jerusalem establishment, on the other. The two functions go together. The wider the gap between the archaic ideal and the actual state of affairs in Jerusalem, of course, the more severe was the critique and the more grand the sectarian claims.

At some juncture in its history the gap widened to the point of mental despair, and apocalyptic visions were entertained as a way to imagine how the impossible ever could happen. The War Scroll is a pathetic example of this kind of fantasy born of sectarian desire. The scroll describes the final battle for the temple in advance, complete with the orders of the priests who would march under their banners, the prayers and blessings all written out, and a plan for the celebration after the victory. It would be a banquet for all the orders of the priests and all the orders of the people with the anointed priest and king properly seated at their heads. The perfection of the plan extended to the prescription that the anointed high priest, not the anointed king, would be the first to take the bread and say the blessing.

Preparation for the apocalyptic turn at Qumran occurred in the reading of the prophets. The books of the prophets were known about generally, of course, and read with greater or less interest by Jewish teachers and literati. But neither the Jerusalem scribes, nor the Pharisees, nor the synagogues of Alexandria, nor, one suspects, most forms of Judaism at the time attributed to the prophets the kind of authority they received at Qumran. Read as oracles predicting their own times, the books of the prophets were the handbooks for the interpretation of all the accidents of history for the almost two hundred years of the sect's existence. Standard interpretations were written into commentaries (called *pesharim*). Verse after verse was taken to apply either to the wicked priest in Jerusalem, his defilements, and the darkness polluting the land, or to the sons of light at Qumran, the holy remnant, the New Israel. A radical sectarian opposition to the temple establishment produced a radically dualistic interpretation of contemporary history by means of an oracular hermeneutic applied to the books of the prophets.

The strategy used to justify the sect's existence in the midst of a contrary history is noteworthy. Because the Jerusalem establishment was held to be in violation of the covenant ideal, the epic history of a Chronicler or a Ben Sira would not do. To make sense of the failure and justify the strange circumstance of having to start all over again, another corpus from the scriptural heritage was inserted between the epic recounted in the books of Moses and the historians ("prophets") of the early kingdoms. The prophets then were read as having known what would happen. This created in effect a new reading of Israel's history. It was coherent from the point of view of the Qumran sectarians, but it was tragic. It was doubly tragic, in fact, for not only was its assessment of the contemporary history of Jerusalem dark, but when that history ended, the sect's own history ended and with it the history of Israel it had imagined.[9]

There is a large scholarly literature on the similarity of early Christianity to Qumran. Points of similarity include sectarian formation, rites of baptism, ritualized meals, an emphasis on the prophets, a claim to the legacy of Israel, the writing of hymns, apocalyptic language, and messianic expectations. Some would also compare the two founders, the Teacher of Righteousness and Jesus. The analogies are helpful, though they apply unevenly as one moves from one early Christian movement to another. They are helpful because certain patterns of sectarian response to social conflict can be discerned. But the foundations of the two movements are quite different. Jesus was not a teacher-priest with claim to the temple theocracy. Nor were Levitical laws of purity the rationale for dissent and claims to perfection among Christians. The Essenes constructed a perfect substitute for the purification of the sacrificial system. That set them apart from all other reform movements, both Jewish and Christian. As those set apart, however, they were linked irrevocably to the destiny of Jerusalem by a principle of opposition that required an inversion of circumstance. The single issue of the legitimacy of the temple establishment meant that the sect was destined to die with the temple's destruction. It does not matter whether the Essenes resisted, fought, or fled when the Romans marched. The end of the temple marked the end of the sect as well. This is quite different than any of the rationales created by early Christian movements. It is, of course, quite possible that erstwhile members of the sect continued to agonize over the destruction of the temple in terms of their grasp of mythic history. The apocalyptic literature produced in the wake of the destruction could easily be read this way (4 Ezra; Syrian Baruch). But the lack of resolution in these

---

9. *Qumran.* For readable introductions to the literature, history, and scholarship on Qumran see Frank M. Cross, *The Ancient Library of Qumran;* and Géza Vermès, in *The Dead Sea Scrolls in English.* For a list of the discoveries, editions of the texts, and select bibliography of studies, see Joseph A. Fitzmyer, *The Dead Sea Scrolls.* The description given is a brief summary of information generally available.

later writings, and the failure ultimately of the angelic authority to convince the troubled seer, is telling. The myth had been destroyed by history and there was literally nothing left for an Essene to do.[10]

---

10. *Jewish apocalyptic*. An introduction is now available by John Collins, *The Apocalyptic Imagination*. Current scholarly perspectives on apocalyptic are given in the proceedings of the International Colloquium on Apocalypticism held at Uppsala in 1979, edited by David Hellholm, *Apocalypticism in the Mediterranean World*. Under debate are questions about the social setting for the production of apocalyptic literature and the prevalence of apocalyptic mentality during the Hellenistic period. The older theory was that apocalyptic appeared as a response to social-historical crises of dramatic proportions, such as the event of Antiochus Epiphanes in 167 B.C.E., the Roman hegemony in 63 B.C.E., or the destruction of the temple in 70 C.E. The difficulty of dating and locating most apocalyptic writings, together with the fact that many later apocalypses invite interiorization and appear in gnostic modes, have led many scholars to question the "historical crisis" approach and interpret apocalyptic mentality as a quest for religious insight and experience. A study by J. Z. Smith, "Wisdom and Apocalyptic," may help. Smith sets early Jewish and Christian apocalyptic in the broader context of ancient Near Eastern scribal activity and traces the developments of "proto-apocalyptic" texts in Babylonia and Egypt into the Hellenistic period when the apocalypse proper appears. The "apocalyptic situation" was, according to Smith, the disruption of temple state order by foreign domination. Scribal response to the situation was a search for archaic paradigms (or order) and ways to imagine their reactualization. The usual pattern was to project a reinstatement of indigenous royalty. It was the absence of kings in the Hellenistic period that set the stage for more imaginative efforts. These produced apocalyptic literature of great variety, all based upon archaic nation state models, while seeking the foundations for a return to order in novel combinations of many systems and classifications of knowledge. Smith's attribution of apocalyptic literature to scribal activity is important. It agrees with the point made by Horsley about the elitist nature of this literature. The evidence from Qumran does show that scribal activity could be dislodged from its primary location at courtly and temple institutions. Apocalyptic in support of sectarian formation was now possible, and with it novel solutions to the problem of where and when the perfect order might again be imagined to take place. Nevertheless, the priests at Qumran did lay claim to the offices of Second Temple institutions. It is necessary, therefore, to locate an apocalyptic writing socially in order to determine the "apocalyptic situation." The great crises of Second Temple history (167 B.C.E., 63 B.C.E., 70 C.E.) are still candidates for apocalyptic situations. But these were not the only situations of social distress and powerlessness experienced by Jewish groups during this period. In the case of Qumran, several apocalyptic situations may have been experienced in the course of its long history, each differently construed depending upon who the "foreigners" were, what social model was perceived under attack, and where the lines had been drawn to define the people in whose behalf the future was to be projected. The problem of identifying (1) national, (2) dislodged, and (3) sectarian scribal activity in the production of Jewish apocalyptic literature has not at all been solved. The evidence suggests, however, that apocalyptic functions where strong social identities are already in place, though threatened. It is questionable, therefore, to speak of a pervasive apocalyptic mentality at large in Palestine that gave rise to new social groupings when triggered by a call for social revolution. Apocalyptic is not a sufficient rationale for novel social formations. The older view is still the best: apocalyptic is a scribal response to a social history that has gone wrong from the point of view of a particular social group. This means that the occurrence of apocalyptic language in early Christian literature makes most sense as the rationalization of failed expectations within movements subsequent to the time of Jesus. As for the nature of those expectations during the earliest phases of social formation, neither apocalyptic mentality, nor a reform of the Second Temple system appear to have been essential ingredients (see chaps. 2–4). Thus the analogy between Qumran (as a Jewish sect) and the early Jesus movements breaks down when pressed to the point of origins and fundamental appeal.

3.2 The Pharisees

Quite another approach to Second Temple institutions was taken by the Pharisees. They also were hasidim concerned about the strict observance of cultic codes and critical of the Hasmoneans. But they did not withdraw to form an apocalyptic sect, choosing rather to emphasize the importance of adherence to the temple system as constituted and stay in the thick of temple politics in Jerusalem. Their historical importance can hardly be exaggerated, for they were the ones who discovered that the observance of ritual rules apart from the sacrificial system could sustain and transmit Jewish culture. The story of how that translation was achieved, however, is very difficult to reconstruct. There are two problems to consider. One is that the sources are unclear about the range of Pharisaic activity and interests. The other is that the extent of Pharisaic influence for the early period lies still in the dark.

There are three major sources for a reconstruction of early Pharisaism: Josephus, the gospels, and the Mishnaic traditions of the Rabbis. In these sources two characterizations intertwine that do not mix easily. One picture is that of lawyers who belonged to some kind of party with political interests, or who represented some kind of "school" of law with institutional interests. The other is that of a class of persons who made a point of keeping ritual codes and were recognized for it. If Pharisees were simply the hasidim of the first century with the nickname "separatists" (i.e., from impurity), both pictures might be possible. But the relationship between the two social roles would still be unclear.

Jacob Neusner has argued that during the early first century the term Pharisee did not refer to an organized school or party, but to a small class of persons who lived according to the laws of ritual purity as a matter of private observance. Such a piety could have been defined in the course of the Herodian period when, after the separation of the temple system from the Roman governance of the provinces, renewed attention to the legal basis for an independent cult occurred. It need not have been a complicated affair at all, that is dependent upon the mastery of a large corpus of legal opinion (halakha). The characterization of the Pharisees in the gospels is limited to a very few matters having to do with sabbath observance, tithing, table fellowship, washings, oaths, prayers, alms, and fasting. These are easily understood as a listing of codes that belonged to the temple cult and its practice in the villages and provinces. Neusner has studied the pre-Rabbinic traditions about the Pharisees and the early schools of legal interpretation in Jerusalem stemming from Hillel and Shammai (late first century B.C.E.). There is striking agreement about the topics taken up for legal discussion in that tradition and the list of ritual codes of importance to Pharisees in the gospels. This must mean that, even if the pre-Rabbinic schools were related in some way to the temple establishment, perhaps as a new forum to study the new situation of cultic authority without royal power, the legal opinion they generated may not have been inordinate. This point is important because of the traditional view among New Testament scholars, derived from a projection of the Mishna back into the time of Jesus, that Pharisees were casuistic legalists delighting in the application of hundreds of picayunish rules to throttle the performance of every natural activity. Huge bodies of legal opinion did accumulate to fill the vacancy after the temple was gone. That phenomenon also is misunderstood, by the way, if one sees it as ethical prescription instead of intellectual activity called for by the need to classify the codes of a community reduced to dependency upon its etiquette for social self-definition. The Pharisees, in any case, were actually building a code to enable Jewish observance applicable to the daily round apart from authorities of enforcement and based on convention ("oral tradition"). If the number of items was manageable, then, a Pharisee would have been one who knew and kept a standard list of ritual codes, primarily pertaining to foods, prayers, and the keeping of ritual occasions. Paul's reference to himself as having been a Pharisee is best understood just in this sense (Phil 3:5).

But the gospels also frequently allude to the Pharisees as teachers who appealed to tradition as law, who represented some standard among the people. So a combination of personal piety and some kind of authority based on knowledge of the laws is assumed. Luke even uses the term lawyers, indicating that the authority stemmed from a recognizable institution or social role. This raises the question of the relation of scribes to Pharisees, and the presence of teaching Pharisees among the people outside of Jerusalem.

It should be emphasized that Josephus' references to Pharisees are limited to Palestine, more particularly to Jerusalem. The Mishnaic traditions about Rabbinic precursors likewise place them in Judea and Jerusalem. The schools of Hillel and Shammai were in Jerusalem, and the hasidic priests who formed the Academy at Yavneh after the war came from Jerusalem. Philo of Alexandria (ca. 20 B.C.E.–40 C.E.), on the other hand, does not mention them, presumably because he had no knowledge of them or their importance. In the Pauline corpus, rife with ideological controversy pertaining to "Judaizers," the law, and cultic codes, there is no mention of Pharisees other than the single self-reference to Paul's own former way of life. Thus the evidence points to Pharisaism as a form of piety particularly associated with Jerusalem.

The references in the gospels are for the most part late, deriving from the last third of the century. The earliest mentions occur in the pronouncement stories of Mark and the woes against the Pharisees in the collection of Jesus' sayings known as Q. Scholarly opinion dates these occurrences roughly in the fifties or sixties, so that one has to assume that Jesus movements encountered Pharisees somewhere around this time as critics and competitors. The most plausible setting for such an encounter would be in proximity to the synagogue as the synoptic stories suggest. The combination of Jesus people, Pharisees, and synagogues presents a very interesting problem in historical reconstruction.

The synagogue in the diaspora was an institution quite different from the places of congregation at the priestly-scribal "stations" in the villages of Judea. Both institutions had evolved long before the Pharisees came on the scene and neither appears to have been of institutional interest to the Pharisees during the Herodian period, although Pharisaic views may have begun to influence the interpretation of cultic codes at the scribal stations in Judea and become issues for debate among scribal interpreters amidst local traditions in the provinces of Palestine outside of Judea. Only in the Herodian period is there evidence of the construction of places for assembly in Palestinian provinces under the temple system, two houses of prayer built apparently under Herod's patronage at Masada and Herodium, one each in Magdala in Galilee and Gamala in the Decapolis, and one at Tiberias, a city founded by Herod Antipas in 20 C.E. Hengel has argued convincingly that the construction of assembly places in Palestine at a remove from Jerusalem copied the construction of assembly places in the diaspora communities. This practice increased dramatically only in the aftermath of the destruction of the temple to fill the vacancy created by its loss. Pharisees, either as a class or as a party, would not have been involved in this development, would not have been "in charge" of congregations. Thus a very fluid situation must be imagined for northern Palestine and southern Syria during the period just before and just after the Jewish War. This would be the most probable location for the encounter of Jesus people, Pharisees, and synagogues, an encounter among three different conceptions of social construction, each traceable to different cultural traditions and institutions that happened to overlap just at this place and time.

Pharisees apparently played an important role in the activities of the hasidic priests after the fall of Jerusalem and into the second century. Toward the end of the first century these priests succeeded in winning the recognition of Rome as the council with authority to represent Jewish interests in Palestine. Galilee then became a favored location for school activities and, though the first century seems a bit early for this council to have worried much about the state of piety in the diaspora synagogues, some presence in the synagogues of northern Palestine is probable. There is one important bit of evidence for the presence in Galilee of a leading hasidic priest even before the war. Yohanan ben Zakkai, who was to be the leading figure in the founding of the Academy at Yavneh, lived for a time in Galilee. Because the traditions about Ben Zakkai are embedded in Rabbinic lore, his relationship to the Jerusalem establishment is unclear. But he was from Jerusalem, and Galilee was a province within the temple system. So Ben Zakkai's move to Galilee shows that the shift in Pharisaic interest toward Galilee may have begun before the war. Legend has it that Ben Zakkai's tenure in Galilee was a mission of sorts to instruct the people in the law. It was not, however, outrageously successful. The Galileans failed to catch on to the importance of strict adherence to the laws of ritual purity, according to these stories. They became legendary for their diffidence and may have been a prime example if not the actual occasion for the Rabbinic-Pharisaic lore about the *'am ha'aretz*, the people of the land who couldn't or wouldn't learn the law.

It is therefore most improbable that Jesus had a running battle with Pharisees in Galilee. Some Pharisaic presence is to be assumed in the last decade before the war, perhaps in those cities in Galilee and southern Syria where an overlap was possible between Jerusalem influence and a Hellenistic synagogue. After the war one can imagine a great deal more Pharisaic activity and some spill over into southern Syria. But even then it would be wrong to think of Pharisees as authorities in control, or even seeking control of the diaspora synagogues. Institutionally, the encounter of the Jesus people with the Pharisees in and around the synagogue had to have been a fair fight, won or lost on its own merits.[11]

---

11. *The Pharisees.* J. Neusner has collected and discussed the primary data in *From Politics to Piety.* On Ben Zakkai's activities in Galilee, see further J. Neusner, *The Life of Rabban Yohanan ben Zakkai.* Neusner does not regard Ben Zakkai's move to Galilee as an official "mission." In his book on *Jesus the Jew,* 56–57, Vermès makes the point that the only Pharisees in Galilee mentioned by Josephus were from Jerusalem. It is well known that Josephus' views on the Pharisees in the *Jewish Antiquities* reflect the importance they had attained after the war toward the end of the first century. The reliability of his reports on Pharisaic Judaism in Galilee at an earlier time has therefore been questioned. See, for instance, M. Smith, "Palestinian Judaism in the First Century." In *Jesus the Magician,* Smith notes the importance of keeping the distinction clear between scribes and Pharisees. Scribes were a professional class of ". . . the middle and lower-middle class schoolteachers, lawyers, and notaries of the Galilean towns, dependent for their status on their limited knowledge of 'the Law,' and therefore devoted to 'the Law,' proud of their knowledge, and pillars of local propriety." While Jesus may well have had occasion to spar with local scribes, it is unlikely, according to Smith, that Jesus would have encountered Pharisees in Galilee. Thus the sayings and stories in the gospels about the Pharisees are to be understood as ". . . the introduction of opponents more important to the later church" (*Jesus the Magician,* 30–31). Seán Freyne agrees that this is the picture available to the historian, though he does so with reticence, *Galilee,* 319–20. He mentions the "sporadic, and apparently unsuccessful Pharisaic presence in Galilee, prior to 70 C.E.," as well as the fact that "the picture of the Pharisees which emerges from the pages of the New Testament is colored by the early Christian community's experiences with Judaism." He argues, nevertheless, that Jesus can hardly be imagined without having held "a genuine confrontation" with the Pharisees. The only support he can bring to this unfortunate conclusion, however, is the picture painted in the gospels.

On the distinction between houses of prayer in the diaspora from the third century B.C.E. and the pattern of assemblage in Palestine, see Martin Hengel, "Proseuche und Synagoge." Hengel argues that the term synagogue came to be used generally for the place of assembly

3.3 The Synagogues

The dispersion and mixture of peoples so characteristic of the Hellenistic age did not leave the Jews untouched. Forced resettlement, flight, and commissioned military service had been the pattern since the sixth century. With the rise of the Hellenistic city, however, voluntary migration occurred as well, and strong Jewish communities formed throughout the Ptolemaic and Seleucid empires. Intensely interested in self-governance, Jews in the diaspora created a peculiar institution called a "house of prayer" (*proseuchē*). Prayers were said there, keeping alive cultural and religious memories and desires. But the buildings served social and civic functions as well, activities that produced a self-conscious society within a society. With an eye both to Jewish interests and to full participation within the life of the *polis*, a diaspora culture began to take shape quite different from that being cultivated in Jerusalem. It was this experiment in negotiating Hellenistic culture within a Hellenistic *polis* but from a distinctly Jewish perspective that created the synagogue, an institution that would prove to be capable of assuming full responsibility even for the cultural heritage of Second Temple Judaism after its demise.

The independence of the synagogue from the temple needs to be under-

---

(rather than for the congregation assembled) only in the course of the first century C.E. under the influence of changes taking place in Palestine. Some combination of diaspora institution, the founding of cities in the provinces of Palestine, and the transformation of the scribal stations at greater remove from Jerusalem would have been the occasion. For a discussion of the prayer houses that began to spring up in Palestine during the Herodian period see E. Meyers and J. Strange, *Archaeology*, 140–41. They note that, while Josephus numbered the "synagogues" of first-century Jerusalem in the hundreds, there is no archeological evidence for buildings, except for the famous "Theodotus Inscription," a plaque for which, however, the building has not been found. Their conclusion is that "it is highly likely therefore, that in the period when the temple still stood, a synagogue could well have been nothing more than a large meeting room in a private house or part of a larger structure set apart for worship." They go on to explain that "when the Jewish population of Judaea and Samaria began to establish themselves in Galilee after the Roman wars, one of the first problems was the issue of how and where to pray. On the basis of archeological evidence from more than one hundred ancient Palestinian synagogues, however, it is difficult to date the earliest evidences of synagogues before the mid-third century C.E." One should keep in mind, however, that there were synagogues in the Hellenistic cities of northern Palestine and southern Syria. Josephus mentions synagogues for Antioch (*Jewish War* 7.44), Dora (*Jewish Antiquities* 19.300, 305), and Caesarea (*Jewish War* 2.285, 289), as well as the *proseuchē* in Tiberias (*Vita* 277, 280, 293ff.). Since the gospels use the term synagogue to refer to the place of assembly, the most probable location for encounter with the Pharisees would be in those cities in and on the fringes of northern Palestine where Pharisaic presence had begun to be felt. This could have happened about the middle of the first century, but would have increased dramatically only after the war.

That the appearance of the Pharisees in the pronouncement stories reflects circumstances of the fifties or later will be discussed in chapter seven below. For the view that the woes against the Pharisees in Q (Luke 11:37–54) belong to a second layer in the history of the Q tradition, and that they arose out of conflict with the synagogue at a later stage in the social history of the group, see John Kloppenborg, *The Formation of Q*, 139–54.

scored. It was an institution created in the diaspora by Jews living in the diaspora. It was not the result of institutional expansion on the part of Jerusalem. Loyalties to the temple were not in question, of course, for diaspora Jews regarded it as the actual manifestation of Jewish epic destiny in Judea. But synagogues were not outposts of the cult on the model of the stations in Judea and Palestine. There were no houses of prayer in Judea until the Roman period and, when synagogues finally did appear in Palestine, they were not built solely under the influence of the temple system, but in the Hellenistic cities of the north, on the model of Jewish diaspora communities. For the period before the war, for instance, Josephus mentions synagogues for Caesarea, Dora, and Tiberias—all Hellenistic cities under strong Seleucid and Roman influence. Local leadership and administration would have been the rule, and it is for this reason that scribal and Pharisaic influence from Jerusalem should not be taken for granted.[12]

In the diaspora, eager exploration of Hellenic culture was pursued by Jews at all social levels. Experimentation occurred with magic and the occult, mystery religions and popular literature, common forms of propaganda and dramatic productions. In the great centers of Hellenization, especially in Alexandria and Antioch, but also in Asia Minor, Jewish intellectuals mastered Greek *paideia*, rhetoric, literature, and philosophy. Schools were established. Literature was produced. Political strategies were devised in the interest of Jewish affairs. And citizenship was a common aspiration. But Jewish identity and sensibility also remained strong. How that was managed has always been a question.

Less is known about ritual practice in the diaspora than in Judea. But a great deal is known about the importance of the books of Moses. Transportable and specifically Jewish, the epic history apparently went along wherever Jews moved. In the cultural climate of the *polis*, Jewish imagination all but exploded as their epic charter was compared with Hellenistic literature, mythology, and philosophical thought. The age-old constraints placed by the Jewish love for the land and sense for creatureliness were

---

12. *Synagogues*. The article by Hengel, "Proseuche und Synagoge," reviews the evidence and sets forth the distinction between diaspora institutions and the stations of the temple system in Judea and Palestine. On the stations, see S. Hönig, "The Ancient City Square." Several studies on the origins and functions of the synagogue are available, including *The Synagogue*, by Carl Kraeling; and *The Synagogue*, by Joseph Gutman. On the foundation of Greek cities in Palestine, see V. Tcherikover, *Hellenistic Civilization*, chap. 2. For Galilee, see Freyne, *Galilee*, chap. 4. On the gradual evolvement of the Rabbinic academy, see J. Neusner, *From Politics to Piety*. The usual view is that Pharisaic-Rabbinic authority had been accepted throughout the diaspora synagogues by the turn of the third century, the traditional date for the codification of the Mishna. Hoffman's study of *The Canonization of the Synagogue Service* documents a much more interesting and laborious process that required several additional centuries.

pressed to the limits. They held. But the mind had been stretched in the meantime to assimilate all that could be comprehended without giving up on certain principles that defined the limits beyond which one must not go. The difference between the human and the divine was one limit. Another was the notion of specifically Jewish identity, a social notion as well as ethnic, for non-Jews could become Jews by being inducted (proselytes, circumcision). In the process of cultural exchange the epic law of Moses was rewritten once again, this time into the very structures of the cosmic orders of things, and they into it.[13]

Philo of Alexandria can be taken as a representative example. The creation story and a Greek conception of the world were aligned. Moses' legislation was seen to correspond to the structure of that created order. The patriarchal legends followed the paths of the mind's quest for virtue. And Moses was therefore regarded as the superior man—author of the laws (a legislator-king), visionary of the hidden *logos* of it all (a prophet), and hierophant of the path to excellence (a priest). Philo and his readers understood themselves to be "in the school of Moses." Ritual observance was not to be given up, according to Philo. But the allegorical reading of the epic law set ritual practice in a universe of meaning governed by Greek conceptuality. Philo's allegory of the books of Moses rationalized the synagogue, not the temple state in Judea. Philo's cosmos was, nevertheless, imagined on the model of the temple and its liturgy, as a great continual sacrifice of prayer in the cosmic house of God. Though fantastic and visionary in imagery, Philo's reading of the epic charter was not sectarian, not apocalyptic. It was cosmopolitan.[14]

Antioch presents yet another combination. If the Wisdom of Solomon and 4 Maccabees are of Syrian provenance, as is likely, they can be used to illustrate what could happen in a thoroughly Hellenistic milieu a bit more affected by the political history of Palestine. Both authors made the equation between Jewish law and Hellenistic concepts of the order in things (*physis, nomos, logos, aretē*). In the case of Wisdom, a fully mythologized cosmos similar to Philo's was used to comprehend the essential unity of the epic and legislative aspects of the Pentateuch. But the hasidim in Palestine had not been forgotten. Political events and persecution were very much matters of concern. The authors of 4 Maccabees and Wisdom both stood in sympathy with the conservatives and against the powers that threatened the practice of piety. The author of Wisdom describes the wicked rulers who look very much like the Hasmonean-Herodian establish-

---

13. *Hellenistic Judaism.* There is now a fine introduction to diaspora Judaism by J. Collins, *Between Athens and Jerusalem.*

14. *Philo of Alexandria.* For an introduction to Philo's life and work see Samuel Sandmel, *Philo of Alexandria.* A bibliography of scholarship on Philo has been prepared by Earle Hilgert, "Bibliographia Philoniana."

ment. But events are viewed from a distance and, though passionately hasidic in attitude, neither author can be called sectarian. The fantasies of resurrection, ascension to rulership, and ultimate victory over one's enemies are all graphically imagined. But the epic and the law do not stand or fall on the existence of a rectified temple liturgy. Moses' codes are about basic ritual identifiers (circumcision, foods, sabbath) on the one hand, and about social codes and ethics fit for the *polis*, on the other. Neither author can be imagined to have given up all hope at the destruction of the temple. The synagogue at Antioch would survive. It might even provide a quiet place after the war for some Essene to reflect on the end by writing an apocalypse (4 Ezra; Syrian Baruch). But after that, even the Essene would have been invited to join in the synagogue business at hand.[15]

3.4 Smaller Sects

The Greco-Roman age was not a time only for dismay and discontent. It was an ecumene that created opportunities for taking one's chances. Many did and found it exhilarating if not lucrative. But the trumpets that were heralds of the *Pax Romana* sounded like bugles to some. Generals keeping law and order for the sake of commerce and taxes alone could not really take the place of divine kings and sacred high priests. As the grand edifice of the Near Eastern temple state suffered sacrilege and settled into ruins, peoples at sea in the choppy waters of the Mediterranean mix of cultures sought one another out to keep alive old national and ethnic traditions. New groups also formed around new human interests. Mystery cults, clubs (*koinōniai*, or "associations"; *collegia*), theosophical societies, communes, gnostic sects, and other forms of social concentrations clustered to fill the void left vacant when the gods departed from the temples. Palestine was not excluded from this form of questing. As the hated Roman presence was prolonged, a restlessness set the climate for smaller sects to form.

There is little descriptive material about such groups. Josephus refused to give much information of a descriptive nature even about such a major sectarian movement as the Essenes, referring only to one or two ideas he thought they held as a "philosophical" school. But there is a wealth of literature remaining that was written just during this period, a literature best classed as sectarian. Known as Pseudepigrapha because scholars classed it first as "inauthentic," this large and growing corpus now appears to be a most authentic clue to the spirit of the times. It includes rewritten histories and epic poetry, quasi-apocalyptic visions, fictional testaments of

---

15. *Antioch*. Scholars generally acknowledge the importance of the Jewish community in Antioch. See M. Stern, "The Jewish Diaspora," 137–42. Dieter Georgi argues for the probability that the Wisdom of Solomon was written in Antioch in *Weisheit Salomos*, 395–97. On the Syrian provenance of 4 Maccabees, see G. W. E. Nickelsburg, *Jewish Literature*, 226–27.

the twelve patriarchs and others, fantastic legends about the early figures of the Hebrew epic, novels, dramas, dialogues, treatises, martyrologies, oracles, magical texts, prayers, odes, and psalms. Most of this literature has not been assigned to social settings, certainly not to any of the groups, movements, or institutions already discussed above. So smaller groups of various kinds need to be imagined. It is important to do this to set the social climate for the followers of Jesus. The description of one small Palestinian sect can serve to illustrate the phenomenon.

The Psalms of Solomon are a precious record of a Palestinian sect of hasidim. Neither purists of the Qumran variety, nor Pharisees of the lawyer type, the people who produced these psalms experienced together the history of Jerusalem from a certain point of view throughout most of the first century B.C.E. The psalms contain some observations about the events of 63 B.C.E. that could be taken as the impetus for the formation of the group. As the history of the sect disappears in the final stage of the collection of its prayers, it is obvious that this group had imagined itself into the future in a most creative way. Briefly, the story is as follows.

Taken off guard by Pompey's approach, the expectation nonetheless was that Jerusalem would not be harmed. The unexpected outcome forced the question why. It was concluded at first that the uncleanness of the temple establishment had been at fault. Much of the poetry is preoccupied with this problem, reflecting on the propriety of the "judgments" that fell both upon the iniquitous leaders (Aristobulus II and Hyrcanus II), as well as upon Pompey (who later was killed, 41 B.C.E.). But in a later layer of psalms the congregations of the righteous steal into the center of attention. Piety and faithfulness become the objects of meditation, and the underlying question is whether one dare think that piety taught and practiced in the "congregations" is enough to lay claim to the legacy of Israel. In the final psalms, an imaginative portrayal of the desire for a perfect restoration of Israel is given. There is no high priest, or temple, in the picture. Instead, a royal teacher of wisdom is at the center, cleansing Jerusalem with his instruction and caring for the congregations of the righteous. Christian scholars have always taken this psalm (Psalms of Solomon 17–18) to be an apocalyptic vision of the messianic hope of Judaism, a precursive desire fulfilled in Jesus as the Christ. It is, instead, an ideal image written by a poet within a small group of pious Jews who had dared to imagine an alternative to the contemporary temple cult. Sectarian mentality had all but given way in the courageous experiment in thinking. The psalmist had begun to consider the possibility that the little congregation itself might be worthy of the name Israel. Something like the houses of prayer of the Hellenistic Jewish communities had been espied and looked upon with great interest. The "royal" figure is hardly an apocalyptic warrior-king. He is a teacher. Any group thinking such a thought, no matter where this teacher might have been placed in the poet's projection of the ideal, would have survived the end of the temple system.[16]

3.5 Prophets and Popular Messiahs

There were, to be sure, "messiahs" popping up occasionally, as there were "prophets," sophists, wandering Cynics, magicians, and those who stepped forth in times of upheaval to cry out woes on all the parties. All of these could be taken as "divine men," figures with charismatic attraction given the proper social circumstances. In addition to sectarian formations, self-appointed spokesmen for seeing things differently, saying what should be done, or would-be leaders for doing something about the state of affairs, were also signs of the times. Individuals as well as sects could function as collectors for the powers dislodged from the sanctuary and the royal throne.[17]

Of particular interest for the study of Jesus are the terms miracle worker, prophet, and messiah. A discussion of Jesus as a miracle worker and prophet will be given in the next chapter. Here a brief word of caution should be given about taking talk of prophets and messiahs too theologically. As used in the first century, the term prophet had little to do with the authors of the prophetic books of the Hebrew scriptures, nor with memories that may have survived in Palestine of the social roles of those and other Hebrew prophets. The scholarly reconstruction of the Hebrew prophets, their messages and functions, needs to be set aside when asking about the meaning of the term in the first century. It was not a social role. No one would have recognized a "prophet" were one to have appeared. The term was used of any person who made a prediction. Some types of persons were known to be able to do that more frequently than others, such as a class of Egyptian priests, the Jerusalem high priest, the Sibyls, and so forth. Moses was a prophet for Philo, because he had privileged information about God's intentions for the universe, wrote "oracles" (that is, the Five Books), and predicted his own death. Josephus called some of the popular leaders of guerrilla bands in Palestine prophets because they announced in advance that God would give them victory.

---

16. *Pseudepigrapha.* The literary sources are available in English translation in James H. Charlesworth, *The Old Testament Pseudepigrapha.* The example given of a sectarian interpretation of the Psalms of Solomon is elaborated in B. Mack, "Wisdom Makes a Difference."

17. *The divine man.* A provocative study by J. Z. Smith, "The Temple and the Magician," sets the phenomenon of the holy man in the context of the cultural fragmentation created by the end of the ancient Near Eastern temple states. In the absence of centralized loci for social and cultural orientation, individuals could experiment with mechanisms traditionally institutionalized. The attraction of a clientele by a local or wandering public figure need not have required fulsome manifestations of charismatic or mysterious powers in order to have been called "divine."

In northern Palestine there does appear to have been a body of lore about the appearance of a prophet like Elijah who was expected to restore Israel to its former glories. But in the synoptic tradition where this motif was picked up in order to garner John the Baptist for Jesus and to garner both for claims to the heritage of hopes for Israel, the genre used was that of the *question* of identity, the enigmatic. Recognition was not automatic according to this tradition, and the debates that raged about these identifications of John and Jesus with Elijah reflect unlikely designation in the first place. People simply may not have thought at first either of John or of Jesus as prophets, given what can be reconstructed of their public postures.[18]

The term messiah is also troublesome. As used in the tradition of New Testament scholarship, messiah refers to an expectation, held more or less generally by all Jews of the time, that God would send a warrior-king to deliver Israel from the hands of its enemies. The basis for thinking that such an expectation was pervasive has been found in the poetic visions of Jewish apocalyptic and quasi-apocalyptic texts such as the Psalms of Solomon 17–18 (which is one of the classic loci). Recent studies have lodged two telling arguments against the traditional view. The first is that, though imaginary figures do appear in apocalyptic visions of the eschaton (the "end" of history), it is impossible to integrate them by assuming that each draws upon a commonly held notion of "the" Messiah. The second is that the texts at hand are not only sectarian but sophisticated, that is, written by intellectuals working at the level of texts and ideas, and whose relation to popular hopes and fears may therefore be one of imaginative distance.

In a fine recent article by Richard Horsley, the distinction between the poetry of the literati and popular conceptions of messianic leaders made it possible to paint quite a different picture. He argued that memories of an old kingdom tradition about the popular leader anointed to be king by the people may have survived in Palestine. Whether that can be demonstrated or not, the old pattern, well illustrated in the stories about David, was found by Horsley to be very helpful in redescribing the so-called messianic pretenders that sought to wrest control of Jerusalem away from the Romans in the period just before the Jewish War, during the Jewish War, and in the Bar Kokbah rebellion of 135 C.E. It is quite important to distinguish these popular leaders from a few earlier leaders of guerrilla bands seeking redress for specific grievances. The popular messiahs were also leaders of guerrilla bands to begin with, but their cause was both more diffuse and eventually more pretentious. They did not appear until the fifties in the wake of the

---

18. *Prophets.* For a careful consideration of the evidence for the notion and social role of prophets in the Hellenistic period and early Christianity see David Aune, *Prophecy in Early Christianity.* Extremely helpful distinctions in social behavior and ideology among popular movements of the time, including those led by "prophets," are available in Richard Horsley and John Hanson, *Bandits, Prophets, and Messiahs.*

famine in the forties, but then their banditry turned to open skirmishes, widespread plundering, and finally escalated into small army wars. Two factions actually had it out in the precincts of the temple, the leader called Simon winning that battle, donning the robes of royal authority, but only as a sign of his opposition to the Romans at the moment of his defeat. He was the one taken to Rome as the king of the Jews and executed. One can see that the relationship between the popular warrior-king and the poetic visions of the anointed of the Lord is tenuous. They do share some features in common. But the difference between the ideal image and the actual manifestation, supposing the two phenomena go together, is painful. The ideal images would not have been helpful in identifying the right messiah to follow, supposing one were expecting a messiah to come along. It is very important to understand that ideal messiahs were ideals, and that popular messiahs did not come along every day. The few thought by scholars to have been "received" as popular messiahs were actually leaders of popular resistance movements that formed in times of critical political unrest, men whose social roles were matters of dispute. Galilee during Jesus' time was not a chaotic social situation. It was very quiet under Herod Antipas. And, one final observation, neither the ideal visions of messianic rulers, nor the actual manifestations of popular messiahs were anti-Jewish, anti-temple phenomena. All were anti-Roman. [19]

---

19. *Messiahs.* The study referred to is Horsley, "Popular Messianic Movements." Horsley argues convincingly that the phenomenon commonly called Zealots did not occur until just before the Jewish War, and that it was a combination of banditry and general civil insurrection caused by the breakdown of the social system at that time. Horsley prefers to reserve the term messianism for political movements on the model of old traditions according to which kings were chosen and anointed by popular acclaim. He argues that several incidents upon the death of Herod the Great, recorded by Josephus, were messianic in this sense, protests caused by particular grievances. Freyne, on the other hand, has argued convincingly that these incidents were politically motivated by residual Hasmonean intrigue accidentally located in Galilee, that they did not arise from indigenous Galilean discontent (*Galilee,* 208–55). A careful reading of Horsley, Freyne, and Hoehner leads to the conclusion that Galilee under Herod Antipas was not the scene of insurrectionist or apocalyptic excitements instigated by messianic prophets and pretenders. Hoehner's statement may be quoted: "In the first century A.D. one can cite many instances of trouble in Judaea, whereas there is no record of any rebellion or anarchy in Galilee or Peraea during Antipas' reign" (*Herod Antipas,* 57).

Horsley's point about the difference between "messianic" texts produced by intellectuals and popular leaders of various kinds of movements is, however, well-taken. See now the studies in J. Neusner, *Judaisms and Their Messiahs.* These studies call into question the scholarly assumption about Jewish expectations of "the" messiah. The several poetic images commonly grouped together as "messianic" texts do not derive from a single conception, but from a mode of scribal activity that is best described as the reimagination of Israel's power and authority. As for the common scholarly assumption of a pervasive expectation of the "eschatological" (re)appearance of Elijah or "a prophet like Moses," see the critical and convincing arguments to the contrary by Horsley, "'Like One of the Prophets of Old.'"

2

JESUS
IN GALILEE

In the gospels Jesus is portrayed as a man of superior wisdom and power.
The nature of his wisdom extends from penetrating insight into the wily
ways of human behavior to knowledge about God and his purposes. Jesus'
divine knowledge includes confidence about his own special relationship to
God and about his singular mission to inaugurate God's kingdom. The
kingdom of God will transform the human situation. Jesus' power contributes to this program mainly by means of miracles. He casts out demons
and heals sick people. Miracles also attend other kinds of activity, however,
providing an aura of divine endowment to all Jesus does and to all that
happens to him. The story ends with a portent at his crucifixion of great
historical and cosmic significance, followed by his miraculous resurrection.
This gospel portrait presents the scholar with a challenge.

The presence of myth and miracle in the gospel was noted as a problem
early in the quest for the historical Jesus. The goal since then has been to
separate the miraculous and the mythic from the historical. By historical,
scholars have usually meant a plausible picture of Jesus unadorned by the
imaginative attributions of the gospel accounts.

Since the gospels are the primary sources for the history of Jesus, and
because they present the problems they do, the quest has been a labor in the
discipline of historical literary criticism. At first it was thought a simple
matter to peel away the illusory and retrieve the plausible lying behind all of
the accounts. In the course of critical analysis, however, the very framework
of the gospel story came unglued, leaving the scholar with a deskful of
fragments and a picture of many diverse memory traditions filling the gap
between Jesus and the authors of the gospels. These fragments are the
pieces of the puzzle with which scholars have to work. They have been
pored over, collected in piles by type, and subjected to many comparative
and critical analyses. It has been found that, in some cases, a particular type
of material may represent a distinct memory tradition. The clearest example of this is given with the sayings of Jesus, a collection of which had
already been made by some group of Jesus' followers long before it was
incorporated into the gospel accounts (the sayings source known as Q).

Other types of memory tradition are given with the miracle stories, the pronouncement stories, the parables, the biographical narratives, and the narratives of the passion. Each type has been carefully analyzed with respect to literary form, modes of transmission, rules of elaboration, reasons for collection, and signs of combination with other types of material in the composition of larger literary units. Each has also been scrutinized for reminiscences of the historical Jesus. All have been thought to derive ultimately from early memories, but none has been found unembellished by very active imaginations. In the process of rehearsal, replication, and elaboration, layers of signification transformed memories into myths. Thus the problem of myth and history has hardly been resolved. It has in fact been compounded. That is because the several traditions of memory cannot readily be merged into a single, coherent picture. Each type of memory tradition requires separate, special handling.[1]

The framework stories of the gospels are the most highly mythologized type of material. They include the narratives of Jesus' birth, baptism, transfiguration, crucifixion, resurrection, and post-resurrection appearances. The transfiguration story is purely mythological, as are the birth narratives, the story of the empty tomb, and the appearances of the resurrected Jesus to the disciples. Critical scholars would not say that these derive from reminiscences. The baptism story is also mythic, but in this case may derive from lore about Jesus and John the Baptist. Lore about John and Jesus is present in the sayings tradition, in a pronouncement story, and other legends both in Q and in Mark. John the Baptist was a public figure whose social role was similar to that of Jesus and whose followers were regarded by some followers of Jesus as competitors. Except for the baptism story, however, there is no indication that Jesus and John crossed paths. As the story stands it serves to link Jesus up with a mythic view of Israel's history and point up the contrast between Jesus and John: Jesus will not baptize with water as John does, but with the spirit. So the lore is mostly legend to confirm Jesus' importance as a figure of epic proportions. It belongs to the later layers of Q, composed not much before the time of Mark, and thus represents a stage of reflection where interest in

---

1. *The Jesus traditions*. The gospels, viewed as biographies during the nineteenth century, came unglued early in the twentieth. Two major works traditionally are credited with the dismantling. In 1901 William Wrede published *Das Messiasgeheimnis in den Evangelien* (*The Messianic Secret in the Gospels*) in which he demonstrated that the theme of secrecy about Jesus' identity was a theological device of the evangelist and could not be used to reconstruct the "development" of Jesus' own "self-consciousness" as nineteenth-century lives of Jesus had assumed. Then, in 1919, Karl Ludwig Schmidt published *Der Rahmen der Geschichte Jesu* (*The Framework of the Story of Jesus*), showing that the gospel was composed of small units of events about which the author had no precise information, and that the overall plan for connecting them together in a single narrative was not an historical memory, but the author's own construction. It was this work that launched "form criticism," the study of types of material independently of the gospel "framework."

the founder of the Jesus movements gave rise to biographical depiction. The biographical narratives do not make a set, do not constitute a memory tradition, and cannot be used to reconstruct the life of Jesus. Their function in the composition of the gospel will be discussed in chapter 12.[2]

The passion narratives are also mythic accounts, containing as they do a ritual meal with soteriological symbolism and a miraculous story of the crucifixion. The account as a whole is so realistic, however, that scholars have been reticent to think of it as fiction. Many have thought it firsthand report. Lore can be assumed, of course, for all Jesus people must have known about Jesus' death. But there were many ways of remembering, understanding, and accepting his death without entertaining ideas about its critical significance as Mark has it. The Q people, for instance, accepted it, regarding it eventually as part of a "prophet's" vocation. There is no evidence in Q for interest in Jesus' death beyond that. Neither is there any interest at all in Jesus' death in the miracle stories or in the pre-Markan pronouncement stories. One might think that at least the anti-temple theme, a narrative element fundamental to the passion account, would be in evidence here and there in other Jesus materials. There is not even a trace of an anti-temple polemic. Neither is there any in all of the Pauline corpus, a large literature prior to Mark stemming from the Hellenistic Christ cult where Jesus' death was central to its myth. So the passion narratives present the historian with a peculiar problem. They constitute a distinctive body of material not integrated with the other Jesus traditions before Mark. They relate, moreover, a series of events in Jerusalem rife with motivational nuance and heavy with christological signification neither of which follows readily upon the kind of activity reported for Jesus in Galilee. Traditions stemming from Jesus' activity in Galilee simply do not contain any narrative lore or allusion to any profound significance of the crucifixion of Jesus. The passion account will have to be discussed later as a separate problem in chapter 9. For now, only the fact of Jesus' crucifixion in Jerusalem can be entered as a datum in the quest for the historical Jesus. The nature of Jesus' activity in Galilee cannot be determined from the gospel account of his decision to go to Jerusalem in the knowledge that he would die there. That account is a Markan design to be discussed in part 3.

The situation is somewhat more hopeful with the sayings, the pronouncement stories, and the miracle stories. All are embellished traditions, however, and each portrays a different role for Jesus. Issues have therefore arisen in the attempts to combine the several social roles espied. Casting out demons is difficult to imagine for one adept at telling parables, for instance.

---

2. *Framework stories.* There is no scholarly discourse about the framework stories as a type or set of narrative material. On evidence in Q that John the Baptist was first thought about in terms reminiscent of Cynic social roles, see Leif Vaage, "To Wear Soft Raiment."

An aphoristic social critique suggests one stance, an apocalyptic pronouncement of doom another, yet both kinds of sayings are included in the collection known as Q. Public performance in the Q tradition, moreover, fits uneasily with the institutional conflicts addressed in the pronouncement stories, and so forth. Thus there are problems given with the different types of material. Opinions vary about the relative merit of each for a reconstruction of the historical Jesus. There is at the moment no firm consensus about Jesus, the nature of his activity, or the reasons for the groups that formed in his name and carried these traditions. Nevertheless, most scholars would agree that what can be known about Jesus will be found among these materials. They have been the object of a great deal of scholarly investigation.

Detailed knowledge has accumulated around each type of material, working forward and backward along the lines of its literary and social histories. Layers and stages have been determined and, in each case, some probabilities about the earlier forms of reminiscence have been established. These need to be taken seriously and brought together in some softly focused characterization of Jesus. Plausibility will be determined by a social role that is recognizable, a stance that is consistent, a mode of address that bears the marks of integrity, and a style that might be understood to have been effective within the social environment in Galilee in the late twenties of the first century.

Under effect, the phenomenon of group formation and movements stemming from Jesus' activity must be included. Since there were many different kinds of Jesus movements, a form of influence must be discerned that can account for that diversity. Diversity is thus a problem and a clue. Sayings collections, pronouncement stories, miracle stories, parables, each appear to have traveled through different configurations of group formation. These are also the types of memory at the historian's disposal for the reconstruction of the historical Jesus. Where overlap or convergence can be determined at the early end of these diverging traditions, something may be said about the man who started it all. It will be important to indicate what the earliest traditions make probable, for the gap to be explored in this study is that between a plausible historical Jesus and the gospel written about him by Mark. The plan for this chapter is to discuss the sayings material first (sections 1–3), then turn to the question of miracles (section 4). Because three of these literary forms will receive concentrated attention in part 2 (parables, pronouncement stories, and miracle stories), the discussions at this point can be brief. They are mentioned here to paint the larger picture for the study to follow. In the case of the Sayings Source (Q), however, a tradition that will not be taken up for detailed study later because of its problematic relation to Mark's composition, a slightly longer introductory discussion will be required.

1. APHORISTIC WISDOM

The teachings of Jesus permeate most of the traditions in his memory. They range in type from aphorisms, proverbs, parables, and pronouncements, to apocalyptic speeches and gnosticizing dialogues and discourses. Q and the Gospel of Thomas consist almost entirely of speech material. Teachings also occur in Mark and in the sources special to Matthew and Luke. The Gospel of John contains discourse attributed to Jesus, and speech material of all kinds extends into a large corpus of extra-canonical and gnostic literatures.

The bulk of this enormous corpus of sayings cannot be authentic. Oral transmission, replication, novel application, the need for authoritative pronouncement, what the Greeks called speech-in-character, and the exercise of mythic imagination are ways scholars have talked about the growth of the traditions of the sayings of Jesus. Elaboration of traditional material and the attribution to Jesus of new sayings are in evidence from the earliest written sources. Sorting through the different types and working back to the earliest forms of this material have been laborious undertakings. Recently, however, three different streams of scholarship, focused on Q, the parables of Jesus, and the pronouncement stories, have offered proposals about the nature of the teaching that Jesus must have given at the beginning. These proposals converge in a very interesting way. The story of that convergence is worth a brief review.

1.1 The Sayings of Jesus in Q

The source for the sayings of Jesus common to Matthew and Luke (Q from *Quelle* meaning source) has been studied with great care in recent scholarship. It was a collection composed by followers of Jesus who thought his message important and who saw themselves called to continue its propagation in public. The contents of the collection is a mixture of wisdom sayings, apocalyptic announcements, prophetic pronouncements, a few parables, a chreia (anecdote) or two, and a touch of biographical narrative about the preaching of John the Baptist and Jesus' temptation. On the surface of it Q appears to be evidence for Jesus' prophetic activity, the proclamation of an imminent if not apocalyptic appearance of the kingdom of God accompanied by a stern call to repentance and harsh warnings of impending judgment on those who refuse the message. Since the turn of the century the prevailing opinion among scholars has been that this picture of Jesus was correct. He was an apocalyptic preacher. The problem has been, therefore, to make sense of the large number of wisdom sayings that do not seem to express that kind of urgency.

The discovery of apocalyptic speech in the sayings of Jesus took place around the turn of the century. Before then, during the nineteenth-century quest, the teachings of Jesus had been understood as instruction in the universal truths of a superior and humane ethic. The enlightenment view was certainly an improvement over the older medieval reading according to which Jesus offered edification in the plan of salvation, the doctrines of the church, and the way to reach heaven. Nevertheless, the improvement was not profound. The nineteenth-century scholars were able to regard Jesus as a superior teacher primarily by means of a translation of the medieval teachings into rationalistic categories. Their conception of Jesus' system of ethic was not based on a careful reading of the texts. The gospels were analyzed rather with the problems of myth and miracle in mind, the deletion of which was thought to free the teacher and his teaching from the bonds of superstition and historical contingency. When the texts were finally read critically at the end of the century, a witch's brew of fantastic prophecies, visions, and woes was discovered. This created considerable consternation and silenced facile references to the teachings of Jesus for a generation while the meaning of apocalyptic was explored.[3]

Many solutions to this dilemma were finally proposed, the most profound and clever of which was that of Rudolf Bultmann. In a little book first published in 1926 (ET *Jesus and the Word*), Bultmann turned the discovery of apocalyptic discourse to good advantage. He argued that Jesus was both a teacher (rabbi) of wisdom as well as a preacher (prophet) of an eschatological message. The tension created by the two modes of address was on purpose, a sign of Jesus' genius. He noted that there was a strange lack of content both to Jesus' wisdom ethic and to his proclamation of the imminent kingdom of God. He concluded that Jesus was not engaged in the transmission of ideas, but in the task of calling for human transformation. Translating Jesus' speech into existentialist terms, Bultmann interpreted the tension as a call to "radical obedience," an ethical demand marked by urgency and openness to the future, but without content or prescription. Bultmann's proposal was to have a deep and lasting effect on New Testament scholarship. He had found a way to accommodate apocalyptic language and retain a view of Jesus that Christians again could understand. Scholars in other countries have debated his program of existential inter-

---

3. *The discovery of apocalyptic.* The apocalyptic hypothesis was proposed in 1892 by Johannes Weiss, *Die Predigt Jesu vom Reich Gottes* (*Jesus' Proclamation of the Kingdom of God*). Schweitzer reconstructed his "life" of Jesus based upon the apocalyptic hypothesis, *The Quest of the Historical Jesus*, 330–403. According to Schweitzer, Jesus imagined himself to be the agent destined to accomplish the apocalyptic reversal and, though he realized that his message would not be accepted in Jerusalem, marched heroically to his death for the cause. This picture of Jesus, so radically different than the nineteenth-century "lives," and so uncomfortable for modern scholars, brought the attempt to write a biography to an end. Nevertheless, transferred to the "teachings" of Jesus, the discovery of apocalyptic was accepted. Since then the problem of apocalyptic has dominated scholarship on the historical Jesus as well as on all aspects of early Christian life and thought.

pretation, and some revisions have been proposed, but few have failed to appreciate the service Bultmann rendered in redeeming Jesus' apocalyptic language as a profoundly prophetic call. Since Bultmann the even balance between apocalyptic speech and wisdom discourse in the teachings of Jesus has been accepted as the rule.

Scholarship on Q has led to other conclusions. The task has been to establish the text common to Matthew and Luke, a text each used somewhat differently as they composed their gospels. Parallels in the Gospel of Thomas also have been found instructive, as has the question of what to do about some overlap between Q material and sayings found in the Gospel of Mark. In the course of these investigations a number of critical issues have emerged that have not been resolved. When and why oral tradition was written down, whether Mark knew Q or some slightly different, parallel or earlier version, and what to make of yet another selection of sayings in the Gospel of Thomas are some of these questions. On two points, however, different theories about Q show some signs of agreement. One is that Q represents a late stage in a dominant tradition of activity oriented to the message of Jesus. The other is that earlier stages in the tradition can be isolated and defined. A number of methods have been used to determine earlier layers in the collection. There is no precise agreement among the results of these efforts, to be sure. Each attempt uses different criteria for the assignment of sayings to this level or that. And yet, just because of the manifold criteria, an emerging consensus about the nature of the earlier layer gains in credibility. The layers appear to break along the lines of aphoristic wisdom on the one side and apocalyptic prediction and pronouncements of doom on the other. Aphoristic wisdom is characteristic for the earlier layer. This turns the table on older views of Jesus as an apocalyptic preacher and brings the message of Jesus around to another style of speech altogether.[4]

J. Dominic Crossan has just published a study of the sayings of Jesus

---

4. *Q.* The most recent study of the "redaction history" of Q is Kloppenborg's *The Formation of Q.* He summarizes a rich scholarship in detail and makes several advances on previous work. One is that, by analyzing the literary genres of the smaller units, the blocks of units, and the overall structure of Q, Kloppenborg is able to exercise a control on the investigation of the growth of the Q tradition. His conclusions support the work of several other scholars who have argued for stages in the tradition on the basis of content as well as redaction-critical indices. Earlier works of importance are Dieter Lührmann, *Die Redaktion der Logienquelle;* H. Koester, "One Jesus and Four Primitive Gospels"; and Arland Jacobson, "Wisdom Christology in Q." Kloppenborg calls the earliest layer "sapiential," the later "the announcement of judgment." A discussion of the growth of the Q tradition in relation to the social history of its tradents is given below in chap. 3, sect. 2.1. Kloppenborg projects the publication of the text of Q in the form of a synopsis, in both Greek and English for Foundations and Facets. For a complete bibliography on Q studies, together with an assessment of the current agreements and issues, see J. Delobel, *Logia.* The Gospel of Thomas is now available for comparison with synoptic materials in English translation in R. Funk, *New Gospel Parallels,* vol. 2.

called *In Fragments, The Aphorisms of Jesus.* His study does not engage the question of Q and its layers of tradition, but it does propose a thesis about the primary characteristic of the sayings traditions. That characteristic is, as the subtitle shows, the aphoristic quality of its formulations. Crossan's approach is an application of a modern theory of criticism to the problem of tracing the transmission of maxim-like materials. Its appropriateness to the sayings of Jesus is astounding. No general truths are proffered. Insights are condensed and the relationships between things that are frequently taken for granted are explored. Depending on context, a critique of cultural conventions is a distinct possibility. But the mode is invitational, exploring seams and discrepancies, or creating them, to clear a space for rethinking. Crossan's work corroborates earlier essays on the proverbs among the teachings of Jesus by William Beardslee, and fits very well with the most recent study of the earliest layer of Q by Kloppenborg. To notice the aphoristic quality of the sayings of Jesus and isolate an early "sapiential" layer in their collection is to define a particular style of speech of great significance for the quest of the historical Jesus.

1.2 The Parables

Crossan's application of a critical poetics to the sayings of Jesus stands in a distinctly American tradition of scholarship associated mainly with the parables of Jesus. Amos Wilder pointed out the possibilities of a rhetorical approach to early Christian language in the early 1960s and Robert Funk demonstrated the difference a poetics would make in his *Language, Hermeneutic, and Word of God* (1966). In this book, Funk analyzed the mode of communication distinctive for several New Testament genres, but it was his chapter on the parables that caught the attention of other scholars. Understanding was not to be gained primarily by comparison with first-century ideas about wisdom and apocalyptic views of history, Funk said, but more by paying attention to formal features and their effect upon the imagination. Wilder, Crossan, Dan Via, and others soon joined Funk in a major project to investigate the narrative structure of the parables and assess their poetic function. This will be discussed more fully in chapter 6.

The critical approach suggests that parables do not convey information. A skillful employment of metaphor casts up an image for consideration. Because parables are narrative in form, the image is about something that happens. Thus the listener is invited to consider the way the story runs in relation to the way in which the listener had been accustomed to thinking about how things go. A wide range of comparisons and contrasts is possible ("parable" means "comparison"), from inviting sharpened observation to imagining just the reverse. Thus parables have their effect in the judgments listeners make as the story is imagined. If the conventional has suffered critique, it is the listener who must decide what to do, how to put the pieces back together.

Scholars have usually assumed that most of the parables came from Jesus. The assumption has been that the parables must come from Jesus because of their original qualities and their lack of specific reference to later matters of concern to his followers. This assumption will no longer do, for creativity cannot be limited to Jesus, and many parables have since been found better explained as later compositions. In a recent essay, Funk acknowledged this problem before proposing a list of those parables that might be considered authentic on the basis of critical scholarly consensus. The list contains six narrative parables and seven metaphors expanded in the direction of narrative. Since the total number of parables transmitted in the synoptic traditions is only thirty nine, Funk's list represents a strong survival. The probabilities are, therefore, that Jesus did speak in parables. The parabolic style of speech matches the aphoristic characteristics of the sayings. Both the parables and the aphoristic sayings suggest the same kind of critical stance toward one's social world, moreover, and the same invitational mode of address to one's audience. Neither suggests a program or a preachment. A lively social setting must be imagined for either to have been heard and remembered. Taken together, then, parables and aphorisms begin to define a very interesting profile of public utterance.[5]

1.3 The Pronouncements

A third class of sayings material is found in the pronouncement stories. These are brief anecdotes in which Jesus finds a clever answer to an embarrassing question or situation. The distinguishing feature of these narratives is the challenge created by the situation to which the pronouncement responds. Robert Tannehill has produced a helpful typology of the relations between saying and setting, noting the various ways in which the pronouncement stories invite the listener to consider the pronouncement. Others have explored the similarity of the pronouncement stories to the Hellenistic anecdote called chreia. It is now possible to describe the logic of response to a challenging situation common to Hellenistic chreiai and the pronouncement stories. Conventional wisdom comes to expression in the

---

5. *Parables.* R. Funk delivered a lecture entitled "The Real Jesus. What did he really say?" at the University of Redlands, California, in May, 1981. His list of candidates for authenticity are: the Great Supper (Luke 14:16–24 pars), the Laborers in the Vineyard (Matt 20:1–16), the Prodigal (Luke 15:11–32), the Samaritan (Luke 10:30–35), the Unjust Steward (Luke 16:1–8), and the Unmerciful Servant (Matt 18:23–24). Funk's conclusion to a consideration of these parables, together with the non-narrative parables and some aphorisms (thirty-six items in all), is worth noting: "As a consequence, Jesus could not have shared the popular apocalyptic expectation of chronological cataclysm." See also the results of the meeting of the Jesus Seminar in Funk, "Poll on the Parables."

challenge. The response turns the tables by means of a clever rejoinder that picks up on the assumptions underlying the challenge and frustrates them by means of another consideration. Invariably, the response cannot apply to the situation without destroying the conventional wisdom thrown up as a challenge. Wit, skillful manipulation of the limits of conventional logic, and delight in repartee are the marks of this manner of conversation.

Authenticity cannot be claimed for most of the pronouncements in the gospels as the stories now stand. But many stories retain the telltale remnants of a rather playful mode of response. These stories have been elaborated in the process of retelling and all fall eventually into very serious preoccupations characteristic of the later Jesus movements. By reconstructing the earlier forms of the stories, however, an approach to discourse and to social critique is manifest that agrees exactly with the style of the parables and the aphorisms of Jesus. This agreement makes it possible to imagine the manner in which Jesus must have addressed his world.[6]

2. SOCIAL CRITIQUE

Jesus was born and raised in Galilee, no doubt from a Jewish family, evidently bright, and apparently educated. His influence indicates that he engaged in some kind of public activity, expressing his views about social circumstances and addressing followers in a challenging way. His followers took what he had to say as a message. Patterns of behavior were changed, conversations started, apparently about something called the kingdom of God, and group movements were formed. The historian's challenge is to understand how all of that happened. It would be helpful, therefore, to know about Jesus' manner of life, message, and effect upon people.

The records, unfortunately, do not supply that kind of information. Only his followers left any record of his activity at all, and those records were not written for the purpose of keeping alive the memory of an interesting person. They were written to authorize matters held to be important and foundational for their cause. Nevertheless, it is from those records and their witness to his influence that some things can be inferred. One bit of evidence is given with the style of Jesus' discourse preserved by his followers. It indicates a certain stance Jesus must have taken toward his social world. Another is given with the content of that discourse. It can be studied for its message. Still another kind of evidence is given with the stories that relate how Jesus affected people. They can be studied for social motives.

---

6. *Pronouncement stories*. Tannehill's typology is worked out in "The Pronouncement Story and Its Types." A detailed discussion is given below in chap. 7. A list of the pronouncement stories in Mark reduced to the form of a chreia is given in Appendix I.

What can reasonably be imagined about the historical Jesus will have to be drawn from a careful analysis of these bits of evidence.[7]

2.1 Jesus' Stance

Judging from the teachings of Jesus as reconstructed above, the subject matter for Jesus' discourse and the source for its imagery was contemporary life in Galilee. The range of observation is fairly spread. It includes the way landed estates operated, the fact of absentee landlordship, householders and their responsibilities, and what servants had to do to please their masters and survive. The discourse addresses the disparity between the rich and the poor. Finery, king's palaces, sumptuous dining, and soft, luxurious living came under review. Less was said about craftsmen and soldiers, but merchants and lesser civic officials such as tax collectors and judges were matters of Jesus' interest. The observation of farming activity yielded a rich supply of images and metaphors. Daily life appears almost to have been a preoccupation. Neighbors and strangers, requests, gifts, and hassles, wages, payments, and basic obligations all were seen as matters that made a difference. Losing things, knocking on doors late at night, and what to do about salt, and bread, and wine took Jesus' attention. Sons and daughters, the way women lived and were treated, and ethnic animosities are only some of the social relationships that centered Jesus' concerns.

Jesus' observation about these things was apparently penetrating. His images are clear and come immediately to the point. The economy of language is noteworthy in light of the insights his speech makes possible. He notes only distinctive characteristics, pinpoints fundamental issues, and describes critical moments. Much is taken for granted, left in place, and all but celebrated simply by being noticed as a piece of a very interesting world. Critical observation slips into social critique quite easily, though, manifesting judgments about the quality of life as lived. It is here that Jesus' peculiar "wisdom" begins to be discerned. Basic considerations about fairness and the consequences of unequal exchange bubble up here and

---

7. *Jesus the Galilean.* There is little evidence external to the gospel traditions that demands locating Jesus in Galilee. Critical inquiry into those traditions nonetheless leads to a firm scholarly consensus on this point. Many of these considerations have to do with the settings, topics, and patterns of behavior characteristic for the earliest layers of the several memory traditions about Jesus. Others have to do with the patterns of group formation that followed, most of which give some evidence of Galilean connections or provenance. That Jesus' family was Jewish is to be inferred from the concerns common to all group formations stemming from him, especially those that appealed to some family connection with him. All Jesus movements, it should be noted, sought to account for their novelty in terms of Jewish questions and answers drawn from epic prototypes. Jesus' Jewishness is, however, not self-evident from the nature of his discourse. His discourse reveals a remarkable openness to Hellenistic culture at a popular level, a stance that makes Galilean provenance quite plausible.

there as if from a strong current flowing beneath the surface of a river. Sources of common anxiety appear to have been subjects of meditation. Behaving simply and out of hand seems to have been something of an ideal felt to be frustrated by the constraints of social convention. The aphoristic quality of his speech shows how Jesus handled the situation. Great pronouncements were not made about the wrong and right of things. Instead, the critical moment, or an aspect of incongruity, or some conflict of interest, set of pretensions, or designs upon others would be exposed. Insofar as social conventions might be viewed as giving structure to such situations of imbalance, Jesus' critical insights could be called a social critique.

Jesus' social critique, though pointed and sharp in particular cases of human event, did not include polemic against specific institutions. He did not name those who were at fault, nor did he suggest an alternative program to set things right. He did not take the Romans to task, nor inveigh against the temple establishment. He did not suggest withdrawal from strife and ungodliness to form a convent. He did not propose to do battle with Pharisees or synagogue leaders for the control or cleansing of a religious institution. He did not philosophize about the *polis*, how to legislate a better law, what to do about tyranny, or the chances of finding a perfect king. He did not suggest a people's revolt to storm the palace in Tiberias, or raise a guerrilla band to march on Jerusalem. He proposed no political program. He did not organize a church.

The basis for his commentary upon the social world in Galilee was some world of wisdom thought. Judging from his way with words, Jesus had an agile mind. But he was not an intellectual at work with the history of ideas. His conversation was not with other schoolmen or authors, and there is no evidence of exegetical interest. He did not spend time searching the scriptures, or using a scriptural mandate or model for making commentary upon his social scene. The occasional occurrence of metaphors, symbols, or narrative themes that may allude to Jewish epic traditions are best understood as taken from lore alive at the level of folk transmission. He may have read some scriptures, just as he may have read Meleager. But his mode of address and mediation was not hermeneutical. His perspective on the whole was from below. Critique began with human experience on the byways and would have to work its way up and out later, by his followers, to encompass kings and commanders, literati, their books, and their systems of thought. Jesus was a peasant with a sense for the precariousness of existence. He assumed a stance on the margins of society and simply invited others to share his view.[8]

---

8. *The "teaching" of Jesus.* The picture given draws upon the sayings traditions, including the parables, bracketing the so-called prophetic and apocalyptic additions by later

2.2 The Social Scene

Those whom Jesus invited to share his perspective on things were Galileans. Galilee had been annexed by the Hasmoneans only in 104–103 B.C.E., then ruled by Roman appointees (kings and tetrarchs) from 63 B.C.E. At the time of Jesus it was a separate tetrarchy under Herod Antipas. Seán Freyne argued for a strong Israelite tradition in Galilee in spite of the cultural mix of its peoples and six hundred years of international designs upon its lands. He did this in order to establish the plausibility of strong loyalties to Jerusalem and, one suspects, claim a thoroughly Jewish context for Jesus and his message. The center for old Israelite traditions centered in Samaria, however, at Shechem and Mount Gerizim, and this center for North Palestinian loyalties was a source of deep hostility toward Jerusalem. Galilee was not Samaria, to be sure, and Jewish pilgrims from Galilee frequently ran into trouble while passing through Samaria. This has been taken as a sign that Galileans and Samaritans were sharply divided over the issue of Jerusalem. It need not be interpreted that way at all.

Galilee was open country, more complex in cultural mixture, and accustomed to accommodation in the face of hegemony. Longstanding communities of Jews are to be expected as part of the cultural mix. Other Jews had recently colonized in the interest of the temple state system. As recently as the first century B.C.E. Herod the Great had settled a colony of Babylonian Jews in Gaulanitis to help protect the overland route for pilgrims. Old Israelite memories were no doubt still alive and may have been quickened in patterns more sympathetic to Jerusalem than happened in Samaria. But Jerusalem did not take Galilee for granted, nor were the rabbis impressed at a later time with Galilean readiness to learn the cultic laws. Worldly-wise and accustomed to diversity, Galileans as a whole were not disposed to take sides in the great dramas of foreign kings and their kingdoms. It had always been a land centered on its own interests and happy not to be in the center of international intrigue. It had survived quite well on the borders of things political. For many Galileans, annexation meant merely that Jerusalem, not Antioch, was now the center of power with which they had to deal.

The land of Galilee was prized for its inland resorts and fine produce. It lay at the southern tip of Phoenicia, crisscrossed by major routes to Damascus, Tyre, Caesarea, Samaria, and the Transjordan. Travel seaward to the ports and northward to Syria and Antioch was at least as important for Galileans as traveling south to Jerusalem. Ideas traveled as well as goods

followers, as well as pronouncements on sectarian matters, also better understood as later additions. The picture is a caricature, helpful nevertheless as a focused summary of recognizable material regularly acknowledged by scholars to bid for early reminiscence if not authenticity.

and officials, and seats of learning were not far away. The land was literally ringed with Hellenistic cities founded by the Seleucids. Many of them aspired to become small centers of Hellenistic culture. Meleager, a well-known Cynic, poet, and epigrammatist of the first century B.C.E., was born and raised in Gadara in the Transjordan to the east of Galilee, then educated in Tyre to the west. Galilee was not insulated from the Hellenistic age. Galilee had its share of social injustice, perhaps, and more than its share of precarious living. But it was of the general kind created by the designs of others upon its land, people and produce, and by the deterioration of the Hellenistic age under the thoughtless Romans. Galilee was in fact an epitome of Hellenistic culture on the eve of the Roman era.

It would be wrong to assume that the fierce infighting, sectarian formations, and anti-Roman hostilities characteristic of Judea were typical for Galilean disaffection as well. Galilee was not Judea. For a Galilean, Roman rule would not have signified a pollution of the land, but only another chapter in hegemony. Once again the legate and his army were stationed in Antioch. Now the king building an ostentatious palace on the Hellenistic model in Tiberias happened to be a Roman tetrarch. Local shrines and traditions were no doubt still alive as well. And there was the constant buzz of crafts, commerce, and conversation from villages to the Hellenistic cities. Judaism was not a monolithic system in control of the culture and state of Galilee. And Galilee was not a hotbed of Jewish apocalyptic fervor.[9]

---

9. *Galilee*. The picture is drawn from standard histories of Palestine during the Greco-Roman period. See Michael Avi-Yonah, ed., *The Herodian Period;* Salo Baron, *A Social and Religious History of the Jews;* Elias Bickermann, *From Ezra to the Last of the Maccabees;* Harold Hoehner, *Herod Antipas;* A'haron Oppenheimer, *The 'Am Ha'aretz;* Emil Schürer, *The History of the Jewish People;* Abraham Schalit, *König Herodes;* and M. Stern, "The Reign of Herod." Descriptions of the social and cultural climate in Galilee written by scholars interested in New Testament questions tend to highlight "religious" phenomena. Some would like to see Galileans as predominantly "Jewish," loyal to the temple, or even Pharisaic in temperament. Others emphasize revolutionary tendencies, messianism, and apocalyptic fervor as peculiarly Galilean. Seán Freyne has recently argued for the "Jewish" hypothesis in a truly major work, *Galilee*. His thesis is that old Israelite traditions still alive in Galilee predisposed Galilean "Jews" to look with favor upon the annexation of Galilee by the Hasmoneans. A critical reading of the considerable evidence he collects about Galilee and its culture, however, leaves one uneasy with the conclusions he draws. Freyne must repeatedly discount the signs of cultural accommodation and compromise in the interest of arguing for his thesis. Appeal to old Israelite traditions is hardly persuasive, given the history of local loyalties and sectarian interests of long standing in northern Palestine. On this see M. Smith, *Palestinian Parties*. Hoehner's conclusions also run counter to a loyalist hypothesis. See his *Herod Antipas*, 53–54. On the basis of archeological evidence, Eric M. Meyers and James F. Strange present southern Galilee as remarkably open to Hellenistic culture and commerce, predominantly Greek-speaking though bilingual, and emphasize that the heavy settlement of Jews in Galilee is documented mainly from the period after the Jewish War (*Archaeology*, 26, 42–43, 65, 78–88, 90). They also call into question the view that Galilee was a hotbed of religious fanaticism (35–37). Thus the principle of selecting and interpreting data is crucial. An illustration of evidence regularly cited for the "messianic" temperament in Galilee would be the lists of

2.3 Social Role

In the light of recent scholarship on the nature of Jesus' teaching, the prevailing opinion about his social role in Galilee needs to be revised. The prevailing opinion has been that Jesus acted as a prophet and was recognized as an eschatological figure. The social historian recognizes traits that suggest another role. The figure that immediately comes to mind is that of the popular philosopher known as the Cynic. Cynics belonged to the broadly Socratic tradition that was generated at the end of the classical age of the *polis*. The topics for conversation among the Socratics and Cyrenaics had to do with life in its social context. Cynics were well-known figures who made a profession of social critique and espoused a life lived naturally. All aspects of social existence were constantly under scrutiny. All forms of conventional authority were disavowed. Appeal was made directly to individuals on the basis of common sense and a vague notion about natural law. The ideal was to live simply, learn to endure hardship, and not get caught doing anything merely to satisfy the expectations of others who treated traditions as laws. The famous Cynics were extremely sophisticated and well-read. The not-so-famous lived on the edges of society, made an art of begging, and looked for opportunities to display the virtues of an unencumbered existence at the expense of stuffy conventions. There was more logic to their lifestyle and non-philosophical philosophy than has frequently been understood. Cynics were a social phenomenon indicative of the times.

The sayings of the Cynics sprang from a frequently unexpressed system

---

"disturbances" in Galilee during the Herodian and Roman periods. A critical reading of these disturbances does not support the hypothesis of religious, eschatological hysteria at all. To take only one instance, it has often been assumed that Judas the son of Hezekiah who led a small revolt shortly after the death of Herod the Great was a "Zealot," and that Zealots were therefore part of the Galilean scene from at least that time on. Horsley has shown, however, that the assumption rests upon a mistaken identification of this Judas with a Judas of Galilee whom Josephus credits with founding the "fourth philosophy" (Zealots), and that the notion of Zealots as a messianic ideology or movement is a misleading, modern scholarly construct. He offers quite a different reading of Josephus' reports in "Popular Messianic Movements." Freyne agrees and goes even further. In a fine discussion he explains the revolt led by Judas son of Hezekiah as a response to the killing of Hezekiah by Herod, and argues that both events were the result of political battles between the deposed Hasmoneans and the Herodians appointed by Rome. Thus the revolt was not a Galilean affair, nor a messianic movement. Freyne concludes that the traditional view of Galilee as the spawning ground for ideological revolutionaries is simply false. See his chapter on "How Revolutionary was Galilee?" in *Galilee*, 208–47. Hoehner takes the same position: "To blame the Galileans for the uprising after Herod's death is unfair" (*Herod Antipas*, 57). During the fifties, to be sure, there was an increase of banditry and peasant revolt throughout Palestine. There were incidents at Jerusalem involving Galileans on pilgrimage, pilgrimage becoming an occasion for seeking redress for wrongs committed by rulers. There were also incidents of outrage against Roman brutality and insensitivity throughout Palestine during the first century. But none of these events was without its social reasons. And none of them supports the view that Galilee was rife with turbulent currents of religious fanaticism.

of thought that was highly rationalized and firmly in place. They also knew, along with others in the Socratic tradition of popular philosophy, about *nomos* (law), *physis* (nature), wisdom, virtue, *paideia* (culture, education), authority, and especially about the difference between kings on the one hand and tyrants on the other. They stood on the edges of society reminding conventional folk of their foolishness. The only program they had to suggest was to join them in their unconventional way of life. But the wellspring for the entire venture was a preoccupation with the question of society and its foundations.

Cynics were best known for their pointed remarks and behavior. A game seems to have been played with them by those daring enough to tackle it. Cynics seem to have delighted in the game, seeking occasions to set it up to their advantage. Finding themselves in a tight situation where accommodation to conventional expectations would seem to make sense or be the easiest thing to do, the Cynic would accept the challenge of exposing the absurdity of the expectations. The Cynic response has seldom been understood to have a logic of its own. It has been called wit, or cleverness, or simply caustic behavior. Marcel Detienne and Jean-Pierre Vernant have rectified that understanding in their study of Greek popular culture. The logic of the Cynic response can now be given a name. It is *mētis*, a term coined by Detienne and Vernant for the practical wisdom required of contingent circumstances that are threatening in some way. The contrast is *sophia*, that kind of knowledge that presupposes stable systems and generates general truths. Professions understood to require *mētis* were, for example, those of the physician, navigator, and rhetor. That is because, in each case, situations to be addressed could not be determined always in advance. The challenge when confronting a disease, storm, or unruly audience required a skillful strategy. Assessing the situation, anticipating the way things might go, a sense of timing, waiting for the opportune moment, dodging, moving in quickly with a forthright initiative were all known about, storied, and practiced by the Greeks. The Cynics applied the logic of *mētis* to the art of living and used it to hone the art of repartee.[10]

Jesus' use of parables, aphorisms, and clever rejoinders is very similar to the Cynics' way with words. Many of his themes are familiar Cynic themes. And his style of social criticism, diffident and vague, also agrees with the typical Cynic stance. Scholars have known about some of these similarities for some time. The chreiai used in the early stages of the synoptic tradition

---

10. *The Cynics.* There are studies of Cynicism by D. R. Dudley, *A History of Cynicism;* and Ragnar Hoïstad, *Cynic Hero and Cynic King.* Cynic influence is the subject in Henry Fischel, "Cynicism and the Ancient Near East"; and in Klaus Döring, *Exemplum Socratis.* Textual studies include a commentary on the famous chapter in Epictetus by Margarethe Billerbeck; and a study of *First-century Cynicism in the Epistles of Heraclitus* by Harold W. Attridge. Editions of Cynic epistles have been published by Abraham J. Malherbe and Edward N. O'Neil. Leonce Paquet has collected the fragments. Cynic chreiai will be discussed in chap. 7.

have been recognized as formally comparable to popular anecdotes about Cynics. The instructions Jesus is said to have given his followers in the so-called "mission" speech in Q have troubled Christian exegetes because they describe Cynic practice so closely. Kloppenborg could find no closer set of parallels for much of the material in Q than Cynic sayings and their type of wisdom. Work now being done at Claremont will demonstrate the extent to which Cynic themes, images, and attitudes pervade Q discourse in its first stages of collection. Jesus' wisdom was neither a Greek philosophical ethic nor a Jewish proverbial instruction, though flavoring from each is evident as one might expect at the end of the Hellenistic age. Jesus' wisdom incorporated the pungent invitation to insight and the daring to be different that characterized the Cynic approach to life.[11]

If Jesus was less a prophet and more a popular sage, the when and the where of his public appearances may need to be reconsidered. An eschato-logical prophet might be imagined addressing crowds in the open, but a teller of tales and one proficient in aphoristic discourse fits best in a smaller, livelier audience. A public figure need not always perform on a large stage. The Cynic style is close and confrontational. Jesus' speech is softly spoken but extremely engaging. The tone is that of common experience to begin with, then an invitation to share the critical insight or perspective, and finally the implicit dare to be different. Situations can be imagined at the market, along the way, or at one's leisure. A social setting at mealtime will be considered in the next chapter as the most appropriate occasion, not only for the type of discourse attributed to Jesus, but for group formation to have occurred.

3. THE KINGDOM OF GOD

In order to imagine the effectiveness of Jesus' proclamation of the king-dom of God, scholars have usually assumed a generally apocalyptic climate in Palestine, including inordinate interest in religious ideals, a bleak

---

11. *Jesus as Cynic.* The proposal that Jesus' public stance would have resembled that of the Cynics requires some supporting argument. Early advocates of a significant relationship between Jesus and Cynicism are Eduard Wechssler, *Hellas im Evangelium*, 42–66; and Carl Schneider, *Geistesgeschichte des antiken Christentums* 1:31–45. Others have pointed out the close parallels between various synoptic materials and Cynic traditions, including: Hans Windisch, "Die Notiz über Tracht und Speise"; W. L. Knox, *The Sources of the Synoptic Gospels* 2:48; M. Hengel, *Nachfolge und Charisma*, 6, 31–37; Paul Hoffmann, *Studien zur Theologie der Logienquelle*, 318–19; G. Theissen, "Wanderradikalismus"; H. C. Kee, *Community of the New Age*, 104–5; L. Schottroff and W. Stegemann, *Jesus von Nazareth;* R. Riesner, *Jesus als Lehrer*, 207, 355–57; and J. Kloppenborg, *The Formation of Q*, 306–25. It should be noted that most of these scholars have been cautious not to draw conclusions about the historical Jesus based on their observations of Cynic parallels. The Cynic hypothesis gains in credibility, however, as soon as the view of Jesus as an apocalyptic prophet is recognized as problematic. The case has been argued for the "mission" charge in Q in a doctoral dissertation at Claremont by Leif Vaage. Vaage has kindly assisted in the compilation of this bibliographical note.

picture of the times, and messianic expectations. According to this scenario, the appearance of a forceful prophet announcing a radical change in the critical situation would have been greeted with excitement. Even if the rulers of "Israel" may have been preoccupied with the temple and the law, it has been thought, the common people would have responded in ways quite similar to the accounts given in the gospels. This tidy solution is questionable for a number of reasons.

In the first place, the apocalyptic reconstruction of the social climate is highly exaggerated if not completely inappropriate. In order to paint the picture that way, concerns more appropriate to sectarian mentality have been used to characterize the public atmosphere. Jews in general were not anxiously waiting for the messiah. There was, in fact, no such thing as a common conception about "the" messiah or "the" kingdom to come. Jews were very busily at work on their social situation and, where apocalyptic notions were entertained, they were derived from definite ideologies and programs related to actual states of affairs and institutional histories. It is not at all clear what effect a general public proclamation of an imminent divine action in history would have had. Many may have thought such an announcement and such an announcer crazy.[12]

Of far greater seriousness for the traditional view, the term kingdom of God does not occur in Jewish texts of the time (with three exceptions to be noted below). It cannot be traced to an apocalyptic worldview, social context, or set of texts anywhere as a technical term. It is quite true that the concept of God as king belonged to ancient Near Eastern mythologies of kingship, and that Jewish piety produced psalms and prayers of desire for God's rule to be actualized in Israel's behalf. In apocalyptic circles, where the preparations for the term have normally been located by scholars, one does find on occasion the imaginative vision of Israel's restoration as the reinstitution of God's reign or rule. But the term kingdom of God does not appear anywhere in the canonical or apocalyptic literature. Where reference is made to God's own intervention at some future time, moreover, messianic figures tend not to appear. The combination of ideas that early followers of Jesus invested in the term kingdom of God just does not correspond to any general Jewish pattern of desire and expectation.[13]

---

12. *Jesus as an apocalyptic prophet*. This has been the dominant view since J. Weiss (*Die Predigt Jesu;* see n. 3 above). Two recent works may be cited to demonstrate the continuing strength of the tradition: N. Perrin, *The Kingdom of God;* and H. C. Kee, *Jesus in History.*

13. *The kingdom of God in Jewish literature.* "Indeed, it may come as a surprise to learn that outside of the gospels the expression 'Kingdom of God' is not very common in the New Testament, while in the Old Testament it does not occur at all." With this statement, John Bright begins his study of *The Kingdom of God*, 18. N. Perrin struggled with this problem in *Jesus and the Language of the Kingdom*. In order to hold onto the traditional derivation of the term from Jewish literature and apocalyptic, Perrin had to develop the

The meaning of the term in the Jesus traditions is also far from clear. It is used in a rather self-evident fashion as if early Christians knew what Jesus intended and what they themselves were about. But a close reading shows that the term was used in a bewildering variety of ways. It pointed to an order of things that could range from the initial effect of Jesus' activity to an apocalyptic appearance of a pre-planned theocracy. In the sayings traditions where the term is most at home, the direction of conceptual development can be traced. The tendency was to increase the apocalyptic projections on the one hand, and to heighten the importance of Jesus as the one who announced them on the other. The greater the discrepancy between the time of Jesus and the vision of the ultimate manifestation, the more imaginative were the efforts to keep the two linked together. The mythology of the Son of Man was introduced into the Q tradition for this reason, for instance. By imagining that Jesus announced the apocalyptic appearance of this mythic figure, and that he spelled out the relationship between his own appearance and that of the coming of the Son of Man, the importance of both events could be heightened even as they were linked together.[14]

Early Jesus movements did see themselves in the light of an ideal order of things designated by the term kingdom of God. That they used it to position themselves within a history that started with Jesus, suffered delay in realizing full potential, thus making it necessary to project an even more momentous manifestation, agrees with the way in which rationalizations occurred (and occur) within apocalyptic sects. This indicates, though, that the technical usage of the term kingdom of God is most probably an early construction of some Jesus movement, not a derivation from a pregiven Jewish conceptuality. As with all symbols, arbitrary as they are, the mean-

---

thesis that, though the term did not appear, the concept was pervasive. Most New Testament scholars have accepted this line of reasoning. A few, however, have registered reservations. To see that the notion of a kingdom of God in Jewish apocalyptic was not combined programmatically with that of a messianic figure in Jewish apocalyptic was the contribution of Philipp Vielhauer, "Gottesreich und Menschensohn." Recently, the Jesus Seminar has decided against the apocalyptic hypothesis. See *Foundations and Facets Forum* 3,1 (March, 1987); and Mack, "The Kingdom Sayings in Mark."

14. *Son of Man in Q.* That the apocalyptic mythology of the Son of Man was a later development of the Q tradition is now accepted by many scholars. See, for instance, H. Schürmann, "Beobachtungen zum Menschensohn-Titel"; and J. S. Kloppenborg, *The Formation of Q*, 159–70. An important argument for later insertion that uses the evidence from the Gospel of Thomas is presented by H. Koester, "One Jesus and Four Primitive Gospels," 186. The crucial text around which all debates ultimately are joined is Luke 12:8–9 and its variant in Mark 8:38. The language of confession is mystifying if the saying is read as authentic. If it is read as a way to link Jesus' authority at the beginning with newly domesticated apocalyptic rationale for the failure of an intransigent world to accept the Q people's message, however, the saying manifests a brilliant logic and clever mythmaking. The Son of Man sayings in Q are conveniently listed and discussed in Richard Edwards, *A Theology of Q*, 39–43.

ing of the term for those who used it of themselves would have arisen in the process of repeated applications to sectarian identity, activity, and social history. This observation does not immediately help to understand the full significance of the term as early Christians used it, but it does allow for a derivation to be sought in social and intellectual contexts much broader than the traditional limitation to Jewish apocalyptic literature.

The attempt to trace the use of the term back to Jesus is a distinctive feature of the scholarly quest. According to a recent listing of the authentic sayings of Jesus (not including parables), however, there are only three sayings among them that contain a reference to the kingdom of God (Luke 11:20; 17:20–21; Matt 11:12). The interesting thing about these three sayings is that none of them requires an apocalyptic interpretation, referring as they do to social history as the arena for encountering the kingdom. The traditional view has been to regard them as claims to a "realized" eschatology, of course, and, overlayed as they are with early Christian nuance, that may be the way in which they were or came to be understood. It is also possible that not even these sayings are authentic. But someone had to start using the term, and Jesus may have been the one. Given the predominantly aphoristic character of his utterance, he must have used it in a way that agreed with that style. Parable studies, for instance, have made it possible to think of Jesus' use of the term in quite a non-apocalyptic way. That to which the parables point is the world as the listener might re-imagine it. A similar result can easily be anticipated for work yet to be done on the aphorisms and activities of Jesus. The unresolved issue, however, is whether Jesus' contemporaries, hearing mention of a kingdom of God in relation to his activities and their purposes, would have understood. Why, indeed, a kingdom symbol at all, unless kings, kingdoms, and social circumstances were up for discussion?[15]

Discourse about kings and kingdoms was not limited to Jewish sectarians during the Greco-Roman period. It was much more prevalent, as a matter of fact, in Hellenistic traditions of popular and school philosophy. Society was imagined still on the model of the *polis*, but the burning issues revolved around kings and tyrants and how to guarantee just rule. Treatises were written on kingship, and philosophers found ways to apply the social metaphor to the problem of ethics in general. The grounds for constructing a just society and for cultivating a virtuous life thus were explored together. Stoics used the cliché about the wise man being the only true king, for instance, both to render political judgments and to propose a path to virtue. Cynics also saw themselves as "kings" standing over against tyrants as well

---

15. *The kingdom of God sayings.* The three candidates for authenticity, referred to in the text, are those proposed in N. Perrin and D. Duling, *The New Testament,* 412–13.

as against a society blindly following unreasonable rules. Using metaphors such as king, overseer, physician, gadfly, and teacher, Cynics understood themselves to be "sent" by God to preside over the human situation. Epictetus even refers to the Cynics' vocation as a reign (*basileia*, "kingdom") in order to catch up the challenging aspects of representing publicly a way of life grounded in the divine laws of nature. An invitation to imagine an order of things other than the actual state of affairs in Galilee, then, would have been quite possible without any allusion to Jewish ideology at all.[16]

The Cynic's self-understanding must be taken seriously as that which many must have expected of Jesus. Not only does Jesus' style of social criticism compare favorably, his themes and topics are much closer to Cynic idiom than to those characteristic for public Jewish piety. One seeks in vain a direct engagement of specifically Jewish concerns. Neither is Jesus' critique directed specifically toward Jewish institutional issues, nor do his recommendations draw upon obviously Jewish concepts and authorities. Unless Jesus' aphoristic address had nothing to do with the kingdom he represented, belonging to that kingdom was based on judgments without respect to prior loyalties, accepting a new ideology, or taking sides in political issues. Jesus' kingdom was not the fulfillment of old epic ideals that history had failed to realize. The social critique was general; the invitation was specific in its address to individuals. The invitation would have been to something like the Cynic's "kingdom," that is, to assume the Cynic's stance of confidence in the midst of confused and contrary social circumstances. Simply translated, Jesus' "message" seems to have been, "See how it's done? You can do it also."

The Cynic analogy repositions the historical Jesus away from a specifically Jewish sectarian milieu and toward the Hellenistic ethos known to have prevailed in Galilee. It reaches its limits, however, when confronted with two additional observations. The first is that the kingdom Jesus represented was theologized. The emphasis upon God as the ruler of the kingdom (kingdom *of God*) strikes a note of seriousness a bit unusual for

---

16. *The kingdom in Hellenistic thought.* The distinction between kings and tyrants is a pervasive topic in Hellenistic literature. Two studies may be mentioned that demonstrate the philosophical vigor with which the topic was pursued: E. R. Goodenough, "The Political Philosophy of Hellenistic Kingship"; and R. Hoïstad, *Cynic Hero and Cynic King.* The pervasiveness of the Stoic commonplace about the sage as king is documented by its frequent occurrence in Philo, for example, *De agricultura* 41; *De sobrietate* 57; *De posteritate Caini* 138. The references to the Cynic's "kingdom" are in Epictetus, 3.22.63; 3.22.76; 3.22.80. The three instances of the term Kingdom of God outside of early Christian literature occur in Hellenistic-Jewish writings. They are the Wisdom of Solomon (10:10); the Sentences of Sextus (311); and Philo of Alexandria (*De specialibus legibus* 4.164). For a discussion of these references, see Mack, "The Kingdom Sayings in Mark."

Hellenistic sensibility. The second is that those who heard him formed groups, all of which understood themselves to be religious movements with claims upon Jewish traditions. A religious piety of some kind must therefore be assumed for Jesus, energized by concerns that can generally be equated with Jewish ethical and theocratic ideals, but lacking interest in specifically Jewish institutions. Such a combination of Hellenistic style and Jewish sensibility is exactly what one might expect at a popular level in Galilee.

One might imagine Jesus doing at a popular level what many Jewish intellectuals did at a more sophisticated and conceptual level, namely, combining Jewish and Hellenistic traditions of wisdom in order to make critical judgments about the times and to propose a religious ethic held to be in keeping with Jewish ideals. Jewish ideals of this nature, not linked immediately to institutional codes and concerns, had been articulated in a wisdom mode of discourse both in Palestine (Ben Sira and Qoheleth, for instance) and in the diaspora (Pseudo Phocylides, Wisdom of Solomon, Philo, Aristeas, and so forth). Avid exploration of Hellenistic popular philosophy took place in these traditions, resulting in creative combinations designed to interpret mainly the essential logic of Jewish religiosity by drawing upon a wide variety of traditions and sources: epic, social conceptions, ethics, religious postures and beliefs.

In the Wisdom of Solomon, for instance, Hellenistic philosophies of cosmology, kingship, law, ethics, and religion were combined with Jewish wisdom ethics and mythology, Jewish religious concerns about idolatry, as well as a retelling of the Exodus story (midrash), to produce a grand affirmation of the sovereignty of God. This was used, then, to criticize contemporary rulers, propose a theodicy for the oppressed righteous ones, project a reversal of the present misuse of power, and envision a perfect society. The perfect society was imagined as the rule made possible by divine wisdom. The author called it the "kingdom of God" (Wis 10:10; cf. 6:3–4; 6:19–21)!

Jesus does not appear to have engaged in such fantasy. The vision in the Wisdom of Solomon was, after all, the studied fiction of an intellectual elite. But the same combination of Hellenistic popular philosophy and Jewish wisdom ethic is quite thinkable at a less literary level of life and thought. If Jesus' "announcement" of the kingdom of god resulted from some such combination of religious sensibility and thought, it would be right to credit him with some creativity and courage, but wrong to overly dramatize the announcement as charismatic proclamation.[17]

---

17. *Popular ethic.* J. Collins, *Between Athens and Jerusalem,* 143–48, gives an interesting description of Jewish popular ethic mixed with Hellenistic moral philosophy. There is still a difference, however, between that and the sayings of Jesus. Jesus was less concerned

4. THE DISPLAY OF POWER

A distinctly different approach to the question of the historical Jesus and his effectiveness has appealed, not to the sayings of Jesus, but to the miracle stories about him. Miracle stories occur in Q and are predominant for the Galilean ministry in Mark's Gospel. Proposals have been made about Jesus as a miracle worker or even a magician, suggesting that his charismatic display of power is necessary to account for his influence. The supporting argument has been to point to the social role of the Hellenistic divine man.

Much has been written about the Hellenistic divine man: magicians, diviners, healers, astrologers, interpreters of dreams, clairvoyants, and workers of miracles of all kinds. It is not clear that all of this applies equally to the way in which people may have perceived a charismatic figure. The magical arts were arts, requiring detailed knowledge and skills. Apprenticeships were the way to learn these skills, and the populace regarded most of these dealers in the divine arts as practitioners, not charismatics. The divine arts filled the void left vacant by the disappearance of the old established institutions of religion, especially the functions of the temple cults in both the ancient temple states and the now archaic *polis*. The complex picture of specializations in the Greco-Roman age is best understood as a fragmentation of the practical aspects of what once were religious systems.

On the edges of the divine arts were those interested in exploring the mysteries of wisdom, holiness, and power as well, for these religious symbols had also become dislodged from the social structures that once gave them meaning and coherence. Those with a sensibility for what moderns call anomie sought to position themselves with regard to the sacred by means of activities that were essentially individualistic, heroic, and potentially sectarian. Recent studies of the social function of the divine man in the Greco-Roman era have suggested that he took the place of the sacred that had been centered until recently in the temple cult. A bewildering variety of secular priests thus was possible, for the combinations among special powers, special knowledge, and special skills were manifold. Popular imagination responded as well to those who claimed to see the hidden truths in ancient texts as to those who knew about the mysterious powers of the natural and cosmic orders of things. A bit of sagacity was as much a mark of the divine as the ability to pursue the forces that seemed to frustrate human well-being.

In this general sense, Jesus could be called a divine man by arguing from the effect that he had upon people and the movements they formed. Appeal to the general phenomenon of divine men cannot be used to argue for any

---

about traditional values and less prone to moral maxims. The aphoristic, Cynic nature of his speech calls attention to itself.

particular miracle-working activity, however. The miracle stories are the only relevant data for such a suspicion.[18]

Studies in the miracle stories in Mark have isolated sets of stories that appear to be pre-Markan collections. These collections bear striking resemblance to a similar collection of miracle stories underlying the Gospel of John. The discussion of these miracle stories in chapter 8 will show (1) that their composition follows a pattern similar to Hellenistic reports, but (2) that their content alludes to Jewish epic themes and figures. Most of the miracle stories in the synoptic tradition occur in these collections, moreover, and the collections can be shown to have functioned as a myth of origins for a group that formed among the followers of Jesus. In addition, Mark can be shown to have exaggerated the power of Jesus to cast out demons for his own narrative purposes. Thus the evidence is that miracle stories functioned in some early Jesus movement to enhance its claim to significant social identity by claiming for its founder miraculous powers. They are not historical reports.

The memory tradition represented by the miracle stories is nevertheless important for the question of the historical Jesus. The stories were a reminder about the effect Jesus had upon people as some remembered him. Rather remarkable changes in conditions, status, and behavior are the points emphasized in most of the stories, exaggerated to be sure in keeping with the miracle genre. They give the impression that Jesus was the source of a divine power capable of effecting radical human transformations. The question is, transformations of what kind? When read closely, all of the miracle stories betray signs of the social circumstance that gave significance to the transformation. That circumstance was the crossing of a social boundary. The perspective on the crossing of social boundaries is oblique, but present nonetheless around the edges of the graphic depictions of physical changes in the lives and circumstances of individuals. If one does not notice the social contexts, the stories read as rather indiscriminate displays of miraculous power. But if a reader does notice the social contexts, the stories suggest that Jesus set something in motion that enabled people to "see," "talk," "walk," "eat," and function freely within a transformed ethos.

What Jesus set in motion was, then, a social experiment. Crossing a social boundary into an arrangement of social relationships sensed as novel

---

18. *The divine man.* See the reference to J. Z. Smith, chap. 1, n. 17, on the social role of the divine man. It is Morton Smith who has proposed *Jesus the Magician.* In an article on the gospel genre, "Good News is No News," J. Z. Smith argues that there was no difference between a "magician" and a "divine man," except for the labeling. Admirers would use "divine man," while skeptics would call such a person a "magician." David Tiede discusses the possibility that the sage could also be considered a "divine man" in *The Charismatic Figure as Miracle Worker.* A discussion of the scholarship on Jesus as miracle worker will be given in chap. 8.

may well have been experienced as transformation. The new arrangement may well have been described as an order of things created and sustained by a new, effective spirit. Fascination with the power to change people, or to display one's own possession of divine spirit, was certainly one of the ways in which some Jesus people and many Christ cult people responded to the spirit experienced in the movements stemming from Jesus. Jesus was held to be the source of the spirit of transformation, and miracle stories were one way to imagine transformations at the beginning.

Nevertheless, neither miracles of healing, nor a life lived as a Cynic sage, is adequate to account for the social nature of Jesus' influence. Some other ingredient needs to be identified that will make it possible to imagine how new social arrangements occurred, and in such a bewildering variety of movements. To track down that other ingredient, the focus of investigation must now shift away from the singular significance of Jesus to the question of group experience among his followers.

3

THE FOLLOWERS
OF JESUS

The gospels picture Jesus calling disciples, instructing them in the mission of preaching, and, according to Matthew and Luke, preparing them for the responsibility of founding the church. This picture belongs to the myth of Christian origins worked out by the authors of the gospels during the last quarter of the first century. It cannot be used to reconstruct what actually happened in the early period. The gospels proposed to even things out, imagining that the congregations for whom they were written were what Jesus had intended. In the case of Luke, a single, mainline development of history from Jesus to the mission of the early Christian church was filled in. The early history did not develop the way Luke tells it. Neither did the later history, for that matter. Luke's little epic erased the histories of a multitude of Jesus movements still in existence in his own time, movements that had taken distinctively different paths. These paths diverged from the earliest times, the early history marked by sectarian movements of very diverse configurations. The notion of "the" disciples does not figure at all in most movements, and only obscurely in one or two early memory traditions. When the gospels were written, the advantage presented by the notion of "the disciples" was that the church could claim to have received its teachings from first-generation leaders taught by the founder-teacher himself. Because the gospels were written by combining different memory traditions taken from various Jesus movements as well as from the Christ cult, "the disciples" also served to combine several earlier notions of group leaders in a common image appropriate to the new, unified view of the church and its history. The disciples do figure prominently in this mythic history, and later came to be known as the twelve apostles with a firm place in the Christian imagination. But the brave souls first to suggest that Jesus' work continue were not trained disciples.

The history of the earliest period, the first forty years, is unfortunately dark. But enough can be traced to know that a variety of Jesus movements were spawned. The spectrum spreads from Galilean itinerants who saw themselves continuing Jesus' public activities, through various groups that thought to accommodate Jewish institutions in different ways, to independent congregations in Asia Minor and Greece. Each harked back to Jesus in a different way, and each formed social units around differing types of leadership. In these movements patterns developed in which leadership roles, views of Jesus' importance as a founder, and the purposes of the movement were conceptualized systematically as coherent rationales for specific social formations. Early designations for leadership roles include "the pillars" (in Jerusalem), "the twelve," "prophets," "apostles," "teachers," and so forth. As for "the disciples," they are not mentioned in the Q collection of sayings, nor in the letters of Paul. They appear for the first time in the Gospel of Mark. If some early Jesus movement understood their leaders to have been disciples of Jesus, it would have been only one of many ways in which leaders in various movements established their credentials.[1]

Jesus certainly must have attracted followers. Only in this way can one account for the Jesus movements. But the extremely diverse types of

---

1. *The disciples.* There are several ways to account for Mark's interest in the theme of the disciples. (1) Theodore Weeden, *Mark,* sees the disciples as representatives of a brand of Christianity oriented to miracles and a divine man christology against which Mark wrote by substituting a christology of the crucified one. (2) The disciples are largely a narrative fiction cast as negative examples to accentuate the martyrological aspects of Jesus' "confession." It is Jesus who serves as the paradigm par excellence for discipleship in Mark's own time. (3) As a narrative fiction, the disciples misunderstand because the "mystery" of the apocalyptic dimensions of the kingdom inaugurated by Jesus can only be grasped retrospectively. The misunderstanding of the disciples serves as a warning to Mark's readers who may not want to consider Mark's novel proposal about this mystery. (4) Mark's portrayal of Jesus as the "teacher" simply requires disciples in keeping with common Hellenistic models of teachers and teaching. This is the view of Vernon Robbins, *Jesus the Teacher.* He demonstrates that Mark used narrative and rhetorical patterns in the composition of the gospel that correspond to Hellenistic literary patterns of instruction.

Thus the disciples in Mark betray thematic interests. Their prominent place in Mark's story of Jesus cannot be used to argue for "discipleship" as a common concept among Jesus movements before Mark's time. It is not unthinkable that Mark was active in turning lore about the "pillars" Cephas, James and John (Gal 2:9) into stories about "disciples" of Jesus. If that is so, however, early Q traditions that were taken up into the Gospel of Thomas may have passed through the Markan milieu or sphere of influence. "The disciples" figure prominently in the Gospel of Thomas also, in contrast to Q, and play a role similar to that in the Gospel of Mark. Their questions to Jesus reveal their ignorance about the true meaning of his teaching, a special understanding given only to Thomas. See GThom (Gospel of Thomas) 13 where this theme is clearly expressed, as well as GThom 61 and 114 where Salome and Mary also are set in contrast to the disciples. That "the disciples" do not figure in Q demonstrates the weakness of the prevailing scholarly assumption that Jesus must have attracted and trained disciples. According to recent reconstructions of Q the term "disciple" occurs only at Luke 6:40 in a proverbial saying about a disciple not being above his master. There is no evidence of a group known as Jesus' disciples in this tradition of the transmission of Jesus' sayings. The importance of the problematic question about "discipleship" for reconstructing early social and gospel history is clearly seen by Werner Kelber, "Apostolic Tradition and the Genre of the Gospel," a paper delivered at the Symposium on Discipleship at Marquette University in April 1983. For orientation to the history of scholarship on the question see Hans-Dieter Betz, *Nachfolge und Nachahmung;* and S. Freyne, *The Twelve.*

movements in the name of Jesus are witness to the fact that Jesus did not set up a program for a new society or religion, train leaders for it, and bequeath to them his legacy. In this chapter the movements formed by Jesus' followers are to be described. A prior question needs to be addressed, though, a question of some importance for making sense of this strange history. If Jesus did not envision a movement and train leaders for it, what might account for the subsequent formations of groups of any kind?

1. MEETING FOR MEALS

A distinctive feature of the gospel accounts is the emphasis placed upon house gatherings, especially for meals, as the occasion for much of the teaching activity of Jesus. As they now stand, these stories reflect the lively imagination of storytellers within some Jesus movement. They probably reflect group practice and they surely take up topics of interest to the members of that movement. They cannot be viewed as historical reports, certainly not in order to theorize a religious "table fellowship" with Jesus, the last supper of which instituted the Christian church. The ritual meal story in the gospels is an etiological legend based upon a tradition (without disciples) taken from the Christ cult. The other meal scenes are for the most part typical settings in the service of the pronouncement stories. But meals did play a very important role in early Jesus movements as well as in the Hellenistic congregations. Though direct evidence is lacking, it would be possible to theorize that gathering for meals was the occasion of social formation for every Jesus movement known, with the possible exception of the Q people. The Christ cult gathered for meals and even ritualized the meal. Those who forged the miracle tradition into sets of stories included meal miracles among them. The pronouncement stories appear to reflect the community practice of those who told them. Several are set at mealtime. The discussion between Paul and the pillars in Jerusalem, yet another Jesus group, was precisely about meal practice. Meals were a topic of intense debate throughout the Pauline mission. And the Didache, an early Jewish-Christian manual, contains prayers for a ritual meal that developed quite independently from the Christ cult meal. A suspicion frequently entertained in scholarship, moreover, is that the issues of most significance in early conflicts between Christians and various forms of Judaism were questions related to meal practice. Meals were apparently very important occasions.[2]

---

2. *Meals*. The main references are: Christ cult ritual (1 Cor 11:23–26; 10:14–22; cf. Acts 2:43–47); miracle chains (Mark 6:30–44; 8:1–10; cf. John 6); pronouncement stories (Mark 2:15–17; 2:18–22; 2:23–28; 7:1–23; 14:3–9); the issue between Paul and the pillars (Gal 2:11–21); other signs of conflict over meals (1 Cor 8:1–13; 11:27–34; Acts 10:9–16; 11:1–10; 15:29; Col 2:21); and the meal ritual in Didache (Did 9, 10). The Q people may not

Gathering for meals was a common social custom during the Hellenistic period. The Hellenistic city owed its attractiveness and success to the opportunities it provided for crafts to expand their markets, dealers to trade, and ethnic traditions to mix. Except for times of political crisis, the energies unleashed by the intermingling of cultures were very constructive. Curiosity about the ways others lived and worked was the rule, and people experimented with new ideas. Life was generally very busy and bubbly. And business was good. But on the other side of the ledger was the desire to stay in touch with the familiar even if only intermittently, far from home, and with a small group of possibly unlikely tradents of one's otherwise grand, archaic culture or craft learned from hoary antiquity. Clubs called associations sprang up on all sides. There was always some interest held in common, whether related to ethnic socializing or craft business. Because of the nature of this social institution there is little in the way of literary remains from which to document its history. But enough is available to be sure about some things. It was a prevalent form of association, organized with officers, rules, and treasuries, named for a patron deity, and conducted as a dinner club. Who was to pay for the wine was a very big issue, written right into the rules with special precautions against admitting members who had not paid their dues. A libation to the god would start things off and after that there was order to keep. Business and pleasure and such repartee as the group could command were poured into the common bowl of what amounted to a middle-class symposium.[3]

Jesus people must have met to talk about their common interests. Since the only model at hand for free association was the gathering for a meal, that must have been what they did. Simple invitations by a patron or householder would have sufficed. But, quite soon in some movements, fully organized congregations appeared that looked very much like Hellenistic associations (koinōniai). The Pauline communities, for instance, can be described as koinōniai in the name of Christ. The social practices within the Jesus movements are less visible, and, judging from their views of Jesus, they did not develop in the direction of cults. But meeting for meals to talk about Jesus and the kingdom would still have been the common practice.

---

have been an exception to the rule, but, because of itinerancy, related to house groups primarily as guests, not as those responsible for the meals. See the instruction about showing up for meals included in the "mission charge" (Luke 10:7–8). Why meal practice may have become a source of conflict with Jews is clear. The meal was significant as a locus of social identity, guarded carefully by the ritual laws of purity. On this and the question of table fellowship among Pharisees, see J. Neusner, *From Politics to Piety*, 83–90. For an anthropological approach, see Mary Douglas, "Deciphering a Meal"; and Gillian Feeley-Harnik, *The Lord's Table*.

3. *Associations*. For evidence for Greek associations see Dennis Smith, "Social Obligation." Smith brings this evidence to bear upon the situation in Corinth as reflected in Paul's first letter.

One has to imagine quite a lively scene as Jesus people got together. In Galilee and the Decapolis the Q people might show up for dinner anytime. In Syria the Jesus people probably went out to dinner "after synagogue." In Jerusalem it would perhaps have been after the temple services of sacrifice and prayers. Householders, deacons, prophets, teachers, patrons, itinerant apostles and all would have tried to get a word in edgewise, no doubt, especially if two apostles had recently been received. But what were the topics of conversation? Why indeed did Jesus people start meeting together at all? In whose name? For what reasons? And why all up and down the eastern Mediterranean seaboard? A social convention was ready for those of like minds or interests to meet together. But what may have been that interest?

The most reasonable assumption would be that eating together was itself the sign and substance of the new order of things. One should not under-estimate the attraction of a group that encouraged novel social experimen-tation during this time in the eastern Mediterranean. If eating together played any role at all in the pattern of Jesus' activity with his followers, a practice may have been started that could have continued quite naturally. It is commonly assumed that Jesus did eat with his followers, of course, but frequently on the basis of an uncritical use of synoptic stories. No one reading the texts critically has found a way to demonstrate that it must have been so. So the argument can only be hypothetical. Its value is, however, that it would explain many uncertainties. Jesus at social occasions would not be difficult to imagine at all, for there would be no need to ask about any grand design or formal recognition of the practice. Taking advantage of invitations from those interested in having a lively guest could fit, as well as rather regular times with friends and close companions. Meals together would be the perfect occasion for aphoristic discourse, parables, reports, poking fun, and serious discussions about staying alert and living sanely in the midst of cultures in transition. A sense of the unconventional may very well have prevailed, supposing the company were mixed and the conver-sation somewhat self-reflective. Even if most were marginal people, without great investments in social status to lose, the risk may have been both poignant and rewarding. The "spirit" of discourse about the kingdom of God as well as behavior appropriate to it may very well have been generated by social formation at mealtime, an experience some did not want to relinquish just because Jesus was no longer present. A little display of wisdom would still be possible. As things developed, ever greater sagacity would have been required to account for what was taking place.[4]

---

4. *The symposium.* There was a formal correspondence between meal practice in Greek associations and meal practice on banquet occasions in homes. The symposium literature, discussed in Dennis Smith, "Social Obligation," focuses upon banquets at a high level of sophistication. It can be used, nonetheless, to complement allusions to meal situations at

Supposing the Jesus movements continued such a social practice, the history of group formation known to have occurred is quite understandable. Without a clear charter and agenda, groups meeting regularly would have to work out the times, purposes, and practices as best they could under the leadership of those willing or eager to assume leadership. Some groups thought that the Jewish codes of clean/unclean would work quite nicely. They did for awhile within the circle that formed in Jerusalem. But others had come to other conclusions. When the leaders of the two groups met finally, only an agreement to disagree could be reached even though a few concessions were granted on both sides in order to keep the fiction of a single Jesus movement alive. Most of the things Jesus people and Christians did happened or could have happened most naturally at gatherings for meals. It was the place for the leaders to be heard, the householders to preside, ideas to be exchanged, the poets to share their pieces, questions to be raised, scriptures to be consulted, and prayers to be said. For the strange thing about the kingdom of God people is that, enamored as they became of the associations they created, they started a new religion by institutionalizing those associations.[5]

2. THE PATTERNS OF GROUP FORMATION

It is very difficult to distinguish clearly the different kinds of groups that formed to keep alive the memory of Jesus. Much of the evidence is secondhand, all of it is later. Some groups died out leaving a single trace

---

other social levels in other types of literature as, for instance, *The Letters* of Alciphron. Such gatherings were seen as social occasions for the exchange of wit, the display of such literary and artistic competence as could be managed, discussion of common interests and concerns, and the engagement of popular philosophical ideas and issues. On the nature of symposium discourse, see David Aune, "Septem Sapientium Convivium." If one looks for settings that could account for the Jesus movements, one sees that gathering for meals was the single most important "generative matrix" for social formation. The "spirit" attending such occasions may have given rise to the use of "spirit" as a primary symbol in early groups. Note that in Paul, "spirit" is a phenomenon manifest on social occasions and understood collectively.

5. *Leadership.* The bewildering variety of leadership roles referred to in early Christian literature indicates two factors at play. One would be the lack of definition at the early stages, due to the lack of program and the need for experimentation. The fierce competition for leadership of the several movements, well known to scholars, would follow from the experimental nature of the situation. "Authority" soon became a major issue. See now Graham Shaw, *The Cost of Authority.* The other factor would be the plurality of official roles already in place in the association model. To "organize" along its lines would have required the assignment and acceptance of various kinds of responsibilities and their ranking according to the importance of functions decided upon by local groups. Many of the offices referred to in early Christian literature correspond to functions common to the association, e.g., deacon (helper, waiter at table), treasurer, householder, supplier, elder, administrator, and so forth. See 1 Cor 12:27–31 for the list with which Paul was working. Paul's account of meeting with the pillars in Jerusalem, their differences and agreements, is in Galatians 2.

assimilated by other groups (Q). Others died out leaving no trace of their own at all (the Jerusalem community). Others produced prized documents but left little information about who they were or where they labored (Didache). Others settled into patterns strong enough to endure for centuries, but are only known from later Christian writers who found them strange and heterodox (e.g., the Ebionites). Some may have produced other varieties, changed drastically in the course of their histories, or merged with movements found to be similar. That there were many, however, is certain. To distinguish several even in partial profile is important in order to set the context for the Gospel of Mark. The points to be made are, first the plurality of social formations and their rationales, and second, the relationship between social histories and the myths that emerged about Jesus.

2.1 The Itinerants in Galilee

The sayings source (Q) may be described as a handbook of Jesus' instructions to his followers emphasizing the main points of his message. It was available as a document sometime in the 70s C.E., for both Matthew and Luke incorporated it into their gospels and Mark also may have used it, or some variant of it. Students of Q have proposed an even earlier dating, however, which is likely, and distinguished layers of kinds of material that suggest a rather lively and complex social history from a very early time. The earliest layer of material is that used to reconstruct Jesus' own aphoristic wisdom, of course, so that those who first collected this material can be understood as early followers. They were those who thought Jesus' teachings important and themselves called to continue their propagation. The idea of the kingdom of God is what they wanted to get across and they apparently went about living much like Jesus had lived, appearing as Cynics to many, except for the note of seriousness, then urgency, that began to creep into the way in which they came to "announce" the kingdom.

It may be difficult to imagine forty years of preaching the kingdom of God by Cynic-like preachers in Galilee and its environs. More than two or three good voices would have been plenty at any one time and people may well have grown weary of their harangue. But perhaps, as Cynics, they spent a good bit of their time simply surviving. In distinction from Egypt where withdrawal from society all but demanded the formation of a convent for survival, the graded topographical and social demarcations in Palestine allowed for the holy man to live on the fringes of society even while "withdrawing" from it. Market days may have been good times both to preach and to beg.

As time went by the Q itinerants learned that some cities were hopeless and not to be bothered. They also learned not to go door-to-door. Instead, they looked for the house that would return the sign of "peace" and "receive" them for dinner. But even that got old. According to the Didache, houses where Jesus congregations formed took the matter up for review and prescribed that a visiting "prophet" could not stay more than two or three days without being put to work. The end of the fiction of public proclamation was therewith sealed and a brief history of semi-sectarian formation ended.

Certain changes took place in the language of the kingdom that mark the stages of this history. Heady promises about divine providence for those who turned their backs on social constraints and labors (such as family ties) turned into calls for repentance, then, finally, pronouncements of judgment and doom upon "this evil generation." It was during the later stages of this history, perhaps during the fifties or sixties, that the rather bleak assessment of the contemporary chances for Jesus' message took over. It was then that the language of the kingdom became apocalyptic and the figure of Jesus at the beginning was matched by the figure of the Son of Man to come at the end. Without a stable social structure to support them, those thinking such thoughts had gone about as far as they could go. "This generation" apparently included everyone and everything. But one detects that, during the course of two generations of activity, preachers of this type had come to think of themselves more and more in terms of lore about the Hebrew prophets of old. They had also turned their guns more and more on Israel, that is Jews living in northern Palestine, as if the message pertained particularly to them. Thus the specifically religious charge to Jesus' notion of the kingdom of God backfired. Originally derived from a generally Hellenistic Jewish religiosity, the ideal came to be used as a judgment upon Jews who did not respond to the construction Jesus' followers put upon it. Were the fire in the preachments left merely to linger in the eyes of these dying prophets, no great harm would have been done. But, alas, householders here and there had thought to copy down the sayings "remembered" by these preachers. In the hands of teachers established in house churches, the experience of these rejected prophets could be used to make sense of the problems the house churches were having with the synagogue.[6]

---

6. *The Q "community."* On the rule about acceptance and rejection at houses, a matter of concern both for the itinerant and for householders, see Luke 10:5–12 and Did 11. The rule in Didache is positioned immediately after the section on the prayers to be said over meals. H. Koester and J. Kloppenborg argue that the language of (apocalyptic) judgment entered the Q tradition at a later stage. See references above in chap. 2, nn. 4 and 14. Two considerations lead to the conclusion that different collections of Jesus' sayings were made at different times by different (settled) communities and transmitted along different paths, some converging, others diverging. One is the difficulty of reconstructing a single text for Q from Matthew, Mark, Luke and the Gospel of Thomas, plus the evidence for other sayings material in the gospels that cannot bid for inclusion in Q as hypothesized. The second consideration is that each of the collections extant (Mark 4; Gospel of Thomas; reconstructions of Q) bears the marks of literary activity. Thus these collections are not simply field notes taken as reports on Jesus' oral performance. People in settled

In the Q collection itself, reflection on the rejection of the prophets in Israel's history had been applied to the experience of the Jesus "prophets" and, by retrojection, to the teachings of Jesus about such rejection. But it had not been applied biographically to Jesus except, perhaps, inversely by emphasizing even more his superior command of the experience of testing (in the late addition of the temptation story) and by an alignment of Jesus with the tradition of the prophets (via snippets of dialogue about Jesus and John the Baptist, also a Cynic-type "prophet"). As the Q material was taken up by those who composed the gospels, however, a theme found in certain Jewish literatures of the time about Israel's rejection and killing of the prophets came to be applied, not only to the failed mission of the Q prophets, but to the fact that Jesus had been killed as well. The function of such a notion was that the experience of failure on the part of Jesus people associated with the synagogue, a failure to convince their Jewish partners to join their group, gained a mythic paradigm.

It should be emphasized at this point that nowhere in this tradition running from Q into the early stages of biographic interest in Jesus is there any evidence for a view of Jesus' death as a "saving event," much less for thinking that Jesus had been transformed by means of a resurrection. The express application of the notion that Jesus had suffered a prophet's fate appears to have been made when the authors of the gospels combined the Jesus traditions with views of Jesus' death and resurrection that had developed in the Christ cults. But the notion of rejection was very near the surface in some of the later oracles in Q, thus preparing the way for thinking of Jesus as the rejected prophet. That Jesus had died a prophet's death would only have meant, however, that he also and especially had been a true prophet in the line of prophets, nothing more. That would have been, in itself, a striking claim about Jesus and his purposes, to be sure, a claim of great significance for the emergence of Christian thought. But it would be wrong to read in any additional Christian nuances about the importance of Jesus' death for those thinking in these terms. Prophets, Stoic philosophers, Cynics, Pharisees—all were widely known to have suffered executions. To have identified Jesus specifically as a Jewish prophet would have been the main point, making it possible for Jesus people to think of themselves as claimants to Israel's history and destiny in spite of the fact that Jews in general had been unimpressed. Beyond that

---

communities from Galilee to Northern Syria must have been party to the collection and transmission of sayings, even though earlier collections took on the form of instructions for the public activity of itinerants. As the sayings traditions evolved, though, the aspect of public announcement either became historicized as in the synoptic gospels, gnosticized as in the Gospel of Thomas, or turned into community codes as in Didache. The Gospel of Thomas shows, for example, that the sayings came to serve some group as a revelation discourse that was not intended for public announcement at all.

one might speculate only that at some point in the Q tradition reflection on Jesus' fate may have contributed to changes in the language of the kingdom, adding to the sense of urgency and underlying the pronouncements of judgment that became characteristic toward the end.[7]

---

7. *The "prophets" in Q.* The current scholarly view is that both Jesus and his followers in the Q tradition were prophets, announcing the kingdom of God and calling upon Israel to repent. M. Eugene Boring develops this view into a thesis about the inspired nature of early Christian prophecy in *Sayings of the Risen Jesus*. Boring's view is that early Christian prophets could have spoken (new) sayings in the name of Jesus only if they knew themselves to be inspired by his spirit (as the resurrected one). It should be emphasized that the term prophet occurs in Q as part of the motif of the killing of the prophets (Luke 6:23; 11:47-51; 13:34). Odil Steck has argued that this motif was a theme in a strand of Jewish literature from Nehemiah 9 on. See his *Israel und das gewaltsame Geschick der Propheten*. Many scholars see the occurrence of the motif in Q as a late stage of reflection, entering the tradition at that layer concerned with woes against the Pharisees, apocalyptic threats, and prophetic pronouncements. See J. Kloppenborg, *The Formation of Q*, 173, 227-29. Still, the prophetic hypothesis persists. Kloppenborg emphasizes the Jewish orientation of the Q material in general, for instance, finding only bits of evidence to suggest that the Q tradents came finally to have some sympathy for Gentiles, *The Formation of Q*, 240-42. Arland Jacobson, "Wisdom Christology in Q," 227, regards Luke 13:34, as well as Luke 13:28-29 and 14:15-24, as evidence that "Israel" had finally been abandoned by the Q prophets. Thus the history of Q presents an interesting case.

Several considerations, in addition to the aphoristic nature of the earliest material already discussed, tell against the prevailing "prophetic" assumption. The activity of the Q itinerants was no doubt public and limited to Galilee, or perhaps northern Palestine. If they followed in Jesus' footsteps, their style would have been similar to his and their social critique quite general. There is no evidence that the early Q people had Jewish institutions specifically in mind, that is, directed their critique against a particular form of Judaism. Neither is the "Jewishness" of the early itinerants more than one might expect of Galilean provincials who had taken up Jesus' ways. The shift to the language of judgment, including the alignment with the precedence of the prophets, points in two directions. On the one hand, a sense of disillusionment and failure is to be noticed. Falling back upon current patterns of thought, such as the motif of killing the prophets, served as a rationale for the failure even as it repositioned the erstwhile itinerants over against the world now as "prophets." The world, for its part, was now a larger scheme of things than had been in view before. That also is a typical move in mythmaking. In this case it was an (apocalyptic) history of Israel that had been called upon, as well as a general (negative) assessment of the present generation, including the central symbol for the culture associated with the prevailing social and political structures, that is, Jerusalem (Luke 13:34). To use these patterns of thought for making sense of a new situation does not mean necessarily that Jews had been or were the principal detractors, although criticism from Palestinian Jews may have been especially painful for followers of Jesus who may have shared both his provincial Jewish roots and his Hellenistic ways.

Of greater significance, however, is the evidence of institutional conflict that does surface just at this point in the history of the tradition. The precedence of the prophets is clearly related to rejection from the synagogue (Luke 6:22-23). The woes against the Pharisees likewise express concerns that can be imagined only for a group of Jesus people in contact with the synagogue. Note that the woes are about table-fellowship, washings, alms, tithes, honor in the synagogues, public recognition, laws of ritual purity, and burial practice (Luke 11:37-47). If one includes considerations such as the confessional issue basic to the Son of Man sayings (Luke 12:8-9 with variant in Mark 8:38) and other indications of sectarian formation in the prophetic and apocalyptic materials at this later stage of Q, the evidence strongly points, not only to a shift in language about the kingdom, but to a social transition taking place on the fringes between itinerants and house groups.

2.2 The Pillars in Jesusalem

In his letter to the Galatians, Paul explained that he thought it wise to compare his understanding of the gospel with views held by the "pillars" in Jerusalem. This is hard evidence for the existence of a Jesus group in Jerusalem already known to Paul. Paul, prone to extremes, wanted to think that the (Gentile) Christianity, to which he had been converted (as a conservative Jew), started in the capital city of Pharisaic religion. Luke picked up on this idea even though by his time the pillars in Jerusalem were no longer there, having fled (to Pella?) it seems when the Roman legions marched on Jerusalem in the late sixties. Thus the tradition of the origins of Christianity in Jerusalem was born, a tradition still very much alive, not only in Christian mythology, but in the scholarship as well. According to this tradition, Peter, the main pillar, was with Jesus in Jerusalem, received the first resurrection appearance shortly thereafter, was responsible for the earliest community of Christians, the first preaching mission, the rudiments of the passion narrative, and the notion of the church as the New Israel. Grave legends, supper traditions, apostleship and all have been traced back to the first church in Jerusalem. There is absolutely no evidence to support these claims, except for Paul's attribution of an "appearance" to Peter in 1 Cor 15:5, a problem to be discussed in chapter 4.

Paul did not say what the gospel according to the pillars was. But he made it very clear, both in Galatians and elsewhere in his correspondence, that his gospel and their gospel did not match. He also names certain things about which they differed. Whether Christians needed to be circumcised was one. Whether Jewish Christians should eat with Gentile Christians was another. Matters having to do with the preparation of foods, especially meats, was another. And then there was the matter of the law, the importance of the temple cult, and the question of Jewishness in general as requisite for membership in the new sect. Except for the orientation of this group to Jesus as founder, nothing is known about it that would not agree with a generally Pharisaic approach to Jewish reform. Thus, instead of providing answers for the origins of Christianity, this strange sectarian formation presents the historian only with a set of very difficult questions.[8]

One can only speculate about what happened. Jerusalem was, of course, the big city for Galileans during this period. Jesus must have gone there on

---

Itinerants became "prophets," then, just at this time. Whether they became "prophets" in their own eyes, or whether in the eyes of Jesus groups interested in their activity and teachings, makes little difference.

8. *The Jerusalem church*. A profile of the early community in Jerusalem and its fate is given in H. Koester, *Introduction to the New Testament* 2:86–89, 198–201. A critical assessment of the traditional view on the origins of Christianity in Jerusalem can begin by noticing the paucity and lateness of the "sources" for the synthetic reconstruction Koester gives.

some occasion, most probably during a pilgrimage season, was associated with a demonstration, and was killed. A reading of Josephus reveals that the temple authorities were beginning to lose control of the situation during this period, that pilgrimage became the occasion for popular demonstrations of dissatisfaction with the way things were going, and that reprisals on the part of the authorities were swift and brutal. Jesus need not even have been the instigator of such a tumult. There is nothing in early traditions about him that would indicate a motivation for doing so. He may, of course, have been trying out a few ideas about the kingdom of God away from home. That would have been a very dangerous thing to do, easily mistaken by Judeans, especially if he dared do so in the midst of pilgrims from Galilee who, according to Josephus, always seemed to have something to complain about at pilgrimage. One dare not overly dramatize, however, thinking the spotlight must have fallen on Jesus as the gospels have it. Only his followers took note, and then, not all of them.[9]

Some of his followers apparently saw a connection between Jesus' activity in Galilee and his fate in Jerusalem. How they put these pieces together, however, and what they concluded from them are hardly reconstructible. They may have concluded that Jesus' fate in Jerusalem was a sign of just how bad things had gotten. Attention could have shifted from the kingdom of God as it sounded in Galilee to very big thoughts about what it might mean for Jerusalem. Jesus may even have been thought of in retrospect as a popular reformer of some kind whose message about the kingdom of God now had to be taken even more seriously. The very fact that the pillars took up residence in Jerusalem does indicate designs upon the religious history of Palestine. For Galilean Jews without credentials that would have been a very pretentious move.

The social codes they adopted, however, agreed with hasidic values. That is very strange. It does not agree at all with the conception of Jesus' importance or intentions shared by the Q people. Perhaps the followers who moved to Jerusalem could find no other way to apply the kingdom idea as a reform program aimed at real Second Temple institutions and issues. In the atmosphere at Jerusalem, hasidic codes may have been the only ones to make sense. What they expected to come of their representation of Israel's destiny as the kingdom of God, however, is not clear. Perhaps they themselves were unclear about it. Their retreat to the Transjordan is suspicious, fleeing before the Romans got there without taking part or sides in the melee that followed. So their designs were, apparently, vague.

Another chapter may have started in Pella for those who fled Jerusalem, but the pillars appear to have fallen even before that time. A Jewish-

---

9. *Pilgrimage.* For a discussion of Galilean pilgrimage with reference to the accounts in Josephus see Freyne, *Galilee,* 287–93.

Christian sect may have been formed in the process, however, eventually producing such literature as the Didache, and influencing such authors as Matthew. Judging from later evidence for Jewish Christianity in general, Jesus was esteemed as the "anointed" teacher of a Jewish ethic of very high standards. He was not revered, held to be divine, or worshipped on the model of the Hellenistic congregations. Confident about claiming Israel's legacy, these sectarians nevertheless quickly settled into postures of containment, drawing the lines firmly both against Jews who did not accept Jesus' way, and against Gentile Christians who held Jesus to be a god and did not keep the law. Thus the "pillars" in Jerusalem may have laid the foundations for a Jewish sect of hasidim who interpreted the law by appeal to Jesus' authority and survived the destruction of Jerusalem as some other sects did not. But they cannot have been the ones who founded the "Christian" church and started the Gentile "mission." Paul was simply engaging in wishful thinking on the grand scale with himself positioned at a crucial juncture in a new holy history.[10]

2.3 The Family of Jesus

Closely related to the hasidic movement that started in Jerusalem, then took root in Transjordan, was another configuration that centered on Jesus' family. One of the pillars of the early group in Jerusalem was James, the brother of Jesus. This means that some family connection was there from the start and may well have influenced the constructions that the Jerusalem group put upon the whole Jesus affair. From later sources there is information about a Jewish-Christian sect called Nazareans closely related to the Ebionites in the Transjordan. Scholars have argued plausibly that there was some connection between these groups and Jesus' family and hometown in Galilee (Nazareth). The early history of these groups is very uncertain and is normally not thought worth discussing as a contribution to the origins of Christianity. But there is mention of Jesus' family already in the synoptic tradition and a very interesting genealogy for Jesus' family in the Gospel of Matthew. Some of the early stories about Jesus and his family in the synoptic traditions follow the Cynic theme of homelessness and the necessity of rejecting one's family. Since the theme is so typical, one must be careful not to historicize. But the impression one has nevertheless is that people in the Q tradition may actually have had a little tussle with Jesus' family and friends over rights to claim his authority. Jesus' importance in the eyes of others may have been taken by his family as a challenge and chance to reverse the proverbial wisdom about a prophet's lack of honor in

---

10. *Jewish Christians in the Transjordan*. For a collection of the unfortunately scanty evidence see H. Koester, *Introduction to the New Testament* 2:198–203. See also Hans Joachim Schoeps, *Jewish Christianity*. For a bibliography accenting recent studies see Bruce Malina, "Jewish Christianity."

his own town. For a presumably peasant family in an insignificant village in the hills of Galilee, a son grown famous would have been a very important event. The normal approach would have been to emphasize the family relationships and speculate about genealogical questions.

The Transjordan would have been an ideal location to nurture a non-Judean, Jewish family tradition with claims to descent from king David and with codes representing the highest standards of enlightenment piety. These claims were taken seriously by many, including other varieties of early Christians in Syria. Contact with other forms of Christianity occurred repeatedly, creating a series of ideological crises well into the fourth century. The history of these groups is therefore dotted with little compromises to accommodate the views of other Christians, while strenuously defending the genealogical and hasidic foundations of the sect. Gentile Christians did not have to live by the law as long as it was understood that Jewish Christians did, and so forth. For such a sect to have evolved was quite natural. Its hasidic character cannot be used to speculate about Jesus' own family and training, of course. But to have drawn Jewish conclusions about him was certainly more legitimate than the conclusions others were to draw. It is very important to see that everyone did not think the same about Jesus. Even among those who thought him very important and especially among those who knew him well there was no agreement.[11]

2.4 The Congregation of Israel

Collections of miracle stories have been discovered among the Jesus traditions used to compose the Gospels of Mark and John. Because they are collections, and because they betray a certain kind of meditation on Jesus' activity, they are evidence for yet another early Jesus movement. Miracle stories do seem an unlikely vehicle for a group's mythmaking. It would be more natural to think that miracle stories simply traveled from group to group as entertainment, or perhaps as supplying just part of the picture of a movement's founder. A collection has usually been thought of, therefore, merely as a stage in the transmission of lore. But the similarity of the Markan and Johannine collections is very striking, indicating some com-

---

11. *The Family of Jesus.* Koester, *Introduction to the New Testament* 2:200, notes the evidence for the existence of a group linked to Jesus by family. Paul knew about James, the brother of Jesus, who was one of the pillars in Jerusalem (Gal 1:19). Important references to Jesus' family in the synoptic tradition are: Mark 3:31–35 (Luke 8:19–21; GThom 99); Mark 6:3 (Luke 4:22–23; Matt 13:55–57); Luke 11:27–28. On the instruction to leave one's family see Luke 9:57–62; 12:49–53; 14:25–26; 18:29–30. A study of the later traditions about James by Scott Brown, "James," demonstrates that none of them can be used to reconstruct an early Jewish-Christian movement since all of them betray either gnostic or Catholic Christian interests. The lack of primary literary evidence for Jewish Christianity in the Transjordan makes it impossible to know what role a family connection to Jesus may have continued to play.

mon milieu or line of intellectual activity lying behind them. The similarity involves quite a distinctive view of Jesus, a view that does not immediately overlap with other characterizations among the early traditions. It extends, moreover, to a particular sectarian claim for which the view of Jesus projected by the stories serves as support or rationale. This claim suggests a particular sense of identity among some early Jesus group or groups.

Anticipating the later discussion of the miracle stories in chapter 8, these collections combine allusions to the activities of Moses and Elijah. The Exodus story appears to be in mind, because each set begins with a sea-crossing miracle and ends with a miracle of feeding in the wilderness. The miracles of healing that are framed by these epic allusions remind one, however, of the Elisha-Elijah cycle of miracles. Other features probably have symbolic significance as well. One is that the people who are healed are socially marginal by first-century standards, and they are ritually impure. Jesus' healings, then, are clearly understood to be an act of "cleansing" these people, but not for Levitical purposes. Instead, they illustrate the process of collecting candidates for the congregation that is constituted by the meal. One can easily imagine a storyteller with a twinkle in his eye taking this way to make a point about the unconventional mix of people who got together for talk about Jesus.

If Jesus was as unconcerned about specifically Jewish traditions as the evidence indicates, this appeal to epic precedence would be another case of followers falling back on available epic models and mythic images of Israel in order to work out a rationale for their social interests and behavior. In this case also, a generally Jewish heritage was apparently taken for granted. But the claim to represent that heritage was made in full awareness of the lack of fit. Boundaries had been violated on all fronts—ethnic, social (class), and Levitical (demarcations of status according to the laws of purity). Thus the group was consciously defining itself over against existing conceptions, especially against hasidic codes and models. Such a point was not made polemically, however. It was, rather, a difference noted with some delight. The delight was due, one suspects, to the clever way in which the traditions of Israel had been applied without falling into Second Temple models. Israel, yes, seems to be the note sounded, Second Temple Judaism, no. Such an attitude would not have been strange at all in North Palestine. It does, in fact, fit in quite nicely.

Miracles, it should be noted, were merely the point of departure for making several connections that served to enhance Jesus' importance as a founder of the unlikely congregation. The images for both Moses and Elijah were taken no doubt from the common stock of lore popular in the north. Elijah was a prophet of the Northern Kingdom, one may recall, about whom rather fantastic stories were still being told, among them some that imagined his reappearance to restore Israel whenever it got into trouble because of forgetfulness. Moses, of course, was the legendary prophet-king of special significance to the Samaritan epic imagination. Neither Moses nor Elijah were the private property of Judea. To have combined features of both in a single characterization of Jesus meant that some group was very close to a myth of origins, justifying its mixed membership, form of leadership ("disciples" performing narrative, scribal, and mealtime functions), and table fellowship, by imagining Jesus to have brought it all about on the grand scale. Jesus had been aligned with highly mythologized epic figures of profound significance for Jewish self-understanding. Thus some claim to the epic traditions of Israel was being made, if only implicitly.[12]

One might note the role played by the epic traditions in this mythologization of Jesus. There is no need to mystify the process, as if this group must first have believed in the resurrection or divinity of Jesus. The divine features of the characterization are fully understandable as a combination of Hellenistic views of the divine man and Hellenistic-Jewish myths of Moses and the prophets that had already been imagined. A Jesus group oriented generally to Jewish-Israelite religiosity, but composed of people with various ethnic and religious backgrounds, could easily have entertained ideas about Jesus like those portrayed in the miracle collections. A reading of Philo of Alexandria, or the Wisdom of Solomon, or any of a great number of Jewish and Samaritan literatures of the period shows that a kerygmatic event was not essential to the kind of epic mythology reflected in the miracle chains. It would be better to understand this mythologization of Jesus as the product of a group's effort to make sense of what actually was transpiring among them. Social formation was taking place and, when asked to say what it was all about, social identity and purpose required some articulation. This group decided in favor of claiming epic precedence for their egalitarian association. It would be helpful to know in what other kinds of activities they engaged, what it was that made that association seem so important. But the really big miracle may simply have been that, within this group at least, differences in social background enhanced rather than hindered the spirit of the conversation about "congregation" at mealtime.[13]

---

12. *Elijah.* A discussion of evidence for the lore about Elijah is found in F. Hahn, *The Titles of Jesus in Christology,* 352–56. A review of this evidence by R. Horsley, "'Like One of the Prophets of Old,'" led him to the conclusion that "there is indeed some solid textual evidence for the expectation of Elijah, as well as indirect evidence that this expectation . . . was alive in popular circles at the time of Jesus." Nevertheless: "There appears to be very little textual evidence of any concept of an eschatological prophet in Jewish society during the early period of Roman domination." And "for the currency in Jewish society at the time of Jesus of an expectation of an eschatological prophet like Moses there is almost no evidence" (p. 443).

13. *Miracles and Moses.* Cosmic mythologies of the Exodus miracles and of Moses as a divine man are a feature of literatures extending from Alexandria through Samaria and into northern Syria. It is important to realize that these imaginative characterizations were achieved in the course of reflection upon the scriptural charter in relation to the times and

2.5 The Synagogue Reform

The pronouncement stories document another very important chapter in the early history of the Jesus movements. In their present form in the Gospel of Mark these stories are highly elaborated and bear the marks of having been interwoven into Mark's narrative designs. Scholars have been able to reconstruct the outlines of a pre-Markan stage of storytelling, however, for which an interesting set of characteristics can be determined. At this pre-Markan stage Jesus was the master of every challenging situation. The challenges came from opponents who questioned his authority and raised embarrassing questions about his activities. These questions are the familiar ones about sabbath observance, eating with unclean people, foods, washings, tithes, fasting, and so forth. One recognizes immediately that Pharisaic laws of purity are at issue and, as one might expect, Pharisees and scribes do figure in the stories as Jesus' opponents. Jesus succeeds in confounding them at every turn, of course, but one sees that his logic and authority depend upon assumptions his opponents would not have shared. The assumptions betray an exaggerated view of Jesus' authority, which means that the stories were told from the point of view of some Jesus movement for which authority had become a big issue.

The settings are typically house-gatherings, with many taking place at mealtime. Since many of the issues raised are appropriate to this setting, one might account for the setting merely as good narrative sense. But since both the setting and the class of issues are so interrelated and of such social consequence, the suspicion would be that they must go together. If so, the most reasonable reconstruction of the social situation addressed by these stories would be meal practice in and around the synagogue where contact with Pharisees may have taken place. If both Pharisees and Jesus people belonged to the same synagogue, one might very well expect fireworks.

For this reconstruction to work, one does have to assume that table fellowship was a very important, distinguishing characteristic for these Jesus people, and that the practice had spread into the Hellenistic cities of Galilee and perhaps southern Syria. One also has to assume that Jesus

---

that the questions raised were about social identity. The occurrence of a similar mythology for Jesus in the miracle stories need not presuppose a prior mythologization of the death and resurrection at all. On the mythologization of Moses in Philo, see B. Mack, "Imitatio Mosis." On the similarity of Samaritan myths of Moses to Philo, see Wayne Meeks, *The Prophet-King*. The cosmic interpretation of the Exodus miracles is elaborate in the Wisdom of Solomon 11–19, probably of northern Syrian provenance. For the logic that underlies this interpretation, see J. P. M. Sweet, "The Theory of Miracles." An introduction to Samaritan literature and thought has been written by James A. Montgomery, *The Samaritans.*

people thought of themselves as a Jewish reform movement of some kind with something to say to Jewish communities in those cities where the synagogue was the institutional form of Jewish identity and activity. That Pharisees became the principal target of polemic does not mean that Pharisees were in control of these synagogues. Not only would they not have been in control, the representation of their views among these Jewish communities would have been as recent a development as the appearance of the Jesus people with their proposals. One has to imagine a lengthy period of encounter from both sides, many arguments, and a slow escalation of the conflict between the two parties. In southern Syria and beyond, both positions may well have been viewed as export ideologies from Palestine, the Pharisees sounding a conservative position, the Jesus people taking the opposite tack. But, of course, the Pharisees had to win, supposing that a synagogue found itself in the position of finally having to choose. Pharisees had arguments, institutional precedents, and practical considerations that made sense, should it come down to the question of Jewish identity. They also had texts, and a bit of practice in how to read them. Jesus people had only their unconventional table fellowship to share, plus the liberal kingdom talk that went along with it, and appeals to a recent sage who had excited the imagination. What sounded good around the table of the Jesus people may not have been convincing in the service at the synagogue.

The elaborated pronouncement stories were a rather late development in this group's history. Scholars date them as a set in the fifties and sixties. The later dating is the more convincing. It gives time for the Pharisaic presence in the synagogue, as well as allows for the contacts and conflicts to run their course. The real debates were over when the pronouncement stories were elaborated. In the process, Jesus people had been forced to give attention to themselves and their claims. Some social coding had taken place, but mostly in weak contrast to Pharisaic standards. Thus Jesus people did not fast on the right days (but they did fast!); they did not keep the sabbath strictly (but they had not given up the notion of the sabbath); they did not accept the Pharisees' proof texts for the laws of purity (but they had found a few other texts that appeared to contradict them). The only authority the Jesus people really had was Jesus. They must have realized this, for the Jesus of the pronouncement stories, though he argues like a non-Pharisaic Pharisee against the Pharisees, always appeals only to his own authority to win the argument. That authority is not clearly rationalized, however, but affirmed. He is simply the one who speaks with authority (for the Jesus people). That would not have been enough to go on, once the Jesus people found themselves unwelcome in a synagogue or two. Having thought of themselves fundamentally as Jews, members of the diaspora institutions, meeting together as those who no longer belonged would have created a very big problem indeed. It was that situation which, most probably, was fresh in Mark's mind when he wrote his gospel.[14]

3. JEWISH REFORM AND HELLENISTIC CULT

The term Jesus movement has been used for those groups that kept the memory of Jesus alive and thought of themselves in terms of Jewish reform. Five types have been distinguished and their differences from one another have been underlined. In actuality the situation may have been a bit more fluid, with some overlapping of people, ideas, activities, and the production of texts. One might imagine a Jesus group in, say, Tyre ca. 55–60 C.E. with copies of Q, a miracle story collection, and some elaborated pronouncement stories in hand. But each memory tradition does stem from distinctive social experience and determined intellectual response localized somewhere. It is important to grasp that, in order to keep from thinking that early Christianity blossomed as a single flower early and overnight. Groups formed as movements, each with its own sense of purpose.

The term Jesus movement is important for another reason as well. By describing these groups as reform movements they can be distinguished easily from the Hellenistic Christ cults that also belong in the larger picture. The usual view of the beginnings of Christianity derives from the Christ cults. There it is that a community can be espied most like the Christian church. Naturally one would like to think that, even though plurality cannot be denied, early Christian groups differed mainly over fine points of christological and soteriological interpretation. Jewish Christianity has not been allowed to intrude, shunted aside as an understandable but mistaken response to what must have been a more dramatic set of events, a set of events more in line with kerygmatic views of the Hellenistic congregations. The sequence should be reversed. Movements in the name of Jesus as a teacher, sage, or charismatic reformer must have been the normal formation, the Christ cults a peculiar aberration. Such a thought is difficult to accept mainly because notions fundamental to the Christian view of Jesus' significance are lacking in the Jesus movements. Though meals were taken together, a ritual in memory of Jesus' death is not in evidence. There is no myth of Jesus' resurrection, no appeal to appearances, no cultivation of his continuing spiritual presence. Jesus did not become the Lord of a new religious society that called for abrogation of the past in order to be transformed and enter a new creation.

---

14. *Synagogue reform.* The reconstruction given will find further substantiation in chap. 7. For positions taken by the synagogue reform movement regarding fasting, sabbath, use of proof texts, and halakhic argumentation see the following pronouncement stories: Mark 2:18–22; 2:23–28; 7:1–23; 14:3–9.

The Christian gospel is as much indebted to the Jesus movements as the Christ cult. Mark borrowed from both traditions and combined them in his narrative. In order to understand what made his gospel work, the Jesus traditions must be studied without assuming Christ cult notions. It was Mark who Christianized them in the writing of the gospel. Before he did that, and of course even after, Jesus people felt no need to think of Jesus as a god or savior. That happened in the Hellenistic communities of northern Syria and beyond.

4

THE CONGREGATIONS
OF THE CHRIST

Paul was converted to a Hellenized form of some Jesus movement that had already developed into a Christ cult. His letters from the fifties, written for the most part to congregations he had founded, gather up an even earlier history during which Paul struggled with the strange new gospel. Thus his letters serve as documentation for the Christ cult as well. They are a precious corpus, for without them the astounding practices of the Jesus people in northern Syria would have been lost. No one would have dared suggest on the basis of the narrative gospel traditions that such a cult could have developed at all, much less as soon as it did.

Still, Paul's letters are to be read with a very critical eye. His own reports of his precipitous turnabout should alert the reader to the possibility that Paul's description of the gospel might be overly dramatized. His first encounters with the Jesus people had angered him. His claim was that his anger stemmed from zeal for the traditions of the fathers (Gal 1:14), but one suspects a special brittleness about that zeal on Paul's part. He told the Galatians that he had "persecuted the church of God violently" (Gal 1:13), drawing the contrast between his former way of life and his Christian vocation as starkly as he could. What persecuting the church of God meant, however, is very difficult to imagine, especially so because nothing is known about any authority Paul might have claimed to have done anything more than to raise a hue and cry. One has to assume that, in retrospect, he pictured himself as a self-appointed terror. His account of his conversion is also suspicious. He claimed a private revelation directly from God in order to disavow that he had learned about Jesus Christ from anybody else (Gal 1:12, 16). These are obvious signs of an unstable, authoritarian person, eager that "his" gospel now be recognized as the standard over against all others (Gal 1:6–9). It should not be assumed, therefore, that Paul's letters provide a clear window into Hellenistic Christianity. His gospel really may have been his own construction, the product of a brilliant mind, a sensitive spirit, and a stimulating but painfully irresolvable conflict of cultures. He was actively engaged in conflict over his gospel and his own position of authority throughout his mission, and the rhetoric of his letters is extreme and impassioned. One suspects that, wherever Paul got his sense of urgency and apocalyptic mentality, it was not from the Christ cult. His preaching was as troublesome for the "Hellenists" in these circles as for the "Judaizers," though for different reasons in each case. Paul, it seems, stood in the middle and carved out a decidedly dialectical theology.

Paul understood his conversion to the Christ cult as a transition from life lived in observance of the law, to freedom enabled by the spirit energizing the new community. From Paul's point of view, the transition may have been just that momentous. What he found when he switched from law to freedom, however, did not grant him peace. He discovered that Jesus people were not all the same and that the issue of law versus freedom had scarcely been raised, much less resolved. His journey to see the pillars in Jerusalem about the gospel was his own idea, one that may not have occurred to anyone except a would-be leader of what Paul took to be a mission of some magnitude. When he got there, however, the pillars confronted him with just those hasidic concerns he had given up in order to become a Christian. His own views, conversely, alarmed the pillars who apparently decided that Paul was a dangerous man. There is evidence of a great deal of conflict between Paul and the so-called (Christian) Judaizers throughout his career, a conflict Paul himself probably provoked. His either/or approach to such matters as Christ and the law, freedom versus bondage, and faith and works, may therefore be due as much to his own experience of a thorny personal issue as to early intra-sectarian conflict. It may have been Paul, not the Hellenistic congregations of the Christ, who decided that Christ meant freedom from the law, on the one hand, and who preached an apocalyptic judgment scene for those who rejected Christ, on the other. One has to admit that such a combination of ideas is contradictory, so much so that only a subtle mind could manage the maneuvers necessary to translate from one to the other quickly. It is doubtful that such preaching was foundational for the Hellenistic congregations. Something else must have carried the day for the Christ cult Paul presupposed, then tried to restructure as a Gentile version of a hasidic sect of perfection.[1]

Paul's gospel was, nevertheless, worked out as an articulation of the Christ cult, not of the Jesus movements. His letters are, in any case, the only window the historian has for peering into the earliest congregations of the Christ. Scholars have rightly concluded that, used with care, quite a number of distinctive features can be determined. The letters are full of small bits of material that bear the marks of cultic formulation. Twice Paul

---

1. *Paul.* From an extensive body of literature, the following studies introduce the issues raised: H. D. Betz, *Galatians;* H. J. Schoeps, *Paul;* G. Shaw, *The Cost of Authority;* J. A. Fitzmyer, *Pauline Theology;* and Krister Stendahl, *Paul Among Jews and Gentiles.*

cites "traditions" he received (1 Cor 11:23–26; 15:3–5). Frequently it is clear from his line of argument that common opinions and practices were in view, some of which Paul agreed with and shared, others of which he argued against. Collecting this material does not produce a single coherent system of belief and practice, to be sure. The scene was very lively, creative, and contentious. But classed as a group of phenomena pertaining to Hellenistic Christians in general, the evidence from Paul's letters is that something quite different happened to the Jesus movements in the diaspora than took place in Palestine. It is with those distinguishing characteristics in general that the present chapter is concerned.

1. THE CHRIST CULT

One of the more startling differences between the Jesus movements and the Christ cult is that a mythology sprang up about Jesus as a divine being. This mythology focused on Jesus' resurrection, understood both as a reward for his obedience and as an ascension to cosmic and community lordship. Jesus the Cynic-sage, whether as teacher or founder of the community by miracles, was erased in the transformation. The title Christ became a personal name used mainly to refer to the one whose death and resurrection founded the community as a saving event. The title Lord was used mainly to refer to the continuing authority and presence of the ascended one. And the terminology of the Son of God was used to imagine the decisive events of Jesus' death and ascension as part of a plan that God had devised, and a pattern of destiny that Jesus had traversed. Thus the saving event of Jesus' death and resurrection revealed to the community the divine power of transformation available to it.[2]

The Hellenistic community was highly conscious of itself as a "gathering together" in the name of the Christ. These people gathered at meals, for Paul took meals for granted, and the primary symbols of the meal (wine and bread) became ritualized moments for remembering Christ's death. But that was not all these Christians did when they met together, nor was the celebration of the meal necessarily a solemn occasion. People talked. And they sang, argued, tried out a new poem, discussed affairs, and listened to guests who brought with them a report, teaching, or prophecy. Hymns, doxologies, prayers, and credos were written. The scriptures were read,

---

2. *The Christ cult.* The term Christ cult is used in a general sense to distinguish the congregations of the Christ from the Jesus movements. The characteristics that invite cultic description are (1) the kerygma of the death and resurrection of the Christ, (2) the production of a myth of cosmic destiny, (3) the mythic ritualization of the meal, (4) the rite of baptism with its symbolic associations derived from the kerygma, (5) the notion of spiritual "presence," and (6) the creation of liturgical materials, including acclamations, doxologies, confessions of faith, and hymns.

interpreted, and applied. People came to be known for certain kinds of responsibilities, and various leadership roles emerged. Rites of greeting and entrance were recognized and practiced. In general, a fully functional religious society can be discerned that celebrated the new spirit of the transcendent Christ.

To account for this surprising phenomenon has been one of the most difficult challenges confronting the historian. Bultmann's formula was simply that the proclaimer of the kingdom of God became the one proclaimed (as the Christ or Lord of the new community). He failed to ask about the reasons for such a significant shift. Others have pointed to the reports of the appearances of the resurrected Jesus as the beginnings of the new religion. In this case the failure has been not to ask about the mythology presupposed by such reports. But the problem cannot be addressed solely at the level of mythology either. The critical difference to be explained is that between the Jesus movements that did not divinize a resurrected founder, and the Christ cult that did.

One has to assume that Jesus people were involved in the beginnings of the Christ cult, of course. The most natural reconstruction would be to project the Jesus people of the synagogue reform northward to Antioch and eastern Syria where another social circumstance and intellectual climate encouraged a more imaginative social formation. The common elements would have been (1) the table fellowship of a cell group on the edges of the synagogue, and (2) a vague sense of being a reform movement with claims to generally Jewish epic traditions and ideals, i.e., to represent Israel. The difference it would make to be in Antioch, then, instead of Galilee or southern Phoenicia, is clear. The farther away from Judea, the less influence came from hasidic Judaism, and the more from a general cosmopolitan ethos.

Antioch was a great seat of Hellenistic culture. Its Jewish community was large, strong and very independent. Jesus people talking about a popular Galilean sage as their founder may have sparked considerable interest. Since their table fellowship was open to any interested person, moreover, proselytes and Gentiles with very little understanding for hasidic concerns could easily have joined in. Paul's Gentile "mission" cannot be understood unless the Jesus Christ people he encountered already included Gentiles. The Jewish-Gentile mix, then, must be considered a very significant factor in the formation of the cult. The myths it generated are ultimately Greek myths, though they were used by Hellenistic Jews to rearticulate Jewish ideals. Such a mingling of ideas was not exceptional in the diaspora. Jewish literature of Syrian provenance demonstrates that Jewish intellectuals were highly Hellenized and very skilled in accommodating Greek thought and mythology to their own ends. Jesus people would have done the same. The cultural climate was simply stimulating, and the imaginative, intellectual production of the Christ cult shows that it was not immune. A new association (*koinōnia*), on the other hand, cultivating a new social vision, may have introduced some stimulus of its own. A vigorous activity of some kind is, in any case, the only way to account for the early origins of the Christ congregations in northern Syria. These were the people Paul did not like upon first encounter. Paul's personal response and his letters have given the impression that the Christ cult was wracked with Christian-Jewish conflict from the beginning. But the opposite seems to have been the case. The Christ association came to a sense of social identity and independence very early on, much before any of the Jesus movements did. It does not appear to have been triggered by an adamant Jewish rejection. The diaspora synagogue may have been, in fact, the chief recruiting grounds as the Christ cult spread.

2. THE CHRIST MYTH

A major stream of New Testament scholarship has born a quest for the earliest christology. By this is meant the earliest designation used to attribute special significance to Jesus as the founder of the new religious society. Most scholars have distinguished between "low" christologies, that is, attributions of social roles that need not have implied divinity, such as that of the prophet, and "high" christologies that did imply divine status or being. Interest has always focused on the "high" christologies where mythological identifications were made.

Among the Jesus movements, the only mythological figure with quasi-divine potential imagined in relation to Jesus was the Son of Man. Scholars have been particularly intrigued by this figure, because it only occurs in utterances spoken by Jesus, though never unambiguously in self-reference. At the narrative level of Mark's Gospel, the context does make it necessary for the reader to make the identification, of course. But in the context of the sayings collection, it seems as if Jesus was referring to some other apoca-lyptic figure destined to come for the final judgment. Those who think that Jesus was an apocalyptic preacher have been particularly interested in these sayings. They have proposed a Son of Man "christology" as the earliest confession of faith, that identification of Jesus which combined his appear-ance as a proclaimer with his final appearance as the judge of those who would not receive his message. Those who propose this reconstruction invariably assume that it was the "experience of the resurrected Lord" that made the christology of the Son of Man thinkable. Unfortunately, there is not a shred of evidence for such a belief in the Q tradition. Unfortunately as well, critical work on the synoptic tradition makes it impossible to regard the Son of Man sayings as early. They belong to that stage of experience within the Q tradition characterized by pronouncements of doom and judgment upon those who rejected Jesus' teachings. Even if the Son of Man christology was an early mythologization in some Jesus movement, however, it could not have stood at the beginning of the Christ cult. It would have provided no incipient basis at all for sectarian formation of any kind, much less for a community gathered in the name of a spiritual presence. That being the case, another line of investigation has been to scrutinize the titles used in the Christ cult and press back to the earliest formulations in that context.[3]

Three titles have received major attention—Christ, Lord, and Son of God. The designation Son of God occurs in formulations that turn on the ideas of "sending," "giving," "giving of oneself," and a return to the father as an exaltation or installation to divine kingship. A fullblown myth of cosmic destiny is therefore assumed with this title. It cannot have been the first myth imagined, for it presupposes other, simpler mythologies, especially those that focus on the reasons for Jesus' exaltation that do not make any appeal to his prior divinity or sonship. The title of Lord also cannot have been the earliest designation. It occurs in liturgical formulations such as hymns (Phil 2:11), acclamations (1 Cor 1:2; Rom 10:13), definitions of cultic ethos (2 Cor 3:17), and ritual etiologies (1 Cor 11:23–26). It evokes both the Jewish idea of God (when in an apocalyptic frame of reference) and the Hellenistic idea of a cultic deity. The jump from Jesus the sage to Jesus the Lord is simply too great to have been taken all at once. That leaves the title Christ, and it is in relation to this designation that the most informative studies have been done.[4]

The term Christ is used in formulations that scholars have called kerygmatic. These formulations are brief statements of credal content bearing the marks of poetic composition and liturgical use. The content refers to Christ's death and resurrection. In some cases the event is emphasized to enhance either Jesus' special status or the pattern of destiny itself. In others, the significance of the event for the community is indicated, as for instance in the addition of the purpose that Christ died "for us," or "for our sins." The tradition cited in 1 Cor 15:3–5 has frequently been in mind as a clear example of the kerygma (see figure 1).

---

3. *Son of Man "christology."* The classic attempt to think through the implications of a Son of Man "christology" at the beginning is the study by Willi Marxsen, *The Beginnings of Christology.* Even though he assumes "the resurrection," making sense of the identification between Jesus and the Son of Man as the first christology of continuing presence leads Marxsen to extremely complicated conceptual problems. His proposal is not convincing. A Son of Man christology at the beginning of the Christ cult simply does not work.

4. *The earliest christology.* A fine exegetical introduction to the christologies of the Hellenistic congregations is Kramer's *Christ, Lord, Son of God.* See also the references cited above in the Introduction, n. 2.

FIGURE 1

THE CHRIST KERYGMA

That Christ died
  for our sins
  according to the scriptures;
that he was buried;
that he was raised
  on the third day
  according to the scriptures;
and that he appeared
  (to Cephas, then to the twelve).
                              (1 Cor 15:3–5)

Critical analysis of 1 Cor 15:3–5 in the scholarship has demonstrated that it is a very complex composition, presupposing several stages of thinking about the significance of Jesus' crucifixion. This analysis has been combined with thorough investigations of all the kerygmatic formulas and other references to Christ, as well as to other statements of the significance of Jesus' death and resurrection in the New Testament. The results of these studies can be summarized quite easily. One finding is that statements about the death and statements about the resurrection originally could be made separately from one another. A second finding is that the earliest references to the significance of the event for the community attached only to statements about the death. Statements about the resurrection, on the other hand, originally referred only to Jesus' own experience and destiny. This was still the case at the level of reflection achieved by the kerygma in 1 Cor 15:3–5. There, Christ's death is said to be for the benefit of the community ("for our sins"); the resurrection, however, is applied only to Jesus' own transformation "on the third day." This results in a certain unevenness in the two rationales combined in the formulation, an unevenness that betrays a prior, separate history of reflection. These findings force further questions about that prehistory. It is obvious that the crucifixion of Jesus captured the imagination, for both statements are interpretations of it. One wonders whether a common set of notions about crucifixions could have given rise to both of them, and why.[5]

---

5. *The kerygma.* That the earliest traditions about Christ's death and Jesus' resurrection were responses to different questions is most clearly worked out in Kramer, *Christ, Lord, Son of God.* For a critical analysis of 1 Cor 15:3–5, together with a demonstration of its composition in Greek, see Hans Conzelmann, "On the Analysis of the Confessional Formula in I Corinthians 15:3–5." Conzelmann leaves open the possibility of some influence from the Jerusalem church, thus continuing the myth of Christian origins there.

The logic behind both views of Jesus' crucifixion can be traced to contemporary conceptions of martyrdom. There is now a strong consensus among New Testament scholars that martyrological ideas were used by early Christians at some time to understand Jesus' death. But the demonstration that a myth of martyrdom lay behind the earliest interpretations of Jesus' death as a saving event must be credited to Sam Williams. He began his study with the isolation of a pre-Pauline formulation behind Rom 3:21–26, a tradition that focused only on the death of Jesus (not on death and resurrection together) and viewed it as a saving event. He also surveyed other early texts, including 1 Cor 15:3–5, the supper texts, and Mark 10:45. Williams' attention was drawn especially to the "sacrificial" language used in these texts, troubled as he was by the traditional scholarly derivation of Christ's sacrificial death from Jewish traditions. A thorough analysis of all the scriptural traditions thought by scholars to have been the source for this idea brought Williams to a negative conclusion. He was surely right about this. The ideas of "vicarious, expiatory suffering, death, or self-sacrifice," to use Williams' terms, were not Jewish ideas. A similar investigation of Greek traditions, however, turned up many analogies. He was able to show, for instance, that the language of "dying for" the *polis* and its laws occurred in accounts of willing self-sacrifice in the Greek tragedies and that the idea of a noble death was pervasive in Greek traditions. These clues led Williams to 4 Maccabees where the Greek traditions surfaced in a Hellenistic-Jewish martyrology. It was there that Williams found language and conceptuality most reminiscent of early Christian interpretations of Jesus' death.

According to this myth, the martyr is one who proves his faithfulness to a righteous cause by refusing to capitulate before enemies who threaten to kill him. The mythologization of the effect of this noble stance runs in two directions: the martyr is vindicated or rewarded by means of a post-mortem destiny, and the cause for which the martyr died is also vindicated, usually by saying that the martyr's death undid the designs of the tyrant and restored the peace. In 4 Maccabees the cause was, of course, the law; the vindication of the martyrs was the granting to them of eternal life; the vindication of the cause was the victory they achieved over the foreign tyrants, understood to be a "cleansing" of the land and a restoration of the community committed to keeping the law. In the mouth of the martyrs one finds prayers to God to "regard" their endurance under persecution and their willingness to "give their lives for" the law as "sacrifices" worthy of both forms of vindication. Williams argued convincingly that the mention of *pistis* ("faith," or "faithfulness") in Rom 3:25 must refer to Jesus' own endurance, the "expiation" to the effectiveness of a martyr's death, and God's "regarding" the crucifixion as an expiation to the mythologization of the event as a whole. Williams' paraphrase of the pre-Pauline tradition is:

God has "regarded" Christ crucified as a means of expiation in order to manifest his righteousness by making righteous the man who has that faith whose source is Jesus (or: the man who shares Jesus' faith).

Williams' philological investigation of these and other terms common to New Testament texts and the martyrological tradition was very careful and convincing. But was he right in emphasizing the incidence and importance of the "sacrificial" aspect to the martyr's death?

That assumption has been challenged by David Seeley. He has shown (1) that the martyr myth does not derive from accounts of human sacrifice, but from the more pervasive Greek tradition of the noble death; (2) that the motivation basic to the noble death idea is not self-sacrifice, but honor and obedience; and (3) that the language used to explicate the vicarious effects of a noble death need not be taken as reference to a theology of cultic sacrifice at all. Seeley has tested his thesis against the interpretations of Jesus' death in the Pauline corpus and shown that the common denominator is the idea of Jesus' obedience. This fits with Williams' exegesis of Rom 3:25–26, with the portrayals of the martyrs in 4 Maccabees, and with the Greek tradition of the noble death, even in the tragedies. The origins of the tradition are to be found in the noble death of the warrior who dies "for the city," or for its laws. In the course of the Hellenic applications of the heroic ideal to kings and commanders, then athletes, and finally philosophers, however, anyone who died for their ideals at the hands of a tyrant could be awarded a noble death. This Greek tradition produced the myth of the martyr in Hellenized circles of Jews which sought to rationalize faithfulness to Jewish piety in keeping with Greek conceptions of virtue. They may have overdone it. Heroism unto death, self-sacrifice, and cults of the dead were not old Jewish ideals.[6]

The emphasis on the vindication of the martyr, however, may belong to a Hellenized version of an old Jewish wisdom tale. George Nickelsburg has collected the evidence for this tale, beginning with the Joseph story in Genesis and ending with 4 Maccabees and the Wisdom of Solomon. According to this tale, a vulnerable righteous one, unjustly persecuted and accused, is finally vindicated in a reversal of the earlier judgment pronounced upon him. In the Hellenized versions, the persecuted one is not just wrongfully accused, but actually killed. The vindication then takes place after death, visualized by drawing upon Hellenistic ideas of immortality, eternal life, and transformation. Both 4 Maccabees and the Wisdom

---

6. *The Martyr myth.* See Sam Williams, *Jesus' Death as Saving Event.* The paraphrase of Rom 3:25–26 appears on 54 in Williams. Others who have emphasized the martyrological influence in the passion narrative will be discussed in part 3. The title of David Seeley's dissertation is "The Concept of the Noble Death in Paul."

of Solomon combine this story with the Greek tradition of the noble death, placing the faithful righteous ones in the hands of tyrants, emphasizing the importance of faithful obedience to the law, and affirming that, though killed, the righteous ones and their cause will prevail. It is probable that both 4 Maccabees and the Wisdom of Solomon were written in Antioch.[7]

Knowing that thoughts such as these were in the air, it would not be surprising to learn that the crucifixion of Jesus also could be understood by his followers in a similar way. Only two "slight" adjustments to the memory tradition of the synagogue reform movement need have been made in order to accommodate the myth. One would have been to imagine that Jesus died true to his own message. If one assumes that the aphoristic tradition had not been forgotten completely by the Jesus people of the synagogue movement, Jesus' style of social critique would have suggested a generally Cynic stance. The chief virtue for Cynics was endurance, just the virtue that, supposing the situation of testing were the threat of execution by a tyrant, would be the mark of a noble death. Jesus people in Palestine had not needed to reflect on the significance of Jesus' death in this way, of course. But, were the occasion to arise in Antioch, a noble death could easily have been imagined.

The other adjustment called for would have been to consider the proposition that Jesus died for a cause. That may have created some consternation, for Jesus' "cause" according to the kerygmatic interpretation of the noble death schema would have been the subsequently formed society of Jesus people continuing his table fellowship and his talk about the kingdom. Paul found this notion very much to his liking, and apparently those who first made the connections took the thought seriously as Rom 3:25–26 shows. But why?

The reasons for being attracted to the martyr myth must be sought in the social experience of the Jesus people in Antioch. The initial success of an essentially open association on the borders of Jewish institutions probably created some problems of its own. One can imagine questions being raised eventually both from within and from without about its status and purpose as a fellowship alongside that of the synagogue. There is no evidence for outright hostility on either part. But the big question that had to be faced was a Jewish question, one that was forced precisely by the difference between the Jesus society and the synagogue. It involved the inclusion of Gentile members in the Jesus association without requiring them to become members of the synagogue as well.

The conceptual problems this would have raised are intriguing. The

---

7. *The vindication motif.* See G. W. E. Nickelsburg, *Resurrection, Immortality, and Eternal Life.*

vague notion about the kingdom of God would have been sorely tested by any early institutionalization of the association. Three issues would have arisen. The first would be the novelty of the Jesus movement when compared to other ways of representing the traditions of Israel. The second would be the difficulty of saying how it could be that both Jews and Gentiles belonged equally to the new association if that association represented the traditions of Israel in any way at all. The third would be that any claim upon the traditions of Israel would be difficult to substantiate as a separate association with none of the traditional authorities or social markers in place. As with the other Jesus movements, the only immediate locus of authority for the association was the significance that could be attributed to Jesus' activity as the founder of the movement. In order to give some account of themselves, Jesus people would have to give some accounting of Jesus.

Answers would not have been easy to find, and the impression should not be given that the martyr myth slipped easily into place. Martyrs died for preexisting institutions and loyalties; Jesus would have to be thought of as dying for a new cause. That new cause would have to be aligned with some concept of Israel; but there was no model that called for Israel's dissolution and transformation into a new non-Jewish society. So a rather convoluted congeries of ideas must have been tried out along the way. But the rationale settled upon does bear striking resemblance to the approaches taken by 4 Maccabees and the Wisdom of Solomon, concerned as those authors also were about reconceptualizing Israel's "righteousness" and its chances in a world where the traditional institutions of righteousness were either threatened (4 Maccabees) or scuttled by the wrong kinds of leaders (Wisdom). In both writings, the little band of the pious was imagined strangely dislocated from the social history of Jewish institutions even as their loyalty to Jewish traditions was idealized. Each author wrote with an eye critically cocked toward circumstances prevailing in Jerusalem, but did not attempt to imagine a restoration on the Second Temple pattern. Instead, Jewish piety was anchored in images drawn from the epic traditions, in the law, and in the inculcation of virtues. Early Jesus people may have felt quite comfortable in such an intellectual climate.

Jesus people in Antioch would not have been able to appropriate the epic images in the same way, to be sure. Some principle of difference would have to be introduced in order to account for the new Jewish-Gentile mixture. They could not appeal directly to the law as the standard for their righteousness, since Jesus' own "teaching" was the basis for the new association. But they might have been interested in elaborating upon the virtues of endurance and faithfulness as they applied both to Jesus' teachings, as well as to Jesus as founder, and to themselves as representatives of a new social experiment under pressure to give an account of itself. The solution proposed by Rom 3:25–26 is, from this perspective, rather ingenious.

In order to grasp the logic, one needs to understand that the distinction between "sinners" and "the righteous" was a common shorthand formula in some Jewish circles for Gentiles and observant Jews. Williams' paraphrase of Rom 3:25–26 leaves out any mention of "sinners," although Paul's appropriation of the tradition saw that distinction as the main point. Williams agreed. In his study he showed that it was the distinction between sinners (Gentiles) and the righteous (Jews) that was addressed by the formula. He argued that the occasion for conceptualizing the formula was the need to justify the inclusion of Gentiles. This was an extremely important and astute observation on Williams' part, for with it a critical juncture in the social history of the Jesus Christ association was identified. Williams did not press this further, but the argument implicit in the application of the martyr myth to Jesus can easily be restated.

The argument was that, if Jesus' death could be regarded by God as a demonstration of Jesus' *pistis,* and the God in question were the God of Israel and righteousness, then all those who shared Jesus' *pistis* also were justified. One sees that the event, thus theologized, points both ways—to Israel's God and history, as well as to the association of Jesus people. Inclusion in the association could be expressed in one of two ways. One way was to use the Greek concept of model (paradigm) and its imitation as Rom 3:25–26 has it ("sharing" Jesus' *pistis*). The other would be to use the Greek idea of the cause or community "for which" the death occurred as in 1 Cor 15:3–5. Either way would solve the problem of the Gentile-Jewish mix by including both equally in the association of "sinners" for which Jesus died. One may note that, even though a claim was made upon Israel's heritage and God, the novelty occasioned by Jesus' death is emphasized. One may also note that the standard for righteousness is left vague by referring it to God's "regarding," and that Jesus' *pistis* is affirmed without reference to the law.[8]

If one sees that the purpose of the martyr myth was to rationalize a social

---

8. *The logic of the saving death.* The argument presented is an elaboration upon S. Williams, *Jesus' Death as Saving Event,* 19–56, esp. 55–56. Williams does not press the logic all the way, thinking still that "the gospel" already had created the Hellenistic congregations so that the martyrological "interpretation" of it was (1) apologetic with respect to the crucifixion of the "Christ," and (2) aimed at the questions Gentiles would have had about also receiving "forgiveness of sins" (55–56, 231–32). The questions answered by the martyr myth, however, are not Greek questions, nor questions Gentile Jesus people would have been concerned with, but Jewish questions about how to include Gentiles. "The gospel" of the crucified Christ is not assumed by the martyrology, but created by it. The logic could not have been worked out piecemeal, but only all at once. Thus the martyr myth is the earliest "christology." On *pistis* as (Jesus') "faithfulness," see Luke T. Johnson, "Rom 3:21–6 and the Faith of Jesus"; and Arland J. Hultgren, "The Pistis Christou Formulation in Paul."

formation already under way, valued for its own sake, the intellectual effort can be understood. Jesus was understood to have intended the formation of that new society, to have lived in keeping with its ethos, and to have died "for" it. Those who needed to justify the new order in terms of Jewish concerns and categories did so by introducing the language of righteousness. But righteousness was redefined in keeping with the makeup of the society. What made the Gentiles (and the Jewish members) righteous was simply belonging to the society "for" which Jesus had died. If the society as constituted was the cause for which Jesus died, however, the death itself had to be construed in its terms. This was achieved by theologizing it from God's point of view. According to this view God acknowledged the event as an authentic manifestation of righteousness. Paul turned the sequence around, to be sure, regarding the founding event as the "cause" that precipitated the new order of faith. Because the group had found no other locus to justify its existence and symbolize its founding, the Christ event actually invited that kind of interpretation. Not only could the community be thought of as the result of that founding event, new members entering into the community could be thought of as being made right because of that event.[9]

The narrative setting for the accusation of the Righteous One in the wisdom tale, as for the persecution of the martyr in 4 Maccabees, was the

---

9. *The motif of righteousness.* The language of righteousness in the formula of Rom 3:25-26 is very important, because the martyrology could not have been imagined without it. According to the noble death pattern, the martyr stood true to the "law" or constitution of that "*polis*" or "land" for which he died, thus could be called *dikaios* ("righteous"). This pattern could not be applied to Jesus' death automatically, for he did not "die for" a law-society already in existence, and could not have been judged righteous on the basis either of Torah obedience or the ethics of a Greek constitutional philosophy. The language of righteousness supplies the ingredient essential to the martyrology. It was a convenient term, for it was capable of linking up three characterizations—of Jesus, of God, and of those belonging to the Jesus people. Thus the martyrology could work as a solution to the social problem defined as a question about the mix of "sinners" and "righteous," i.e., Gentiles and Jews. To formulate the martyrology from God's point of view solved two problems at once. The theological perspective provided the necessary link with the notion of Israel, even while mythologizing the event, that is, making it possible to imagine its new significance from God's point of view. According to the formula, the *pistis* of Jesus is the middle term that makes it possible to say that both God and those who share Jesus' *pistis* (those who belong to the cause for which he died) are "righteous." To characterize Jesus, *pistis/pistos* has been used instead of *dikaios* as the term more appropriate to the manifestation of virtue in the face of such an eventuality. Thus Jesus also has been viewed implicitly as *dikaios*. The term *dikaios* is firmly embedded both in the Greek traditions of the noble death of Socrates, as well as in the Hellenistic form of the wisdom tale (in the Wisdom of Solomon). In both cases, the "law" according to which the victim is judged to be *dikaios* describes an order of things displaced from and in tension with the laws of the city that condemn him. Thus an extremely interesting intertextuality marks the fabrication of the earliest christology. That the motif of righteousness does not derive from Paul's own theological persuasions, but from the Hellenistic congregations, is argued, though for other reasons, in John Reumann, *"Righteousness" in the New Testament.*

court of trial. The narrative (mythic) resolution to the time of testing was also imagined on the model of the trial. It was a vindication or justification of the blamelessness of the falsely accused. In the Christ cult, a narrative embellishment of Jesus' trial did not develop, presumably because the Jesus group in Antioch had no interest or reason to fill in an account of who the "tyrant" was. That would have created tremendous embarrassment, implicating unnecessarily either the temple establishment or the Romans. It wouldn't have achieved any purpose, in any case, because the memory tradition of the Jesus people did not include those kinds of political, institutional conflicts, and no conflicts of that kind impinged upon them as the myth was being conceived. So the matter of the persecutors was left vague, as vague as the whole ecumene that Jesus and the Jesus people had placed under critique. Vindication, however, was still imaginable, belonged to the myth, and was, of course, the narrative concomitant to righteousness. One might even argue that the language of righteousness (justification) was at hand because of the myth about vindication (justification). The myth vindicated the martyr by means of a postmortem transformation, status, or honor, on the one hand, and by means of a manifestation of the rightness of his cause, on the other. Jesus was understood, therefore, to have been awarded spiritual sovereignty over the "kingdom" for which he died, and those who belonged to his kingdom were understood to have been vindicated as right. Both mythic notions were combined in the pre-Pauline kerygma in Rom 4:25 where Jesus' resurrection was "for our justification."

At some early point, reflections along these lines were found to be irresistible. Jesus came to be imagined as the patron deity of a religious association that took on a cultic nuance. People like Paul could continue to struggle with the Israel-Christian tension. But others found the cultic association exciting simply as a new religion on the model of the Hellenistic cults. The title Christ must have been introduced by Jewish members in the course of trying out ideas about Jesus as the sovereign ("king") of the "kingdom" he had founded. But very soon the term became simply the name of the god of the cult. Greeks would have had no trouble interpreting what it was all about. A fellowship to celebrate the presence of the spirit of one transformed and ascended was appealing. Hymns to the god of cosmic descent and ascent were written. The languages of vision, mimesis, and transformation were used to describe the experiences available in this new order of things. The display of personal powers of creativity and wisdom marked the meetings. The memories of the founder-teacher from Galilee, however, seem to have been erased by the new myth.[10]

---

10. *The death as martyrdom.* Kramer makes the point that, in contrast to Paul's interpretations of them, the kerygmatic formulations do not refer expressly to the crucifixion, but to Christ's "death." See *Christ, Lord, Son of God,* 28–29. Christians have

New Testament scholars regularly refer to Easter as the event that marked the transition from the historical Jesus to the Christ of faith. This formula is understood, however, to include all of the attributions of authority to Jesus along with views of his person as special or divine. The assumption has been that the "scandal" of the cross would have canceled out any chance that Jesus and his message would have survived, that a new society could have formed, without the miraculous impetus of Easter.

Critical scholars do realize that the attributions of superior or divine authority to Jesus by his followers were expressed in terms of myths that can be traced to ideas already present in the contemporary cultures. Since none of these background myths fit the early Christian myths exactly, however, and most have no need of a resurrection motif, Easter has been regarded frequently as a distinctively Christian ingredient. It should now be clear that the idea of the resurrection of Jesus was not a commonly shared datum among all forms of the Jesus movements. It was an idea limited to the Christ cult and derived from the Christ myth. In the kerygmatic formulas, the preferred expression is that Christ "was raised" (from the dead). The slightly narrative, reportorial nature of these expressions corresponds exactly to the way in which Christ's death or crucifixion was imagined. The function of the motif is the same as the affirmations of vindication in the martyrologies. To be raised means to have overcome, been vindicated, granted divine reward, status and destiny in spite of the death. The idea that the persecuted righteous one, though slain, would be transformed, receive eternal life, and rule in judgment over his persecutors is depicted graphically in the Wisdom of Solomon. The rather rare term for "resurrection"

---

always preferred the language of death, rather than of execution, to express the significance of the founding event. Thus the dialectic between life and death in the Christian myth has been understood to address the human condition of mortality in general, rather than the issues of power and violence. It should be emphasized that the kerygmatic formulations are not about death and life as natural (or supernatural) phenomena at all. The common scholarly reduction of the kerygma to the statement "that Christ died and was raised" is dangerously misleading if taken to refer to death and (a symbol of after-) life. The kerygmatic statement in 1 Cor 15:3 is not "that Christ died," but "that Christ *died for*. . . ." The phrase "died for" is the kerygmatic formulation of the martyr myth in respect to the resolve of the martyr and the vicarious effect of his death. That the death in question was not a natural death, but an execution, had not been lost. It was precisely the crucifixion as a martyrdom that had been interpreted. Because the kerygma was not firmly anchored in social history, however, the Christ myth that evolved took on Hellenistic patterns of cosmic destiny and transcendence. Then it was that the myth could be interpreted symbolically as the dialectic between "death" as a condition of living in this world, and "life" as extrication from its constraints. This move took place early in the Hellenistic congregations and was further developed in, for instance, the Johannine community and Christian Gnosticism. But even in these developments, the nature of "transformation" as "eventful" reveals the martyrological and kerygmatic origins of the Christ myth. Paul's repeated mention of the crucifixion shows, then, that he understood the original intention and reference of the kerygmatic formulations about Christ's death. For the new community, the kerygma was not about death and dying, but about social conflict and martyrdom.

(anastēsis) used in the Christ cult occurs also in the martyrological tradition as the proper reward for a righteous and noble death (2 Macc 7:14). Because the notion was mythic, "raised from the dead" meant the same thing as "vindicated," "exalted," "ascended," "enthroned," and could be elaborated by calling upon other myths of cosmic destiny (Wisdom, Son of God) or cultic sovereignty and presence (Lord). The "spirit" of the Hellenistic Christ cult was subsequently understood to have been unleashed by this event, creating the environment for interpreting many social and personal experiences as having been effected by the one who was (crucified and) raised from the dead.[11]

---

11. *Resurrection as vindication.* Hans Conzelmann, *An Outline of the Theology of the New Testament,* sees correctly that "originally, resurrection and exaltation are identical. . . . The meaning of the resurrection is from the beginning the appointment of Jesus to his heavenly glory" (67). Conzelmann does not consider, however, that resurrection and exaltation were narrative symbols for a martyr's vindication. That demonstration is the contribution of G. W. E. Nickelsburg, cited above, n. 7. In order to avoid the conclusion that the notion of the resurrection was a product of mythmaking in the Hellenistic congregations, scholars have frequently taken recourse to the "early" evidence for the "appearances" of the resurrected one. This persuasion is doubly convenient, for it traces the beginnings to an "experience" that cannot be questioned further, and it locates the first such experience in Jerusalem in agreement with the Christian myth of origins. It should be emphasized that this "evidence" finally reduces to (1) Paul's claims to have received a revelation of God's Son (Gal 1:12, 16; cf. 2 Cor 12:2-7), and (2) the appearances tacked on to the Christ myth in 1 Cor 15:5-8. It is on these verses attached to the kerygma that the entire edifice of the origins of Christianity (as a Christ cult) in Jerusalem ultimately must rest. The first appearance mentioned in this list is to Cephas, the foremost "pillar" according to Paul's account in Galatians 2. Since Galatians was the earlier of these two letters, the proper order in which to read the two accounts is given. In Galatians Paul is caught in a horrible dilemma. He claims on the one hand not to be dependent upon any human instruction for his gospel, a gospel derived solely from a private vision of God's Son. Nevertheless, he admits that his subsequent trips to Jerusalem were for the purpose of clearing his version of the "gospel" with the pillars (Gal 2:2). The conversation reported, however, was not about the kerygma, but about freedom versus the laws of circumcision. There is no mention of appearances or revelations or christological debate. The list of appearances added to the kerygma in 1 Cor 15:5-8 is therefore odd. The "last" appearance is Paul's own, of course, which means that that appearance at least could not have belonged to the "tradition" Paul "received." Working back through the series of appearances, each added by the term "then," one arrives at the statement, "And he appeared to Cephas, then to the twelve. . . ." One should note that the statement "And he appeared" does not require further qualification, any more than the statement "And he was buried." Both of these statements function primarily to illustrate and support the truth of the kerygmatic phrases "that he died" and "that he was raised," that is, "literally." If one suspects that Paul was the one to add the list of appearances to the kerygmatic formula, it can be seen that he resolved the question of his authority and linkage to the first pillar in a most interesting way. The chain of "tradition" in which Paul himself stands is not a passing on of the kerygma as teaching or preaching, but of a series of revelations that now include Paul's own visitation. Thus his claim to private revelation was preserved, enhanced even, by special status as the one "untimely born" and "unfit," and by special authority as the "last" to have received such. His own addressees will therefore not have been so fortunate, dependent as they have become upon the gospel of the man of vision. And the gospel? Note that the kerygma set forth as "tradition" is exactly Paul's own, the content of his preaching learned in the Christ cult. Thus Peter's "appearance" serves to validate Paul's own gospel, not Peter's view of the

3. THE RITUAL MEAL

A remarkable verification of social experience as the matrix for early Christian mythmaking is given with the ritual for the Lord's meal. Scholars are in agreement that Christians met to share a common meal, but the relationship of that meal to the ritual of the Lord's supper continues to be disputed. Some would like to think the ritual meal was "instituted" by Jesus himself as the "last supper" with his disciples in anticipation of his forthcoming passion. A more reasonable account would be to recognize the common meal as the important thing, the occasion for social formation, and the ritual meal as evidence for the way in which early Christians noticed its importance.[12]

The practice of meeting regularly to eat together would not have been unusual at all, for it belonged to the normal pattern of Greek association as discussed above in chapter 3. Dennis Smith has shown that the meetings of the Christian community in Corinth bear many striking similarities to the normal pattern. The similarities, interestingly, include much more than the meal practice. Meals were very important social occasions for Greeks, around which a certain type of discourse, etiquette, and entertainment was customary. The pattern was to gather, eat together, then sing a hymn and pour out a libation to the patron deity in preparation for the party or meeting to follow. The symposium literature offers the clearest picture of the Greeks at mealtime, but does need to be toned down a bit. Authors of this literature had fun describing philosophers at party, and so the genre tends toward parody and is limited to gatherings of the intellectual elite. Not every householder would have been able to provide entertainment that ran from song and dance through witty repartee and the rehearsal of poetry to hot and heavy philosophical discussions. Popular literature indicates, though, that even at a less sophisticated level hosts chose guests with care, wanting to be sure of lively conversation. Ranking of several kinds was customary, including honored positions among guests, entertainers who knew their place and thus did not expect to share in the more sumptuous

---

matter. One has to be suspicious of such a clever solution to what otherwise would have involved Paul in an impossible set of claims for the authenticity of his authority. William Baird also has taken note of the strange shift in argument from Galatians to 1 Corinthians 15. See his "What Is the Kerygma?" Baird seeks, however, a more conservative resolution, one that ultimately does not satisfy. Therefore, both Paul's own revelations, and his attribution of a kerygmatic appearance to Peter, presuppose the Christ myth. Conzelmann is absolutely right to say that all references to the resurrection presuppose "exaltation," that is, the mythic datum of vindication. None should be used to argue for a private vision at the beginning instead of a social experience in need of rationalization.

12. *The Lord's Supper.* For the conservative position, that the Lord's Supper was "instituted" by Jesus, see J. Jeremias, *The Eucharistic Words of Jesus.* For a more critical perspective and introduction to the problem of the supper traditions see W. Marxsen, *The Lord's Supper as a Christological Problem.*

dainties of the banquet, and servants. This social custom was formalized during the Hellenistic period as the *koinōnia* or club. Ranking was institutionalized in the hierarchy of offices and assigned places at the table. Dinner was followed by meetings at which official business was conducted. And room was made for socializing. It is important to realize, nevertheless, that heroes and gods were recognized as the patrons for these associations. Even those clubs that were organized primarily for socializing were named after a god, and the etiquette required the customary libation.[13]

Early Christian meal practice would not have been much different, except for the topics of conversation that distinguished it from other associations. Meeting in houses, patrons and servants (deacons) would have had their roles to play. After-dinner discourse would have turned to talk about affairs of interest to the group. Prophets, teachers, and apostles were the names given to the intellectual leaders that arose. Instead of Homer and Theognis, the Jewish scriptures became the sounding board for literary citation and interpretive ingenuity. Trying out a poem or a newly composed hymn to the Christ would have been in order. A symposium atmosphere is not at all unthinkable, given the picture of the Corinthians retrievable from Paul's correspondence. And the "spirit" of the occasion may well have been the most attractive and challenging feature of the association. To have been invited to a *koinōnia* that cut across conventional barriers would in itself have been a slightly enticing experience. To find oneself in mixed company, having a good time talking about mixed company, might have been all the challenge one could stand. For the business of this association was just about itself as a new social configuration. It took its place on the borders of traditions breaking down, and filled in the spaces left vacant by the institutional fragmentation that was becoming obvious at the end of the Hellenistic era. People who felt lost or displaced may have found the association in the name of Christ appealing. Intellectuals without a cause or home, that is, without a lively cultural tradition of discourse, also may have been attracted. But just because the business of the society was its own formation rather than any public function, self-reference had to occur.

The Christ myth, it should be emphasized, was not the result of a merely speculative adventure on the part of visionaries. Real people were involved, struggling to define a new social configuration not based on ethnic, cultural, or personal identities. The very constitution of the social group was at stake in the efforts to imagine an order of things in which they had their

---

13. *Mealtime practice.* See the reference to Dennis Smith, "Social Obligation," above, chap. 3, nn. 3 and 4. Classical studies include those by Erich Ziebarth, *Das griechische Vereinswesen;* Franz Poland, *Geschichte des griechischen Vereinswesens;* and Mariano San Nicolò, *Aegyptisches Vereinswesen zur Zeit der Ptolemäer und Römer.* See also Martin P. Nilsson, "Die Götter des Symposions."

place. The Christ myth gave an account, a rather strange and dislocated account to be sure, of history, cosmos and a founding event that, looked at from God's point of view, defined the community as a new, divine creation. Christians were busy constructing a symbolic world in which to live. The rapidity with which this happened, over against the lengthy struggles of the Jesus reform movements, is astounding. It was the brokenness of the cultural terrain in northern Syria, then in Asia Minor and Greece, combined with the availability of mythic models and the imaginative energy invested in applying them to a table fellowship set free from its moorings, that invited the new creation. That the meal itself was noticed in the process, and marked as a Christian occasion, would only have been natural.

The tradition Paul cites in 1 Cor 11:23–26 is the text available to the historian for the ritualized meal in the Hellenistic congregations of the Christ. Paul calls this meal the Lord's Supper, and the text refers to the Lord, rather than to Christ. That agrees with the community's preference for the term Lord when thinking of itself as a religious society constituted by some immediate presence or practice. But the symbolism of the supper was not the result of reflection upon the Lord, but upon the Christ. The text is given in figure 2.

FIGURE 2
THE LORD'S SUPPER

For I received from the Lord what I also delivered to you,
    that the Lord Jesus on the night when he was handed over took bread,
    and when he had given thanks, he broke it, and said,
        "This is my body which is for you.
        Do this in remembrance of me."
In the same way also the cup, after supper, saying,
        "This cup is the new covenant in my blood.
        Do this, as often as you drink it, in remembrance of me."
For as often as you eat this bread and drink the cup,
you proclaim the Lord's death until he comes.

                                         (1 Cor 11:23–26)

A brief analysis of this tradition is in order, focusing mainly on the relation of the symbols both to the common meal and to the Christ myth (see figure 3).

Common meal practice is not difficult to discern as the occasion from which two special moments were lifted up for symbolic attribution. Eating bread and drinking wine were a shorthand reference to meals taken together. The thanksgiving over the bread is probably a Christian substitution for the Jewish practice of saying a blessing. But both Jewish and early

FIGURE 3
THE RITUALIZED MEAL

Common Meal Practice	Symbol- ization	Mythic Reference	Ritual- ization	Etiological Reference	Terms	(Mark)
				x	The Lord	
				x	Handed over	
x	x		x		Took bread	
x			x		Gave thanks	(Blessed)
			x		Said, "This is . . ."	
		x			My body	
		x			For you	
			x		Do this	(Take)
				x	For my memorial	
x					After dinner	
x	x		x		The cup	
			x		Similarly	(Took . . . gave thanks)
			x		Said, "This cup is . . ."	
		x			New covenant	(Of the covenant)
		x			In my blood	(My blood)
		(x)				(Poured out for many)
			x		Do this . . . when you drink	
				x	For my memorial	

(1 Cor 11:23b–25; Mark 14:22–24)

Christian meal practices were versions of the more general Hellenistic pattern. The wine gesture after dinner and before the meeting was traditional. In Hellenistic context, the gesture would have been a libation accompanied by some reference to the patron deity. To identify the meal as the meeting of the Christ people by framing it with appropriate words and gestures over the bread and wine is simply the way in which any association would have gone about it.[14]

14. *Blessing and thanksgiving.* J. M. Robinson argues that early Christians substituted a thanksgiving for the traditional Jewish blessing at meals. See his "Die Hodajot-Formel in Gebet und Hymnus des Frühchristentums."

From these moments, two symbols arose—bread and cup (or wine). Both were capable of bearing rich and far-reaching metaphorical significance. Attempts to identify particular nuances or references that might have started the process of thought are frustrated, however, just because they are primary symbols. Each is laden with complex connotations in the narrative, poetic, and allegorical literatures of the Judaisms of the time. Each also could evoke trains of thought leading zigzag through the lore of the Greeks. Though many of these standard metaphorical uses are very suggestive, and some did occur as important to later Christian theologians in relation to the supper symbols, scholars have not been able to identify any particular cluster of ideas that could easily have produced the meanings assigned to them in the meal ritual. If a metaphor stood at the beginning, it was soon lost in the new identifications. But perhaps there is another way to understand what transpired.

If one assumes that the meal was ritualized in the process of working out the Christ myth, a quite reasonable explanation can be given for the symbols. The identifications that were made focus upon two figures. One is "my body for you"; the other is "the new covenant in my blood." Both of these figures belong to the myth of the martyr, although the addition of the idea of the new covenant would be the specifically Christian appropriation of that myth. The combination here of the terms body and blood as symbols for a death is an important clue. They only make sense within the tradition of martyrological thought. The otherwise normal combination when refer-ring to a self would be body and soul; flesh and blood are the terms that go together when referring to the physical body. But both body and blood occur in martyrological texts. The martyr gives his body or his soul into the hands of the tyrant "for the sake of" his cause. The tyrant tortures the martyr's body and spills his blood in the act of taking his life. In the Markan version of the ritual symbols, the martyrological derivation is made explicit by reference to the blood being "poured out for many" (Mark 14:24). In Paul's text, the death as a founding event for the community has been emphasized, not by the spilling of the blood, but by using the idea of a "new covenant." Since the mythic references are so focused, and since they agree with the earliest stages of the Christ myth, one has to imagine that that set of ideas was in mind as the symbols were identified. How could that have happened?

The identification of the meal symbol with the mythic reference to martyrology was made by means of the simple formula "this is." Because the immediate reference of the pronoun is not clear, meticulous analysis of this and the parallel texts has been the scholarly challenge. Especially in relation to the bread-body identification, the "this" has been understood to refer to (1) the bread, (2) the act of breaking the bread, (3) the event of blessing, breaking, and eating the bread, and (4) the community as the corporate "body" present. This approach to the problem has not produced a consensus, but it is better than the metaphorical suspicion mentioned above for one reason. The identification formula "this is" carries a certain weight of its own. It was used, for instance, in the typological and allegorical interpretation of texts in Qumran and by Philo of Alexandria. It certainly need not be limited to texts, but it is there that an important aspect of arbitrariness in its use is apparent. While it is frequently the case, and always desired by interpreters, that an image or term in a text held to be coded contain some clue to its new interpretation, decoding with specific intention ultimately must simply be stated. It is as if the formula means "this clue, however slight, will be taken as significant, none of the other associations counting for the moment." This consideration does not immediately help to determine which reference is intended in the usage of the formula at the meal, of course. But it does allow for a less direct equivalency between symbol and reference than has usually been assumed necessary.

Applied to the situation of the meal, then, one should really set aside the extravagant embellishments the symbols obviously received in the course of replication. The etiological features, for instance, that imagine the Lord Jesus presiding and saying the words, must be recognized as cult legend. The reapplication of that scene to those in the present by means of the imperatives to "do this in remembrance of me" also need to be set in brackets. What remains, if one does reduce the tradition in this way, is some connection made between the two special moments of the meal and the death of Christ according to the myth of the martyr. This would not be inappropriate for an association meeting in the name of Christ. All associations had patron deities. The libations were poured out with that deity in mind, as were other gestures of acknowledgment. One does not get the impression that these were solemn moments. They belonged to the etiquette of recognition and, in the case of divinized heroes, memorial. Experimenting with the special moments of the common meal as proper occasion for acknowledging the Christ as the community's patron deity, early Christians chose to recall the two essential moments of the martyr myth. One was the death itself; the other was the resolve that turned the death into a founding event "for" the community. The cup of wine would more easily be associated with the death, especially if the earliest practice were a libation; the thanksgiving and breaking of the bread as the signal for the dinner-association to begin would have been the appropriate moment to remember the founding event. One could imagine an early thanksgiving to the effect that Christ handed his body over "for" the gathered community. At some point the breaking of the bread could be thought of as pointing in both directions, that which reminded of Christ's resolve and that which constituted the community as gathered. The rather awkward (and audacious) shorthand formula might then be used ("this is [my] body"), drawing perhaps upon various symbolisms of the bread, all of which pertained to "life," most of which evoked the idea of gift, and some of which recalled classic images from the epic tradition and its lore such as manna, miracles, wisdom, Torah, bread of the presence, and so forth. Early Christian literature, indeed Paul's letter to the Corinthians, shows that these metaphoric possibilities were familiar. But they were not allowed to surface in the formula, leaving the enigmatic symbol of the bread, its breaking, thanksgiving, and distribution only to serve as reminders of the vicarious death of the founder.

One needs to be careful not to interpret this early evidence for the ritualization of the meal in terms of later Christian eucharistic theology. The Corinthian Christians certainly did not interpret it in that way. And the text itself is an etiological legend. There is no evidence that it was performed as written, with some "priest" daring to take Jesus' place and say those words. Paul referred to it as if it were the historicized form of the community's foundational martyr-meal myth. He used it to remind the Corinthians in general about the ethical dimensions of their gatherings, not to instruct them in the liturgy. But the text is evidence, nonetheless, for the ritualization of the common meal, using its two special moments to recall the founder's death. It is this evidence for an early social formation as a strictly religious society, complete with myth, ritual, and symbol system, that makes the Hellenistic Christ cult distinctively different from the groups formed by the Jesus movements.[15]

---

15. *The ritual meal.* There is a huge bibliography on the Lord's Supper in the New Testament and early church. The prevailing assumption, read back into the early texts from later Christian interpretation and practice, is that the ritual depends upon a sacrificial theology and memorializes Jesus' death as sacrifice by reenacting the Last Supper. There are two category mistakes underlying this discourse. One is the notion of a "sacrificial meal." A recent monograph by Hans-Joseph Klauck, *Herrenmahl und hellenistischer Kult,* pursues exhaustively the "background" material only to find that the early Christian ritual is a strange combination of many diverse practices and ideas, no one of which could have served as sufficient model. He concludes, oddly, that there must have been a Last Supper with Jesus along the lines of the gospel accounts in order for such a unique practice to have begun. The second mistake is the assumption that there was such a Last Supper, an occasion fraught with the significance of Jesus' impending death. The position taken in the present study is that the ritual meal in the Hellenistic congregations was not a "sacrificial meal." Neither was the supper text a script intended for reenactment. As an etiology it served a mythic function to supplement the kerygma. Because the kerygma could not be located historically without indicating who the tyrant was, the mythic event was in danger of floating off into a timeless and cosmic order of the imagination. The supper text could anchor the event in human time without running into that danger, because it viewed the event, not as a report on the martyrdom itself, but only from the perspective of the martyr's *resolve* "on the night of his arrest." The story of the Last Supper in the gospel is to be explained as the result of historicizing the Hellenistic etiology in the process of composing the gospel narrative. This will be explained and argued in chapter 11.

The supper text in 1 Cor 11:23–26 documents a ritualization of the meal peculiar to some early Christian communities with which Paul was familiar. It was not the only way in which meals were formalized as significant occasions in early movements in the name of

4. THE NEW CREATION

Paul's letters were written in the fifties, removed from the time of Jesus by a full human generation and its history. During those approximately twenty-five years an improbable society was formed. It was an amalgam of essentially irreconcilable cultural sensibilities, an emergent growth on the jagged edges of Greek and Oriental traditions intertwining in the daily life of the Hellenistic *polis*. The new society was new because, though skillfully put together from the pieces of cultural tradition at hand, as if by Lévi-Strauss' *bricoleur*, it could not say which pieces were more essential. The social unit bore some resemblance to the Jesus movements of reform and to other non-Jesus conventicles of Jewish reform as well (for instance, the sect responsible for the Psalms of Solomon). But it also took on features from the diaspora synagogue and especially from the Hellenistic pattern of free association. Its intellectual leaders must have been Hellenistic Jews, to be sure, for the new rationales betray prevailing Jewish notions of the social, and deeply embedded Jewish concerns for linkage with the past. But the past, the epic traditions and the scriptures for instance, could not really be thought of naturally any longer as the cultural genealogy of this unrecognizable hybrid. The claims upon those traditions were all the more adamant, of course, but no systematic exegesis ever developed that did not begin with the discrepancy between the old and the new. None could develop, because the epic traditions, to say nothing of the Torah as ritual code, had been replaced by an essentially alien imagination. The Christ cult claimed its own generation in a fantastic moment of volition, violence, and vindication. A rupture erased the past in effect, and fixed the vision on a single event of transformation. Ever after, Christian eyes would dance around that haunting diptych (cross and resurrection) hoping to catch sight of the source of the power to change one thing to another.

Separated from the synagogue, constituted by a mix in need of justification, Christians decided upon an event instead of a teaching to say how things got started. The event was, mythically imagined, the crucifixion and

---

Jesus, nor the only way in which significance was interpreted and symbolized. There may have been many forms of meal practice and ritualization during the early periods. One very important bit of evidence that such was the case comes from the eucharistic prayers included in the Didache 9 and 10. In this case, the prayers customary for Jewish mealtime were formalized, rephrased, and ritualized in place both at the beginning and at the end of a meal taken only by those who had been baptized in the Lord's name. The prayers are thanksgivings for the knowledge that this group belonged to God's kingdom, a knowledge made known through Jesus, God's child. Both the cup and the bread are mentioned, the cup reminding them of "the Holy Vine of David," the bread of some "scattering" and "gathering" that symbolized the hope for the *ekklesia* to become one. There is no mention of the death and resurrection of Jesus the Christ. Meal practice and its ritualization can thus be imagined to have taken on any number of forms among the early Jesus movements without the influence of the Hellenistic martyr myth.

resurrection of Jesus Christ. The event was imagined to have happened in history, "on the night when Jesus was handed over," but nothing more would ever be said in these circles about the human history that led up to that event, or away from it, that was not determined by the event itself. After things settled in a bit, and the cult's own human history became more obvious, the problem of linking up the new history with the old epic history would surface as the major challenge to an apologist for the new religion. The intellectual history of Christianity in the second, third, and fourth centuries can be read as the attempt to solve this problem. Desperately needing to domesticate the Hebrew epic without relinquishing the claim to the new truth manifest in Jesus Christ, an astonishingly circular hermeneutic was worked out, essentially with the aid of Platonic allegory, that eventually lifted both the epic, the Christ event, and the history of the church into that never-never land of the medieval imagination. But all of that came later. At first the break between the times was underscored in order to define the new community as new. Paul already saw the problem that created, but, committed as he was to a conversionist mentality, fastened on the Christ event as if it were a formula to be applied to every personal and social ill. Christian self-definition took place in this application.

The formula followed the sequence from death to resurrection, or from everything tyrannical, conflictual, judgmental, legal, constraining, traditional, old, past, and painful, to release into the imagined realm of pure spirit, absolute power, free grace, and eternal transcendence. An equation of inversion from one extreme to the other was derived from the myth of an event into which all of human history had been condensed. The old now applied to Israel's history before the Christ event, but also to all human history. It also applied to personal human histories, the lives members had lived before joining the association, as well as the experiences of everyday, especially those aggravated by discord. A mythic principle of spontaneous generation fired the desire for a new humanity imbued with love of the kind Christ had extended in the giving of his life "for sinners."

The process of application can be visualized as a dislodgment of the Christ event from its originally "historical" placement, to become the sign marking every community event of exchange. Thus baptism, the crossing of the border into the community, was a Christ event. So was the Lord's Supper, bringing the event right into the middle of the circle. And from the myth and ritual traditions Paul even worked out an ethic all the community's own: "Have this mind . . . which you have in Christ Jesus" (Phil 2:5), "present your bodies as a living sacrifice" (Rom 12:1). But the definitive border was that between the church as now defined and the world, between the realm where the spirit of Christ reigned and all that lay outside. Cosmic claims affirmed the original impulse to open out and include those on the outside. The claim was that God's decisive revelation and rule applied universally and forever. But the facts of the case were that the little sect hardly matched the perfect dream. And so the borders below were narrowly defined and the vision of the new creation was carried along like a bubble on a turbulent stream. Though the Christ myth was born in the desire to justify a novel experiment in social inclusiveness, its cultivation was in danger of creating a desire for personal transcendence as if the world were not worthy unless transformed.[16]

---

16. *The new creation.* See the classic study of Pauline Christianity, organized according to the categories old/new, by W. D. Davies, *Paul and Rabbinic Judaism.*

5

THE PATTERNS
OF SOCIAL CONFLICT

The importance of social experience for the beginnings of Christianity has been demonstrated by emphasizing two developments: (1) the followers of Jesus formed movements of exceptionally diverse configuration; and (2) group identities were rationalized in the production of surprisingly different kinds of myths. A few common factors do need to be kept in mind. All groups may have formed around gatherings for meals, as has been suggested. All seem to have been energized by some social notion that some groups referred to as the kingdom of God. And all recognized Jesus as their founder. Diversity begins immediately, however, from this point on. The reasons for the diversity both at the social and at the ideological levels need now to be looked at in a more systematic way. One organizing principle for such an overview would be to chart the nature of the social conflicts encountered and sustained by these new groups in the course of their histories. It will have been noticed that self-definition, the more obvious function of mythmaking, took place in order to distinguish from others a group's particular constituency and sense of purpose. By comparing the several reactions to other groups during the first forty years, several typologies can be discerned that will be helpful as a preparation for Mark's own particular response.

1. FROM SOCIAL CRITIQUE TO
SOCIAL FORMATION

The story of the first forty years begins, it should be remembered, with the appearance of Jesus, a rather piquant critic of his social world in general. It ends with several different groups that had defined their boundaries against the larger social arena, thus becoming social worlds of their own. Criticism had, moreover, not only been given, but received. It was in the course of that give and take that the boundaries had been established and hardened. No longer free simply to bring charges against the way in which society at large worked, each group had to defend its own emerging social practices, and each escalated its claims. The claims were different, not only because different constituencies clustered around the memory of Jesus, but because each group found itself in different social circumstances, addressing different configurations of the world outside. Two observations can be made about these groups as a set. One is that a similar pattern of shifting attitudes internal to each of these groups can be discerned. The other is that the external circumstances in which these groups found themselves can be sketched as a gradient curve describing types of conflict with various forms of Judaism.

The shifts in attitude can be described as the sequence from an early period of optimistic activity, through a period of tussle and setback, to a later period of polemic and compensatory reaction. This was true for the prophets in Galilee, where an earlier stage of the Q tradition contained aphoristic and instructional material, a later stage polemical pronouncements of doom, and a final stage compensatory biographical mythology. It was also true for the synagogue reform movement, where the chreiai underlying the pronouncement stories made their point teasingly, hence with optimism, whereas the elaborated versions looked back upon a period of tussle and compensated for a lost battle by attributing superior cleverness and authority to Jesus. In the case of the congregations of the Christ, sectarian independence was achieved with such rapidity that an early sequence of optimism and struggle was all but erased in the compensation achieved by the Christ myth and meal. But a second round of conflict began, one in which Paul was involved. This cycle of conflict ran from early optimism about the Christ cult, through the battles with the (Christian) "Judaizers" in the fifties, to the highly self-referential post-Pauline communities represented by Colossians and Ephesians. The miracle stories in the pre-Markan tradition of the congregation of Israel do not contain signs of overt social conflict, hence may be placed toward the end of a period of optimism. But the miracle stories in John show that conflict had been experienced by some group that continued to use this genre, that the battle had been lost, and a theory of substitution had developed. Stages for the pillars in Jerusalem and the family of Jesus cannot be determined in the same way. Nevertheless, the legend about the martyrdom of James, and the report about the flight to Pella, show that, after a brief period of activity marked by expectation, the group(s) experienced resistance in Jerusalem and had to withdraw from the scene. It is important to emphasize the signs for an early period of buoyancy in all of the movements, and that conflict developed gradually in the course of social experience and construction.[1]

---

1. *The stages of social history.* The outline proposed is not a standard datum in New Testament studies, but does agree with conventional scholarly observations when organized around the questions of social formation and conflict. Additional argumentation for two

The span of time under consideration should not be compressed in the desire to overcome the gap between the texts in hand and the historical Jesus. Forty years represent approximately two generations of social activity. Divided in half to accommodate the shift in attitude described, the year fifty can serve as a convenient marker of the midpoint of this history. Much can happen in twenty years and each movement appears to have been very busily engaged with activity. Many persons would have joined who did not know Jesus "according to the flesh" as Paul expresses it. It is also true that changing attitudes and developing rationales would have occurred at different paces determined by the varying circumstances.

Two circumstantial factors of significance have been touched upon— geographical-cultural location and relationship to Jewish institutions. In Jerusalem both Pharisaic piety and the institutions of the temple cult would have been encountered by the pillars. The family of Jesus in the (northern) Transjordan would have been in contact with self-confident Jewish communities generally loyal to Jerusalem, but self-conscious about their Jewishness quite apart from the temple-state history. The congregations of Israel manifest in the miracle stories are best imagined in northern Palestine, drawing upon local lore and relatively undisturbed by Judean authorities. The synagogue reform behind the pronouncement stories pushes the spread of Jesus people into the Hellenistic cities of Galilee and southern Syria. And the congregations of the Christ can be situated in Antioch and other cities of northern Syria and Asia Minor. The thoroughly Hellenized synagogues experienced by the Christ people in northern Syria define a Jewish institution quite distinct from the temple establishment in Jerusalem. Thus each movement experienced contact differently with different Jewish institutions.[2]

Jesus movements, the "synagogue reform movement" and the "congregation of Israel," will be given in the course of the chapters to follow. The question of the "Judaizers" who gave Paul so much trouble, whether Jewish or Jewish Christian, and of what ideology, is far from resolved. There is a great deal of evidence that inner sectarian conflict among Christian groups played a far more significant role than has normally been recognized. Evidence for this has not been collected and analyzed, but mention of some of the pertinent material will be made as the study proceeds.

Josephus reports the martyrdom of James in *Jewish Antiquities* 20.200, written during the nineties of the first century. The legend of the flight to Pella is from Eusebius, *Preparation for the Gospel* 3.5.3, written around 300 C.E. Eusebius, interestingly, shifts the cause for the destruction of Jerusalem from the crucifixion of Jesus, as Mark tells it, to the murder of James. This follows the general pattern during the patristic period according to which the apostles, instead of Jesus, become the models for martyrdom. It also demonstrates that the gospel plot was capable of reapplication to other paradigms of persecution.

2. *Geographical locations.* The placements indicated follow the consensus of scholarship. On the family of Jesus and Jewish Christianity in the Transjordan, see H. Koester, *Introduction to the New Testament* 2:200–203.

2. THE PATTERNS OF CONFLICT
WITH JUDAISM

Each of the early Jesus movements drew upon a conception of "Israel" in order to imagine its place in the scheme of things. These conceptions determined the stance each took in relation to some form of Judaism encountered directly in its particular environment. All developed the confidence at first that they belonged somehow to the larger picture of Jewish presence and destiny at the time. The modes of address to their contextual worlds ranged from invitations to join, through calls to reform, to the formation of alternative social structures that were imagined as appropriate perfections of Jewish models, if not modern substitutes for existing Jewish institutions. There was no common form of address, just as there was no common Jewish response. The customary scholarly construction put upon this history has summed up the conflicts by using the term persecution. The critical historian should be disabused of this simplification. The term persecution came to be used by many of the early movements as a way to interpret rejections and the failure to convince others to join them. The idea belonged to prevailing schemes for rationalizing such conflicts and should not be taken as descriptive. Most conflicts with Judaism were quite understandable competitions, initiated in this case by the Jesus movements themselves. Because of their novelties, positions taken that threatened Jewish symbols and social markers of long standing, it is no wonder that Jewish reaction was for the most part negative. The quarrels that developed were at first family quarrels.

The itinerants in Galilee do not appear to have tangled with a specific Jewish institution. References to Pharisees and to Jerusalem in the later stages of the collection (Q) show that a broadening perception of the worlds of Judaism did eventually take hold, perhaps in combination with the experiences of the settled groups of Jesus people upon which the prophets increasingly became dependent. But the address was still quite general, coming to focus upon "this evil generation." One has the impression that an early activity of generalized social criticism followed upon Jesus' own style of critique, then shifted by degrees as the movement thought of itself more and more in terms of metaphors taken from Jewish traditions and lore. These metaphors had to do with the role of the prophet, calls to repentance and reform, and a deuteronomistic view of the restoration of Israel fully compatible with northern Palestinian provenance. Because their preachments were delivered scatter-shot, institutional conflict is improbable. It was disillusionment, not persecution, that set in when their message failed to achieve its goal.

In Jerusalem, on the other hand, the pillars apparently specified their sectarian intentions purposefully under the shadow of the temple cult.

Pretensions thus were imagined in institutional terms, but without any recognizable credentials of power, without any real foothold within the institutions either of Pharisaism or the temple establishment. Occasions for conflict would have been created by intrusions on the part of the Jesus people into a very complex and tensive political history of long standing. As the situation in Jerusalem worsened in the 60s, withdrawal from the scene was really the only option this group had.

In the Transjordan, the family of Jesus probably took its place simply as one among many traditions of memory and identity that traced histories back to earlier chapters in the Hebrew epic. Social markers definitive for all forms of Jewishness (circumcision, foods, basic rituals, codes for things clean or unclean) were probably accepted by the family of Jesus as well. Conflict, if at all, would have taken the form of denominational grousing.

The conflict of major significance for the separation of Jesus movements from Jewish institutions, and the eventual formation of a distinctively Christian society, took place within and around the Hellenistic synagogue. Two brief histories of conflict can be distinguished, the experience of the Jesus people and that of the Christ cult. The Jesus people tried to remain within the traditional structures, failed to convince Jews who were committed to the traditional signs of identity, ran afoul of the Pharisees who were able to articulate the reasons for the importance of those social markers, and found themselves ousted without much of an alternative conception in place. This cycle probably did not run its course until late in the fifties or sixties.

The Christ people, on the other hand, were apparently able to achieve a self-confident identity rather quickly by borrowing Hellenized conceptions of Israel and leaving the synagogue on their own accord. The bitter battles recounted in the Pauline corpus have more to do with conflicts internal to the several competitive Jesus and Christ movements than to direct conflict between Christian societies and Jewish synagogues. (The schematic picture Luke paints in Acts is unreliable. It is a combination of lore about the Pauline mission with the characterization of the Pharisees and the synagogue created in the gospel accounts.) Issues in the Pauline congregations were second-generational conflicts precipitated most likely by Paul's visit to Jerusalem, the so-called apostolic council, and the growing awareness of the huge gap that separated a conservative (Jewish) Jesus movement from the free, Hellenized congregations of the Christ.

3. INTRA-CHRISTIAN CONFLICTS

Because there was no charter to guide the Jesus movements, each had to construct its own. Models had to be chosen and rationalized, responsibilities for common activities assigned, and authorities agreed upon. With mixed constituencies and social roles undefined, one has to imagine a very lively group dynamic at the beginning. Leadership roles were not prescribed and who was in charge must have been a nagging question. For the early period, evidence for experimentation with positions of leadership is all but gone, except for the Q prophets, the pillars, and whatever role James may have played as Jesus' brother. It cannot be, though, that householders, patrons, "deacons," presiders, "teachers," and other social roles failed to appear at a very early time. Within the constraints set by a group's particular social circumstances, the stronger voices will have prevailed, and their leadership roles and "gospels" accepted.

Each of the gospels centered upon Jesus as the founder of the movement. That might be considered natural but for the diversity of images that emerged and the tendency toward extravagant claims. The extravagance can be understood, however, as a compensation for the lack of any other authority to which to appeal. Only as a secondary reflection would it have been possible for these groups to start the process of appropriating other forms of authority that underlay Jewish identities and institutions. The most important of these was the scriptures. Except for the pillars and the family of Jesus which may have viewed the scriptures in accordance with Judean traditions of cultic law and genealogy, Jesus movements seem to have taken up the scriptures as epic history. Narrative images, figural typologies, and allegories will have been the means by which pointed but unsystematic connections were made. Psalms and didactic hymns (*hodayot*) provided patterns for original creations in the Christ cult from an early period. Gradually, especially evident in Mark, then refined in Luke-Acts, the prophets also were domesticated by reading them much the same as had been done at Qumran. The ritual codes, however, that served all forms of Judaism as a common set of authorities for social identity, were not as easily managed, hermeneutics being one thing, behavior another. The poignancy of the conflicts both within and without the several movements took its edge on the issue of ritual purity. Who came to dinner, who served it, and what was served were truly decisive questions. Those movements that decided in favor of keeping the Jewish codes became Jewish sectarians; those who decided against them eventually had to construct a whole new system of authority.[3]

---

3. *Scriptural interpretation.* For introductions to Jewish interpretation of the scriptures during this period see Daniel Patte, *Early Jewish Hermeneutic in Palestine;* and Merrill Miller, "Targum, Midrash and the Use of the Old Testament." J. D. M. Derrett, *Law in the New Testament,* offers a fine set of studies showing that early Christians learned to exegete the law in their favor. For a general survey of early Christian hermeneutic see Richard Longenecker, *Biblical Exegesis in the Apostolic Period.* There is, unfortunately, no systematic study of the patterns of scriptural accommodation among early Christian movements. As in the case of mythmaking, however, one suspects great diversity in

The Pauline corpus gives some idea of the intensity with which leaders of the various Jesus movements competed for authority during the second generational period. It also provides a picture of the several social functions that developed in the congregations of the Christ. Activities with functional significance for the practical maintenance of the group meetings were the more easily designated. Even within a single working community, however, ranking and the prioritization of roles was a problem. This problem was compounded to the point of outright hostilities when leaders from other groups or those eager to introduce another gospel appeared on the scene. Paul sought to rank the various functions: "first apostles, second prophets, third teachers, then workers of miracles, then healers, helpers, administrators, speakers in various kinds of tongues" (1 Cor 12:28). Judging from this list and the general tenor of Paul's concerns for the conduct of Christian meetings, (community) leaders could appeal to a wide range of authorization: commissioning, representation, hermeneutical skills, superior wisdom, charismatic display, and direct experience of the spirit of God. Paul himself had to vie with local leaders and contend with other apostles. He appealed to direct revelation, ecstatic experience, knowledge of the traditions, a visit to the pillars, winning the case for Gentile Christianity, his success as a founder, skill at typological and allegorical interpretation of the scriptures, wisdom in theological argumentation, an appearance of the risen Lord, and his self-sacrificial mode of life. Those who opposed him were "false apostles." The question of authority was obviously a burning issue in the fifties, and the authorities were not yet in place.[4]

The exigencies of social experience and the failure to resolve certain conflicts both within and without the Jesus movements eventually produced a series of withdrawals from the fray. The sayings tradition was domesticated by settled sectarians on the one hand, gnosticized by those who composed the Gospel of Thomas on the other. The pillars fled from Jerusalem, and the family of Jesus withdrew to the Transjordan. Gnosticizing enclaves appeared in the second generation after Paul. The history of the Johannine community follows the pattern of competition, withdrawal, and the formation of an exceptionally cozy conventicle cut off from the outside world. Mark also shows the signs of withdrawal. A "teacher" in his community no doubt, Mark defined his group apocalyptically by severing the ties with Judaism, as well as ties with the past history of the group, and with other competitive forms of early Jesus–Christ movements. His

selection of texts and their interpretations as one moves from group to group and from stage to stage of their social histories.

4. *Authority conflicts.* Three recent works take note of the problem: John Howard Schütz, *Paul and the Anatomy of Apostolic Authority;* Bengt Holmberg, *Paul and Power;* and Walter Schmithals and Antonius Gunneweg, *Authority.* For a much more incisive description of the problem see Graham Shaw's *The Cost of Authority.*

authority in his community is not expressly evident. But he wrote as one omniscient, using authorship as his vehicle of influence. The gospel he composed addressed the issue of authority in a very provocative way. All contenders were crushed or subsumed in the single figure of Jesus. And Jesus' authority was such that only by reading Mark's Gospel would anyone ever have imagined it so. It is impossible to tell whether Mark saw signs of the fruits of his labor or what his personal sense of reward may have been. But the history of the synoptic tradition and the history of the Christian church are evidence that Mark's story eventually won the day. It was Mark's solution to the question of conflict. That solution must now be analyzed with care.

PART II

STORIES IN
THE GOSPEL TRADITION

> All you need for a founder figure is a name and a place.
>
> Jonathan Z. Smith
> Claremont, 1986

6

THE PARABLES
OF JESUS

The parables of Jesus have exercised the Christian imagination from the beginning. Lively and provocative, these little stories have provided major themes for Christian art, divine instruction in the gospel's message, and favorite texts for homilies and sermons. The first intrigue has been that Christian truth appears presented in the language of the everyday. The second is that the gospels, which are stories about Jesus, also contain accounts of the stories Jesus told. Since the gospels are stories about Jesus, the stories Jesus told have always been read as gospel stories, stories that offer instruction in the Christian gospel about Jesus. To the modern sophisticate this presents a curiosity. The strange thing is not that Jesus told stories, but that, read the way they have been read throughout Christian history, Christians have imagined Jesus telling stories about himself. This has not been a bother, apparently, to the Christian imagination. The gospel itself merges myth and history in its story of the Christ. If Jesus was the Christ, what other story could he have told?

The history of reading the parables as little gospels has not been without its excitements. From the beginning Christian interpreters of these texts have been aware that their stories did not refer directly to Jesus and the gospel about him. The challenge was to discover the connections and work the figurative meanings out to correspond with Christian truths. To regard a brief and simply told story as a condensed intimation of the gospel was already titillating. To have to probe its surface meaning in order to discover its hidden intention was inviting. And to discover for one's efforts at the end of the quest some facet of the gospel story was nothing short of revelation. To discover the Christ's story lurking beneath the everyday has seemed a confirmation of the Christian's claim to truth.

Christian theologians have not understood the matter exactly in these terms, to be sure. Parables were merely part of the scriptures, and the scriptures, it was understood, contained the word of God. That understanding came about at a very early time, articulated clearly during the patristic period in the process of domesticating the Hebrew epic. It was then that the allegorical method was pressed into service in order to find the Christian *logos* embedded in the sacred story of events before the appearance of the Christ. The desire was to trace the Christian lineage back through sacred history to the beginning when God created the world. But on the surface of it, the scriptures told the Jewish story, not the presentiments of the Christ. Fortunately, the Greeks had learned about translating epic verse into concepts that belonged to systems of thought, primarily cosmologies and philosophical ethics. The Stoics, for instance, used etymologies, metaphors, word plays, and typologies to discover the outlines of their own worldview encoded in the Homeric epic. Philo of Alexandria used the Stoic method and educed from the Mosaic epic a story of the Jewish soul fit for telling in the first century. Christians found the *logos* of the Christ in the Hebrew scriptures by the same methods. At the literal or epic level, the scriptures told the story of Israel, a largely negative preparation for the coming of the Christ. At the allegorical level, the timeless truths of God's plan of salvation were nevertheless revealed.

How the texts came to be encoded was never explored as thoroughly as how one went about decoding them. The ancient scholars gave names to various procedures for making the connections from text to the order of truth. Technical terms came into being through constant use. Theories were developed about the twofold sense of the scriptures (literal; allegorical), then expanded to the three (historical) and four (moral) senses. For almost two thousand years allegory was the queen of the hermeneutical sciences. An elaborate discourse filled its treasuries as Christian scribes searched and researched the scriptures, and the philosophers explored the nature of the truth that was at once hidden and revealed, historical and eternal, embedded in a text yet ordering the world.[1]

The parables were simply there on the surface of the scriptures after the New Testament took its place beside the Old. That the Christians had two stories, one to be read in the light of the other, was a literal manifestation of the allegorical principle. The parables, for their part, were noteworthy just because they were contained in the New Testament, but contained no reference to the Christ. The tension between the everyday of the parables and the gospel truth they contained was the same as that between the written scriptures as a whole and the divine *logos* they contained. It was also

---

1. *Allegory in antiquity.* The standard work on the history of allegory during the classical period is Jean Pépin, *Mythe et allegorie.* For a critical survey of studies on allegory in Jewish and Alexandrian provenance see B. Mack, "Philo Judaeus and Exegetical Traditions in Alexandria." A detailed study of the function of allegory in a treatise of Philo's commentaries is available in B. Mack, "Weisheit und Allegorie." For a brief survey of the patristic period see Robert M. Grant, *The Bible in the Church.* On Origen, see R. P. C. Hanson, *Allegory and Event.* For a comparative study of Irenaeus, Tertullian, and Clement of Alexandria, see Hamilton B. Timothy, *The Early Christian Apologists and Greek Philosophy.*

the same as that between the Jesus who appeared in Galilee and the Christ he really was, or between history and the eternal orders of God's creation. Allegory played the gaps and led from the lesser to the higher truth. Both the parables and the Christ seemed to profit from the arrangement, a miniature case of the mystery of the incarnation. To the Christian interpreter, the allegorical encounter with the parables was an event of Christian revelation.[2]

The modern New Testament scholar, however, came to see allegory as an illegitimate hermeneutic. The story of the Christ to be educed from the parables or from the Hebrew scriptures by means of allegory was, the scholar emphasized, already known to those who set out to educe it. To use the Christ story as the key to decode the encoded text, then claim to have found the deeper meaning of the text, appears to post-enlightenment mentality to have been a meaningless if not naive procedure. The example used to demonstrate how superficial allegory could be is Augustine's treatment of the parable of the Good Samaritan (Luke 10:30–37). According to Augustine, the traveler is Adam, whose fall from Jerusalem, the heavenly city, down to Jericho, the sign of the moon and mortality, makes him vulnerable to the thieves. The thieves are the devil and his angels, who strip him of his immortality, pummel him into sinning, and leave him half dead in his sinful state. The priest and the Levite represent the ministry of the Old Testament which should provide for salvation, but are not sufficient. The Good Samaritan is the Lord himself, who renders aid and places Adam in the hands of the Apostle Paul. Paul keeps the inn until the morrow when the resurrection will occur. In the meantime, Christ provides the two pence of the precepts of love and the promise of eternal life. So the little story of the man who fell among thieves was found to rehearse the grand scheme of the Christian plan of salvation. It was the legitimacy of allegory that made that reading possible. Christian imagination had no trouble at all with the procedure or the results. A parable of Jesus could implicate the entire sweep of holy history from Adam through Christ and Paul to the eschaton because the realm of truth was timeless. But allegory came under suspicion when the texts over which it ruled were read again as epic, and a critical approach to history was devised.[3]

---

2. *Theory of allegory*. Recent studies on allegory as a literary design suggest that its attraction lies just in the tension created between poetic (imagination) and discourse (rationality; reference). See Angus Fletcher, *Allegory*.

3. *Critique of allegory*. The history of modern parable studies began with the enlightenment critique of the allegorical method of interpretation. The watershed event was the publication in 1888/89 of *Die Gleichnisreden Jesu* by Adolf Jülicher. Norman Perrin recently summarized the story of parable research in *Jesus and the Language of the Kingdom*. Perrin selected the parable of the Good Samaritan to illustrate the development of modern critical methods and the difference each new turn made for understanding the story. His paraphrase of Augustine's allegory, used to contrast modern with medieval

1. PARABLE THEORY

1.1 The Discovery of the Parables as Parables

About one hundred years ago, during the last two decades of the nine-teenth century, Adolf Jülicher noticed the anomaly presented to enlighten-ment mentality by the allegorical interpretation of the parables of Jesus. The battles that had raged for over a hundred years around the miracle stories had subsided for the time being. The conclusion was that Jesus had been a superior teacher of humane morals. This comfortable characteriza-tion was soon to be challenged by the discovery of apocalyptic and the problem of the relationship between the Jesus of history and the Christ of faith. But in the calm before the storm, Jülicher had the leisure for a careful consideration of the teachings of Jesus from a rationalist point of view. The parables caught his attention and he devoted two huge volumes to the task of setting things straight. Parables, Jülicher argued, were not allegories, and should not be read as allegories. They were instead teaching devices used to illustrate moral principles. The parable of the Good Samaritan, for in-stance, was a "story of compassion in which even a Samaritan is approved as neighbor if he acts compassionately." This manner of teaching, Jülicher found, agreed with Greek traditions where *parabolai* ("comparisons") were understood rhetorically to make a single point.[4]

The effect of Jülicher's work on the parables had to wait for almost two generations while the furor about apocalyptic ran its course. Then, in 1935, C. H. Dodd proposed a thesis that established the directions modern parable studies were to take. Dodd accepted Jülicher's distinction between parable and allegory, but preferred a more literary definition for parables in the place of Jülicher's emphasis upon rhetoric and instruction. Dodd's definition of a parable, now a well-known statement, was "a metaphor or simile drawn from nature or common life, arresting the hearer by its vividness or strangeness, and leaving the mind in sufficient doubt about its precise application to tease it into active thought." With this definition secured, Dodd went to work on the question of what Jesus may have intended his hearers to think about.

Jülicher's conception of ethical instruction had been canceled out by the image of Jesus as an apocalyptic preacher. Dodd agreed that Jesus' proc-lamation of the kingdom of God was grounded in an apocalyptic view of history. Most of the parables, however, did not seem to share this view, confronting the interpreter with a conundrum. Dodd solved the problem by

---

interpretation, was taken from C. H. Dodd, *The Parables of the Kingdom,* 1–2, and appears in *Jesus and the Language of the Kingdom,* 94. Perrin's study was used as a guide for the discussion to follow.

4. *Adolf Jülicher.* His discussion of the Good Samaritan appears in *Die Gleichnisreden Jesu* 2: 585–98.

arguing that the eschatological language in the teachings of Jesus did not intend a foretelling of the end of the world. Instead, Jesus announced the realization of apocalyptic expectations in his own life, time, and teaching. The parables, then, were metaphors of the "realized eschatology" taking place in Jesus' ministry. By putting this theological construction upon the parables of the kingdom, Dodd intended to diffuse the more dramatic depictions of Jesus characteristic of continental scholarship and retain a view of Jesus more compatible with British sensibilities. What he achieved, however, was a relocation of the dramatic events of apocalyptic from the arena of history to the realm of the imagination. Thirty years later Robert Funk would put two and two together, arguing that the imaginative experience invited by the parable as metaphor would be, at the same time, the experience of the realized kingdom of God intended by the teaching of Jesus.[5]

During those thirty years two additional chapters in the history of parable studies were written in Germany. In 1947 Joachim Jeremias published a major work in the form critical tradition. His goal was to reconstruct the original forms of the parables by deleting the accretions that had accumulated in the course of their transmission. He then placed the earliest forms among the teachings of Jesus and asked about their intention. For Jeremias, Jesus was the church's Lord who had come to inaugurate the way of salvation. He used the parables as example stories to illustrate and commend aspects of that teaching. Classified by topics, in Jeremias' hands the parables as a class illustrated a full complement of teachings not unlike the traditional Lutheran scheme of soteriology. The lesson from the parable of the Good Samaritan, for instance, was that no one was beyond the reach of charity, a theme that belonged to Jesus' teaching on discipleship. Jeremias' work is still the standard form critical effort, but his view of parable as theological paradigm (example story) has not worn well.[6]

The other development took place under the influence of Rudolf Bultmann. In his work on the history of the synoptic tradition, Bultmann had not paid any particular attention to the parables of Jesus. His interest in Jesus and his teachings was soon to wane, in any case, coming to focus instead on the *Theology of the New Testament.* According to Bultmann, Christian faith could only be understood as a response to the proclamation of the kerygma (the death and resurrection of Christ), not to the proclamation of Jesus. The first sentence in his *Theology of the New Testament* was that "the message of Jesus is a presupposition for the theology of the New

---

5. *C. H. Dodd.* The quotation frequently cited is from *The Parables of the Kingdom,* 5.

6. *Joachim Jeremias.* For a fine discussion of the importance of Jeremias' work on *The Parables of Jesus,* together with observations on its methodological limitations, see Perrin, *Jesus and the Language of the Kingdom,* 101–7. A more recent critique has been lodged by Ronald Hock, "Another Look at Jeremias' *Parables of Jesus.*"

Testament rather than a part of that theology itself." As he developed his program of demythologization, it was the kerygma Bultmann had in mind, not what Jesus said. Nevertheless, in his *Jesus and the Word* Bultmann had laid the foundations for an existentialist interpretation of Jesus' message. In the fifties, Ernst Fuchs, one of Bultmann's students, and Fuchs' own students Eta Linnemann and Eberhard Jüngel, moved from the kerygma back to the teachings of Jesus fully armed with Bultmann's existentialist hermeneutic.[7]

The "new hermeneutic" was a conscious departure from Bultmann's own position on the insignificance of the historical Jesus for Christian faith. The parables, according to Fuchs and his students, expressed Jesus' own faith on the one hand, and made that faith available to his listeners on the other. Faith meant a response to the call to deny determination by the cares and constraints of the world, and to dare an uncertain future in freedom. They did not regard the parables as metaphors (as Dodd had suggested), or as example stories (as Jeremias had proposed), but as "language events." Read closely, however, one is not quite sure whether it was the parables that created the situation of faith, or the presence of Jesus who spoke them. Hearing the parables and encountering Jesus were one and the same thing. Parable as parable, therefore, was not fully explored. Neither were Fuchs and his students able to work out a rationalized theory for their existentialist program analogous to Bultmann's program of demythologization. That was because the literary form of the parable is quite different from that of kerygmatic forms. This was not sufficiently noticed and, lacking a literary critical theory, the new hermeneutic devolved into a dense meditation marked more by pious sentiments than clarity about linguistic functions. Fuchs and his students had nonetheless made it possible to imagine a parable's effect apart from ideation. They introduced to parable studies the imposing influence of Bultmann's hermeneutic and prepared the way for the American school soon to follow.[8]

1.2 Parables and Poetics

American preoccupation with the parables began in the late sixties with Robert Funk's *Language, Hermeneutic, and Word of God*. Drawing on the work of Amos Wilder, Funk decided to read New Testament materials as literary critics read literature. Paying attention to formal features, as well as

---

7. *Rudolf Bultmann.* The citation is from his *Theology of the New Testament* 1:3.

8. *The new hermeneutic.* The discussion follows Perrin, *Jesus and the Language of the Kingdom*, 110–27, with special reference to Ernst Fuchs, *Studies of the Historical Jesus;* Eta Linnemann, *Jesus of the Parables;* and Eberhard Jüngel, *Paulus und Jesus.* The new hermeneutic blossomed, then withered in the sixties, failing to find a congenial soil and climate in America except for its modified application to parable studies. The bridge was made by Robert W. Funk, *Language, Hermeneutic, and Word of God.*

to the functions of poetic language, Funk was able to give an account of the way in which various compositions achieved their effect. This rescued the new hermeneutic from the morass of existentialist soundings, introduced a critical discipline to control scholarly discourse, shifted the focus of attention away from Jesus and onto the listener's understanding, and positioned the parables centrally for the question of Christian origins. In Funk's view, the parable was a narrative metaphor that led the listener to the point where a judgment had to be made about the conventional world of the everyday. Since the parable suggested that there might be another way for things to go in the world of human experience, the decision with regard to the conventional world was also a decision for or against the challenge to entertain the parable's suggestion. Placed in a first-century Jewish milieu, the surprising turn taken by the story of the Good Samaritan would have created a "primary shock," according to Funk. Were one to entertain the possibility of the new storyline, one's accustomed lifeworld would come under judgment and, daring to imagine another order of things, the listener would have ventured into the kingdom of God.[9]

One year later, Dan Via's study on *The Parables* was published. He also sought to control an existentialist interpretation of a parable's effectiveness by means of a critical theory of literature. In keeping with the school of thought known as the "New Criticism," Via argued that parables were "aesthetic objects." According to this theory, a text should be regarded as having its own integrity, discerned by careful attention to its internal system of signs, not read in the light of reference to some external world. The hermeneutical task was to help the reader see the view of human existence presented by the parable and contemplate its aesthetic qualities. This could happen in the twentieth century as well as in the first, according to Via, so that there was no need to situate the parables in their first-century settings in order to understand what they offered. What they offered, Via said, was a view of human existence fraught with the impingements of God and invitations to Christian faith.

Christian theologians found Via's work compelling. A strong stream of anti-historicism was running and a desire to make the biblical texts relevant again was becoming adamant. The aesthetic object approach seemed to be the answer. Rooted in the Romantic tradition, the imaginative effect described by the New Critics was easily associated with traditional types of

---

9. *Robert W. Funk.* Parable studies in America began with Funk's discussion of "The Parable as Metaphor" in *Language, Hermeneutic, and Word of God,* 133–62. From that point on, a steady and widening stream of publications documents the enormous interest and energies unleashed. Funk continued to give leadership to the discussion as his founding editorship of *Semeia* and his own publications show. Selections from his many contributions include: "Saying and Seeing"; "Structure in the Narrative Parables of Jesus"; *Jesus as Precursor;* and *Parables and Presence.* See J. D. Crossan, "A Basic Bibliography for Parables Research."

Christian experience. Two problems soon surfaced, however, as soon as others made the attempt to replicate Via's hermeneutical essays. One was that Via's discussion of the imaginative existential effect of a parable frequently introduced theological categories not immediately derivable from his discussion of the parable's aesthetic aspects. The other was that Via's analysis of a parable's internal system of signs invited contemplation of a story the object of which was not always clear. More work had to be done on the narrative structure of parables.

In 1973 Funk organized a national Seminar on the Parables in order to explore the way in which narrative parables achieved their effect. The seminar formed under the aegis of the Society of Biblical Literature and brought together Wilder, Funk, Via, Dom Crossan, Norman Perrin, and others in common forum. They left a record of their work in the early issues of *Semeia*, the experimental journal of the society launched by Funk at the same time. Structuralism was then in vogue and theories of mythic structure (Lévi-Strauss) and narrative structure (Vladimir Propp, Roland Barthes, A.-J. Greimas) were applied. The structuralist approach was rationalized in terms of linguistic theory, not poetics, and it sought to penetrate beneath the surface patterns of a story in order to disclose the "deep structure" of the narrative pattern that a particular story shared with others of its set. Debates raged about the proper way to collect a set of stories, whether from the same genre and culture, or across type and cultural lines. Critical differences of opinion arose in the attempt to identify narrative components of a given parable in accordance with a given model of narrative structure. All were concerned to assess the distinctive quality and function of the parables of Jesus, and several attempts were made to classify the sub-genres of the parables as a set. Still, nagging questions constantly intruded about where uniqueness was to be located. Lévi-Strauss had argued that the structuralist method of analysis put one in touch ultimately, not with culture specific patterns, but with the way in which the human mind functioned in general. The more abstract the analysis of the parables, the more difficult it was to see why they had created such a fuss.[10]

Early in the 1970s John Dominic Crossan entered these discussions with several articles, one on the Good Samaritan ("Parable and Example") and a book, *In Parables*. In them he announced a theme that would be pursued by him in an increasingly productive investigation. He argued that the parables of Jesus were distinctive and that their distinctive quality could be defined. He found it in the challenge presented by the parables to look at the world differently, so differently in fact, that expectation about the way

---

10. *Structuralism.* J. D. Crossan, "A Basic Bibliography for Parable's Research," includes a section on structuralism. See also the statement and introductory bibliography in the Introduction n.6.

things normally go might have to be completely reversed. The reversal took place in the imagination of the listener, according to Crossan, in the space between the listener's "world of expectation" and the story world of the parable. Because he was interested in a parable's effect upon a listener's prior view of things, and because he understood the parables to have been the creative vehicle of a unique Jesus, Crossan insisted on placing the parables in the world of the first century and in the life of Jesus. The parables, Crossan said, used imagery first to evoke the listener's view of the world, in order then to introduce the telling critique. The imaginative effect of the parable of the Good Samaritan, for instance, was just the way in which the hearer was forced to consider the shocking combination of the ideas "good" and "Samaritan." To allow that thought to be thought, according to Crossan, would be to have one's older world shattered, and to experience the challenge of reimaging how one then might live.

Crossan came to parable studies well versed in criticism and poetics. He thus stood closer to Funk than to Via on two issues. The imaginative effect of a parable was understood situationally and dramatically. And the situation of significance would be the social and cultural world in which the parable first was told. Crossan was nevertheless intrigued by structural analysis and set to work on the problem of demonstrating how parables achieved their effect in terms of narrative structure. He proposed a theory that combined a structural analysis with situational concerns in a popular book entitled *The Dark Interval*. This parable theory deserves a brief description.

Crossan introduced the notion of living in a language world and showed that the dominant narrative patterns in a culture form the hearer's world of expectation. That world can be called the culture's myth, the way things are understood to be arranged. The myth is in mind when listening to any story. What happens in the hearing is that correlations are made between the myth and the story, noticing places where things fit or do not fit between the two storylines. If the story agrees essentially with the cultural patterns, the hearer is gratified and supported in his worldview. If not, adjudications have to be made, ranging from slight adjustments to critical confrontations. A typology of stories results, with myths on one end of a spectrum and parables on the other (see figure 4).

FIGURE 4
CROSSAN'S THEORY OF STORY TYPES

Myth	Apologue	Action	Satire	Parable
establishes world	defends world	investigates world	attacks world	subverts world

To show how parable "subverts world," Crossan used a modified version of Greimas' theory of narrative structure. Greimas' theory reduced all narrative elements to six fundamental functions called actants. The actants are related to one another in a formula or equation as in figure 5.

FIGURE 5
GREIMAS' THEORY OF NARRATIVE STRUCTURE

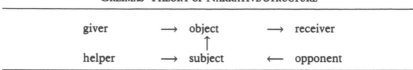

Helpers and opponents assist and complicate the subject's purpose, which is to gain some object originally at the disposal of another (giver, or ordainer) and in the interest of some receiver. Since actants are functions, not characters, a given person or thing can serve more than one actantial function, and a given function can be distributed among several narrative elements. Structural analyses of the parable of the Good Samaritan undertaken in the Parables Seminar had shown that the Samaritan was the subject in only one of three episodes of the story, but in that episode he was both subject and giver. Because the story set up a contrast between the priest and Levite on the one hand, and the Samaritan on the other, Crossan suggested a modification of Greimas's formula capable of expressing the comparison. He then filled in the formula in terms of the hearer's world of expectation. It would have been an apologue, supposing such a story could have been told and found interesting (see figure 6).

FIGURE 6
APOLOGUE: STORY OF THE GOOD PRIEST

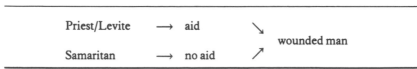

Against this background, Crossan argued, the parable as told actually cancelled out the conventional view of things, reversing both patterns of expectation as in figure 7.

Parables, reversal, and the subversion of world thus were joined in a definitive theory of the principal effect of Jesus' "teaching." Not all of the parables were to be classed formally as parables of reversal, to be sure. In his

FIGURE 7
PARABLE: STORY OF THE GOOD SAMARITAN

Priest/Levite	aid	↘	
	✕		wounded man
Samaritan	no aid	↗	

book *In Parables,* Crossan had proposed two other classes of parables. There were, he said, also parables of advent, and parables of action. Nevertheless, the effect of all three classes in the context of the first-century world was, according to Crossan, parabolic, that is, a world-shattering invitation to live without myth.

Not satisfied to make the point only with a parable of reversal (the Good Samaritan), Crossan produced yet another study to show that even such a simple theme as that of the treasure became, in the hands of Jesus, a parable of reversal when judged against the world of conventional wisdom. In his *Finding Is the First Act,* Crossan collected an immense reference to treasure stories from many cultures. He reduced their narrative structure to a certain pattern in which the quest for the treasure always precedes the finding. He then showed that Jesus' parable reversed this pattern. The result was a story about finding a treasure without looking for it, by surprise. Crossan concluded that Jesus had done it again, that the kingdom he announced in parables canceled quest stories, and appeared as an unexpected treasure.[11]

1.3 Parable Theory and Christian Origins

Parable studies in America are now a recognized sub-discipline of New Testament criticism. A large bibliography has been produced in the last ten years and the energies unleashed by the Parables Seminar show no signs of subsiding. Crossan's parable theory has not been accepted by everyone without revision, others preferring slightly less dramatic, more aesthetic, psychological, or theological articulations of the parable effect. These revisions have not introduced a fundamental criticism, however, the general tenor of more recent studies tending to support the view that parables are to be placed at the beginnings of things Christian, and that their function was primarily to open up the new world that dawned with Jesus. The influence of this discourse is such that scholars in related disciplines now regularly use the terms parable and parabolic to designate any critical inversion of perspective held to be in the interest of Christian critique of the

---

11. *John Dominic Crossan.* See his 1972 study of the Good Samaritan, "Parable and Example." In addition to those works mentioned in the discussion, there are two subsequently published studies of importance: *Raid on the Articulate;* and *Cliffs of Fall.*

world. Parabolic now substitutes for the older term prophetic to name the genius of Jesus and the peculiarity of a Christian's stance toward the world. Parable studies have produced a theory of Christian origins.[12]

The reader of this scholarship on parables will not find much discussion of the importance of parable studies for the quest of the historical Jesus, however, nor of the importance of parables for Christian origins. The importance of the parables for Christian origins has simply been assumed and scholars have been satisfied to elaborate on the parabolic effect without arguing for those assumptions. There are several reasons for this, one suspects. One reason is that scholars in the Anglo-American tradition have seldom felt it necessary to defend the supposition that Christianity started with Jesus, a very superior person. The agony on the Continent over the difference between the message of Jesus and the kerygma about the Christ did not take root in America where the preference has always been to bracket the whole matter of mythologization as embarrassing. Lines have always been drawn from Jesus the teacher straight into the history of the church, conveniently bypassing the messy business about the passion and its myths and rituals. Part of the attraction held by the parables is just that a dramatic inauguration of the Christian time can be imagined without having to reconsider those other events as the source for the Christian notion of transformation. If the critical sequence of death to the old world (shattering) and invitation to the new (as an imaginative creation) can be attributed to the parabolic effect of Jesus' utterances, there is no need for the death and resurrection of the Christ to account for Christian origins. Or so the assumption seems to be.[13]

Another reason for the general lack of discussion about Christian origins in this scholarship is that the authenticity of the parables has been taken for granted. One suspects a strong influence at this point of Jeremias and his student Norman Perrin, both of whom accepted the authenticity of the

---

12. *Recent parable research.* Major works published since Crossan's bibliography of 1974 include: Sallie McFague, *Speaking in Parables* (1975); Madeleine Boucher, *The Mysterious Parable* (1977); Mary Ann Tolbert, *Perspectives on the Parables* (1978); Pheme Perkins, *Hearing the Parables of Jesus* (1981); James Breech, *The Silence of Jesus* (1983); Amos Wilder, *Jesus' Parables and the War of Myths* (1983); and Bernard Brandon Scott, *Jesus, Symbol-Maker for the Kingdom* (1985).

13. *Jesus versus the kerygma.* An attempt to reconstruct early Christian history from Jesus to the gospels that denies the necessity of kerygmatic influence is argued by W. Kelber in *The Oral and the Written Gospel*, chap. 5, "Death and Life in the Word of God." Kelber is deeply in touch with American sensibility in this study. He is also right in his criticism of scholarly assumptions about the passion narrative as very early, kerygmatic in intent, and fundamental for all movements stemming from Jesus. This will be borne out in part 3. Kelber's solution to the origins of Christianity and the gospel cannot be supported, however, for he must mystify what he calls Jesus' continuing "Oral Presence" as a substitute for the kerygma and its power to symbolize transformation. The position taken in the present study, against Kelber's thesis, is that the Gospel of Mark could not have been imagined apart from knowledge of the kerygmatic tradition of the Hellenistic congregations.

parables and worked hard to situate them in the life and teachings of Jesus. Many reservations have been expressed about this or that particular parable in recent scholarship, but no scholar has seriously questioned that Jesus taught in parables, or that "the parables" of Jesus are the parables "of Jesus." The thought that the parables put one in touch with the essential significance of Jesus has been too comfortable not to take it for granted. The comfort is understandable. Not only are the authentic teachings of Jesus found to be devoid of myth, they are lacking in propositional didactics. Jesus looms large as a very sage individual, superior in creativity and skilled in rhetorical finesse. He is, moreover, inaugural in just the right ways. His critique of the old order is devastating. His invitation to the new time is demanding. And when it is seen that the parables are stories, not preachments, or apocalyptic pronouncements, a most humane nuance is given to an encounter that reaches down to the very fundamentals of human experience mediated by a primary mode of human articulation.

Human foibles being what they are, it is even possible on this suspicion of the way Christianity got started to account for the failure of Jesus' followers to stay perched on the brink of novelty. To make of a parable an example story, an allegory, or even a gospel, would be an understandable, if regrettable, return to the human securities of codes and conventions. An implicit apologetic thus can be discerned in the originary hypothesis. Since the parables were retained, however, though tarnished and misinterpreted, the possibility of recovering the pristine parable is given. Parable studies have been devoted to such a recovery. The desire has been not only to reconstruct the earliest and therefore original form of a parable, but to make it possible to listen in on the first time it was told. Every theory of parable interpretation has aimed at recapturing that moment. Once recaptured, there is usually a shift into a hermeneutical discussion of the relevance for a post-modern Christian style. Listening in on the first time has seldom been suggested as a means to historical reconstruction, certainly not as an effort in understanding social history. It has been an effort to isolate a critical moment available to the modern interpreter. The effect upon the first (hypothetical) listener has been understood solely as the effect of the parable's language upon the individual's imagination. Conveniently, the modern interpreter has access to the same language. Setting the first-century scene has functioned, therefore, as an historical "once upon a time," allowing twentieth-century individuals to imagine the proper time and place for hearing the parables afresh and participating in their challenge. Thus the language event can be reproduced by reconstruction and the original generative effect reexperienced. The marks of the Christian imaginative scheme on modern parable theory are therefore obvious. The desire is to be present at the beginning by reconstructing the first parabolic effect of Jesus' speech.

1.4 Parables and Social Contexts

Modern parable theory leaves the social historian with a host of unanswered questions. The scholarly demonstration of thoughtful and skillful composition in the parables is, of course, persuasive. The call for analyses of narrative structures is also compelling. The appeal to imaginative effect is eminently compatible with a social historical approach to discourse and literature as well. Questions arise, however, at the point of situating the parables in some particular social context and assessing their effect in light of yet larger cultural frames of reference. It is not that some sense of the need to position the parables in a first-century context has been lacking in this discourse. Funk, especially, has consistently reminded parable scholars of this need. It is that a rather superficial notion of first-century culture has prevailed, presumably in the interest of working out a single theory of effectiveness adequate to account for the novelty Jesus is understood to have introduced. Problems arise when one sees that the "worlds of expectation" in Palestine were diverse.

The parable of the Good Samaritan, to take only that example, could have worked the way Crossan suggested only under certain very narrowly prescribed circumstances and in a very specific social context. Given the complex social and cultural terrain within which the parable of the Good Samaritan might be placed, the assumption of circumstances optimal for the parabolic effect is questionable unless additional argumentation can be marshaled for the specific occasion. Were the optimal circumstances readily imaginable for Galilee in the twenties, the beginnings of a case might be made. But the story is about a priest, a Levite, and a Samaritan on the road from Jerusalem to Jericho. A Galilean would have had no trouble imagining that, of course. But would the loyalties from a distance have been so strongly pro and con as the theory requires? Only in a context where priests and Levites were highly regarded, animus against Samaritans shared, and both attitudes figured prominently in a rationalization of cultural identity, would the parable work just the way parable theory says it would. Might not a Galilean, hearing the story about Judean cultic personnel and a Samaritan, have enjoyed a tinge of satirical delight? It would clearly have been possible for a Syrian or Greek to have taken it satirically. In Samaria, on the other hand, the story may well have worked parabolically, not by making the point at the expense of one's loyalties as Crossan proposes, however, but at the expense of one's disloyalties or hostilities. Still, supposing the Samaritans were not as evil as made out to be, and thought of themselves on occasion as compassionate, the story might even be taken as a hero's tale, exploring a certain action quizzically if not with pride. Domesticated far from the scene in Luke's Gospel, the parable could be taken as an action story (scholars would say an example story), or it could be taken as an apologue, defending the claims of the non-Jewish church to the legacy of the myth of Israel. At what point it was read as myth, whether allegorized expressly or not, is not important here. The point is that, on the surface, told in different contexts, the story of the Good Samaritan might function now as parable, now as satire, now as action, apologue, or myth. There is really no compelling reason to argue for its authenticity and interpret it parabolically. Its composition and occurrence in Luke as a Christian example story make good sense, though not the kind of sense a parable theory of Christian origins would demand.

To the social historian, then, parable theory seems to require the effacement of complex social circumstance. It also appears to exaggerate the effect of a parable upon a listener's "world of expectation." Many of the parables do employ images that evoke Jewish themes and ideals only to challenge them. It is not clear whether Jesus or his followers are to be credited with this interest in every case. But placing them in an essentially Jewish context for the sake of argument, many of these stories do turn the tables on basic Jewish values. Parable theory goes on to interpret the imaginative effect of these parables as the challenge of an either/or, a call to leave the old behind and venture forth. This interpretation appears to be a Christian value, however, delighting in the Christian myth of origins. It is not at all clear, supposing such stories to be authentic and that Jewish listeners heard them told by a Jewish Jesus from within or at most on the borders of a shared sense of identity, that Jewish ears would have felt the effect in the assumed Christian way. Certain features of *The Art of Biblical Narrative,* as Robert Alter has explored it, are quite similar to the way in which Jesus told stories. Alter noted, for instance, that in the Hebrew Bible the story of the two sons, one elder, one younger, rides on the theme of election, specifically the law of primogeniture. The stories invariably set up a conflict between the two sons, and then relate the transmission of privilege to the younger. This inversion of expectations, Alter argued, does not destroy the law. Neither does it destroy confidence in the idea of election. What it achieves is circumspection, a kind of awareness and honesty about the irregularities that actually accompany application to the real world. In Crossan's terms, the genre would be parable, but the function would be action. If one translates this Jewish sensibility into the situation of Jesus among Jewish ears in Galilee, caution is required in assuming that his parables shattered Jewish myth. The parable of the Good Samaritan may be a dangerous prime example for theorizing on parables, because it trades more in an ethnic hostility than in an epic ideal. Those parables that do evoke the epic and ethical ideals may not have brought myth to an end at all, but applied it by pointing out the incongruity between the ideals and the quality of life actually observable in the contemporary society. The general tenor of Jesus' social critique needs to be kept in mind as well. It does not appear to have been institutionally specific. Those parables that do announce the new at the expense of the old, that divide between those inside and outside, that threaten exclusion for those who do not hear, are probably not the parables of Jesus, but Christian apologues written some time after Jesus told his stories.

One need not deny that Jesus told parables, nor that his parables were effective vehicles for daring thoughts and new behavior. But a twice-told/twice-heard parable can be a very tricky thing. Heard for the first time, the Good Samaritan comes as a surprise. Domesticated, however, and listened to again, the hearer already knows how the story will end. As with jokes, it is not impossible to listen attentively the second time as if for the first time. Still, one does need to ask whether first-time hermeneutics are adequate for domesticated rehearsals. A critical shift in perspective automatically invites hearing the story as apologue or example. Theoretically it would be possible to imagine the followers of Jesus becoming the tellers of the story in situations of invitation similar to that imagined for Jesus, thus addressed always to first-time listeners. But in the synoptic tradition the stories, though attributed still to Jesus, thus "heard" as if "told" for the first time, are actually read from the perspective of their already having been heard. If, then, the parables are understood to have inaugurated the new time and society, the new time and society have become the arena of domestication. Since the parables have been placed for hearing imaginatively just before the beginning of the new time, just beyond the borders of the new ethos they generated, however, they no longer function to recreate the surprise of imagining the new at all, but to defend the new world already imagined against those who were not surprised but offended. A voyeuristic perspective on the "first" time the parables were told is thus a distinct possibility. But to watch Jesus confound with a parable those known to have decided against the invitation of the parables would be a devastating application of the parabolic function.

2. THE PARABLES IN MARK

In the Gospel of Mark Jesus is pictured telling parables at two important junctures. In chapter 4, after Jesus' appearance in Galilee and the appointment of the twelve, Mark introduces Jesus' discourse on the kingdom of God. It consists entirely of parables. In chapter 12, after Jesus' entrance into Jerusalem and the action in the temple, Mark introduces Jesus' discourse on issues of conflict with the temple leaders. The discourse includes the parable of the Tenants. The parables in Mark have attracted a great deal of scholarly attention. The plot of the parable of the Tenants so closely follows an early Christian view of Jesus as the last of a line of rejected prophets that one can hardly read it without seeing that connection. It is so finely crafted, however, that one need not take it allegorically in order to imagine its parabolic effect. The result has been a heated scholarly debate about its authenticity. The parable discourse in Mark 4, on the other hand, is the classic depiction of Jesus "speaking in parables." The chapter contains several peculiar features of great interest to scholars. It emphasizes that the hidden message of the parables is the kingdom of God. It is the earliest occurrence in the synoptic tradition where a parable (the Seeds) is given an ("allegorical") interpretation. It also contains the only explanation given in the gospels for teaching by means of parables. And, because the several parables are united by a common theme (seeds), the chapter seems to be evidence for an early, pre-Markan interest in collecting the parables of Jesus. These matters need to be reviewed.

2.1 The Collection in Mark 4

The place to begin is with the parables in chapter 4. The chapter lends itself easily to the outline given in figure 8.

FIGURE 8
THE PARABLES IN MARK 4

4:1–2a	Setting by the sea
4:2b–9	The Seeds
4:10–12	The reason for parables
4:13–20	The explanation of the Seeds
4:21–23	The Lamp
4:24–25	The Measure
4:26–29	The Seed Growing Secretly
4:30–32	The Mustard Seed
4:33–34	Conclusion

There is some consensus that Mark is responsible for the setting, conclusion, and the reason for parables. There is less clarity about the extent of a pre-Markan collection. H.-W. Kuhn's exhaustive analysis had finally to settle on only the three major seed parables. Because they shared the common theme of the eventual success of the Christian "mission," Kuhn argued that they belonged together and that they stemmed from a period prior to Mark when the failure of the mission had become a problem. He pointed out that the emphasis in the Seeds was on their adverse fate, that the Seed Growing Secretly did so "automatically," and that the Mustard Seed promised a success yet to be realized. Using the principle of thematic consistency to establish the collection, Kuhn excluded the explanation of the Seeds, the Lamp, and the Measure. These are usually regarded as pre-Markan also, however, so that a complex history of the parables prior to

Mark can be imagined. Because the reason for parables is so closely related to the explanation of the Seeds, and because the explanation of the Seeds is obviously secondary to the Seeds, some scholars have thought Mark added the explanation, while others have argued that Mark was not the first to have given the reason. Many scholars would like to think that all of the parables were authentic, then transmitted and collected in various stages, finally to be integrated into the Gospel by Mark. Thus there is no scholarly consensus.[14]

The question of authenticity should probably be handled on a parable-by-parable basis. A thorough discussion of all the parables need not be given in order to position them for the study to follow. It will be enough to grant that the memory tradition represented by the parables in Mark 4 may contain some authentic reminiscences in spite of what would then be forty years of transmission. The parables least under suspicion would be the Lamp and the Measure, simply because they can be imagined most easily in the situation of the aphoristic Jesus. They need not apply to great undertakings, but to behavioral issues arising from the kind of social critique Jesus lodged. Memorable because of their oddness and pithy qualities, each could also easily have been reapplied to many other situations without internal revision.

The Mustard Seed also generally has been understood to be authentic. It was certainly in circulation before Mark used it, as its occurrence both in Q (Luke 13:18–19) and the Gospel of Thomas (GThom 20) attests. In his book *In Parables* Crossan argued convincingly that the earliest of the three textual instances is that found in the Gospel of Thomas, for there, in distinction from the variants in Q and Mark, apocalyptic nuances are completely lacking. Still, authenticity is questionable even for the variant in GThom 20 because it already presupposes a social history. Someone took note of the small beginnings of a group that had become a movement with great expectations. The expectations reflect the optimism one can imagine for the early stage of some Jesus movements. It is significant, also, that the ethos of the movement may have been designated by the term kingdom of God already at this early stage. In Q, then, the great expectations were specified apocalyptically by means of an outrageous allusion to the great tree of apocalyptic vision (in Ezek 17:23–25; 31:6; Dan 4:10–12). In Mark the parody created by the association of the mustard shrub with the apocalyptic tree lost whatever humor it may have had, though, in the very serious prediction that the kingdom of God Jesus announced would

---

14. *The parable collection in Mark 4.* The reference is to H.-W. Kuhn, *Ältere Sammlungen im Markusevangelium,* chap. 2. Further discussion will be found in W. Kelber, *The Kingdom in Mark,* 25–43; and in B. Mack and V. Robbins, *Patterns of Persuasion in the Gospels,* chap. 6.

eventually become the greatest dominion of all. The history of resignifi-cation shows that the analogy was popular among Jesus movements for some reason, but the reason had more to do with the appropriateness of the metaphor to the movements' own sense of history than to an inaugural announcement of some grand program by Jesus. If Jesus did use the metaphor of the mustard seed, its occasion and thus its point has been lost.

The Seed Growing Secretly occurs only in Mark. It is neither very provocative as a parable, nor apt as an image of the kingdom of God. Its point is appropriate within its present context, as will become clear, but probably only there. It is best therefore to regard it as a construction composed just for that context.

That leaves the Seeds, the most provocative of the five parables and one that many scholars hold to be most important and most probably authentic. It deserves a separate discussion.

2.2 The Parable of the Seeds

Reconstructions of the original form of the parable have been guided by two criteria. One is that several phrases describing the growth of the seeds disturb both the theme and the narrative flow (5b, 6b, 7c, and the phrase "growing up and increasing" in 8). The second is that, by deleting them, a finely crafted aesthetic object results. The text reconstructed by Theodore Weeden can serve as a basis for discussion (see figure 9).

FIGURE 9
THE PARABLE OF THE SEEDS

Look:

A sower went out to sow, and while sowing it happened:

Some seed fell along the path	and the birds came	and devoured it.
Other seed fell on rocky ground,	and when the sun rose	it was scorched.
Other seed fell among thorns,	and the thorns grew up	and choked it.
Other seed fell into good earth,	and it gave fruit	and yielded
thirtyfold,	sixtyfold,	one hundredfold.
		(Mark 4:2b–9)

The arrangement of the text demonstrates the care taken with its com-position. The balance of members is even. The rule of three pertains throughout. There are three main episodes. These are countered by the threefold yield in the contrastive episode. Each line also is triadically composed, the first unit describing the fall, the second the entrance of an agent, and the third reserved for the action. Repetition is used to establish the pattern, but is relieved by slight suggestions of serial progression (cf.

along, upon, among, into). The actions are portrayed with extremely vivid verbs. But each action is "natural," as is each of the agents. A troubling nuance is created by the fact that none of the agents is an unambiguously negative symbol. Because the agents are neutral the fate of the seeds is all the more noteworthy. The reversal is also hardly a surprise, except as contrast to what has gone before. The disturbance of the progression thirty, sixty, ninety, in order to end with one hundred gives a twitch to the upbeat intended by the final stroke that reverses the progression and swiftly concludes the story. The listener is left with a mild relief. But it cannot cancel out the imagery already etched in the background. Chanciness means that the joyous ending will have to be an invitation to pensive reflection.

Post-modern sensibility might be content to leave it at that, a contemplation on the natural order of things troubling enough to trigger reflection back upon the listener's own attitude toward life and death, chance selection, forces of destruction and generation, and so forth. First-century sensibility was not lacking in aesthetic capacity, of course, but it is questionable whether even such a sensitive poetic as this parable would have been taken romantically. Some translation from the natural to the human orders must have been intended, and first-century listeners would have looked for the reference and connection. Scholars have been satisfied to think that the reference must have been to the kingdom of God just as Mark says it was. With that assumption in place, Crossan could then emphasize the surprise at the end of the parable and relate it to the "advent of the kingdom" as "surprise." Weeden thought reversal was the point of the parable and that the parable was therefore a profound invitation to optimism about God's ways in the world in spite of all appearances. Others have been content to imagine Jesus telling the parable as a riddle whose point about the kingdom of God was purposefully unclear in keeping with the necessarily vague status of a call to an open future. All seem to agree, however, that the story was original with Jesus and should be read as an invitation to imagine a novel order of things as if for the first time.[15]

The problem with these views is that the parable introduces a full screen of eventualities upon which to reflect, and the point about eventual fruition is made only against the background of a thorough acknowledgment of threats to those eventualities. Some entire history, complete program, or final destiny is under review, not an announcement of a new insight or beginning. If the parable is about the kingdom of God Jesus announced,

---

15. *The Parable of the Seeds.* Theodore Weeden's reconstruction is found in "Recovering the Parabolic Intent." His text is won in debate with J. D. Crossan, *In Parables,* 39–44; and "The Seed Parables of Jesus." Crossan thought that deletion of phrases showing interest in the theme of growth a sufficient reconstruction. Weeden was impressed by the possibility of reconstructing a perfectly balanced poetic structure.

and if it is regarded as authentic, the story would reflect a high degree of self-consciousness about his mission, experiences of rejection, and futuristic projections about eventual success quite out of character for his otherwise non-programmatic style. There would also be an unguarded invitation to allegorize by self-reference were one to get serious about its application in this manner. But perhaps the story is not about the eventual fate of the kingdom of God Jesus announced. Perhaps it is about the fate of Israel.

The imageries of the field, sowing, seeds, miscarriage, and harvest are standard metaphors for God's dealing with Israel in Jewish apocalyptic, wisdom, and prophetic literatures. Depending on the context, the use of such imagery would automatically have suggested a statement of theological import about Israel's destiny. In the mouth of Jesus, however, what could that statement have been? It could only have been a rehearsal of some negative results of God's "instruction" to Israel in contrast to some positive results when the "seed" fell upon the "good earth." Such a general reference raises a host of distracting questions, however, such as: which instruction, by which teacher(s), and which Jewish responses? Distracting questions about the story's intention hardly enhance the aesthetic effect, and the contrasting fates could not have been used to imply a self-reference to Jesus in this scheme without offending Jewish ears and normal logic. That is because the story is not about two different teachers or instructions, but about two different kinds of fate or soil. Thus the point of the story would hardly have been found clever, surprising, or comforting as a parable of Jesus told in reference to his own novel program.

Such a highly theologized review of Israel's history, complete with an implicit claim to know how the story would end, what the divine instruction had been, and how absolute the distinction between the two types of destiny would be, might be imagined for a later Christian thinker, but not for the historical Jesus. Since the parable only works when the listener is concerned about the fate of the seeds, and since the fate of the seeds is calculated to heighten that concern by imagery of loss through destruction, the most plausible reference is not directly to the history of Israel, but to the early history of the Jesus movements. The parable makes good sense about the kingdom of God Jesus announced, but only in retrospect upon some adverse history of its failed attempts to take root. Facing up to rejection and finding ways to compensate for it were characteristic of the fifties and later in most Jesus movements. Thus the parable of the Seeds is most easily understood just in that situation.

2.3 Teaching in Parables

The parables in Mark 4 transmit a memory tradition about Jesus' mode of discourse and raise it to the level of programmatic statement: "He taught them many things in parables. . . . He did not speak to them without a parable" (Mark 4:2, 34). The memory tradition that Jesus spoke in parables can be granted. If the term parable is taken in broad connotation to refer to imagistic language used metaphorically or analogically, a connotation that agrees with its use in general in the synoptic tradition, the programmatic statement might be understood as an astute observation on the part of the author regarding the nature of Jesus' discourse known to him. The particular parables Mark used as examples of Jesus' teaching, however, suggest that something more was at stake. These parables are not only difficult to read as first-time announcements of a newly imagined kingdom of God; they actually reflect upon the hidden history of a purpose not yet realized. Carefully composed and consciously interpreted as enigmatic, the parables Mark selected to illustrate Jesus' teaching betray deeply embedded concerns about the destiny of some Jesus movement that thought of itself as the bearer of the kingdom Jesus had announced. Social history is under review, history whose "harvest" is being imagined and affirmed by means of the parables about the seeds.

A very complex literary history would need to be untangled in order to identify every juncture of social history through which this material had passed. Several views of the kingdom and its destiny have accrued. The sequence from an earlier, optimistic application of the Mustard Seed (in Q) to the later more prophetic and apocalyptic allusions (in Mark) is understandable. What to make of the theme of growth inserted into the Seeds, on the other hand, is not certain. It fits neither the overall thrust of the parable, nor Mark's own interpretation of it. Addition at a later time to soften Mark's essentially apocalyptic view of things would be the easiest solution. Whether there was a pre-Markan collection of seed stories on the theme of the kingdom, therefore, is far from clear. What is clear is that a rich reflection on a lively and troubling social history had been managed before Mark by the use of parables attributed to Jesus. Mark fastened upon that practice, contributed substantially to it, and raised it to the level of a program.

The odd thing about the collection of parables in Mark 4 is that, with the exception of the explanation that the parables refer to the kingdom of God, Jesus' teaching according to Mark consisted only of parables. This indicates more than astute observation on Mark's part. He was not taking up the parables because he was impressed with the effective function of parabolic discourse as modern parable theory purports. He was not suggesting that Jesus' teaching in parables inaugurated the kingdom. The parables were about the kingdom, but they did not function "parabolically." Their "secret" was known only to those already on the "inside" of the kingdom by means of explanations. For those on the outside, the meaning of the parables remained a mystery. What then might be the function of "parables" according to Mark?[16]

2.4 Parables and Paideia

In first-century parlance, the term parable (*parabolē*) did not refer to a story that subverted myth, but to a "comparison." Marsh McCall's book, *Ancient Rhetorical Theories of Simile and Comparison*, offers a thorough philological investigation of *parabolē* and related terms (*eikōn, homoiōsis, eikasia, simile, similitudo, comparatio*) in Greco-Roman literatures of rhetoric and criticism. The term refers in general to an "illustrative comparison" or "analogy." It was discussed in these literatures both under the rubric of "style" or "poetics" on the one hand, and under the rubric of "proof" or "argumentation" on the other. Stylistic observations recognize (1) that *parabolai* range from metaphors, through similes, to nonfigural comparisons between similar things. One also finds discussions of (2) the length appropriate to various literary contexts, (3) degree of detail in the explication of points of comparison, and (4) what difference it makes whether the two things compared are basically the same, similar but from different orders of reality, or different in all respects (i.e., contrastive). Appropriateness to the speech situation is always in view in these discussions, "heightened" and "poetic" forms of comparison thought to be distracting in forensic and deliberative situations, and so forth. Aesthetic and literary critical observations are therefore not lacking in discussions of *parabolē*, but nowhere is there evidence of what moderns would consider a genre critical definition. By definition, *parabolē* was understood to be a matter of content.

In the rhetorical tradition, a *parabolē* was understood to function as an "argument." From Aristotle on, *parabolē* was regularly paired with *para-*

---

16. *The mystery of the kingdom.* H. Koester, "History and Development of Mark's Gospel," finds that the use of the term mystery in the singular in Mark 4:11 is suspicious, given the plurals in both parallels (Matthew and Luke). The clue is found in the singular form of the "mystery of the kingdom" in the account of the midnight baptism in M. Smith's reconstruction of a secret gospel of Mark. See his *Clement of Alexandria and a Secret Gospel of Mark.* Koester finds the singular form supported by the use of the singular elsewhere in esoteric baptismal contexts. Koester argues that the original Mark 4:11 used the plural "mysteries" in keeping with the practice of the allegorical interpretation of parables, but that it was changed to the singular at that point when Mark was esotericized as the secret gospel. Finally, shorn of its offending parts, canonical Mark appeared, but with the singular mystery left intact in Mark 4:11. Koester's observation on the appropriateness of the plural to hidden matters requiring decoding is helpful. Cf. the plural in Wis 6:22, and GThom 62. It is not clear, however, why it would have occurred as important to the author of the secret gospel to introduce a baptismal usage at Mark 4:11. In either case, singular or plural, the "mystery" of the kingdom provides the clue, not only to the meaning of the parable of the Seeds, but to Jesus' teaching in Mark 4 as a unit. This will become clear as the discussion proceeds.

deigma (paradigm, example) in discussions of the "topics," or sources from which rhetorical arguments could be taken. Both were important for exploring and addressing the world of human affairs where principles of order and arrangement were not always obvious, and "logic" had to be content with establishing "probabilities" through "inductive" reasoning. Both offered ways of pointing to incidents, events, and describable phenomena that could provide at least one case for the rhetor's contention about "the way things go." Brought to bear upon some subject under discussion, *paradeigma* and *parabolē* could furnish either a primary or a supporting argument, depending on their place in the development of an argumentation. A *parabolē* differed from a *paradeigma*, not in respect to its logical function, but in respect to its source and content. The *paradeigma* was taken from "history" (and thus depended upon a certain literacy for its effectiveness). It was understood as "fact," i.e., a specific (and precedent) case in actuality. The *parabolē* was taken from the generally familiar world of human observation and experience. It was understood as "fiction," i.e., "invented" by the author to illustrate the point to be made. It did not refer to a specific and actual case, but generalized a common and recurring phenomenon. Its subjects were cast as abstractions (e.g., "nature"), classes (e.g., "farmers"), or indefinite subjects (e.g., "a certain one"). A *parabolē* could be set forth as a proposition about the way things go, then supported by additional considerations. Or it could be used as an argument in support of a proposition made some other way. One thing was never lacking, and that was the subject under review, the proposition or phenomenon for which the *parabolē* offered an instructive analogy.

Mark's statement that Jesus "taught with *parabolai*" is a rhetorical observation. The observation is strangely appropriate to the aphoristic and figural use of language characteristic of the Jesus traditions. But a problem immediately arises. Most of the aphoristic sayings of Jesus lack explicit reference. They are *parabolai* without the comparison stated. This characteristic may be illusory in part, the intended reference having been to social situations addressed, but lost in the process of collecting sayings and writing them down. But it also may be true in some ways. It may be descriptive of a discourse that combined the *mētis* of the Cynic with the playful wisdom characteristic of the Jewish *mashalim*. Neither form of "wisdom" knew the constraints of the Greek penchant for explicit definition. Mark may have taken note and heightened the cultural contrast by calling Jesus' metaphors *parabolai*, "analogies" that failed to include the comparison intended. That Mark wanted to make such a point, however, cannot be explained at the level of a literary critic's delight. [17]

---

17. *Parable as analogy.* For a discussion of the function of *parabolē* in the Greek

Mark, at any rate, supplied the object of reference. The parables were analogies, offering instruction about the kingdom of God. On the surface of it, that should take care of the matter. If Mark was right, offering merely an observation that accurately described the historical realities, the mystery of the analogies without reference would simply disappear. In supplying the reference, however, Mark was not offering a banal observation. The parables remain enigmatic to those who do not "know" the reference. And the reference, though named, remains a "mystery" known only to those to whom it is "given" (Mark 4:11). Savvy about the function of *parabolai* in the Greek rhetorical tradition, Mark manipulated the aphoristic quality of the sayings tradition to account for two ways in which Jesus' message had been taken. He described a single occasion in the life of Jesus when "teaching" in parables worked both ways at the same time, i.e., "mystified" as well as "instructed." The question is whether the mystery of these parables was really all that mysterious.

2.5 Sowing Seeds and Paideia

The content of the parable of the Seeds makes one suspicious. That is because the image of agricultural endeavor, especially that of sowing seed, was the standard analogy for *paideia* during this period. *Paideia*, it may be recalled, was the name regularly used for both teaching and culture. Mark portrayed Jesus teaching about the kingdom of God with a *parabolē* about sowing seeds. Ears acquainted with Hellenistic culture to any degree at all would immediately have recalled the stock image for offering instruction with a view to the inculcation of Hellenistic culture:

> The views of our teachers are as it were the seeds. Learning from childhood is analogous to the seeds falling betimes upon the prepared ground. (Hippocrates, *Law* III)

> As is the seed that is ploughed into the ground, so must one expect the harvest to be, and similarly when good education is ploughed into your persons, its effect lives and burgeons throughout their lives, and neither rain nor drought can destroy it. (Antiphon, fr. 60 in Diels, *Vorsokratiker*)

> Words should be scattered like seed; no matter how small the seed may be, if it once has found favorable ground, it unfolds its strength and from an insignificant thing spreads to its greatest growth. (Seneca, *Epistles* 38:2)

---

traditions of rhetoric and education, in relation to the *paradigma* and other ways of constructing an argument, see B. L. Mack and V. K. Robbins, *Patterns of Persuasion in the Gospels*. *Mētis* as a form of wisdom typical of Cynic response to situations will be discussed in chap. 7. The term *mētis* is a coinage by Marcel Detienne and Jean-Pierre Vernant, *Cunning Intelligence in Greek Culture and Society*.

If you wish to argue that the mind requires cultivation, you would use a comparison drawn from the soil, which if neglected produced thorns and thickets, but if cultivated will bear fruit. (Quintilian, *Institutio oratoria* 5.11.24)

The "sower" was a stock analogy for the "teacher," "sowing" for "teaching," "seed" for "words," and "soils" for "students." The *parabolē* Mark chose to illustrate Jesus' enigmatic teaching was itself a standard image for offering instruction! Since for Greek ears teaching (*paideia*) was the inculcation of culture (*paideia*), neither the imagery of the analogy nor its standard reference to culture (ethos, "kingdom") would have been mysterious. Thus the mystery does not reside in the parables as parables, but in the nature of that culture or kingdom they illustrate. Merely by using the *parabolē* of the Seeds, Mark set up a study in contrastive comparison of his own. One was to think *paideia*, but listen to the parables. Any differences detected might help define the "secret" of the kingdom of God to which they referred.

In order to work out the traits of the kingdom Mark had in mind, all of the parables in chapter four must be read in sequence. They form a set, composed in accordance with a standard outline for elaborating a thesis. Before taking up Mark's elaboration of the Seeds, however, one clue to the mysterious kingdom can already be mentioned. For the Greeks, *paideia* was a matter of labor. Education was a process in the cultivation of virtue or culture. The analogy of cultivation made its point precisely by emphasizing the necessity of discipline, work, and the relationship of these to the quality of the eventual harvest. The parable of the Seeds and its elaboration delete the essential moment of labor. In its place, the moments of sowing and fruition are emphasized as events definitive for the new *paideia*. Everything has been brought to focus on beginnings and endings, events of consequence for they determine the fate of the seed, but of consequences essentially beyond the control of the sower.[18]

---

18. *Sowing as metaphor of paideia.* The analogy of *paideia* to sowing seed is pervasive in the educational literature of the Greco-Roman period. Another metaphor widely used, also taken from agriculture, is that of the farmer's labor. Labor (*ponos, ergasia*) was understood to be essential in the "cultivation" of virtue. Treatises were written on the subject of *de agricultura* as a symbol for exercising the life of virtue, as for example in Philo's commentary on Noah as a farmer, husbandman, and vintner (*De agricultura; De plantatione*). David Flusser, *Die rabbinischen Gleichnisse,* studies the parables of Jesus in relation to parables in the Rabbinic tradition and traces both to Hellenistic influence (141–60). He makes two very important observations. One is that both "Jesus" and the Rabbis turn Greek analogies into "epic stories" (155). The other is that, while the Rabbis accepted the Greek virtue of "toil" and its rewards, the parables of Jesus excised this theme (143).

The chreia chosen by Hermogenes to illustrate the elaboration (*ergasia*) pattern in his handbook (*progymnasma*) for teachers of rhetoric was the saying of Isocrates that "the root of *paideia* is bitter, but the fruit is sweet." In the elaboration of this chreia, the point is first made that "bitterness" refers to the "toil" required for truly successful accomplishments. At the point in the elaboration pattern where an(other) analogy was required to lend support

2.6 Parables and the Kingdom of God

Mark 4 is a literary unit with a narrative setting. The introduction sets the scene and announces that Jesus will teach. The conclusion forms a period in which both the narrative setting and the teaching in parables again are acknowledged. After the first parable, the problem created by the fact that its subject of reference was not expressed is acknowledged by having the disciples ask Jesus privately what the parables are about. He tells them that they are about the kingdom of God and explains to them that only they know this secret. This is followed by the explanation of the Seeds and the other parables. A bit of narrative confusion is created by this private audience because Mark does not bother to say whether the rest of the parables are given privately or publicly. But in the conclusion he again sums up Jesus' teaching in parables as public appearance with the notice that explanations were given privately to the disciples. In spite of this infelicity at the level of narrative setting, the pattern of the literary unit is clear. It follows a standard miniature speech form that teachers of rhetoric called an elaboration. The pattern consists of (1) an introduction to the speech situation, (2) a statement of the thesis, (3) a rationale for the thesis, (4) a testing of the rationale by setting up a contrast or showing that the converse also is true, (5) providing an analogy (*parabolē*), (6) giving an example (*paradeigma*), (7) offering a pronouncement, maxim, or precedent judgment from some authority, and (8) summing up in a conclusion.

Three observations need to be made about this outline before applying it to the parables in Mark 4. The first is that the items 5–7 were considered supporting arguments and need not be given in that order. The second is that, should the thesis be given in figurative language, the rationale could be used to make the reference or point clear. The third is that an elaboration of a thesis not only demonstrated its plausibility, but developed its theme as fully as possible. Ideally, an elaboration would show that the principle pertained in all of the orders of conventional knowledge: philosophy (3), logic (4), nature and society (5), history (6), and literature and cultural tradition (7). Two additional considerations should be mentioned about peculiar aspects of the employment of this pattern in Mark 4. One is that the illusion of the enigmatic character of Jesus' teaching is achieved by using analogies throughout. This is in keeping with the theme of teaching (only) in parables. It does not destroy their distinct functions in the elaboration pattern. The other is that, lacking a full complement of cultural

---

both to the interpretation given and to the truth of the original saying, Hermogenes suggests using, "Just as farmers must work the soil before reaping its fruits, so also must those who work with words." For the text of Hermogenes' elaboration of the chreia, together with translation and notes, see "Hermogenes of Tarsus" in Ronald Hock and Edward O'Neil, *The Chreia in Ancient Rhetoric*, 153–81.

conventions specific to the kingdom, ingenuity would have been called for to find good examples. Authoritative statements other than those of Jesus also would be highly problematic. Nevertheless, Mark was up to the challenge, producing a very cogent and clever elaboration of the parable of the Seeds:[19]

(1) *Introduction*

Again he began to teach beside the sea. And a very large crowd gathered about him, so that he got into a boat and sat in it on the sea; and the whole crowd was beside the sea on the land. And he taught them many things in parables. (4:1–2a)

(2) *Thesis*

And in his teaching he said to them: "Listen!"

"A sower went out to sow. And as he sowed, some seed fell along the path, and the birds came and devoured it. Other seed fell on rocky ground, where it had not much soil, and immediately it sprang up, since it had no depth of soil; and when the sun rose it was scorched, and since it had no root it withered away. Other seed fell among thorns and the thorns grew up and choked it, and it yielded no grain. And other seeds fell into good soil and brought forth grain, growing up and increasing and yielding thirtyfold and sixtyfold and a hundredfold."

And he said, "He who has ears to hear, let him hear." (4:2b–9)

(3) *Rationale*

Request for rationale

And when he was alone, those who were about him with the twelve asked him concerning the parables. (4:10)

Rationale given as direct statement

And he said to them, "To you has been given the secret of the kingdom of God. But for those outside everything is in parables; so that they may indeed see but not perceive, and may indeed hear but not understand; lest they should turn again, and be forgiven." (4:11–12)

Rationale given as paraphrase of the parable

And he said to them, "Do you not understand this parable? How then will you understand all the parables?

The sower sows the word. And these are the ones along the path, where the word is sown; when they hear, Satan immediately comes and takes away the word which is sown in them. And these in like manner are the ones sown upon rocky ground, who, when they hear the word, immediately receive it with joy; and they have no root in themselves, but endure for a while; then, when tribulation or persecution arises on account of the word, immediately they fall

---

19. *The elaboration pattern.* A study of the elaboration pattern in the *progymnasmata* is given in B. Mack and V. Robbins, *Patterns of Persuasion in the Gospels*, chap. 2.

away. And others are the ones sown among thorns; they are those who hear the word, but the cares of the world, and the delight in riches, and the desire for other things, enter in and choke the word, and it proves unfruitful. But those that were sown upon the good soil are the ones who hear the word and accept it and bear fruit, thirtyfold and sixtyfold and a hundredfold." (4:13–20)

(4) *Converse*

And he said to them, "Is a lamp brought in to be put under a bushel, or under a bed, and not on a stand?

For there is nothing hid, except to be made manifest; nor is anything secret, except to come to light.

If anyone has ears to hear, let him hear." (4:21–23)

(7) *Authoritative pronouncement*

And he said to them, "Take heed what you hear. The measure you give will be the measure you get, and still more will be given you.

For to him who has will more be given; and from him who has not, even what he has will be taken away." (4:24–25)

(6) *Example*

And he said, "The kingdom of God is as if a man should scatter seed upon the ground, and should sleep and rise night and day, and the seed should sprout and grow, he knows not how. The earth produces of itself, first the blade, then the ear, then the full grain in the ear. But when the grain is ripe, at once he puts in the sickle, because the harvest has come." (4:26–29)

(5) *Analogy*

And he said, "With what can we compare the kingdom of God, or what parable shall we use for it? It is like a grain of mustard seed, which, when sown upon the ground, is the smallest of all the seeds on earth; yet when it is sown it grows up and becomes the greatest of all shrubs, and puts forth large branches, so that the birds of the air can make nests in its shade." (4:30–32)

(8) *Conclusion*

With many such parables he spoke the word to them, as they were able to hear it; he did not speak to them without a parable, but privately to his own disciples he explained everything. (4:33–34)

The introduction (1) mentions items that were standard for the description of a speech situation: the occasion, any special characteristics of the speaker, and a brief encomiastic remark. Jesus is described as a teacher of the sort that used analogies, and the "very large crowd" provides the encomiastic touch.

The thesis (2) is presented as a *parabolē*, framed by the imperatives to listen (4:2b) and hear (4:9). Attentive ears would suspect that it was about some teaching and its troubled fate. But why is the subject of the teaching not given, and what could the subject be—an ethic, a philosophy, an epic *aggadah,* a ritual code, a program, a wisdom?

The rationale (3) answers these questions. The teaching is about the kingdom of God. Readers in Mark's community would have understood what that meant, but they may also have been interested in hearing what Mark's Jesus had to say about it. Two boundaries are established. Jesus' teaching about the kingdom stands to Mark's community (the "insiders" of the teacher-listener circle) as *paideia*-culture does to the Greeks. It also is to be distinguished from instruction in Judaism, as the citation of Isa 6:9–10 makes clear. The citation is strangely atavistic, preferring the stronger statement of the "original" saying (with "lest"), rather than the more mild rephrasings found in later citations, translations, and targumim.[20]

The rationale is made explicit in the explanation of the Seeds. The explanation has regularly been viewed as an allegorical interpretation of the Seeds. It is not an allegory at all, because it merely explicates the implicit meaning of the analogy intended by the parable of the Seeds. The seed is the teaching (*logos*) about the kingdom (*paideia*); the fate of the seeds is the fate of the teaching; and the fate is determined by the reception of seed in different kinds of persons (soils). The explication does move the elaboration along, however, by adding several new ideas. One is that the reception of this instruction is more than a matter of insight and understanding. The list of things that can hinder the acceptance of the teaching is impressive: Satan, tribulation, persecution, cares, riches, and desires. At first the listener may think that these merely spell out the difficult circumstances under which the cultivation of the new *paideia* has to take place, the measure of its toil, achievement, virtue, and eventual reward. Cultivation is not what the story is about, however. Decisive moments distinguish two kinds of receptions, two kinds of eventualities. The new *paideia* is not a culture, it is a movement in conflict with other cultures, borne of a threatened *logos* that marks the boundaries between those who remain in the cultures of convention and those who accept the secret promise of an eventual "harvest."

The converse (4) introduces the image of the Lamp, extending the metaphor of the seed equals *logos* in the direction of enlightenment. The opposition is between "hidden" and "manifest." The point is that, as with

---

20. *Lest they should turn again.* A comparative study of the targums and citations of Isa 6:9–10 in early Jewish and Christian literature has been made by Craig Evans, "Isaiah 6:9–10 in Early Jewish and Christian Interpretation." A targum is an Aramaic translation of the Hebrew scriptures characterized by paraphrastic constructions and the interweaving of clarifying comments in the interest of contemporizing interpretations. In comparison with all extant rearticulations of Isa 6:9–10 in which the harsh tone of the "lest" in the Masoretic (Hebrew) text is rephrased, and thus explained away, Mark's atavism stands out as exceptional.

lamps, so with the *logos* and with the kingdom. In both cases one can be sure that the kingdom will not remain secret forever.

The authoritative pronouncement (7) is given next. This reverses the normal sequence of the second half of the elaboration pattern, creating a chiastic structure that pivots on this important statement. Two shifts in emphasis occur at this point. One is that the teaching is suddenly applied personally to the listener by using direct address: "Take heed what you hear." The other is that, should one not have tumbled to the apocalyptic destiny encoded in the hidden secret of the seeds, the future tense is used. The image of the Measure is appropriate to the parable of seeds sown and harvested. But now the listener is addressed as one whose destiny is involved in the process of "giving" and "getting." At the harvest the division between those who have and those who do not have will be made absolute.

The example (6) underscores the contrast between the present time when the kingdom is hidden and the harvest time when it will be manifest. Now it is clear why the parable of the Seeds emphasized only the moments of sowing and fruition. Everything else occurs "automatically," left to the mysteries of the natural process, that is, to God.[21]

The analogy (5) completes the elaboration. As with the Mustard Seed, so with the kingdom of God. A small beginning does not mean that the ending can't be great. The point is assurance. Ears attuned to the theme of cultural conflict coursing throughout the discourse, however, will have heard more. The parable of the Seeds sets up a contrast with Greek *paideia*. The Mustard Seed clearly evokes traditional imagery of Israel's destiny. The point of the parable, then, is that the kingdom of God eventually will succeed in displacing both of those presently competitive cultures. The "mystery" of the kingdom is not a matter of mystique at all. It is simply an apocalyptic persuasion.[22]

3. PARABLES AND THE GOSPEL

The parables in Mark compose a speech that, according to Mark, was given on a certain occasion by Jesus to his disciples and others. The

---

21. *The concept "automatic."* In Philo's allegories, Isaac regularly represents the one who attains virtue "by nature," making a triad with Abraham ("by teaching") and Jacob ("by practice"). To strike the contrast, Philo often says that Isaac is "self-taught" (*automatēs*). References are given by J. W. Earp in the Loeb edition of Philo, 10:324–30. It is also the case that "nature" (*physis*) is personified in Philo as "divine." The odd but pointed use of *automatē* in Mark 4:28 would receive some clarification, were it also derived from a discourse on education similar to Philo's. The contrast with *paideia* as toil, the Greek notion, would be underscored even while making the apocalyptic point.

22. *Parables of the kingdom.* For a more detailed discussion of Mark's apocalyptic interpretation of the kingdom of God, see B. Mack, "The Kingdom Sayings in Mark."

narrative setting for the speech situation makes that clear, as does the placement of the speech in the gospel just at the point where instruction to the disciples is appropriate. The teaching of the parables is presented as the teaching of the Jesus about whom the gospel account is written. Teaching in parables is a gospel event, an event that takes place within the story about Jesus.

3.1 The Teachings of Jesus in the Gospel

The teaching of the parables is an apocalyptic instruction in the fate of the kingdom of God inaugurated by Jesus. The Gospel of Mark as a whole is also an apocalyptic instruction in the fate of the kingdom of God inaugurated by Jesus. This will become clear as the study of the gospel text unfolds. Mark's situation in social history was thought by him to be critical. He wrote in the aftermath of two unnerving events. The more recent was the destruction of the temple in Jerusalem, an event that required reassessment of one's expectations about Israel no matter what one may have thought before. The slightly less recent event was the failure of the synagogue reform movement on the part of Jesus people in Mark's circles. This also will be clarified as the study proceeds. Both of these events created confusion for Mark's community. The signs of disintegration including loss of loyalties, diversity of leadership, and competitive christologies and ideologies are manifest in the little apocalypse in Mark 13. Mark's approach to this situation was sectarian and conservative. Part of the answer was to acknowledge the failures and define the borders clearly between those inside and those outside of the Jesus movement. Another part was to imagine the embattled enclave in the midst of an apocalyptic history, a time of trials just before the end when the truth of the Jesus movement would be vindicated by God. A third factor in the solution was to imagine all that had transpired as planned, as part of the design from the beginning. The gospel was written with these rationalizations in mind. They belong to Mark's apocalyptic mentality.

Mark's apocalyptic imagination was generated in the seventies as a reaction and response to contemporary social history. There were certain advantages, however, in presenting his views, not as a new revelation in the traditional genre of apocalyptic, but as the teaching of Jesus. Not only could the authority of Jesus be called upon to give the instruction legitimacy, the import of Jesus' appearance could be aligned with the apocalyptic scheme. All of the events at the beginning could be cast as powerful, mysterious, and absolutely determinative for the subsequent course of history in spite of the fact that the intervening history was not all that glorious. Reasons could be given for the rejection from the synagogue and for the confusions within the community by linking them, not to the failure of the movement, but to the nature of the kingdom and the enigmatic manner and authority of Jesus himself. If Jesus knew and predicted the way it was going to be, those on the inside could understand, take heart, watch for the end, and perhaps endure. If Jesus' own fate was rejection and violence, the troubled history of the Jesus movement was to be expected. Evidence in support of the seriousness of the times was given with the destruction of the temple. If that could be understood as an act of judgment by God upon an intransigent Israel, the seriousness of the Jewish rejection of Jesus and the kingdom could be imagined. Mark made the connection at the level of social history and its rationalizations. He projected them back upon the time of Jesus by creating a narrative setting of conflict and rejection for the teachings and activities of Jesus. Before Mark, the memories of Jesus had not been given, had not needed, such a setting.

The apocalyptic instruction presented by the parables in Mark 4 was not the teaching of Jesus, but of Mark. It does not matter to what greater or lesser extent snippets of this parabolic material may be traced back through two generations of retelling to an origination with the historical Jesus. The instruction spoken by Jesus in Mark is historical fiction. Mark created the fiction in accordance with the apocalyptic schemes of (1) prediction and fulfillment, (2) secret revelation and eventual manifestation, and (3) orig- inary plan/negative history/final resolution. To imagine Jesus' teachings as predictive apocalyptic instruction solved social historical issues nicely, but it did create a serious narrative problem.[23]

3.2 The First Listeners

In order to create the fiction that Jesus taught the mystery of the apocalyptic destiny of the Jesus movement and the kingdom of God, Mark introduced the division between those inside and those outside as having occurred already in the presence of Jesus. The disciples served as repre- sentatives of those on the inside. Those familiar with the discipleship theme in the gospel will know, however, that not even the disciples were able to comprehend the teaching. The reasons for this are quite complex, because Mark used the theme of the misunderstanding of the disciples creatively to introduce a series of studies on discipleship for the edification of his readers. Against the background of the imperious loyalty of Jesus to his mission and destiny, the disciples present an image of uncertainty, fear, and disloyalty, lessons of urgent consequence for Mark's own community. Thus the fact that the disciples are given the privilege of knowing the secret

---

23. *The parables and apocalyptic gospel.* That the parables in Mark 4 are to be read in the light of "the theology of the gospel as a whole," and that both are apocalyptic, is the thesis of a recent dissertation at Columbia University by Joel Marcus, "The Mystery of the Kingdom." Marcus' demonstration, though argued differently than in the present study, may be taken as a corroboration of Mark's apocalyptic intention in the composition of the gospel.

teaching does not mean that they will "understand" it (cf. Mark 4:13). But this narrative design is not sufficient to relieve the conundrum of a teacher who fails to get his instruction across, not only to those who can't understand its encoded utterance, but to those granted plain instruction privately. The conundrum is due partly to the implausibility of Mark's fiction about the content of Jesus' teaching, a teaching about the future quite out of keeping with the grand and glorious events that accompanied the teacher's appearance. Thus a double layer of misunderstanding hides the meaning of the teaching from Jesus' first listeners. Jesus is pictured "teaching" them then, but only the readers of Mark in Mark's time would ever get the picture.

It is the same with the parable of the Tenants in chapter twelve. The parable is given publicly as part of Jesus' instruction in the temple in the overhearing of the temple authorities. Just as the content of the parables in Mark 4 pertained to the disciples and was spoken to them, so the content of the Tenants pertains to those addressed. Mark states that "they perceived that [Jesus] had told the parable against them" (Mark 12:12), but of course they were not able to accept or understand it. To the reader, the parable is clearly a thinly veiled rehearsal of the history of Israel (the vineyard) and its rejections of the claims of God upon it. Violence toward the owner's son will result in the transfer of the vineyard to others. By telling it, Jesus predicts not only his forthcoming death, but the destruction of the tenants as God's punishment for killing him (that is, the destruction of Jerusalem in 70 C.E.), as well as the legitimacy of the claim of the Jesus movement to the "vineyard" (that is, the kingdom of God as the legacy of Israel's epic history). Attempts to redeem the parable as an aesthetic object simply wilt in the light of the transparent purposes of the author. Mark did not have Jesus tell the parable to the temple authorities to instruct them in the gospel, but to provoke the fruition of the plot of the parable which was at the same time the plot of the gospel. "And they tried to arrest him, but feared the multitude" (Mark 12:12). The only persons "edified" would be Mark's readers, those by whom Jesus' authority was already accepted. The "edification" would have been apologetic, the confirmation achieved by imagining Jesus' foreknowledge and prediction of events and their consequences that reached even into their own time and beyond.[24]

---

24. *The Tenants.* Most scholars agree that the story in Mark bears literary allusions to the Septuagint of Isa 5:1–5. Since that, plus the citation of Ps 118:22–23 in Mark 12:10–11, betray the signs of literary activity, several scholars have made the attempt to reconstruct an earlier, less allegorical form of the story. Crossan especially, *In Parables*, 86–96, argues strongly on the basis of the variant in GThom 65 that the story was originally not allegorical, either with respect to Israel's destiny, or with respect to Jesus' destiny, and that it was authentic, "a deliberately shocking story of successful murder" (p. 96). Crossan does not go on to explain the "parabolic effect" this might have created, except to say it may have been a commentary upon the times. To follow Crossan in this attempt to retrieve the

As with the parables, so with all of the "teachings" of Jesus in the Gospel of Mark. Nowhere are the first listeners instructed. Nowhere are they depicted as learning correctly what was told to them. They react, but in ways that contribute to the rejection of Jesus and to his violent end. The "new teaching" in the synagogue in Capernaum (Mark 1:21–28) is not instructive, but a display of power and a claim to authority. It results in the plot to destroy him (Mark 3:6). The pronouncement stories do not offer instruction. They assume an authority beyond the adjudication of discourse, an authority only Christians would recognize. The discipleship sayings in chapters 8–10 all but redeem the violent plot of Mark's story. They stem from a daring and deeply pious meditation on the consequences of just such a gospel for the quality of life within the Christian movement. Both Mark and Mark's Jesus knew, however, that this instruction also could not be heard until a later time. It is the same with the teaching of Jesus in the temple in chapters 11 and 12 and the apocalyptic discourse in chapter 13. Those who are to be instructed by Jesus' teaching are not those to whom he speaks in the story, but those who read the story in Mark's time. Mark addressed his readers by attributing his message to Jesus and letting them overhear Jesus' instruction to others.

3.3 The Readers of the Gospel

The readers of Mark's Gospel would have had no trouble understanding Jesus' instruction. To imagine that Jesus offered such instruction at the beginning would enhance his authority even as his authority would invite attention to the teaching. All predictions would have been fulfilled except for the final manifestation of the kingdom. One might conclude that it, therefore, was assured. For a bedraggled conventicle, the apocalyptic mystery may have been comforting indeed.

The cost of the comfort appears, however, to have been staggering. The community was now possessed of an esoteric teaching stemming from a

---

parable for Jesus, one has to imagine a situation in which listeners would not have been tempted to pick up on allusive suggestions to other stories and histories at all. The tightly constructed story, however, with its motifs of "sending," "servants," in series, to "tenants" of a "vineyard" for its "produce," to say nothing of the negative fates of the servants, that the tenants knew who the servants were, that the last one sent is different (the son), and that he was killed, is literally packed with invitations to think of Israel's epic history from a Christian point of view. Images and narrative schemes that come immediately to mind include the vineyard as a traditional metaphor for Israel (even if the literary allusion to Isaiah in Mark 12:1 is deleted), the sending of the prophets, the rejection and killing of the prophets, and perhaps wisdom's envoys (Wis 7:27). The parable betrays a reflection on Israel and the negative fate of the prophets that is greatly advanced over Q. Because the special status and destiny of the last emissary is both emphatic and climactic, the story is surely a product, not of the historical Jesus, but of a much later Christian claim. The story fits best just in Mark's milieu where Jesus traditions, including Q, were combined with meditations upon Jesus' death as a crucial event. Mark's additions merely explicate the allegorical significance contained within the story itself.

founder teacher who did not address the world authentically. His "instructions" were not meant to be understood by those he addressed. He entered the arena of discourse as one destined not to be understood, and he played it out "so that they may indeed see but not perceive, and may indeed hear but not understand; lest they should turn again and be forgiven" (Mark 4:12). To imagine that happening at the beginning would be to watch an event of singularly tragic proportions take place from a very safe distance. The time of the event was "prior" to the Christian time; the place was "outside" the Christian domain. Christians watched as others were "instructed," and thus they learned about their secret destiny at the expense of those who reacted to Jesus without having been instructed.

Some aspects of the historical setting had been erased in the intervening history. The temple, the temple establishment, and that form of Judaism defined by the temple system were things of the past in Mark's time. Perhaps, then, the historical fiction should be thought harmless, a revision of little consequence, since the parties portrayed were gone from the scene. That would be to misinterpret both Mark's story and its commentary on Mark's times. In the story, Mark took pains to initiate the conflict in the synagogue and unite the synagogue leadership with the temple authorities in the plot to destroy Jesus. The subsequent history had not erased the synagogue nor the Jews with whom until recently the most vociferous arguments had taken place. Mark's story marked the end of those debates. It explained in effect that, from the beginning, there had been no point in addressing the Jews. The Jews who did not accept the teaching of the Jesus people about Jesus and his kingdom are pictured in the gospel as those who conspired to kill him because of a teaching encoded against them. Set forth as a self-fulfilling prophecy, the gospel actually is a retrojection of subsequent failure upon the point of the community's origin. As a result, the teaching of Jesus in the Gospel of Mark enlightens no one except the Markan reader willing to entertain an apocalyptic imagination.

For Mark and his readers there was a *logos* of the kingdom of God. But, according to Mark, the *logos* of the kingdom, which Jesus did introduce, and the kingdom itself, which Jesus did not inaugurate, were two different things. Neither did Mark understand the parables spoken at the beginning to have offered an aphoristic critique of Jesus' world, or a parabolic invitation to imagine things differently and thus make a difference then. For Mark, the apocalyptic process started with a demonstration of power, a claim to absolute authority, and a conflict of tragic propositions that was predetermined. Events were what mattered, judged solely on the basis of the acceptance or rejection of Jesus' self-referential claim. Words were a matter of charge and countercharge. Scholars have wondered what happened to the tradition of Jesus' teaching in Mark, why he did not make use of Q. The answer must be that Q was simply unusable, given Mark's narrative plan. Mark did not wish to portray Jesus addressing his generation publicly with instruction about the kingdom of God as if his world could have accepted it and changed. What Jesus says in Mark's Gospel is not instruction to those within the story at all. What Jesus says in the story functioned as pronouncement, a sign of his imperious authority, a behavior that triggered and sealed a predetermined fate of ultimate consequence both for the Christian community and for the opponents of Jesus. What Jesus said then is instructive only for the reader in Mark's own time.

The parables of the kingdom in Mark are not stories that invite one to enter into the kingdom. They are stories about a *logos* of the kingdom, to be sure. But the *logos* they are about is the apocalyptic Gospel of Mark, a gospel that presupposes the decisive events of Jesus' appearance, his violent end, the social history of the Jesus movement, the destruction of the temple, and the eventual manifestation of the glorious kingdom in power. The parables are therefore mini-gospels. Placed within Mark's myth of origins as they are, the parables can only function allegorically. They are told by the teacher about the teacher and the consequences of his appearance in history. The sower in the story of the Seeds will, in the context of such a gospel, have to be Jesus. The son in the story of the Tenants will, in the light of the plot of the gospel, have to be Jesus. Augustine, therefore, was not misreading the parables. He was reading the parables as the gospels invite them to be read. The most devastating mode of domesticating the parables occurred already in the earliest gospel. It occurred when the parables were claimed as esoteric teaching, yet placed outside the boundaries of understanding in order to precipitate the very events they encoded.

7

THE PRONOUNCEMENT
STORIES

The gospel is composed of many small stories about Jesus in settings where he is surrounded by others in conversation. Jesus is seen answering questions, addressing issues, parrying criticisms, and offering instruction. Scholars call these pronouncement stories. They are the stories Christians have always had in mind when imagining Jesus as the teacher. They, together with the miracle stories, make possible the dominant image of Jesus portrayed by the gospels. They are also the source for the scholarly image of Jesus as a remarkable teacher of things that inaugurated the Christian era.

These stories have only recently been subject to scholarly investigation. During the long quest of the historical Jesus, miracle stories were the preoccupation. If miracle stories could be explained, scholars of the nineteenth century thought the gospel portrait of Jesus as a superior teacher fit quite nicely with the framework stories that outlined the major moments of significance in his life. Only after the embarrassment about apocalyptic subsided during the first generation of the twentieth century did scholars turn their attention once again to the question of Jesus' portrait and the narrative material in the gospels. By then, however, the framework stories could no longer be used naively, for William Wrede had shown that the overarching themes in Mark were Mark's own, and K. L. Schmidt had demonstrated that Mark was responsible for the way in which all of the smaller story units had been connected together to tell the larger story. The fragmentary disarray of the individual stories and sayings that resulted called for another approach.

1. THE DISCOVERY OF THE
PRONOUNCEMENT STORIES

The pronouncement stories were noticed as a particular form of the synoptic tradition by the form critics Martin Dibelius (1919), Rudolf Bultmann (1921), and Vincent Taylor (1933). Each had taken note of the different kinds of memory traditions and set out to classify them by type. Bultmann's *History of the Synoptic Tradition* still stands as the standard work produced during this period and can be used to describe the first judgments made about the pronouncement stories in the light of form critical methods.

The major principle in Bultmann's system of classification was the difference between the sayings of Jesus on the one hand, and the stories about him on the other. That created a problem in the case of the pronouncement stories. In his discussion of the narrative materials (miracle stories, "historical" accounts, and legends), Bultmann was content to assign most of it to the imaginative propaganda of the early Christian communities. In his work on the sayings of Jesus ("Words of the Lord"), Bultmann treated each as an isolated, free floating unit of speech in order to regroup them as (1) wisdom sayings, (2) prophetic and apocalyptic announcements, (3) pronouncements of legal matters and community rules, (4) words of self-reference, and (5) parables and "related material" (by which Bultmann meant other unclassifiable aphoristic and metaphorical sayings). The purpose of this classification was to get at the question of authenticity. Words of self-reference and community rules were automatically out. Prophetic and apocalyptic announcements were most authentic in keeping with Bultmann's view of Jesus as the proclaimer of the kingdom of God. Wisdom sayings were difficult to judge. Only those that could be imagined to have contributed to Jesus' announcement of the kingdom were thought possibly to be authentic. Thus Bultmann's approach to the sayings material determined his assessment of the pronouncement stories.

Because the pronouncement stories contained sayings of Jesus, Bultmann classified them with the sayings, not with the narrative materials. In order to do that, however, he was required to enter a major division within the section on the sayings. Strangely, Bultmann chose to discuss the pronouncement stories first. He called them apothegms (from the Greek meaning "saying" or "maxim"), and distinguished between (1) controversy and scholastic dialogues, and (2) biographic apothegms. In case after case the same point was made. The sayings of Jesus at first traveled freely; the narrative settings were later contrived. Shorn of their narrative settings, the sayings could then be evaluated with respect to authenticity. Not many sayings stood the test. Those pronouncements thought by Bultmann to have some claim to authenticity are decidedly aphoristic. They are desperately in need of some context in which to make their points. Bultmann tried to place them in the context of Jesus' proclamation of the kingdom of God, but none were found that added anything of significance not already known from the prophetic words.

Martin Albertz, working with these stories at the same time, thought all of the pronouncements "prophetic" on the model of criticisms registered by the prophets of the Old Testament on their own situations. Dibelius called them paradigms. He thought they were taken from early Christian preaching, incidental to the Christian message, but supportive of its main points about Jesus' authority as the Christ. Thus the first attempts to understand these stories were not very instructive. A marked advance was made, however, by Vincent Taylor.

Taylor noticed that the saying was the climax of the story and that the story, therefore, was essential to the way in which the saying was to be taken. He coined the term "pronouncement story," a designation American scholars later would find intriguing. Taylor did not distinguish between controversy stories and biographical apothegms as Bultmann had done. He saw the structural element common to all of them, thus classed them together. He identified twenty-three such stories in the Gospel of Mark. The pronouncement story was discovered.[1]

In 1975 a working group on the pronouncement stories was formed within the Society of Biblical Literature under the leadership of Robert Tannehill. The aim of the project was to collect examples of pronouncement stories from literatures of the Greco-Roman period outside of the New Testament with which stories in the gospels might be compared. Taylor's designation was accepted and the integrity of the two-part structure (narrative setting plus pronouncement) was clearly seen from the beginning. In order to guide the collection of parallels, Tannehill submitted the New Testament stories to a careful analysis of the several ways in which a saying was related to its setting. He discovered six different relationships which he termed rhetorical, and proposed a typology. (1) Correction stories are those in which the speaker responds to someone's actions or words by correcting them. (2) Commendation stories offer commendation by the speaker. (3) Objection stories are those in which criticism is raised by others and then countered by the speaker. (4) Quest stories tell about someone in quest of "something important to human well-being," to which the speaker responds. (5) Inquiry stories place a question to the speaker instead of a criticism. (6) Description stories introduce a situation that the speaker aptly sizes up in some descriptive comment.[2]

The results of the first phase of the work of the group were published in *Semeia* 20 (1981). In an article in that issue, Tannehill identified thirty-two pronouncement stories in the Gospel of Mark, expanding Taylor's list by nine. A quick review of the gospel, using Tannehill's list, shows that roughly two-fifths of the narrative material in the first twelve chapters of

---

1. *The form critics.* The earlier form critics and their works are: Martin Dibelius, *From Tradition to Gospel;* Martin Albertz, *Die synoptische Streitgespräche;* Rudolf Bultmann, *History of the Synoptic Tradition;* and Vincent Taylor, *Formation of the Gospel Tradition.*

2. *Tannehill's typology.* See Tannehill, "The Pronouncement Story and Its Types." The quotation on the quest story is from p. 9.

Mark consists of pronouncement stories. They were obviously a major source for the composition of the gospel. They are also very important for the quest, because they are the earliest stories about Jesus. A list of the pronouncement stories in Mark is given in an appendix as a guide for the discussions to follow in this chapter. An example of a pronouncement story may already be given, however, as an introduction to the study.[3]

In the second chapter of Mark a chain of pronouncement stories is used to characterize Jesus' activity in Galilee. The first and last of these are combinations of a miracle story with a pronouncement story form. But the three stories in the middle are fine examples of pronouncement stories at various levels of complexity or elaboration. The first is the simpler. It is the story about Jesus at table with sinners (Mark 2:15–17).

> And as he sat at table in his house, many tax collectors and sinners were sitting with Jesus and his disciples; for there were many who followed him. And the scribes of the Pharisees, when they saw that he was eating with sinners and tax collectors, said to his disciples, "Why does he eat with tax collectors and sinners?" And when Jesus heard it, he said to them, "Those who are well have no need of a physician, but those who are sick; I came not to call the righteous, but sinners."

One sees that the setting provides the theme. Both the question raised about Jesus and his answer to the question address the activity described. Jesus' answer accepts both the scene and the judgment upon the scene made by the questioners, but evaluates them differently. It is in this sense that Jesus' answer is a "pronouncement" upon the situation.

1.1 The Didactic Interpretation

The pronouncement story group collected a large number of examples from literatures of the Greco-Roman age. This established the pronouncement story as an identifiable form current in the first century. Most of the parallels were found in literatures with biographic interest, such as *The Lives of Eminent Philosophers* by Diogenes Laertius and the *Lives* of Plutarch. Only three examples of the quest story had been found, however, and most of the examples fell into the class of correction stories. The assumption had been that the purpose of the pronouncement story was didactic. The large number of correction stories made it necessary to look closely at the manner in which they may have offered instruction.

In his introductory essay to *Semeia* 20, Tannehill proposed a hermeneutic based on a narrative poetic to explain the preponderance of conflict

---

3. *Pronouncement stories in Mark.* The list of pronouncement stories in Mark given in Appendix I has been gleaned from Tannehill's identification of pronouncement stories throughout the synoptic gospels. The title of his article is "Varieties of Synoptic Pronouncement Stories."

situations in these stories, but interpreted the tension between the situation and the response constructively. He spoke of an "attitude shift" made possible as the reader contemplated now the situation, now the pronouncement that implied a new perspective on the situation.

The pronouncement story in Mark 2:15–17 cited above was classed by Tannehill as an objection story. It was an example of that subtype of objection story that used an analogy in the response (the physician) to present "a judgment which implies a new way of viewing the matter under debate." The addition of a formal statement of principle ("I came to call . . .") was also a common feature of objection stories. This feature moved from the specific case at hand to a "general disclosure of God's will or the meaning of Jesus' mission." In most cases, then, Jesus "appeals for agreement" and the reader is invited to share Jesus' view. "Both the power of the words and their story help them take root in the memory and imagination of the reader, where they may provoke new thought."

Tannehill recognized that those within the story who raised the objection were lost to sight toward the end. Their own response is not given, so that the story as story seems to be incomplete. He suggested that this formal feature supported the didactic function of these stories by making it necessary for the reader to supply the ending. It should be noted that Tannehill is consistent throughout in taking the perspective of the reader. It should also be noted that the reader Tannehill has in mind would have to be a Christian or very sympathetic to Christian views about the authority of Jesus in order to supply an ending appropriate to the pronouncement. In Tannehill's words, "The powerful wisdom and authority of Jesus stand out as they are put to the test. Thus these stories are also indirect praise of Jesus." For Tannehill, Jesus is the praiseworthy teacher and the pronouncement stories are instructive because they invite the reader to make those judgments.[4]

Other scholars, however, working independently of the pronouncement story group during the same period of time, were not as comfortable about the way the objectors were treated in these stories. In the works of H.-W. Kuhn (1971), Arland J. Hultgren (1979), and Joanna Dewey (1980), the same issue surfaced repeatedly. If one asked about the terms of the controversy internal to the story, and tried to assess the persuasive power of the pronouncements from the objectors' points of view, Jesus' responses did not appear all that enlightening. These scholars used a more traditional approach to the critical analysis of the stories as literary forms, and two of them were interested in the social sources for the topics of controversy contained in the stories. This scholarship came to a conclusion quite the opposite of Tannehill's. It needs a brief discussion.

---

4. *Didactic interpretation.* The citations are from Tannehill, "Varieties of Synoptic Pronouncement Stories," 110–11.

1.2 The Controversy Stories

Bultmann had used the term controversy and scholastic dialogue to identify one class of the apothegms and distinguish them from biographical apothegms. Because the class of controversy stories was so large, many scholars have used this term (or the term conflict story) instead of the term pronouncement story to refer to the kind of story under discussion. It may be noted (Appendix I) that Tannehill's classification of the pronouncement stories bears out this judgment. In Mark, no description stories were found. Only two quest stories were identified ("What must I do," Mark 10:17–22; "Which is the first commandment?" Mark 12:28–34), but neither of them is told without that tensive moment that turns the question into a tryst. Four commendation stories were identified, but all of them were found to have been combined with the correction motif. There were five inquiry stories, but three of them had to be qualified by the addition of the term "testing" because the inquiry did not function naively. It was put to Jesus just in order to test him. The bulk of the stories were correction stories (nine) or objection stories (twelve). This means that, of thirty-two stories, only two stories were found that did not contain an element of controversy. These were the inquiries about parables in Mark 4:10–12, and about the withered fig tree in Mark 11:20–25. Readers of Mark's Gospel will know that these inquiry stories do not function innocently. They also are designed to contribute to the theme of conflict in the gospel.

The major studies of the controversy stories by Kuhn, Hultgren, and Dewey carefully reviewed a larger body of scholarship on these stories and took up the question of pre-Markan tradition and provenance. Kuhn and Hultgren were especially interested in placing the stories in some social historical context. Dewey decided to test critically some of the methods used to determine pre-Markan forms of the stories and theses about collections of such stories available to Mark.

Kuhn and Hultgren marshaled considerable evidence for the existence of these stories before Mark. They differed slightly on matters of dating them and on the constitution of the Christian groups within which the stories and their collections were composed. Agreements in general are nonetheless strong and a scholarly consensus can be discerned in their reports of the judgments many others have made. This consensus may be summarized. There is general agreement that (1) the Jesus of the stories is the Jesus as early Christians came to see him; (2) the issues addressed were Christian issues, matters of importance for the social formation of early Christian groups; and (3) the challenge to Jesus that invites his address in the stories reflects in general the actual challenge that other Jewish movements posed for these early Christian communities. Thus the controversies related in the stories arose out of cultural conflict.

Two troubling questions arose in the course of these investigations. First, Jesus' pronouncements are "merely asserted," to use Hultgren's words. No rationale is provided for their acceptance. Christians will already have known they were true on the basis of other instruction. This raises the question of the purpose of the pronouncements. What do they contribute to early Christian knowledge? The second question relates to the nature of the arguments used in the controversy dialogues. The argumentation, according to Kuhn, would have been "completely unintelligible for Jews outside the Christian community." Kuhn therefore sought to limit the controversies to an inner community debate. This raises the question of the function of the stories within the Christian community. Do they offer any kind of instruction at all?

Dewey's work showed that the issues under debate came to focus on the question of the authority of Jesus and that the controversy story, though certainly used by Christians before Mark's time, nevertheless was still a living and pliable form for reimagining Jesus in Mark's time. She was able to show this by a detailed analysis of the collection of the five stories in Mark 2:1–3:6. The five stories were not really a collection, but forged into a single unit of composition in order to present a full picture of the issues under debate between Jesus and the leaders of the synagogue. Dewey was convinced that the unit was pre-Markan, but she uncovered a very interesting and troubling datum in the course of her investigation that made it difficult to sustain her thesis. Her thesis was based on formal and stylistic evidence for the unitary nature of the collection in distinction from Mark's own style and use of the material. The problem arose with the last story (Mark 3:1–6). It was obviously part of the five-story unit, and yet it was formally different from the others and clearly Markan in style and theme. She decided that the pre-Markan unit must have contained only four stories even though the four did not make as nice a unit as the five. These five stories in Mark will be discussed later. For now the significance of Dewey's work should be underscored in relation to the question about the function of these stories still in Mark's time. The stories belonged apparently to Mark's milieu. If the unit was pre-Markan, it was only slightly so. The terms of the controversy reflected in the stories as a set reflect, then, a rather recent experience among those who composed them. Mark is surely to be included among those who used controversy stories to address that experience. If that is so, the function of these stories at such a remove from Jesus does need to be better understood.[5]

---

5. *Controversy stories*. The references are to: H.-W. Kuhn, *Ältere Sammlungen im Markusevangelium*, 96; Arland J. Hultgren, *Jesus and His Adversaries*, 33; and Joanna Dewey, *Markan Public Debate*. Hultgren's conclusion to his investigation is worth repeating: "They [the controversy stories] have been formulated and preserved by early Christian traditionists for purposes which we can scarcely determine. Our study has shown, however, that previous assumptions concerning the *Sitz im Leben* of the conflict stories

2. THE PRONOUNCEMENT STORY AS CHREIA

At a meeting of the Society of Biblical Literature in 1981 the pronouncement story group reviewed its work and compared it with studies undertaken at Claremont in 1978 on the chreia (anecdote) in Greco-Roman
education and literature. Most of the stories collected by the pronouncement story group were recognized by Claremont scholars as chreiai, the
term used for these stories in handbooks for teachers offering beginning
instruction in rhetoric (*progymnasmata,* or first exercises). Very few parallels had been found in Jewish literatures of the period. This narrowed the
cultural context within which this type of story traveled and heightened the
significance of the rhetors' discussions of them. If the Greeks had taken
notice of these stories by type and used them for instructional purposes,
something important might be learned about the way listeners of the first
century would have taken them. It was time for a pause.[6]

2.1 The Chreia in Hellenistic Culture

The chreia or anecdote was very popular among the Greeks. They took
delight in maxims, aphorisms, telling insights, witty and well-turned
phrases, and clever rejoinders. The chreia was the form in which a
memorable saying by some person was repeated. Most were occasional,
coined in response to specific situations. Many were set with another well-
known person playing the part of the straight man. Situations could easily

---

cannot rest unchallenged. There are some conflict stories of a unitary nature which clearly
could not have been formulated to preserve a statement of Jesus useful for preaching. . . .
There are others which clearly could not have been formulated in rabbinic-styled debates
within the church on points of law—either among church leaders, or between church
leaders and those outside. . . . What is common to them, rather, is that they offer for the
primitive church a justification for its beliefs and practices in response to Jewish criticism.
. . . There is no attempt in these stories to argue for the legitimacy of belief or conduct on
the basis of contemporary procedures of structuring an argument. . . . They center not in
law, but in the person of Jesus and his conduct and attitude" (87–88). Had Hultgren
explored the "procedures of structuring an argument" given with the Greek rhetorical
tradition, his assessment of the failure to engage the positions taken by the objectors in
these stories would have been even sharper. For a comparison of the controversy stories
with Rabbinic debates, see J. Neusner, *Early Rabbinic Judaism,* 115. He notes that,
whereas the opposition gets only a single argument in the controversy stories, Jesus
regularly gets two arguments and thus overwhelms his opponents.

6. *The pronouncement story as chreia.* That the chreia was not a common convention in
Jewish literature of the time is the conclusion to be drawn from the studies in *Semeia* 20 by
James C. VanderKam, "Intertestamental Pronouncement Stories"; Leonard Greenspoon,
"The Pronouncement Story in Philo and Josephus"; and Gary G. Porton, "The Pro-
nouncement Story in Tannaitic Literature." It may also be mentioned that where chreiai
have been identified in early Rabbinic tradition, Greek influence has been obvious. See
Henry Fischel, "Studies in Cynicism and the Ancient Near East." In an unpublished paper
delivered to the Pseudepigrapha Seminar of the Society of Biblical Literature in 1979,
Fischel distinguished two types of stories told about Hillel. The majority cast Hillel as a
Rabbinic sage; a few, however, were chreiai of the Cynic type. The latter were, according
to Fischel, the earliest stories about Hillel.

be typical, however, with unnamed persons creating the occasion by means of a remark, question, or their own manner of behavior. The settings were very often everyday affairs familiar to everyone. The occasions were frequently activities of the most mundane variety.

The records available to the historian for documenting the popularity of chreiai among the Greeks limit them to well-known persons in the history of the Greek philosophical schools. The fact that they were told of leading philosophers, however, is a mark of their general popularity and respectability. It is also a very important evidence for what might be called the oral tradition of Greek school philosophy in distinction from the high level of discourse characteristic for written treatises produced by Greek philosophers. In the *Lives* of Diogenes Laertius, the publications of the leaders of the philosophical schools were carefully listed as one of the items for which they were known. Other matters were also of interest, however, such as biographical reminiscences, the place of a philosopher in the succession of teachers and students describing the history of the schools, and some evaluation of the content of one's philosophy. Of interest to the present study is that Diogenes regularly included a section of anecdotes as well.

By using anecdotes, Diogenes achieved two purposes. They were the way in which characterization was created. They were also the way in which differences among the various philosophical schools could be illustrated. That is because many of the chreiai were exchanges between exponents of two different schools of thought. One has the impression that Diogenes' collections of chreiai derived ultimately from living discourse and tradition among the schools of philosophy. Each would tell stories on the other and treasure those that were exemplary for a particular philosophical perspective on a situation. Thus the function of these little stories may have been more than entertaining. There is some evidence that chreiai were used as the principal ingredient for the composition of lives of the philosophers as early as the third century B.C.E. These were written in the "Aristotelian" tradition, the tradition from which Diogenes Laertius drew his material.[7]

There are a number of fine discussions about the relationship of speech

---

7. *Chreiai in biographies.* The distinction between the "Aristotelian Lives" that used anecdotal material and for which Diogenes Laertius is a late example, and the "encomiastic" biography that did not accentuate chreiai and for which Cornelius Nepos is a good example, is discussed briefly in Thomas Lee, *Studies in the Form of Sirach.* Lee provides a full documentation for the encomiastic tradition and type of speech together with a fine historical introduction. The distinction between the encomium and the Aristotelian lives must be inferred due to lack of texts prior to Diogenes Laertius. The *Lives* of Plutarch clearly manifest a mixed form, however, when compared with Cornelius Nepos and Diogenes Laertius. In Plutarch's *Lives* the chreiai appear within an encomiastic framework, frequently elaborated in order to serve the purposes of the larger narrative themes. See V. Robbins, "Classifying Pronouncement Stories in Plutarch's *Parallel Lives.*"

to character among schoolmen and authors of the first and second centuries. The main idea for the Greeks was that a person's speech revealed the person's character. This could be turned into an ethic to the effect that one should live in accordance with one's espousals. But in the case of well-known persons whose espousals were clear, their character was assumed to be known from their sayings. One function of the chreia was to establish and project the speaker's character. Another was to see the person in action, noticing how a particular philosophical stance made a difference where speech and behavior worked their way out in application to situations.

The collections of chreiai attributed to the various philosophers in Diogenes Laertius can be analyzed with the question of characterization in mind. Every philosopher got a few pungent apothegms of the "know thyself" variety. Even the legendary seven sages at the hoary beginning of the grand history of the Greek philosophical tradition were honored with a maxim or two. Chreiai also were attributed to as many different philosophers as possible including rather somber figures like Plato. But the chreia was clearly more at home in the Socratic and Cyrenaic traditions, then took its place as the major means of characterization and memory with the Cynics. Reading closely one can discern the distinctive features of the Cynic chreia. The sagacity of the response is of the *mētis* variety, a clever extrication from an embarrassing conventional situation. The chreiai attributed to Stoics on the other hand, though witty as well, often express a moral judgment.

Two examples of Cynic chreiai are the following:

> To one reproaching him (Diogenes the Cynic) for entering unclean places he said, "The sun, also, enters the privies but is not defiled."
>
> (Diogenes Laertius, *Lives* 6.63)

> When one of his students said: "Demonax, let us go to the Asclepium and pray for my son," he replied: "You must think Asclepius very deaf, that he can't hear our prayers from where we are."
>
> (Lucian, *Demonax* 27)

Two examples of chreiai attributed to Zeno the Stoic are the following:

> To a stripling who was talking nonsense his words were, "The reason why we have two ears and only one mouth is that we may listen the more and talk the less."
>
> (Diogenes Laertius, *Lives* 7.23)

> He used to say, "Well-being is attained by little and little, and nevertheless it is no little thing."
>
> (Diogenes Laertius, *Lives* 7.26)

An aspect of cleverness attends all four sayings. In the case of the Stoic chreiai, however, one can easily see that a moralism lies behind the response. The Cynic chreiai, on the other hand, address themselves to the conventional logic implicit in the situation and turn it upside down.

In the first chreia, Diogenes is reproached for visiting "unclean places," that is, socially unacceptable locales such as places of prostitution. The response uses an analogy in which an "entrance" into an "unclean place" happens all the time without affecting the entrant. The force of the analogy lies in its shrewdness, not its persuasion. By switching orders of discourse from the social to the natural, the definition of "unclean" and its effect is changed. In the space provided by the humor and in the hesitation created by the momentary confusion, the Cynic escapes unharmed.

The second chreia, of Demonax, is a bit more difficult to resolve. It might appear at first that Demonax was correcting an inadequate understanding of religious belief by suggesting that the gods were omnipresent and could hear prayers everywhere. It would be most unusual, however, for a Cynic to be found recommending piety or propounding religious teaching. A closer look shows that Demonax has been put in a very uncomfortable situation, since the request is for his companion's son and includes taking a religious institution seriously. Demonax's response counters the suggestion as in figure 10.

FIGURE 10
A CHREIA OF DEMONAX

Suggestion:	Let us go	to the Asclepium	and pray.
Rejoinder:	You think	where we are	he is deaf.

Three contrasts are made and aligned. The first is the point of departure, that between the Asclepium (there) and where we are (here). Since the companion wants to go there and pray, the first contrast results in the second, that between praying there (as if Asclepius hears) and not here (as if Asclepius were deaf). That leads to the third contrast between the companion's practice (Let us go) and his belief (You think). The result is the insinuation that "the action you propose is not supported by the beliefs you hold." The result is a momentary confusion about the contradiction, and that is just the point. A moment of confusion is long enough for the Cynic to get out of the trap.

The pronouncement story in Mark 2:15–17 has the structure of a Cynic chreia and uses the same kind of logic. The setting has been expanded slightly in order to specify the objectors as scribes of the Pharisees and explain that the table fellowship with tax collectors and sinners should be understood as a custom of Jesus with his disciples and his many followers.

To the response has been added the pronouncement about Jesus coming to call sinners, not the righteous, an obviously theological explication. If the embellishments are deleted, the chreia reads as follows:

> When asked why he ate with tax collectors and sinners, Jesus replied, "Those who are well have no need of a physician, but those who are ill."

The response counters an assumption that underlies the objection. The alignment of the objection and the response can be visualized as in figure 11.

FIGURE 11
A Chreia of Jesus

Objection:	(For the righteous)	to eat with	sinners (defiles).
Response:	For the Physician	to treat	the sick (does not defile).

The category that links the two statements is that of uncleanness. The issue under debate is the status of the code of clean/unclean as it pertains to table fellowship. A Jewish code underlies the objection. Jesus' response shifts the order of discourse from the social to the natural. The sick also are unclean, but physicians regularly attend them. This confuses the situation because it appears that Jesus agrees with the objectors. Yes, these people are sick and in need of help. But then it occurs that the shift in orders of discourse lets Jesus off the hook (does not defile). It also introduces a subtle counter-proposal, namely that Jesus' role is legitimate and that, if that is so, the crowd with him is legitimate also.

The saying about the physician was proverbial. The image of the physician was a favorite among Cynics. Thus the chreia corresponds fully with other early evidence for Jesus' aphoristic style. It is not the only case of Cynic influence among the pronouncement stories. The style of response is the same everywhere, and some of the themes that occur were traditional with Cynics. The list would include: the saying about Jesus' family (Mark 3:33), the play on *patris* in the saying about the prophet's honor (Mark 6:4), the scatological humor in Mark 7:15, the image of the dogs and crumbs (Mark 7:28), and the evasion of well-wishers in Mark 1:38. Many other pronouncements could easily be imagined in Cynic ethos, though the themes are so general they cannot be limited to Cynic stock. The list would include: the saying about the first and the last (Mark 9:35; 10:44), only one is good (Mark 10:18), the camel and the needle's eye (Mark 10:25), Caesar's coin (Mark 12:17), the widow's mite as more (Mark 12:43), and the woman's "good deed" (Mark 14:6). A conclusion is not difficult to reach.

The pronouncement stories in the Gospel of Mark are constructed on the model of the Cynic chreia and many of them use Cynic themes.[8]

2.2 The Chreia in Literature and Education

Thus far the discussion has been about the chreia as a small, independent unit of composition. When placed in a larger literary context, chreiai were frequently amplified and elaborated. In Diogenes Laertius the chreiai come in collections, one after the other, and thus do not illustrate the variety of changes possible when used in a biography with greater narrative or thematic interest. In Plutarch's *Lives*, however, chreiai can be detected at the core of longer stories. The ways in which chreiai were elaborated into these richly developed illustrations of a person's characteristics can be described.

Some grammatical changes would be required merely to introduce the chreia into a certain mode of discourse. Settings also could be expanded by adding descriptive details or explaining items of significance to the point of the story. Instead of a single saying or exchange, dialogue could lead up to the pithy insight. Or, conversely, an aphorism could give rise to additional questions or comments within the story. Of particular interest are the ways in which an author might comment upon the significance of a story. Comments might include a statement explaining the point of a difficult chreia, the use of an image of contrast to heighten the profile, a helpful analogy to the point of the story, the addition of some other examples of the same kind of behavior, speech, or virtue, and perhaps some eulogistic remarks.

The type of material one finds surrounding a chreia in a biography might be understood as commentary upon the essential point of the story, or merely descriptive embellishment, or an author's manipulation of traditional material in the interest of his larger narrative themes. All of these modes of amplification occur. But patterns of elaboration can frequently be discerned that serve rhetorical functions as well. Since most of the chreiai in the Gospel of Mark are elaborated, and since most of the elaborated pronouncement stories involve conflict and argumentation, the rhetorical function of elaboration needs to be understood.

In the Hellenistic schools of rhetoric the first lessons were performed on small units of familiar material taken from classical literature. Teachers were advised to comb through the classical texts, from Homer through the

---

8. *The Cynic chreia.* For a more detailed discussion of the moral and Cynic types of chreiai in the first century see B. Mack and V. Robbins, *Patterns of Persuasion in the Gospels*, chap. 2. On the proverb about the physician, frequently in Cynic context, see: Plato, *Republic*, 1.332D–E; Ovid, *Ex ponto*, 3.4.7; Diogenes Laertius, *Lives*, 6.6 (*Antisthenes*); Plutarch, *Sayings of Spartans* 230F; Dio Chrysostom, *Discourses*, 8.5 (*Diogenes*); Lucian, *Demonax* 146–47. Additional references are given in Johannes J. Wettstein, ʽΗ Καινὴ Διαθήκη 1.358–59.

poets, historians, and sages, to Aesop's fables, and collect good examples of various types of discourse for rhetorical analysis. Particularly graphic descriptions, condensed narratives of an event, fine speeches, and so forth, were lifted out of the texts, subjected to criticism, and used as models to practice a variety of compositional skills. Rhetoric was understood as a useful preparation for the practice of law, any vocation that required public performance, and also for teaching and writing. The chreia was chosen as the small unit of speech for the very first exercises.

Cynic chreiai were very helpful for the first exercises in analyzing the rhetorical effectiveness of all forms and figures of speech. That is because the chreia presented a "speech situation" in miniature—speaker, speech, and audience or setting. Since the setting in Cynic chreiai represented cultural convention and its logic, moreover, the Cynic response could be viewed as taking the other side of a debatable issue and studied for its rhetorical value as an argument. Long lists of things to look for (*topoi*) were in hand as chreiai were analyzed. *Topoi* included matters of logic, style, grammar, and figures of speech. Analysis could be extremely detailed and demanding. At some point, however, the student was required to begin the process of composing his own material. The process began by amplifying given material, and then moved to the development of little paragraphs called theses or declamations, the object of which was to support the contention of a given maxim or chreia by bringing other material to it. At that point, the Cynic chreia was found to be less useful.

Theon, a teacher of rhetoric in the first century, worried about the difference between Cynic chreiai and those that derived from a moralism. In his lengthy discussion of the exercises to be performed on the chreia, Theon used examples predominantly of the Cynic variety. This documents their "usefulness" (chreia means "useful") in the rhetorical tradition of education. But he made a distinction between the types of chreiai appropriate for the two approaches to any proposition, refutation on the one hand, and confirmation on the other. He explained that one should take care to select chreiai for use in the composition of theses (confirmation) by making sure that they were from "approved" persons of well-known character. He even defined the chreia with this preference for constructive sayings, by calling it a *maxim* attributed appropriately to a specific character. Exercises in the confirmation of approved chreiai included amplification, the composition of theses, and the development of supporting argumentation called elaborations.

Theon's *progymnasmata* is a very important witness to the merger of literary and rhetorical sensibility that was taking place in the first century. Not only were teachers of rhetoric turning to literature and its criticism, authors were becoming highly conscious of the rhetorical functions of all kinds of speech. It was a literary culture whose *paideia* had already turned the corner on the way to the Second Sophistic. The marks of rhetorical education and skill can already be detected in such authors as Philo of Alexandria and Plutarch. They can also be detected in the Gospel of Mark. Mark's pronouncement stories bear comparison with the way in which Plutarch used chreiai and sayings material in the composition of his *Lives*. Taking a cue from Theon's discussions on preliminary exercises in composition, several observations can be made about the way in which chreiai appear in an expanded form in a narrative context.[9]

One observation is that the saying of a chreia may have been analyzed by the author from a rhetorical point of view. Another is that even figural and aphoristic sayings were understood to have persuasive power, functioning as theses or arguments. A third would be that the amplification of a chreia was a normal procedure and that every item added in its expansion including descriptive details of the setting may have been thought important for making the point of the story as clear and strong as possible. A fourth observation is that the clustering of additional sayings tacked onto a chreia should not be thought a haphazard procedure. They should not be accounted for as free-floating sayings that were added at a convenient location merely in order to conserve them. They probably were intended to develop the point (thesis) of the chreia, or to support its argument. A fifth consideration would be that patterns of elaboration did exist that used just this kind of material in order to construct tight but complete arguments.

The pattern of elaboration referred to briefly in the last chapter ("The Parables") is one of the more important ways in which aphoristic and imagistic material was used to compose a full argumentation. It consisted of (1) an introduction, (2) the chreia, (3) a rationale, (4) a contrast, (5) an analogy, (6) an example, (7) an authoritative pronouncement, and (8) a conclusion. In a biographic narrative, not every chreia had to be expanded into a full argumentation. Many could be given in brief if the point was clear and they fit into the narrative theme appropriately. Others might be expanded in various ways short of developing a full episode of debate. But some might be selected to demonstrate the full range of argumentation available to the thesis, as well as the consummate skill of the speaker. In the Gospel of Mark, some chreiai have been fully elaborated.

2.3 Elaborated Chreiai in Mark

The elaboration of Markan chreiai is surprising. Since the chreiai are

---

9. *The chreia in literature and education.* See the "General Introduction" in R. Hock and E. O'Neil, *The Chreia in Ancient Rhetoric,* 1–78. On Theon's concern about "approved" chreiai for confirmation in theses see C. Walz, *Rhetores Graeci* 1.212.12–15 (L. Spengel, *Rhetores Graeci* 2.103.2–5); 1.243.16 (Spengel 2.121.2). A critical edition of the Greek text of Theon, together with an English translation and notes, has been prepared by James Butts, "The Progymnasmata of Theon."

predominantly Cynic, the logic they contain is that of critique. Such a logic does not easily lend itself to elaboration. The materials at hand for developing elaborations, moreover, would have been meager. With only two generations of social history to call upon, well-known examples (paradigms) would have been scarce, and those from either Greek or Jewish traditions inappropriate. The citation of authorities from the past, a very important element in the construction of rhetorical argumentation, would have been impossible. Only the sayings of Jesus were available for this strange, new culture. So the elaborations in Mark consist mainly of Jesus' sayings, parceled out according to the various functions required by the elaboration pattern. Metaphors predominate for contrasts and comparison (*parabolai*). The problem of the paradigm appears to have been solved by creating a new way to picture exemplary behavior without appeal to an actual case. The sayings about "the one who . . . ," or "everyone who . . ." frequently function as paradigms in an elaboration. The result was that the "cultural history" of the Jesus movement was created in the imagination at the level of mythic ideal even as the stories of Jesus were elaborated. That is because the persuasive power of the pattern of elaboration lay in its capacity to position a particular thesis firmly in alignment with commonly accepted values and views given with cultural tradition. Three examples of elaborated chreiai in Mark will illustrate this process of retrospective rationalization.

2.31 Mark 2:15–17. Mark 2:15–17 is an example of a slightly expanded chreia. The logic of the chreia has already been discussed. Here the logic of the expansion may be given. The setting was expanded to specify the opponents as scribes of the Pharisees, and the followers of Jesus as a society. Thus the issue up for debate now pertains to this social conflict. To the saying about the physician a rationale was added ("I came not to call . . ."). The rationale was derived from the logic implicit in the original chreia. It makes explicit that the issue about clean/unclean was a social conflict that could also be expressed in terms of the distinction between the righteous (unexpressed in the chreia) and sinners. Such a clarifying rationale was a standard item for "difficult" chreiai even in the collections. The person who added the rationale in the case of this chreia, however, took the opportunity to develop and apply the theme as well. That also was frequently done and would have received high marks by a teacher of rhetoric. The author picked up on the image of the physician, erased any ambiguity about purpose that may have accompanied a purely Cynic reading, and justified Jesus' behavior as founder of the new society composed of "sinners" who were nevertheless "right." The ironic employment of terms continues the Cynic style of critique. The critique is no longer Cynic, however. The teasing invitation to reconsider things has been transformed into hardened polemic in the course of the domestication of the chreia. A system of rationalization for the new movement has been read into the situation. One might note that the opponents are depicted as asking, not Jesus, but his disciples, about the practice of table fellowship. Jesus' function now is to answer for the disciples as their champion.

2.32 Mark 2:18–22. The second pronouncement story in chapter two is an example of a slightly more complex expansion. In Mark 2:18–22 the objection raised is that Jesus and his disciples do not fast. There is a great deal of evidence that Jesus was remembered as a Cynic of the hedonistic variety, not of the ascetic type. Some of the evidence uses the contrast between Jesus and John the Baptist to make the point, and this story also sets the scene with a contrast between the disciples of Jesus and those of John. The original chreia is easily reconstructed:

> When asked why he and his followers did not fast, Jesus replied, "Can the wedding guests fast while the bridegroom is with them?"

If the saying is authentic, a bit of Cynic impertinence cannot be avoided in the self-reference. But perhaps the chreia stems from an early period of buoyancy when the importance of Jesus as instigator of the new movement was being explored. In either case, the logic is clear. The question of fasting was countered by shifting focus to an occasion on which fasting was fully inappropriate. The shift turns the question back upon the objectors by suggesting that they may not have interpreted the occasion correctly.

At some later time a rationale was given to this chreia, explaining that the time of the wedding was during the time of Jesus. The domestication that occurred by adding this rationale all but scuttled the point of the chreia, however, for lo and behold, the Jesus people now are fasting. Not to leave it there, however, two *parabolai* were added about the patch and the wineskin. The point is that, even if the Jesus people are fasting now, they are doing so for reasons altogether different than others may have. The separation between the old and the new inaugurated by Jesus' unconventional behavior still stands. The last saying about "new wine is for fresh skins" serves then as an authoritative pronouncement. Only the example and the author's conclusion are missing from the elaboration pattern. A sufficient contrast was given with the expansion of the setting by including both the disciples of John and Jesus. The theme of the wine was derived from the chreia, for wine and weddings go together quite well. By mutually subverting these two metaphors, the essential point of the chreia could be retained and reapplied. That point was the novelty of the group, a novelty that placed it beyond traditional classification.[10]

---

10. *John and Jesus.* The contrast is drawn in Luke 7:24–26, 31–35. It corresponds to the distinction customary in the Hellenistic period between two types of Cynics, the

2.33 Mark 7:1-23. In chapter 7 a very elaborate expansion of a chreia is presented. Reconstructing the original chreia has been difficult because the process of its domestication was quite complex. Following the logic of the resulting elaboration has also been problematic because, in the process of expansion, new themes were interwoven into an increasingly complex argumentation. Nevertheless, two remarkable rhetorical moves can be identified that largely account for the confusion. One is that, when the setting was redescribed, the original focus upon the disciples who did not wash before eating was shifted to fall upon the Pharisees who washed regularly. This shift allowed for the question to be raised about the "tradition of the elders," thus creating a new issue and the necessity of crafting a new response from Jesus to that issue. The second shift followed from this. Since the original retort was no longer appropriate as a response to the newly phrased objection, the original chreia was effaced in its elaboration and a new chreia was created by having Jesus counter with the quotation from Isaiah.

The original retort was not lost in this process, however. It was merely displaced and used later in the elaboration. Scholars have frequently noted that verse 15 is odd and enigmatic, and that much of what follows it appears to be an attempt to tone down an otherwise risqué rejoinder. By putting this saying together with the original objection about eating with unwashed hands, a fine chreia can be reconstructed.

The original chreia can be given in paraphrase:

> When asked why he ate with hands defiled, Jesus replied, "It is not what goes in, but what comes out that makes unclean."

The humor is scatological, typically Cynic, but should not detract from the clever logic employed. The issue is, again, the matter of clean/unclean. The topic is table manners. The objection registered in verse 2 is that Jesus and his disciples are violating the ritual laws of purity. The response shifts the order of discourse about things unclean from table manners to what happens to the food one eats. The usual confusion of categories occurs. For a moment the thought is allowed that it doesn't matter whether one washes one's hands or not, since putting food into the mouth is not where uncleanness resides. In the process of domestication the saying was too risqué to use for the thesis, but too good to dismiss altogether. A later scribe, afraid that it might be buried in the elaboration, knowingly added a scholion: "If anyone has ears to hear, let that one hear" (vs 16).

The shift in issue from "eating with hands defiled" to "keeping the tradition of the elders" may have happened not much before Mark's time.

"ascetic" and the "hedonistic." On John the Baptist as a Cynic of the ascetic type, see Leif Vaage, "To Wear Soft Raiment."

In fact, Mark's own hand may be suspected in the composition of this chapter, for the confusion in audience that results is handled in a way similar to that in chapter 4. Here in chapter 7 there is a change of audience in verse 14, and in verse 17 the disciples ask Jesus privately for an explanation. The elaboration pattern continues to give structure to the unit as a whole, however, just as in chapter 4. The saying from the original chreia now serves as the *parabolē* in the pattern of elaboration that works with the new chreia created by the enigmatic citation from Isaiah.

The chapter now can be outlined as follows:

Introduction

Now when the Pharisees gathered together to him, with some of the scribes, who had come from Jerusalem, they saw that some of his disciples ate with hands defiled, that is, unwashed.

For the Pharisees, and all the Jews, do not eat unless they wash their hands, observing the tradition of the elders; and when they come from the market place, they do not eat unless they purify themselves; and there are many other traditions which they observe, the washing of cups and pots and vessels of bronze. (vss. 1–4)

Chreia setting

And the Pharisees and the scribes asked him, "Why do your disciples not live according to the tradition of the elders, but eat with hands defiled?" (vs. 5)

Chreia response

And he said to them, "Well did Isaiah prophesy of you hypocrites, as it is written,
This people honors me with their lips,
but their heart is far from me;
in vain do they worship me,
teaching as doctrines the precepts of men." (vss. 6–7)

Rationale

"You leave the commandment of God, and hold fast the traditions of men." (vs. 8)

Contrast

And he said to them, "You have a fine way of rejecting the commandment of God, in order to keep your tradition.

For Moses said, 'Honor your father and your mother'; and, 'He who speaks evil of father or mother, let him surely die.'

But you say, 'If a man tells his father or his mother, What you would have gained from me is Corban' (that is, given to God)—then you no longer permit him to do anything for his father or mother, thus making void the word of God through your tradition which you hand on. And many such things you do." (vss. 9–13)

Analogy

And he called the people to him again, and said to them, "Hear me, all of you, and understand:

There is nothing outside a man which by going into him can defile him; but the things which come out of a man are what defile him." (vss. 14–15)

Explanation of the Analogy

And when he had entered the house, and left the people, his disciples asked him about the parable. And he said to them,

"Then are you also without understanding? Do you not see that whatever goes into a man from outside cannot defile him, since it enters, not his heart but his stomach, and so passes on?" (Thus he declared all foods clean.) (vss. 17–19)

Examples

And he said, "What comes out of a man is what defiles a man. For from within, out of the heart of man, come evil thoughts, fornication, theft, murder, adultery, coveting, wickedness, deceit, licentiousness, envy, slander, pride, foolishness. (vss. 20–22)

Pronouncement

All these evil things come from within, and they defile a man." (vs. 23)

The introduction was necessary in order to shift the objection away from Jesus and back onto the Pharisees. The problem now is not that Jesus and his disciples do not wash, but that the Pharisees do. In the shift, the basis for Pharisaic law is specified as the "tradition of the elders." That sets things up nicely for Jesus' countercharge. It will ride on the distinction between oral and written tradition.

The objection raised in the chreia setting can now include, not only the original issue of hands defiled, but the specification that the tradition of the elders is at stake.

The chreia response is a well-chosen prophecy, a text that requires elaboration. The procedure is perfect. Instead of Jesus expounding upon his own saying, he will develop a thesis taken from a chreia of a well-known author just as a student of rhetoric would have done. The choice is devastating, because it is taken from the opponents' own tradition, but can be used against them. Rhetors would have called this "invention," or finding a text just right for the purpose. In this case two sets of contrastive images are combined in a single saying that will allow both the original chreia and the new chreia elaboration to be combined. One set is the lips/heart contrast. The other is the contrast between the worship of God and the precepts of men. Both will be elaborated thematically and intertwined.

The rationale explains that the text is about the distinction between God's commandments and the traditions of the elders. It is applied immediately to the practice of the objectors. The commandments of God are not yet specified as written tradition, but the way has been prepared to do that in the contrast.

The contrast sets the written word of God against the traditions of the Pharisees in a specific case.

The original chreia can now be used as a *parabolē* (analogy). The shift from hands to foods and mouth given with the original saying in response to the original objection can now be used, for the text cited has introduced the themes of lips for teaching and heart for worship as substitutes for mouth and stomach.

The explanation of the analogy is designed to make that substitution stick. The logic is hard-pressed, since the obvious meaning of the *parabolē* has to be acknowledged. But the point is clear: defilement is a matter of the heart, not the stomach.

Examples can then be given of defilements of the heart.

The pronouncement is a bit weak after such a hot polemic and laborious argumentation. Nevertheless, it does make sense and sums things up as well as one might expect.

Three pronouncement stories in Mark have been analyzed in relation to chreiai and their elaboration in Hellenistic literature and education. They are not the only pronouncement stories in Mark that lend themselves to such an analysis. All of the pronouncement stories betray knowledge of rhetorical functions, and many of them manifest skill in rhetorical composition. The logic is invariably informed by the requirements of polemical argumentation. In the three analyzed, it could be shown that an original chreia had been amplified according to the principles of rhetorical elaboration. In their form as elaborated chreiai, these pronouncement stories reveal the stress of the process of domestication. The social critique and apology implicit in an original response was not relinquished. But the aphoristic style hardened into pronouncements of a decidedly polemical nature. The delight in unconventionality and newness gave way to the justification of distinctions between a social movement and its critics. This sequence agrees with the thesis presented in chapter 5 about the general development of the social history of the Jesus movements. If the stages through which the pronouncement stories passed can be made a bit more precise, a social history of one Jesus movement active in Mark's environment might come into view.

3. THE SYNAGOGUE REFORM MOVEMENT

The detection of Cynic-like chreiai lying at the base of three pronouncement stories is sufficient to excite the historian's imagination. The first thought might be that all of the pronouncement stories could be reduced to original chreiai and that, making a set of them, the earliest stage in the synagogue reform movement could be recovered, if not some entrée found to the historical Jesus. This hope founders on principle, unfortunately, when knowledge of the ways of rhetorical education is in hand. Training was given, not only in the amplification and elaboration of chreiai, but in how to reduce them, paraphrase them, and create them as well. There is no reason to suppose that a fully elaborated chreia could not have been created from scratch, chreia and all. The creation of chreiai should not be evaluated by modern sensibility. There need not have been any sense of daring or ecstasy in the creation of a brand new saying or pronouncement attributed to Jesus. Students were taught how to go about that, and the creation of an appropriate speech-in-character for a well-known person in a particular circumstance was considered to be an accomplishment.[11]

Many of the pronouncement stories in the Gospel of Mark appear to have been created long after the time of Jesus, some as late as the time when the gospel was composed. Mark's own hand is to be seen or suspected in many of them. Some brief exchanges that Tannehill identified as pronouncement stories, such as the cleansing of the temple, the prediction of the destruction of the temple, and the incident of the withered fig tree, do not make good chreiai at all. There is a touch of the enigmatic still, and of course there is the ever-present correction, but the point is not made by a well-considered phrase addressed to an obviously challenging situation. Oddness frequently resides in the fact that not enough of the story has been told to get the point no matter who Jesus' interrogators were. Snippets such as these do show that Mark thought of episodes on the model of the chreia. But this kind of episode cannot be imagined to stand alone and make sense. Each of the above examples draws upon the larger narrative to create its suspense. These were created in the course of composing the gospel just with the narrative needs of the gospel in mind.

Nevertheless, the isolation of three fine chreiai that appear to have been given before being taken up for elaboration is significant. They are not the only instances where the core of the pronouncement story makes a good chreia when seen as a singular response to the challenge. The core pronouncements have been identified in the appendix. Approximately one quarter of them are weak, without enough bite to ride on rhetorical effectiveness alone. But roughly three-fourths of them are rather strong chreiai, judged rhetorically, not on the basis of content. Many of them

---

11. *Speech-in-character*. The *progymnasmata* regularly contain a chapter of instruction on *ēthopoïa*, or *prosopopoiia*, that is, how to create a saying or speech appropriate to the character of a well-known person, or create a character by means of the attribution of speech.

appear to have been elaborated in a second reworking. It is that phenomenon that suggests a tradition of telling chreiai behind the pronouncement stories in Mark.

One needs to keep in mind that the creation of speech-in-character for a known person was judged on the basis of the appropriateness of attribution. That means that the "character" of Jesus known to the group would have been in mind when any new saying was crafted. This does not mean that the image of Jesus could not have changed, as indeed it did, nor that the creation of new chreiai would not have contributed to changing images. But it does draw attention to the fact that a Cynic style of response continued to be attributed to Jesus even after his authority had been charged with pronouncements that led to claims no Cynic ever would have imagined for himself.

The Cynic humor upon which many of the core pronouncements ride also is suspicious. At the stage of elaboration, humor was effaced by a very serious, if not hostile tone. Humor is an evidence for some of the underlying chreiai being early. One cannot imagine that the scatological saying in Mark 7:15, for instance, would have been created for Jesus after the serious business of polemic was underway. Other considerations, then, begin to fall into place. The thematic shifts that sometimes occur between the chreia and its elaboration are telling. So are some uneven seams where additions have been belabored. The logic changes as well, from appeal to common sense and insight as sufficient for the good chreiai, to rather far-fetched arguments and attempts to garner traditional authorities (e.g., scripture) in the elaborations. The conclusion must be that, on the whole, chreiai were created, and then in the process of transmission, elaborated.

The set of core pronouncements contains a sizable number that could be imagined for a pre-Markan stage of social history. Examples would be: the physician (Mark 2:17); the wedding (Mark 2:19); the sabbath for man (Mark 2:27); Jesus' family (Mark 3:33); prophet without honor (Mark 6:4); hands defiled (Mark 7:15); children and dogs (Mark 7:27–28); children and the kingdom (Mark 10:14); why call me good (Mark 10:18); camel's eye (Mark 10:25); taxes to Caesar (Mark 12:17); and the woman's beautiful deed (Mark 14:6). A few could even be understood as "authentic" in the sense that they capture Jesus' circumstances and style without an eye to his importance for the movements stemming from him. But most of those retained were told originally, not in the interest of keeping Jesus' memory alive, but to claim his precedence for practices of importance to the movements stemming from him. The table fellowship, the wedding metaphor, plucking grain on the sabbath, the pervasive concern about violating the basic codes of ritual purity, and so forth, all attest that even at the chreia stage the stories were told with a high degree of self-consciousness about the group that had formed and its needs. It needed to affirm its unconventionality not only as a distinctive trait, but as the purpose for its existence. It needed as well to fend off any reservations that might arise within, or criticisms that might come from without. The chreia helped by inviting a reimagination of strong moments when Jesus created the space for unconventional thoughts and behavior. One could also take heart and delight in the humor chreiai created. The earlier stages of chreiai-telling in the synagogue reform movement are marked by a distinctly convivial tenor.

3.1 Conflict with the Synagogue

Approximately two-thirds of the pronouncement stories in Mark are set as conflictual situations between Jesus and Jewish leaders. In many of the settings a place has been made both for the disciples and the Pharisees. The questions are sometimes addressed to the disciples about Jesus, sometimes to Jesus about the disciples, but always about issues that divide the syna-gogue reform movement from the synagogue. One has to assume that the chreiai were elaborated by a group whose social history merged for a time with that of the synagogue and eventually brought it into conflict with proponents of Pharisaic Judaism. These conflicts were projected back upon the time of Jesus in order to claim the founder's authority for new argu-ments that had to be devised.

The role of the disciples in these stories is strange. Mark may have introduced them into several of the stories in order to keep his discipleship theme alive. He needed their frequent appearance because they were very important to his plot. Still, some of the stories seem to require that the disciples be mentioned in the setting. This is especially true of those stories in which the question was cast in terms of the behavior of the disciples. Other than draw criticism and questions, however, the disciples never have anything of consequence to do or say. (This does not apply to a second class of stories, approximately one-third of the collection, in which Jesus' con-flict is not with the Jewish leaders, but with the disciples.) The suspicion would be that the amplified settings for the elaborated chreiai purposefully included both disciples and Jewish leaders. In Mark the disciples ("students" or "followers" of Jesus) would represent leading figures of the synagogue reform movement, just as the scribes and Pharisees would represent the leaders of the contemporary synagogue. By constructing the setting to reflect the social institutions at odds, the purpose of Jesus' pronouncements could not be mistaken. He would be arguing against the Pharisees in favor of the practices of the synagogue reform movement at every turn.

The issues up for debate tell the tale. They break unevenly into two classes. The larger class pertains to the constitution of the group, its unconventional behavior, and the question of codes by which to judge obligations. The smaller number, including some that are most likely

Markan, revolve around the question of Jesus' authority and identity. The larger class presents a very interesting profile. There are no earth-shattering experiences at stake, no strange practices that divide the groups. The matters of concern are, actually, rather banal. But they all share one thing in common: charge and countercharge about social identity. The Jesus people have not accepted Pharisaic codes of obligation, ritual purity, and halakha. The problem centers in the constitution of the Jesus group as mixed, and the behavior of the Jesus people as unclean (from a Pharisaic point of view).

The attitude of the Jesus movement is obvious and its social history can easily be inferred. The members of the Jesus movement rejected the Pharisaic critique, but they did take it seriously because they believed that they had some place in the Jewish scheme of things. Criticism could not merely be dismissed if both critics and those criticized shared for a time the same sense of heritage and institutional turf. Sharp exchanges must have been the rule when Pharisaic views and influence entered the picture, with many caught in the middle between Jesus' table fellowship and synagogue membership. In the course of these exchanges, some counterarguments were found to defend the practices of the Jesus people against Pharisaic criticism. Some countercharges were lodged as well. Mostly, however, the pronouncement stories reveal a posture of adamant affirmation of their own way of doing things in the face of Pharisaic criticism.

The Jesus people could not meet the Pharisees on their own ground, because the ground rules would have required some accession to the traditional authorities lying behind the ritual laws of purity. The only alternative was to appeal to ground common to both, namely the larger corpus of epic traditions and its function as source for narrative paradigms (aggadah) and ethics (Torah). This would have been a natural move, given the role of the scriptures in the synagogue where the battle took place. Unfortunately for the Jesus movement, most of the narrative paradigms of value for the debates had to be negative examples for polemical use, illustrations of Pharisaic inconsistencies, or sets of texts where scripture could be set against scripture. Torah could be marshaled in support only in very general terms, such as "the greatest commandments." The appeal to scripture did not succeed. The Pharisees won the battle both for the synagogue and for the scriptures as Torah.

In the course of the conflict, Jesus people did learn a few tricks, make a few accommodations, and establish a few social markers that could be used to identify the group as a separate society after its separation from the synagogue. But there is no evidence for the creation of a new, complete system of symbols, myths, practices, and codes in this material. There was mainly a high degree of self-consciousness about the gatherings and their importance, a sense that they belonged somehow to the grand history of Israel, and constant appeal to the importance of Jesus, his activity, and views as the one who made it possible for the Jesus people to eat together. Nothing else was required as long as the movement thought of itself as fully franchised in the social structures of the diaspora synagogue. When the separation occurred, probably only in Mark's recent past, the task of constructing an independent society and rationale would have been very difficult.

Stories that address the constitution of the group as a mixture of peoples whose social relationships were in need of some justification include: table fellowship with sinners (Mark 2:15–17); forgiveness of the paralytic (Mark 2:1–12); Jesus' family (Mark 3:31–35); the Syrophoenician woman (Mark 7:24–30); the question about the resurrection (an issue of social import, not of belief, Mark 12:18–27); and the woman's good deed (a social issue before elaboration, Mark 14:3–9). The question about divorce might also be included in this list. There are also signs of social tensions and questionable relationships under observation in the background of many of the other stories.

Unconventional behavior under criticism includes: table fellowship (Mark 2:15–17); fasting (Mark 2:18–22); washings (Mark 7:1–23); and failure to keep the sabbath (Mark 2:23–28; 3:1–6). The theme of clean/unclean is present in the background of many stories.

Issues of obligation are also pervasive. The codes were unclear, most of the effort having been directed against the Pharisaic principles. Stories that center on these issues include: the question about fasting (Mark 2:18–22); the sabbath controversies; the tradition of the elders (Mark 7:1–23); divorce (Mark 10:2–9); the commandments (Mark 10:17–22); taxes (Mark 12:13–17); and the greatest commandment (Mark 12:28–34). One might also include the debate about alms and good deeds in the anointing story (Mark 14:3–9).

The stories show that Jesus was the only real authority the Jesus people had. There can be no doubt that a good bit of criticism also was received because the Jesus people were just Jesus people. It would be wrong, however, to think that the question of Jesus' authority had given rise to "christological" claims and debates. The stories that introduce conflict over Jesus' identity in christological terms are very late, most likely Markan or composed by others like Mark in his immediate circle. These include: the authority of the Son of Man in Mark 2:1–12 and Mark 2:23–28; David's Son (Mark 12:35–37); and the question of authority (Mark 11:27–33).

The stories about Beelzebul, Elijah, and the Pharisees' request for a sign (Mark 3:22–30; 9:9–13; 8:11–12) also center on Jesus' identity, but appear to be Markan reworkings of materials and themes already present in Q. Mark upgraded these materials to mesh with his highly christological narrative designs, but they need not have been understood that way in their pre-Markan context. The Beelzebul controversy was about the source of

Jesus' effective spirit (imagined as power to exorcize demons), whether an alien spirit (Beelzebul, "Lord of the Heights," probably a Syrophoenician deity), or one that had to be taken seriously as arising from within Judaism. (In Q: "By whom do your sons cast them out? Therefore they shall be your judges. But if it is by the finger of God that I cast out demons, then the kingdom of God has come upon you," Luke 11:19–20.) The request for a sign was likewise taken from Q where mutual rejection of and by "this generation" was the issue, and the authority of Jesus was imagined still in the genre of the power of the miracle worker. The question about Elijah coming first also derived from the Q tradition and its preoccupation with the image and role of the prophet, rather than from the synagogue reform movement where the controversy pronouncements were created.

Within the synagogue reform movement, Jesus' authority came to be imagined in terms appropriate to the conflict. He steps forth as a scribe, interpreting the scriptures. He appears as a Pharisee, debating points of halakha. His approach, of course, is Cynic, based upon a wisdom that frustrates the principles of scriptural and halakhic interpretation used by his opponents. His wisdom is such, in fact, that, as the master rhetor, his arguments and pronouncements override the authority of scripture itself. Where he can use the authority of Moses for the sake of his argument, he will do so (Mark 7:9–13). But if it should turn out that Moses can be set against Moses, as in the debate about divorce (Mark 10:2–9), Jesus has no trouble deciding which side to take, then going on to offer his own authoritative pronouncement on the issue (Mark 10:9). His authority for the synagogue reform, therefore, was just that of the strange rhetor whose pronouncements were binding because he won the arguments decisively. The way in which those argumentations run now needs to be looked at quite carefully.

3.2 The Nature of the Argumentation

The pronouncement stories are elaborated chreiai. They follow patterns of embellishment and argumentation customary to rhetorical training and practice in the first century. In the culture at large the normal practice would be to debate a traditional thesis, or confirm a chreia, maxim, or apothegm from some well-known person. The resources (arguments) for supporting a thesis would be taken from lore, literature, and history common to the culture. The authorities cited would be other well-known "approved" persons whose wisdom, logic, or precedent judgments were trusted. The conclusion would point out that the thesis had been sustained, its importance recognized, and that its guidance should be accepted. In the "culture" represented by the synagogue reform movement the normal practice would have been impossible.

In the first place, the chreiai at hand were of the Cynic variety. They were designed to celebrate the unconventional, the clever critique of customary logic, and the new climate opened up for thinking and behaving differently. In the second place, the resources for argumentation were not only meager, such sayings as there were stemmed from the same source as the sayings in the chreiai, that is, from Jesus. In the third place, appeals to authorities in either the Jewish or the Greek cultural traditions were blocked on principle, leaving only, again, the words of Jesus from which to construct a supporting argument.

An exceptionally odd thing happens. Jesus becomes his own authority. Everything is attributed to Jesus: chreia, rationale, supporting arguments, and even the authoritative pronouncements. Jesus elaborates his own saying and ends up pronouncing authoritatively upon it. The weird effect for Hellenistic ears would have been the image of a Cynic sage preoccupied with proving his wisdom authoritative. The circle closes. There is no point of leverage outside the sayings of Jesus to qualify or sustain the argumentation and its conclusion. Jesus' authority is absolute, derived from his own Cynic wisdom, and proven by his own pronouncements upon it.

The chreiai of Jesus contained an implicit critique of society. In the early stages of chreiai creation and retelling, a culture slowly came into view over against which the Jesus people saw themselves identified. It was society as Jews idealized it. Domesticated, the chreia now could be situated specifically on that social-cultural border. When the Pharisaic criticism was encountered, elaboration was undertaken specifically with that conflict in view. A mode of argumentation was devised to support and sustain the Cynic effect. Because there were real opponents now, a more forensic, less deliberative style of argumentation was used. The logic was heavily dialectical, dealing in contrasts, oppositions, and either/ors. Nevertheless, the pattern was still that of the elaboration of the "thesis" given with the Cynic chreia. The result was that the pronouncement stories painted a picture of interrogation, dialogue and debate. It was, however, a debate the questioners had no chance to win. Objections are raised in order to set things up for Jesus to win. The objectors get one statement. Jesus gets at least two pronouncements, the saying in the chreia of response, and the authoritative pronouncement at the end. At the end there are only two alternatives available to those who have overheard: amazement or silence. By the very simple means of manipulating the sayings of Jesus rhetorically, the synagogue reform movement turned a Cynic sage into an imperious judge and sovereign. He rules by fiat.

3.3 Mark 14:3–9

The story of the anointing at Bethany (Mark 14:3–9) will serve as an example of the nature of argumentation found in the pronouncement stories. The story only makes sense where it is situated in the gospel, during the events of the passion week with the reader's foreknowledge of what is in store for Jesus assumed. It is therefore a very late creation, unlike all of the other pronouncement stories in regard to its theme of Jesus' death. It was most probably composed by Mark or a colleague in his community. Nevertheless, the pattern of elaboration was used to construct the argument, and the style of argumentation is the same as in the other stories. Because it is a late creation, composed in the process of imagining the gospel as a whole, the anointing is evidence for the pervasive and persistent use of rhetorical savvy in the synagogue reform movement within which Mark worked.

The story is put forth as a commendation of the woman's good deed, justified in the face of some who took offense. Strangely enough, however, the deed is called good because it was an "anointing beforehand for burial." What that could possibly mean, whether the woman could possibly have known, and how that answers the objection raised, are the problems over which interpreters have fretted. It does not seem as if the woman's action, unannounced and unexplained, could have led anyone to such a conclusion.

J. D. Derrett is the only scholar who has noticed that the objection raised against the woman's action is contrived. There must have been something else about the woman's action that was objectionable in an earlier version of the story. He noted that the companion story in Luke 7:36–50 shares the scene, but enters an entirely different objection. He concluded that both stories were versions of an originally shorter one in which Jesus responded directly to the challenge of some embarrassment created by the deed. The deed, he thought, would probably have been considered risque by most social codes of the first century.

Derrett is undoubtedly right. The original story would have been a chreia in which a woman, unannounced at a meal with guests, entered to pour out a perfumed oil on Jesus. That could have caused a stir even in a Cynic's symposium. Luke may have retained some of the original flavor in his elaboration by playing on the woman's status as a "sinner," and developing the theme of love. Mark may have retained something of the original response in that Jesus calls the action *kalon,* that is, both "beautiful" and "good." A humorously ambiguous retort using such a term would have made a fine chreia. Paraphrasing, the chreia may have run as follows:

> When Jesus was at table, a disreputable woman entered and poured out a jar
> of perfumed oil upon him. He said, "That was good."

The elaboration in Mark situated the scene at Bethany, related that the perfume was poured out "over his head," and introduced an objection to the deed to set Jesus up for a fine little speech. The elaboration can be outlined as follows:

Setting

While he was at Bethany in the house of Simon the Leper, as he sat at table, a woman came with an alabaster jar of ointment of pure nard, very costly, and she broke the jar and poured it over his head. (vs 3)

Objection

But there were some who said to themselves indignantly, "Why was the ointment thus wasted? For this ointment might have been sold for more than three hundred denarii, and given to the poor." And they reproached her. (vss 4-5)

Response as elaboration

Introduction

But Jesus said, "Let her alone; why do you trouble her?" (vs. 6a)

Rationale

"She has done a beautiful thing to me." (vs. 6b)

Contrast

"For you always have the poor with you . . .; but you will not always have me." (vs. 7a, c)

Analogy

"And whenever you will, you can do good to them." (vs. 7b)

Example

"She has done what she could; she has anointed my body beforehand for burying." (vs. 8)

Authoritative pronouncement

"And truly, I say to you, wherever the gospel is preached in the whole world, what she has done will be told in memory of her." (vs. 9)

The woman's action puts both her and Jesus in a bad light. The original chreia vindicated both of them in a single response. The elaboration also will have to vindicate both of them even though attention is shifted immediately away from the embarrassment and onto a specific objection that some raise. The indignation and reproach of the objectors give Jesus the opportunity of questioning them first. The debate will be about motivations.

The objectors charge that the anointing was a "waste," and give a reason for thinking so. It would have been "better" if the ointment had been sold and "given" to the poor. The better use agrees with conventional Jewish piety.

Jesus' thesis is that the woman's deed was "good," not wasteful. In the rhetorical tradition, *kalon* was a technical term for one of the standard "objectives" in a deliberative argumentation. Jesus now must demonstrate that the action was good. If he can do so, his thesis will have been sustained. Jesus' argument turns on a series of contrasts designed to confound the objection that giving to the poor would have been a better deed. One needs to know a bit about Jewish codes in order to understand the argument. Briefly, both giving to the poor (alms) and anointing for burial counted as good deeds. The difference was that alms-giving responded to a general need and could be performed at any time. Anointing for burial was an occasional need classified with specific cases of obligation. Specific cases took precedence over general cases.

One can already see how the argument will go. The setup is clever, but it is also dishonest, if read as a real debate. Jesus is not a corpse, so the argument will ride on the plausibility of the notion that the anointing was done "beforehand." Neither the woman, nor the objectors, could have suspected that intention. Only the reader might find himself bemused. Scholars have been troubled. Jeremias and Derrett, for instance, resisted the conclusion of rhetorical chicanery even though they both saw how the argument ran. Both agreed, therefore, that the story really happened, that it was enough to think that Jesus knew what lay before him, gospel and all. That is exactly what the story wants the reader to think, of course, but the critic should be aware that the point is made at the expense of Jewish objectors who could not have known the Christian meaning of the action used as argument against them.

The first contrast is that between Jesus (not always with you) and the poor (always with you). The objectors would have to agree about the poor. The allusion to Deut 15:11 would not have gone unnoticed: "The poor will never cease out of the land."

The analogy is "doing good works," conceptualized as a general and habitual practice. It is applied to the objectors, however, in order to set up the second contrast, that between what the objectors could do anytime and what the woman actually did on a specific occasion. Because the analogy is applied in this way, it loses some of its power as a statement of the ways things generally go and borders on being a description of the objectors (perhaps a contrastive example). They are not described as having performed good deeds, however, but merely as those who could "whenever" they would. That is intentional.

What the woman did is the example. It also serves several other rhetorical functions, drawing the argument to its moment of insight. Her deed can be called an "anointing for burial" because Jesus is "not always with you." She fulfilled an occasional obligation, "doing what she could . . . beforehand" in contrast to the objectors who could "do good to the poor . . . whenever." Thus her deed is "good," and it is "better" than the alternative suggested by the objectors.

What more could the objectors have to say? A fully mythic view of Jesus' authority provided the clinching proof, an assumption fully foreign to the original terms of the debate. They are not heard from again and Jesus turns to his authoritative pronouncement. The woman's deed will be her memorial wherever the gospel is preached. What Mark means, of course, is wherever his gospel is read. The woman is not even given a name. She is carefully de-faced, for Jesus does not even turn to her to address her. She, as well as the objectors who are also not specified, are props for a portrayal of Jesus as the dismissive sovereign whose forthcoming death will be of such significance that it will be preached throughout the world. Objections are clearly no longer in order. It is just as well. No one could possibly win against such an opponent. Only devotion will do.[12]

The pronouncement stories in the Gospel of Mark do not record debates Jesus had with the Pharisees. Neither do they record the way arguments ran between the synagogue reform movement and the Pharisees. They record the way Jesus people wanted to imagine the conflict and its resolution in retrospect. The real debates are a thing of the past. In their place are imaginary fictions. They are fictions because they violate the basic ground rules of human discourse and dialogue. Not even a Cynic would approve. A Cynic would at least have caught his questioners in their own juices. Jesus catches them in his own juices by using assumptions that his questioners did not share or could not have known. The significance of Hultgren's judgment can now be seen: Jesus' pronouncements are "merely asserted." No rationale is given for accepting his authority to make them. Kuhn's words also come home: the argumentation would have been "completely unintelligible for Jews outside the Christian community." To use Bultmann's words, the argument, followed closely, leads *ad absurdum*. So the break has occurred. Conversation has broken down. There is nothing more to say. The Jesus people are out on their ear.[13]

The value of the fiction for those in need of rationalizing their separate social identity should be acknowledged. The stories say, not only that they were right, but that they had been right all along, from the beginning.

---

12. *The argument.* A more detailed discussion of the argumentation in the anointing story is given by B. Mack in Mack and Robbins, *Patterns of Persuasion in the Gospels.* The Rabbinic codes underlying the argumentation have been worked out by J. Jeremias, "Die Salbungsgeschichte Mark 14:3–9"; and J. D. M. Derrett, "The Anointing at Bethany."

13. *Inauthentic logic.* See the references above, n. 5. Bultmann's *ad absurdum* is found in his *History of the Synoptic Tradition,* 45–46. Bultmann argues that such logic is characteristic of Rabbinic controversies as well. A more careful comparison of the Rabbinic chreiai with the pronouncement stories of Jesus shows, however, that, whereas the Rabbinic tales continue to delight in the absurdity of a Cynic-style *mētis,* Jesus' pronouncements assume an authority inappropriate to the "dialogues" in which they are set. It is the seriousness of Jesus' pronouncements, and the fact that they assume an authority not shared by his opponents, that make the logic of the "dialogues" inauthentic.

Jesus' pronouncements attest the legitimacy of the staggering claims they had to make about him. They articulate principles that can be used for beginning to construct an independent system of codes by which to identify the group. A myth is all but in place, quite by accident. Without any speculation, great imaginative leaps, visionary moments, or experiences of ecstasy, a figure of absolute authority emerged from his sayings to champion their cause against all criticism. A critical view of the world can now be seen as a sufficient justification for the formation of a new and distinctive society.

The cost of the new myth of origins was, however, high. The claim to have won the debates had to be made in the face of having lost them. The fiction that Jesus won them all compensates for the failure of the synagogue reform movement to have won any. In the stories, Jesus wins at the expense of the movement's erstwhile opponents. His face is turned outward, toward them, but not to invite them in, not even to agree to disagree. With models of logic such as these in place, fair fights and exchanges in the marketplace are unthinkable, to say nothing of negotiations whereby arrangements might be imagined for both the insiders and the outsiders to exist side by side in the world. Common ground has been relinquished. The insiders are so right because the outsiders are so wrong. The stories prove it by a devastating fiction of authority against which there can be no appeal. Not even his followers will have had much more to say for themselves. Jesus will speak for them, and his word will be final.

If this view holds, it will not be possible to imagine Christian beginnings in terms of human discourse. Origination cannot be imagined as a call intended to be comprehended, whether as an aphoristic, sapiential, prophetic, apocalyptic, parabolic, persuasive, inviting, instructive address, or a call to some new, expansive and better vision of the way things might go. It will rest on a word that does not derive from persuasion, but from the marvelous fiction of the power of self-identification.

4. CONTROVERSY AND THE GOSPEL

Mark belonged to a circle of Jesus people who had access to some form of the sayings tradition (Q), some miracle stories, and many pronouncement stories. In addition to these materials from the Jesus movements, Mark had access to some traditions from the Hellenistic Christ cult. It is difficult to determine whether others in his circle also had taken note of Christian myth and ritual with its orientation to Jesus' death. It is possible that Mark was not alone in exploring ways to accommodate and merge the two diverse traditions. Some of the highly elaborate stories in his gospel may have been written by others in his circle as contributions to a common effort in reimagining the origins and foundations of a movement set adrift in very

high seas. Some stories, such as the anointing, need not have been composed by Mark himself. If not composed by Mark, however, these stories
must have been composed by others in his milieu who generally shared his
views about the value of making the merger.

Mark composed his gospel by forging these materials together into a
narrative on the model of biographic literature. The pronouncement stories
were used as a major element for the characterization of Jesus. Mark's
competence in the pronouncement story tradition is demonstrated by his
skillful reworking of many stories, and by the many stories best explained as
his own creations. These include most of the pronouncement stories
featuring the disciples, stories designed to carry his discipleship theme. His
interest in the pronouncement stories is shown by their use in his gospel.
They are the stories from the traditions that contributed two major narrative
themes. One was the theme of Jesus' authority. The other was the theme of
conflict.

Mark accepted the image of Jesus' authority given with the pronouncement stories, ironies, enigmas, and all. He enhanced it even more by
specifying that the identity of Jesus was more than that of an authoritative
teacher. Drawing upon the mythology of the Christ cult, Mark introduced
Jesus into the world as the Son of God. Drawing upon the apocalyptic
visions of the later Q tradition, Mark identified Jesus as the Son of Man.
The final judge had already appeared. With credentials like that, Jesus'
pronouncements were not only authorized rhetorically, their self-referential oddity was now transformed into a revelation of the divine. As Jesus
comes on the scene, his first words are an announcement of the nearness of
the kingdom of God (Mark 1:15). This defines the content of his "teaching." It also justifies all of his pronouncements as announcements of the
gospel. "Repent," he adds, "and believe in the gospel." Thus Jesus
announces the "gospel of Jesus Christ, the Son of God," that Mark has
written (Mark 1:1). Jesus' authority is such that he can proclaim his own
appearance as the beginning of the gospel.

In order to make this point more clearly, Mark crafted a number of stories
that combined miracles with pronouncements. The theme Mark took from
the miracle story tradition was that of Jesus' power. By combining miracle
stories and pronouncement stories, Jesus' authority was specified even
more precisely. It was the authority residing in the power to effect change.
Mark announced this theme in the very first story about Jesus' "teaching" in
the synagogue in Capernaum (Mark 1:21–28). "They were astonished at his
teaching, for he taught them as one who had authority, and not as the
scribes" (Mark 1:22). But he does not teach. Instead, Jesus exorcizes an
"unclean spirit." The people say, "What is this? A new teaching! With
authority he commands even the unclean spirits, and they obey him" (Mark
1:27). For Mark, Jesus' authoritative pronouncements are those of the Son

of God. They do not invite a reimagination of the world, offer instruction in the new order, or engage the world in argumentation. They command. Their power to effect radical transformation means that the only proper response is to obey.

Nevertheless, there is conflict. The theme of conflict in the gospel also was derived from the pronouncement stories. They served Mark well in his project, for they contributed the narrative theme that made it possible to join the Jesus traditions with a narrative of the crucifixion. The conflict of Jesus and the Pharisees, given with the pronouncement stories, was portrayed as the reason for a plot against Jesus to destroy him. The plot is introduced early in the gospel in the following way. After the first appearance in the synagogue at Capernaum, Jesus performs two other miracles leading to the generalizing remark that "He went throughout all Galilee, preaching in *their* synagogues and casting out demons" (Mark 1:39; emphasis given). The chain of five controversy stories comes next (Mark 2:1–3:6), the first and last of which combine miracles and pronouncements. At the end of the chain Mark explains the response of the Jewish leaders to Jesus' effective power and authority: "The Pharisees went out, and immediately held counsel with the Herodians against him, how to destroy him" (Mark 3:6). From that point on someone is always showing up from Jerusalem, to lodge a charge against him (scribes from Jerusalem, Mark 3:22), raise a critical question (Pharisees and scribes from Jerusalem, Mark 7:1), argue (Pharisees, Mark 8:11), or test him (Pharisees, Mark 10:2). Upon entering finally into Jerusalem, Jesus "cleanses" the temple, "and the chief priests and the scribes heard (what he said) and sought a way to destroy him" (Mark 11:18). In the temple, the chief priests, scribes, and elders question his authority (Mark 11:27–28), Jesus tells the parable of the Wicked Husbandmen (Mark 12:1–11), and they make the first attempt to arrest him (Mark 12:12). Failing in this attempt, they then send the Pharisees and some of the Herodians to "entrap him in his talking" (Mark 12:13). Another set of controversy stories is given which brings them to silence (Mark 12:34), and the stage is set for the passion. "The chief priests and the scribes were seeking how to arrest him by stealth, and kill him; for they said, 'Not during the feast, lest there be a tumult of the people'" (Mark 14:1–2). Judas then hands Jesus over and the trial and crucifixion are on.

The position of the controversy stories in the gospel narrative is further evidence of intentional narrative design. They cluster at the beginning around the theme of Jesus' entrance into the synagogues in Galilee. Then they cluster for Jesus' "teaching" in the temple after he entered Jerusalem. Jesus' conflict with the synagogue authorities was linked by design to a conflict with the leaders in Jerusalem. The plot to kill Jesus was hatched in the synagogue. The series of attempts to take Jesus follow the theme throughout the gospel and allow Mark to mention various combinations of leaders. The effect is to create the impression of a major collaborative effort. The reason for the plot is that the Jewish leaders would not accept Jesus' authority. Jesus is not at fault for the entrance and provocation, because he is the Son of God with full rights to his domain. He came to cleanse it of unclean spirits. Thus the Pharisees, not Jesus, are those who initiated the violence. The conflict of the synagogue reform movement with the synagogue was read back into the myth of origins and presented as the cause for Jesus' crucifixion.

Mark's use of the parables of Jesus created the strange circumstance of a teaching not designed to teach. In his hands the pronouncement stories do not lead to enlightenment, but to violence, blame, and judgment. The plot thickens.

8

THE MIRACLE STORIES

The reader of Mark's Gospel cannot avoid the question of miracle. After Jesus appears on the scene announcing the kingdom, his first deed is a miracle. His second deed also is a miracle. So are his third and his fourth. In the first eight chapters, Jesus performs not less than fifteen miracles. Fully one half of the narrative material in this first section of the story is taken up with miracles. On the way to Jerusalem two more miracles are performed. In Jerusalem Jesus does not perform a miracle, but miraculous events do not cease. Predictions are made that come true. The temple veil is rent from top to bottom and there is darkness at noon when Jesus dies. Afterwards the women visit the tomb only to find that he is not there. A miraculous aura attends Jesus from the very beginning to the very end of his story.

Miracle stories are the source of the impression Christians have that an explosion took place at the beginning of the Christian time. They are also the source of the scholarly imagination about Christian beginnings and the assumption that, if not an explosion, something quite dramatic must have happened. Scholars and miracles don't mix well, though, so the effort has been to shunt them aside. How much better it would be to see a powerful message at the start. Most of the effort devoted to Christian origins has therefore been to locate the miraculous in what Jesus said. Unfortunately, the miracle stories have not gone away.

In very recent debate the miracle stories have forced their way into the center of attention again. They had been there once during the nineteenth century, but that was when the gospels were thought to be biographies. The solution was easier then. Miracles were simply the mistaken perceptions of credulous persons amazed with the appearance of the superior man. From a distance, seeing Jesus on the other shore could readily have generated sea stories and fish stories. Then the critical view broadened its horizons. Miracle stories were miracle stories. Greeks told them, Jews told them, and Romans told them. What could be the point of Christians telling them as well?[1]

---

1. *The nineteenth-century view.* A review of A. Schweitzer, *The Quest of the Historical*

1. MIRACLE STORIES AND PERFORMANCE

Around the turn of the century scholars in the history of religions school started to make collections of miracle stories from the literatures of the Greco-Roman period. Comparison with the miracle stories in early Christian traditions led to the conclusion that early Christianity was another Hellenistic religion. Since miracle stories were not unusual for certain kinds of cults, there was nothing unusual about the stories Christians told. Bultmann took care of the problem quite nicely. The stories about Jesus were late, a product of the cultic imagination. Miracles and the historical Jesus had nothing to do with one another. Since Bultmann's time scholars have taken another look and the judgments have fallen the other way.[2]

Bultmann's judgment was based on the formal similarity of miracle stories in the synoptic tradition and in pagan literatures. Similarity has generally been conceded by other scholars, though fine points of distinction have been made. Where Bultmann drew the conclusion that the stories about Jesus were contrived, however, others have argued that they therefore must be true. The argument has been that miracle stories would not have been told in general unless miracles happened, or were believed to have happened. If so, formal similarity should not be used to deny that Jesus performed miracles. Formal similarity must mean that, like others of the period, Jesus did work miracles and that early Christians reported them in the same way believers in other miracle workers did.

This argument from the incidence of miracle stories in the cultures at large has been combined with a closer analysis of the formal characteristics of the synoptic stories than Bultmann was able to do, or interested in doing. Form-critical studies have pushed miracle stories back to early stages in the pregospel traditions, stages as early as can be managed for the sayings of Jesus. Bultmann's consignment of the miracle stories to late stages has therefore appeared facile. The evidence is just as strong for miracles, on this view, as for Jesus' teachings. What to make of these findings, however, has not yet been fully determined.[3]

Two problems have persistently worried this discourse. The one is that a convincing argument for inferring miracle working activity from miracle stories has been difficult to find. Caution competes with impatient pronouncements. The other is that the import of such activity in the case of Jesus resists definition. These problems are versions of the usual concerns

---

Jesus, demonstrates the fixation upon the problem of miracles by authors of the many "lives" of Jesus written during the nineteenth century. David F. Strauss used the heading "Sea Stories and Fish Stories" for the "nature miracles," cited in Schweitzer, 83.

2. *Rudolf Bultmann.* Bultmann's discussion of the miracle stories is in *History of the Synoptic Tradition,* part 2A.

3. *The current view.* In recent scholarship it has become customary to characterize Jesus not only as "prophet," and "wisdom teacher," but as "exorcist" as well. See, for example, H. Koester, *Introduction to the New Testament* 2:77.

of New Testament scholars about history and myth on the one hand, and about the uniqueness of Christianity on the other. If miracles are miracles, are Jesus' miracles any different than those of others? The closer one comes to the spectacular, the less significance there seems to be. Various positions have been taken in recent scholarship with regard to Jesus' miracles and their significance. A brief statement about four of the more prominent proposals can set the issues and the context for the study of these stories in this chapter.

1.1 Jesus the Magician

Morton Smith has produced a number of studies to the effect that Jesus must have been a worker of miracles no different than others of his time. According to Smith, the miracle worker was a popular form of the hero, a well-known figure during the Greco-Roman period. The evidence extends from accounts of miracles in the lives of divine men, such as Apollonius of Tyana, through gnostic texts, to the magical papyri. The high proportion of miracle stories in the Gospel of Mark, the earliest record of Jesus' life, means that Jesus must have been a common magician, nothing more.

Smith has been more interested in exploring the trajectory that runs from Jesus the magician into gnostic sects than the question of the emergence of the Jesus movements and the Christ cult. How to account for either of the latter on Smith's reconstruction is therefore quite unclear. In a now-famous debate with Howard Kee at a meeting of the Society of Biblical Literature in 1970 this issue was engaged, though obliquely. Kee has been a proponent of the Jewish and apocalyptic backgrounds to much of the synoptic tradition. He challenged Smith's use of only Hellenistic sources for comparison, suggesting instead that early Christians saw Jesus as an eschatological prophet and themselves in the light of Jewish epic and destiny. The stories of Jesus' miracles cast him in the role of Jewish prototypes, according to Kee, not that of a Hellenistic divine man. The debate created an impasse. It also set the stage for a number of studies on the question during the seventies. The debate revealed that simple appeal to Hellenistic parallels was not enough either to determine the form and function of the Jesus stories, or to draw conclusions with respect to Jesus' social role. Miracles were still mysterious.[4]

1.2 Jesus the Power of God

In 1974 Gerd Theissen published a major work on the miracle stories. Using a structuralist approach, Theissen collected all of the miracle stories

---

4. *The Smith-Kee debate.* The papers of the 1970 debate have been published: M. Smith, "Prolegomena"; and H. C. Kee, "Aretalogy and Gospel." Smith's *Jesus the Magician* was published in 1978.

in the New Testament to make the set, including the stories of Jesus' epiphanies and post-resurrection appearances. A comprehensive list of narrative roles, motifs, and themes was worked out, and the "virtual genre" of the whole defined. Jesus represents divine power in confrontation with a sphere of demonic power. People are caught between these two spheres in various positions of possession, awareness, and volitional states. Liberation from the power of the demonic is what Jesus can offer. The sick are healed, opponents confronted, crowds provisioned, disciples rescued, demons cast out, and the miracle worker revealed.

Theissen's evaluation of the virtual genre of New Testament miracle stories involved a discussion of miracles in the Greco-Roman world. He pointed out that miracles functioned constructively for the lower class, not only providing help, but becoming a form of political critique and resistance to oppressive institutions. The fact of miracles thus established, Theissen then took up the question of the distinctive characteristics of the miracles of Jesus. They were unique because of their manifestation of divine power. They were accompanied by amazement because of their improbability, and they were rightly defended by early Christians against comparison with all other claims to the miraculous. Only by assuming that Jesus worked miracles, cast out demons, and introduced the eschatological spirit of God can one account for early Christian miracle workers, the success of the Christian mission, the formation of the church, the composition of the gospel, and the cultural victory Christianity finally achieved.

One does wonder how Theissen knows such things to be true. Backing up a bit to look for those statements of his that define the peculiarity of Jesus' miracles over against others, the troubled mind is not set at ease. According to Theissen, pagan miracles only did what their reports said they did; Christian miracles did more than could be told. People were not only healed, but transformed. Jewish messiahs were not even as effective as pagan miracle workers. They only announced typical miracles, miracles that did not in fact take place. Jesus actually performed unique miracles. Jewish messiahs announced miracles to be performed by God. Jesus performed miracles by means of a power he himself possessed. And these are only some of the considerations Theissen enters toward the end of the book in support of Jesus' uniqueness. Critical discourse is no longer in evidence as Theissen brings his work to a conclusion. If one wonders why, the answer surely must be that the study is at fault from the moment the set of stories includes myths and cultic legends. It stands as a monument merely to the desire for a miraculous origination of a unique Christianity.[5]

---

5. *Gerd Theissen.* The English translation of Theissen's work appeared in 1983, *The Miracle Stories.* Theissen's discussion of the uniqueness of Jesus' miracles appears on 244–45, 276–86.

1.3 Jesus the Exorcist

Paul Achtemeier took another approach in an article called "Miracles and the Historical Jesus: A Study of Mark 9:14–29" (1975). He applied form-critical and redaction critical methods to lay out three stages in the transmission of two intertwined stories. He warned that later interpretations should not be used to evaluate "the historic events which gave rise to the traditions." At the earliest layer of the tradition Achtemeier found two "uninterpreted" stories, one about a boy with a dumb spirit (Mark 9:17–18, 20?, 26b–27), the other about a boy with an unclean spirit (Mark 9:20–22, 25–26a). Because there were so few stories in Mark without interpretation (only Mark 1:29–31 and 8:22–26), the reconstruction of these exorcisms was important. He was prepared to argue that they were historical.

A discussion of an institution of healing (the sanctuary of Asclepius at Epidauros) and the general belief in miracles during the Greco-Roman age (Apollonius of Tyana) led Achtemeier to caution modern liberals about hasty dismissals of the "reality" of the cures reported. "Human beings react to reality as they perceive and understand it." "What functions as reality" in a concrete historical period is what counts. Therefore, "the miracles of Jesus . . . may not be affirmed or denied on the basis of the Christian interpretation which has been given to these stories, as though that interpretation allowed one to make a different historical judgement on the miracles of Jesus than, say, the miracles of Apollonius of Tyana. . . . One must therefore either judge all reports of such miracles from the Hellenistic age as false, including those reported in the gospels, or one must allow for the reality of more Hellenistic miracles than simply those reported of Jesus."

Achtemeier's argument is interesting and noble. He does not want to play favorites, and thus agrees that, at the uninterpreted level, it is all or nothing. He himself is prepared to conclude "that the historical Jesus did in fact perform deeds such as the exorcism reported of him in the early traditions underlying Mark 9:14–29." Nevertheless, because they are uninterpreted, "the miracles had little if any probative value with respect to Jesus." One may wish to pause here for some pondering.

Achtemeier has grandly relinquished the distinctive and particular from the miracles of Jesus in order to establish their historical plausibility. But what he has left is a generalization about uninterpreted deeds ("*such as* the exorcism reported") without probative value, that is, without significance. Achtemeier does not go on to tell the reader how this should be taken. He ends by saying only that ". . . any historical picture of Jesus that does not include his activity as exorcist will be a distortion." No one wants a distortion, of course. But neither will the traditional quester be satisfied to learn that, once one has broken through the ring of fire, the originary event will be found banal and without meaning. Perhaps Achtemeier has gone too far.

The story of the boy with the dumb spirit, in any case, may not be totally without significance. It has as its point that the disciples could not cast the spirit out. The story of the unclean spirit also may be quite significant. Unclean spirits are exactly what Mark thought Jesus was after for very big reasons. But that would mean that the stories are not innocent with respect to interpretation after all and, according to Achtemeier's schema, would not be historical. Thus the form-critical approach has not produced a convincing entrée to the historical Jesus. It appears best to leave the question of uninterpreted activities to the philosophers, acknowledge that the stories are not devoid of signification, and seek to place them in some context where that meaning can make sense.[6]

1.4 Jesus the Enabler

In "The Structure of the Gospel Miracle Stories," published in 1978, Anne Wire expressed interest in knowing more about the social function of the telling of miracle stories. Wire noted that miracle stories are either second- or third-hand reports. But they were told for the sake of persons, both the person about whom the story was told, and the person to whom the story was told. Because they were "whole" stories, moreover, they reveal the "exchange" that took place between the miracle worker and those forces that impinged upon the person in need. She classified the miracles of Jesus in four types according to the forces and exchanges they reveal. Exorcisms dramatize Jesus' "expelling of powers which possess and enforce their will over people." The exposé pits Jesus against religious authorities who represent "standard procedures and exalted egos." The interaction results in "a fissure in an otherwise closed legal system." The provision story is about "situations of hunger, scarcity or oppression where people have lost hope in their ability to provide for themselves." And the demand story relates an interchange between the miracle worker and the person in need as an individual. It functions in retelling to call "the hearer to break out of a closed world and to demand, struggle and realize miracle in human life."

Wire does not say how she understands the difference between "miracle in human life" and the miracles as recounted in the stories. The typology shows that her interest lies in the human life miracle, however, and that the human situation addressed by Jesus was oppressive. This appears to be the distinctive feature of Jesus' miracles. They were performed in the interest

---

6. *Paul Achtemeier.* The citations are from "Miracles and the Historical Jesus," 471, 488–91.

of liberating people from the "oppressive restrictions" of a "tragic" human condition. The miracles of Jesus as a whole tell of "a transforming event that changes the human condition."

Wire's interpretation is romantic. In her view, the miracle stories are not about miracles, but about a mysterious power of human transformation that originated with Jesus. Situating the miracle stories in this way, however, clarifies neither the question of the historical Jesus, nor the question of their social function. Society is in view only as the oppressive other, the context from which individuals need to be set free. One therefore looks in vain for a reflection of the Jesus society within which these stories were told.[7]

1.5 Jesus the Leader

Recent attempts to argue for the miracle-working activity of Jesus and the function of miracle stories for the origins of Christianity are not convincing. Some knowledge has been gained along the way, nonetheless, and can be summarized. Miracle stories are a recognizable genre. Compared with other examples, early Christian stories exhibit a few distinctive features. Among these are (1) a little test of faith or fear as a precondition in some of the stories; (2) a high incidence of socially marginal people; (3) a tendency toward the improbable; (4) a tone of seriousness about the matter; and (5) a high number of exorcisms. All of these features can be taken as signs that those who told the stories invested them with social concerns.

Theissen saw that the test of faith (1) symbolized the crossing of a social boundary. Several scholars have noted that the people who figure in these stories were socially marginal (2). It should be emphasized, however, that the selection does not constitute a profile of the average poor. Neither is there any strictly humanitarian program discernible. Marginality is more a matter of social stigma than poverty or oppression, and the lack of overlap in the set of marginal types is most surprising. It is as if some principle of selection were at work. Helplessness is exaggerated in keeping with the desire to portray the improbable (3). The stories do not appear to be a study in a sociology of hunger, sickness, misfortune, and physical disability. If the story is about a woman with a hemorrhage, it will be a hopeless case. If it is about a ruler's sick child, she will be at the point of death. Total helplessness, extreme deformities, demonic possessions are the rule. The impression given is that even stupendous miracles are child's play for Jesus. Nevertheless, what Jesus is about is serious business (4). Theissen noted that the impression one has from Epidauros is that "miracles are an everyday event here." Jesus' miracles are not an everyday event. They are

---

7. *Antoinette Wire.* The references are to "The Structure of the Gospel Miracle Stories," 83–84, 96, 110.

dramatic and freighted with consequence. The number of miracles attributed to Jesus is also without parallel in ancient accounts of miracle
workers. Moses, the prophets, rabbis, Apollonius of Tyana, each performed
a few miracles along the way. Jesus performed many. The result is a
heightened sense of the marvelous, the powerful, and the paradoxical. This
sense is concentrated in the high number of exorcisms recounted (5). And
the exorcisms have to do with spirits that are unclean, just that category of
social classification known to have been at issue among the early Jesus
movements.[8]

Were it possible to place these stories more precisely in their social
settings, the intention assigned to these expressive features might become
clear. In the following section another tradition of scholarship on the
miracle stories will be reviewed. Collections or sets of miracle stories have
been isolated at the pregospel stage of the Jesus traditions. These sets are
highly selective in the kinds of miracles reported, use the Greek genre, but
are full of allusion to Jewish epic prototypes and can easily be interpreted as
intentionally symbolic. Since features of these sets coincide with the list of
distinctive features outlined above, an impressive weight can be given to an
alternative thesis. The earliest miracle stories were not reports of the
miracle-working activity of Jesus. They were carefully composed sets of
stories about Jesus as the founder of the "congregation of Israel." Miracle
stories served some Jesus movement as its myth of origins.

2. MIRACLES AND MYTH

The prevailing opinion among scholars is that miracle stories were
widely disseminated in early Christian circles as oral tradition. Wandering
charismatics made use of them according to this view, but no one collected
the stories until Mark worked some of those he knew into his gospel. The
phenomenon of independent units traveling separately has been imagined
on the model of Bultmann's view of Jesus' sayings as free-floating logia. A
cluster of notions has given a special aura to this mode of transmission:
Jesus' power, the excitement of miracle working activity, various means of
imagining the transference of Jesus' spirit to his charismatic followers,
contact with the resurrected Lord, demonstrative preaching in the Christian mission, and the transformation of persons in keeping with the new era
that had dawned. As recently as 1971 this view was rearticulated fully by H.-
W. Kuhn. He was able to find pre-Markan collections of parables (Mark 4)
and pronouncement stories (Mark 2:1–3:6; 12:1–44), but he was not able to
find evidence for a pre-Markan collection of miracle stories. Wandering

---

8. *Peculiar characteristics*. The list is derived from points made regularly in current
studies of the miracle stories. The reference to Theissen is from *The Miracle Stories*, 284.

charismatics had to fill the space, therefore, from the time of Jesus until the time of Mark.

In an article published in 1970 (not available to Kuhn), Paul Achtemeier came to a different conclusion. He showed that Mark had used two sets of miracle stories, each of which followed a similar pattern of composition. The discovery of a collection of miracle stories used by Mark to compose his gospel compares with a proposal Bultmann had made earlier about miracle stories behind the Gospel of John. John also, according to Bultmann, had used a collection of miracle stories (Signs Source) as a basic building block for his story of Jesus. These three collections change the picture of miracles in early Jesus circles. They document a very interesting social history that appears to have had little to do with charismatic activity.[9]

2.1 The Miracle Chains in Mark

In his essay, "Toward the Isolation of Pre-Markan Miracle Catenae," Achtemeier was able to assign ten of the seventeen miracle stories in Mark to two sets of stories with the same pattern. Each set consisted of five stories, the first of which was a sea-crossing miracle, and the last of which was an account of feeding the multitudes. In between were an account of an exorcism and two healing miracles. Achtemeier explained the slight rearrangements of sequence by carefully showing Mark's reasons for rearranging. Material inserted between some of the stories could be laid to Mark's account. And, of course, Achtemeier resolved the old problem of doublets (two feeding miracles, for instance). The two sets were reconstructed as in figure 12.

FIGURE 12
THE MIRACLE CHAINS IN MARK

Stilling the storm (4:35–41)	Walking on sea (6:45–51)
Gerasene demoniac (5:1–20)	Blind, Bethsaida (8:22–26)
Jairus' daughter (5:21–43)	Syrophoenician (7:24b–30)
Woman with hemorrhage (5:25–34)	Deaf-Mute (7:32–37)
Feeding 5000 (6:34–44)	Feeding 4000 (8:1–10)

---

9. *Sets of miracle stories.* Kuhn's study of the miracle stories in Mark is in *Ältere Samm-lungen im Markusevangelium*, 191–213. His negative conclusion regarding a pre-Markan

Placed side by side, the pattern stands out visibly. All are miracle stories, but miracles are not all that matters. Some interest determined a particular selection of kinds of miracles and a specific arrangement of their order. Content is as suggestive as form and perhaps even more important. Achtemeier promised to have a look and share his assessment of the significance of the pattern in another article.

The essay appeared in 1972 ("The Origin and Function of the Pre-Markan Miracle Catenae"). Achtemeier had not been able to find similar "chains" of miracle stories in Hellenistic literatures. Some deities were known for sea rescues and for presence at cultic meals, such as Serapis, but there was no evidence for sea rescues and meal miracles being combined in a small collection of miracle stories. In the Hebrew scriptures, however, and in Jewish literatures of the Greco-Roman period, suggestive parallels began to appear. Narrative motifs were found that could shed light on the content, and combinations of similar motifs as well as stories in sets were found that helped explain the chain effect. The individual stories were Hellenistic in form and style, but the narrative themes pointed to familiarity with the epic of Israel.

The clue was given by seeing that the first and last stories went together. A miraculous sea crossing and a miraculous feeding of the people in the wilderness were standard items in the Exodus story. Evidence was plentiful that the Exodus story was much in the minds of first-century Jews. Sea crossing and miraculous feeding had, in fact, become shorthand codes for the whole story when referred to in psalms, poems, and other types of writing. The miracles of the ten plagues were also still very much alive in the Jewish imagination and, of course, Moses had been reimagined in every conceivable posture of importance as the leader of the people out of Egypt toward the promised land. The first thought was, therefore, that Jesus had been associated with the figure of Moses for some reason.

The three miracles in the middle did not seem to fit at first. But scholars had often noted features of the stories, especially the stories of the Syrophoenician and Jairus' daughter, that recalled accounts of miracles performed by Elijah and Elisha. For them also, small collections of stories were in evidence. Achtemeier explored the possibility that small sets of stories about certain figures may have been a Jewish idiom of some kind. He did

---

collection contrasts starkly with Achtemeier's finding in "Toward the Isolation of Pre-Markan Miracle Catenae." Bultmann's proposal of a Signs Source for the Gospel of John was made in the course of his commentary on *The Gospel of John*. That both Mark and John used sets of miracle stories in the composition of their gospels will be argued below. The sets are hypothetical in the same way that Q is hypothetical, that is, must be reconstructed as a source from the gospels within which they were embedded. An early scholarly consensus is therefore not to be expected, although both the Signs Source and Achtemeier's miracle catenae have won adherents. The value of working with these reconstructions will become clear in the course of the chapter.

find some examples of small collections in Hebrew, early Jewish, and Rabbinic texts (he was looking for sets of five), but was not able to establish a practice firmly enough to account for a set of just five miracles like those attributed to Jesus. The allusions to the prophets Elijah and Elisha were found to be very strong, however, so that some combination of Moses and Elijah seemed to lie behind the set. Achtemeier knew that there was evidence for popular lore about the return of Elijah for the purpose of restoring Israel when threatened. He also thought that there was some evidence for popular lore about the "prophet like Moses" promised in Deut 18:15. In other early traditions of the Jesus movements Moses, Elijah, and "eschatological prophets" were much in mind as folk figures with which the memory of Jesus was compared. Achtemeier concluded that the miracle story chain was intentionally allusive to these epic prototypes for Jesus and that the set had some significance for the community he founded.

Community is a big word. When combined with "miracle," "eschatological," and "prophet," moreover, charismatic ethos could be imagined right at the center of a group's practice. Achtemeier could not resist the temptation to link the miracle chain up with the old charismatic hypothesis. He found the linkage in the eucharistic nuances of the meal miracles and proposed a cult tradition in which the spiritual presence of Jesus was celebrated, not by reference to his death, but by participation in his resurrection through the symbols of bread and water alone.

Achtemeier's reconstruction of a cultic setting for the miracle chains brought together a number of older scholarly hypotheses in a novel arrangement. Among them were the notion of Jesus as a divine man, charismatic phenomena in the Hellenistic congregations, the relation of the resurrection to early Christian experience of the spirit, and an old scholarly suspicion about an early meal ritual in which bread, rather than the combination of bread and wine, was the important symbol. The force of Achtemeier's thesis lies in the combination of these several motifs and their linkage to a text held to be of liturgical significance. The apparent attractiveness of the thesis, however, is just the nuance of mystery attributed to that spiritual experience now positioned at the center of a very early Christian community.

It should be noted that the cultic interpretation of the function of the miracle chains rides on the "eucharistic" allusions in the feeding stories, and that these are recognized as "eucharistic" only by comparison with the ritual texts in Paul, Mark, and Didache. The similarity is given with the sequence of Jesus' actions in "blessing" (or "giving thanks"), "breaking," and "giving" the bread and fish to the disciples to distribute to the crowd. These actions do portray meal practice. The emphasis placed upon them in the feeding stories indicates that the person responsible for the stories wanted the signs of meal practice to be clearly visible in them. The question is how to interpret these signs. If they belonged to the earliest form of the feeding stories, the meal practice of some group of Jesus people may have found its reflection in the stories about Jesus in this way. Such a procedure, however, need not be understood as the product of a cult of spiritual presence at all. Even the highly formalized liturgy of the meal in the Didache lacks any such reference. The prayers give thanks for the knowledge about the church that Jesus "made known."

If, on the other hand, the actions of Jesus were introduced (later) into the stories as intentional allusions to the meal practice or meal texts of the Hellenistic congregations, their function at that level of composition would need to be clarified. Scholars have not found a way to control such an investigation, however, either at a pre-Markan stage, or at the level of Markan composition. In his book, *Loaves and Fishes,* Robert Fowler has argued that even the narrative of the last supper in Mark, though derived from some ritual tradition, was not intended as an "institution" of a ritual practice, but was Mark's way of bringing his theme of discipleship to a climax. According to Fowler, Mark's great interest in the feeding stories is also related to the theme of the disciples and their misunderstanding, not to a coded reference to eucharistic traditions. Fowler's work is a helpful caution about the danger of superimposing notions taken from the Pauline tradition upon the feeding stories. He did not account for the similarity in the actions of Jesus in both kinds of story, however, nor consider the possibility that diverse meal traditions may have come together at the level of Markan composition. Mark's uneasiness with the Hellenistic ritual meal (of presence) will be discussed in chapter 11 in relation to the Last Supper. Anticipating that discussion, the point may now be made that Mark therefore would not have understood the actions of Jesus in the feeding stories on the Hellenistic model. If that was not Mark's intention, Achtemeier's thesis is questionable, for it borrows the cultic interpretation of the feeding miracles from the Hellenistic practice even while distinguishing the form and function of the ritual from that practice.

If the miracle chains are not liturgical texts for a cult of the resurrected divine man, some other function needs to be worked out. Achtemeier's focus upon the eucharistic nuances of the feeding stories, and his attempt to reconstruct a community setting on the model of the Hellenistic cult, all but erased the significance of his discovery of the miracle chain as a set. The set of stories does have something to say about the social history of the group within which it was composed, but that social history does not appear to have held esoteric rituals of spiritual presences. Instead, a set of stories on the model of epic prototypes was composed to portray the origins of a most unlikely congregation in the process of formation. This alternative proposal needs now to be developed. But first the question of a similar set of stories within the Signs Source of John's Gospel should be asked.

2.2 The Signs Source in John

In the course of writing his commentary on the Gospel of John, Bultmann noticed that two types of material had been combined in various ways to create the effect of episodes in an otherwise very uneventful narrative. One type was the enigmatic and circular discourse of Jesus. Bultmann called it "revelation discourse." The other type was the narration of the scenes in which Jesus came to speech. Because many of these stories related miracles, and because the miracles were called signs (*semeia*), Bultmann called this material the Signs Source. Moody Smith collected Bultmann's references to the Signs Source in a later study. Robert Fortna built upon it to theorize an early edition of the gospel in the Johannine community composed almost entirely of miracle stories (*The Gospel of Signs*). Since then the theory has had a bumpy history.

Many scholars have not registered conviction about the Signs Source because the compositional history of John is so difficult to unravel that caution is always in order. All critical scholars agree that Johannine material passed through many stages of reworking. The amount of material reworked was relatively small, however, so the layers seem all but impossible to sort out. This material was pored over, rearranged, associated with symbolic signification, then given a decidedly ethereal cast by imagining Jesus to have "explained" it all in enigmatic, self-referential discourse appropriate only for a deity appearing incognito on earth. Since all of the miracle stories at this final stage are interpreted as manifestations of the glory of this revealed figure, some scholars have argued that it is impossible to separate out an earlier source for the miracle stories alone.[10]

The theory of the Signs Source should not be given up. The miracle stories are easily identified by the literal style of description used in their narration. There is also evidence of serializing at some stage prior to the gospel as it now stands. The wine miracle at Cana is called the "first sign" (John 2:11), and the healing of the official's son is called the "second sign" (John 4:54). Enumeration is not continued for the other stories, though the designation "sign" was picked up by those who reworked the material by

---

10. *The Signs Source*. See Moody Smith's reconstruction of the Signs Source in *The Composition and Order of the Fourth Gospel*. Smith's study is important for two reasons. One is that, since Bultmann did not bother to collect the pieces he assigned to the source in his commentary on John, Smith's reconstruction serves both as a reconstruction of Bultmann's text and as a critical analysis of the arguments for its existence and isolation from John. The second is that Smith provides a full discussion of the scholarly debate on the Signs Source and the Revelation Discourse up until 1965. Smith notes that, whereas scholars in general had been reticent to accept Bultmann's proposal of a pre-Johannine source for the Revelation Discourse, the Signs Source had commended itself to many. Robert Fortna's attempt to expand Bultmann's source in the direction of a mini-gospel is worked out in *The Gospel of Signs*. Fortna's reconstruction has not produced a strong following.

turning "sign" into a major motif for distinguishing between the miracles as miracles and the miracles as symbolically significant. Many scholars have proposed a sevenfold structure to the first twelve chapters of John, and some have made a list of the miracle stories that belong to the sevenfold structure. The suspicion is that the Signs Source originally contained seven miracles. Because the original set of stories was expanded somewhat in the course of composing and embellishing the gospel, scholars have proposed lists that differ in respect to one or two items. A number of complicated theories have been devised in order to include the post-resurrection miracle in chapter 21, for instance. The more conservative and less complicated listing is the most interesting. It includes the following:

FIGURE 13
THE SIGNS SOURCE IN JOHN

---

1. The wedding at Cana (2:1–11)
2. The official's son (4:46–54)
3. The lame at Bethesda (5:1–9)
4. Feeding the five thousand (6:1–14)
5. Walking on water (6:16–21)
6. Healing the blind man (9:1–34)
7. The resurrection of Lazarus (11:1–44)

Two stories draw attention to themselves as differing from the others. The wedding at Cana is different because the problem is hardly a matter of great importance when compared with the other miracle stories of Jesus. The point has to be derived from the symbolism of the story, a symbolism that sets allusions to Dionysus and his wine over against the Jewish rites of purification. Even the steward of the feast did not know that a miracle had taken place, the perception of Jesus' "glory" being reserved for the disciples and the reader. The story of Lazarus is so extravagant, so macabre in its humorous depiction of burial rites, and so obviously suggestive of Jesus' own resurrection to come, that it also appears to have been added when the idea occurred to treat Jesus' miracles as "signs," that is, symbolically significant deeds. With the first and last stories deleted, then, the set of miracle stories reduces just to five.

The five stories bear comparison with the pre-Markan chains. Overlooking the fact that the order is not the same, one sees that there is a sea crossing, a feeding of the multitude, and three healings. Two of the healings are similar in theme to stories in each of the pre-Markan sets. Persons with debilitating deformities are healed, in this case a lame man and a blind man. The other story, that of the official's son, has often been compared with the stories of the Syrophoenician's daughter (Mark 7:24b–30) and the Centurion's servant in Matt 8:5–13 (Luke 7:1–10). The parallels are suggestive. Both feature the healing of a Gentile. In the case of the Syrophoenician's daughter, the healing is an exorcism. That the official in John's story is a Gentile is not stated, but the designation *basilikos* makes it probable. If so, a set of five miracle stories following the pre-Markan pattern can be imagined for the earliest stage of storytelling in the Johannine tradition.

Three sets of stories on the same pattern invite scrutiny. The pattern relates in some way to themes reminiscent of Jewish epic and lore. Those themes suggest interest in the figure of Jesus as founder of a movement conceived on the model of Israel as a congregation in the making. If the outlines of a social history for such a movement can be determined, the function of the earliest miracle stories can be clarified. One might bear in mind that the fifteen stories under consideration form the bulk of all candidates for the earliest miracle stories in the Jesus traditions.

2.3 Miracles and Social History

The pattern of five stories replicates in miniature the story of the Exodus from the crossing of the sea to the formation of the congregation in the wilderness. Jewish imagination might have assumed that the congregation of Israel was already formed in Egypt and ready to go. Nevertheless, Passover was celebrated the last night before the crossing and provided rich imagery for the people (*laos*) to be gathered together just at that time. The wilderness way was also a time for the people to be tested and formed into a congregation. Haggadic traditions also abounded that would have made it possible to imagine the formation of the community after the crossing. The signs of the fully formed congregation were the divine guidance of the Shekinah, the provision of the daily "bread" (manna), and the organization of the people and its leaders under Moses. The bread, the organization of the people, and the leaders under "Moses" are alluded to in the feeding stories.[11]

---

11. *The congregation in the wilderness.* For a fine midrash (interpretive retelling) of the Exodus story and the wilderness way see the Wisdom of Solomon 11–19. Of interest is the fact that the miracles of the Exodus and the miracles of the wilderness way have been merged in the study of God's providence and testing as a paradigm for "all times and all places" (Wis 19:22). The critical moment of departure thus includes both the great light in the midst of the darkened night and mention of the pillar of fire to guide the way (Wis 17:20–18:4). It was at this moment that the holy ones "offered sacrifices, and with one accord agreed to the divine law, that the saints would share alike the same things, both blessings and dangers, and already they were singing the praises of the fathers" (Wis 18:9). Thus the congregation was imagined to have been formed at a moment impinged upon by the meaning of miracles taken both from the Exodus story and from the wilderness way. In Philo's *Life of Moses* the congregation is actually formed under Moses' leadership after the

The wilderness way was also a time for other miracles (quails, water from the rock, the serpent that saved, and many others including the recognition of Israel's right to the "king's way" by other kings and peoples along the route). In the case of the miracle chain, the miracles along the way visualize the gathering of unlikely people into the new congregation. This congregation did not make its crossing en masse, but one by one. The boundaries crossed were social boundaries. The motifs of testing, hesitation, courage, and faith highlight the seriousness and consequence of each venture. The unlikely mixture of peoples is given profile in the selection of individuals portrayed: a Gerasene, a Syrophoenician, an official, women, children, the blind, lame, deaf, and dumb. These are socially incongruous, socially marginal, and from the Jewish point of view generally "unclean" people, that is, in need of ritual purification or healing before (re)entering the "congregation" and participating fully in the daily round of activities. The selection of extreme cases (blind, lame, deaf, incurable hemorrhage, etc.) accentuates the point that the new congregation was not formed by attention to Jewish rituals, for these people are impossible cases and need something more. They are figures chosen to represent the unthinkable aspect of the new social arrangement, its difference from the prevailing models. Jesus heals and cleanses them (the point of the exorcisms of unclean spirits) without any precondition based on social status governed by the laws of purity. (Mark will make a point of that difference in Mark 1:44.) The miracles attest the formation of the new congregation as the congregation of Israel in spite of unconventionality by imagining a new set of miracles on the wilderness way. The feeding of the multitude by companies, then, takes place away from home, in a lonely place, on the other side of the sea (Mark 8:2–3; 6:35; John 6:1–3), that is, on the other side of the social boundaries that had been crossed.

Jesus, the founder and leader of the new movement, is like Moses (as leader) and like Elijah (as restorer). Likeness is not identity, however. The difference between Jesus and his prototypes is as great as the difference between the new congregation and the old. The Jesus movement is fully conscious of its novelty. Those without any claim to membership in Israel are nevertheless included. It is not really "Israel" that is being renewed or restored. Jesus does not stand in the office of Moses as a "new Moses." He does not perform a prophetic critique of Jewish institutions from within as a call to repentance or reform. He marches under his own banner without polemic, effecting those changes in people that had to be made if the new congregation was to form. Jesus is the founder of the new society, and the set of stories is its myth of origins.

---

crossing of the sea. See *De vita Mosis* 1:158–59. For a discussion see B. Mack, "Imitatio Mosis."

The model for imagining the formation of a congregation would have been available in Galilee. Galilean provenance for the stories suggests that the social formation celebrated in the myth took place in Galilee or its immediate environment. In Galilee, social formation of this kind could have continued the table fellowship with Jesus in a relatively conducive atmosphere. The stories do not contain a hint of institutional conflict. There is no sense of hostility against representatives of the "old" Israel. The set of stories marks the differences between the new congregation and traditional views of Israel, not as apology or polemic, but merely as definitional. The idea of ritual purity is used, for instance, to make a positive point about the distinctiveness of the new group that is not based on such prerequisite, not to counter charges of illegitimacy or raise the question of conflict between Jesus' authority and the authority of the law. The choice to imagine what was happening on the model of the Exodus story was natural, given the Galilean climate. The model was taken from the epic and haggadic readings of the scriptures, perhaps even at the level of local lore, not from the conceptualized model of Israel as a temple state based on cultic law. The exodus, that is, was not at first understood to be an exodus from Judaism.

3. MIRACLES IN THE JOHANNINE TRADITION

In the Johannine tradition, the myth of the congregation of Israel was reworked several times, each time making more explicit the contrast between the new movement and the old. Institutional conflict, hostility, and outright polemic eventually entered into the picture. There is some question whether the reworking of the myth took place within the same movement responsible for the first set of stories, a movement whose own social history would then be reflected in the changes, or whether the myth traveled to find a new home among Jesus people in other circumstances. One does have to imagine a parting of the ways at some point, perhaps about Mark's time, in order to account for the different treatments this myth received in Mark and in the Johannine tradition.

It will be helpful to outline the stages of interpretation in the Johannine tradition, for each of the earlier stages throws some light back upon the significance of the original set of stories. Interpretation in the Johannine tradition will also provide a helpful control for evaluating Mark's own particular interest in the stories. Control by means of comparing John and Mark cannot be firm, to be sure, for the relation between the two texts and their pre-histories is disputed. It would be plausible, however, to imagine that the miracle stories were more at home in the Johannine community where they were cultivated and resignified several times in a continuous social history stemming from the "congregation of Israel." Mark, then, would have been the one to have borrowed stories from this movement before it took that turn which set it on the Johannine course. If the authors in the Johannine community were aware of the Gospel of Mark, a possibility remarked upon in recent scholarship, many features of the Gospel of John where it is clearly distinct from Mark could be explained as intentional. Conversely, Markan peculiarities in the signification of the miracle stories might be discerned simply by their absence in John. The comparison is worth the effort in any case, for the Gospel of John, though later than Mark, demonstrates that the miracle stories were capable of sustaining a community's myth of origins through several stages of elaboration. The elaborations attest that the conception of social formation fundamental to the Johannine community was indeed that of the Exodus.[12]

3.1 The Stages of Resignification

Three distinctly different significations of the miracle stories in John can be isolated: (1) the embellishment of the miracle stories to reflect a conflict with Judaism; (2) the designation of the miracles as "signs"; and (3) the use of the stories to manifest Jesus' "glory" and provide the occasions for his revelation discourses. The discourses treat the "signs" as symbols of the manifestation of a fully mythic revealer who entered into the world to shed light upon its darkness and bring life to those willing to be transformed. These three employments can be arranged in sequential order as junctures in a social history that follows the general pattern outlined in chapter 5. An extremely complex literary history will be violated somewhat by this simple proposal of three stages in the resignification of the miracle stories. It agrees

---

12. *Mark and John.* The literary relationship between the two gospels has been very difficult to determine because of striking differences in style, form, and content. There is overlap, however, and in the case of the two passion narratives, the similarities have always caught scholarly attention. A recent set of studies on *The Passion in Mark,* edited by W. Kelber, touched upon the problem at several points. The conclusions drawn by the several scholars involved were that John did know Mark, but that he did not slavishly "depend upon" Mark. Kelber noticed the consistency with which this judgment surfaced in the articles, and in his concluding essay he provided an additional bibliography of scholars who have argued for a relationship between the gospels (p. 159, n. 4). One would hardly expect a "slavish dependence" upon precursors where authorial intention is in evidence. A very wide range of writing activity must be imagined for the time in both Jewish and early Christian circles. Writing activity ranged from making copies of texts, to various modes of interpretive rearrangements, to outright compositions of materials in various degrees of remove from texts and genres that may have served as precursors. The John-Mark question should not be engaged at the level of scribal activity, if by scribal is meant copying. Obviously, the Johannine community drew upon other texts, markedly reworked material originally shared with other Jesus groups, and produced material of its own. The critical issue concerns the plot common to both Mark and John. It consists of a link, fundamental to the narrative design, between the miracles of Jesus and the decision of the Jewish leaders to have him crucified. Since the link is forged externally to the miracle stories included in the chains, John's use of just this narrative design apart from knowledge of Mark would constitute a coincidence of fantastic proportions.

in general with more elaborate theories on the formation of John's Gospel, however, and can be very useful for the determination of social issues addressed by this literature in the course of its evolution.[13]

At some point in the history of the Johannine community there was a conflict with Judaism. This conflict was written into the miracle stories just as the synagogue reform movement had written its experiences into the pronouncement stories. The two clearest examples of miracles as the occasion for conflict are the story of the lame man at Bethzatha and the healing of the blind man. They are the only stories of the three chains of stories that take place in Jerusalem, indicating most probably that the setting is new and intentional. Each of the stories is embellished differently, but in both cases the recasting is distinct from the original story.

The story of the lame man (John 5:1–18) is given much as it might have read in the original chain of stories set in Galilee (perhaps at Bethsaida instead of Bethzatha). The story concludes, however, with the information that "that day was the sabbath" (John 5:9c). Because it happened in Jerusalem on the sabbath, "the Jews" can then be introduced to raise an objection. They object to the man that he should not be carrying his pallet on the sabbath. This develops into a conflict over Jesus and his authority to have told the man to carry his pallet (1), at the end of which the statement is made that "this is why the Jews persecuted Jesus, because he did this on the sabbath" (John 5:16). To this point the story functions as do the controversy-miracle stories in Mark 2:1–3:6. There is no indication that Jesus is the revealer, nor need there be. The symbolic significance of the miracle is indicated in the very next verse, however (3). Jesus "answered" them, "My Father is working still, and I am working" (John 5:17). Before the narrator lets Jesus proceed with a revelation discourse on the topic of "working" the "works" of his Father (a wisdom theology of continuous "creation" used to imagine the new "life" created by Jesus' appearance), he adds the comment, "This was why the Jews sought all the more to kill him, because he not only broke the sabbath, but also called God his Father, making himself equal with God" (John 5:17–18). The twofold rationale clearly reflects two stages in the reworking of the story. Each was simply tacked on to the story, the first addition occasioned by controversy over sabbath observance, the second reflecting a much later time when the community had developed its own private discourse and mythology.

More interesting is the way in which the story of the blind man was retold (John 9:1–34). Two layers of reinterpretation can still be distinguished, but in this case, the symbolism of the revealer (3) was placed at the

---

13. *The Johannine trajectory.* An introduction to the problem of tracing the history of the Johannine community and its literature is available in J. M. Robinson, "The Johannine Trajectory"; and Raymond E. Brown, *The Community of the Beloved Disciple.*

beginning in order to enhance the significance of the healing as Jesus' work of bringing "light" into the world (John 9:3–5). Then follows the miracle story, after which a sabbath controversy with the Pharisees ensues (1). The controversy is fully developed as a dramatic dialogue and ends with the blind man's confession which results in his being cast out of the synagogue.

3.2 Miracles and Conflict

Conflict with Judaism was a chapter in the social history of the Johannine community. The issues do not appear to have been as pointed as those experienced by the synagogue reform movement. Rejection of claims to Jesus' authority seems to have forced a hermeneutical conflict over the scriptures rather than debates about the full range of codes related to the laws of ritual purity. Interest in Jerusalem and the cycle of feasts and festivals means that the community came to see itself over against a more generalized picture of Judaism. At the later stages of the composition of the gospel, Jesus is portrayed as substituting a spiritual presence for every Jewish practice. But Pharisees and scribes were in the picture as opponents, and that probably represents firsthand experience with Jewish leaders outside of Judea. Some contact with the synagogue or acquaintance with the synagogue reform movement surely lies behind the story of the blind man and much other material in the gospel dealing with scribal interpretation and authority. However the conflict was engaged, that chapter of social history ended by being "cast out," just as the history of the synagogue reform movement had ended.[14]

The experience of conflict and separation was retained in the memory of the Johannine community, but not as a discrete phase of its experimentation with social formation, a chapter of the past over and done with. Written into the myth of origins, conflict with the synagogue and being "cast out" became part of the community's rationale for separate existence. The sense of being right was worked out in contrast to those who were wrong. The distinction between Judaism and the Jesus movement became definitional for the Jesus movement as the true congregation. The borders crossed to form the new congregation were now defined as those between Judaism and the true formation. The transition was imagined as eventful, born of conflict, with hostility, rejection and violence nipping from behind, and transformation to a new life waiting on the other side of the crossing. The event of origination for the new order was the transformation of the old into the new. The miracle stories could be reread from that point of view.

---

14. *Conflict with the synagogue.* The major study of conflict with the synagogue in the history of the Johannine community is by J. Louis Martyn, *History and Theology in the Fourth Gospel.*

3.3 The Miracles as Signs

Calling the miracles "signs" (2) and adding the stories of the wedding at Cana and the raising of Lazarus probably happened at the same time. The wedding at Cana, at any rate, came to be called the "first sign" and, if the collection of seven had a separate existence in some form, bracketing the chain of five with two new miracles would have been one way to achieve a resignification of the set as a whole. The term *sēmeion* (sign) has normally been taken to refer to the miracles as miracles. It is a term that was used of miracles as "signs" of the divine power manifest by them. But *sēmeion* was not a term limited to miracles, nor was it the standard technical term for designating miracles. It meant sign in the sense of a mark, trace, or indicator of something else intended. If the term is taken in this sense, two very interesting possibilities are given for the significance attributed to these miracles.

One is that their function as allusions to the (new) Exodus was brought to expression in this way. This possibility can be supported by the use of the term in Greek-language Jewish literature of the period including the Greek translation of the Hebrew scriptures (LXX, Septuagint). Raymond Brown has shown that *sēmeia* (in the plural) was used particularly of miracles associated with the Exodus tradition. The double formulation "signs and wonders" frequently occurs as a reference in miniature to the Exodus event as a divine occurrence. Because *sēmeion* carried this connotation, a remarkable attestation of the significance implicit in the original miracle chain is given.[15]

The addition of the wedding at Cana and the raising of Lazarus show, however, that even more may have been intended. The exodus from Judaism has been accomplished and the new miracles are signs of its distinctly Christian character in contrast to the old. The old order from which the exodus took place is no longer left unspecified. The six stone jars "were standing there for the Jewish rites of purification." Jesus turns their water into new wine. The Jews have come to console Martha and Mary for the loss of their brother. Jesus brings the dead man out and commands that they "unbind him and let him go." A wedding at the beginning of the series and a burial at the end make a nice period of ritual occasions left behind. In their place are the new wine and life of the highly self-conscious community of Jesus.

Regarded as signs, that is, significant miracles marking the emergence of the new order from the old (2), each of the miracle stories could now be

---

15. *Signs and wonders.* Raymond Brown, *The Gospel According to John* I–XII, 525–31, provides a collection of references to "signs" and "signs and wonders" in early Jewish and Christian literatures, together with a fine discussion of the usage of the term "sign" in John.

explored as encoded (3). Decoding was possible by developing the controversy dialogue between Jesus and his opponents to draw out the symbolism. Wine signifies the new Spirit (in the dialogue with Nicodemus which follows upon the miracle of the wedding as its explication); sight becomes Light, bread indicates the True Bread from heaven that Jesus is, life restored to Lazarus is a sign of the Life Jesus gives, and so forth. This is a late stage of reworking. The Johannine community had learned about the meaning of the death and resurrection of Jesus, either from the Hellenistic Christ cult or from Markan circles. A complete redeemer-revealer myth had been imagined by using wisdom mythology to connect the significance of the miracles with the death and ascension destiny pattern of the Christ myth. There was now a private language of discourse, a fund of local knowledge, a fully developed ethic ideal of reciprocity for inner community application, and hermeneutical principles in place. There is some evidence as well of peculiar ritual and liturgical practice. According to the myth, the miracle worker now knows who he is, what the miracles mean, and what will happen to him because he does them. He is the prophet-king like Moses on the one hand; he is a god passing through on the other, bringing light to the world by inverting all valencies. The miracles are all signs of the one big miracle of his own crossing from death (at the hands of the world, the Jews) to life eternal. Irony abounds, and the little band has learned to look for life through death at every turn, in every human encounter. Alas, it is hermetically sealed off from the wicked world without, a gnostic sect withdrawn within in order to define the life that came with exodus.[16]

The tragedy of this social history is that the community could not extricate itself from the trauma of separation from Judaism. The rationalizations all emphasized the opposition between Judaism and Christianity as part of the self-definition. Written into the myth of origins based upon the idea of Exodus and imagined as miracle, the opposition dramatized the event by defining it as a conflictual moment. Assimilation to the Christ myth meant that the creation of light and life was radicalized as a passage from death to life. Death was the sign of the old order. The gospel that introduced the leader of the new Exodus into the world, a leader full of grace and truth, also marked the world for judgment because it lay in darkness. The plot of the gospel shows that the traumatic experience long past was not resolved by the visions of transformation. The plot now casts the Jews as the agents of the darkened world. Light, life, and love only come through the miracle of a crucifixion to a community behind closed doors. The miracles mark a transition from determination by the "world"

16. *Myth and symbol in John.* The major studies have been: C. H. Dodd, *The Interpretation of the Fourth Gospel;* R. Bultmann, *The Gospel of John;* W. A. Meeks, *The Prophet-King;* and "The Man from Heaven"; and E. Käsemann, *The Testament of Jesus.* On the use of irony see Paul Duke, *Irony in the Fourth Gospel.*

(Judaism, darkness, literality, the mundane) imagined as hostile and demonic, to an ethos generated by desire for transformation and transcendence. The new congregation made possible by the miraculous would be a cultivation of otherworldliness.

4. MIRACLES IN MARK

Mark used two sets of miracle chains in the composition of his gospel, plus seven more miracle stories. Miracles were obviously of great interest to Mark and the way he positioned them in his story indicates purpose. Fifteen miracle stories comprise one-half of the narrative material about the Galilean phase of Jesus' activity. The impression this creates is overwhelming. The reasons Mark wished to create this impression can be inferred by paying attention to miracles as a narrative theme.

4.1 Miracles as Theme

There are several indications that Mark was aware of the function of the miracle chains as myths of origin for the congregation of Israel. One of these is the use he makes of the miracles as the occasions for the crowds to gather. The image of the crowds gathering to and around Jesus is a Markan creation, for they are mentioned for the most part around the edges of the stories and fill in the background against which all of the foreground events of the gospel take place. The crowds come to Jesus because of the miracles he performs. The performance of a miracle results in the spreading of reports about Jesus (Mark 1:28). The crowds gather and he heals their sick (Mark 1:32–34, 45; and often). Some of the miracle stories are used to accentuate the function of the miracles in spreading the word about Jesus (for instance, the Gerasene demoniac); others describe the "press" of the crowds around Jesus. The press of the crowds is so great that some people in need have trouble getting through to Jesus (for instance the paralytic, Mark 2:1–12; and the woman with a hemorrhage). The crowds function in Mark's Gospel as the multitude functioned in the miracle chain. And yet, the crowds do not form a congregation.

The crowds at first think that Jesus is a prophet come to restore Israel (Mark 6:14–15; 8:27–28). They are on the right track, but have missed something. Mark helps the reader see that it would have been more accurate to have concluded that Jesus was the Messiah, come to reign as king over Israel. He does this by contrasting the view of the crowds with the confession of Peter (Mark 8:29). The reader is not told how the crowds come to their senses, yet they do. It may have been because of the march from Caesarea Philippi to Jerusalem, the city of the kings. As Jesus approaches the city, at any rate, riding upon the mysteriously acquired colt, the people are there to cry, "Hosanna! Blessed be he who comes in the name of the Lord! Blessed be the kingdom of our father David that is coming! Hosanna in the highest" (Mark 11:9–10). Now they have it right, almost. Jesus is the king of the Jews, according to Mark, and will be crucified as such. But that presents a problem. Jesus will not automatically assume his rightful office, for there are other kings and priests in place who will not allow it. The crowds have received him, but they have not understood about the problem and are not capable of "following" Jesus to the end. At the trial they fall under the influence of those in power and end up against what Jesus is for, crying out to have him crucified (Mark 15:8–14). The miracles do not result any longer in the formation of the congregation of Israel. According to Mark, the crowds did not want to relinquish the established state of affairs.

Perhaps, then, those that stepped out from the crowd will join with Jesus to form the new congregation. The woman with a hemorrhage steps out, and the blind Bartimaeus steps out (Mark 10:46–52). Unfortunately for this view, miracles do not result in a collection of followers distinguished from the crowds. All of those touched by Jesus' miracles vanish after the episode, subsumed again by the crowds. Neither are miracles the way in which disciples are called. The disciples are called by words after the announcement of the kingdom and before the first miracle is performed (Mark 1:16–20). Disciples do figure in the miracle chains, however, and Mark used the motif of miracles and the disciples to great advantage. Thus a second narrative theme was derived from the miracle myth of origins. But this theme also merely used the miracle stories to make a Markan point. The point was not about the formation of the congregation of Israel in Jesus' time.

In the miracle chains, disciples figured in the sea crossings and the feeding stories as leaders of the congregation. Mark took note and developed the theme of disciples as understudies of Jesus. He introduced them into other settings and some of the stories as observers and questioners (Mark 5:37, Jairus' daughter; Mark 5:31, woman with a hemorrhage). When "the twelve" were "appointed" it was for the purpose of preaching and casting out demons, that is, doing exactly what Jesus was doing (Mark 3:14–15). When they were sent out, it was to preach and to cast out demons (Mark 6:7–13). One might think that since they received such attention from the master, those called to be leaders of the congregation would understand. But the miracles were too much for the disciples as well. On the first sea crossing they are afraid and Jesus chides them for not having faith (Mark 4:40). On the second sea crossing they are terrified even though Jesus has already shown them how to multiply the loaves. Mark explains that their hearts were too hard (Mark 6:52). By using two miracle chains Mark could show just how dense the disciples were. Even after a repeat performance they do not have the foggiest notion about the meaning of the meals (Mark 8:17–18). How could they, when the "broken pieces" hinted at a later meal to be held in anticipation of Jesus' death, a meal meant to remind them to beware of the "leaven of the Pharisees and the leaven of Herod" (Mark 8:15)? As with the parables, the disciples are privy to private instruction, but it does no good.

A glance at Achtemeier's reconstruction of the two miracle chains (figure 12) shows that Mark made one major change in the sequence of the stories. In the second chain he removed the story of the healing of the blind man from its position in second place, and put it after the feeding story. One can now see why Mark did that. It was the story most appropriate to carry the theme of the blindness of the disciples into the next major section of the gospel. It set up a contrast by making the point that Jesus' miracles should help people "see." Mark placed it immediately after the discussion about the broken bread and the leaven, and immediately before the turn in the story known as Peter's "confession" (Mark 8:27–30). The turn in the story is indicated by the switch from parables to "plain" instruction, the announcement of the destiny of the Son of Man in Jerusalem, and the beginning of the march toward Jerusalem (Mark 8:31–34). It is this section that contains the "discipleship sayings." The would-be leaders are to learn that the first must become last, and so forth. Now the disciples are in serious trouble, because the instruction is put forth plainly. They squirm. Peter will simply not accept it and proposes instead that shrines be erected already (Mark 8:32; 9:5). James and John are ready for the cup, but think it means ready access to positions of power in the kingdom. They want those positions of power (Mark 10:35–40). The others are repeatedly amazed, afraid, or indignant as they accompany Jesus on the way.

Only two more miracles are performed after Caesarea Philippi. They were used to heighten the tensions created by this section of the story. The first is the exorcism of the unclean spirit from the deaf and dumb boy. Mark placed it after the private instruction to Peter, James and John about Jesus' true nature and destiny (transfiguration, resurrection, Mark 9:2–13). The point of the miracle story is that the disciples left behind were still trying their hands at casting out demons, but failed. This was especially embarrassing, because the scribes were looking into the matter. Jesus casts the unclean spirit out in order to set the contrast, but it is clear that the time for exorcisms is past. This story, Achtemeier thought, was a combination of two stories derived from historical reminiscence. A more reasonable view would be that the story is contrived, made up of clichés accented by exaggeration and accentuating the impossible, implausible, and unbelievable. There is no reason not to think that Mark constructed it just for this purpose on the model of the exorcisms in the miracle chains. That was to underscore the helplessness of the disciples when confronted with the impossible task of setting the world right without realizing just how intransigent the forces of opposition were.

The other miracle that appears out of place in this phase of the story is the healing of the blind Bartimaeus as the crowd comes along for the triumphal entry to Jerusalem (Mark 10:46–52). This story also is best understood as Mark's composition. It lacks many of the formal features of miracle stories (such as a description of the problem and a description of the means by which the miracle was performed), yet it clearly forms a doublet with the healing of the blind man at the beginning of the journey to Jerusalem. Many scholars have remarked on this, the consensus being that the two stories were intended to bracket the section on the way to Jerusalem with sight miracles in contrast to the blindness of the disciples. The consensus is undoubtedly correct, for the conclusion of the story has it that "he received his sight and followed him on the way" (Mark 10:52), as if to remind the reader that the discipleship theme of "following" should not be forgotten just because the disciples were doing such a poor job of it.

Markan purpose for the story of blind Bartimaeus is also apparent in the presence of a number of other themes. The story starts when the blind man hears that it was Jesus of Nazareth who was approaching. The reader has not heard mention of that name since the baptism (Mark 1:9) and the demon's recognition of Jesus in the synagogue at Capernaum (Mark 1:24). That was the occasion for Jesus' first deed in Galilee. The demon cried out, "What have you to do with us, Jesus of Nazareth? Have you come to destroy us?" Now on his entry into Jerusalem, Jesus is recognized by the blind man. Jesus' first deeds upon entry will be to curse (and destroy) the fig tree, and to cleanse the temple (Mark 11:12–18). When the blind man cries out, he twice calls Jesus the "Son of David." The reader will not recall any mention of Jesus as the Son of David, but will recall that the gospel is about Jesus Christ (Mark 1:1), and that Peter had concluded as much from the miracles when asked at Caesarea Philippi. Thus the blind man's "sight" reminds the reader about miracles and the Messiah-king even as it prepares the reader for the triumphal entry to follow. Alas, the blind man gets lost in the crowd even as Jesus' messianic entrance will only result in his death.

Twelve of the seventeen miracle stories in Mark have been touched upon as vehicles for two themes derived from the miracle chains. In neither case have the miracles of Jesus achieved results comparable to their original intention. The crowds do not form a congregation and the disciples do not learn how to be leaders. The spotlight falls on Jesus. Perhaps the miracles are meant mainly to reflect on the leader's authority.

4.2 The Authority of Jesus

Jesus' first miracle takes place in the synagogue at Capernaum (Mark 1:21–28). His entrance into the synagogue is also the first occasion for teaching. The people are astonished at his teaching, "for he taught them as one who had authority, and not as the scribes" (Mark 1:22). The response comes from a man with an unclean spirit who recognizes that Jesus is "the

Holy One of God" who has "come to destroy us." Jesus casts out the unclean spirit and the people say, "What is this? A new teaching! With authority he commands even the unclean spirits, and they obey him" (Mark 1:27). The term authority is used twice, once for Jesus' teaching, once for his power over the unclean spirit. Both forms of authority are combined in the phrase "a new teaching." The new teaching is not a matter of instruction (for the content of Jesus' teaching is not given). It is a matter of power. The term used is *exousia,* the kind of authority magistrates have to decide and execute matters. Mark used an exorcism to introduce the man of authority and power.

Mark's choice of an exorcism to define Jesus' power was intentional. The sequence of the events immediately following is: (1) Jesus' fame spreads because of the new teaching (Mark 1:28). (2) While that is happening, Jesus goes to a disciple's house and performs another miracle, this time a healing (Mark 1:29–31). (3) That evening, however, the people show up with both their sick and those possessed of demons. Jesus heals the sick and casts out the demons (Mark 1:32–34). (4) In the morning everyone is searching for Jesus, but he explains that it is time now to go through the towns of Galilee on a preaching mission. Mark's summary statement at this point must be taken very seriously: "And he went throughout all Galilee, preaching in their synagogues and casting out demons" (Mark 1:39). What happened in the synagogue at Capernaum set the program. The unclean spirits are emphasized again in another summary statement about Jesus' activity in Mark 3:7–12. Preaching and casting out demons is what the disciples are appointed to do. The word authority is used in respect to the exorcisms (Mark 3:14–15). When the disciples are sent out, it is again to preach and to have authority over the unclean spirits (Mark 6:7). From among the several types of miracles reported of Jesus in the miracle chains, Mark chose exorcisms to develop the theme of Jesus' authority. The question is why.

Exorcisms have to do with unclean spirits. Jesus' authority over the unclean spirits demonstrates that his power is extraordinary. It is, in fact, divine. After the first round of Jesus' activity the question of the source of Jesus' power is raised by his friends at home, who think him crazy, and by the scribes, who say that he is possessed by Beelzebul, the prince of demons. Jesus responds by arguing that Satan cannot cast out Satan, for a kingdom divided against itself cannot stand. Then he warns them against blasphemy against the Holy Spirit (Mark 3:20–30). The reader will know what to make of it. Jesus' authority derives from the Holy Spirit. Suddenly the significance of the baptism snaps into place. A prophet's attempt to wash away Israel's sins with water gave way in the case of Jesus to another medium. Not only does the Spirit descend upon Jesus in the baptism, God attests that he is his Son. He is now ready to "baptize" with the Holy Spirit, that is, to rid the land of unclean spirits. Jesus' authority over the unclean spirits is derived from God. Unclean spirits and Holy Spirit make a pair in opposition.

In the synagogue at Capernaum Jesus demonstrates this authority by casting out an unclean spirit. The people, however, call this demonstration a new teaching. The combination is bizarre. One normally distinguishes between the kind of authority teachers have and the kind that belongs to men of power. Scholars have never been able to accommodate Jesus the miracle worker and Jesus the teacher in a single configuration that makes sense. That has not hindered many from taking delight in the announcement that Jesus' teaching was "not as the scribes," of course. Many meditations have been devoted to the exploration of this difference as if it signaled a profundity. One needs to be cautious, however, because the difference hangs on the word authority, the same word used for Jesus' power over the unclean spirits. The combination is very strange. If Mark had not made a point of it, no one ever would have dared imagine such a thing. But what is that point?

The point begins to come clear when it is seen that Mark's portrayal of Jesus in general was achieved by combining miracle stories with pronouncement stories. The large bulk of narrative material through chapter 12 consists of both kinds of stories one after the other. The function of both kinds of stories in their traditions prior to Mark, however, was precisely to claim the authority of Jesus as founder for the Jesus movements. Mark's genius was to understand that and find a way to combine the two images of Jesus just at the point that mattered most. Jesus the teacher was the same as Jesus the miracle worker because his authority to perform miracles was the same as his authority to teach, according to Mark. The combination is announced in the first story and illustrated by his authority to command the unclean spirits. They obey him. The combination occurs again in the chain of five controversy stories (Mark 2:1–3:6). Two of the stories report miracles; three are pronouncement stories. The first is literally a combination of a pronouncement story and a miracle story. It is the controversy-miracle story about the paralytic, the story of the first event when Jesus returns home to Capernaum after his mission throughout Galilee. It follows, therefore, directly on his first appearance in the synagogue at Capernaum. It is also about authority.

The story of the paralytic (Mark 2:1–12) begins as a miracle story. Jesus is at home surrounded by so many that those bringing the paralytic to be healed cannot enter. When they remove a portion of the roof and lower the paralytic to the presence of Jesus, instead of performing as a healer, Jesus pronounces that the paralytic's sins are forgiven. The scribes think to themselves that this is blasphemy because only God can forgive sins. This turns the scene into a controversy and Jesus responds with a chreia, "Which is easier, to say . . . 'Your sins are forgiven,' or to say, 'Rise, take up your pallet and walk?'" Not waiting for an answer to this impossible choice, Jesus continues, "But that you (scribes) may know that the Son of Man has authority on earth to forgive sins . . . I say to you (paralytic), rise, take up your pallet and go home." When the paralytic does that, all are amazed. The reader also may be amazed. According to Mark, Jesus speaks for God. What he says happens.

Joanna Dewey has shown that the story of the paralytic was very carefully composed. The combination of controversy story and miracle story was crafted in such a way that the two cannot be separated. The intention is clear. Jesus' pronouncements are as effective as his miracles. As if the narrative itself did not make that obvious, Mark used the authoritative pronouncement of the elaboration pattern as the place to have Jesus command the cure and pronounce on his own authority in a single saying. Jesus uses the word *exousia*. He has *exousia*, pronounces authoritatively that he has it, and proves it by performing the miracle. Mark was not at all bothered by the fact that the authoritative pronouncements in all of the pronouncement stories were self-referential, the product of an elaboration that derived all of its sayings from the same source, not amenable to dialogue, question, or accountability. He saw that feature in the pronouncement stories and turned it to good advantage. Jesus' "teachings" were not teaching. They were authoritative pronouncements. The authority of pronouncement was no different than the authority to command. Mark put the two authorities together at the level of absolute determination. What Jesus says will be. What Jesus commands will be obeyed.

The combination of pronouncement story and miracle story, teaching and power, was made possible in part by the evolvement of the elaborated pronouncement story and its attribution of a peculiarly self-referential authority to Jesus. The combination of types may also have been thinkable because of the combination of prototypes for Jesus in the miracle chains. The miracle chains recalled Moses and Elijah, a teacher and a prophet. Thus the imagination of Jesus as the founder of the congregation of Israel already combined implicitly the two forms of authority. Both Moses and Elijah were quasi-mythological figures in the haggadic lore used to create the miracle myth for Jesus. For Jesus to walk on water and multiply the loaves was, therefore, already a sign of his divine powers. Anyone interested in drawing out the implications of that kind of power for the question of Jesus' authority would have been able to do so by putting together ideas given with the combination of prototype figures in the myth. There would have been no need to have knowledge of the Christ myth and the spiritual transformation of the resurrection, for instance. By upgrading the mythological aspects of the miracle myth of origins, Mark easily could have merged teaching with authority, prophetic pronouncement, and effective performance in the execution of miracles.

From this point of view the choice of a baptism by John to introduce the man of power is very interesting. John was cast in the role of a prophet, an interpretation in retrospect of the same kind as early Christian reimaginations of Jesus. Prophets and spirit go together, for prophets speak by the spirit of God. And John was not just any prophet. He is depicted in the role of Elijah. The crowds wondered whether Jesus was not Elijah. Herod wondered whether Jesus was not John returned from the dead. That is where they were wrong. Jesus explains to the disciples that Elijah (John) has already come (Mark 9:9–13). If in Mark's scheme of things the role of the prophet Elijah was fulfilled by John, one wonders what he had in mind for Jesus. According to the miracle chain, Jesus could be thought of both as an Elijah as well as a Moses.

Wayne Meeks has shown that Moses was regarded as the "prophet-king" in Samaritan and Hellenistic-Jewish haggadic traditions of the time. He was interested in just this combination of roles attributed to Jesus in the Gospel of John. He concluded that in the Johannine tradition, Jesus was imagined on analogy to Moses as the prophet-king. A remarkable mythology of divine knowledge and power explicated this configuration of roles. To have moved from the characterization of Jesus in the miracle chain to another level of mythological reflection about Jesus' divine nature and power would have been quite possible in the atmosphere of such haggadic lore. Mark already made that move. In the transfiguration story Jesus is manifest as a divine being and appears in the presence of Elijah and Moses, just those prototypes imagined for Jesus in the miracle chain. The story is told, however, not to underscore the similarity, but to mark the difference. The difference is that Jesus is more than the prophet-king. He is the Son of God.

It may not be possible to work out all of the distinctions between roles, functions, sequences, and levels of divine status that Mark imagined within this cluster of characterizations. But his desire to draw upon the similarities while claiming for Jesus a superior status is obvious. In order to do so he upgraded roles and functions by selecting nuances that could bring teaching and power together in a single conception of authority. The conception was that of the Son of God, a royal status, whose word was the world's command.

The mythology of the Son of God was widely known during the time, with roots in ancient Near Eastern cultures, but imaginable in a variety of conceptualities. Philo of Alexandria, for instance, imagined Moses as the divine Word of God, a personified figure in second place of authority in the cosmic orders of creation and governance, a "second God," God's Son. So there is no need even at this level of titulature to think that Mark must have borrowed the idea from the Christ cult. He was capable of manipulating mythological figures for his own purposes merely by (re)imagining them.

The introduction of the figure of the Son of Man into the controversy-miracle story is proof of this mode of mythologization. The Son of Man was an apocalyptic figure whose role was imagined as the royal judge at the end of time and whose decisions would be final on the question of rewards and punishments. To imagine that Jesus was the Son of Man who had authority to forgive sins was a stupendous manipulation of imagery. But it can be understood without appeal to the normal scholarly opinion about "christology" explicating an implicit meaning to the event of Jesus' resurrection. It can be understood as Mark's desire to claim for Jesus absolute authority.[17]

Mark's use of titles, roles, and mythologies to enhance the importance of Jesus is a novelty in the Jesus traditions. Unless one takes this development merely as speculation, the entertainment of flights of fantasy for their own reward, it reveals the pressures upon Mark for another rationalization of a new set of social circumstances. Before going on to explore those social circumstances more fully, two observations can be made about the level of mythologization Mark achieved. One is that, at this level of mythological characterization, linkage with the mythologies of the Hellenistic Christ cult was possible. Mark made that connection, as the next chapters will show. The other is that, in the effort to enhance Jesus' authority in this way, Mark showed preference for royal power over priestly-teaching forms of status. The importance of the study on the temple-state model in chapter 1 now begins to surface. Inner Jewish movements developed leadership roles on the priestly model, not on the model of royal power. Priestly functions were teaching functions. Authority was located in texts such as wisdom texts, epic texts, legal texts. The teacher's authority was that of interpreter, thinker, lawyer. The roles were those of the scribe, the sage, the Pharisee, all to congeal in the rabbi. Mark chose the other option, to follow the lead of the pronouncement stories and locate authority in the author of speech that did not interpret, but pronounced judgments. Royal mythology was therefore preferred. The teacher is the royal Son of God. "Listen to him!" (Mark 9:7). No wonder there is no content given for Jesus' teaching in the synagogue.

4.3 Miracles and Conflict

The myth created by the chain of miracles had as a subtheme the motif of cleansing. The people healed were unclean. Jesus' miracles made them

---

17. *Title and roles.* For the most recent study of Mark's "christology" see J. D. Kingsbury, *The Christology of Mark's Gospel.* It presents a discussion of the titles. The essays in Kelber, *The Passion in Mark,* also demonstrate the importance of the titles and the christological themes for deciphering Mark's narrative schemes. The study referred to by Wayne Meeks is *The Prophet-King.* The relation of the christological titles to the narrative designs in Mark will be explored more fully in chap. 10.

clean by inducting them into the congregation of "Israel," a congregation without need, therefore, for the laws of ritual purity. Mark chose the miracle of exorcism to develop the theme of Jesus' authority. Exorcisms were extreme cases of cleansing, however, so that Jesus' authority was illustrated just in terms of his power to cast out demons. The problem of clean/unclean was also the major issue for the synagogue reform movement, written into the pronouncement stories it had produced. The combination of concerns resulted in a major narrative theme for Mark's story of Jesus.

Jesus' entrance into Galilee was imagined as a crusade to cleanse the land of unclean spirits and revoke the laws of ritual purity. The theme is developed programmatically in the first eight stories. Five of these stories are miracle stories, the five Mark added to the ten in the miracle chains. All of the five can easily be explained as Mark's own fictions. Each has a very definite function in the development of the narrative theme. The first eight stories describe the sequence given in figure 14. All stories address the issue of clean/unclean. There are three interwoven periods. (1) Activity in the synagogue at Capernaum on the sabbath begins and closes the cycle as a whole. (2) Activity starting at Capernaum moves out to sweep through Galilee, then returns to Capernaum. (3) After the return, the sequence from Jesus' home, to the house of a disciple, to the fields, to the synagogue, forms a cycle similar to that of the first four stories, except that the difference between Jesus' home and the synagogue, both in Capernaum, disturbs the symmetry. Within these periods certain combinations of types of miracle with types of persons and different locations are significant. There is also a development of the theme of Jesus' authority and an escalation of the conflicts that result.

Conflict was announced immediately after Jesus' baptism. The Spirit

FIGURE 14
THE STRUCTURE OF MARK 1:21–3:6

1. An exorcism on the *sabbath* in the *synagogue at Capernaum* (1:21–28)
2. A healing in the house of the disciples (1:29–31)
3. Summary: Healings and exorcisms for the whole city (1:32–34)
   Departure for the mission throughout all Galilee (1:35–39)
4. Cleansing a leper in the countryside of Galilee (1:40–45)
5. Controversy: Healing the paralytic *at home in Capernaum* (2:1–12)
6. Controversy: Eating with sinners in Levi's house (2:15–17)
7. Controversy: Feasting not fasting (in Levi's house?) (2:18–22)
8. Controversy: Eating forbidden grain on the sabbath (2:23–28)
9. Controversy: Healing on the *sabbath* in the *synagogue at Capernaum* (3:1–6)

drove him into the wilderness to be tested by Satan. When Jesus entered Galilee it meant that it was the time for the kingdom of God to dislodge the forces of evil reigning in the land, for the land was occupied by unclean spirits. The unclean spirit in the synagogue at Capernaum recognized Jesus as the Holy One of God and realized the import of his appearance. "Have you come to destroy us?" he cried. The answer, not expressed, was yes. A battle of spirits for the control of the people was announced with this exorcism. That the demons knew who Jesus was is emphasized in Mark 3:11 and 5:7. Jesus placed them under the interdiction of silence, however (Mark 1:25; 3:12), just as he did those who had been healed (Mark 1:44; 5:43; 7:36; 8:26), or were privy to his true identity (Mark 8:30; 9:9), for there was another conflict about to erupt between Jesus and the institutions of the land. The issue would be about the new teaching and the authority of Jesus. The decisions would be either for or against. The consequences would be in the hands of the spiritual forces impinging upon the fateful entrance of God's Son into the land.

Jesus came "from Nazareth of Galilee" to be baptized (Mark 1:9). When he "came into Galilee preaching the gospel of God," however (Mark 1:14), he was no longer "from" Galilee, but "from" God. His preaching of the gospel and his announcement of the kingdom were pronouncements with the full authority of God's Spirit and sonship invested in him as the pronouncer. Jesus announced himself, in effect, as the king of the kingdom. Those in charge of the institutions of the land were to be confronted with a contender for their positions of authority.

In the first encounter in the synagogue (Mark 1:21–28), the leaders are not mentioned. Only the people are there to explain quite innocently that the teaching was not like that of the scribes, and announce unknowingly that the issue will be one of authority. That a man with an unclean spirit makes the response to Jesus' teaching, however, is ominous. Mark would have the reader see that the synagogue will be the scene of the first battle, and that the synagogue is possessed of people with unclean spirits. Mark composed this story with purpose. Every phrase is either a cliché taken from the common stock of miracle stories (unclean spirit, crying out, convulsing, rebuking, came out, amazement), or a Markan construction (immediately, authority, be silent, a new teaching).

The healing of Peter's mother-in-law (Mark 1:29–31) hardly rates as a miracle story. Its purpose is to set the contrast quickly between the synagogue where conflict will break forth, and the "house" where healing and ministry take place. Mark made it up as the tight cluster of Markan interests, themes, and stylistic traits shows (immediately, house, mention of the disciples just called in Mark 1:16–20, immediately they told him, raised up, served). A very cozy picture is painted with a few brief strokes to fill in the interlude while Jesus' fame spreads. It is a picture of the way things might be were there no conflict in the world: the master, disciples, at home, a slight bit of fever taken care of quickly, women in attendance, a meal together. Mark slipped it in before the conflict broke. It was the only space he had to give expression to his dreams.

The healing of the leper was chosen to illustrate the import of Jesus' healings throughout Galilee. Healings also were to be understood as cleansings. Clichés and Markan traits are the ingredients once again. The conclusion is very suggestive. The leper is not to tell about the healing. But he is to present himself to the priest and offer the proper sacrifice "for a proof to the people." The first story only hinted that scribes were in the background. This story hints that priests also are part of the larger picture. The reader may not know yet, but Mark knows, that the scribes and the priests will get together with the Pharisees and Herodians to thwart Jesus' kingship.

The healing of the paralytic introduces, finally, the scribes (Mark 2:1–12). They are not on home turf, but with the people gathered in Jesus' house. Healing is a sign of restoration into the congregation. Since the congregation of Jesus is composed of "sinners," the man can be pronounced "forgiven." Jesus does so and the scribes think to themselves, "Blasphemy!" As in all controversy stories, Jesus' authoritative response puts them down. They are silenced, just as the unclean spirit had been silenced in the synagogue. They do not speak again, and the story ends with the people again expressing amazement. This time they even glorify God. But the reader will have taken note of the scribes' thoughts. Blasphemy will be the charge upon which Jesus is eventually condemned. The horrifying thought is already intimated. Jesus makes pronouncements with the authority of the Son of God to command demons and with the authority of the Son of Man to render judgments on earth. The scribes hold such pronouncements to be blasphemy. The two authorities are already in deadly opposition.

In the story of the meal with sinners and tax collectors the scribes are present again (Mark 2:15–17). This time they raise their objection out loud, and this creates a bit of escalation in the encounter taking place. By means of another hint, the background is enlarged as well. The scribes are "scribes of the Pharisees."

The people ask the question in the next story, the question about not fasting (Mark 2:18–22). They phrase it, however, as a difference they have noted between Jesus and his disciples and the disciples of John and the Pharisees. The principal antagonists are coming more clearly into view. The people's question concerns the ritual laws of purity.

The Pharisees finally enter the picture when the disciples are seen plucking grain on the sabbath (Mark 2:23–28). They question Jesus about the disciples. Jesus' response is swift and pointed. He and his disciples may be compared to David and his men who entered the temple to eat the forbidden bread of the presence! As for the sabbath, it is less important than human need. And as for authority, "The Son of Man is lord even of the sabbath." The Pharisees are silenced.

In the synagogue, then, the Pharisees watch to see if Jesus would heal on the sabbath so that they might accuse him (Mark 3:1–6). Jesus asks them whether it is lawful to do good or ill on the sabbath. They remain silent. Jesus gets angry and heals the man with the withered hand. "The Pharisees went out, and immediately held counsel with the Herodians against him, how to destroy him." Jesus came to destroy the demons. The Pharisees plot how to destroy Jesus.

The Markan passion plot was set in the first cycle of eight stories. Miracles were used to demonstrate Jesus' incomparable authority. The cause is humane (healing, doing good, restoration, salvation, Mark 3:4), but the means divisive. The people will be set against their leaders. A little band will be separated out from among the people. Two powers, one with claim to absolute representation of God's will, are opposed. They will do battle for allegiance of the people and the control of the social institutions. The entrance of the man of power provokes the conflict, but he cannot be at fault. Those opposing him will be the offenders.

Jesus' entrance into Galilee was an invasion of the land and the synagogue in the interest of the kingdom of God. The first section of the gospel unfolds this conquest in a dramatic display of miraculous powers and teachings. The plot against Jesus is not mentioned again, though scribes and Pharisees from Jerusalem keep showing up to test him. Then Jesus announces at Caesarea Philippi that he will go to Jerusalem. Miracles all but cease and the topic of conversation turns to his fate at the hands of the powers in the city. The city is the citadel. There Jesus will confront not only the scribes and the Pharisees, but the priests, elders, Sadducees, Herodians, and chief priests as well (Mark 11:18, 28; 12:13, 18, 28; 14:1–2, 43; and at the trials).

As with his first entrance into Galilee, then into the synagogue, so Jesus will enter Jerusalem, then the temple, to cleanse it. The entrance into Galilee was under the sign of the kingdom of God. The entrance into Jerusalem will be under the sign of the king, the Son of David. His first two deeds are the cursing of the fig tree (Jerusalem, Israel) and the cleansing of the temple. Jesus' action in the synagogue precipitated conflict with the scribes and Pharisees over his authority. Jesus' action in the temple will precipitate conflict with the authorities there over his authority. Jesus' response to the scribes and Pharisees in Capernaum was portrayed by a set of controversy stories. Jesus' "teaching" in the temple is described by means of a series of controversy stories. Thus the entrance into Jerusalem follows the pattern of the entrance into Galilee. The purposes and issues are the same. In Galilee, however, Jesus silenced his opposition. In Jerusalem the opposition will put Jesus to death.

The stark contrast between the power of the man of miracles in the first section of the gospel and his utter helplessness in the hands of the temple authorities is the enduring problem of Mark's portrayal of Jesus. Mark was aware of the problem. His answer to it cannot be fully addressed until the passion narratives are analyzed. Three considerations can be given here, nevertheless, for they bear on the question of the miraculous and follow from the discussions of Jesus' power in this chapter. One is that the crucifixion of Jesus will not be the end of the story, according to Mark. There will be yet another entrance into the world for the Son of Man. He will come with power, and the kingdom of God will be manifest and established. This is the apocalyptic resolution to the violent fate of the man of power and his kingdom upon his first entrance. The promise of the kingdom coming with power is emphasized repeatedly after the first announcement of the forthcoming passion (Mark 9:1; 13:26; 14:25, 62). Jesus' authority and power were not canceled by failure to establish the kingdom in Jerusalem.

The second resolution to the problem of thwarted power was to link the crucifixion of Jesus to the destruction of the temple in Mark's own time. He did this by transferring power from Jesus back to God. In the parable of the Tenants the conclusion is that the owner of the vineyard "will come and destroy those tenants" (Mark 12:9). The cursing of the fig tree is also symbolically predictive, not of cleansing, but of condemnation and destruction (Mark 11:12–14, 20–21). A plain prediction of the destruction of the temple is given in Mark 13:1–2, followed by a cryptic apocalyptic vision that it will occur (Mark 13:14). Jesus' threat to destroy the temple plays a role at the trial. The rending of the veil from top to bottom at the crucifixion aligns the two events, for the rending is a miraculous portent of what will happen to the temple because of Jesus' treatment at the hands of the chief priests. Thus Mark interpreted the destruction of the temple as an act of God's judgment upon Jerusalem for its rejection of Jesus as rightful sovereign.

The first two resolutions work by relocating power and authority outside the story in order to vindicate the claims the story made but cannot realize about Jesus. The third resolution is less obvious than these, but more interesting as a device to redeem the storyline from within. It is that, when miracles cease, predictions begin. The turn in the story is, in fact, accomplished by means of a prediction, the first prediction of the passion (Mark 8:31). From that point on Jesus predicts the passion two more times, where the colt will be found for the triumphal entry, how the room will be found for the meal, Judas' betrayal, the flight of the disciples, Peter's denial, the resurrection, the proceeding into Galilee, the exclusions from the synagogue, the divisions in the families of believers, the martyrdom of James and John, the rise of false messiahs, the destruction of the temple, the coming of the Son of Man with power, the kingdom with glory, and the meal to be celebrated when it arrives. Pronouncement took the place of miracles as Jesus approached Jerusalem. Many of the predictions come true within the story; others had come true by Mark's time. Only the prediction of the advent of the kingdom in power was left outstanding. So Jesus' miraculous power was not forfeited by the turn of events that destroyed him. He took charge even of the course of his destruction by means of his power to effect change through pronouncement. A weird logic to the mastery of a path of action destined to defeat was created by Mark's choice of exorcisms to demonstrate Jesus' power. The way in which both Jesus' history and the history of the synagogue movement had ended told against such claims. In order not to give up such claims, Jesus had to be imagined also in control of his rejection and vindication. The events in Jerusalem are therefore determined by an unexplained necessity: "It is necessary that the Son of Man suffer many things, and be rejected by the elders and the chief priests and the scribes, and be killed, and after three days rise again" (Mark 8:31). The necessity is not grounded in some inexorable fate, however, nor in some mysterious, apocalyptic plan of salvation. Those are second-level rationalizations. They never would have dawned upon anyone as helpful ways to understand Jesus' crucifixion, had not Mark decided to portray Jesus as the man of power in the face of all appearances to the contrary. The necessity that Jesus be rejected is announced by making the prediction. It is Jesus' pronouncement of the necessity that makes it so. Prediction is too weak a word for this function of Jesus' words. Predictive causation would be better. It is not merely that what Jesus knew and predicted happened. It is that it happened because he predicted it. The cursing of the fig tree is the parable that tells. The measure of Jesus' authority to cast out demons is, according to Mark, the measure of his power to destroy. Jesus' miraculous power did not cease on the way to Jerusalem. It was redirected.

Mark's myth of origins was written to vindicate the synagogue reform movement after its exclusion from the synagogue. He did that by imagining the authority of Jesus, to which the movement appealed, to have been from God. He demonstrated Jesus' divine authority by using the miracle myth from the congregation of Israel. By using it, Mark could picture Jesus' purposes and power as part of God's design for Israel's cleansing and perfection. Alas, the trauma of the exclusion, the terms of the conflict, the definition of the new group by opposition to the old, and the patterns available to imagine vindication all determined that the claim to be right would not be made except at the expense of those who were wrong. Vindication was achieved, not only by making Jesus' pronouncements the words of God, but by directing them back as the words of God upon those who had already rejected them as the words of Jesus. Vindication was achieved by shifting the locus of conflict from the synagogue to the temple in Jesus' time (by narrative device), in order to claim the destruction of the temple in Mark's time as the judgment upon those who rejected Jesus' words. Unfortunately for the Jesus people, the cost of vindication included becoming an apocalyptic sect. The fault of the myth was that the destruction of the temple was an inappropriate way to imagine God getting even with the synagogue. The synagogue was not destroyed. Thinking that it should have been, Mark's direction for his group of Christians set a disastrous course. The need to huddle while the horsemen rode would pass. But the apocalyptic mechanism that made Mark's myth work would remain, written into the structure of the Christian gospel. And the reasons for the judgments yet needed to be brought upon the wicked world were also written into the gospel. Miracles would be the only way Christians would have to imagine supporting their claims and making things right. Apocalyptic judgments on those who reject Jesus would be the only way to imagine vindication.

PART III

NARRATIVES OF THE PASSION

The generations of men, throughout recorded time, have always told and retold two stories—that of a lost ship which searches the Mediterranean seas for a dearly loved island, and that of a god who is crucified on Golgotha.

Jorge Luis Borges
"The Gospel According to Mark"
Doctor Brodie's Report 19

9

THE ENTANGLEMENTS
OF HISTORY AND MYTH

For most of the rather long history of New Testament scholarship, the passion narratives remained critically unexamined. Only recently has this situation changed markedly. The reasons for tardiness in coming to this text are complex, no doubt, but underlying all of them one suspects a certain hesitation to scrutinize those events crucial for Christian myth and ritual. This suspicion would be difficult to establish, to be sure, for there has been so little discussion from which to judge. A general acknowledgment of the distinctiveness and privilege of this portion of the gospel appears to be quite modern.

Traditionally, the events memorialized in the Christian liturgy of the Eucharist have been imagined visually by means of iconography with its epic and framed settings, and supported textually by means of a confluence of gospel and Pauline readings. The significance of the crucifixion likewise has been available primarily in various kerygmatic, creedal, iconographic, and theological formulations, rather than specifically referred to the gospel account. Nevertheless, the Christian understanding of both the supper and the crucifixion contains the claim that they happened at a particular time in human history. The passion narrative identifies that particular time. The Christian imagination, therefore, is ultimately indebted to the passion narrative as it recalls those events historically. The passion narrative is the only New Testament account of that history that combines the supper with the crucifixion in a single narrative. Although the church has not acknowledged the fact formally, the passion narrative is the primary myth-ritual text for Christianity. For that reason it holds a privileged status. Probably for that reason also it has been less rigorously analyzed than other portions of early Christian literature.

Although the passion narrative must serve as the primary account of those incomparable Christian events basic to the myth and ritual, its style is strikingly realistic. The account is certainly not devoid of reference to the transhistorical significance of the events it relates, but there is far less manifestation of the transcendent in this merger of myth and history than one might expect. Christians do not appear to have found this strange, however, even though the history of the theological explication of the Christian imagination clearly documents the necessity of bringing many other mythic and philosophical notions to bear upon these accounts in order to derive from them their saving, that is, Christian significance. Instead, the accounts have been appreciated precisely for their lack of the fantastic, serving instead as an evidence for the historic claim Christians make for their myth. Dates, places, and historical agents are given. Jesus is suddenly depicted, not as the special man of power, but as human, subject to the vicissitudes of real social forces and procedures. The set of social agents seems to represent a rather complete picture of institutions and interests with some stake in the question of a reformer's activity. And the sequence of events unfolds according to plausible patterns of motivation. Because the narrative is so coherent, and so graphically portrays human events, the tendency has been to accept it, regard it as the (historically) true but (mythically or theologically) incomplete account of those momentous events foundational for Christianity.

Scholars generally seem to have agreed with the popular Christian perception. The passion narrative was long considered to be the earliest continuous account of important events in Jesus' life, based on historical reminiscence and providing the core narrative material around which other memories of Jesus then were collected in the formation of the gospels. Martin Kaehler's formulation was that the gospels were passion narratives with extended introductions. It was convenient to hold this view, because all of the New Testament materials, not just the synoptic traditions about Jesus, could then be arranged around the events of the passion for the purposes of historical reconstruction. There was no other text, in fact, no other set of events in view that could substitute for the narrative of the passion. Its reliability as historical report was accepted simply because it had to be. Were it ever to be questioned, the fixed point in the historian's image of early Christian history would be threatened and the outline of that history seriously disturbed.

Uncertainties eventually entered into the arena of scholarly discourse, however, at first focused upon a few details. The question was raised about the plausibility of the trial before the Sanhedrin in view of the fact that, according to Rabbinic tradition, it was conducted illegally. Then there was the matter of discrepancies in dating, whether the supper account agreed with Passover practice, and reservations about the plausibility of the charge, and so forth. With the form critics, then, the individual story units began to fall out of the main storyline. The British discovered evidence of scribal activity in the composition of the story of the crucifixion and "theological tendencies" were unearthed in every little story. Thus the quest was on to recover the history lying behind a text that looked more and more to be put together from fragments and highly interpretive in conception.[1]

The story of this scholarship can be told as a series of efforts to be critical about the composition of the text while refusing to give up its claim to historical report. The massive and detailed accumulation of studies since the war is evidence of great interest and concern about this. A privileged text, that is, is currently under review. It would be impossible to report fully on all of the fascinating twists and turns this scholarship has taken. But the essentials can be sketched. (1) The form critics set the agenda for the entire enterprise by imagining a development of the "passion tradition" from early reports to the final gospel form. (2) The observation of Christian scribal activity, especially the importance of the scriptural references for the characterization of Jesus, made it necessary to acknowledge apologetic motives at some stage in the formation of the tradition. (3) With much of the material colored by Christian interpretations, the quest began in earnest to isolate the earliest layer of historical report. (4) Finally, however, a few scholars had to admit that the concerted efforts had not produced a convincing text or argument. American scholars gingerly suggested an alternative: Perhaps Mark made it up.

A brief discussion of these scholarly efforts will introduce the issues that accompany a critical reading of the passion narratives and prepare for the study to follow. A table listing the individual units of the passion narrative will serve as a point of reference (see figure 15).

1. DEVELOPMENT BY STAGES

The first critical analyses of the passion narrative happened in the course of studies on the Jesus traditions in general. The form critics, Dibelius and Bultmann, did not take the synoptic materials up primarily with the passion narratives in mind. Their work with the small story units of the Jesus traditions alerted them to the signs of compositional activity in the passion narratives as well, however, and they concluded that some of the stories had traveled independently just as other synoptic material had. They encountered two problems. One was that the stories of the passion did not lend themselves to form-critical definition as easily as other types of material for which there were many examples to make a set. The other was that neither Dibelius or Bultmann could imagine only individual stories traveling separately from the beginning, because many seemed to presuppose the events reported by others and the whole seemed to have as its basic struc-

---

1. *Historical discrepancies.* For a brief summary of the earliest questions raised about the accuracy of the passion account see John R. Donahue, "Temple, Trial, and Royal Christology," 61–62. Martin Kaehler's famous dictum is mentioned also by Donahue in his "From Passion Traditions to Passion Narrative," 1.

FIGURE 15
THE PASSION NARRATIVES IN MARK

11:1–11	Entrance into Jerusalem	Entrance doublet
12–14	Cursing the fig tree	
15–19	The temple act	
20–25	The withered fig tree	
11:27–12:44	Teaching in the temple	
13:1–2	Prediction of the destruction of the temple	
3–37	Apocalyptic predictions	
14:1–2	Conspiracy against Jesus	
3–9	Anointing at Bethany	
10–11	Betrayal by Judas	
12–16	Preparation for Passover	
17–21	Prediction of betrayal	
22–25	The supper	
26–31	Prediction of denial	
32–42	Temptation in Gethsemane	
43–52	Arrest	Arrest as betrayal
53–65	Trial before the Sanhedrin	
66–72	Peter's denial	Peter's denial
15:1–5	Trial before Pilate	The two trials
6–15	Sentencing	
16–20	Mocking	
21	Road to Golgotha	
22–39	Crucifixion	Crucifixion cluster
40–41	Women looking on	
42–47	Burial	
16:1–8	Empty tomb	

ture a definite sequence of narration. Each concluded that there must have been an earliest, shorter account to which other independent units later were added.

The solution Dibelius proposed was quite simple. He regarded the entire account as pre-Markan with the exception of the anointing, the preparation for Passover, the temptation in Gethsemane, and the trial before the

Sanhedrin. He argued that these were "inserted" into the longer account mainly because, by deleting them, a sequence resulted that read much more smoothly. Dibelius did note several other places where connections were rough. He also saw that many of the narrative themes were developed by reference to the scriptures and realized that the account was composed by Christians deeply interested in the theological significance of the events. But these observations did not force a reconsideration of the assumption of an early report of the passion as a whole. This means that the sense of a story as an uninterrupted sequence of closely related events influenced Dibelius' judgments as much as did form-critical observations.[2]

Dibelius illustrates the dilemma inherent to the form-critical approach. An earliest connected narrative was to be reconstructed by deleting independent story units that also may have been early. Two forms of memory clashed, the memory of an episode and the memory of a series of events. The problem has always been, therefore, where to stop the process of fragmentation. The problem is serious, because any reconstruction of the original account can only consist of a set of conjoined stories. One scholar's connections have been another's seams.

Bultmann's approach was more daring. In his *History of the Synoptic Tradition,* Bultmann took the process of form-critical analysis almost to the point of dismantling the entire account. Most units could be regarded as independent traditions, leaving Bultmann with the task of explaining how they then had been put together. His proposal was that four stages of development could be established. (1) The kerygma of Christ's death and resurrection must have been the earliest form of the account of the passion. (2) From this developed an early historical account consisting of the arrest, hearings before the Sanhedrin and Pilate, sentencing, and crucifixion. This he called the "brief" account. He was honest enough to say that the existence of this account could only be "suspected," but that the "nature of the affair" required it and it did agree with early Christian iconography. (3) Embellishment by adding narrative clusters occurred at a third stage. He noted that there was a complex of stories surrounding the supper, including the preparation and the prediction of denial. Since the prediction of denial formed a cluster with the denial stories, and since the prediction of betrayal formed a link with the arrest and betrayal stories, interlocking of clusters was also a mark of the major expansion. (4) Finally, some additions were made at the level of gospel composition, such as the anointing.[3]

Bultmann's scheme, worked out in less than twenty-seven pages, became

2. *Martin Dibelius.* His form-critical work on the passion narrative is found in *From Tradition to Gospel,* 178–217.

3. *Rudolf Bultmann.* The reconstruction of the four stages is given in *History of the Synoptic Tradition,* 262–84.

the standard model for the development of the passion tradition, the model other scholars would use to try for greater clarity about the earliest, brief account. Because it assumed a straight-line development from the historical events to the gospel, however, conservative as well as liberal scholars found it attractive. Bultmann was content to demonstrate the largely legendary character of most of the narratives. It is therefore something of an irony that conservative scholars could take the same scheme, include more material, and conclude just the opposite. A particularly embarrassing example of this can be found in the work of Joachim Jeremias, a conservative scholar severely critical of Bultmann's views on legend and myth. Jeremias was able to use the four-stage scheme, reverse Bultmann's judgment about the legendary nature of the later clusters, and conclude, "On the whole this long account may well represent a reliable account of the historical sequence of events."[4]

Another strange conclusion reached during the early stages of the form-critical approach appeared in Vincent Taylor's commentary on Mark (1952). He used the incidence of Semitisms (lexical and grammatical peculiarities best explained as translations from an Aramaic original) to verify the historical accuracy of the earliest layer of tradition. What happened was that many of the stories thought by Bultmann and Jeremias to belong to later stages popped up in the list of stories with Semitisms, stories Taylor thought must be Petrine reminiscences. This was true for the anointing, the supper, Gethsemane, the denial, the Barabbas episode, and the mocking. This list did not make a story. The remaining material, in better Greek, made a fine running account. In the light of these findings, Taylor should have revised his original hypothesis. Instead, he proclaimed that both accounts must therefore have been early, one because of the Semitisms, the other because of coherence, two independent traditions later combined by Mark. His conclusion was that "almost at once primitive Christianity began to tell the story of the Cross."[5]

This obvious lack of control on the material was due both to theological conservatism and to a serious confusion about myth and history inherent in the developmental scheme. All form critics worked with the assumption that the kerygma documented the first stage of the tradition and that the second stage was an early historical account (reconstructible from the passion narratives). The confusion lies in the notion of development from kerygma to historical account. The kerygma was a mythic formulation without need of further narrative embellishment. It contained no flaw

---

4. *Joachim Jeremias.* His views are stated in *The Eucharistic Words of Jesus,* 89–96. The citation is from 96.

5. *Vincent Taylor.* For Taylor's study of the passion narratives see *The Gospel According to Mark,* 644–67. The citation is from 664.

needing further adjustment, no gaps that still had to be filled. Recalling the discussion in chapter 4, moreover, the kerygma worked just because questions arising from historical placement and motivation had been bracketed. Thus the kerygmatic interpretation of Jesus' death actually resisted historicizing, and therefore could not have been the first stage in a development of the passion narrative.

The notion of the second stage, then, also becomes problematic. If it occurred as a development of the kerygma, it is difficult to imagine why the nature of the event would have been portrayed so differently, that is, as historically motivated and without obvious kerygmatic allusions. If, on the other hand, such an account derived directly from historical reminiscence, one wonders why it has to be a second stage. Bultmann's proposal for this stage is troubling, moreover, just because of its brevity and a lack of reason for its existence. Why twentieth-century scholars might be interested in such an account needs to be distinguished from why early Christians would have been interested. No reason can be found. Bultmann did not even try to find one. The historian can only conclude that the scholarly suspicion of an early account stems from a desire to document the credibility of the kerygma, that is, the historical reality of the event as significant in ways Christians are used to imagining it as significant.

A statement Dibelius made about the historical significance of the crucifixion (which he called simply "the Passion") is revealing: "It was not in the healings, or in the parables, . . . but in the Passion that the eschatological event manifested itself which was to point immediately toward the turning of the ages. The Passion is the beginning of the end time." Dibelius' statement may appear somewhat naive and dramatic in retrospect, but it documents the assumption underlying all of the form-critical efforts on the passion narratives. That assumption was, and has continued to be, that the crucifixion of Jesus was a truly amazing event of unique theological significance. With that presupposed, the quest for the earliest account could not really be an effort in historiography, but in Christian apologetics. The kerygma was not to be disturbed as the first report and truest guide to what happened.[6]

2. SCRIBAL APOLOGETICS

A theory of social setting and function arose in the course of advanced studies in comparative midrash (Jewish methods of interpreting scripture) and Christian apologetics. Dibelius had already taken note of the scriptural

---

6. *The kerygmatic interpretation.* The citation from Dibelius is taken from J. R. Donahue, "From Passion Traditions to Passion Narrative," 5.

citations in the passion narratives and concluded that the passion narratives must have been used in sermonizing. His insights were followed up by a number of scholars in the period after the war, including C. H. Dodd, Christian Maurer, J. Jeremias, and Barnabas Lindars. They collected the scriptural citations, allusions, and themes appearing in the passion account and subjected them to painstaking analysis. They discovered that the selection of scriptural loci, mainly the Psalms of lamentation, particularly Psalm 22, had been governed by a common interest. That interest was the theme of the suffering of the Righteous One at the hands of enemies.

FIGURE 16
JESUS AS THE PERSECUTED RIGHTEOUS ONE

(1) Clear references to the Psalms

Mark 14:18	Betrayal by friends (at meal)	Ps 41:9
Mark 14:34	A soul full of sorrow	Pss 42:6, 11; 43:5
Mark 15:24	Garments divided	Ps 22:18
Mark 15:29	Derision of onlookers	Pss 22:7; 109:25
Mark 15:34	"My God, my God ..."	Ps 22:1
Mark 15:36	Vinegar to drink	Ps 69:21

(2) Thematic allusions

Mark 14:1	Conspiracy to kill	Pss 31:4; 35:4; 38:12; 71:10
Mark 14:56, 57, 59	False witnesses	Pss 27:12; 35:11; 109:2
Mark 14:61; 15:5	Silence before accusers	Pss 38:14–16; 39:9
Mark 15:20, 29	Mocking	Pss 22:7; 31:11; 35:19–25; 69:20; 109:25

(3) Characterization as a whole

	Enemies	
Markan plot	Persecution	Pss 22, 27, 31, 34, 35, 38,
Predictions	Vulnerability	39, 41, 42, 43, 55, 69, 71, 109
Mark 9:12: "It is written"	Silence	Isa 52:13–53:12 (LXX)
		Wis 2–5
Passion account	Prayer	
	Obedience	
	Trust	

None of these scholars drew the conclusion that the passion narrative was therefore unreliable as historical account. But they did recognize that a preexistent profile of the innocent sufferer had been interwoven into the material by Christian scribal activity. They noted that details such as the betrayal by friends at the meal, Jesus' silence at the trial, the mockery of the soldiers, and the distribution of Jesus' clothes at the crucifixion were motifs taken from the Psalms. This meant, in Lindars' words, that the scriptures became "a quarry for pictorial detail in writing the story of the passion. Every detail of the tradition has its counterpart in prophecy." Lindars' statement reveals the mythology that allowed these scholars to claim historical reliability for the account while exploring its correspondence to Jewish prototypes. It was the Christian myth of promise and fulfillment according to which the passion of Jesus could be viewed as the historical realization of earlier prophecies. But why from the Psalms? And why such an emphasis upon Jesus' innocent suffering?

The function was, according to these scholars, a Christian apologetic for the crucifixion. Christians would already have known about the saving significance of Jesus' death as the Christ, but Jews would not. Jews would have stumbled when presented with the idea that the Christ had been crucified. Jews would have questioned how a criminal and shameful death implying guilt could be imagined for the Messiah. (The proof text for this Jewish view was found in Deut 21:22–23.) Since the victim of suffering in the Psalms was not guilty, but innocent, showing that Jesus died as the Righteous One would have made the apologetic point. The crucifixion was not a scandal as the Jews may have thought. And thus the kerygma was acceptable.[7]

The reader may well revolt at the logic of this self-serving apologetic. It assumes that the "scandal of the cross" (1 Cor 1:23) was a matter of misunderstanding, easily cleared up by showing that Jesus died as the innocent one, as if that demonstration (via scribal fiction) could redeem for the Jews a story in which they were cast as the perpetrators of the crime. A critique of greater importance for the historian, however, is the assumption of a scandal in the first place. Jesus' death was not a scandal until Christians made it so by claiming that Jesus had been the Christ (Messiah) and was crucified as such. The story the apologists thought written to correct the scandal was the very creation of the scandal. The death of Jesus became an

---

7. *The apology of innocence.* The comprehensive study is by Barnabus Lindars, *New Testament Apologetic.* The citation is from 90. The other references cited above are: C. H. Dodd, *According to the Scriptures;* C. Maurer, "Knecht Gottes und Sohn Gottes"; and J. Jeremias, "παῖς θεοῦ." For a review of the work of other scholars in this area see J. R. Donahue, "From Passion Traditions to Passion Narrative," 2–6.

intellectual scandal when the ideas of martyrdom and Messiah were joined in the Christ cult and the crucifixion was imagined as a saving event. It became a social scandal when preached to the Jews as kerygma and written up as history with the Jews cast as those who put the innocent one to death. The theory that the passion narrative was a Christian apologetic is itself an apologetic, an apology for Protestant views of the reliability of the scriptures as the firm foundation for Christian faith in saving history.

If one brackets the theological bias, however, credit can be given to these scholars for working out the element of midrashic activity in the formation of the passion narratives. The citations and allusions to the Psalms are surely there, and they are no doubt a very significant clue to the reasons for which the narrative was written. The lasting achievement of the apologists would be, then, quite contrary to their own intentions, to have demonstrated scribal and authorial activity in the fabrication of the passion account.

3. THE EARLIEST ACCOUNT

In the seventies many studies on the passion narratives appeared in Germany. All of them were aimed at recovering the earliest layer of the tradition, struggling always with the question of myth and history. They used form-critical methods and shared in the assumption that Christianity somehow started with the events recounted in Jerusalem. They brought a formidable, new arsenal of critical skills to bear upon the task of making stylistic, syntactical, linguistic, and literary-critical distinctions. The list includes works by Johannes Schreiber, Eta Linnemann, Ludger Schenke, Gerhard Schneider, Wolfgang Schenk, Detlev Dormeyer, and Till Arend Mohr. Each (except Linnemann) proposed a reconstruction of a pre-Markan account. Alas. Not one looked like the others. Something had gone wrong. Schreiber had reduced the crucifixion story to its minimal, declarative form: "And they led him out to crucify him. And they compelled a passerby. . . . And they brought him to a place called Golgotha. . . ." He could not say why early Christians would have bothered with such a report. Mohr, on the other hand, after 427 pages of discriminating observations, concluded that every place where Mark and John could be made to agree must be accepted as historical, miracles and all. Schenke isolated a layer in which Jesus was portrayed as the suffering Righteous One. He argued that it must have been the earliest report, for it fit the point of Jesus' death as the Messiah so well. It was also, by the way, the interpretation Mark preferred, bringing Mark's story conveniently close to the earliest account. The historian despairs.[8]

---

8. *The quest for the earliest account.* The references are to J. Schreiber, *Die Markus-*

Two studies from this period are, however, worth reading. They are those by Eta Linnemann and Detlev Dormeyer. Neither solves the problem, but each makes a fine contribution to the history of efforts to do so. They may serve as examples of the latest chapter in the form-critical approach to the passion.

Linnemann's work is something of an anomaly, since her purpose was not to assume an early account, but to push the form-critical approach as far as it would go on each separate story. She studied the arrest, the temptation in Gethsemane, the two trials, and the crucifixion. This selection was designed to test the assumption of a brief historical account behind them. She did not find any evidence for such an account. Each story could be read as an independent unit and make sense. The point in each case, moreover, presupposed views of the significance of Jesus' death as exemplary for Christian faith and life. They were, all of them, theological constructions based upon the identity of Jesus as the Christ. She concluded, therefore, that the passion narratives were not based on historical reminiscence, and that there had not been a connected narrative prior to Mark. The appearance of connected sequences was Mark's own contribution.

The value of Linnemann's work lies in her demonstration of the theological nature of the stories at their minimal narrative level. (Her reconstructions are given in an appendix for reference.) The striking thing about the way in which these stories make their point is that all of them draw either upon obviously Christian themes, or upon motifs belonging to the picture of the persecuted Righteous One. This is the case even when the citations to the Psalms are removed, a deletion Linnemann consistently made where possible. Since she nowhere referred to the works of Dodd and Lindars, the agreement of her finding with theirs is the more noticeable. At the basic level of narrative sense, she concluded, all of the stories depicted Jesus as the suffering one, a depiction much like that found in the scriptures.

According to Linnemann, the arrest makes its point by scriptural citation. The arrest as betrayal combines the motifs of conspiracy and betrayal in the duplicity of (the kiss of) friendship, all documented in the Psalms of lament. The point of the trial before Pilate is just Jesus' silence, a characteristic of the persecuted Righteous One. Linnemann found two stories interwoven in the trial before the Sanhedrin. The first makes two points. One is Jesus' confession, a Christian motif. The other is that of the false witnesses, a motif taken from the Psalms. The second story of the Sanhedrin trial contains three points: false witness, silence, and the temple

passion; Die Theologie des Vertrauens; E. Linnemann, Studien zur Passionsgeschichte; L. Schenke, Studien zur Passionsgeschichte; Der gekreuzigte Christus; G. Schneider, Die Passion Jesu; W. Schenk, Der Passionsbericht nach Markus; D. Dormeyer, Die Passion Jesu als Verhaltensmodell; and T. A. Mohr, Markus- und Johannespassion.

charge. The false witness and silence are fictional motifs. Only the crucifixion story is difficult to align with motifs of the righteous sufferer at its
minimal level. But its highly mythological character is obvious. It was not a
reminiscence, but a fantastic portrayal of cosmic (darkness at noon) and
historical (temple veil rent) convulsion. All of the material interwoven into
the single narrative structure, moreover, expresses motifs taken from scriptural portrayals of the suffering Righteous One.

Linnemann's conclusion was that these stories arose at different times
and places in the early history of the church. She compared this to the way
in which form critics had understood other kinds of stories about Jesus to
have arisen and traveled independently. The passion narratives could be
told without larger narrative context because all Christians knew about the
significance of Jesus' death. They were lessons for preaching and instruction, setting forth illustrations of Jesus as the "man for others," paradigms of
faith and faithfulness for Christian imitation. She expressed astonishment
that, given this rather long history of independent storytelling, all stories
agreed in a single characterization of Jesus.

Linnemann could think of the stories functioning that way because she
held a view of Christian origins typical for German kerygmatic theologians.
Faith in Jesus as the Christ was definitional for all Christians from the
beginning, and it was linked necessarily to the saving significance of the
crucifixion. Because such an all pervasive Christ faith is no longer thinkable, Linnemann's conclusion has to be revised. The astonishment she
registered at the consistency of characterization in all of the stories would
have been her better conclusion. The consistency points, not to a monolithic Christianity as context for the stories, but to the storyline of the
passion narrative itself as literary context, and some definite circle of
Christians as social context. Still, her conclusions per story unit are
important and could have been reached only by doing what she did.
Reducing each story to its minimal form, the narrative sense in each case
was nevertheless strikingly similar. What Linnemann demonstrated was not
the pervasiveness of the kerygma in narrative form, but "the unity of these
stories in structure and character."[9]

Dormeyer worked with the problem of the storyline, and sought to
isolate the pre-Markan stages of a running account. His method for
determining Mark's hand in the shaping of the passion narrative was a
statistical analysis of Markan vocabulary throughout the gospel. This
analysis was then combined with a form-critical approach to story units. He
distinguished three elements in the composition of brief narratives: declara-

---

9. *Eta Linnemann*. For her statements regarding the unity of the stories see *Studien zur
Passionsgeschichte*, 176: "Das eigentlich Erstaunliche ist aber nicht ihre Fülle, sondern die
Einheitlichkeit dieser Erzählungen in Struktur und Charakter. . . ."

tive statements, description, and dialogue. He understood declarative statements to belong to historical report, description and dialogue to be secondary embellishments. Non-Markan description and dialogue was assigned to the middle stage of the passion tradition. Three stages in the development of the tradition could then be separated: (1) The earliest layer (T) was an account that bears similarity to the genre Acts of a Martyr (a reconstruction is given in Appendix III); (2) An embellishment (Rs, for Redactor); and (3) Mark's account (RMk).

Dormeyer recognized that the earliest account was a literary fiction, not a verbatim account. He nevertheless argued that its main points were based on reminiscence. It differed from Jewish martyrologies by including a trial, from Hellenistic martyrologies (that conclude with the sentencing) by going on to report the execution. These differences, Dormeyer thought, argued for the reality of the events reported.

Dormeyer's separation of the Markan account into stages is not convincing. There is no reason to think that the primary (declarative) and secondary (descriptive) elements in a story correspond necessarily to the chronology of its composition. Dormeyer's interest in reducing each narrative to its basic, uninterpretive level of declaration is astonishing. Anyone can do that to a story, should one wish to do so. To think that one has gotten to historical bedrock by means of such a procedure, however, is most naive. At some point, Dormeyer simply lost perspective in his desire to contact history amidst all of the linguistic details at his command. The function Dormeyer assigned to the earliest report is, moreover, completely incomprehensible. Dormeyer acknowledged that it would not have served well for preaching or liturgy and that it made its point about Jesus' stance toward trial only indirectly. He suggested, therefore, a catechetical purpose. Catechumens would be told the story and asked to say what they thought it meant! The secondary expansion (Rs) contains the sense this Jewish-Christian community made of the early report. The sense they made of it, according to Dormeyer's reconstructions, was that Jesus was the suffering Righteous One. This strangely staged history illustrates the lengths to which one must go in order to preserve the notion of an earliest historical account. There is no reason to accept it.

In the course of his form-critical work, however, Dormeyer collected an impressive documentation of motifs from martyrological literature that compare with those found in the passion narratives. This demonstration of dependence upon a martyrological genre was an advance. He also worked out the differences between the profile of the martyr and the profile of the Righteous One in relation to the incidence of motifs in the passion narratives. This also was an advance. That he intended this difference to establish the separation of layers of tradition was unfortunate, however, because there is no reason why both models could not have been in the mind of a single author. His discussions of the differences between the two profiles is, nevertheless, usable and important.

Elaborating somewhat on the observations scattered throughout Dormeyer's study, the following summary can be given. Both the Righteous One and the martyr find themselves pressed by enemies. There are taunts, charges, and threats of death. The Righteous One, however, complains of a plot, betrayal, and false charges, for he is innocent. He prays for protection in his hour of need, but is brought to silence in the presence of his accusers. There is no formal trial, and the plot against him does not result in his death. He is rescued. The martyr, on the other hand, comes to speech before his enemies who have power to charge him with civil disobedience and execute him. He does not complain, refuses solace, and dies with honor.

Jesus is, according to the passion narrative, charged, tried, and executed as a martyr. But the charges are false, resulting from a plot and betrayal as in the case of the Righteous One. He performs an act of civil disobedience, yet is innocent. The political claim, "King of the Jews," fits neither model, according to Dormeyer, for the grounds of the charge are not given. One might press Dormeyer at this point, however, for the charge "King of the Jews" actually unites both models by giving the reason why the "innocent" Jesus was "martyred." He was innocent with respect to the "laws" of the "kingdom of God." He was martyred as an offender against the laws of the Jews. Dormeyer would not find this composite reading comfortable. Should his separate layers collapse into a single narrative design, however, the point of Mark's story may lie just there.

4. FICTIONAL THEMES

American studies set a new course in the 1970s. Scholars trained in the criticism of literature decided to collaborate on an investigation of the passion narratives with the questions of authorship and composition in mind. Fully aware of the continental traditions, the possibility of Markan authorship was nevertheless entertained. The passion narratives contained just the right mixture of history, tradition, and redactional nuances to test the difference compositional criticism might make. Their collection of essays, *The Passion in Mark* edited by Werner Kelber, amounted to a declaration of independence. There were other American studies of significance as well, one by John Donahue (*Are You the Christ?*), another by Donald Juel (*Messiah and Temple*), each troubled by traditional scholarly assumptions about the nature of pre-Markan material. Then, in 1980, George Nickelsburg published "The Genre and Function of the Markan Passion Narrative," which demonstrated that the passion narrative as a whole followed the pattern of a known genre, the wisdom story of the persecuted Righteous One. All of these studies overlap and complement one another in ways that suggest a solution to the question of the complex interweaving of themes in Mark's single storyline.

The Kelber volume presented exegetical essays by John Donahue, Vernon Robbins, Norman Perrin, Kim Dewey, Theodore Weeden, John Dominic Crossan, and Werner Kelber. The theme was announced by Donahue in his introduction to the volume: "Mark as Author and Theologian." The set of studies is remarkable for the high level of agreement it achieves. It is the more remarkable in that each of the major story units of the passion account was studied independently. There is some unevenness from author to author on the question of Mark's sources and how to go about showing Mark's hand at work. Some referred regularly to pre-Markan traditions. Others were more comfortable with the idea that Mark made some stories up. All were in agreement, however, that each story gained its narrative significance only when read in the context of the gospel as a whole. Looked at closely, narrative themes and devices, even details of these stories, could be accounted for in terms of the author's own creativity and intention.

In his essay at the conclusion of the volume, Kelber noted that all of the major Markan themes had come to climax in the passion account. Paraphrasing somewhat his list of these themes, they include the question of Jesus' identity, the plot against him, the nature of the kingdom he announced, the anti-temple theme, the failure of the disciples to understand, and the portrayal of the communal codes relative to such things as meal practice, ranking, and patterns of discourse. Most of these themes were developed in the gospel as issues in need of clarification or resolution. They were resolved finally in the passion narratives by various combinations of motifs that revealed what had been at stake all along. Taking the theme of Jesus' identity as an example, the three christological titles Mark had introduced, Son of God, Christ, and Son of Man, were finally brought together at the trial (Mark 14:61–62). This point in the narrative is climactic. The problematic secret about the titles is disclosed in public confession, and the confession immediately becomes the ground for Jesus' condemnation. Thus the trial scene takes its meaning only when placed in the context of the gospel as a whole and serves as the narrative climax it was designed to be.

The notion of a pre-Markan passion narrative suddenly becomes very problematic. Kelber put it succinctly: "Thematically, it is difficult to identify a major non-Markan thrust or theme in Mark 14–16, let alone extrapolate a coherent pre-Markan source." His own conclusion was that there was none. He did think that there must have been a few individual stories floating around prior to Markan usage. These include the anointing, some tradition of the meal, a story about Jesus' presentation before Jewish officials, a short story of Peter's denial, and "traditions" about a lament or prayer of Jesus (as basis for the Gethsemane story) as well as about the crucifixion. This shows that, even though the developmental scheme of stages has been given up, confusion still exists about "traditions" and about free-floating reminiscences. Kelber could not imagine that Mark had made the story up entirely from scratch. Nevertheless, he was able to ask the right question with a good bit of precision. "The issue," he stated, "is not why Jesus' passion demanded an early pre-Markan connected narrative form, because it did not, but the issue is why Mark created the Gospel whole in its present form."

Kelber may have supplied his own answer to this question in the remaining sections of his essay. If so, his question is better stated than his answer. What Mark achieved, according to Kelber, was a clear narrative portrayal of Jesus as "the crucified King." Kelber seemed to think that this was true to something, a position carved out from among competing views that resonated with what Kelber had called "Jesus' passion." How the meaning of Jesus' passion got to Mark, Kelber did not say. He worked out Mark's position as a "christological" statement, however, and one suspects that some kerygmatic history was in Kelber's mind. Perhaps Bultmann's kerygmatic view of Christian origins had not yet been fully exorcized after all.

All of the essays in the Kelber volume were oriented to the "christological" problem of the gospel. Jesus' identity, the titles, the characterization and behavior of Jesus as clues to the way in which Christians might have imagined their founder, Lord, and coming judge, were the focus of attention in every chapter. As for references to the Christian "community," it was defined and discussed solely in relation to matters of "faith." There was no attempt to place Mark, the gospel, or his community in any social history. It is therefore of great interest to note that the Markan theme that caused the most trouble throughout the volume was that of the anti-temple incidents. Disconcertion and disagreement about this plagued almost every essay. The relation of the "kingdom" to the temple, the relation of Jesus' death to the destruction of the temple, and especially what to make of the "temple word" ("I will destroy this temple . . . ," Mark 14:58), were problems no one could solve on the grounds of compositional observations alone.

Donahue argued that the temple word was an ironically placed statement expressing Mark's view that Jesus' death and the end of the temple were very closely related events. (Donahue is undoubtedly right.) Weeden thought that the saying was to be understood as a false accusation, that Mark wanted to dissociate Jesus' death from the destruction of the temple. Kelber fastened upon this disagreement in his concluding essay to agree with Weeden against Donahue. Kelber states:

> For Mark the fall of the Temple is in no way related to Jesus' resurrection or parousia. . . . For Mk, Jesus dies because he reveals his full identity which includes, but is not limited to, his authority to take action against the Temple. In the last analysis Jesus dies because he confesses to be the Christ and Son of God who as the Son of Man claims authority for the future.

This is a shocking conclusion to this set of studies. Kelber would like to see the significance of Jesus' death apart from any contaminating relationship to the messy history of Second Temple Judaism. The figure of the Jesus with authority has even been lifted out of the story, leaving all the naughtiness, plottings, taunts, warnings, and reciprocal condemnations behind as if Mark had not brought Jesus to the revelation of his identity precisely by means of these narrative devices. Kelber's disappointing conclusion to a remarkably fresh set of essays may indicate the inadequacy of the literary approach taken. The text was treated as if in a bubble, thus the Christ characterized also was imagined extricated from the entanglements of myth and history to exercise "authority" over a demythologized "future." The text needs to be put back into the human worlds of social and cultural history. The essay by Nickelsburg pushes in that direction.[10]

Nickelsburg would agree that Mark was the author of the passion narrative. His approach differs from that taken in the Kelber volume, however, by suggesting that Mark's narrative design followed the pattern of an existing genre. It was the wisdom story of the persecution and vindication of the Righteous One. Nickelsburg's work on the wisdom story reaches back to his Harvard dissertation, *Resurrection, Immortality, and Eternal Life,* published in 1972. In it he identified a narrative pattern consisting of eighteen functions (revised and expanded to twenty-one in his "Genre and Function of the Markan Passion Narrative") a pattern he called "The Wisdom Tale," or "The Story of the Persecution and Exaltation/Vindication of the Righteous." He traced this story, called a "genre" in his essay, from its earliest record in Genesis 37–50, through Ahikar, Esther, Daniel 3 and 6, Susanna, Wisdom 2–5, 2 and 3 Maccabees, and other Jewish literatures. Functions fell on either side of a scene of trial or judgment. The sequence of functions was fixed generically, though transpositions were possible. Different performances (new stories told according to the pattern of the genre) could be related to differences in social, literary, or theological contexts.

In "Genre and Function of the Markan Passion Narrative" Nickelsburg argued that the passion narrative was another performance of this genre.

---

10. *Werner Kelber.* The concluding essay by Kelber in *The Passion in Mark* is "From Passion Narrative to Gospel." The references are: on the Markan themes that come together in the passion, 157; on the problem of the origin of the passion narrative, 158; on "the crucified king," 158; and on the temple, 171–72.

Working through the Markan text he was able to identify seventeen of the twenty-one functions and account for much of the material basic to the Markan plot. His thesis has several advantages. One advantage would be that motifs in the passion narratives that allude to the figure of the Righteous One, as demonstrated in earlier scholarship, can now be promoted as potentially functional within the larger narrative (not merely characteristics of a figure, but functions within a narrative). The Psalm citations, for instance, a feature of the passion narratives Nickelsburg did not discuss, might serve narrative functions other than characterization.

A second advance is that Jewish martyrologies can be accommodated. Since the wisdom story lies behind both Jewish martyrological literatures as well as depictions of the rescue of the Righteous One, Dormeyer's distinction between the two can be corrected, and his separation of layers in the pre-Markan tradition on that basis dismissed. Dormeyer did not recognize that motifs of the suffering Righteous One could serve as narrative functions, nor did he even cite the close parallels to Mark in Wisdom 2–5.

Nickelsburg's thesis also sheds new light on the episodic nature of the passion narrative and its formation by connecting small story units. While there is no necessary correlation between a function and a single story unit, it is quite possible to imagine story units composed with a particular function in mind. Thus the temple act serves primarily as the provocation, Gethsemane as the obedient decision, the arrest stories as critical for the plot and betrayal. The sentencing is developed in a scene separate from the trials, as is the taunt, and so forth. The fact that the individual story units appear to be so disparate in form, description, setting, and detail, might also be accounted for in terms of functional requirements within the genre. Nickelsburg's discussion has been put in the form of a table for review (see figure 17). Additional entries have been made in the interest of illustrating the extent of the correspondence between the wisdom tale and the passion narrative.[11]

---

11. *The passion narrative as fiction.* The article by G. W. E. Nickelsburg on "Genre and Function of the Markan Passion Narrative" is a revision of a section of his dissertation that was not included in its publication, *Resurrection, Immortality, and Eternal Life.* The table of correspondence between the wisdom tale and the passion narrative was prepared by Brenda Hines. Nickelsburg's demonstration of the correspondence between the passion narrative and the wisdom tale can be read as a companion piece to Frank Kermode's study of Mark's Gospel in *The Genesis of Secrecy.* Kermode reads the passion narrative as a *fabula* generated mainly from Old Testament texts, and explains that literary critics, in distinction from New Testament scholars, would not find such a procedure difficult to understand at all. Kermode distinguishes a first stage of augmentation that created characters to fulfill functions suggested by Old Testament texts, primarily the Psalms, from a later stage in which the characters were fleshed out as "persons." Kermode does not speculate on the origin of the pre-Markan *fabula* itself, the simple plot that invited augmentation. Nickelsburg's wisdom tale supplies an answer to that question.

FIGURE 17
THE MARKAN PASSION NARRATIVE
AS THE STORY OF PERSECUTION AND VINDICATION

( ) Component out of usual order   [ ] Additions to Nickelsburg's Chart

	Mark
Introduction	Chaps. 1–10
Provocation	11:15–17, [12:1–11], 14:3–9 [?]
Conspiracy	11:18, [12:12–13], 14:1–2, 14:10–11
Decision	[14:3–9], [14:35–36], [14:41–42], 14:62?, 15:29–32
Trust	[14:35–36]
Obedience	[14:3–9], [14:35–36], 14:62?
Accusation	14:57–61, 15:2–3
Trial	14:53–64, 15:1–15
Condemnation	14:64, 15:15
Protest	Eliminated when accustion is true
Prayer	[14:35–36], 15:34
Assistance	15:9–14, [15:21]
Ordeal	[14:65], [15:16–20], 15:29–30, 15:31–32, 15:36
Reactions	14:63, 15:5
Rescue	(14:62)
Vindication	[12:10–11], (14:62), 15:38, [15:39], [16:4–7]
Exaltation	(14:62), [15:26?]
Investiture	(15:17)
Acclamation	(15:18), 15:26, 15:39
Reactions	[15:39]
Punishment	[12:9], [12:36], [12:40], [13:2], [14:21], [15:38]

Nickelsburg thought that Mark had reworked a pre-Markan story of Jesus as the Messiah by using the genre of the suffering Righteous One. He argued that there must have been such a pre-Markan narrative because he could not fully explain the anti-temple theme with his thesis. By assuming the correlation of Messiah and the Righteous One, Nickelsburg was able to show why certain actions and sayings of the persecutors should be taken ironically, and to explain features of the failure of the disciples during the ordeal. These observations are most helpful. Care needs to be taken, nevertheless, not to limit the identification of the Righteous One with a particular christological title or role, as if such a role preexisted. The reason this approach will not work is because Mark intentionally recast every pregiven profile associated with the titles he used for Jesus. This is particularly clear in the case of the role given to the Son of Man, but it is also true for the Son of God, the Christ, as it was for the worker of miracles, and the teacher. Mark did not prefer one title over the others, nor think of the Righteous One as a new and better characterization of Jesus with its own distinctive profile. It is not the case that Mark used the story of the Righteous One to enhance a suffering servant role for a pregiven view of Jesus as the Messiah-king.

Markan composition raises a problem more serious even than can be expressed by a discussion of recharacterization or reidentification of roles. Nickelsburg might well concede that a pre-Markan narrative is improbable, and that that role for Jesus as the Christ is not what Mark had in mind. One suspects, though, from the way in which Nickelsburg treats the Markan account, that some other configuration called Jesus Christ would have to take its place. Like Kelber, Nickelsburg approaches the text of Mark as if Mark had the "passion of Jesus Christ" already in mind before he wrote the gospel, the passion of a figure already associated with the historical events to be recorded in his gospel story. The impression given is that Mark "merely" used the genre of the wisdom story to give the passion of Jesus Christ narrative form. This circular reasoning does save the day for a kerygmatic view of the history of Jesus' passion, but at tremendous cost to normal logic. If there is no evidence for a passion narrative before Mark, and no need for one among the only circles known to have been interested in Jesus' death, it is simply inadequate to assume that the events recorded in the gospel account were somehow charged with meaning before Mark gave them narrative expression. Creativity is denied to Mark in the interest of investing the events of his story with prior significance (divine creativity).

A possibility more interesting than Nickelsburg's suggestion, and more reasonable than Kelber's conclusion, therefore, would be that the story of the Righteous One provided Mark with a basic narrative design capable of accommodating the integration of a number of previous characterizations of Jesus as well as a number of other narrative themes. The prior characterizations of Jesus would have been given with the materials and social histories of the various Jesus traditions known to Mark, as well as mythological configurations taken from the Hellenistic Christ cult, for Mark also was acquainted with that tradition. The several narrative themes in the gospel, then, would be credited to Mark's authorial decisions about how to combine different views of Jesus, how to construe Christian origins, and what he wanted his narration of those events to effect for his readers. This suggestion will be explored more fully in the next chapter.

10

THE NARRATIVE DESIGNS

Major studies by scholars of all persuasions have repeatedly stumbled upon traits of characterization in the passion narratives that correspond to a certain ideal type. The type is that of a figure, variously depicted in Jewish literatures before Mark's time, that may be called the Righteous One. Opinions about the specific literary locus of derivation have diverged, preference being given now to the Psalms, now to the suffering servant of Isaiah 53, now to the wisdom literature, especially Wisdom 2–5, and now to the martyrologies. There have been differences of opinion also about the importance of these traits in the passion account, whether constitutive, ornamental, or a later stage of reinterpretation of an earlier account. These differences of opinion should not cloud the consensus about the fact that the traits are there. They need to be accounted for some way.

Nickelsburg is the only scholar who has suggested that there was a story about the Righteous One, and that the passion narrative followed its pattern. Others have considered the narrative aspects of the passion account to have derived from "the nature of the affair," as Bultmann put it, and treated characterization as a separate matter. Characterization is, nevertheless, what the passion narratives are about. All scholars have acknowledged this by returning constantly to the question of Mark's "christology," and struggling with the "layers" of characterization that pile up upon Jesus at the end of Mark's Gospel. The essays in the Kelber volume are an evidence for this phenomenon. Setting out to identify the signs of Markan composition, each article settled finally on the function of the pericope under study for the development of Mark's "christology," that is, characterization of Jesus. Since the story of the Righteous One was about nothing if not characterization, the solution to the narrative design of Mark's passion account is really quite obvious. The traits of characterization belonging to the figure of the Righteous One, and attributed to Jesus in the passion account, belong to the plot. And the plot is about the trial of that figure. The conclusion should be that Mark composed the passion account on the model of the story of wisdom's child, the persecuted, innocent one.

A simple demonstration of this thesis cannot, unfortunately, be given. That is because attempts to correlate the wisdom story with the passion narrative on a function-by-function basis run into two unmanageable problems. One is that the story Mark told is about Jesus, not about "the" Righteous One. It is assumed by the author that readers will recognize the plot of the story about the Righteous One, and see the significance of allusions to the familiar character from the Psalms. But Jesus is still Jesus, and titles taken from the Jesus and Christian traditions are still the way in which Jesus is designated. If the new characterization is to be demonstrated, it must be done so in terms of Mark's manipulation of preexistent Christian views associated with these titles, and his forging of connections with the new storyline about the persecution of wisdom's child. Studies in the Kelber volume demonstrated how important the various titles were as narrative themes reaching back into the gospel and coming to climax in the passion account. These narrative themes need to be distinguished, studied in relation to the titles Mark used to designate them, and related to one another at the level of functions within the persecution story. If that can be done, the fundamental importance of the story of the Righteous One for the design of the whole will have been demonstrated.

A second problem frustrates this program, however, for a cluster of stories in the passion narrative does not seem to fit the story of the persecuted Righteous One. The meal, for instance, was not mentioned by Nickelsburg, nor could it have been. It does not fit the plot. The meal was also one of the stories Kelber thought must have existed before Mark wrote his account. Others were the anointing, Gethsemane, and Peter's denial. These stories introduce other perspectives on the basic set of events that constitute the plot. They need to be accounted for some other way. Were it possible to do that, however, the design of the passion narrative as a complex but coherent story might be clarified.

In this chapter, Mark's narrative design for the passion account will be explored as an interweaving of "christological" themes and traditions with the fundamental plot of persecution.

1. NARRATIVE CLUSTERS AND PLOTTING

Fundamental to the passion narrative is the sequence from the arrest, through the trials, to the crucifixion. This sequence corresponds to the story of the persecuted Righteous One. All scholars interested in isolating an "earliest layer" of the tradition have proposed some combination of this sequence. Dormeyer and Nickelsburg added to this sequence one other episode. They were able to show that the temple act belonged to the basic plot as the inaugural event of provocation. They were certainly right about this. The essential episodes of the basic plot are, therefore, temple act, arrest, trials, and crucifixion.

The rest of the material is related to this basic sequence in different ways. Some narrative units function as elaborations of the plot, fully dependent upon one of its major episodes, explicating the plot's own narrative logic. A cluster of stories around the crucifixion function this way. Other stories are only loosely linked to the plot, occurring in its shadow as it were and taking their meaning from it as counterpoints. Some of these counterpoint stories are fully independent episodes. They could be removed without disturbing the logic of the main narrative sequence. Others, especially those that cluster around the meal, are related to the meal and to one another by various means of interlocking. They describe a sequence that runs parallel to that of the main plot. These stories also require the main plot to have their significance, but, with one exception, do not contribute to the logic of the plot. If one distinguishes between independent counterpoint stories and those that cluster, the passion account can be arranged in columns for visual reference (see figure 18). The logic of the various relationships among stories will then need some discussion.

1.1 The Overall Pattern

Using the table as a guide, important features of the composition can be seen. The basic plot contains the pivotal events that change the situation and move the story ahead. All other material is brought to it for meaning. Of that material, four independent counterpoint stories attract attention (meal, anointing, Gethsemane, empty tomb). The meal stands out as that story around which other narrative units cluster. The narratives clustered around the meal are structured by a logic different from that at work in the persecution sequence. These stories highlight Jesus and the disciples. In them fulfillment "follows" upon a prediction. This kind of narrative logic is at work throughout the gospel also, even in relation to the persecution sequence, as the earlier predictions of the passion show. But the persecution plot, once set in motion by the temple act, unfolds as determined without further announcement. The unfolding of these plotted events is the context within which the second series of events focusing upon the disciples takes place. Of the five predictions made in the meal sequence (preparation, betrayal, kingdom, flight, denial), four are fulfilled within the story as narrated. One is not. The day of the kingdom is yet to occur. That day will also be a day of drinking wine, however, so that the meal event is strangely capable of attesting visually (by reverse allegorization) the fulfillment even of that prediction.

On the surface of it, then, the principal design would be the interweaving of the meal and the sequences dependent upon it with the persecution plot. One of these narrative units, the prediction of betrayal and its fulfillment, provides an important link to the persecution plot. The arrest as betrayal actually contributes to the development of the plot. This means that, at the level of the logic of composition, the meal and the five major episodes

FIGURE 18
The Structure of the Passion Narrative

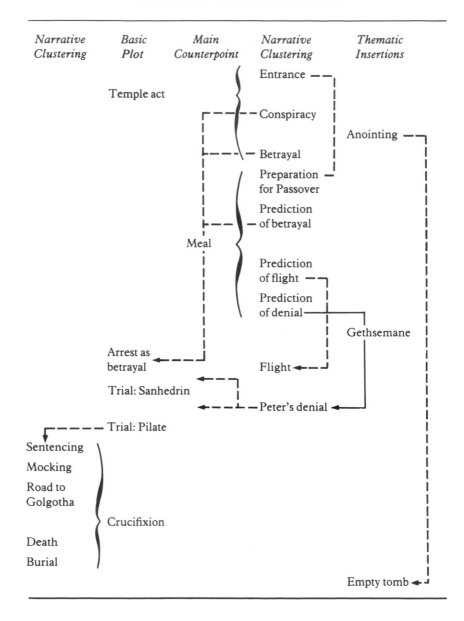

belonging to the persecution plot are the narrative units fundamental to the structure of the whole. All other material is dependent upon or subservient to these six episodes.

1.2 The Narrative Clusters

There are several small narrative units that cluster around the crucifixion. They provide further narrative description for that major event and may be considered embellishments of the event itself. They are the sentencing, mocking, road to Golgotha, death, and burial. They are subordinate to the plot, some of them serving as connectors between the trial and the crucifixion. It would be difficult to imagine them as independent stories or "traditions," for they presuppose the narration of the trial before Pilate and the crucifixion as these appear in the present account.

The stories that cluster around the meal function differently. They are the preparation, the prediction of the betrayal, and the predictions of the flight and denial. Following upon these predictions as their fulfillments, then, are the arrest as betrayal, the flight (at the arrest), and Peter's denial. Each sequence of prediction and fulfillment presents a study of the response of the disciples to the events transpiring in the persecution plot. They take place reactively but, with the exception of the betrayal, do not contribute to the movement of the plot. Because they all share the same (discipleship) theme, one may speak of a second storyline running through the passion account. This second storyline is dependent upon the meal for its place in the overall structure of the account, but each prediction/ fulfillment sequence is related to the meal only artificially. None would make good independent stories, each presupposing the larger context to gain its meaning. They do that by filling in the space between the plot on the one hand, and Jesus' own attitude toward it on the other. It was the meal that Mark chose to describe Jesus' attitude, making it the counterpoint of greatest opposition to the plot. The artificiality of the meal as occasion for the several predictions of inadequate response should be taken, not as a sign of sloppy workmanship, but as an indication of craftsmanship fully aware of its purposes.

A word should be said about a less obvious third clustering of narratives at the beginning of the passion account. The inaugural phase of the plot is triggered by Jesus' temple act. The account of the arrest and the charges at the trial show that this is so. Nevertheless, much intervenes between the temple act and the arrest. The intervening material is essential to the integration with the persecution plot of several narrative themes from the earlier phases of the gospel. This material is not introduced haphazardly, however, for the entrance into Jerusalem was structured on the same pattern as Jesus' entrance into Galilee at the beginning of the story. As with the exorcism in the synagogue at Capernaum, so here in the temple, Jesus' action is interpreted as a "teaching." This significant teaching-event is followed in both sequences by a period of instruction consisting mostly of controversy stories. Just as the set of controversy stories in Mark 2:1–3:6 plays upon and develops the theme of authority announced in the synagogue act, so does the second set of instructions in the temple (Mark 11:27–12:44) elaborate upon the significance of the temple act. In this elaboration two reversals are announced. One is that the plot to destroy Jesus, announced at the end of the first round of "teaching" in the synagogue (Mark 3:6), will now be matched by Jesus' prediction of the destruction of the temple (Mark 12:9–10; 13:1–2). The other is that the kingdom Jesus announced at the beginning, a kingdom that was to draw near by means of the "new teaching," is now specified as that to be realized apocalyptically after the temple has received its just rewards. Noting this craftsmanship, the following narrative units can be understood as yet another kind of cluster, this one dependent upon the temple act for its significance. The cluster includes the entrance, the teaching in the temple, the conspiracy, and the plans for the betrayal.

Because the temple act is a major episode in the persecution plot, the persecution plot is essential to the structure of the gospel itself at the very point where the Jesus traditions and the passion narratives are joined. Those stories clustering around the temple act and dependent upon it are very important thematically as well. The entrance makes the transition from the preceding sections of the gospel to the events in Jerusalem. It also is the story where the messianic motif is made explicit. The teaching, first in the temple, then privately to the disciples (Mark 13), transposes the theme of the kingdom from parabolic discourse (Mark 4) into apocalyptic prediction (Mark 13). The conspiracy alerts the reader to the fact that the time for action has arrived because the place for action has been sighted and Jesus has entered that place. The betrayal announces the point at which the theme of Jesus and his disciples will mesh with the plot of the leaders against Jesus. Thus the temple act triggers other events that serve to conjoin unresolved narrative themes that have been developing throughout the gospel. Two of these are major, the plot of the leaders against Jesus, and the following along of the disciples. One is a minor theme, but of great importance for the sense to be made of Jesus' presence in Jerusalem after the other themes are conjoined, namely the crowd's view of Jesus. The leader's plot was frustrated by the people, even though the people had no idea about what was abrewing. The people first took Jesus to be a prophet, but now greet him as the Messiah. The crowds will drop from sight until the trial, but there the question of Jesus' identity as the Messiah will surface with them and trigger the charge. The disciples' story, however, will come to climax round and about the event of the meal. Jesus will end up facing his accusers alone, just as the persecution plot of the one innocently charged requires. The temple act is pivotal to the integration of all three narrative themes: the crowds, the leaders, and the disciples.

1.3 The Importance of the Meal

The meal is the only counterpoint story essential to the plot in any way. The disciples gather together for the meal and hear Jesus announce the betrayal. The betrayal is essential to the plot. The leaders have repeatedly sought to take Jesus, but have failed because of the crowds, that is, because Jesus was always in public view. Mark uses the betrayal to join the two major narrative themes of the gospel, each of which had been developed separately until this point. If the theme of discipleship is as important as the theme of conflict for the gospel as a whole, the meal, though only a single event, is as important to the passion narrative and its rhetorical designs as is the persecution plot. Two fundamentally diverse images of Jesus' death are thus set side by side and related by narrative interweaving. The meal brings one image to focus; the plot develops the other. The parallel correspondence is indicated clearly in the doublet created by the two entrance stories, one leading to the temple act, the other leading to the meal.

This is a rather surprising find. Coming upon the story of the meal after reading through the gospel, the first impression is that it does not fit in with the surrounding narration. The sudden change in atmosphere is strange. Jesus' demeanor and his words about the bread and cup are alien in the context of both the gospel that has gone before and the passion about to unfold. The scene floats uneasily on the surface of the story, a momentary reflection of some other way of being with Jesus, some other story, some other Jesus. The response of the critical scholar has always been to overlook the "insertion" of the meal as some awkward attempt in etiology. The meal, as has been suggested, was Mark's way of reminding the reader of the true significance of Jesus' death given with the eucharistic ritual as practiced in Mark's community. According to this theory, the meal allowed the reader a momentary respite in the midst of a story full of morals with much less gracious intent.

It is now possible to suggest another reason. The meal is important to the historian because it is the only story in the passion account for which there is evidence of a precursor within early Jesus Christ traditions. The evidence for a precursor is the account of the Lord's Supper in 1 Cor 11:23–26, a ritual text from the Hellenistic Christ cult. Mark's use of this cultic tradition is positive proof of his acquaintance with Hellenistic Christianity. That he used the ritual text the way he did, that is, as the scene of counterpoint to the persecution plot in the composition of the passion narrative, means that the Hellenistic cult was a major source for Mark's ideas about the significance of Jesus' death. It also means that he was interested in making the source of his appropriation obvious, because the ritual symbolism was allowed to stand. One should not take the occurrence of the meal scene for granted. One should not assume that Mark's community celebrated the Hellenistic Eucharist. Jesus people may have been shocked. It would have been one thing to have imagined just how bad the Pharisees and temple authorities had been, thus introducing the theme of Jesus' death into myths of origin growing out of the Jesus tradition. It would have been another thing altogether to suggest a saving significance for that death on the pattern of the Hellenistic Christ cult.

Mark appears to have positioned himself between the Jesus movements and the Christ cult. His passion narrative may have been fabricated on the model of the persecution plot. But his knowledge of the significance of Jesus' death appears, now, to have been gotten, not from an early wisdom tale about Jesus' persecution and death (a pre-Markan account of the passion), but from Christ myth and ritual. The presence of the meal text and its structural importance within the passion account is the proof. If that is the case, however, the process of composition is disclosed. Mark used the pattern of the wisdom story to conjoin myths of origin stemming from the Jesus movements on the one hand, with the myth of origin stemming from the Christ cult on the other. Those traditions were the only pre-Markan precursors from within early Jesus or Christ movements. The wisdom tale was the narrative device used to merge them. The gospel is the product of that accommodation.

2. REWRITING THE CHRIST MYTH

By inserting the meal scene into the story of the plot against Jesus, Mark positioned himself between the Jesus movements and the Christ cult. He may have been walking a very thin line. The Hellenistic idea of Christ's death as saving event would have been strange if not obnoxious to many people in the Jesus movements oriented to Jesus myths of origin. Yet, there it was as big as life in the center of the meal scene: "This is my blood of the covenant which is poured out for many" (Mark 14:24). There is absolutely nothing comparable to this in any of the Jesus traditions. To notice that the meal creates an anomaly, yet is structurally foundational to the passion narrative, changes the question one must ask of Mark. The question is not why he joined Jesus traditions (miracle stories, for instance) with "the" passion narrative, but why he joined Jesus traditions with the Christ cult traditions.

There are two bits of evidence that indicate Mark was well acquainted with the Christ myth and the ritual of the Hellenistic communities. One is the meal scene, a ritual text. The other is the way in which the predictions of the passion are formulated. They correspond to the kerygmatic formulations of the Christ myth. That Mark knew what he was doing is evident by the use of the three predictions to structure the phase of the story on the way to Jerusalem. Three times Jesus announces what will be (Mark 8:31; 9:31; 10:33–34). The announcement is rebuked (Mark 8:32), or creates fear (Mark 9:32), or leads to impossible pretension and desire (Mark 10:35–41). Following these "misunderstandings" Jesus then "instructs" the disciples in what it means to "follow" him to Jerusalem. These are the well-known sayings on discipleship (Mark 8:34–9:1; 9:35–50; 10:42–45). The sayings are a call to "take up one's cross and follow" for the sake of Jesus, saving one's life, and the final manifestation of the kingdom in power and glory. The predictions of the passion are carefully constructed as a pre-script for what will happen in Jerusalem. The sayings instruct the reader to see the passion plot as a model to be imitated. The notion of a noble death is Greek. The notion of imitation is Greek. The logic of "losing one's life in order to save it" is Greek. Thus the discipleship sayings move the Jesus myth of origins into the arena of making martyrological sense of Jesus' death by persecution. That sense has been pressed to the limits of its acceptability for Jesus' followers. Not until the final saying in these three sets of instruction is there any need to entertain the notion that Jesus' death was vicarious. There, however, in the last saying, Mark has Jesus say that "the Son of Man came . . . to give his life as a ransom for many" (Mark 10:45).[1]

This and the cup word in the meal scene are the only declarative references in the entire gospel to the saving significance of Jesus' death. Mark 10:45 is obviously a Markan creation, derived from the ritual text, but attributed to the Son of Man whose mythic destiny has been laid out in accordance with the plot of the gospel. That cannot have been an accident. The saying is positioned as an argument (*gar*, "for . . ."), as well as an authoritative pronouncement at the end of an elaboration pattern. It comes, therefore, both as a conclusion to all of the reasons that have been given for seeing Jesus' death as a paradigm for imitation (Jesus' death will be a truly noble obedience), as well as a surprise (Jesus' death will be a true martyrdom, that is, "for others"). Because the groundwork was laid so carefully in chapters 8–10, the new and surprising thought may well have been found acceptable also. Mark, at any rate, had to hope so. The pronouncement about the "ransom for many" was barely mentioned, then left there to work its way into the imagination of the reader while working through the rest of the story. Mark 10:45 was the only preparation the reader would have before coming upon the startling saying about the cup in the meal story. If the reader was not to be overly offended at the saying at that point, the meaning of the "for many" would have to have been discharged of its cultic

---

1. *The Hellenistic milieu.* On the noble death as a Greek tradition, see above, chap. 4, n. 6. On mimesis, see Elizabeth Castelli, "Mimesis as a Discourse of Power." On "Saving One's Life By Losing It," see William A. Beardslee's article by that title.

and participatory connotations, and resignified as a statement of the vicarious death of a martyr. The vicarious death of the martyr might be acceptable to Jesus people, whereas rituals celebrating the presence of a deity of
self-sacrifice would not.

The care with which Mark constructed the three prediction units is
evidence of conscious appropriation from the Christ cult traditions. Mark
10:45 shows that Mark knew about the correspondence of myth and ritual
in the Christ cult. It is a saying that explicates the predicted destiny of the
Son of Man kerygmatically, while pointing ahead to the cup word of the
meal, thus combining the myth (of Jesus as the Son of Man) with the ritual
(of Jesus at meal). It also shows that he purposefully shifted the kerygmatic
core of the Christ myth to his own characterization of the Son of Man. The
idea of giving his life as a ransom was foreign to the figure of the Son of
Man. "Creative borrowing" is thus in evidence on both fronts. Both the
Christ myth and ritual as well as the traditions about Jesus, his authority,
and its vindication when the Son of Man appears apocalyptically, were
manipulated, twisted out of shape in order to create a new character at the
beginning of the community's time. Bracketing for now the question of why
Mark would have wanted to create a new figure, that he did it, and how,
needs to be demonstrated.

2.1 Kerygma and the Son of Man

There is a strong scholarly consensus that Mark formulated the predictions of the passion and that they relate in some way to the kerygmatic
formulations of the Christ myth. Using the kerygma in 1 Cor 15:3–5 as a
control, Mark's appropriation of the Christ myth can be discerned by noting
how the predictions differ from it. The kerygma is given on page 104. The
predictions of the passion are given in figure 19. There are five observations
of significance that follow from a comparison of the two modes of formulation.

The first difference is that the predictions are given as sayings of Jesus,
not proclamations about him. They occur in the midst of narrative discourse, have the quality of condensed narrative about them, and function to
prepare for the full narration of the events they predict. The kerygma
(proclamation of a completed event) is erased as soon as the event is taken
up into a story for narration. Proclamation and storytelling are two different
modes of communication. Mark understood that in his own way, making
sure that the kerygma was fully subsumed by his narrative treatment of it.

A second difference is that the predictions contain no reference to the
saving significance of Jesus' death and resurrection. This is an extremely
important point. Mark was aware of the soteriology attached to the myth in
Hellenistic circles. He allowed its mention in Mark 10:45, but only after

FIGURE 19
THE PREDICTIONS OF THE PASSION

First Prediction: Mark 8:31

And he began to teach them that

The Son of Man
must suffer many things
and be rejected by the elders
and the chief priests
and the scribes,

⌈and be killed,
⌊and after three days rise again.

Second Prediction: Mark 9:31

For he was teaching his disciples, saying to them,

The Son of Man
will be delivered into the hands of men
and they will kill him;

⌈and when he is killed,
⌊after three days he will rise.

Third Prediction: Mark 10:33–34

He began to tell them what was to happen to him, saying
Behold, we are going up to Jerusalem,

And the Son of Man
will be delivered to the chief priests
and the scribes,
and they will condemn him to death,
and deliver him to the Gentiles;
and they will mock him, and spit upon him,
and scourge him,

⌈and kill him;
⌊and after three days he will rise.

(Brackets highlight the kerygmatic core.)

three formulaic predictions were given without any trace of the death's effectiveness. The predictions are presented, rather, with the effectiveness of Jesus' pronouncement about the death in mind. Other reasons for the death are left at the level of enigma. Jesus only says that it must be so (*dei*, "it is necessary that . . .").

A third observation is that the terms used to predict what will happen are descriptive: "rejected," "handed over," "condemned," "mocked," "killed." Kerygmatic traditions do not reveal interest in exploring the treatment

Jesus received, nor in deriving significance from the motivation of those who killed him. Paul gave the matter some thought after the kerygma had been conceived and accepted. He said once that the Jews killed Jesus as they had killed the prophets; he said another time that had the rulers known they would not have done it (1 Thess 2:14–15; 1 Cor 2:8). But neither of these statements intends an explanation about how the death came to be significant in the first place. Both assume its significance already. The reason the rulers would not have done it had they known, for instance, was that they would not have chosen wittingly to contribute to the plan of salvation and their own undoing. Paul's meditation shows just how dangerous it would be to historicize the kerygma. It also shows the circumstances under which one might be tempted to do so. The circumstances are those of conflict with Judaism or with Christian Judaizers. Mark took the next step (for reasons related to the situation of the ousted synagogue reform movement, not that of the Christ cult). His introduction of motivational considerations altered radically the nature of the account. If one asks from whence these terms derive, the answer is simple. These descriptions of motivation belong to the persecution story. Mark turned the kerygma of Christ's death and resurrection into a formulaic prediction of the persecution plot. For Mark, the meaning of Jesus' death was to be taken from the wisdom story, not the Christ myth and ritual.

A fourth consideration can now be given. The intention of the rewriting was not innocent. It was not merely a matter of giving narrative form to the kerygmatic report. It cannot be explained as the natural desire to flesh out the historical point of contact for the cosmic event, as if the kerygma implicitly invited such explication. The predictions of the passion changed the kerygma into a script for writing an account of Jesus' death as a geopolitical event. Read in the light of the predictions, the passion plot unfolds exactly according to its prescription. The sequence of events given in the predictions (each prediction expanding a bit upon the previous statements) is the same sequence that unfolds on cue in the passion account. The agents, those who will play their roles as determined, are already indicated in the predictions. The elders, chief priests, and scribes will reject him (Mark 8:31). He will be handed over into the hands of men (Mark 9:31). He will be handed over to the chief priests and the scribes, and they will condemn him to death, and deliver him to the Gentiles, and they will mock him, spit on him, scourge him, and kill him (Mark 10:33). Time, place, agents, and consequences are all spelled out in the predictions and identifiable in the passion account. They purport to be the ingredients of a historical event, but this story does not derive from history. History was written according to the script of the persecution story.

A fifth comparison is noteworthy. The destiny is not to be suffered by the Christ, but by the Son of Man. The mythic pattern of death-resurrection thus was transferred from the Christ who, in the Hellenistic cult mediated life and power presently to the community, to a figure of authority who functioned only at the beginning and at the end of a history imagined on the apocalyptic model. The death of the Son of Man became in this way a manifestation of the evil in human society that needed to be set right. It also provided justification for imagining that it must be set right and therefore would be. The resurrection showed that the rulers had not had the final say, did not possess lasting power. Mark's application of the Christ kerygma to Jesus as the Son of Man violated earlier notions both of the Christ and of the Son of Man in order to plot a novel myth, one that inaugurated an apocalyptic history for the synagogue reform movement.

2.2 Christ and the Messiah

In the Christ cult, Christ was exalted to reign over a new order of things. This order was sometimes conceptualized as a new "creation," at other times (primarily by Paul himself) it was visualized as the kingdom of God to appear at the end of human history. But the Hellenistic communities did not use the term king (*basileus*) for Jesus Christ, nor develop the notion of the kingdom of God. At some early or fundamental level, the term Christ must have retained the connotation of kingship in accordance with its Jewish derivation. All of the other mythic titles and roles for the Christ were royal. Nevertheless, the Christ cult had no interest in going back over the history of Jesus to imagine the ways in which he may have fulfilled popular messianic roles. Mark is the one who did that.

The term Christ appears first in the incipit (Mark 1:1), then in the confession of Peter (Mark 8:29). At that point in the story, the title comes as something of a surprise for there has been no preparation for it in the narrative. It is put forth as Peter's idea in contrast to that of the crowds who hold Jesus to be a prophet. Jesus' response is twofold. He charges the disciples not to tell anyone, then goes on to give the first prediction of the passion of the Son of Man. Because of the double remonstrance that follows, Peter's rebuke and Jesus' harsh rejoinder, scholars have debated whether Peter's identification of Jesus as the Christ was intended by Mark to be taken constructively. The answer surely must be yes, as the secrecy charge shows. Nevertheless, the meaning of the term is unclear and may be quite different in the context of Mark's Gospel than in the Christ cult. The term Christ does not occur in any of the Markan predictions of the eschatological kingdom, for instance. The term Christ nowhere is allowed to take on the connotations of a cultic deity, present or transcendent. The saving significance of Jesus' death was transferred from the Christ to the martyrdom of the Son of Man.

Nevertheless, the term Christ reappears at the trial where Jesus' confesses that he is the Christ. This identity obviously is important, for his confession becomes the basis for his condemnation and he is crucified as the "King of the Jews." This cannot be what Peter had in mind, to be sure, since his remonstrance was to the point of rejecting any idea that Jesus must die. If this is what Mark had in mind all along, however, there should no longer be any mystery about why Jesus' identity had to be kept secret. As soon as Jesus' identity becomes known, the situation will change and events will unfold according to another script—the script of the persecution plot. But what has the Christ to do with this persecution plot?

In Mark, the term Christ must mean (popular) Messiah. This would be a reduction of the cultic connotations of the term to the level of its popular and political meaning. This would explain why the term is introduced just at the point in the story where Jesus intends to begin his way to Jerusalem. There can be no doubt that Mark's readers were acquainted with such a scenario. Between the time of Jesus and the time of Mark there had been several popular "messianic" movements, two or three of them successful enough to have precipitated the Jewish War. All leaders of popular king movements zeroed in on Jerusalem and the temple as the object of their maneuvers and final object of their guerrilla wars. All of these leaders ended badly. Mark's readers would have had no trouble imagining a popular king who got killed. The thought would have been depressing, but not scandalous. Peter's remonstrance would have made sense and been greeted with sympathy.

Everything about the Markan use of the theme Christ-Messiah fits the popular model and the recent history except for one thing. The messiahs marched against the Romans, not against the temple. With Jesus, it is the temple itself that must fall. The crowds did not understand that. They greeted him with hosannas (Mark 11:1–10) and heard him gladly when he proposed a conundrum to the scribes about a Davidic Messiah and Lord (Mark 12:35–37). They were foolish to do so. When the full significance of what Jesus was up to came out at the trials, so did the understanding of the crowds. They wanted instead an insurrectionist against the Romans (Mark 15:11) and thus joined the chief priests in crying out for Jesus' crucifixion. Mark's fiction of an anti-temple messiahship (a contradiction in terms) could have worked only after the temple had already been destroyed. The gospel theme must therefore be a post 70 C.E. fabrication. Before that time the scenario would have appeared ridiculous.

Mark's fabrication of the narrative theme was not without its purposes. Three can be given. One was to empty the Christ title of its cultic connotations. Another was to provide a narrative theme to link the Jesus traditions with the account of his death. The persecution plot could not achieve this, could not motivate Jesus' march to Jerusalem. And a third was to counter enthusiasm about "popular messiahs" by showing that Jesus had already done that, leaving the future for another kind of appearance altogether. In the apocalyptic instruction, the appearance of "false Christs" is strongly counseled against (Mark 13:21-22). This counsel reflects recent memory for Mark and his readers, as well as a period of confusion in the late sixties about taking sides in the Jewish War. Mark's story answers these questions by saying (1) that "messiahship" had already occurred with Jesus, (2) the war was hardly a time for salvation, rather for woes and judgments, and (3) that the next appearance would be one of glory.

2.3 Son of God and Miracles

Christ, Son of Man, Son of God—these are the titles of significance for the "christology" of the Gospel of Mark. The way in which Mark recast earlier configurations of the Christ and the Son of Man has been sketched. The same kind of purposeful appropriation can be shown for the title Son of God.

The term Son of God occurs in the gospel in two distinctly different types of story, the framework stories (baptism, transfiguration, and crucifixion), and the stories of exorcisms (Mark 3:11; 5:7; in Mark 1:24 the term is "Holy One of God"). The framework stories indicate that Mark had a mythological figure of cosmic destiny in mind. The stories of exorcisms, however, lead one to think of the Hellenistic divine man. He also could be called a son of God. Scholars are undecided about which meaning to prefer.

The normal procedure has been to survey the meaning of the term in the literatures of the period. The problem with this approach is that the use of the term during the Greco-Roman period lacked specific profile. That is because it was applied to a wide range of special figures, including gods, ideal types, and personifications of human capacities held to be divine. Ultimately, the source of the notion was in ancient Near Eastern mythologies of divine kingship. Kings were the point at which social order constituted through sovereignty was joined with the mythic world of the gods and the stories of their creation of order by sovereign power. The king was imagined to be the son of (the high) god. The drama of royal succession could be storied in the realm of the gods on high, imagined as an intercourse between the family of the gods and the royal dynasty, or focused upon rituals of the palace that treated the king with the deference due the gods. Some of these mythologies and rituals were still alive during the Hellenistic period. The Greeks took them up both playfully and with some seriousness, reconceptualizing the divine figures by combining them with their own myths and translating the mythic figures into concepts. They understood that sonship was the mythological articulation for the generation, representation, and (re)constitution of order in the world. They interpreted the myths as narrative descriptions of the forces held to be fundamental to the structure of the world (*physis, nomos, logos, pneuma, dynamis*), and these forces as the "nature" of the divine and human in the world. Thus the term son of God can be found as a designation for second rank deities and powers with stories of marvelous missions to earth, of battles in the realms above and below, and victories involving cosmic ascent and enthronement. It could also be used, however, to designate the man of special endowment, the sage or thaumaturge, whose wisdom and power were held to be "divine."

As for the Jewish tradition, the term son of God could be used for the king, Israel as a people, special messengers such as angels, or even the ideal, true Israelite. In Alexandrian imagination, special figures of mediation between God and the people, such as the divine *logos* (Word), or Moses (mythologized), could be called a son of God or even a "second God." In the Wisdom of Solomon, the Righteous One knows himself to be a son of God (Wis 2:18), and the people waiting for their deliverance from Egypt are called the son of God (Wis 18:13).[2]

Attempts to move directly from this rich background to the Markan texts, therefore, have not succeeded in pinpointing a specific figure with which Jesus may have been identified, or found any reason for Mark to have done so. His use of the term in double connotation, for a worker of miracles as well as a divine figure of destiny, is hardly a clue, for neither meaning is extraordinary and the combination is not unthinkable.

The better question would be about the meaning of the term within the Jesus and Christ movements before Mark's time. The thought of Jesus as a son of God was hardly necessary or appropriate within the Jesus movements. There is no evidence for its occurrence in these circles before Mark. From their perspective, then, Mark's attribution of the term to Jesus would have been a novelty. But in the Christ cult, the term Son of God had come to be used for Jesus as the Christ in respect to his divine nature and the father's approval of his mission into the world. Jesus' divine sonship was one of the ways to think the thought that the Christ event and its consequences originated with God. With that thought came a pattern of destiny on the model of Hellenistic deities and their missions. Thus Jesus as the Son was "sent" into the world by the father, accomplished his task in obedience, returned to the father, and was rewarded with an enthronement to lordship over the world as his kingdom. The most reasonable way to imagine where Mark got the idea of Jesus as the Son of God would be from

---

2. *Son of God*. The ancient Near Eastern and Hellenistic "background" to the notion of the Son of God has been investigated repeatedly by scholars writing monographs on New Testament christology. The references are endless. Discussions of the range of meaning can be found in R. H. Fuller, *The Foundations of New Testament Christology;* and the articles on "Son" (Greek, *huios*) in *The Theological Dictionary to the New Testament,* vol. 8.

the Christ cult. The introduction of a novel mythology taken from the larger world of Hellenistic thought does not make sense when a point of departure is known to have existed in early Christian circles.[3]

Derivation from the Christ cult would mean that special attention should be given first to the use of the term in the framework stories. Each of these stories makes some reference to movements of ascent and descent. Each accentuates the idea of the divinity of Jesus. Each contains notice of a cosmic event coterminus with the historical moment under description. In each of them God plays a decisive role. And they are those in which Jesus is attested and recognized as God's son. Mark positioned them, one at the beginning, one in the middle at the turning of the story, and one at the end, in order to "frame" the two phases of Jesus' activity with the myth of divine entrance into the world.

Philip Vielhauer noticed that these stories formed a set, framed the two major sections of the gospel, and employed the title Son of God. He was reminded of Egyptian mythology about the installation of a newly selected king. The myth recounted the inauguration of a new era from the divine point of view. It consisted of three acts. The first was an announcement by God to the king-to-be of his selection. The second was a presentation of the king to the heavenly court. The third was a public presentation at which the divine selection would be confirmed by the people in acclamation. The correlation of the three gospel stories with the three acts of the Egyptian pageant is uncanny. The Egyptian script articulates a precise mythology: the king is the son of (the high) God.[4]

Vielhauer's proposal is attractive because it allows some sense to be made of the framework of the gospel. According to this view, the three stories superimpose a script of divine approval and involvement for all of the activities and events in the gospel. They mark the story of Jesus as the point at which the flow of human history was interrupted by powers from on high. In the Christ cult, the cosmic myth could be imagined without much concern for description. The Christ hymn in Philippians 2, for instance, gets by with the terminology of the "form" of one divine who took the "form" of the human. For Mark, integrating a figure of cosmic destiny with the picture of Jesus was more difficult to imagine. He joined the two

---

3. *Christ as Son of God.* References to the cosmic myth of the Son of God in the Hellenistic Christ cult are given in H. Conzelmann, *An Outline of the Theology of the New Testament,* 76–82.

4. *Philipp Vielhauer.* His thesis is set forth in "Erwägungen zur Christologie des Markusevangeliums." An Egyptian pattern lying behind the myth of the Son of God is not at all unthinkable in Jewish-Christian circles familiar with Jewish wisdom thought. On the Egyptian derivation of wisdom mythologumena in Sirach 24, see H. Conzelmann, "The Mother of Wisdom." For the Wisdom of Solomon, see James Reese, *Hellenistic Influence on the Book of Wisdom.* For Philo of Alexandria, see B. Mack, *Logos und Sophia.*

configurations by using the euphemism of the Spirit to suggest both generation and endowment. Accompanied by the voice from heaven, the divine sonship was imaginable without depicting a cosmic descent for the son. The euphemism was, in fact, more satisfactory to Mark than the cosmic myth would have been. Mark's plan in general was to reassign the symbols of cosmic presence either to the inaugural period or to the final consummation of a thoroughgoing apocalyptic history of the Jesus people. In the Christ cult the myth of the Son of God supported the sense of divine presence mediated through the new world created by the Christ event and ruled by the world's new sovereign. Mark diffused the myth of cosmic (lordship and) presence by reducing its moment to the level of divine kingship. This reduction meant that the myth could be played out as the drama of the king's installation. The act of selection was imagined as the bestowal of divine spirit. The "enthronement" took place, not in heaven, but in history, an enthronement that could be managed within an apocalyptic view of that history. The enthronement of Jesus as the Son of God would be the same as his death as the messiah-king of the Jews.

Mark's story of Jesus as the martyr for the kingdom of God could not accommodate the myth of the Son of God as the Christ cult imagined it. Mark's story could barely accommodate the pageantry of divine kingship. That is because the kingdom over which the Son was to rule was rejected upon announcement in a world ruled by a hostile power. As soon as the Son was selected, the Spirit that entered the world upon him drove him into a confrontation with his archenemy, Satan (Mark 1:12–13). Demonic forces were already in control of the world, according to Mark, and the Son's destiny was to be involved in a conflict of gigantic proportions with those forces. He had the power to cast out demons, to be sure, and they acknowledged that he had power over them because he was the Son of God. But as the scene of conflict shifts from demons to the synagogue and the temple, it is clear that Jesus' authority to rule will not be recognized at large. Thus the installation of the king could not run according to script. The acclamation would have to come from one who saw how the Son of God died, not from the crowds who might have celebrated his enthronement.

It was the centurion who, "when he saw that he thus breathed out his last," said, "Truly this man was a son of God" (Mark 15:39). Howard Jackson studied this story to find out why Mark thought the centurion could have inferred that. The clue is to be found in the rending of the temple curtain at the moment of Jesus' cry. Jackson demonstrates that the "thus" refers to the rending, not to the way in which Jesus expired. The emphasis upon "breathing out," however, is also important. It is a sign to the reader that a connection is to be made between Jesus' spirit (leaving him) and the rending of the curtain. Jackson calls the rending of the curtain a prodigy, and relates the spirit of Jesus here in this story to the spiritual power Jesus demonstrated earlier in his miracles and exorcisms. Jackson is willing to leave it there, to say that Mark saw Jesus as a thaumaturge.[5]

If the rending of the temple curtain is Jesus' last exorcism, it is peculiar. The miracle occurs at the moment of Jesus' death. It is effected by the exit of his own spirit in a cry. It is directed at the temple, not the demons, exactly that symbol of the kingdom Jesus confronted with his claim. The rending of the curtain and the cry do recall the exorcisms with their convulsions and cries. The rending also recalls the splitting of the heavens at Jesus' baptism, however, and the descent of the Spirit from heaven upon him. There was a voice heard then also, the voice of God. So the symbolism at the crucifixion is compounded of both cosmic myth and inverted exorcism. The exit of God's spirit from Jesus and the world is marked by a prodigy signifying destruction. A figure of manifest destiny, approved and empowered by God, before whom the demons cried out, was destroyed in the city. There will now have to be wars and rumors of wars, nations rising up against nations, before he comes in power and glory. The certainty of his appearance and the measure of his power and glory is already sealed by a narrative prolepsis. God's prodigious rending of the temple curtain to end three hours of darkness over all the land is the signature of judgment upon the city that refused to receive its king.

---

5. *The prodigy.* See Howard Jackson, "The Death of Jesus in Mark."

11

THE COMPOSITIONAL PROCESS

Four narrative designs have been uncovered, each closely associated with a particular christological theme. Each converges with the others in the formation of the passion narrative. (1) The framework stories introduce Jesus as the Son of God and climax at the crucifixion. (2) The messianic scenario underlies the journey of Jesus to Jerusalem and comes to climax at the crucifixion. (3) The persecution plot is basic to the sequence of events of the passion narrative itself, beginning with the entrance into Jerusalem. The conspiracy that belongs to the plot, however, was triggered by the first appearances of Jesus in the synagogues of Galilee. This means that all of Jesus' activity is to be understood as part of the provocation. The christological theme is that of the Son of Man. (4) A fourth narrative design is the use of prediction/fulfillment sequences throughout. This is a very complex, but important and pervasive device. At its most obvious level it occurs in the predictions that Jesus makes as the teacher, predictions that come true within the story as told. There are, however, a number of other ways in which prediction and fulfillment are used to give events significance. One is that the prophets are cited as oracles that come true in the life of Jesus. Another is that a given incident is patterned in such a way that it recalls or anticipates a companion event somewhere else in the story. Everything seems to happen twice in Mark. The piling up, bracketing, and formation of doublets are all ways to correlate patterned events separated in narrative time, and thus play with the notion of prediction and fulfillment typologically. Jesus' predictions of the kingdom coming in glory and with power are supported by the events narrated in the gospel, because the gospel as a whole is inaugural and predictive in relation to the events at the end of history. The four narrative designs are given in figure 20, and will be indicated in the discussions to follow by the designation "D" (D1, D2, . . .).

None of these designs came with the christological traditions Mark inherited. All of them were, nonetheless, common plots and devices, readily recognizable to anyone familiar at all with Hellenistic-Jewish culture in general. Prediction/fulfillment was customary for apocalyptic scripts. The wisdom story lay behind a variety of compositions including martyrologies and poems. The messianic scenario may not have been available in literary form, but would have been recognized when seen, allusions to the epic motif of the entrance into the land and all. The framework stories might have seemed far-fetched to some, but the mythological motifs would have been familiar. Even the placement of the transfiguration story in the middle of the gospel would not have seemed strange to those familiar with Hellenistic versions of the story of Moses. Philo's *Life of Moses* is structured very much like the Gospel of Mark, with a marvelous transfiguration story in the middle, dividing an earlier period of miracles in Egypt from an account of the wilderness way of testing that lay before. Moses' transfiguration also is imagined as an ascent into the presence of God. There his divine nature and kingship is confirmed in order to make legitimate his leadership of the people.[1]

FIGURE 20
MARK'S NARRATIVE DESIGNS

	Jesus' Role	*Literary Device*
D1.	Son of God	Framework stories
		Exorcisms
D2.	Christ	Miracle Stories
	(Messiah)	Crowds
		Journey to Jerusalem
D3.	Son of Man	Pronouncement stories
		Persecution plot
		Passion narrative
D4.	Prophet	Predictions/
	(Seer)	Fulfillments

To structure a story about Jesus by means of these narrative designs was, therefore, to create a new story out of familiar plots. The new story was truly new, for none like it had been told about Jesus before. But the plots were not new, nor were they selected without consideration for the nature of the received Jesus materials and the Christ myth. For each narrative design

---

1. *The transfiguration.* On the structural significance of a transfiguration story in both Mark and Philo's *Life of Moses,* see B. Mack, "Imitatio Mosis," esp. nn. 6 and 9.

there was a definite point of departure given with the traditions. The framework stories were appropriate to the Hellenistic Son of God mythology. The messianic scenario took its rationale from the popular meaning of the Christ title. The persecution plot was a reduction of the Christ myth to the logic of martyrdom at its core. The prediction/fulfillment sequence was suggested, no doubt, by the apocalyptic schemata that came with the sayings of Jesus (Q) and the figure of the Son of Man. The narrative designs were selected, therefore, in order to merge Jesus traditions with Christ cult traditions at the point of an account of Jesus' death.

This was cleverly done. The miracle stories were used to demonstrate the power of the Son of God, on the one hand, and to collect the crowd for the Messiah on the other. The pronouncement stories were used to provoke the conspiracy and support the persecution plot against the Son of Man. The parables and discipleship sayings were fit into the prediction/fulfillment design, creating the new image of Jesus as an apocalyptic angelus. Thus the several plots govern all of the material. There is even a correlation between the plots and themes associated with character types. The crowds follow the miracle worker–Messiah. They know nothing of the plot against the Son of Man until it is too late. The leaders, offended by the reaction of the crowds, know nothing about Jesus except his threat to them. The disciples are those who have to struggle with meaningless predictions of strange events not yet fulfilled. Only the demons know Jesus' true identity. And only the reader knows what the framework stories mean. Given the bizarre congeries of materials available to him, and the complexity of narrative designs decided upon to integrate them, Mark's story of Jesus is amazingly unified and coherent.

1. THE CONVERGENCE OF THE DESIGNS

Each of the four narrative designs has the crucifixion of Jesus in view as its climax. The designs converge, therefore, as soon as Jesus reaches Jerusalem. It can now happen that a single event functions in relation to two or more designs. The trial before the Sanhedrin, for instance, gathers up themes from all four designs, each element in the narrative unit having some major consequence for the resolution of one of the designs. The result is that many narrative units of the passion account are charged with significance just because of the concentration of thematics within them and because of the multiple resonance they sustain with other events and other designs. A brief discussion of each episode will demonstrate Mark's compositional activity and account for the function of themes within the four narrative designs. This section of the chapter focuses on those episodes fundamental to the persecution plot. The next section deals with episodes clustering around the meal.

1.1 The Temple Act

The temple act is composed of four units: (1) the action of driving out those who sell and buy; (2) the teaching from Isa 56:7 and Jer 7:11 contrasting house of prayer with den of robbers; (3) the response of the chief priests and scribes who seek a way to destroy Jesus; and (4) a mention of the amazement of all the crowd. Two narrative designs finally mesh, the plot against Jesus by the leaders (D3), and the messianic scenario of the crowd (D2).

This is Jesus' first public appearance in Jerusalem, following upon the triumphal entry of the day before. The crowd continues that theme, and its amazement is the typical response throughout the gospel to Jesus' miracles and teachings. That the amazement is now directed to the temple act as an instruction recalls the first "teaching" of Jesus in the synagogue at Capernaum. There also an action of casting out was combined with an authoritative pronouncement. The two stories form a set. The difference between the first entrance act and the temple act is that, with the change of scene and the merger of plots, this act will provoke the execution, not just the plan, of the plot to destroy him.

The leaders are still afraid to make any move. That gives Mark a chance to let Jesus teach in the temple for a day. The teaching makes public the issue of Jesus' authority, alludes to the theme of sonship in the parable (D1), and ends with a private instruction to the disciples on the future of the temple and the kingdom of God (D4). Thus all four narrative designs are touched upon in the temple in the wake of the temple act.

The act itself is contrived. Some gesture was required that could symbolize both casting out and taking charge with some semblance of legitimacy. Demons would be too much, since Jesus is about to be taken. It would, in any case, have been implausible. But filthy lucre would do just fine. Taxes and the temple treasury had been hot political issues underlying much of the history of conflict between Jerusalem and Rome. The citations from Isaiah and Jeremiah could put Jesus on the safe side of the conflict, motivated by righteous indignation. Jewish authorities (scripture) could be used against Jewish practice. The subtheme of temple robbery, moreover, given with the citation from Jeremiah, was also most convenient. Temple robbery was a stock image of degradation in the popular imagination, combining criminal activity with impiety. The first use of the theme in Mark is Jesus' application of Jeremiah's charge to those who bought and sold in the temple (that is, animals for offerings and money at foreign rates of exchange). This subtheme recurs at the arrest where Jesus chides the arresters for coming after him as though he, not the money changers, were the temple robber (Mark 14:48). This develops the theme somewhat, playing on the symbolic significance of the temple act and putting the countercharge in his opponents' mouth. At the trial the question of Jesus' authority is the more important theme, but the temple act has not been forgotten. Jesus' authority is related to the kingdom, the substitute for the temple, thus builds upon the temple act as symbolically having taken charge. The hearsay about destroying the temple pushes the symbolism of the act in the direction of an exorcism (casting out as destroying). And underlying the charge of blasphemy is the notion of desecration, also related allusively to the temple act. When Jesus is crucified, then, he is positioned between two robbers, that is, as one who desecrated the temple (Mark 15:27). Thus the subtheme is carried through to the end. It is a fictional theme derived from the scriptural citations.

The temple act cannot be historical. If one deletes from the story those themes essential to the Markan plots, there is nothing left over for historical reminiscence. The anti-temple theme is clearly Markan and the reasons for it can be explained. The lack of any evidence for an anti-temple attitude in the Jesus and Christ traditions prior to Mark fits with the incredible lack of incidence in the story itself. Nothing happens. Even the chief priests overhear his "instruction" and do nothing. The conclusion must be that the temple act is a Markan fabrication.

1.2 The Arrest

The narrative unit consists of (1) the crowd's coming with swords from the chief priests, scribes and elders; (2) Judas' leadership to the secluded spot and his betrayal; (3) seizure and scuffle; (4) Jesus' response; and (5) the flight.

The arrest follows naturally upon the temple act. It is the critical moment for the plot (D3), for Jesus must be placed into the hands of his persecutors. It is also the point at which the story of the disciples (D4) merges with the plot. There is a hint of a change in the constitution of the crowds (D2), and the sonship motif is now introduced for the first time under the sign of humiliation instead of exaltation (D1). Thus all four narrative themes are touched upon.

Jesus is the Righteous One, betrayed by friends and seized unjustly by enemies. The Righteous One under duress does not cease to be God's "child," "servant," and "son" (Wis 2:13, 16, 18). The traits are concentrated within a few very brief strokes: the kiss, the suggested irony about seizure for temple robbing, and Jesus' willingness that the "scriptures be fulfilled."

That a crowd comes with Judas from the temple establishment, bearing swords and clubs, is a remarkable touch. Temple police or Roman guards would have been the reasonable detachment. Jesus is away from the crowd when the chief priests send to take him. That is according to their plan, enabled by the betrayal. They had feared a tumult should the crowd witness the arrest. But now it appears that those they send are a "crowd." They are armed and a small tumult results. At the seizure someone with a sword strikes one of the high priest's men. The text does not say that it was one of the disciples. The swords enter the picture with the "crowd." So Mark is making a point. The tumult feared occurs whenever Jesus is taken. It does not happen, however, because of the crowd's partiality to Jesus, or because of anything Jesus did. The crowd with swords is the priests' own doing.

Jesus turns the irony to good advantage in his chiding. He reminds them that he had been teaching daily in the temple. To come for him as a robber was quite unnecessary. Suddenly the tables are turned on the private/public theme (secrecy motif). Since his entrance, Jesus had been a public figure. It was the high priest who now had to deal in stealth. The exchange at the arrest is literally layered with innuendos that deal in reversals, inversions, sarcasm and irony. These are tropes created by a concentration of narrative themes at the very point where the plot finally turns.

That "all" forsake him and flee is not a historical reminiscence. The Righteous One is the forsaken one, without helpers and alone before his accusers. In the prediction of the flight, moreover, Jesus had used another image, the scattering of the sheep at the smiting of the shepherd (Mark 14:27). This prediction is a citation from a messianic oracle in Zechariah (13:7), and the oracle also mentions that the shepherd is to be struck by a sword. This is an example of a typical scholarly ploy when referring to well-known scriptural passages, that is, evoking a cluster of images with only a brief citation. The motif of flight, therefore, is called for by the persecution plot, supported by a scriptural allusion, and narrated in accordance with the messianic theme. The story of the arrest is a Markan fiction.

1.3 The Trial before the Sanhedrin

The trial narrative consists of (1) the setting (Jesus taken to the high priest where the whole council is assembled); (2) the false witnesses; (3) the question of Jesus' identity; and (4) the condemnation and abuse. A trial lies at the very heart of the story of persecution. This scene is Jesus' trial, his encounter with his accusers. In the story of the trial of the Righteous One the accusations are false. The trial, then, would have been Mark's greatest challenge. To produce the record of a judicial proceeding in which the accusations were false but the charges credible enough to warrant condemnation would have required a bit of forethought.

The search for witnesses was used to scandalize the proceedings. Specifically, since Jewish law required that two witnesses agree, the failure to produce agreement meant that the trial was illegal. The ploy was doubly shrewd, for witnesses who did not agree would be false witnesses, or accusers only. Because their accusations were false, Jesus should have been declared innocent.

The specific accusation is something they heard Jesus say, a hearsay, an overhearing. It is the famous "temple word," Jesus' threat: "I will destroy this temple that is made with hands, and in three days I will build another, not made with hands" (Mark 14:58). A great deal of ink has been spilled over this enigmatic saying. The following are some of the questions that have been asked: Could Jesus have said it? Why did not Mark report it earlier? Was it a prophetic word referring to an action to be taken by God? What "destruction" of the temple is meant? What is the temple "not made with hands"? Does Mark intend for it to be a true statement? If so, why is it put in the mouth of false witnesses?

The saying is crafty. It seems to be a prophecy of some kind that could unlock the apocalyptic logic behind the entire passion narrative (some scholars would say history). It makes absolutely no sense, though, because the apparent parallelism is deceptive. In order for the two lines to run parallel and remain in the same order of discourse or refer to the same order of reality, some change has to be made. Either the subjects are different (Jesus says one, God the other), or the perspectives are different (literal, spiritual), or the reference is compound (temple, Jesus' body, Christian community), or the times don't match ("destroy"/build now, or destroy/"build" later?). The problem is that changes entertained in the interest of making sense also ruin the correlation of lines. That, of course, is the point. The accusation is a hearsay loaded with fragmentary truths that can't make sense in this formulation. It is obvious that, if this is what the witnesses overheard, they would not be able to agree.

Thus the accusation cannot be the charge. Mark used the motif of the false witnesses to create the illusion of a trial and develop a riddle of comparison between two contrasting kingdoms. Naturally Jesus will remain silent when asked to respond to such an accusation, a very clever introduction of the motif of silence before one's accusers. When the high priest goes on to ask Jesus' identity, however, Jesus is not silent.

Jesus acknowledges that he is the Christ, the Son of the Blessed, then adds the prediction about the coming of the Son of Man. Three of Mark's four narrative designs (D1, D2, and D3) merge in this threefold identification. It is Jesus' (only) public "confession" of the "secret." Upon the confession of his identity, the condemnation follows immediately.

The charge is blasphemy. Blasphemy was a slander against God, thus it had to be spoken. The high priest underscores the point, "Why do we still need witnesses? You have heard. . . ." Nevertheless, there is little to be gained in trying to figure out just what it was Jesus said that could have been labeled blasphemy. Popular messiahs did not get charged with blasphemy. Apocalyptic visionaries did not get killed for impiety. Sons of God were not considered profane. So something else is at work in this charge. The clue was given in the first response of the scribes to Jesus' claim to authority in Mark 2:7, 10: "It is blasphemy. Who can forgive sins but God alone?" The issue is not just Jesus' authority. It is much more serious than that. It is the old distinction between the Jesus people who admit "sinners" into the group and the synagogue people who hold to the codes of ritual purity. Social contamination is the charge against Jesus. In the Beelzebul controversy the scribes charged that Jesus had an "unclean spirit" (Mark 3:30). Jesus' response to them was a warning about blasphemy against the holy, that is, clean or pure spirit (Mark 3:28–29). Thus the high priest's charge was one Jesus people had heard before, apparently, leveled at the movement that laid claim to the religious heritage of Israel and yet was "unclean." Mark found the charge useful because it could reflect upon Jesus' confession of identity as sovereign of the kingdom of God while expressing the reasons for the Jewish rejection. Those reasons had to put a construction upon Jesus' words that would make them deserving of death, that is, regard them as a slander against the fundamental legitimacy of Judaism as a religious system. Again one must supply the temple act as the provocation in order to make sense of the charge. Mark took the Jewish point of view for the moment. As one unclean, taking charge of the temple as his sovereign right, the king of the kingdom of sinners, Jesus' entrance into the temple would have been a desecration, a profanation. Jesus' confession to sovereign identity makes it clear that it was. So Jesus' "cleansing" of the temple was turned into a threat of desecration in order to find a charge worthy to condemn him to death. The horrible irony is that the council must "accept" Jesus' "confession" as true in order to condemn him for it as false. The trial is really a very vicious fiction. Not only are the proceedings scandalized purposefully, the manipulation of the charge means that the Jews condemn Jesus to death on the basis of claims only Christians would accept.

1.4 The Trial before Pilate

The trial before Pilate was necessary simply because historical credibility demanded it. The Romans, rather than the Jews, executed criminals by means of crucifixion. The trial consists only of (1) the question about Jesus' identity; and (2) Jesus' silence before the accusations of the chief priests. The Barabbas episode and the sentencing follow the trial.

Mark took advantage of the necessity for a second trial by introducing a slight shift in the charge. Pilate's term for Jesus' role is king of the Jews. Questioned about this, Jesus' answer ("You have said so") amounts to, "That is what you, a Roman procurator, might call me." The Roman perspective on the situation is therefore used to great advantage. By falling back from the high christological titles used in the Sanhedrin trial, a semblance of political realism is gained without giving up the essential claim. Pilate is not threatened by this king, seeks to release him to the people, and knows that he has done no evil (Mark 15:9, 14). It is the envy of the priests and the adamancy of the crowd that force Pilate to his decision. The horrifying result is that Jesus will be killed as the king of the Jews at the insistence of the Jews. That, of course, is the very point Mark wished to make. One sees now why it was that Mark worked so hard to interweave a popular "messianic" scenario into his gospel (D2). Only so could the whole be given any semblance of a claim to historical credibility.

1.5 The Crucifixion

The account of the crucifixion is, at first glance, an accumulation of snippets of unrelated information. The traditional view has been to see it layered, the result of many insertions in the long course of many retellings. Deleting the insertions, however, does not produce an account that can be called early. The narrative structure is clearly that of an apocalyptic event of six hours duration divided into halves by darkness over the land for the second three hours. The times are given together with the events that occurred: third hour (9:00 A.M.), crucifixion; sixth hour (noon), darkness over the land; ninth hour (3:00 P.M.), cry, exhalation, rending of the temple's curtain. The symmetry of threes is obvious, as is the correlation of the crucifixion events with those transpiring in the natural and institutional orders of things. The schema is mythic. There is no "earlier" report extractable from the story, no reminiscence. This is the earliest narrative there is about the crucifixion of Jesus. It is a Markan fabrication.

The details are interwoven into the structure with some care. The first three-hour period follows the theme of derision. The second follows the motif of abandonment. The details can be accounted for either as allusions to (or citations from) scriptural depictions of the persecuted Righteous One, or as Markan themes. The scriptural allusions are the division of garments (Mark 15:24; cf. Ps 22:18); the mocking (cf. Ps 22:6–8); the cry of abandonment (Mark 15:34; cf. Ps 22:1); and the offering of vinegar (Mark 15:36; cf. Ps 69:21). The Markan motifs and themes are visible in the inscription (Mark 15:26), the robbers (Mark 15:27), the taunt about the temple (Mark 15:29–30), the chief priests' taunt (Mark 15:31–32), the question about Elijah (Mark 15:35–36), the tearing of the temple curtain (Mark 15:38), and the centurion's statement (Mark 15:39). There is nothing left over except information about the name of the place, Golgotha, also a Markan narrative device.[2]

---

2. *Golgotha.* An emphasis upon places and place names is a Markan characteristic. Certain things happen in certain kinds of place (as, for instance, cities, houses, open country, and places of withdrawal). Meaning is invested both thematically (as, for instance, in the double entrance, first into a city, then into a house) as well as symbolically. Kelber has worked out the symbolism for "Galilee" in *The Kingdom in Mark.* Proper names frequently give specificity to places. Golgotha ("skull") is an example of a particular place

All four Markan narrative designs climax in this scene, as well as many Markan themes. It is for this reason that the accumulation of motifs is dense. The extravagant use of the Psalms can be explained as an attempt to continue the characterization of Jesus as the innocent sufferer who suffers to the end (D3). Derision belongs to the pattern and the crucifixion was the place to exploit the motif. Derision was a perfect narrative device with which to formulate ironies. The messianic climax is indicated in the superscription (D2). The centurion's statement aligns the event with the framework stories (D1). And the apocalyptic prodigy serves as a sign that Jesus' predictions come true (D4).

The anti-temple theme is present in much of the material. It is the reason for the taunts and the focus of the miracles. Jesus' death is the sign of the end of the temple's time. The rending of the temple curtain anticipates the destruction of the temple in 70 C.E. There is no other sense to be made of the concentration of suggestions than that the reader associate the two events. Apocalyptic mentality would have understood the destruction of the temple as an act of God's judgment in any case. Mark stacked up the reasons for seeing it related to the crucifixion of Jesus. The reason he could not make the point explicit in a direct statement is because to have named a single cause either of the crucifixion or of the temple's destruction would have ruined the multimotivational interpretation of the events he had in mind and the reciprocal dynamics of conflict he needed in order to carry out his fiction.

---

name that bears symbolic potential. The addition of a Greek translation of an Aramaic transliteration is not unusual in Mark. It occurs in Mark 3:17 (*Boanerges*—Sons of Thunder); 5:41 (*Talitha cumi*—arise little lamb); 7:11 (*corban*—given to God); 7:34 (*Ephphatha*—Be opened); 14:36 (*Abba*—Father); 15:34 (*Eloi Eloi la'ma sabachtha'ni*—My God, My God, Why have you forsaken me?); as well as at 15:22. A compromise "translation" of an Aramaic-Greek wordplay may also provide the clue to the problematic identification of the blind Bartimaeus. The text now appears to read "son of Timaeus, Bartimaeus, a blind man" (Mark 10:46). The Aramaic appears to have been *"bar tamea"* which means "son of the unclean." The information that Bartimaeus was the "son of Timaeus" is most probably the Greek "translation" that, however, because *timaios* means "honored," introduces a clever inversion: not "son of the unclean," but "son of the most honored." Since the Greek *huios timaiou* was not a true translation of the Aramaic nickname it could not be placed following *bar tamea* as if it were. Originally, the Greek transliteration alone would have been enough to name the blind man in this clever way. But only one who was bilingual or acquainted with the nickname would have gotten the chuckle. One need not conclude that all of these Aramaisms betray early, authentic traditions. A predominantly Greek-speaking social milieu with some bilingual aspects would be sufficient to account for the delightfully mystifying wordplays. This describes the Markan situation exactly, according to H. C. Kee, *Community of the New Age*, 101. Every event in the passion narrative has been located somewhere as specifically as possible in relation to Jerusalem and the temple. Golgotha is an appropriate location (outside the city) with an appropriate name (in Mark: "the place of a skull") for the crucifixion.

2. THE CONNECTION WITH THE MEAL

The meal cluster consists of (1) the preparation, (2) the prediction of the betrayal at table, (3) the breaking of the bread and the distribution of the cup, and (4) the prediction of new wine in the kingdom of God. Closely related is the following prediction of flight and denial. The importance of this narrative cluster for the structure of the passion narrative has already been stressed. It carries the theme of Jesus and his disciples into the Jerusalem setting in order to study the response of the disciples not only to Jesus and his teachings, but to the events that will befall Jesus. The core unit is the breaking of the bread and the distribution of the cup. This unit is the only story in the entire passion narrative for which a pre-Markan tradition can be established. It is therefore a text of great significance for understanding the composition of the passion account.

2.1 The Meal

The scholarly quest for the earliest tradition of the ritual meal has dealt with five New Testament texts. Two of them are found in Paul and are considered to be pre-Pauline (1 Cor 10:16; 11:23-26). Two are from the synoptic tradition (Mark 14:22-25; Luke 22:17-20). One of them is from John (John 6:51c). Matthew's account is of less significance because it copies Mark. Each of these texts has been thought by some scholar to provide important clues to the earliest Christian practice. As with Mark's witnesses, however, no two can agree. Jeremias was the most notable proponent of the value of the synoptic tradition over the Pauline, but that was because he wanted very much to think that Jesus started it all at his last Passover with his disciples just as the narrative relates. In order to reconstruct the original account exactly, though, Jeremias was forced to combine fine points taken from all five texts. His attempt can safely be discounted in favor of a more reasonable approach.[3]

In general, the Pauline texts must be given priority and the discrepancies of the Markan and Lukan traditions must be accounted for. Origin in the Hellenistic cult is what matters. Paul's account is representative, formulaic, and can be used as evidence for the Hellenistic tradition with which Mark was acquainted. The Markan text does differ from that of Paul and the differences need to be assessed. Luke's account is most easily understood as a combination of the Markan and Pauline versions. John's account is simply aberrational ("flesh" for "body").

---

3. *The supper texts.* For excellent, brief summaries of the problems confronted with the several textual traditions, as well as the history of scholarly attempts to resolve them, see Eduard Schweizer, *The Lord's Supper;* and W. Marxsen, *The Lord's Supper as a Christological Problem.* Jeremias' study is *The Eucharistic Words of Jesus.*

The Markan text differs from Paul's in several respects. Assuming that Mark made some changes in the process of turning an etiological myth into historical narrative, discrepancies between the two accounts can provide clues to his intention. The two texts are given in a table for convenient reference, along with the Lukan version as a control (see figure 21).

(1) The first difference is that Paul's setting of the scene ("on the night he was handed over") is not found in Mark's text. Scholars interested in a Palestinian origin for the ritual meal have suggested that Mark's simpler introduction ("as they were eating") was the earlier tradition. By assuming the priority of the synoptic account, then, the term *paradidonai* ("handed over") in Paul's text could be translated as "betrayed." The sequence should be reversed. Paul's use of *paradidonai* does not refer to betrayal, but to the martyr's fate. Nowhere in Paul is a third party involved in the "handing over," the subjects being either Jesus himself (cf. Gal 1:4; 2:20), or God (explicitly in Rom 8:32; understood as subject of the passive in Rom 4:25). It was Mark who supplied another human subject (Judas) when he decided to make the meal part of the historical narrative of the passion. That would not have been difficult to imagine, since *paradidonai* was commonly used in Greek parlance, not as a technical term for martyrdoms, but simply as the standard term for "transfer." It could be used for any transfer of goods, persons, or teachings into the keeping, protection, or power of another. Mark expanded upon the possibilities given with the term in a very conscious and creative way. By letting *paradidonai* mean "arrest" (transfer of one accused into the hands of the civil authorities), a connection could be made between the meal etiology and the wisdom tale without destroying the martyrological substrata both shared in common. By letting *paradidonai* mean "betrayal" (transfer by a friend into the hands of an enemy), a connection could be made between the wisdom story (persecution plot), the meal sequence, and the gospel theme of Jesus with his disciples. That Mark was aware of the narrative potential of the term *paradidonai* is demonstrated by its occurrence in the predictions of the passion (which serve as scripts for the passion narrative, Mark 9:31; 10:33), as well as repeatedly in the narrative itself (Mark 14:10, 11, 18, 41, 42, 44; 15:1, 10, 15). The conclusion must be that Mark's text does not at all lack the etiological reference to "the night he was handed over." It was the very phrase in the Pauline text that made it possible to embellish the etiology. The scene in Mark 14:17–21 shows Jesus at meal with the disciples making the prediction of the betrayal. This scene immediately precedes the symbolic gestures and words. It is Mark's amplification of the Pauline "on the night he was handed over." A single word and complex concept lies at the intersection of the Jesus traditions with the Christ traditions in Mark's Gospel.[4]

---

4. *"Handed over."* That the term *paradidonai* did not mean "betray" in the Pauline

FIGURE 21
THE MEAL TEXTS

Paul: 1 Cor 11:23–26	Mark 14:22–25	Luke 22:14, 17–19d	Luke 22:19e–20
On the night he was handed over	And as they were eating	(14) And when the hour had come	
The Lord Jesus took bread	he took bread	(19) he took bread	
and when he had given thanks	and blessed	and when he had given thanks	
he broke it	and broke it	he broke it	
	and gave it to them	and gave it to them	
and said	and said	saying	
	Take		
This is my body	This is my body	This is my body	
for you			(19e) which is given for you
Do this in memory/ memorial of me			Do this in memory/ memorial of me
And in the same way			And in the same way
also the cup	And he took a cup	(17) And he took a cup	also the cup
after supper			after supper
	and when he had given thanks	and when he had given thanks	
	he gave it to them	he said Take this	
	and they all drank of it	and divide it among yourselves	
saying	and he said to them		saying
This cup	This		This cup
is the new covenant	is		is the new covenant
in my blood	my blood of the covenant		in my blood
	which is poured out for many		which is poured out for you
Do this			
whenever you drink it			
in memory/ memorial of me			
	Truly I say to you	(18) For I tell you	

Paul: 1 Cor 11:23–26	Mark 14:22–25	Luke 22:14, 17–19d	Luke 22:19e–20
For as often as you eat this bread			
and drink this cup			
you proclaim the Lord's death			
until he comes		that from now on	
	I shall not drink again of the fruit of the vine until that day when I	I shall not drink of the fruit of the vine until	
	drink it new in the kingdom God	the kingdom of God comes	

(The order of the Lukan text is, first the cup, then the bread. This agrees with Paul's statement in 1 Cor 10:16 and Did 9, leading some scholars to posit this order as the "earliest." The order in 1 Cor 10:16 is governed by the logic of Paul's argument, however, and the Lukan text is governed by a narrative logic of eschatological reference, not a desire to depict the institution of a ritual. The "longer text" of Luke [19e–20] is missing in some early manuscripts, best explained as a later scribal conflation of Mark, Paul, and the shorter Lukan accounts in the interest of agreement.)

---

(2) The second difference between the Markan and Pauline texts is that the symbols are separated by the dinner in Paul, but joined together in Mark. Scholars have thought this difference to be important for the question of when Christian ritual separated from the communal meal. Mark's text cannot be used as evidence for early liturgical practice, however, because putting the two symbols together was simply a narrative requirement. Mark emphasized the common meal and dish in the preceding narrative unit. By placing the two symbols after the meal with its prediction of betrayal, the impression could be given that the betrayer knowingly was offered the bread and the cup ("They all drank of it"), thus drawing the betrayal theme right through both of the symbolic moments of the meal. The additional "and he said to them" in verse 24 may very well be the seam that resulted when the Pauline tradition was rearranged.

(3) A third difference supports this view. Mark's text does not contain mention of memorial, any command to repeat the symbolic meal, or any indication that other meals like this one should "proclaim" (as Paul has it) or be performed in reference to the crucifixion. The obvious connection between the symbols and the forthcoming crucifixion are made at the

---

context is clear, according to R. Fowler, *Loaves and Fishes*, 136–38. The importance of the term *(para)didonai* for the development of the Christ myth in the Hellenistic congregations can be inferred from a study by N. Perrin, "The Use of (Para)didonai." Perrin, however, did not trace the term to its martyrological context, and assumed a kerygmatic intention for the Markan predictions and passion narrative.

narrative level only and left there. The meal in Mark is not an "institution." It is the last supper of Jesus with his disciples.[5]

(4) Paul's text associates the announcement of vicarious significance with the bread-body symbolism ("This is my body for you"). Mark's text lacks the mention of "for you" in relation to the body, but adds "poured out for many" to the cup word. This may be significant. In the Hellenistic communities, cultic presence was associated with Christ's "body," and the saving significance of Christ's death was expressed by using the "for you/us" formula. Mark may have deleted the "for you" from the body word on purpose. It would agree with his manner of appropriation of Christ cult traditions in general. Mark was consistently cautious not to allow cultic nuance to continue to attach to the Christ materials he used.

(5) There is more stress upon the cup in the Markan text than in the Pauline tradition. The addition of the rationale "poured out for many" is just one of several indications of a special interest in the cup. Another is the deletion of the adjective "new" for the covenant in comparison with Paul. A third sign that changes were made is the infelicitous construction that resulted, literally "the blood of me of the covenant." An oddity of the Markan text may also be related to a shift in attention away from the symbolism of the bread and onto the cup. Where Paul has a thanksgiving for the bread, Mark has a blessing. A blessing would be the more Jewish formulation. Nevertheless, Mark specified that a thanksgiving was said over the cup where Paul mentions only that Jesus treated the cup "in the same way."

Scholars have thought that Mark's attention to the cup word revealed an interest in sacrificial soteriology. Exactly the opposite must have been the case. The shift from Paul's text is a shift away from the Christ cult and toward a more primitive notion of martyrdom. Blood is exactly what martyrs give, so that a martyrological significance could be retained for Jesus' death by signifying the wine as well as the bread. With the bread symbol so laden with Hellenistic connotation, Mark deemphasized bread and accentuated the symbolism of the cup. In the Hellenistic tradition, the cup was the symbol for the death as a violent end, the bread a symbol for the resolve of the martyr. Mark worked out the resolve of Jesus narratively, thus could afford the shift in emphasis. In the Hellenistic cult, Jesus' death was pictured in such a way as to invite a celebration of the cosmic victory announced in the resurrection. In Mark, endurance unto death in the midst of social conflict was selected as the more appropriate theme.

With the shift two additional advantages may have been gained. One

---

5. *The last supper.* R. Fowler, *Loaves and Fishes,* 138–47, has argued convincingly that the last supper in Mark is not intended as an "institution" of the Eucharist, but is a narrative employment of a eucharistic text to bring to climax the theme of the disciples at meal with Jesus. He is surely correct in this judgment.

advantage may have been a subtle alignment of the ritual meal with Jewish texts and institutions of a ritual nature. There is a very strong possibility that "blood of the covenant," a rare and strange phraseology, was intended as an allusion to its occurrence in the story of Moses sealing a covenant between the people and the "book of the covenant" in Exod 24:3–8 (note "blood of the covenant" in Exod 24:8). That Mark was interested in making allusions of this kind can hardly be doubted. He expressly made the connection between the meal and the Passover, for instance (Mark 14:12). The intention in each case surely must have been to suggest that a substitution was taking place, Christian events dislodging Jewish covenants and practices.

Another advantage gained by focusing attention upon the cup symbolism would have been the creation of an overlap with an interpretation of Jesus' death entertained in Q. In Q the theme of the killing of the prophets was taken up at some point as a way to charge Israel with intransigence and, presumably, reflect on Jesus' death as having been like the prophet's deaths. It should be underlined that this theme is the only evidence of reflection upon the significance of Jesus' death in the Jesus traditions, and that it was not a soteriological significance, but a homiletic rationale that was derived from the identification. Mark would not have been uncomfortable with the thought, though he had decided on casting Jesus as the Righteous One persecuted rather than as the prophet slain. He may have been looking for all of the bridges between the Jesus and Christ traditions he could find. It is of some interest, in any event, that the term "poured out" (*ekchunnomai*) occurs also in the oracle of wisdom about the deaths of the prophets: "That the blood of all the prophets, shed (i.e., poured out) from the foundation of the world, may be required of this generation, from the blood of Abel to the blood of Zechariah, who perished between the altar and the sanctuary" (Luke 11:50–51). To find a point of agreement between the martyrological tradition of the Christ cult and the homiletic topos of the Jesus people would not have been unimportant for Mark, especially if the homiletic tradition brought along with it a clear sense of Jewish responsibility for Jesus' crucifixion.

All of the differences between the Markan text and the Pauline tradition point toward the same conclusion. Mark toned down the cultic nuances of the Hellenistic meal tradition, just as he had reduced the Christ myth, by allowing the martyrological identifications basic to the Christ event to show through again. It was this reduction that allowed the Christ traditions to be taken up into a narrative about the persecuted Righteous One and thus connected to the Jesus traditions. One might say, therefore, that the passion narrative was conceived as a possibility by the discovery of the martyrological substrata of the Christ myth and ritual. The meal was not "inserted" into a preexisting account of the passion. It was the first text on Mark's desk to crack wide open. As soon as the narrative possibilities suggested by the term *paradidonai* were seen, the passion narrative was as good as written. Mark's passion narrative is essentially an elaboration of the etiological myth of the Hellenistic cult meal through combination with the wisdom story of the persecuted Righteous One as martyr.

2.2 The Betrayal

The story of Judas' betrayal is a Markan fiction. There is no evidence that betrayal was a problem under consideration in Jesus or Christ circles before Mark's time. Mark found the notion convenient for two reasons. Betrayal solved a big problem in narrative design, on the one hand, and it addressed a certain problem Mark's community was having, on the other.

Mark played with the double meaning of *paradidonai* as "arrest" and "handing over" (betrayal) through the entire gospel story. When Jesus is introduced at the beginning, coming into Galilee, the information is given that it happened "after John was arrested (*paradidonai*)." Later one learns what that meant for John (Mark 6:14–29). In the meantime Herodians had been mentioned with the Pharisees in the plot to destroy Jesus (Mark 3:6), and Judas had been designated in an aside as the disciple who would "hand Jesus over" (Mark 3:19). The theme is then developed through the predictions and up to the arrest as betrayal. It is always the Son of Man who is betrayed. At the end of the Gethsemane scene, Jesus declares that "the hour has come, the Son of Man is handed over into the hands of sinners." The "hour" is the moment that has been forestalled since the beginning of Jesus' activity. When Jesus immediately goes on to say, "See, my betrayer is at hand," all nuances of the term *paradidonai,* developed separately until this point as narrative themes, collapse: arrest, betrayal, handing over, persecutors, enemies, power transferral, preparation for martyrdom. One might note that the term for "is at hand" is the same as that Jesus had used at the beginning when announcing the "nearness" of the kingdom of God (Mark 1:15). He used it as well of the coming of the Son of Man in the apocalyptic parable of the fig tree (Mark 13:29).

From this point on two terms are used to show that Jesus is in the hands of those who will dispose of him. Now he is "led" from place to place as well as "handed over" from power to power. The crowd leads Jesus to the high priest (Mark 14:52); the chief priests lead Jesus and hand him over to Pilate (Mark 15:1); Pilate hands Jesus over to the soldiers (Mark 15:15); and the soldiers lead him into the praetorium, then out to be crucified (Mark 15:16, 20).

One becomes suspicious about Mark's interest in *paradidonai* as betrayal when reading the apocalyptic discourse in chapter 13. There the term *paradidonai* is used to warn the disciples that they would be delivered up to councils and trials (Mark 13:9, 11). Because the discipleship sayings have been given, one knows to think of the similarity between what will happen to Jesus in the story ahead and what will happen to the disciples in the future ahead. Still, one might wonder who the "betrayer" might be. As if Mark knew that would be the next question, he has Jesus add the sobering explanation that "brother will deliver up brother to death, and the father his child, and children will rise against parents and have them put to death. And you will be hated by all for my name's sake" (Mark 13:12–13). Making some room for Markan exaggeration, it does appear that his community was experiencing some defections to say the least. One may very well worry, therefore, about the name of the betrayer in the Jesus story. If Judas is a fiction, the Jews have become Mark's scapegoat. Not only are they the enemy on the outside, they are the enemy to be warned about from within as well.

2.3 The Denial

The story of Peter's denial consists of (1) the prediction on the way to the Mount of Olives (Mark 14:29–31); (2) the following into the high priest's courtyard (Mark 14:54); and (3) the accusation, denial, and remembrance (Mark 14:66–72). Many scholars have thought to see a "Petrine" reminiscence in this story, finding it difficult to believe that Mark imagined all of it. The evidence that he did, however, is overwhelming.

Features that point to Markan composition are the prediction/fulfillment design, the separation of the story into three episodes (cf. the betrayal episodes), the threefold structure of the denial unit, the placement of the story as a bracket around the Sanhedrin trial, the emphasis on the Jerusalem-Galilee tension, the use of graphic detail with symbolic potential (e.g., the cock crowing), and the interweaving of narrative themes developed elsewhere in the gospel. These include the figure of Peter, the contrast with Peter's earlier confession and rebuke, the theme of following, the motif of denial (cf. Mark 8:34), and the motif of shame (cf. Mark 8:38).[6]

Some story had to be told to bring the discipleship theme to a conclusion. The theme was one of misunderstanding instruction or failing to perform. Peter's denial is the only story in the passion account that brings this narrative design to a fitting climax. It does so by concentrating upon the problem of discipleship as a trial. By interlocking the story of Peter in the courtyard with the story of Jesus in the high priest's council, a sense of simultaneity is created on the upstairs-downstairs model. As Jesus is led to the high priest, Peter follows into the courtyard. There the maid's observations are set forth as accusations, the temple guard becomes a (silent) council, Peter's identity is at issue (as Galilean and follower of Jesus), his denial is an oath, the cock crowing signals the decision (change of guard at

---

6. *Markan narrative devices.* For a summary of literary devices characteristic of Mark, see H. C. Kee, *Community of the New Age,* 50–64.

the fourth watch, prediction fulfilled), and Peter goes out to weep (has excluded himself from the Jesus group by his own denial of identity and failure to follow all the way to the crucifixion). The contrast between Jesus' "confession" upstairs and Peter's denial downstairs is the point of the story.

There is nothing in the story that reflects historical reminiscence. The story is about denial. Denial is about undergoing trial. Trial is the point of the wisdom story of the innocent martyr. Application of the wisdom story to discipleship depends upon the application of the story to Jesus. The narrative of Peter's denial was composed when the gospel was composed. Peter's denial does not throw light on the circumstances of 30 C.E., but upon the circumstances of 70 C.E. Mark's community must have been under considerable duress.

3. THE COUNTERPOINT STORIES

Three counterpoint stories are yet to be reviewed, the temptation in Gethsemane, the story of the empty tomb, and the anointing. These stories are not integrated into either of the two major narrative designs (persecution plot and discipleship sequences) in the same way as other stories. They have often been regarded as independent traditions because, while they are dependent upon some account of the passion, they seem to have been merely inserted into the account as Mark now has it. Each has a peculiar feature or two, seems a bit jumbled, and strikes the form critic as layered, that is, the result of accumulations received over a long period of retelling. However, the functions of these stories in the Markan passion narrative can be explained. Those functions, moreover, can account for the jumbled texture and the appearance of independence. The stories do belong to Mark's passion narrative.

3.1 The Temptation in Gethsemane

The story of Jesus and the disciples in Gethsemane, like the story of the meal, comes as a surprise to the reader. The very human characterization of Jesus is startling, especially his express desire that the hour and cup be removed. The behavior of the disciples is also past believing, given the tense atmosphere just at this point in the story. The jerky movements, now focusing on Jesus, now on the disciples, now on the cup, now the hour, now distress, now resolve, give one the impression that a very early poignant reminiscence proved to be too popular and was ruined in repeated retellings by the addition of too many good ideas.

Markan features are not lacking, however, and need to be listed. Mark was partial to triads, so the threefold structure is suspicious. The motif of withdrawal to be alone with the disciples is not unusual for Mark. Singling out Peter has a Markan ring to it. The combination of Jesus' instruction and the disciples' failure to comprehend it is peculiarly Markan. The cup was mentioned earlier in Mark (10:38–40), as was the charge to watch (13:35–36). The story is, after all, a trial scene, both for Jesus and the disciples, recalling the discipleship sayings about Jesus as the example to be followed. Its position in the story is correct, placed here before the trials of the persecution plot. So perhaps the proper question would be to ask what difference the story makes for the passion account as a whole.

The persecution plot, based on the wisdom story, combined two characterizations of the Righteous One. One was that of the innocently accused Righteous One who fears falling into the hands of his persecutors and falls silent before them, vulnerable and helpless, calling upon God for his rescue. The other was that of the warrior who marches into the line of fire for a righteous cause, accosts his captors, and faces death with resolve as a martyr. Throughout the gospel, Jesus has been cast as an aggressive warrior for the kingdom of God. But the plot against him is now about to be executed. Jesus will come into the hands of accusers and captors. The warrior and the vulnerable one need at some point to be combined, since neither can handle the tricky case of Jesus' crucifixion alone. It cannot be that to fall into the hands of the plotters will silence the warrior's strength and confidence before the ungodly tyrant. But neither can it be that the warrior's sovereign mien makes sport of the tyrant's real power to dispose of the helpless and innocent one.

Gethsemane is the place where the two attitudes are merged into a single stance. The prayer is the typical request for deliverance of the Righteous One in distress. Jesus is greatly troubled and asks that the hour and cup be removed. The decision, "Yet not what I will, but what thou wilt," however, is the martyr's resolve. The decision is made to proceed as a martyr even though "sorrowful unto death": "It is enough. Get up, let us go." Both attitudes are kept in view through the remainder of the passion narrative, as if Mark knew that the balance might easily be lost. In the two trials, Jesus is both silent (stance of the suffering Righteous One) and confidently outspoken (sign of the martyr). On the way to the cross, Jesus is both weak (so that Simon of Cyrene must carry his cross) and strong (refusal of the wine as they arrive). On the cross Jesus is both destitute (the words of desolation) and imperious (the outcry as he dies). The Gethsemane story prepares the reader for this. The cup is the cup of martyrdom; the hour is the hour of innocent suffering. If the reader did not know that Jesus had resolved to march ahead, the theme of being led and passed along as one handed over would have been simply overpowering. No king could die like that. So Jesus' resolve in the garden is absolutely crucial to Mark's narrative design. It is the story in which the saying about the Son of Man giving his life as a ransom comes to narrative expression. The resolve makes it clear that, though he is about to be taken, Jesus will hand himself over to the tyrant for the sake of the cause for which he will die.

3.2 The Empty Tomb

Mark's story of the empty tomb is the earliest narrative evidence for Easter and has been the object of very vigorous exploration by scholars. The later post-resurrection appearance stories in Matthew, Luke, and John all depend upon the Markan account in the sense that they seek its revision. In the Pauline correspondence there is no narrative of or reference to a narrative of the resurrection, just as there is no narrative of the crucifixion. There are, however, references to visions and revelations of the resurrected Christ or Son of God. In the case of the tradition cited in 1 Cor 15:3–5, a list of appearances was appended to the kerygma of the death and resurrection of Christ. It is probable that Mark knew this tradition. It is obvious, at least, that he knew the Hellenistic Christ myth in some tradition that mentioned the three days, for each of the passion predictions mentions rising "after three days." Mark must have known as well that the visions and appearances of the resurrected Christ or Son of God were a cultivation of the Christ cult, and that they presupposed the Christ myth with its orientation to patterns of transformation, spiritual presence, and transcendence. Mark was not interested in pursuing a cult of spiritual presence, but he was interested in justifying an apocalyptic view of history on the side of the Jesus people set adrift in what had become an alien cultural climate. He had found a way to realize the value of the Christ myth for an embattled community by reducing it to its essentials as a martyr's death, approved by God, and thus vicariously effective for the cause (kingdom of God) yet to be fully vindicated. So he had also to find a way to retain the moment of vindication for Jesus without creating the impression of a spiritually transformed, cosmic presence emanating from the cross or tomb. Resurrection as vindication was an acceptable notion, for it belonged to the story of wisdom's child. It was also an interesting notion, for it could be used to forge the link between Jesus and the future coming of the Son of Man. But it was a dangerous notion because, were a cosmic presence to be inferred, the apocalyptic concerns for vindications, judgments, and the eventual manifestation of the kingdom of God in human social history would be threatened. The story of the empty tomb is Mark's answer to this dilemma.

The story of the empty tomb is a poor appearance story since Jesus does not appear. It is also a poor cultic legend of any kind. The young man explains that the women have come to the wrong place. "He is not here." "Go." ("Don't come back.") According to the story, a resurrection has occurred, of course. It fulfills Jesus' own predictions that it would be so.

The question has always been, what kind of a resurrection did Mark have in mind?

In his last reference to the resurrection, Jesus had mentioned "going before" the disciples into Galilee (Mark 14:28). This prediction followed closely upon the prediction about drinking new wine in the kingdom of God (Mark 14:25). If one does not supply a Christ cult assumption to the form of the manifestation of Jesus intended by the young man's announcement, "There you will see him as he told you" (Mark 16:7), the reference must be to the eschatological appearance of the Son of Man coming with power. That would mean that Mark stripped the Hellenistic notions of transformation, appearance, vision, and spiritual transcendence from the myth of the resurrection of Jesus. He reduced the mythic idea of resurrection to its fundamental meaning as a martyr's vindication, and used the historicized event in support of his apocalyptic scheme. According to this scheme, the final judgment and victory of God's kingdom would be determined by the appearance and fate of Jesus at the beginning of the Christian era. Resurrection merely meant that Jesus' final appearance was assured.

The narrative consists of (1) the women looking on at the crucifixion (Mark 15:40–41); (2) the burial (Mark 15:42–47); and (3) the visit of the women to the empty tomb (Mark 16:1–8). The women are the principle of continuity for the three days (Friday through Sunday morning). Burial was reported, but the lateness of the hour on Friday (onset of the Sabbath) meant that the body could not be anointed properly. This supplied a motivation for the visit to the tomb on Sunday. Without such a rationale the visit to the tomb would have been a very strange incident, wanting to anoint a body after the tomb had been sealed. The women do not get to anoint the body. They get only to see the place where Jesus was. Thus Mark's story of the resurrection is like Mark's story of the crucifixion. Both are prodigies, proleptic miracles pointing ahead to events governed by an apocalyptic plan for the manifestation of the kingdom of God.[7]

3.3 The Anointing

The story of the anointing disturbs the conspiracy sequence because it is inserted between the report about the chief priests' and scribes' anxiety to find a way to take Jesus before the feast (Mark 14:1–2) and the solution that

---

7. *The empty tomb.* The theme of absence has been mentioned throughout the study in order to point up Mark's sense of the location of Jesus between the times in contrast to the language of presence used in the Christ cult. The story of the empty tomb is an important evidence for Mark's apocalyptic interpretation of kerygmatic traditions. J. D. Crossan has also seen that the empty tomb has its point in the absence of Jesus. See his "Empty Tomb and Absent Lord." Support for this view is found in the strong arguments put forth by V. Robbins in his study of the Markan intention in the last supper story: "Last Meal."

FIGURE 22
THE WEEK OF THE PASSION

Day		Events	Account
1	Sunday	Triumphal entry	11:1–11
2	Monday	Temple act	11:12–25
3	Tuesday	Teaching in the temple and on the Mount of Olives	11:27–13:37
4	Wednesday	Anointing at Bethany	14:3–9
		Conspiracy	14:1–2, 10–11
5	Thursday	Preparation for the meal	14:12–16
	Thursday Evening	The meal	14:17–25
	Thursday Night	Gethsemane	14:26–42
		Arrest	14:43–51
		Trial: Sanhedrin	14:53–65
		Peter's denial	14:54, 66–72
6	Friday	Trial: Pilate	15:1–20
		Crucifixion	15:21–41
		Burial	15:42–47
7	Saturday	—	—
8	Sunday	Visit to the tomb	16:1–8
	Passover		14:12–16

(Note that, according to Jewish reckoning, "a day" began at sundown. There is some uncertainty, both in Mark and in ancient sources, as to whether the "first day" of the Passover week referred to the day of preparation when the lambs were slaughtered and the meal made ready, or the "day" of the meal itself that was eaten after sundown. If Mark intended Jesus' meal with his disciples to be a celebration of the Passover meal, his account of the trial and crucifixion on the [night and] first day of Passover is an outrageous insinuation.)

Judas offered to them (Mark 14:10). It is another of Mark's surprising changes in social climate and mood. Most scholars have thought it ill placed, a "late" addition to the passion narratives of an "early" independent tradition. In chapter 7 this story was discussed as a late elaboration of an early chreia. The suggestion can now be made that Mark performed the elaboration with a particular purpose in mind.

Mark's decision to rewrite the Christ myth as history was made possible by the availability of a number of narrative designs that could explicate

Jesus' death in a way appropriate to merge with the Jesus traditions. The same was not true for the resurrection. Since the story of the crucifixion ended with a body on a cross, certain things had to happen before the resurrection could occur. The Hellenistic tradition for the time of the resurrection was "on the third day." Mark had decided to schematize the passion account, first by following the cycle of a week, and second by correlation with a Passover festival (see figure 22). The combination of constraints meant that burial would have to occur hurriedly between Jesus' death at 3:00 P.M. and the beginning of the Sabbath at dusk, or else the timing would go awry. Mark used the challenge creatively by turning the lack of proper burial into a reason for the women's visit to the tomb on the first day of the week. The failure to anoint Jesus' body either at the burial or at the tomb, then, left a motif free for another very interesting set of reflections. The story of the anointing was the result.

At the end of the story five ideas are pressed into the pronouncement: (1) anointing, (2) beforehand, (3) body for burying, (4) gospel, and (5) memory (Mark 14:8-9). Each of these is a very big idea. The fact that all of them come together in a solemn prediction, not about eschatological vindication, power, and glory, but about the manner of the gospel's transmission in the meantime, should not be overlooked.

"Anointing" is what the story is about. The question is how this motif is intended to fit with the other concepts in the pronouncement. Since Jesus' body will not be anointed at the burial, this is the only anointing Jesus' body will receive. Since it occurs "beforehand," it can only be "for" burying, not the anointing that accompanies a burial. The woman's deed, moreover, will become part of the gospel to be preached. Preaching the gospel and the Christ kerygma are, of course, concepts that belong together. Body, burial, and memorial also belong together in the martyrological tradition. Thus it appears that the purpose of the story is to resignify terminology taken from the Christ cult.

In order to make any sense of this odd interpretation of the woman's deed, Mark's attitude toward the kerygma (gospel) of the Hellenistic Christ cult needs to be kept in mind. The passion narrative was written as a martyrology, thereby countering the enthusiasm of the Christ cult for symbols of otherworldly power. A new danger had to be avoided, though, for the passion account could be (mis)taken as an etiology for a martyr's memorial. Mark's view was apocalyptic. He would not have been any more comfortable with a cult of Jesus as martyr than he was with a cult of Jesus as the cosmic Christ. The woman's deed is a kind of substitute for the burial of the martyr and the anointing of the Christ. Her deed is final, so there need be no other form of memorial. Her deed is also proleptic, thus predictive, not celebrative. The gospel will no longer be an etiological ritual of memorial or a myth of present vindication. It will be a story of the fate of the

Son of God in the world as the martyred Messiah with a future destiny. The story of the woman's sacrifice belongs to that larger story now, because of its position in the narrative gospel. To "preach" the gospel is not to proclaim the kerygma for Mark, but to make the stories about Jesus memorable. The gospel is no longer the Christ myth, but the myth of origins.[8]

---

8. *Anointing as memorial.* V. Robbins has taken note of the relation between the anointing and the last supper in Mark in respect to the themes of absence ("You do not always have me with you," Mark 14:7) and memorial. He suggests that, if Mark knew the Pauline tradition, Mark appears to have shifted the occasion for memorial from the meal to the anointing. Remembrance is now a function of the gospel Mark has written. See his "Last Meal," 36.

PART IV

THE GOSPEL ACCORDING TO MARK

Even if our gospel is veiled, it is veiled only to those who are perishing.

The Apostle Paul
2 Corinthians 4:3

12

THE GOSPEL
AS MYTH

1. THE SOCIAL SETTING

Southern Syria in the seventies would be about right for such an intellectual labor as the Gospel of Mark. Jesus' apocalyptic instruction in Mark 13 is the important bit of evidence for a post-70 C.E. date and for a place from which the events of the Jewish War could be closely observed, yet without immediate involvement. The Jewish War was in very recent memory and rather vividly so. It had, moreover, created confusion about what it could mean for Judea, for Palestine, for Jews, and for the Jesus people. Jesus people were not the only ones confused.

The story Josephus tells of the sixties is one of famine, social unrest, institutional deterioration, bitter internal conflicts, class warfare, banditry, insurrections, intrigues, betrayals, bloodshed, and the scattering of Judeans throughout Palestine. Josephus was in Galilee for a time trying to raise an army for the anti-Roman cause, then surrendered to befriend the conquerors. Simon, the zealot leader who rose to the top by routing other contenders, had a following of soldiers, women, and malcontents. He was the one who ruled the city toward the end of the war and was then executed by the Romans after the war as the chief instigator and king of the Jews. During the years of siege (66–70 C.E.), stories spread of popular messiahs, prophets crying out woes on the city and temple, mock trials, and crowds creating tumults at the times of pilgrimage. There were wars and rumors of wars for the better part of ten years and Josephus reports portents, including a brilliant daylight in the middle of the night. Two Roman generals were in the field, coming and going. Jerusalem fell bit by bit, and the end did not finally come until 72–73 C.E. at Masada.[1]

---

1. *The Jewish War.* Josephus wrote *The Jewish War* during the seventies. The construction put upon the war is generally that the Romans did what they had to do in the face of a very chaotic and unreasonable series of incidents caused by the deterioration of Jewish institutions. Some scholars have drawn the conclusion that Josephus laid the blame for the war solely, if not primarily, upon the Jews. A more cautious reading detects

Jesus' apocalyptic instruction follows this history closely, with one exception. Tucked into the middle of it there is mention of expulsions from the synagogue. These also, according to Mark's Jesus, belong to the signs of the woes that will take place before the coming of the Son of Man with power. If one reads Jesus' apocalyptic predictions in light of the histories actually experienced by Mark's community, one can imagine its effectiveness as a powerful rationalization of catastrophe. The apocalypse easily falls into four periods as outlined in figure 23.

Jesus people in Southern Syria would have been abuzz for several years about rumors of wars in Jerusalem, popular messiahs on the march, and the Roman armies coming and going along the coast highway. If ever there was a need for a warrior-king to rise, now was the time. How to get that together with Jesus, the Jesus movement, and the talk about the kingdom of God, though, was the problem. Could the message of Jesus and the crisis in Jerusalem have anything to do with one another?

Southern Syria is a probable location for Mark's activities for other reasons as well. Synagogues are in the picture and Mark wrote his story with the problems of the synagogue reform movement in mind. Galilee is not probable because, while Mark championed Galilean traditions, he made a few descriptive errors about Galilean locations, enough to raise the question whether he lived there and knew the territory intimately. Antioch would be an attractive site because of its intellectual atmosphere. But it also must be suspect because that is where the Christ cult took its rise, and Mark was not eager at all about the spiritual enthusiasms of Hellenistic Christianity. There is nothing that would tell against Tyre, Sidon, or Byblos, however, eminent cities with strong cultural resources and traditions, close

---

Josephus' dismay at his inability to account both for the disintegration of Jewish society and for the ruthlessness of the Roman response. The style of the report is straightforward, but the accounts of slaughterings, unfortunate coincidences, and devastations are numerous and exaggerated. It is true that Josephus regards the various popular Jewish leaders of the insurrections and rebellions to be "impious" and their followers foolish. He tends to blame them for the Roman reprisals. Interwoven into the history, however, are descriptions of Jerusalem, the temple, and the Jewish institutions around which all of the battles revolve, descriptions that let one intuit just how great the loss was for Josephus. The very fullness of the account, lingering over each detail, decision, and move, betrays a certain trauma, an unwillingness to bring the story to an end. As the story does finally reach its climax in books 6 and 7, Josephus cannot resist including phenomenal occurrences that, as he says, belonged to the reports, stories, and rumors of the last months of the war. Even if one greatly discounts Josephus' accumulation of gory and marvelous lore, the impression remains that the picture he paints must have been shared by many. References to examples of phenomena cited in the discussion above include: *Jewish War* 5.21–26, 371, 424–38 (famine); 5.446–52 (crucifixions); 6.285–87 (false prophets); 6.288–300 (portents, including the light at midnight); 6.300–309 (the crying out of "woes on Jerusalem" by a certain Jesus); 6.310–15 (oracles of doom); 6.420–34 (the mass slaughter of pilgrims at Passover); 7.26–36 (capture of Simon in his purple robes); 7.153–57 (Simon's execution in Rome).

FIGURE 23
THE APOCALYPSE IN MARK 13

1–2   Jesus predicts the destruction of the temple.

3–4   The disciples request a sign to know when it will happen.

5–37   Jesus responds by predicting the future as follows:

I.   5–8   *Early Signs*

                  Wars and rumors of wars
                  Nation rising against nation
                  Earthquakes and famines

                  Warnings

                  Messiahs will lead many astray
                  Do not be alarmed, the end is not yet

II.   9–13   *Suffering in the Diaspora*

                  You will be delivered up to councils
                  You will be beaten in the synagogues
                  Brother will deliver up brother to death

                  Advice

                  Do not worry about what to say
                  The one who endures will be saved

III.   14–23   *Desolation in Jerusalem*

                  (Let the reader understand)

                  Advice

                  Flee
                  Do not go after false messiahs and prophets

IV.   24–37   *Desolation in Creation*

                  Sun, moon, and stars will fall
                  The Son of Man will appear

                  Advice

                  Learn from the fig tree
                  Watch

---

enough to Palestine to feel the vibrations of the troubled history in Judea, yet far enough away to account for the painful history Jesus people had with a conservative diaspora synagogue. That history of hostility was also of recent memory. The Jesus people of the synagogue reform movement were therefore in serious trouble. Having thought of themselves as sons and daughters of Israel, failure to find an acceptable arrangement with the diaspora synagogue meant that the kingdom they talked about hardly represented the sect they had become. The Jesus people to whom Mark belonged were in need of figuring things out some other way.[2]

2. THE AUTHOR'S CONCERNS

Mark tackled the problem of the right of the Jesus movement to exist independently of the synagogue. The terms in which the failure/rejection had been couched were those of the basic codes of Jewish identity. The Jesus people had violated the ritual laws of purity. On the basis of their memories of Jesus and their experiences as a social entity, Jesus people had argued that the ritual laws of purity did not apply. They had pitted Jesus against the Pharisees to authorize a claim to Israel's heritage and they lost the debate. Mark set about the task of turning that failure into a sign for the legitimacy of the claims Jesus people had made.

A comprehensive rationale was needed for the enclave of the unclean as the true inheritors of the promises to Israel. The traditional identifiers had been disputed. Now it was necessary to claim them for the newly independent movement. Jesus' authority would have to be shown greater than that of the Pharisees. The epic history would have to be channeled in such a way as to come to fulfillment in Jesus and the Jesus movement. The Jesus movement would have to be distinguished clearly from other alternative Jewish institutions as the only legitimate heir of the promises of the epic history. Israel's God would have to bless Jesus and his kingdom at the

---

2. *Date and provenance.* Howard Kee also argues for southern Syria as the most reasonable location for Mark and his gospel, *Community of the New Age,* 100–105. Kee does not include Mark's knowledge of the Jewish War as a consideration in determining provenance. He leaves the impression that the power of the apocalyptic imagination could have created the Gospel of Mark even before the end of the Jewish War and the destruction of the temple. One detects a growing tendency in recent scholarship to agree with this position. The pre-70 C.E. date is convenient, for it (1) supports traditional sensibilities about the priority of *logos* over history, (2) does not threaten the sense that some modicum of insight or truth may reside in the predictions after all, whether made by Jesus or by Mark, and (3) keeps the earliest gospel pressed back as far toward the beginning as possible in the hope of closing the gap between Jesus and the stories about him. For a much more convincing approach to the problem of dating the Gospel of Mark see W. Kelber, *The Kingdom in Mark.* Kelber shows that the gospel makes most sense in post-70 C.E. circumstance. This perspective is missing, unfortunately, in Kelber's more recent work, *The Oral and the Written Gospel.*

expense of others who mistakenly thought they belonged to his plans for the world.

Problems internal to the Jesus movement made Mark's task very difficult indeed. Though at home in the erstwhile synagogue reform movement, Mark was aware of other groups with claims upon the name of Jesus, groups that understood things quite differently. He knew about the prophets of Q, the twelve in Jerusalem, the family of Jesus, the congregation of Israel, and the Christ cult. He also knew about ways in which several of these movements had rationalized their histories and worked out their authorities. He knew, for instance, about Peter, "disciples," James (and John), "the twelve," visions, appearances, and ritual etiologies. Worse than that problem of pluralism, though, within the Jesus movements he knew there had been confusion about the times, messianic excitements, betrayals, denials, and apostasies. The little band set free into an unsympathetic if not hostile world was faced with a most critical situation.

Mark was worried about working out the conceptual foundations for the continued existence of the Jesus movement. He was also concerned about the social practices that identified the Jesus people and gave the movement its distinctive place in the world. He had some very definite ideas about what these practices should be and projected them onto the story of Christian origins. Table fellowship was the important occasion. An egalitarian principle was to prevail, disallowing distinctions in status and contravening claims to higher positions. There was a *logos* about the kingdom of God that should be the subject of discourse, and an ethic about service that should be the rule of behavior. Strangely, in light of the extravagant myth of origins Mark imagined, there appear to have been some other more normal codes in place as well such as fasting, keeping the great commandments, doing good, and staying married. Jewish sensibility had won a few rounds. Watching out for the "cares of the world, the delight in riches, and the desire for other things" on the one hand, and for the appearance of the Son of Man to render judgment on the other, Mark's idea was to withdraw from the fray for the meantime, but hope nonetheless for a social historical vindication at the end.

3. MARK'S NEW MYTH OF ORIGINS

For Mark the figure of Jesus as the founder of the new movement was the place to start a new reflection, and the place to end it. The importance of Jesus had been settled upon during the intervening forty years as the Jesus movements returned again and again to their beginnings in order to say what it was they intended to be and do. To give an account of themselves under question, Jesus people could not simply point to the constitution and experience of their group activities for there were no conceptual categories available for describing and justifying social formation as merely human derring-do. In the process, Jesus had been accommodated to images of leadership and authority, then set apart from others in the class to underscore distinctiveness. Mark accepted fully the logic underlying the creation of the myths of origin in the Jesus movements. What had been worked out was available to him in materials composed and transmitted by the movements, namely the sayings (Q), parables, miracle stories, and pronouncement stories. From these Mark was to craft a composite picture of the man of authority at the beginning of the endtime for Israel.

From Mark's point of view, the common denominator where all Jesus and Christ traditions might agree was a characterization of Jesus as a royal figure. To enhance the royal authority of Jesus was, moreover, a timely consideration. Jesus movements could be aligned with epic traditions over against Second Temple models with their orientation to priestly figures. Because the Pharisees derived their codes from the ritual laws of the Second Temple system, to pit against them a royal figure with epic precedent would be a *coup de maître*. What could they say, now that Jerusalem was in shambles and the temple in ruins? Mark decided to do it. He brought the Jesus materials together to create the image of Jesus as the king of the kingdom of God, predicted by the prophets and acknowledged by his Father as the legitimate heir of all the promises ever made for Israel among the nations. Packed into this sovereign figure, suddenly appearing on the scene just before Jerusalem's sorry end, was absolute authority (pronouncement stories), power (miracle stories), and knowledge (Sayings Source). Alas. With such a manifestation of rupturous revelation needed to justify the little band, rejected and confused about its place in the scheme of things, the question of credibility was now internalized. With that kind of origination, what had gone wrong?

A second set of reflections focused on the reasons for rejection. Again, Mark's point of departure was found within the Jesus traditions. Prophets in the tradition of Q had already made the connection between their failure to win "this generation" for Jesus, and the homiletical *topos* of Israel's rejection of the prophets. Putting the two together, Jesus people in this tradition had already dared the thought that Jesus' death had been a sign that he and his message and his followers would be rejected. Mark could use that notion, for it explained the failure of the reform movements in terms of the "hardness of heart" of those who refused the message, rather than calling into question the message or the messengers (cf. the theme announced in Mark 4:12). *Voilà.* Another masterstroke was also close at hand. The people of the Q tradition were not the only ones to have given thought to the significance of Jesus' death.

Mark was aware of the meaning of Jesus' death in the myth and ritual traditions of the Hellenistic Christ cult. He was not interested in the way in which that meaning had been elaborated culticly. But there were two aspects of the Christ myth and ritual that could be used to great advantage. One was the logic fundamental to the entire system of rationalization, namely, the logic of martyrdom. That could easily be combined with the rejection motif by turning those who rejected Jesus (and the synagogue reform movement) into the tyrants of the martyrological schema. The other aspect of interest to Mark was the logic of martyrdom as a vicarious and effective event. The synagogue reform movement was desperately in need of a charter document to put a constructive rationale upon its independence. The purpose of Jesus' resolve to die for the cause, or "for many," could be understood as effective for the Jesus movement as well as for the Hellenistic cult. Mark was obviously intrigued by this possibility, though he approached it cautiously. If Jesus' martyrdom were not complemented by a fully cosmic myth of vindication and present exaltation, the effectiveness of his obedience could be regarded as constitutive for the new movement as the social form "Israel" was to take. The pattern of Jesus' resolve could be seen as the model for the group's ethic and practice. Mark decided to work out the possibilities. Just as the martyrological pattern had commended itself to the Jesus people in Antioch in the forties as a way to justify a new social constituency, so it commended itself to Mark in the seventies as a mythic charter to claim legitimacy for the newly ostracized society of the unclean followers of Jesus. To hit upon an interpretation of Jesus' death that lent itself both to an apologetic and to a constitutive mythic function was irresistible. The only problem was how to compose a narrative based upon that kind of logic.

The wisdom tale made it possible to integrate the martyrological reduction of the Christ traditions with the Jesus materials to form the gospel story. The overlaps, combinations, reinterpretations, and rearrangements of all the Jesus and Christ traditions have been indicated in the preceding chapters. It is now possible to emphasize that Mark's accomplishment was an authorial, intellectual achievement. In modern critical parlance, Mark's Gospel is a very richly textured story. Its most distinctive feature is the complexity of what critics call intertextuality, the domestication and integration of diverse texts, genres, and patterns of perception in the formation of a novel literary performance. Mark's Gospel stands at the intersection of many streams of cultural, literary, and social history. It was created by effort, intellectual effort, and it is marked by conscious authorial intention. Mark was a scholar. A reader of texts and a writer of texts. He was a scribe in the Jesus tradition of the synagogue reform movement.[3]

---

3. *Intertextuality.* The nature of the intertextuality of Mark's Gospel calls for a brief digression. The traditional scholarly approach to intertextual relationships among early Christian literatures has been to trace single line dependencies starting from discrete (and

Mark's Gospel was not the product of divine revelation. It was not a pious transmission of revered tradition. It was composed at a desk in a scholar's

preferably single) points of origin. This results in a "stemma" or family tree arrangement. The desire has been to see junctures in the history of a textual tradition as interpretive developments of the essential ideas, insights, or implicit structures at the core of a tradition. All traditions eventually converge at the point of origin. The single trunk, naturally, has been imagined rooted in Jesus, or stemming from very early reminiscences about him. The approach to intertextuality taken in the present study differs from the traditional in two respects. One is that, since social history and experience have been emphasized as the human situation within which literature is generated, novelty is to be expected at every turn. This is especially the case with the early chapters of the Jesus and Christ movements where experimentation was required. Vigorous intellectual effort has been seen at every juncture documented by literary production, intellectual effort that sought to accommodate or use a wide variety of views, experiences, traditions, authorities, and genres, all "texts" pressed into the rationalization of new circumstances. Thus "creativity" or "originality" has not been located solely at the beginning of a "trajectory," but dispersed and distributed among the many moments.

The second difference is that a given moment of composition has been viewed as the (momentary) intersection of multiple textual, cultural, and social "traditions," not the "development" of a single tradition. Each composition analyzed was found to be the result of "translations" from among many given systems of signs in the interest of a new (composite) arrangement. Even the earliest, "simplest" rationalizations among the Jesus movements were complex coordinations of memory traditions, observations on social experience, and various patterns of imagining "Israel" taken from generally available lore outside of the tradition of memory. While some traditions are invariably given privilege over others in any new arrangement, texts not so privileged may actually contribute more to new composition. Ranking, resignifying, even erasing the traces of textual traditions of influence and other ways of manipulating linguistic conventions occur in the process of rearticulation. Mark is an interesting case in point. In addition to the written texts he pursued he must have known about a great many genre pervasive in the culture at large. He knew, for instance, about Hellenistic biography, about rhetoric, chreiai, and their elaboration, the notion of the noble death, the pattern of the wisdom tale, apocalyptic schemata, and so forth. The object of the study has been to identify some of the major textual traditions of importance to Mark's composition, ponder their diversity, and marvel at Mark's skill in their combinations. The aim has been to demonstrate the fact of mythmaking in this way, and to ask about its purposes. Because the myth of Christian origins has been the theme, however, the pre-Markan traditions about Jesus and the Christ have been focused upon, primarily, leaving other aspects of Mark's intertextuality largely unexplored. These deserve exploration, if for no other reason than to demonstrate the impingement of texts not indigenous to the privileged tradition, texts that describe a cultural fabric, not a family tree. If they are not in the picture, one might still have the feeling that Mark's Gospel was the product of an evolvement stemming mainly from the influence of Jesus.

A clear case of Mark's use of a written corpus not adequately discussed in this study might be mentioned here in order to indicate the range of his scholarship. H. Kee counts fifty-seven scriptural quotations in Mark 11–16 of which thirty-three are from the prophetic books. Of one hundred sixty scriptural allusions in Mark, half are from the prophets (*Community of the New Age*, 45). Such an excessive interest in the prophetic corpus is unusual when compared with the way in which other early groups went about reading the scriptures. It reminds one of the hermeneutic practiced in Qumran where the prophets were given privilege as in no other Jewish sect. Since one does not normally imagine the Hellenistic synagogue paying this kind of attention to the prophets, one wonders where and when Mark would have learned to do so. Both Paul and the tradents of Q had entertained apocalyptic imagination, to be sure, each for different reasons. But Mark's systematic

study lined with texts and open to discourse with other intellectuals. In
Mark's study were chains of miracle stories, collections of pronouncement
stories in various states of elaboration, some form of Q, memos on parables
and proof texts, the scriptures, including the prophets, written materials
from the Christ cult, and other literature representative of Hellenistic
Judaism. It would not be unthinkable that Mark had a copy of the Wisdom
of Solomon, or some of the Maccabean literature, or some Samaritan texts,
and so on. One "text" he did not have was a copy of the passion narrative
because there was none until he wrote it. One might imagine Mark's study
as a workshop where a lively traffic in ideas and literary experimentation
was the rule for an extended period of time. Colleagues may well have
contributed ideas and experimental drafts for many of the little story units
used throughout the gospel in a common effort to think things through on
the new storyline. The passion narrative is simply the climax of the new
storyline. The story was a new myth of origins. A brilliant appearance of the
man of power, destroyed by those in league against God, pointed nonetheless to a final victory when those who knew the secret of his kingdom would
finally be vindicated for accepting his authority.[4]

---

approach to the construction of a thoroughly apocalyptic view of (Christian) history, and
his literary dependence upon the prophetic corpus, especially the Book of Daniel, is
different. Mark, or someone in Mark's milieu, spent a considerable bit of time searching the
scriptures in the interest of establishing a certain relationship between them and the
emerging gospel-story of Jesus. One wonders how that energy and direction of research
came about, under what circumstances the hermeneutic was learned, and whether his
readers would immediately have shared his assumptions about the oracular authority of the
prophetic texts. Similar questions could be asked about Mark's readership of the many
other textual traditions with which he obviously was acquainted. The point would be that
Mark's literary accomplishment is not adequately assessed when seen only as a poetic and
creative achievement. To relate a variety of "traditions" not brought together before should
be acknowledged as scholarly labor. His gospel is not the germination of a single kernel of
truth finally flowering, nor the product of "collecting" and "passing on" early traditions
about Jesus. Neither is it simply the confluence of parallel but essentially compatible
traditions about Jesus. It is, instead, a highly conscious scholarly effort in fabricating a new
text by taking up strands from textual patterns that belonged to the multifaceted cultural
fabric of his times.

4. *The Markan milieu.* The confluence of early traditions in Mark's Gospel may
document more than a single author's facility in research and creative composition. The
kind of vigorous activity in which Mark engaged can be imagined for many others like him.
This period of activity was localized loosely in southern Syria and marked by the authors'
awareness of each other's labors, if not the exchange of ideas and materials. Extrapolating
from Mark's manner of work, some characteristics seem worthy of note: (1) The authors
took interest in several Jesus and Christ traditions other than their own. (2) They appear to
have gained a fair amount of critical knowledge about these other traditions by some
means. (3) Some notion of integration seems to have been at work in the effort to merge or
conflate diverse traditions in a new and unified charter. (4) An amazing amount of freedom
was exercised in the recasting of traditions toward this end. (5) In spite of the desire to
accommodate a great variety of disparate material in a unified charter, consciousness of
taking a position over against other Jesus and Christ movements is also in evidence.

(6) Contact, recognition, and exchange took place in the absence of any mechanism by which social identity, beliefs, and practices among the various groups could be normalized.

The point has repeatedly been made throughout the study that much of the material in Mark not usually identified as "Markan" nevertheless shares the author's overall perspective on Jesus and his program for the gospel. Examples of stories that create problems when judged according to the usual list of "Markan" characteristics (of style, vocabulary preference, and so forth) would be the set of miracle and pronouncement stories in chap. 2, the story of the anointing, or some of the other passion narratives. "Markan" authorship has been emphasized nonetheless in order to exhibit both the intentional fabrication (or recasting) of the many stories as well as the coherence of that intentionality when assessed in relation to function within the overall plan for the gospel. One might well imagine, however, many hands at work on the common project in the course of working out together the new rationale. A lively intellectual atmosphere can easily be imagined. The Gospel of Mark appears to have been the stellar production during this period, for its dissemination and subsequent influence seem to be assured. Nevertheless, other solutions to what may have been an intellectual crisis experienced by most Jesus movements also may have been forged during this time. Examples would be the shift that took place in the Q tradition that produced the Gospel of Thomas, the accommodation of the Q tradition that produced the Gospel of Matthew, and the peculiar merger of miracle stories and sayings that underlay the Gospel of John. Each of these new arrangements and resignifications of Jesus materials bears the marks of intellectual labor, drawing upon new myths, patterns of characterization, and other "texts" carefully selected from the rich variety available in the culture. Each can be related to a distinctive sectarian identity, and understood as a product of the construction of that sect's symbolic world.

Two observations follow from this hypothesis. If the Markan milieu is imagined both in a narrower sense, a circle of those that worked out the gospel solution, and in a more general sense, a network of exchange that allowed for others to have worked out other solutions, the old problem of the relationships among these various texts might be reimagined as well. There is really no reason to think that the Markan circle did not "know" about the tradents of Q and some collection of their sayings just because Mark did not incorporate them into his story as Matthew decided to do. Those who produced the Gospel of Thomas may well have been aware of the picture of "the disciples" and their bad image about Mark's time in the Markan milieu. That John's community passed through the Markan milieu, collected the same kinds of material as did the Markan circle, and knew about the Markan solution, is a much more reasonable assumption than that the gospel produced by John was an independent creation. The radically different solutions to the post-70 C.E., postseparation crisis, solutions that range from Matthew's scribal community, through Mark's apocalyptic solution, and John's community of spiritual transformation, to the group that decided for a private interpretation of the teachings "to Thomas," is enough to account for the discrepancies among the textual traditions they share when compared. The rule in general was not the "transmission" of "received" (sacred) tradition, but creative reworking and creative borrowing, that is, intellectual labor best understood on the model of intertextuality.

The second observation is that the exchange did not produce a unification of "Christianity" either institutionally or symbolically. Positions were taken and groups went their way. The various solutions that pop up textually later in the course of the late first and early second centuries, many of them best located in Syria and thus not far apart, show this to have been the case (for example: Q, Matthew, Gospel of Thomas, Didache, Gospel of John, Luke-Acts?, Epistles of Ignatius). Each textual documentation of a sectarian rationale bears the marks, nonetheless, of contact with others at some point in their social histories. Mark's time and milieu bids high as the occasion when contact was made and positions were taken. Mark's Gospel also bids high as a well-known product of the intellectual activity that must have been characteristic for that time.

13

THE GOSPEL
AS APOCALYPSE

1. THE APOCALYPTIC STRUCTURE

Compared with other apocalyptic literature of the times the Gospel of Mark does not appear to be an apocalypse, but only to contain an apocalyptic speech (Mark 13). The speech, moreover, is more matter of fact than visionary in its description of the events to befall the end, and Jesus is not portrayed as a seer, that is, one whose primary importance is related to the reception of revelations of privileged information. Were chapter 13 deleted from the gospel, it would be difficult to argue that the gospel was written by an author of apocalyptic mentality. Thus debates have raged about Jesus' message of the kingdom of God (Mark 1:15), whether it was intended as an apocalyptic pronouncement, an announcement of a "realized" eschatology, or of an order of things without any apocalyptic nuance at all. Serious differences of opinion define the current state of discussion on the transfiguration as well (whether an apocalyptic vision, or a pre-dated Easter appearance), the crucifixion (whether an apocalyptic moment of fulfillment, or a cosmic event of obedience and sacrifice), and the promised appearance of Jesus in Galilee (whether referring to the eschaton, the birth of the church, or a post-Easter appearance). In spite of apocalyptic language throughout, whether to portray the time of Jesus as a time of fulfillment, or to predict yet another eschaton, the story at first reads as a myth of origins for the new time of the followers of Jesus, not as a visionary revelation of the future end of the world.

A study by Norman Petersen points toward the solution of this problem. He distinguished between the "plotted time" actually recounted in the gospel as written (the narrative account from John the Baptist to the empty tomb), and the larger sweep of history assumed by the narrative, a history reaching back into the time of Israel and the prophets, and ahead to the destruction of the temple and the coming of the kingdom in power. He called this history the "story time." Connections between the two narrative times could then be visualized as a complex set of interlocking predictions and fulfillments. Thus, Isaiah and Malachi point to John the Baptist who fulfills their predictions and makes a prediction of his own. John points to Jesus who fulfills the Baptist's prediction and becomes a predictor as well. Jesus' predictions are final, the beginning of the end. He predicts what will happen in Jerusalem (plotted time), as well as what will happen in the future (story time). Thus the prediction/fulfillment mechanism is the device used to connect the plotted time of Jesus to the story time of Israel's history. It is also the device that made it possible to imagine the eschaton as determined by the appearance of Jesus and his fate. Chapter 13 is critical, therefore, for the composition and intention of the gospel as a whole. It is in chapter 13 that the predictions of the coming of the kingdom in power and glory are placed clearly at the end of the story time of the history of Israel.[1]

Building upon Petersen's proposal, the apocalyptic intention of Mark's story of Jesus can be specified quite easily. Apocalyptic means the imagination of divine intervention in history. An apocalypse unfolds under the signs of crisis, conflict, judgment, and transformation. An ideal or desire has not been realized in a history contrary to its expectations. Those who hold nevertheless to the plan have no alternative but to account in some way for the sorry state of affairs and project another time and place for the realization of the perfect order of things. There are several ways in which a compensation for the evils of the world can be managed, an apocalyptic vision of the end of the present social order being only one of them. Apocalyptic projections are usually made by sectarians whose failed expectations lay in the order of realizable social history. On the other end of the spectrum would be Gnostics, those who project the ideal order in some transcendent realm and hope to realize perfection via otherworldliness. There are many combinations of apocalyptic and otherworldly realms possible, each relatable to a particular view of social identity and its definition vis-à-vis some larger (usually dark) cultural context. Mark's apocalyptic view of the end of Israel's history and the fate of the synagogue reform movement was a complex interweaving of the judgmental aspects of divine intervention (to destroy what Israel had become), and the redemptive aspects of divine intervention (the inauguration of the gloriously perfect kingdom).

The normal sequence in contemporary apocalyptic visions was for woes to precede battles and the rendering of judgments, upon which the vindications appropriate to a little band of righteous survivors would coincide with the restoration of the perfect order of things. An apocalypse was written and read in the midst of the troubled times. The Jewish apocalypse

---

1. *Norman Petersen.* See "Story Time and Plotted Time." In a recent essay, "The Reader in the Gospel," Petersen positions the implied reader of the gospel within the "storytime."

gained perspective on the times, however, by the fiction of authorship at some time in the distant past when a seer, frequently also found in troubled circumstances, was granted a vision of the drama yet to be played. The ending, of course, still future even to the readers, would be God's mighty act of judgmental destruction and the creation of a new and just world. The reader of such an apocalypse was, therefore, not asked to evaluate the credibility of a novel revelation in his own time, but to affirm the (ancient) seer's assessment of the intervening history, position oneself toward the end of the script, and agree to the future projection on the grounds of the script's accuracy of prediction up until the reader's time. A sense of determinism about history, rightness about the judgments that must fall, privilege for receiving the revelation, and passive obedience and gratitude toward the sovereign power above generate a strong sectarian persuasion.

Mark's fiction attributed the vision of the script to Jesus, thus casting him in the role of seer. Jesus also was involved in troubled times, thus qualified to receive an apocalyptic revelation. In this case, however, different from Jewish apocalypses, the trouble in which Jesus was involved was not an episode from a past, paradigmatic cycle of conflict and judgment, but the first sign of the final cycle of woes he was predicting. Thus Jesus was not only seer, but the first casualty of the wars of conflict between the powers at the end.[2]

Jesus was, of course, even more. According to Mark, Jesus appeared as the king of the kingdom destined to be established in place of the evil kingdoms of the world. This role was necessary in view of the claims of the synagogue reform movement to be the people of the kingdom of God. Jesus had inaugurated the time of the new kingdom destined to substitute for the old demonic order. To imagine the inauguration of the kingdom of God before the apocalyptic script of the woes and final judgments had run its course, however, inverted the normal sequence of apocalyptic drama and meant, in effect, that the divine interventions of judgment and restoration had overlapped. The announcement of judgment and the announcement of the new kingdom coincided in the appearance of Jesus in Galilee. His battle with the demons demonstrated the eventual victory. Still, in the meantime, the forces in opposition to God's righteous reign would arrange themselves to do battle, demonstrating by their wickedness that they were deserving of the destruction in store for them. The compounding of roles for Jesus resulted in the strange circumstance that, in the midst of his own conflict with the institutions of the world, the king-designate predicted his

---

2. *Mark as apocalypse.* Several scholars have come to the conclusion that Mark should be read as an apocalypse. Among them are: N. Perrin, "The Gospel of Mark," chap. 7 in *The New Testament;* and H. C. Kee, *Community of the New Age,* esp. 64–76. On apocalyptic as a response to the failure to realize new expectations, see Adela Yarbro Collins, *Crisis and Catharsis,* 106.

own death as the first casualty in a series of conflicts destined to vindicate his claim, bring destruction upon those who killed him, and guarantee the absolute execution of righteous power when the kingdom was manifest in its glory.

From this point of view, the debate about the kingdom of God Jesus announced should not be staged as an either/or between a "realized" eschatology and an imminent future apocalyptic eventuality. A both/and approach would be better. Mark superimposed an apocalyptic script, starting with the appearance of Jesus in Galilee, on top of a myth of origins according to which Jesus was the inaugurator of the new group to whom the secret of the kingdom was given. The superimposition was achieved by using the framework stories to depict divine intervention in the appearance and destiny of Jesus. Double connotation is discernible in all of the framework stories, but especially in the account of the crucifixion. It had to serve both as the validation of Jesus' claims to be the king, as well as the apocalyptic prodigy pointing to its sequel in God's judgment upon the temple. A threefold vindication was called for. Jesus' own vindication was assured in the resurrection that follows. The destruction of the temple in 70 C.E. answered the establishment's destruction of Jesus. And the yet-to-occur manifestation of the kingdom in power would vindicate the kingdom announced and represented by Jesus at his appearance in Galilee, temporarily postponed by the forces still lodged for a time in Jerusalem. The apocalyptic structure of the gospel can be visualized in figure 24.

2. THE PERSPECTIVE ON THE TIMES

The position of the first readers of Mark's Gospel is indicated on the chart. The history of the end of Israel and the beginning of the people of the kingdom of God engulfed the reader while the completion of the story still lay before. The desire for full vindication and the manifestation of the kingdom of God demanded, therefore, a stance toward the future. Nevertheless, what could be known about the future was encoded only in the gospel account, and the gospel was an account of the time of Jesus in the past. The reader will have viewed the time of Jesus by peering back through the intervening history into an epoch that had literally come to its end. The story of Jesus' activity was set in the old epoch, but as the account of those momentous events that spelled its demise. The events were set in motion by the intervention of divine activity from outside the normal flow of human history. This divine activity was not to be viewed as arbitrary, a chance or surprising inbreaking of transcendent power, but as determined, fulfilling a purpose of long-standing and effecting a necessary conflict (cf. the *dei*, "it is necessary . . .," Mark 8:31). From the reader's point of view, the intervening history had borne out the inaugural signs. A critical attitude toward Mark's

FIGURE 24
The Gospel as Apocalypse

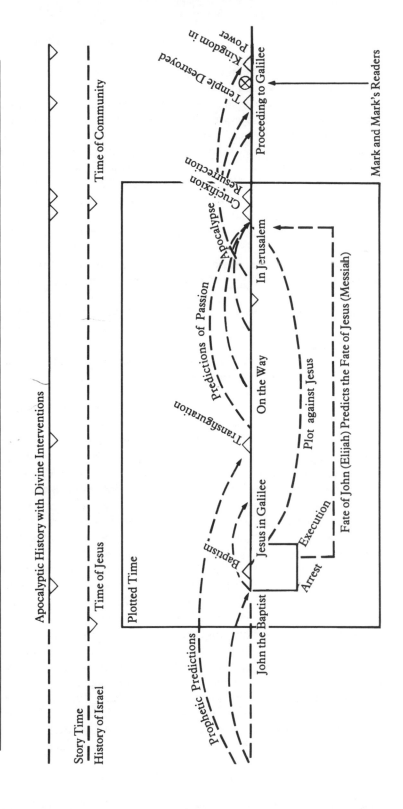

fantastic reconstruction of the past may have been very difficult to support, supposing one had wanted to be cautious.

Not only had the end of the epoch of the temple come as announced, the intervening history had erased by degrees whatever historical reminiscences there may have been toward the beginning. All of the people who figured in Mark's story were, moreover, long since dead. Pilate had been dead for over thirty years. Caiaphas, whose name Mark apparently did not know, had also been dead for over thirty years. Peter had died; James had died; Paul had died. There were no followers of Jesus in Jerusalem. It is probable that Mark's group did not contain anyone who had known Jesus. The past was ripe for reconstruction, full of various fantasies and mythic imageries. By writing the story the way he did, Mark determined that the appearance of Jesus be viewed as a particular past event of astounding consequence for the history of Israel and the beginning of the Christian time.

Looking back to that time, the reader of Mark's Gospel became an uninvolved spectator of events that determined destiny. The events were manifestations of incomprehensible powers in battle for the control of a human history over which the reader was powerless. Spectating was complemented by the phenomenon of listening in, overhearing the words of Jesus to others. A sense of knowing privileged information would have been inevitable, for the reader knew more about the meaning of Jesus' words and the accuracy of his predictions than anyone in the story could possibly have known. The "secret" of the kingdom of God would not have been a secret for the reader, though it would have been an esoteric knowledge, a *logos* that made sense only within the borders of the sect. To watch Jesus "teach in parables" without teaching, or speak predictions openly that no one then could understand, would not have seemed strange, given the apocalyptic import and seriousness of the entrance of the Son of God on the scene. Mark's Gospel did not just happen to contain an apocalyptic speech, it forced an apocalyptic view of the reader's history and times.

From within the sect privileged to read this gospel, the world beyond the borders came under the judgment of God. While the fixation of hostility was focused on Judaism, that which Judaism represented, history, tradition, law, and structured society, all fell under the sign of the inadequate if not depraved. Encounter with those outside was conceived as confrontation. One had to be careful, for the possibility of conflict was inherent in the world. Beware was the watchword with regard to those outside. Stay awake was the watchword with regard to the imminent appearance of the Son of Man. In the meantime, within the cell, patience, humility, and mutual service were to be the signs of perfection and preparation. Mark did not give up the desire for a manifestation of the kingdom of God in the social orders of human history, but his gospel left no room to be hopeful about its achievement except by means of a yet more fantastic intervention of divine power and sovereignty. The group his gospel rationalized was actually cut off from the social orders of human history, isolated from social reality, without even a history of its own, waiting between appearances of Godot.

3. COUNTING THE COST

Mark was willing to consider some of the costs accruing to an apocalyptic assessment of the chances for the kingdom of God in a hostile world. He indicated his understanding of those costs in the discipleship sayings about willingness to lose one's life for the sake of the gospel. He knew that the costs were high, and that the "weakness of the flesh" could be expected to engender fear, flight, or denial instead of "confession." But these costs were predicated on a persuasion of the reality of the ideal and its apocalyptic manifestation. They did not acknowledge that the ironies created in order to justify the group's constructive visions were double-edged swords. The ironies surrounding the crucifixion were designed to play the gap between the extremes of destruction and salvation, and function as weapons against those who destroyed the savior and therefore would be destroyed. The ironies came back upon their creators, however, for they only work when the fantastic is posited, and they seal off the chances for the realization of any less fantastic salvation. The desire originally underlying the whole program was for social reform, open borders, the presence of the new social spirit, the affirmation of plural pasts, and invitational discourse. The apocalyptic solution to the failure of the program meant that all of the original desires were abrogated, sacrificed to the new desire for self-justification. In the place of a social experimentation and its constructive visions, sectarian existence was now governed by absolute loyalty to a power effective only in events of vindictive transformation. These events were imaginary and could only be viewed from afar. The reader looks on, is a voyeur, not only upon an event in which God justified Jesus and his followers, but also upon an event in which those who created the need for that justification are seen as God's antagonists. The cost of such a salvation is extremely high. One need not become a martyr in order to have lost everything for the sake of such a gospel. One big loss was not having anything left to say to the world, those who inhabited the synagogue down the street. "Don't worry what to say," was Mark's advice, "when they deliver you up . . . it is not you who speak, but the Holy Spirit" (Mark 13:11).

14

THE GOSPEL
AS PARABLE

1. THE PARABOLIC STRUCTURE

A strictly apocalyptic interpretation of the Gospel of Mark is uncomfortable for modern sensibility. Attempts have therefore been made to determine the essential message of the gospel in other terms. An apocalyptic dimension cannot be denied, according to these views, but it should not determine the definition of Christian self-understanding made available by the (plotted time) story of Jesus and the disciples. One important attempt to redeem the gospel for more constructive meditations has been to read it as a parable. The story lends itself to this interpretation because of the turn taken in chapter eight where, in spite of Jesus' previous demonstrations of power to change things, the themes of suffering and the passion are introduced. This turn comes as a surprise both to the reader and to the disciples. As the story continues, moreover, much of the discourse plays on the contrast between miracles and power on the one hand, and the passion and servanthood on the other. This indicates that the author intended for the turn to plunge the disciples and the reader into a troubled reflection on the enigma of the crucifixion. The parabolic interpretation sees this reflection as an invitation to question conventional institutions of power and imagine a new kind of power, the influence that flows from self-sacrificial leadership.[1]

The division of the gospel into two phases, pivoting on the events at Caesarea Philippi, appears in figure 25. A chiastic structure is discernible, so that narrative elements and themes in each of the two parts correspond.

---

1. *Mark as parable.* See the remarks of J. D. Crossan at the conclusion of his book on *The Dark Interval,* "The Parabler becomes Parable," 123–28. A recent example of the parable theory at work is W. Kelber's "Parabolic Gospel—Oral Tradition—Jesus, The Parabolist," 211–26, in his *The Oral and the Written Gospel.* See also D. Via, *Kerygma and Comedy.* Via does not use the term parable, preferring various expressions of the dialectic between life and death as the way to fathom the *logos* of the gospel's structure. His treatment of the inherent tension in the dialectic corresponds well, however, with the parabolic function others have described.

A comparison of the corresponding elements shows that various kinds of contrast have been developed to set the two phases of the story in opposition. By folding the story in the middle so that phase one layers over the events in phase two, the oppositions come to climax in the crucifixion where Jesus' vulnerability and exit from the world describe an ending to the story that inverts completely the expectations raised at the beginning of the story. At the beginning, Jesus was baptized with the spirit and entered Galilee with authority and power.

FIGURE 25

THE CHIASTIC STRUCTURE OF MARK

A John the Baptist (points back to old story expectations)

 B Jesus' baptism (mythic "transition")

  C Temptation (encounter with demonic)

   D Call of disciples (positive response)

    E Teaching in synagogue (cleansing)

     F Mission in Galilee (power)

      G Jesus' transfiguration (mythic "transition")

     F' Way to Jerusalem (passion)

    E' Cleansing the temple (teaching)

   D' Response of disciples (negative)

  C' Temptation and trial (encounter with authorities)

 B' Crucifixion (mythic "transition")

A' Angel at tomb (points ahead to new story expectations)

Scholars have pointed to several thematic oppositions between phase one and phase two: miracles and institutions; power and powerlessness; success and failure; the kingdom of God and the kingdoms of the world; taking charge and being taken in charge; leadership and servanthood; and so forth. If the gospel is read as a chiasm, beginning with the baptism and stopping with the crucifixion, the sequence from power to powerlessness describes a single inversion that sets normal expectations about kings and the uses of power on their ear. It is this inversion that has been understood as the parabolic structure of the gospel.

2. THE PARABOLIC EFFECT

The parabolic interpretation of the gospel is a modern reading. It depends upon a comparison of the literary structure of the gospel with other genres of literature, primarily parables and hero tales. Parable theory has been discussed in chapter 6. The gospel is parabolic because of the unexpected twist in the plot and the questions that such an incongruous fate raises about power and its execution in human societies. Because the story is about a king or hero, however, comparison with hero tales has also been suggested. The hero tale generally follows the pattern of quest and trials, the hurdles to be overcome before reaching the goal and returning home. The homecoming may be tragic, but, if tragic, it is usually because of an action taken in ignorance, the consequences of which destroy the hero and his plans. If the ending is not tragic, the homecoming celebrates the hero's achievements by attributions of honor and office. Jesus' story seems to run in reverse. It begins with attribution of office and power, then descends to trials and humiliation. Jesus is fully conscious of the consequences of his deeds and he resolves to accept them. Mark appears to have invited just such a comparison in Mark 10:42–45 where reference is made to Gentile rulers who lord it over their subjects. In the Markan community, by contrast, leaders should serve, because even the Son of Man came (a narrative notion), not to be served (as one might have expected from phase one), but to serve (as phase two describes). Compared with the hero tale, then, the story of Jesus inverts sequences and themes and is, that is, a parable.

Parable theory suggests that the expectations raised in part one of the gospel belong to the myth of the hero or divine man. A superior person solves human ills by extraordinary powers, is honored for his abilities to master every situation, and is therefore granted first rank in return for the benefits bestowed upon the people. These expectations can be identified in the gospel story by asking about the reasons for the excitements of the crowd, the misunderstandings of the disciples, and the contrast made in Mark 10:42–45 between Jesus' mission and rulership among the Gentiles (Greeks). The crowd's desire for miraculous solutions to human ills is frustrated, so they turn against Jesus. The disciples hope for positions of power in the kingdom, are chastised, and flee before the "enthronement." Thus the expectations raised in part one are dashed in part two.

According to the parabolic interpretation, the reader is invited to reflect on the challenge the gospel presents to expectations and desires that are impossible, naive, and self-centered. The mythic world of heroics is shattered by the parable of Jesus' new kind of kingship. Another kind of power is intimated as a better and alternative vision. It is the power released in a martyrdom for the sake of others. The intended effect upon the reader is mirrored within the story by the challenge Jesus brings to the crowds and to the disciples. In part one, Jesus' challenge is to refine the misunderstandings that accompany the expectations that have been raised. The reader is caught in the middle, according to this reading, just as the disciples and the crowds are, between Jesus and the status quo. The caughtness does not go away, thus the parabolic function is preserved. It can be illustrated in a chart, the two phases of the story described as two sets of sine waves in opposition to one another (out of phase 180 degrees), crossing at the major points of transition in the chiasm (see figure 26). One sequence represents Jesus' activity and destiny. The other represents the expectations that are raised, only to be challenged within the story.

3. THE PARABLE AS IRONY

A fundamental criticism of the parabolic interpretation of the Gospel of Mark needs now to be introduced. The parabolic interpretation is possible only if three conditions are met: (1) The apocalypse in chapter 13 must be deleted and the apocalyptic history of the larger story world must be stripped away. (2) The plotted time of the gospel must be dislodged from the social history in which it is embedded and read as if it happened once upon a time. (3) It must be read, then, by Christians who assume in advance the importance of Jesus, some saving significance to his death, and some continuing sphere of influence or meaning within which the story as parable can function. (This new world of spiritual truth or Christian experience substitutes for the Markan apocalyptic history as the large arena of world context.)

The reason for insisting that the gospel must be read by Christians in order to work as a parable is that the myth to be dashed is not really an old-order, pagan, status quo, nor a universal human desire for authority, divine kingship, or power at all, but instead the Christian myth itself. The expectations that are raised in part one of the gospel are the form human desires take when it is Jesus, the Son of God, who appears on the scene. The expectations, that is, are Christian fantasies generated by the Christian myth of origins. The desire awakened is to imagine a unique breakthrough of God's power to transform the world. This desire is never really called into question by the parabolic inversion, nor given up in the parabolic interpretation. The desire is sobered and refined by the thought that, having gone through suffering and loss, the kingdom is the more glorious.[2]

---

2. *The kerygmatic assumption.* Since parable by definition works from within a world of discourse, the tension created is that between the myth assumed and the parable that calls it into question. Parable theory was developed, however, in order to account for the effect of Jesus' parables as the occasion for leaving the myth (of Judaism) behind. Modern sophistication is fully capable of imagining parabolic utterance to continue to function in relation to the Christian myth that resulted, to be sure. In this case, though, a dialectic is imagined according to which Christian existence is defined as living in the tensive space between myth and parable, both of which are understood to belong to the strange new kerygma at the heart of the Christian vision. The kerygma, it is assumed, functions both as myth and as parable—a uniquely dialectical creation. All interpretations of the gospel as

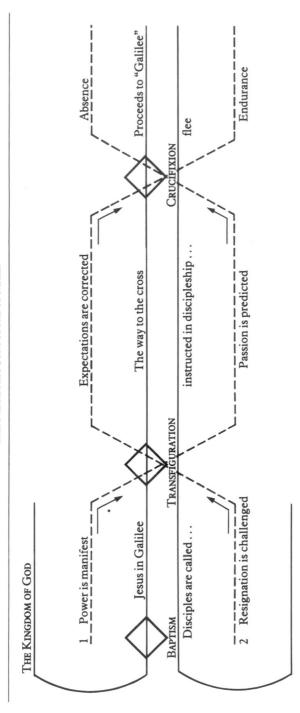

FIGURE 26

THE PARABOLIC STRUCTURE OF MARK

THE KINGDOM OF GOD

1 Power is manifest

Expectations are corrected

Absence

Proceeds to "Galilee"

Jesus in Galilee

The way to the cross

BAPTISM   TRANSFIGURATION   CRUCIFIXION   flee

Disciples are called . . .   instructed in discipleship . . .

Endurance

2 Resignation is challenged

Passion is predicted

1. Jesus appears with power to inaugurate the reign of God; this creates conflict and the world puts him to death; he will be vindicated fully only when the kingdom of God comes in power.

2. The disciples (and the people) are amazed at Jesus' authority; they conclude that he will inaugurate God's reign; but they underestimate the conflict and find themselves chided about the high cost of the kingdom of God.

1 and 2. Because the phases are out of sync the reader is always caught in the middle between great expectations and sobering resignations.

If the parable is applied internally, the gospel might become a critique of triumphalism, pride, or inordinate desire, of course, but always only as a pious reading made possible because it is one of several other readings, all of which are valid simultaneously. Applied to the world without, the gospel ceases to be a parable, reminding the Christian instead of the contrast between the kingdoms of the world and the kingdom of God. Even as parable, that is, the gospel functions as myth. Somewhere on the other side of the violence depicted a sequel is posited if not projected, something else is imagined that keeps the story from stopping at the parabolic point. That to which the story opens out at the end is not left to the imagination to be filled in even though it is not narrated. It is already filled in before the "parable" is read as the Christian myth.

This means that the gospel does not function parabolically at all, though it does create irony. Irony is created because the mythic order evoked by phase one is carried forward and allowed to glorify the death of Jesus in phase 2. It should be acknowledged that irony generally has been interpreted as a parabolic function by New Testament scholars. Interpreters of irony in the New Testament have wanted to see it as a mark of primitive Christian profundity, the appropriate trope for pointing to the mystery of transformation lying at the core of the Christian vision of hope and salvation. One should be clear about the mythic foundations for the ironic vision in the gospel. The irony is created by the superimposition of a Christian mythology upon a purportedly historical execution that becomes in the process a raw act of violence. Thus the perspectives of opposition are extreme and radical. Because the crucifixion is climactic for several narrative designs, all hands are in on the action: God is implicated (Mark 14:36); Jesus purposes it (Mark 10:45; 14:24, 36); the chief priests carry out the plot; a disciple hands Jesus over; the rest of the disciples participate by failing to take any measures; the crowd forces Pilate's hand; Pilate renders the sentence; and the soldiers knowingly do their work. Such being the case, the combinations of ironic perspective on the event are endless. Mark took advantage of many of them, but he preferred to end on the most dialectical of them all, the opposition between "salvation" and "destruction." Ultimately, this opposition rides on the extreme contrast between the beneficent use of God's power and the destructive use of human power. In order for such an irony to work, some notion about the saving significance of Jesus' death must already be in hand. It is this ironic vision of the king

---

parable assume some form of the Christian understanding of the dialectic between death and life stemming from the mythic event of Jesus' crucifixion and resurrection. D. Via's study of the Gospel of Mark in *Kerygma and Comedy* is a good example of the kerygmatic assumption, that is, the inability to read Mark, even as parable, except against the background of the Christian myth of transformation.

who rules by becoming a savior that has exercised the Christian imagination and been taken as the parabolic effect of the gospel.[3]

4. IRONY AS WEAPON

If the gospel Mark wrote is not to be misread, the apocalyptic intention
cannot be placed in brackets. There was in Mark's mind a particular sequel
to the crucifixion that reversed the play of powers once more, and finally.
The irony of the crucifixion was only a temporary illusion. God would
surely have the last word. The expectations raised in part one of the gospel
were not, according to Mark, fantastic desires evoked only to be crushed.
They were merely to be postponed until after the exchange of human
power and divine retribution had run its violent course. The story about
Jesus does not come to an end at the crucifixion. It empties out into the
larger storytime that ends only when the kingdom fully appears. When it
does, the Son of Man will come in power and glory. To use Crossan's
typology, the Gospel of Mark is not parable, it is (apocalyptic) myth. The
irony it contains functions solely in support of that myth. To those on the
inside the irony does not call the glory of the sheer power of God into
question, it justifies the need for that power to be manifest even more
decisively both in judgment and in salvation, in destruction as well as in
new creation, by giving an account of the demonic in the world of human
institutions.

Just as the parables were given so that those outside would not understand (Mark 4:12), so Jesus' resolve to die for "the many" was made known
only to the disciples. Mark did not understand the irony of the crucifixion as
a description of the public event, but as a private perspective. The reader
was invited to watch those who unknowingly got caught in the glare of
God's glory work their way out into judgments and actions that told against
them as ignorant articulations of the truth. When the chief priests who
consigned Jesus to the cross say "he saved others; he cannot save himself.
Let the Christ, the King of Israel, come down now from the cross, that we
may see and believe" (Mark 15:31–32), the essential irony is clearly

---

3. *Irony*. The reader of current interpretations of New Testament texts from a literary
critical point of view will find the discussions of irony to be pervasive. The recent study of
the Gospel of John by Paul Duke, *Irony in the Fourth Gospel*, focuses entirely upon this
trope. For a very interesting commentary upon the emergence of irony in the Johannine
trajectory see Alan Culpepper, *Anatomy of the Fourth Gospel*. Culpepper notes that the
earliest stages in the tradition did not use irony. The appropriate investigation then would
be, it seems, to determine the social circumstances and mythic precursors that gave rise to
the ironic mystifications. One suspects that such an investigation would reveal a
combination of sectarian withdrawal with the cultivation of patterns of transformation
somewhat similar to the Markan model.

expressed. It is, however, only available for the reader to see. Those in whose mouth the profundity has been placed do not know what they say, cannot know what they say. The irony depends upon their not knowing. The irony is a weapon used against them. It works vindictively. The terms are absolute and the judgments already sealed. It is impossible that such an irony could generate a parabolic transformation, either for those on the outside who are made to say the truth, or for those on the inside who are allowed to witness the fabricated mockery.

Whatever else irony may be asked to do in a narrative context, the trope itself functions, it should be remembered, not to create meaning, but to destroy it. A German theologian in the dialectical tradition, such as Schenke, might say that, because the crucifixion of the Messiah was a paradox that destroyed rationality, it was able to call Christian faith into existence. The historian, however, fails to discern that kind of paradox either at the beginning of the Jesus movements or in the composition of the gospel. The irony Mark created was paradoxical, certainly, but it was not intended to create faith. Neither was it a creation born of piety. It was a result of the need to rationalize the failure to persuade Jews of Jesus' authority. Mark's community found itself cut off and powerless in the midst of a social world torn by the exercise of power. The gospel was an imaginary compensation for the loss of connection to that social history. Schenke's paradoxical reading of early Christian history, like the modern parabolic interpretation of early Christian literature, depends upon Christian interpretations of the gospel that could have developed only later than Mark's time. In order for either the theological or the poetic reading to work, the gospel must already be functioning as the myth-ritual text of an institutionalized Christianity with standing, power, and connections in the larger cultural scheme of things. It would be then that a meditation on irony, paradox, and parable might be dared as an exercise in pious self-criticism. Mark was not that far along.[4]

---

4. *Ludger Schenke.* The reference is to his hermeneutical reflections in *Der gekreuzigte Christus*, 135–45, a booklet following upon his scholarly, exegetical work in *Studien zur Passionsgeschichte*. Reading Schenke is a very painful but revealing experience. The apologetic motivations that guided the scholarly work, though unacknowledged in that context, are fully disclosed in the popular book. It is a clear case of rational dialectic in the service of the Christian kerygma, said to be true just because of its power to destroy reason by virtue of its own dialectic.

15

THE GOSPEL
AS PARADIGM

1. JESUS' DEATH AS MODEL

The troubling sequence from Jesus' activity in Galilee to his fate in Jerusalem, the sequence that gives the gospel its appearance of being a parable, was developed thematically by Mark at two points in the story. One was the study of the crucifixion as an ironic event. The other was the implication of Jesus' crucifixion for discipleship given in the instructions to the disciples on the way to Jerusalem. According to these instructions, Jesus' death was a model to be imitated. Applied to the situation of the disciples, losing one's life was to be understood as the price to be paid if one wanted to save it. This irony works somewhat differently than that placed in the mouth of the chief priests and soldiers, because the reader is asked to view Jesus' death knowingly under a double perspective (the loss-that-saves), and consider it definitional for those who would be Jesus' followers. The disciples in the story are not able to grasp or measure up to these instructions, thus serve as negative examples. That being the case, the sayings function as Mark's positive statement about the paradigmatic purpose of the gospel for his own time and community. They describe, in effect, Mark's own solution to the conundrum of Jesus' fate, the way in which he intended for his readers to make sense of the gospel and the crucifixion as irony. They are Mark's instructions as to what, then, one was to think and do in the meantime. The instructions read as follows (see figure 27). They describe the situation in the world (first column) in light of the apocalyptic appearance of the kingdom of God (third column). The instructions in discipleship are given in the middle column.

There are three sets of instructions, each following upon a prediction of the passion and some indication of the disciples' misunderstanding. The first saying of the first set (Mark 8:34) establishes the theme of model and mimesis, the last saying of the third set (Mark 10:45) makes the period by returning to the idea of the death of the Son of Man as the standard and major argument for defining discipleship. Each set begins with a succinct statement of the requirement for being a disciple, followed by arguments in its support and application. The first section develops the irony of losing one's life in order to save it. The second section, a less coherent line of reasoning, uses the contrast of accepting and rejecting (or offending) to define the community of disciples. The third section defines the community of disciples in terms of service by appealing to the Son of Man who gave his life as a ransom for many. The progression of topics from discipleship in the first section, through the constitution of the community in the second, to the definition of servantship as the community's ethic, shows that Mark intended the gospel to be read as a charter document for social definition. The way in which he understood the gospel story as a model for each of these identifications requires a brief discussion.

2. DISCIPLESHIP

The requirements for discipleship are condensed formulations that draw their power from the narrative context. Because the disciples have followed Jesus through the Galilean activity, their expectations have been raised. Peter concluded that Jesus was the Christ-king and that Jesus' announcement of his fate in Jerusalem was therefore inappropriate. The disciples on the way were already discussing who was the greatest (in the kingdom). James and John even dared to request of Jesus the highest positions of honor in the kingdom of God he was to establish. The instructions respond to these misunderstandings.

The first statement of requirement takes place just after the turn of the story and continues the narrative theme: if anyone wants to follow Jesus (as the disciples did), he must continue with Jesus all the way to the cross. The second and third requirements compress the narrative sequence of the two phases of the gospel into statements of the contrast between Jesus' two roles, first as man of power, then as one who accepts obediently a destiny of rejection and service. The disciples are stuck at the point of desire for power and need to be instructed in the necessity of becoming last, servant, and slave (if they want to be first, great, and lord). The principle of inversion is used to state the requirement that the disciple not escape the master's fate. Not all of the arguments given in support and application of these primary statements are as poignantly condensed, but each subsequent saying does develop some aspect of the fundamental irony expressed.

The first set of instructions is the clearest elaboration of the irony, because the meaning of Jesus' death is applied specifically to the question of the fate of the individual disciple. The terms of the dialectic are saving (or gaining) and losing one's life. These terms anticipate the expression of the irony of the crucifixion placed in the mouth of the chief priests ("He saved others, he cannot save himself," Mark 15:31). In both the discipleship

FIGURE 27
INSTRUCTIONS IN DISCIPLESHIP

Circumstance	Requirement	Consequence
FIRST SET OF INSTRUCTIONS: Mark 8:34–9:1		
The Principle		
If anyone would come after me	let him deny himself, and take up his cross, and follow me.	
The Arguments		
Whoever would save his life		will lose it.
	Whoever loses his life for my sake and the gospel's	will save it.
What profit is there if one gains the whole world		and forfeits his life?
What can one give		in return for his life?
Whoever is ashamed of me and my words in this sinful generation		of him will the Son of Man be ashamed when he comes in the glory of the father.
SECOND SET OF INSTRUCTIONS: Mark 9:35–50		
The Principle		
If one wants to be first	he must be last of all and servant of all.	
The Arguments		
Example: Accepting a child:	Whoever accepts a child in my name,	accepts me.
	Whoever accepts me,	accepts him who sent me.
Example: Rejecting strange exorcists:	Do not forbid him.	

Circumstance	Requirement	Consequence
	Whoever gives a cup of water because you bear the name of Christ	will not lose his reward.
Whoever causes a little one to sin		it would be better to drown by a millstone.
If your hand/foot/eye offends you	cut it off.	Better to enter life maimed than go to hell.
If salt has lost its saltness		how will you season it?
	Have salt among yourselves and be at peace with one another.	

THIRD SET OF INSTRUCTIONS: Mark 10:42–45

Negative Example

Gentile rulers		lord it over their subjects.

Principle

Whoever would be great among you	must be your servant.	
Whoever would be first among you	must be slave of all.	

Positive Example

The Son of Man came not to be served	but to serve and to give his life	as a ransom for many.

---

sayings and the saying at the cross the notion of being saved is introduced rather unexpectedly. Given the theme of the necessity of the cross, being saved from that fate makes sense as a desire and problem. That association cannot be all there is to it, however, for if one does not save one's life in this sense, some other kind of salvation is in store. For the disciple, his own life is "saved." In the case of Jesus, others are "saved." Because the irony of the disciple's salvation depends in some way upon the irony of the crucifixion, the meaning of Jesus' death as a saving event with ironic aspects needs to be specified as Mark understood it.

The ironies created by the crucifixion of Jesus are most complex, the result of a multilayered set of interests invested in the event. At the level of apocalyptic history, Jesus' death is set forth as a manifestation of the extreme case of resistance to the (bearer of the) kingdom of God on the part of the kingdoms of the world. Because Jesus was destroyed in Jerusalem, Jerusalem would be destroyed by God. Only a crass irony is possible at this level of meaning, created by contrasting Jesus' knowledge of the consequences of the deed with the ignorance of those who perform it. Otherwise, the two destructive events would be related only as a reciprocal exchange of power, one defensive, the other retributive.

A slightly more complex view is given when the constructive use of (divine) power is allowed consideration alongside its destructive capacity. Mark did not highlight this dialectic because, as an apocalyptic event, the crucifixion belonged to the period of woes with its wars and destructions. Nevertheless, the "temple word" referred both to a destruction and to a construction of "temples" in ambiguous contrast, so that the intimation of some inversion or substitution by reversal was allowed. It is only with the introduction of the "saving" significance of Jesus' death, however, that the irony Mark had in mind is fully developed.

Mark's reduction of the Christ myth to its martyrological core meant that the notion of salvation could be used in either of two senses. If Jesus was not to be saved (rescued) from the hands of his persecutors as the wisdom tale preferred to end things, he could still be saved (vindicated) by means of some post-mortem honor, immortality, or transformation in accordance with the martyr myth. Mark did not dare an elaboration of Jesus' resurrection or transformed status, because he wanted to emphasize Jesus' absence from the world during the period of woes and his brilliant reappearance at the eschaton as the Son of Man. Still, Jesus' resurrection and his future role as Son of Man verified his salvation, that the Jerusalem leaders did not, in fact, succeed in destroying him.

The other use of the term salvation applies, not to Jesus' own destiny, but to the survival of the cause "for which" he died. The cause was the kingdom of God imagined as a collection of those who accepted God's rule as Jesus had represented it. As in the case of Jesus as the Son of Man, Mark chose to reserve the full manifestation of the kingdom of God for the future hour of power and glory. This created a problem, for those "for whom" Jesus had died were still living in the world. In one sense the followers of Jesus were already saved ("He saved others"; "In three days I will build another [temple] not made with hands"). In another sense, however, salvation would have to wait until the kingdom appeared ("He who endures to the end will be saved," Mark 13:13). Thus the irony of the crucifixion is compounded by a double inversion. "He saved others" is ironic because, though meant facetiously, it is true. It is doubly ironic because the means by which Jesus saves is just the fact that "he cannot save himself." Moreover, the salvation in view is manifest both in the present under the sign of the community of disciples and in the future under the sign of glorious fulfillment. That Jesus "cannot save himself" is ironic because, though it is meant in mockery, it is true. Yet it is not true, for he also will be saved just by means of his rejection and "rescue," that is, his obedient death and vindication.

The discipleship instruction dares to apply the irony of the crucifixion to the case of the follower. As with Jesus, so with the disciple who loses his life, there will be salvation. It is noteworthy, though, that two features of the model do not apply. The disciple's death is not said to be effective for the salvation of others, but for his own life. And the disciple's salvation is conditional and derivative in a way in which Jesus' vindications are not. Were it not for Jesus' inaugural martyrdom, there would not even be the possibility for the disciple to consider salvation. Looked at closely, then, the disciple's self-denial is patterned after a truncated version of the martyrdom of Jesus. The disciple denies himself for the sake of Jesus, or the gospel (Mark 8:35), and his salvation is manifest only at the appearing of the Son of Man. The saying about gaining the whole world and still not having enough to buy back one's life serves merely to support the radical claim that salvation will only be granted to followers of Jesus (Mark 8:36–37). The warning that follows makes this clear. The one ashamed of Jesus now cannot be honored when the Son of Man comes in the glory of his father (Mark 8:38). This statement is not ironic. It is thoroughly apocalyptic, a single level, reciprocal exchange conditioned by the faithfulness of the disciple during the period of the adulterous and sinful generation. Thus the sense of the ironic that is achieved by the timeless, condensed formulation about saving and losing one's life evaporates on a ledger of strict accounting yet to be disclosed.

The saving significance of Jesus' death, then, is limited to the kingdom of God as the cause for which he died. He was the supreme and inaugural martyr, set apart from all others by virtue of his special relation to God as his Son and his special role at the eschaton as the Son of Man. Mark did not interpret the effectiveness of his death "for many" as a sacrifice with power to guarantee the forgiveness, transformation, or eventual salvation of any given follower. It established the *logos* of the kingdom of God and the mystery of its eventual manifestation. Salvation for followers was conditioned upon their own loyalty to the cause, a loyalty exemplified by the willingness to lose one's life for it. Thus the negative examples of "denial," "betrayal," and "flight," all underscore the positive example of Jesus' "confession." It is Jesus' confession, not his divinity, power, transformation, or eventual position of honor that is the model for imitation. When James and John ask about positions of honor in the glorious kingdom, Jesus asks them whether they are prepared to drink the cup. They reply that they are and Jesus assures them that they will. He adds, however, that that does not mean they can count on positions of honor in the kingdom (Mark 10:39–40). Discipleship under the sign of martyrdom, then, is mainly a matter of absolute loyalty to the cause of the kingdom of God which entered the world with the appearance of Jesus.

3. OBLIGATION

Mark's application of the charter document is thus far consistent. During the time of woes and powerlessness the model for discipleship was to be taken from that phase of Jesus' destiny characterized by obedience unto death. In sections two and three of the instructions, however, Mark took another step. He made the attempt to apply the gospel paradigm to the structure of relationships within the community of disciples. Because the Son of Man came to give his life as a ransom for many, the sign of leadership within the community was to be that of service, not of lording it over the little ones. The notions of receiving (and being received), and giving (and being given to), cluster up in a variety of reciprocal formulations as definitive for the followers of Jesus during the meantime. It is here that a sympathetic reading might hope to find the redeeming feature of the Gospel of Mark. According to such a reading, the constructive attempt to define the community of the kingdom along egalitarian lines would be the value of the gospel. A hierarchy of leaders with authority and power within the group would be denied on the ethical principle of all being servants to all. Perhaps, so this reading might be construed, Mark's unfortunate apocalyptic exaggerations could be excused if his real intent was to work out a charter for a truly gracious community capable of survival in an ungracious world.

It is probable that Mark gave considerable attention to the question of social formation and behavior appropriate to his gospel of the kingdom. It would be possible, for example, to read the gospel through with the theme of the constitution of the community in mind. Different from the characterizations of the crowds alone, or of the disciples solely in their role as negative examples of leadership, the vignettes could be noticed in which those who gather around Jesus may have reminded his readers of their own constituency and behavior. Those stories in which houses, meals, discourse, and social mix are thematized may be much more important in this regard than scholars have realized. Supposing that Mark's community continued some form of table fellowship, a suspicion that seems fully justified, the series of settings that run from eating with sinners in Levi's house to the disciples' last supper with Jesus may reflect a high degree of consciousness on Mark's part about the shape of his community. The significance of table fellowship as the occasion when his community actually knew itself to gather, be constituted, talk about its purposes, and work out its codes would be mirrored in this way in the myth of origins he wrote. If so, the occurrence of the terms *diakonos* (servant) and *diakonein* (to serve) in Mark 10:43,45 may be important clues to Mark's thoughts as he worked up the discipleship sayings. *Diakonos* was the Hellenistic term used for household servants and was especially associated with waiting table. Linked here as it is with (1) the definition of Jesus' death as a vicarious martyrdom and (2) the definition of leadership in the community as service, one has to consider the possibility that meal practice was the middle term that gave rise to the notion of service in the first place. Waiting tables apparently had become a major metaphor in some circles of early Christianity, for working out codes of etiquette, ethic, and social roles. Mark fastened upon the idea in order to relate his picture of Jesus to the self-understanding of the community and gain its support for his proposals. Modern Christians might well find such an ethic attractive and regard Mark's Gospel worth it if, in the last analysis, the ethic is what the gospel was about.

Alas, one needs to keep in mind that Mark's ethic of service applies only within the boundaries of the threatened community, while the paradigm appealed to is set on events that take place outside. The Son of Man may have died "for many," but the rule of service pertains only "among you" (Mark 10:43). Mark's drawing of the boundary between those inside and those outside cannot be forgotten. If the Jesus movements began with various open invitations to table fellowship, thus were energized by an optimistic, inclusive ideology, the process of self-definition during the forty years had closed the borders. This switch from a focus upon the world at large as potentially capable of kingdom behavior to a concentration upon the codes that distinguished the little kingdom society from the rest of the world has to be seen as a very costly forfeiture of the exuberance that brought the movement into being in the beginning. The fact that the borders had been closed may not seem to make much difference as long as the quality of the ethic (reciprocal exchange) is so clearly expressed. Under scrutiny, though, the obligation to give service is not anchored in a social notion of give and take based upon the mutual enhancement of the quality of life lived together in this group. As Mark lays it out, service is a sign of understanding and a confessing of one's loyalty to the gospel of the kingdom Jesus announced. To serve is required of individuals who desire to be saved. They must do it not for the sake of one another, but for the sake of Jesus, the gospel, and being saved. They must do it, moreover, as a "following" of Jesus' example.

If Jesus set the example, one might think that the theme of service or "giving his life as a ransom for many" may have been elaborated elsewhere in the narrative. It appears that such is the case. The reader will recall the earlier discussion of Mark's use of the term *paradidonai* (hand over) and its thematic development into the passion narrative where Jesus is repeatedly handed or led from one to another of his enemies. One suspects that it was this theme that received additional nuance throughout Mark's story by playing upon a series of verbs having to do with touching or taking Jesus. Seizure is in any case emphasized at the arrest. The one who handed Jesus over had instructed the armed crowd to "seize him and lead him away" (Mark 14:43). Thus, "they laid hands on him and seized him" (Mark 14:46), something the rulers had wanted to do frequently, but had not been able to do until this point in the story. This means that the result of Jesus being "handed over" is, according to Mark, that he was "taken." The counterpart to this theme, then, is that of Jesus' obedience unto death, emphasized in both Mark 10:45 and the supper saying as the "giving" of himself for others. Since this is so, the notion of service is modeled on the case of Jesus' martyrdom as a reciprocal giving and taking of his life. The irony of the crucifixion is, in fact, based upon this doubling of perspective and motivation upon the single event.

Christian piety has always marveled at this radical irony and sought to understand the saving significance of Jesus' death in the transformation of the event achieved by the inversion of the two perspectives: a taking that turns into a gift received, or a grace that, when realized, includes the moment of judgment upon the one who accepts it. Requisite to such a pious reading, however, is a dislocation of the story from its social history, an erasure of Mark's distinction between those outside and those inside the world in which the story applies, and some modulation of the passion narrative into the order of metaphor or symbol so that the Christian reader can "identify" as well with Judas and the rulers as with the disciples and the crowds. Then, and only then, can the give and take of the passion narrative invite the imagination to consider its irony both as a saving event (grace) and as a model to be imitated (obligation) at one and the same time. It is questionable whether Mark could have dared such a thought. The reason he could not have is because, according to the pious reading, those who "take" Jesus are those who then receive his gift of life, that is, are or will be saved. Mark's myth demanded that those who "took" Jesus were not the disciples, but those outside the circle loyal to him. It is not said that they will be saved.

The crucifixion of Jesus is, therefore, not ironic because of the reciprocity of gifts exchanged at all. It is ironic because of the double incongruence between what the rulers do and think they do on the one hand, and what Jesus does and thinks he does on the other. This irony, which is really a vindication of Jesus (who does the giving) and a condemnation of the rulers (who do the taking), is the model Mark set forth for service within the community. It cannot work as a paradigm for mutual service because it does not describe an exchange of "service" at all. It remains a violent exchange on or outside the borders, left at the level of charge and countercharge. Jesus' "gift" is not given to those who take him, but to those who belong to the kingdom, the cause "for which" and "to which" he died as an obedient martyr. That death is inaugural and unrepeatable. It founds Jesus' absolute authority and guarantees his eventual exercise of absolute power. It cannot function as a paradigm for others, but only as a standard for measuring loyalty to the cause Jesus represents. Both service within the community and loyalty in the face of persecutors without are, on this model, obligations required by anyone who desires ultimately to be saved. The apocalyptic frame cannot be subtracted from Mark's Gospel without destroying its logic. Mark's "community" is, in the last analysis, a collection of those who hope to endure until the end. The apocalyptic resolution is necessary because Mark gave up on the possibility of imagining a society fit for the real world.

IMAGINATION AND THE MYTH OF INNOCENCE

> If you must write about killings and war, don't compose a poem or a hymn.
>
> Elie Wiesel
> On the lesson from the Book of Judges
> Claremont, February 22, 1984

IMAGINATION AND
THE MYTH OF INNOCENCE

1. MARK'S GOSPEL AND CHRISTIAN ORIGINS

It was Mark's fiction of a fantastic infringement on human history that created Christianity's charter. Mark was not the first to imagine Jesus as founder, of course, nor the only one to invest in Jesus an authority that, historically, Jesus could not have possessed. Each sectarian formation stemming from Jesus had found it necessary to claim that Jesus had laid the foundations for what the group had become. Some notion of novelty at the beginning of each movement was thus held by all of them. This study has touched upon some of the ways in which novelty was attributed to Jesus in early circles. Each can be understood as an exaggeration required to rationalize novel behavior and answer embarrassing questions about identity experienced within the social history of some group. The projections back upon the figure of Jesus were in part called for by the lack of any other recognizable means of authorization for unconventional practice, in part by a need to adjudicate internal conflicts over authority, and in part by a feedback mechanism whereby, once accountability had been transferred to the champion, the champion was there to assume ever greater burden for the new. In the process, the very stupendous claims for Jesus encountered in the gospels came to be made.

The images of Jesus as founder were, however, various, and the notions of novelty uneven. Before Mark, Jesus had been imagined in several different kinds of role, including that of wisdom's child (Q), the last of the prophets (Q), a man of power like Moses (miracle chains), an enigmatic teacher (parables), and the authoritative lawyer (pronouncement stories). Each role had as its correlate some conception of the social entity the group wished to be or represent. Beginnings were in view in all of these movements, but before Mark the notion of the new had not produced a rationalization for departure from the "old" as a radical necessity that required violence.

In the Christ cult, to be sure, the focus upon the event of Jesus' crucifixion had described an originary moment. At first this moment was imagined as a founding event in order to justify the new social formation in the eyes of the diaspora synagogue and in the eyes of the new social formation itself. Then, however, the myth was applied to the new beginning marked by an individual's entrance into the community and to other moments thought to correspond to its model. At this point the idea of transformation was fastened upon, the "old" placed under the judgment of death while celebrating the "new" as the gift of life. It has often been thought that the radical break with Judaism occurred in this context. This view needs to be corrected. Gentiles simply saw in the myth a paradigm for release into "freedom" from social constraints, understood by some to be an invitation to charismatic and esoteric experience. It was Paul who was attracted to the negative sign of the kerygma and who emphasized the necessity of suffering and obedience as the condition for authentic membership in a new society. Reapplied to the origins of Christianity and the question of Israel's history and legitimacy, however, the transformational model didn't work. The crucifixion could not simply be interpreted as a sign of cancellation upon Israel as the "old" from which Christianity emerged by radical opposition and transformation. For Paul, Christian claims to the legacy of Israel were much more ambiguous and dialectical than that. So the kerygma as a transformational pattern was not applied to social history, but to the experiences of individual converts and to the internal ethos of the new society as having been generated out of a rather vague and very mythic "old" order of ethnic identity. In the Christ cult the kerygma functioned as a myth of origins in the same way that the several portraits of Jesus functioned for the Jesus movements. Within the context of the Hellenistic congregations, though, the kerygma did not become a double-edged sword. The crucifixion had been mythologized, stripped of any historical motivation, and internalized as a paradigm for understanding the repeatable moment of Christian con-version.[1]

---

1. *Attitude toward Judaism.* The novelty claimed for Christians did result in a series of contrasts between the old and the new in Pauline interpretation. Many of these contrasts were phrased in keeping with Paul's own Jewish past, as for example, that between works of the law and faith in Christ, or between the old Adam and the new creation in Christ. Such contrasts were handled at the level of powers impinging upon human existence in general, however, not concretized historically as descriptions of the determination of social destinies. This is clear, for instance, in Paul's letter to the Galatians where the old order of constraint is described both as law and as "the elemental spirits of the universe" (Gal 4:3). Where Paul does confront the problem of applying his mythicized epic of the old time/new time to social history, as in Romans 9–11, he cannot bring himself to consign his Jewish brothers to condemnation. It was the lack of historical placement that allowed the kerygma of crucifixion its mythic function for the Christ cults without having to consider making absolute judgments upon social historical institutions. Roy Harrisville, *The Concept of Newness*, struggled with this odd incongruence between claims to newness and lack of specific social location. He concluded that "the locus of the New Testament concept of

Mark appropriated the Christ myth and linked it with the Jesus traditions. By doing that he radicalized the appearance of the man of authority and power. Jesus' appearance marked the absolute beginning of the end, his activity the sealing of the borders, and his death the violent event of decisive significance for history and its goal. By locating the Christ myth precisely as an originary event complete with social historical motivation and consequence, Mark created the story that was to give to Christian imagination its sense of a radical and dramatic origin in time.

According to Mark, Jesus' appearance in Galilee was a dazzling entrance of God's Son into the world with the power and authority to set things right. The world was wrong, set against the rule of God and in league with powers under the control of Satan. Ultimately, these forces could be no match for the rightful rule of God. Unfortunately, however, the evil forces were still firmly enough in control to plot against the Son of God and kill him. That sealed the fate of the temple of the Jews and all it stood for, and inaugurated the time of the end. Judgments were called for and woes unleashed. The citadel of opposition would be destroyed and another brilliant appearance of Jesus as the Son of Man with power and glory would be necessary to bring the hostilities to an end and vindicate with finality the cause of God's kingdom. Those who understood that secret and endured until the end belonged and would belong to the new and perfect order of things.

The reason Mark wrote the story of Jesus in this way had little to do with the historical Jesus, much, however, with the recent history of the Jesus movement to which Mark belonged. A failure to reform the diaspora synagogues, from which this group or groups had finally found it necessary to withdraw, resulted in confusion about the group's purposes, hostility against Judaism, and withdrawal into a sectarian mentality and enclave. Mark associated the death of Jesus with the group's rejection by the synagogue and then linked both to the destruction of the temple. The end of the temple was, according to Mark, a righteous judgment, a vindication of the rightness of the cause and kingdom for which the group stood. Before Mark made that connection, neither the Jesus movements nor the congregations of the Christ had imagined Second Temple institutions as their

---

newness" was therefore "the eschatological aspect of the kerygma" (p. 106).

Although Paul saw fit to exercise an unbelievable authority within the Christian communities he addressed, judgments upon the fate of those outside were, graciously according to him, left in the hands of God. This slight bit of advantage in attitude is the result of the mythic dislocation of the kerygmatic event from social historical context. Bultmann's preference for the kerygma over the gospels as the myth more adequate to modern times is due, no doubt, to his Lutheran tradition. It was also, however, intuitively correct. His approach to the kerygma may be compared to the recent work of René Girard on the gospels in *Le bouc émissaire,* except for that intuition. On the difference it makes when the shift from kerygma to gospel occurs as the point of departure even for a radical hermeneutic, see B. Mack, "The Innocent Transgressor" in *René Girard and Biblical Studies.*

nemesis. When Mark did make that connection the Christian myth of succession or substitution was born. Jesus had been the rightful heir to a kingdom in conflict with Second Temple Judaism. Its leaders had sought to destroy him, but had succeeded only in destroying themselves. Jesus, the once and future king, now was to reign in the place of the vanquished high priests. It was a myth written during a brief period of threat to a particular Jesus movement in danger of losing its bearings, its confidence, and its cool.

In order to integrate the several traditions about Jesus and the Christ into a single and comprehensive narrative, Mark used the story of the obedient martyr. His narrative design was such that the story of wisdom's martyr provided the warp into which the traditions of Jesus and the Christ could be interwoven to result in a new mythic tapestry. Thus the Son of God became the innocent victim at the hands of tyrants who used their power to bring God's rightful king to naught. As Mark portrayed the appearance of Jesus, everything he said and did was right as became wisdom's child, but nothing worked to change the minds of those in charge. Indeed, so adamant was Mark about the intransigence of the Jewish leaders that Jesus' deeds and teachings, though explosive, were recounted as veiled and ineffective. The bizarre effect of this narrative design is that Jesus is depicted as a master teacher who could not teach, a super rhetor who could not persuade, a divine authority who was rejected, and a savior who got killed.

Every manifestation of Jesus' superior powers is set on conflict. The conflict was public and obvious from the beginning and Jesus was fully aware of its consequences. He performed as a solitary figure, a superhero who knew that his inaugural announcement of the time of the kingdom would involve his crucifixion as an unavoidable prelude to an eventual, final vindication and victory. Thus the story of the martyr was incorporated into an apocalyptic view of history. The result was a grand beginning, so grand that history was broken open by intersection with the eternal purposes of God and the entrance of his Son from the heavenly realm, yet so tragic that history must now lie under the sign of violence until God comes again. In the Christian imagination informed by the gospel story some sequel is required to answer the unbelievable expectations raised at the beginning about the kingdom of God. That kingdom should obviously have been established when God's Son entered with power to transform the world. Because the world refused to be transformed, a judgment must fall upon it as fallen.

Viewed in retrospect, from the point of view of what the later institutional church was to become, Mark's Gospel was the most important mythology constructed during the early period of Christian beginnings. It is quite true that the church came to prefer other versions of the gospel story that did not accentuate the apocalyptic frame. But it is also true that the other preferred gospels were dependent upon Mark. This was certainly the case with Matthew and Luke. Though not yet established by means of a scholarly demonstration, the most plausible hypothesis would be that John also was indebted to Mark's achievement. Each of the other three gospels made the attempt to recast Mark's portrayal of the man of power by shifting attention to his teachings. Matthew and Luke did this by integrating the Sayings Source (Q) into Mark's story and adding other teaching materials such as parables. Matthew emphasized Jesus' wisdom and used a mythology of wisdom to soften the sense of radical rupture with the past. Luke used the notion of the Spirit of God to bridge between the times and accentuate a constructive and compassionate ministry for Jesus. John used the myth of the *logos* to claim for Jesus a full revelation of the eternal purposes of God for the enlightenment of the world. But none of them changed Mark's plot nor his account of the crucifixion in any fundamental way. In some sense their myths of origin were less vindictive than Mark's, for they were less concerned to dwell upon a political and apocalyptic history of judgment and vindication. But in other ways the irony of originary violence was exacerbated, for now it appeared that Jesus was killed not only because his power and authority was found threatening by the leaders, but because his acceptable teachings could not be withstood. Because Mark's plot provided the narrative logic for the other gospels, then, Mark's Gospel must be seen as the origin for the Christian view of Christian origins. That is because it was Mark's plot that Christians settled upon when contemplating those events foundational to Christianity.

2. MODIFICATIONS OF THE STORY LINE

For the next two hundred fifty years of early church history one loses sight of the role played by the Markan conception of Christian origins. Gospels came to be accepted in one form of telling or another, as the foundational mythology granting Christians of all stripes their legitimating charter. Judging from the burgeoning literature produced during this period, however, horrendous battles had to be fought on several fronts before the church could agree upon its canonical selection of gospel accounts and construct upon them the edifice known now as Christendom. Three arenas of intellectual and social conflict can be identified: the challenge of Gnosticism, the appropriation of the Jewish epic, and the domestication of Greek philosophy. The outcome of each of these battles set the stage for the Constantinian revolution and the emergence of the synoptic gospel as the myth and ritual text for Christianity.

The gnostic challenge was critical because it focused upon an issue integral to early Christian social formation and its rationalization. The parting of the ways between a gnosticizing option on the one hand, and a claim upon the goals of world history on the other, can already be discerned in the late first century. In a sense, Mark's preference for orientation to world history, even if only in apocalyptic stance, was a rejection of the Christ cult with its cultivation of spiritual or philosophic presence as the hallmark of its ethos. The difference between the two orientations thus became the harbinger of the battle that would rage for the next centuries. Because Mark's solution to the question of the historical role for the Christian group turned out to require an apocalyptic view of history, however, the Markan solution was actually another form of withdrawal from the public fray. Only in the cases of Matthew's and Luke's revisions of the gospel does one catch sight of movements that had survived the crisis of failed expectations and dared project a universal mission to the world.

That the gnosticizing alternative was attractive and strong in the period just after Mark's apocalyptic proposal is demonstrated by developments in several streams of early tradition. In circles cultivating the sayings of Jesus, for instance, the apocalyptic tendencies of the later layers of Q contrast with the gnosticizing interpretations of those same traditions in the Gospel of Thomas. The group responsible for the Gospel of Thomas had withdrawn to ponder the sayings of Jesus as secret revelations of an invisible spiritual order. This already pointed toward the gnostic developments in the next centuries. In the post-Pauline tradition, Colossians and Ephesians are evidence for the construction of huge imaginative worlds of "wisdom" within which to live, ethereal bubbles with no discernible contact with the real world. In the gospel tradition the Johannine community cultivated a small set of private symbols and rituals in order to create a sense of being within a realm of absolute light and life. According to John's Gospel, Jesus came mainly to proclaim his own true identity, a mission even less engaging of the world than Mark's messianic incognito. The crisis this created was, nevertheless, held to be absolute. Jesus' pronouncements were the judgment upon the world for its darkness. The controversy dialogues with "the Jews" failed completely to enlighten. Jesus' crucifixion was therefore the disclosure of the measure of the world's darkness as well as of Jesus' "glory." Irony pressed the symbol of transformation to its limits, the point at which God's creative power fused with the depths of human depravity. Only the elect were able to perceive this glory, of course, the crucifixion becoming the source of their own light and life.

Gnostic Christianity flourished during the second and third centuries. Enclaves marked the retreat from social history, and schools of thought cultivated the secret gnosis of unimaginable eons filled with bits of psychic powers and desires. Thus the real was located in some transcendent realm beyond the reach of worldly existence. Jesus became the revealer of esoteric knowledge about the world above and about the paths that led back to it from the fallen world below. Corresponding to the break between the realms of light and darkness, the gospels written by these sectarians

relocated the moment of Jesus' instruction to the period after his resurrection. There, in some serene setting devoid of any earthly traits, precious
confirmation of the reality of the hidden realms was said to have been
imparted to the chosen few. The great debates about the nature of the
Christ were thus gospel debates, battles about how the gospel story should
go and how it should end. Read in one way, a gnostic view of the world
came into place to rationalize a particular sectarian disdain for the world of
human intercourse and enterprise. Read another way, the church took its
place amidst the landscape of more recognizable human endeavors and
institutions. The credos that emerged to control the Christian imagination
were actually little gospel epitomes of the synoptic variety. They were
crafted to meet the gnostic challenge by those who chose to reengage the
world. The gnostics left their imprint on the Christian imagination, nonetheless, for the gospel as credo now was understood to point the way to
heaven.[2]

The second battle that raged throughout these same centuries was about
the right to claim the Hebrew scriptures as the church's epic inheritance.
The gnostic challenge was an affair internal to the Christian movements, a
serious conflict about where to locate the perfect kingdom Christians had
espied and what that location implied for human existence in a world held
to be hostile. The aggressive requisition of the epic of Israel, on the other
hand, took place on the borders between Christians and Jews. The major
weapon used by Christians in this battle for the right to read the epic text as
"promise" that came to "fulfillment" in Christ was allegory. No one could
deny that, at the literal level, the scriptures told the story of the Jews. By
means of allegorization, however, the literal level became a negative prehistory that demonstrated how unworthy the Jews had been and were of the
promises made to them. Because the promises could be read as prefigurements of the full revelation in Christ of God's intentions for "Israel," the
Jewish rejection of Christianity came under the judgment of their own
scriptures and demonstrated the right of Christianity to the true if hidden
meaning of that holy history from the beginning. In effect, the allegorical
reading of the "Old Testament" positioned the Christian gospel as the story
of that event of manifestation through which as a singular lens Christians
would view all of human history, the standard by which judgments could be
rendered upon all inadequate responses to their claim to truth. Mark's story
of the entrance of God's Son into the world suffered modulation in this
expansion of historical horizon, for that revealed in Christ was now less a
matter of power, more a matter of meaning. Nevertheless, the dramatic
aspects of the revelation were not eroded, for it was storied still as a

---

2. *The gnostic challenge.* For an introduction to this intriguing history see Elaine Pagels,
The Gnostic Gospels.

breakthrough event imagined narratively as the result of a cosmic destiny of descent and transformation.[3]

A third arena of intellectual effort was the struggle to domesticate the cultural traditions of the Greeks. The sharp contrast Mark had made between the kingdom of God and Hellenistic *paideia* was blunted as the church found ways to accommodate philosophy to its own ends. Greek *paideia* was pressed into service as a pedagogy, as a means to rationalize a Christian system of ethic, and as a means to construct a view of the world appropriate to the purposes of the church. The translation of the language of the kingdom, or the language of revelation, into the language of philosophic presence infused the heavenly realm revealed in Christ with an additional sense of reality, a sense provided by the nuance of rationality given with the philosophic language itself. The church took the place of the *polis* in the Hellenistic pattern whereby *cosmos, polis,* and *anthropos* could be aligned ideally by mimetic correlations. Gnostics were forced to retreat as the bishops worked out the mechanisms by which the church could be linked to the cosmic realm of salvation.

The bishop functioned both as a *pater familias* within his province, caring for the social needs of his flock, and as a guardian of the gateways to salvation within the divine topography represented by the church. Baptism defined the crossing requisite to participation in the social and heavenly orders over which the bishop presided. Because it promised so much and was understood to be the effective means of making those promises come true, baptism was the public rite of prominence during this time, apostasy the occasion for the most painful theological consternation. It was difficult to imagine what to make of anyone who relinquished the heavenly and earthly treasures promised by the bishop once those treasures had been claimed and savored.

Corresponding to the bishops' station, the iconography of the period suggests that the Christ was imagined primarily as the great Good Shepherd of the church, instructor in the way of salvation and guarantor of eternal life in realms beyond the grave. Strangely, in view of the rhetoric of persecution said to be suffered by Christians in conflict with the kingdoms of this world, the Good Shepherd does not appear to have been imagined as a martyr, or as the crucified one portrayed by Mark and Paul. He was, rather, the incarnation of a beneficent, inviolate, and divinely gracious power. He was imagined mainly as the one untouched by the machinations of the world. He was the alien Son of God who had come into the world to reveal the realm of eternal life and open the way to salvation. His other-

---

3. *The Old Testament.* For a telling discussion of the church fathers' arguments to claim the "Old Testament" for the church, see David Efroymson, "The Patristic Connection."

worldly serenity and power assured the believer that such a salvation was real.

Mark's Gospel portrait is difficult to discern any longer in the imagery used of the Christ in the homilies, treatises, and art of the period. Still, in the exhortations to Christians imagined at the point of being forced to make the great "confession," as well as in the martyrological literatures of the period, the martyr became the model for faithfulness. Luke's Gospel can be read as an early evidence for such a bifocal view of Christian paradigms. To the Lukan account of Jesus, who appeared to be more the teacher than a Markan martyr, Luke appended the Acts of the Apostles. Because of their preaching of Jesus as the Christ, the apostles were constantly threatened by martyrdom. Thus Mark's image of the innocent victim was dislodged from the imagination of the Christ and focused upon the apostle confessor. The church greatly exaggerated the threat and incidence of persecution by the Romans in order to pose as being at the mercy of those in power. In fact, however, by the end of the third century the church had grown large and strong. When that circumstance was disclosed with the conversion of Constantine, the rhetoric of martyrdom was no longer possible. Now blessed as the religion of privilege with entrée into the places of power, the church would have to read its gospels differently.

3. A TEXT FOR MYTH AND RITUAL

With the conversion of Constantine, Christianity gained access to worldly power. The borders of Christ's kingdom could now be imagined to coalesce with those of the state. The times of persecution were past and the witness of the martyr was no longer needed. Christians held the sword at last, and the age of the holy empires began. Buildings, art, councils, the "law of Christ," and bishops at the rulers' courts blossomed at once to inaugurate the age of Christendom.

One can only be amazed at the ease with which this transition was made, given the charter documents, and given the rhetoric by which the church had justified its lack of worldly power in the period recently past. Christ was now depicted gloriously as the king, ruling from heaven over his kingdom on earth. Rulers marched under his banner. Rival religions within the realm would eventually be extinguished. Barbarian tribes from the north would be civilized and Christianized, Christianized and civilized in concert. A Christian culture was to emerge and last a thousand years, holding together the many shifting configurations of heterogeneous peoples, powers, and kingdoms that would come under the aegis of the staff. The staff had won its place beside the scepter. Rulers would rule only in the name of Christ whose rule on earth it was their charge to guarantee.

Apparently the kingdoms of this world had been transformed. Apparently the apocalyptic Gospel of Mark was now passé.

Basilicas announced the construction of the new reality, first at Rome, then at Constantinople, and finally at Jerusalem. Why Constantinople? Why Jerusalem? Real buildings at central loci in the real world were the signs of Christendom taking place. At Rome, earlier Christian designs upon the ecumene meshed with the emperor's primary place of power and display. Constantinople was imagined next, an appropriate symbol of the New Jerusalem to make concentric the novel alignment of two this-worldly orders. Construction at the old Jerusalem was a further display of Roman patronage on the one hand, the marking of the church's claim to real origination on the other. It was here that the gospels were given their new role. They provided the charter document as well as the chart to find the way back to the sites most sacred and foundational for the new religion. The church of the holy sepulchre would have preeminence, built as it was on the very spot where Christ had assumed his sovereignty, but other places reminiscent of his birth, life, and death were soon to be enshrined as well. Scriptural loci were to be read at the proper time and place to reenact the story where the church had its beginnings. Pilgrimage began, and Christians started to worship where the Christ had been and the church had been founded.[4]

When Palestine fell to the (Persians and then) Islamic empire in the seventh century, pilgrimage was no longer possible. By then, however, Christians had learned to model churches and the conduct of worship elsewhere on patterns informed by the pilgrimage ideal. Basilicas, then cathedrals, were shaped to recall the gospel story. Cycles of liturgies and scriptural readings were arranged to celebrate the gospel events in order. Symbols were used to mark the gospel topography spatially within the walls, and artistic embellishments recreated upon the walls the great moments of the epic history of the Christ, flanked by his Old Testament prefigurements, his apostles, and the saints of the church. The baptistry, recalling the baptism of the Christ, was positioned near the threshold of the main entrance to the cathedral. Portals positioned the entrant under the figure whose story was about to be reimagined, the figure of Jesus who centered the symbols of the human history arrayed on either side. Inside, the life of Christ unfolded by depiction, procession, and liturgical symbols and practices. The liturgy of the church literally reproduced the gospel story within the space constructed according to its plan.

As Christians became accustomed to power, a strangely compensatory revision of the Christ slowly came into view. The shepherd-king gave way

---

4. *Constantinian construction.* This amazing transition has been analyzed incisively by J. Z. Smith in *To Take Place.*

to the portrayal of Jesus as the crucified one. Cruciform architecture provided the mass with its proper place, focusing upon the altar with its triptych of the Christ event. Entering in, the faithful found themselves approaching the scene that centered time and transfixed space. The figure of the crucified Christ was the point at which a static epic history hinged, and the *axis mundi* pierced through to heaven above and hell beneath. The crucified Christ became an object of devotion, a sign of humility, inverting the privilege actually enjoyed by the church in the world at large. A piety of grace and graciousness evolved, inculcated by the practice of meditation upon the sufferings of the one who gave himself as a sacrifice for the sins of the world. The exalted Christ as crucified became a symbol of power ruling under the sign of suffering and service.

Mark's narrative of the passion had combined Pauline traditions of the kerygma of the Christ and the supper of the Lord. By situating the account of the supper in his story as he did, by linking the supper to the crucifixion at the level of narrative sense, and by portraying Jesus as the savior who presided over his own symbolic enactment of his own forthcoming death, Mark created the myth that eventually was read as script for ritual reenactment in medieval Christianity. The gospel now became the church's myth and ritual text. Mark's climax to the story of Jesus as God's Son surfaced finally in yet another nuance to position the symbol of radical transformation right at the heart of a monumental construction of cosmic vision and social reality.

Two symbols of the death of Christ were displayed within the church, the table and the cross. The cross recalled the gospel account of the crucifixion, the table the story of the last supper. Liturgically, however, the two symbols collapsed in the moment of transformation that happened at the table, the moment that celebrated the climax of Mark's story. When the gospel became a script for reenactment, the priest took the place of Jesus presiding over the supper. It was then that the symbolism of the supper turned the table into an altar and the meal became a sacrifice. The mass was a symbolic reenactment, not only of the supper, but of the crucifixion as well. Thus Mark's fiction of the passion, contrary to his own intentions, provided inadvertently the text for a marvelous ritual system designed to enact in the present those events at the beginning that marked the origination of the church.

The exception taken to this system by the reformers did not destroy the core construct of Christian myth and ritual. It is true that the reformers were restive about the church's sacrificial theologies, its authorities, institutions, and the traditions upon which Christendom was based. They sought to reposition the Christ at the center of another view of the world, a view of the world in its vastness that had awakened the spirit of renaissance. But the image of the Christ was available mainly in the icons and the scriptures of the church, not in the natural orders. The reformers could leave the icons behind, but not the scriptures. When they ventured forth to explore the vistas coming into view, they took the gospel with them.

Coming out with the text was a social occasion. Not only did the text have power, it gave power to those in charge of it. The one who could read and translate the text had great authority. So did the one who could interpret its meaning in keeping with new forms of social formation. The preacher became the priest of the pulpit, presiding over the enactment of the new liturgy, a liturgy of linguistic transformations. Christian experience now took place in the aural imagination of the listener. It was called salvation by faith based solely on scripture.

The shift from icon to text was fortuitous. The text was that form of human discourse that would dominate intellectual questing for the next four hundred years. The biblical Christ gave his blessing. At first found lurking everywhere behind the allegorical signs in all the scriptures, the Christ soon became a symbol for the creative and redemptive power of God in all of the orders of reality. One by one, the critical disciplines of the modern academy were pressed into the service of the investigation of the Christ as the *logos* of God in the nature of the world and in human history. The text had to provide the point of departure, however, and became the very Word of God at the close of every circle of investigation and interpretation. Thus the gospel as the Christian myth remained in place for Protestants and has retained its position of privilege wherever Christianity has spread throughout the modern world.

As for the eucharist, the reformers could not deny its efficacy. Attempts were made to strip the ritual symbols of their power to change one thing magically into another. But the rule prevailed that the church was actual only where the Word was preached and the sacraments performed. To have the authority to preside over the enactment of the Eucharist, and to say what happens when it is performed, even yet determines both status and power within Protestant as well as Catholic Christianity. To have that right recognized by other communions is the fundamental issue in any cross-denominational dialogue. Reducing the system of Christian symbols to essentials, the reformers settled on the myth and ritual of the crucified Christ as presented in the gospel.

This means that Christianity can be defined as the cultivation of the Christ symbols, symbols that present a certain pattern of transformation and evoke a certain desire for seeing that transformation occurs. Cultivation involves the establishment of the symbols as shared objects for proclamation, meditation, and public enactment.[5]

---

5. *The Christ as symbol.* For a history of the ways in which Jesus has been imagined as the Christ see Dennis Duling, *Jesus Christ through History.* Duling also places the views of scholars within this history of imagination.

4. THE SYMBOLS OF DESIRE

And so it is that a single event, composite and complex, has haunted the Christian imagination for nearly two thousand years. That event is the manifestation of divine authority and power breaking into human history, coming to a violent climax in the crucifixion of God's Son. His vindication by resurrection, then, envisages the radical transformation of human society intended, and guarantees the eventual actualization of the perfectly just and peaceable kingdom. The tale is told in the New Testament gospels, the early martyrologies, the meditations of the Christian monastics, the creeds and symbols of the church, the history of Christian architecture, the dominant themes of Christian art, the forms of the Christian liturgy, the pattern of the Christian year, the rationale given for Christian mission, and the volumes of sermons, theologies, studies, and commentaries produced by Christian thinkers. All are documents of the fascination which the Christ event has held for Christian imagination. The history of the Christian religion can be told as the history of re-imagining the event of the Christ.

The Christ event is a symbol of radical transformation. The transformation it presents is, moreover, spectacular. The perfect one is rejected and disposed of, only to be raised from the dead to assume his rightful place over all of the orderings of creation and history. The meaning Christians give to this event is, in addition, absolutely astonishing. Occurring within human history, the Christ event generates a new kind of time, inaugurates a new human community, and transforms people who enter this community, making them fit for heaven itself. The mission of this new community is also determined by the event. That mission is to re-present in the world the power of the event to change the world. Under mandate and destiny to expand until the whole world has been transformed, the church calls upon the world to receive its redemption. The history of Christianity can be told as the history of the representation of the Christ event as the vision and vehicle of what the world must become.

The church represents the Christ event with exceptionally vivid images. Two interlocking systems of symbols have been dominant. One set of symbols revolves around the image of the crucified and exalted Christ. The other centers on the Last Supper. The image of the Christ concentrates symbols of transformation on the singular destiny of one who is human and divine, historical personage and cosmic presence, pattern and power, brother and Lord at one and the same time. The Last Supper depicts a social moment wherein the believing community is constituted. The Eucharist does not portray the symbols of the crucifixion and resurrection directly. It portrays instead the moment when the benefits were made available and received by those who dared to come to the table.

The function of these interlocking symbols is to evoke the imagination of the origins of Christianity. The historical placement of the symbols is not ornamental. They provide the only rationale the Christian church has for existing, and they establish its mode of existence as historical, that is, as having itself a history. Whether in the form of the gospel, the creed, or the eucharistic liturgy, the symbols of the Christ draw the Christian imagination back to the originary event even as they make the significance of that event available for personal meditation. To imagine the Christ event is to imagine the originary event that generates personal faith even as it generates the history of the church.

To imagine the Christ is to meditate upon a social moment. The symbols are social both because of their primary intention as social historical events, and because of the cultural context within which they are encountered in the subsequent history of the church. The symbols of the Christ are, in fact, a cultivation of the church as a social institution. They function as a memory of those events understood to have brought the church into existence in the first place, as well as the symbols and scripts of those events the church is called upon to replicate. The church is a social historical institution that defines itself in the act of replicating its origination by means of the symbols of its origin.

Replication is more than memory and memorial. By means of complex, imaginative maneuvers, the first time is recalled in order to be relived, made present. There is thus a decidedly dialectical twist to the Christian experience of the Christ and his moment. The symbols express unique, originary and unrepeatable moments, first times that supersede all later imitations. Nevertheless, Christians repeat those moments regularly, and all reenactments are understood to be fresh actualizations of the first time in present experience. In order to comprehend how this can be, Christians have developed intricate systems of rationalization at a second level of discourse. All of the so-called authorities of the church—scriptural canon, institutional tradition, sacramental theologies, psychologies of experience, and philosophies of religion—have been created in order to bridge the gap from the symbols of origin to the actual existence of the church in some specific culture. The history of the church demonstrates the capacity of the symbols to survive cultural change and bless new cultural formations. They call for change even as they demand alignment with the history of Christianity from the beginning.

Christian symbols are not abstract, subtle objects of meditation. Death is literally death, and the resurrected Christ is vibrant. The action at the meal is portrayed so that no one can mistake its intention. It is shocking and provocative to normal sensibility: the savior about to be crucified presiding at his own memorial. To imagine the perfectly innocent one condemned to death for the world's salvation creates consternation. To be invited to partake of the symbols of that gift creates humiliation. The exchange is uneven and the passage from humiliation to exaltation, whether of the Christ or of the Christian, is unaccounted for. That is because the moment of transformation crucial to the symbols is grasped absolutely as a miracle that creates life immediately simply by inverting its opposite. There is no principle of mediation.

The symbols provide a kind of guidance for their imaginative exploration nonetheless. That is because the images of opposition are juxtaposed and superimposed upon one another in just a certain way. At first the terms of extreme opposition are blurred by composite characterization. But then each term stands forth as in a geometric illusion of reversible design, first one and then the other as the focus of attention. The space between the focus now upon the passion, now upon the glory, now upon the grasp, now upon the gift, provides no respite for the imagination. The space between is the place of mystery to which the Christian imagination is invited. But it has no mechanism to carry from the one focus to the other. Attention is merely forced to shift suddenly from the one moment to the other, creating the illusion of merger again whereby neither term is the same any longer. The life imagined in this way, for instance, is no ordinary human life. It is the life created by inverting the sign of violence and raising it to the higher power.

Nevertheless, a narrative logic prevails that determines the fundamental sequence. The direction is from negative to positive sign. If the sequence of signs is reversed, a kind of imaginative darkness is produced. Christians have been known to explore the negative sign, meditating on the darkened condition of natural or fallen humanity, but always in the hope of coming again to see the signs of resurrection. Applied to the orders of human observation and the levels of human experience, the Christian symbols demand that the world be given a certain sense of direction lest the negative sign prevail.

Applied to the interiorized moods of the soul, for instance, the symbols of the Christ may plunge the sensitive mystic into the descending vortex of darkness, a descent created by accelerating the ironic inversions of extreme oppositions to the point of blur. This horror occurs, however, only against the desire, ultimately, to gain perfection by means of a new vision of transcendent light.

Applied to the daily lives of average Christians, the effect of the Christ symbols has been to dramatize crises and give privilege to eventful and extraordinary occurrences. Positioned as a banner of the Christian mission to the world, the Christ event marks the borders between those outside the fold as unenlightened and those inside as redeemed. It is expected that those outside convert, that is, pass through the event of transformation, the moment of judgment upon the past and its forgiveness, in order to be recognized as socially accepted.

The symbols of the Christ can be applied to events occurring at every level of human activity and experience within the kingdom, at its borders, and wherever the agents of the kingdom find themselves throughout the world. The symbols have sustained a great desire to make the world over into conformity with the Christian vision of the kingdom of God. They are the imaginative scheme Christians use to interpret all that happens.

5. THE COST OF THE MARKAN LEGACY

The Christian gospel is the lens through which Western culture has viewed the world. This means that a refraction of the symbols of transformation has determined the way in which the world has been imagined. Translated into secular systems of human thought and observation, the imaginative scheme has given rise to notions and categories that appear to be self-evident, yet continue to support the Christian construction of reality from which they are derived. Self-evident categories are difficult to expose because they stem from the matrix of fundamental interests and attitudes that govern social identities and the sense to be made of human activity and intercourse both at the intellectual and the practical levels of endeavor. The example used to investigate this phenomenon in the present study is the notion of origin, a self-evident category that has determined the scholarly quest to understand how Christianity began.

The scholarly investigation of Christian origins has proceeded in terms of critical methods drawn from the humanistic disciplines. The guiding vision, however, has been some imagined event of transformation that might account for the spontaneous generation of the radically new perception, social formation, and religion that Christianity is thought to have introduced to the world. Because this notion of origins has been assumed as self-evident, its derivation from Christian mythology has not been examined. The results of this scholarship, therefore, have been secular apologies for the truth of the Christian claims to unique foundations, even though the purpose of the enterprise as a whole has been purportedly self-critical. The object of this book has been to explore the unacknowledged influence of the Markan legacy upon the scholarship dedicated to a critical analysis of that legacy. By noting that the unique, in distinction from that which is merely different, is essentially beyond analogy, and therefore functions as a hyperbole for the incomprehensible, the irony of a scholarly discourse in quest of the incomparable can be noted.

The Markan legacy should not be thought of as a problem limited to New Testament scholarship, however, for the gospel lens, secularized in the enlightenment academy, has determined the way in which questions have been phrased and categories formed in many disciplines. Another example of the influence of Christian mythology would be the academic quest for the origins of human culture in general. During the nineteenth century developmental schemes were proposed that correlate nicely with the stages outlined in the Christian epic. The domestication of the Hebrew scriptures meant that the Christ event as a new creation could be juxtaposed to the Genesis account of the creation of the world itself. The Genesis account could be read both as a glorious event of divine *creatio ex nihilo* as well as a fall into sin and degeneracy on the part of the first human pair. The Christ event could then be seen as a renewal of God's creative activity focused upon the redemption of fallen humanity. Many nineteenth-century thinkers used the analogy of creation to interpret the dawn of reason in the enlightenment. Applied to the reconstructions of the history of human culture, then, the developmental scheme regularly featured three phases: the primitive (read Old Testament), the religious (read Catholic Christianity from a Protestant point of view), and the rational (read the Protestant recovery of the originary revelation of God in creation and in Christ). This scheme was used to collect, classify, rank, and interpret the anthropological data that began to be amassed. To get at the very beginning, moreover, scenarios were repeatedly reconstructed that portrayed some momentous event, either of the elevating (read origins a la the Christian myth) or of the degenerative (read origins a la the sin of Adam) variety. By degrees, the accumulation of data in the human sciences has forced reassessment of the more obvious and naive assumptions derived from Christian bias. These reassessments have been vigorously resisted, however, at the level of popular culture. That is because the Christian gospel continues to function as the lens by which the world is viewed, ordered, and interpreted.[6]

In America, especially, popular culture and Christian mythology have intertwined to produce a strong, secular sense of destiny. The combination of new land, new people, and the challenge of constructing a new society along egalitarian lines seemed to justify the sense of fulfilling a divine mandate. The analogy with Christian origins seemed natural, except that, in this case, the divine intentions for the people of God were finally coming true. Every invention, achievement, and success could be interpreted as divine approval. Freedom, risk, dint, can-do, vision, progress, and righteousness won the day for God and country. Woes and the wrath of God did provide some times of testing, but mainly during the wars for independence, unification, and the subjugation of Indian resistance. Each war was remembered from the perspective of the victors, thus falling into place as signs that the American spirit was a flowering of manifest destiny making a break with the sins of the past. The sense of beginning anew in the new

---

6. *Myth and category formation.* For a lucid discussion of a nineteenth-century quest that was burdened by categories rooted in Christianized ethnocentric myth see Léon Poliakov, *The Aryan Myth.* On New Testament scholarship as a hero's quest, and how it came to be, see B. Mack, "Gilgamesh and the Wizard of Oz."

world meant that the times of trial, exodus, and redemption had been accomplished. The pristine had been regained, and with it the innocence and exuberance of paradise before the fall.

The gospel of new beginnings blessed the call to live adventurously and produced a truly amazing chapter in human history. Americans have expended enormous energies to make all things new. Ingenuity, valorized as creativity, focused on experimentation, invention, and new technologies. The forward thrust of the Christian scheme has seemed, therefore, to have been vindicated in the success Americans have had in building the great society.

During the last forty years, however, Americans have lost their innocence. Inability to solve the problems of the world abroad and the suspicion of impurities at home have proven to be most unnerving. Up against limits and constraints felt to thwart the American mission, a troubling introspection has emerged. Blame has been laid at the door of every conceivable institution and center of human interest within, and charges leveled at enemy forces threatening from without. Parties have formed around special interests to call for reform in the name of justice and human rights. A sense of helplessness in the face of powers concentrated in the hands of cold, giant institutions sets the mood. Predictions of the future, when dared, are frequently bleak. There is no social notion to lead the way, despite the horror of having learned that societies are what they are. Unwilling to join the human race, to settle for less than the kingdom of God, an apocalyptic mentality is again in evidence.

Those frightened by the apocalyptic vision have renewed the quest for the sources of human transformation. The churches have found their public voices again, calling for spiritual changes. Fundamentalist Protestants want people to be born again. Conservative Presbyterians are organizing for church renewal. Catholic pronouncements call for shifts in moral alignments. A few liberal theologians still hope for some recurrence of enlightenment. Theologies of liberation abound. These voices are discordant, though, and there is no agreement even on what the world should be like were the Christian missions to prevail. The only factor shared in common is concern. There is a sense that something fundamental is wrong with the world, something that must be destroyed or transformed to assure the peaceable kingdom. Each church wants to be the answer, of course, but projects its global vision only from within a fully sectarian perspective.

The quest for religious experience is rampant in the secular culture as well. On the fringes of the Christian churches a magnificent intensification of the desire for personal transformation by means of some kind of charismatic, psychic, therapeutic, or "spiritual" experience is the order of the day. Meditations undergird the required mystifications: the redemptive powers of art, the priestly function of the artist, the ritual potential of theater, the intentionality of changes in lifestyle. From psycho-dynamics through the quest for universal symbols to new wave philosophies of science, auras, time-warps, astrology and the occult, the search is on for the source of the mystery behind it all. Most of these searches are guided by the notion that the mystery is a power capable of making things other than they are, that the power resides hidden in reified transcendence or in the depths of the nature of the world. Contact as breakthrough is what is desired. The Markan legacy is not too difficult to discern.

Publicly, however, neither the invitation of the churches to Christian renewal, nor the private moods of dis-ease and longing, can be acknowledged. The posture that has been taken in Washington is rather to rekindle the American myth and stubbornly proclaim that it is still true. This attitude and its rhetoric have tapped the well-springs of popular desire sufficiently to silence critique and set the eagle flying for a time. As Scott Johnson explained in May of 1985, the American myth has taken the form of the desire to be "the innocent redeemer of the world." His essay is worth repeating:

> The image of American innocence is central to our country's consciousness. It is the leitmotif of Aaron Copland's "Appalachian Spring" and George Gershwin's "An American in Paris." It tints the primitive landscapes of Grandma Moses and the folksy allegories of Norman Rockwell. Writers such as Mark Twain title us "Innocents Abroad," while Henry James calls us "Daisies" that wither and die when moved to foreign soil. "We are," in our own eyes, Niebuhr says, "the most innocent nation on earth."
>
> This sense of our own innocence is coupled with messianic visions of our role in history: the revolutionary redeemers of a Europe corrupted by kings, the blessed heirs of a destiny made "manifest," the all-bearing defenders of a Free World at any price. We are the new refuge of an Old World's huddled masses, the "liberators" of two world wars, the rebuilders of a war-torn Europe, the world's "policeman" against "yellow hordes" and "evil empires."
>
> Even our failures, such as Beirut or Southeast Asia, seem merely to persuade us that, like all messiahs, we may be at times too good, too eager with our help, and so become the victim of an undeserving or ungrateful world. In one sense this may be a "lesson" that we believe we have learned from Vietnam, and justifies our increasing impatience with those who—UNESCO or New Zealand, for example—appear not to appreciate the "goodness" of our works.
>
> It is clearly this conception of ourselves as humankind's white-hatted savior that President Reagan drew on two years ago when he revealed his plan for what was later named the Strategic Defense Initiative. "My fellow Americans," he announced, "tonight we are launching an effort which holds the purpose of changing the course of human history." A declaration laden with messianic intent.[7]

---

7. *Scott Johnson.* His article, "'Star Wars' Trusts in Our Innocence, Not Our Nightmares," appeared in the *Los Angeles Times*, Opinions, May 7, 1985.

So the gospel plan is back in place, though cast in terms of national mission and character rather than as a religious call for human transformation.

Johnson's portrayal is not intended as a eulogy for the messianic spirit. By lifting up just those aspects of the American self-image that may stem from the gospel of innocent power, Johnson intends for his readers to wonder how it could be that such naïveté is still possible in the light of the last forty years. According to Johnson, the rhetoric of innocence is dangerous and the policies rationalized by it are foolish, a combination that can no longer be afforded. Given the sense that makes, a reflection is called for on the Markan legacy. Could it be that the Christian gospel continues to inform the taking of such a posture?

The Markan legacy is a myth of innocence that separates those who belong to the righteous kingdom within from those without. The boundaries, however, are not at all static. The borders shift as conflicts arise both within and without. Separation occurs when the mission to convert the other is thwarted. Judgments fall to support the righteous cause as justified and the recalcitrant other as wrong. A period of time is devoted to patient proclamation, but an either/or approach to issues excludes the middle range of compromise. Conversion means loyalty to the cause of the righteous; rejection means consignment to the forces of opposition. Ultimately, should the mission be threatened with failure, victims may be sacrificed. That is because the cause is righteous and must somehow prevail. The sign of failure, a crucifixion, also serves as the sign of victory. If all else fails, both martyrdom and the destruction of the wicked can be imagined as the means for vindicating the cause and trusting in the power of God to resurrect a new creation from the ashes.

This coarse description of a modern Markan myth does not do justice to the civil sensibilities that mediate competition and conflict much of the time in actual practice in the modern world. But the reduction of the myth to its apocalyptic rationale does illustrate the essential inadequacy of the plot as a means of rationalizing social encounters in the late twentieth century. Insofar as it describes a fundamental structure of American mentality, the Markan myth is no longer good news. That is because the costs of maintaining such a mentality are much too high. Not only does the need always to be right involve devastating denials of normal flaws and failures, such a posture makes it impossible to appreciate others in their difference. Fair exchange can hardly be imagined, much less delight in a multicolored world, if the borders are defined by a Markan rationale.

Within the realm of righteousness, the symbols of transformation set an awesome standard for evaluating life in the daily round. The messiness of the actual give and take of social existence is hardly blessed with great significance. The routine is held to be uninteresting. Only eventful moments capable of high dramatization seem to be worthy of extra attention. Devoid of eschatological moments, the normal breeds malaise, and a dull seriousness about one's duty threatens all other perspectives. To compensate for the lack of truly spiritual crises, sensationalism will (have to) do.

On the boundaries where encounters take place, the Christian lens is the forfeiture of the capacity to engage the other in his difference as a remarkable human being. Those on the other side have always been ranked as inferior and in need of changing, or prior and in need of development. Difference is deviance from the high standard set by the Christian ideal of the kingdom. To the Markan mentality, the world is not a richly woven tapestry, interesting and elegant precisely because of its many, patterns, worthy of its wisdoms.

So the borders have been crossed at will, without a wink or hesitation. Invitations have seldom been thought necessary. A right to be there is the impression given by Americans in other countries, whether representing business, industry, the military, cultural embassies, the state, the churches, or one's own pleasures as a tourist. A profoundly tensive double bind ensues. On the one hand, American interests are at stake and the sense of presence infused with rightful expectations. On the other, American presence is held to be good for the other country, a sign of the expansion of the American way of life. Largesse rejected thus creates dismay. Then it is that thoughts turn ugly, to the use of force to save the world from its demons. The tale has been told in Southeast Asia, Vietnam, the Middle East, Chile, and the Caribbean. It is now being told in Central America, a pathetic example of irrational reaction to messianic failure.

It is the combination of innocence and power that is dangerous. The great man view of history, mythicized according to the gospel of redemption, results in a justification of violence if the power to smash the enemy is placed in the hands of the perfectly pure and righteous ruler. Scott Johnson continued:

> Even beyond the President's stated purpose, it is obvious that visions such as Star Wars require what the 17th Century's George Alsop called the "Adamitical" image of America for their base. For no one contemplates wielding ultimate power, as the ability to render nuclear missiles "impotent and obsolete" surely is meant to be, unless he sees himself as pure enough to draw out of the stone the sword denied the older, tainted warriors of the world.
>
> But such a purity, as with Arthur's legend itself, exists only in myth, and that is the most serious danger of Star Wars—that in it we may mistake our images for our reality. We may too readily believe, as we've imagined in the past, that it is virtually our birthright to hold powers unmatched. We may convince ourselves as we have done so dangerously before that it is our real purpose in the world to save humanity, and that our nature is too peaceful, our character too good, to ever be the source of tragedy.

Johnson is surely right about this self-understanding and its danger. In a series of studies on popular American culture, Robert Jewett has traced the themes of innocence and power through the popular literature and stories in America from the Virginian through the Lone Ranger and Superman to Star Trek and into the present decade. In these stories redemption is placed in the hands of the pure and purely altruistic man of superior power. Interdiction against intrusion or intervention in the affairs of others, a theme for instance in Star Trek, is consistently broken when evil threatens from an alien source. The solution is invariably the use of one's superior power to eradicate the evil in the name of making peace. The Markan savior is still about his business.[8]

It is time, according to Johnson, to set the myth against the history Americans have actually lived. Focusing upon moments intended for glory, the discrepancy between the two story lines is stark indeed. Johnson explained:

> But we are not always the bearers of divine beneficence, and our dreams are often tangled with our nightmares. Our eyes have seen the glory of the coming of the Lord, but they have also seen our Shilohs, our Wounded Knees, Dred Scotts, Nisei, Dresdens, Hiroshimas and My Lais, events that, though they've changed the fate of man, are surely closer to damnation than a glimpse of future earthly paradise.

One might think that such a contrast between the fiction of glory and the history of tragic consequences would call the Markan legacy into question. Unfortunately, the Markan plot centers on catastrophe to justify the righteous cause. It does so, moreover, in just a certain way. The wars that flatten the wicked city in the present are only signs to be read by reference to events that determine the present but take place outside of it. One is the originary event in the past; the other is the final event in the future. Both are violent moments, eruptions of God's power to destroy and to renew. They function as paradigms to clarify critical moments of the history in between. They do not call these moments into question. How can they, when the "glory of the coming of the Lord" celebrates in anthem the loosening of "his terrible, swift sword"?[9]

The clarification that occurs when history is read against the backdrop of myth allows for considerable slippage in the alignments of the two. By assuming positions that enable reading both from a given perspective,

---

8. *Popular myth.* See Robert Jewett and John Lawrence, *The American Monomyth.* R. Jewett has also published *The Captain America Complex,* another study of the devastating effects of biblical myth on American self-understanding.

9. *The apocalyptic solution.* See R. Jewett's chapter on "To Convert Them or Destroy Them" in *The Captain America Complex.* A confirmation of the self-evident status of apocalyptic logic in American culture is James Watt's naively phrased retort to those concerned about how his proposals for the exploitation of natural resources would have lasting effects on the ecology. He said in effect that it did not matter what we do, since the world will soon end anyway.

however, the narrative logic of the myth can be applied. The narrative logic of the Markan plot is clear when read in retrospect from a later point in history. The Christian reader looks on as his innocent and rightful king is rejected and crucified by others, those outside the kingdom of God, those undeserving of its benefits, those whose fate is already sealed.

The plot itself is quite familiar to the historian of religion. The collective decision of the Jews to rid their land and kingdom of an alien intrusion and impurity follows the pattern of the apotropaic sacrifice, better known as the expulsion of a scapegoat. Normally, those who rid their land from the plague in this way think to reap the benefits, a return to peaceful order. It is the logic that lies behind excommunication and the execution of criminals even in the kingdoms of righteousness. But in this case, the Jews do not reap the benefits of their sacrifices. Christians do, though they have not performed the deed. Their righteousness is attested by innocence while the blame for the violence is laid to the account of the enemy of God. The sacrificial reading of the gospel offers Christians their redemption at the expense of the damnation of the Jews. It is a strikingly voyeuristic mode of vicarious experience.

The scapegoat plot reverses with a vengeance when the originary violence is answered by the apocalyptic resolution. Then the enemies get their due. Read together as two perspectives on a single critical moment, the passion plot in retrospect and the apocalypse in anticipation, the logic of any catastrophe perpetrated by the righteous is given. Innocence is assured and blame heaped upon the doubly deserving scapegoat.

This sorry plot lies at the very foundations of the long, ugly history of Christian attitudes and actions toward Jews and Judaism. The destruction of their city was only a sign. They did not vanish as was their due and thus were there to reap repeatedly the wrath of God in anticipation of the final, apocalyptic resolution. No thinking person can justify this long history, nor doubt that the gospel has justified it in the eyes of Christians. Boring and distasteful, the documents pile up from the time of the early church, through the *adversus Judaeos* literature, to the crusades, reactions to the plagues, Catholic doctrine, Luther's pronouncements, German tracts of the nineteenth and early twentieth centuries, common clichés in New Testament scholarship, and the anomaly of anti-Semitic attitudes that emerge throughout the third world wherever the gospel is read today. The Nazi enactment of the final solution forty years ago may have been tainted by pagan desires. But the rationale was Christian. The holocaust was also a gospel event.

Scott Johnson did not mention the holocaust in his litany of sacred tragedies, perhaps because he was writing only about the American myth. Hiroshima and the holocaust belong together, however, for they mark the beginning of the last forty years of innocence, its horrors, and its loss.

Neither did Johnson bring his essay around to a final reflection on the gospel as the source of the American myth of innocence. He chose instead to call to mind another myth residing in the Anglo-American tradition. He chose it because of the way it ends. It does not support the Christian gospel:

> Dreams of innocence die hard, but always finally die. King Arthur's stainless Camelot ends on a blood-soaked battlefield, without a breath of victory or life. The dying king, ringed by corpses, learns as we one day may that there are no human messiahs, no innocent souls. Wise at his death, he orders Bedivere, the lone survivor of the carnage, to throw Arthur's Excalibur, the "invincible" weapon that in the end saves not a soul, back to the Lady of the Lake, beyond the dangerous grasps of men. Bedivere hesitates, but finally heaves the sword into the waves. It is an act, if we are wise, to imitate.

Some readers of this book may want to concur with Johnson's final statement. Given the kinky logic with which apocalyptic Christian mentality has rationalized authority, power, innocence and violence, however, the reader may also want to ponder whether King Arthur's wisdom will have a chance, will be enough as long as the Markan myth is in place. The lesson he learned, according to Johnson, was that "there are no human messiahs." In view of the Markan legacy a slight correction might be considered. Perhaps the sentence should simply read that "there are no messiahs." It may be time to give up the notion. Neither Mark's fiction of the first appearance of the man of power, nor his fantasy of the final appearance of the man of glory, fit the wisdom now required. The church canonized a remarkably pitiful moment of early Christian condemnation of the world. Thus the world now stands condemned. It is enough. A future for the world can hardly be imagined any longer, if its redemption rests in the hands of Mark's innocent son of God.

APPENDICES

THE PRONOUNCEMENT STORIES IN MARK

(A Table of Classification)

x indicates that the pericope is admitted by each author
(*Controversy Dialogues* [Bultmann] and *Pronouncement Stories* [Taylor]).

	Tannehill	Bultmann	Taylor	The Core of the Chreia *(Challenge/Response)*
Mark				
1:35–38 Jesus departs from Capernaum	Correction			C: Everyone is looking for you. R: Let us go on. (1:38)
2:1–12 Healing the paralytic	Objection-Quest	x	x(2:3–12)	C: Who but God can forgive sins? R: Which is easier, to forgive or to heal? (2:9)
2:15–17 Eating with tax collectors and sinners	Objection	x	x	C: Why does he eat with sinners? R: Those who are well do not need a physician, but those who are ill. (2:17)

	Tannehill	Bultmann	Taylor	The Core of the Chreia (Challenge/Response)
2:18–22 The question about fasting	Objection	x	x(2:18–20)	C: Why don't your disciples fast? R: Can wedding guests fast while the bridegroom is with them? (2:19)
2:23–28 Plucking grain on the sabbath	Objection	x	x(2:23–26)	C: Plucking grain on the sabbath is not lawful. R: The sabbath was made for man, not man for the sabbath. (2:27)
3:1–6 Healing on the sabbath	Objection	x	x(3:1–5)	C: Unlawful to heal on the sabbath. R: Is it lawful on the sabbath to do good, or to do harm? (3:4)
3:22–30 Beelzebul controversy	Objection	x	x(3:22–26)	C: He casts out demons by Beelzebul. R: How can Satan cast out Satan? (3:23)
3:31–35 Jesus' true family	Commendation (Correction)		x	C: Your family seeks you. R: Who is my family? (3:33)
4:10–20 The reason for parables	Inquiry		x(4:10–12)	C: Why do you speak in parables? R: To you (the twelve) has been given the secret of the kingdom of God, but for those outside everything is in parables. (4:11)

	Tannehill	Bultmann	Taylor	The Core of the Chreia (Challenge/Response)
6:1–6 Rejection at Nazareth	Objection			C: Is not this the carpenter? R: A prophet is not without honor except in his own country. (6:4)
7:1–15 Eating with hands defiled	Objection	x(7:1–23)	x(7:5–8)	C: Why do your disciples eat with unclean hands? R: Nothing which goes into a man can defile him, but what comes out of a man can. (7:15)
7:24–30 The Syrophoenician woman	Objection-Commendation (Quest)			C: Request for an exorcism. R¹:Let the children first be fed. (7:27) R²:Even the dogs eat the children's bread. (7:28)
8:11–12 Pharisees seek a sign	Correction		x	C: Pharisees seek a sign. R: Why does this generation seek a sign? (8:12)
8:31–33 The Son of Man must suffer	Objection			C: Peter rebukes the prediction of suffering. R: Get behind me Satan! (8:33)
9:9–13 The coming of Elijah	Objection			C: Why do scribes say Elijah must come first? R: Elijah does come first. (9:12)

	Tannehill	Bultmann	Taylor	The Core of the Chreia (Challenge/Response)
9:33–37 Dispute about greatness	Correction			C: Who is the greatest? R: Whoever wants to be first, must be last. (9:35)
9:38–40 The strange exorcist	Correction		x(9:38–39)	C: Forbidding the strange exorcist. R: Who is not against us, is for us. (9:40)
10:2–9 On divorce	Inquiry (Testing) (Correction)	x(10:2–12)	x	C: Is it lawful to divorce? R: What God has joined, let not man put asunder. (10:9)
10:13–16 Blessing the children	Commendation (Correction)		x	C: Disciples rebuke the children. R: The kingdom belongs to the children. (10:14)
10:17–22 The rich young man	Quest		x(10:17–27)	C: Good teacher, what must I do . . . ? R: Why do you call me good? (10:18)
10:23–27 Entering the kingdom of God	Objection			C: Can the rich be saved? R: It is easier for a camel . . . (10:25)

	Tannehill	Bultmann	Taylor	The Core of the Chreia (Challenge/Response)
10:35–45 The sons of Zebedee	Correction		x(10:34–50)	C: Request for position in glory. R: Whoever would be first, must be a slave. (10:44)
11:15–17 Cleansing the temple	Correction			
11:20–25 The withered fig tree	Inquiry			
11:27–33 The question of authority	Inquiry (Testing)	x	x	C: Who gave you this authority? R: Was the baptism of John from heaven or from men? (11:30)
12:13–17 Paying taxes to Caesar	Inquiry (Testing)		x(12:13–16)	C: Should we pay taxes to Caesar? R: Give to Caesar the things that are Caesar's. (12:17)
12:18–27 On the resurrection	Correction	x	x	C: Which of the seven (dead) men will have the woman as wife? R: He is not God of the dead, but of the living. (12:27)

	Tannehill	Bultmann	Taylor	The Core of the Chreia (*Challenge/Response*)
12:28–34 The greatest commandment	Quest		x	C: Teacher, you are right about the greatest commandment. R: You are not far from the kingdom of God. (12:34)
12:35–37 Question about David's son	Correction or Inquiry (Testing)		x	C: The scribes say Christ is David's son. R: David himself calls him Lord, so how can he be his son? (12:37)
12:41–44 The widow's mite	Commendation (Correction)		x	C: Many rich people put in large sums. R: The poor widow has put in more than all the others combined. (12:43)
13:1–2 The destruction of the temple	Correction		x	C: Look, what wonderful stones. R: Not one stone will be left upon another. (13:2)
14:3–9 Anointing at Bethany	Commendation (Correction)		x	C: The woman does an unseemly thing. R: She has done a beautiful thing to me. (14:6)

LINNEMANN: THE TRADITIONS OF THE PASSION

The texts follow the reconstructions in *Studien zur Passionsgeschichte,* 178–82.

The English translation is given according to the Revised Standard Version.

[   ] indicates reconstructed additions by Linnemann.

(   ) indicates secondary insertions according to Linnemann.

JESUS IN GETHSEMANE

Mark 14

The original story

32   And they went to a place which was called Gethsemane; and he said to his disciples, "Sit here, while I pray."

35   And going a little farther, he fell on the ground and prayed that, if it were possible, the hour might pass from him.

37a   And he came and found them sleeping.

39a   And again he went away and prayed.

40ab   And again he came and found them sleeping, for their eyes were very heavy.

41ab   And he came the third time, and said to them, "Are you still sleeping and taking your rest?"

40c   And they did not know what to answer him.

41c   [And he said] "It is enough; the hour has come."

First-level additions

33   And he took with him Peter and James and John, and began to be greatly distressed and troubled.

34ab   And he said to them, "My soul is very sorrowful, even to death;"

. . . . . .

36   And he said, "Abba, Father, all things are possible to thee; remove this cup from me; yet not what I will, but what thou wilt."

Second-level additions

34c   ". . .remain here and watch."

37b   And he said,

38   "Watch and pray that you may not enter into temptation; the spirit indeed is
          willing, but the flesh is weak."

Markan additions

37bc   (And he said) to Peter, "Simon, are you asleep? Could you not watch one
          hour?"

. . . . . .

41d   "Behold, the Son of Man is handed over into the hands of sinners.
42   Rise. Let us go. Behold, the one handing me over approaches."

THE PREDICTION OF DENIAL

Mark 14

27   And Jesus said to them,
          "You will all fall away, for it is written,
          'I will strike the shepherd, and the sheep will be scattered.'"
29   Peter said to him,
          "Even though they all fall away, I will not."
30   And Jesus said to him,
          "Truly, I say to you, this very night, before the cock crows twice, you will
          deny me three times."

THE ARREST

He was reckoned among the robbers

Mark 14

43b   [A] crowd [came] with swords and clubs from the chief priests and the
          scribes and the elders.
48   And Jesus said to them,
          "Have you come out as against a robber, with swords and clubs to capture
          me?"
49b   But [it happened so that] the scriptures be fulfilled.

The sign of denial

Mark 14

1   It was now two days before the Passover and [the feast of] Unleavened
          Bread;
          And the chief priests and the scribes were seeking how to arrest him by
          stealth, and kill him;
2   For they said, "Not during the feast, lest there be a tumult of the people."
10   Then Judas Iscariot, who was one of the twelve, went to the chief priests in
          order to betray him to them.
11   And when they heard it they were glad, and promised to give him money.
          [And he led them to the place where Jesus was.]
44   Now the betrayer had given them a sign, saying: "The One I shall kiss is the
          man; seize him and lead him away safely."

45   And when he came, he went up to him at once and said, "Master."
        And he kissed him.
46   And they laid hands on him and seized him.

The flight of the disciples (a fragment)

Mark 14

47   ... But one of those who stood by drew his sword, and struck the slave of the
        high priest and cut off his ear.
        ......
50   And they all forsook him and fled.
51   And a young man followed him, with nothing but a linen cloth about his
        body; and they seized him.
52   But he left the linen cloth and ran away naked.

THE TRIAL

Jesus' silence before the Sanhedrin

Mark 14

55a   [The chief priests and the whole council sought testimony against Jesus to
        put him to death, and found none.]
57   And some stood up and bore false witness against him, saying,
58   "We heard him say, 'I will destroy this temple (that is made with hands), and
        in three days I will build another (not made with hands).'"
61b   [And] the high priest asked him,
60b   "Have you no answer to make? What is it that these men testify against
        you?"
61a   But he was silent and made no answer.

The condemnation of the Messiah

Mark 14

55   The chief priests and the whole council sought testimony against Jesus to
        put him to death, but they found none.
56   For many bore false witness against him, but their witness did not agree.
60a   And the high priest stood up in the midst and asked Jesus,
61c   "Are you the Christ, the Son of the Blessed?"
62   And Jesus said, "I am."
63   And the high priest tore his mantle and said, "Why do we still need
        witnesses?
64   You have heard his blasphemy. What is your decision?" And they all
        condemned him as deserving death.

THE CRUCIFIXION

Mark 15

22a   And they brought him to the place called Golgotha.
24a   And they crucified him.

25a   And it was the third hour.
33   And when the sixth hour had come there was darkness over the whole land
        until the ninth hour.
34a   And at the ninth hour
37   Jesus (uttered a loud cry and) breathed his last.
38   And the curtain of the temple was torn in two, from top to bottom.

APPENDIX III

DORMEYER: THE ACTS OF THE MARTYR

Dormeyer's reconstruction is summarized in *Die Passion Jesu als Verhaltens-modell*, 238, 297–301. The reconstruction consists only of verse portions. In order to visualize the range of material included in the Acts, the verses have been assigned to the various narratives of the passion as designated in the present study.

	Mark
The temple act	11:15b, 18a
Anointing at Bethany	14:3
Betrayal	14:10–11a
To Gethsemane	14:32a
Arrest	14:43b, 46, 50, 51–52, 55
Trial: Sanhedrin	14:55
Trial: Pilate	15:1b, 3, 5
Sentencing (Barabbas' release)	15:6, 11, 7, 15
Road to Golgotha	15:20b, 21
Crucifixion	15:22a, 23, 24a, 26, 27, 31a, 32c
Death	15:34ab, 37, 38, 40
Burial	15:42b, 43ac, 46a

THE GOSPEL OF MARK: AN OVERVIEW

Preparation (1:1–8)
        John the Baptist in the wilderness

PHASE ONE:
EVENTS IN GALILEE
(1:9–8:21)

I. The Appearance of the Man with authority (1:9–3:12)
    1. *His commission* (1:9–20)
        (Baptism, temptation, message, disciples, and authority over unclean spirits: "What is this?")
    2. *His Galilean mission* (1:21–45)
        ("Preaching in their synagogues and casting out demons.")
    3. *His encounter with the leaders* (2:1–3:12)
        ("The Pharisees went out and immediately held counsel with the Herodians against him, how to destroy him.")

II. The people take note and gather (3:13–6:5)
    1. *The people are divided* (3:13–35)
        (Leaders, people, disciples, friends, and family— each draws a different conclusion. "A kingdom divided.")
    2. *Jesus' teaching discriminates* (4:1–34)
        ("To you has been given the secret of the kingdom of God, but for those outside everything is in parables.")
    3. *Jesus' deeds affect social arrangements* (4:35–6:5)
        (Miracles beyond the borders of Galilee. "A prophet is not without honor, except. . .")

III. The disciples are charged with the mission (6:7–8:21)
    1. *The disciples are sent with authority* (6:7–33)
        (And the reader learns that prophets like John the Baptist are killed.)
    2. *Jesus exemplifies power to change people* (6:35–7:37)
        (And the reader learns that the Pharisees are wrong to follow the traditions of the elders.)

3. *The disciples fail to understand* (8:1–21)
(And are compared to the testy Pharisees whose "leaven" is dangerous.)

TRANSITIONAL PHASE:
ON THE WAY TO JERUSALEM
(8:22–10:52)

Flash: A blind man is given sight (8:22–26)

I. *The question of Jesus' identity is raised* (8:27–9:1)
   (The views of the people and the "confession of Peter")
   The first prediction unit:
   1. The first prediction of the passion (8:31)
   2. Peter's misunderstanding (8:32–33)
   3. Teaching about discipleship (8:34–9:1)

II. *Jesus' true identity is revealed* (9:2–29)
    (Transfiguration; relation to "Elijah"; "O faithless generation, How long am I to bear with you?")
    The second prediction unit:
    1. The second prediction of the passion (9:30–31)
    2. The disciples' misunderstanding (9:32–34)
    3. Teaching about discipleship (9:35–37)

III. *Jesus explains the kingdom of God* (9:38–10:31)
     ("It is better to enter the kingdom of God with one eye than with two eyes to be thrown into hell.")
     The third prediction unit:
     1. The third prediction of the passion (10:32–24)
     2. The disciples' misunderstanding (10:35–40)
     3. Teaching about discipleship (10:41–45)

Flash: A blind man is given sight (10:46–52)

PHASE TWO:
EVENTS IN JERUSALEM
(11:1–16:8)

I. *Jesus' appearance in Jerusalem* (11:1–13:37)
   1. Actions directed toward the temple (11:1–25)
   2. Controversy with the leaders (11:27–12:44)
   3. Private instruction to disciples (13:1–37)

II. *The last supper with the disciples* (14:1–52)
    1. Preparations (14:1–16)
    (Including being anointed "beforehand for burying")
    2. The meal (14:17–31)
    3. The arrest and the flight (14:32–52)
    (Including Gethsemane and the betrayal)

III. *The trials and crucifixion* (14:53–15:47)
    1. The trials (14:53–15:5)
       (Including the "trial" of Peter)
    2. The crucifixion (15:6–39)
    3. The burial (15:40–47)

Sequel (16:1–8)
        The empty tomb and the messenger

BIBLIOGRAPHY

Achtemeier, Paul J. "Miracles and the Historical Jesus: A Study of Mark 9:14–29." *Catholic Biblical Quarterly* 37 (1975): 471–91.
————. "The Origin and Function of the Pre-Markan Miracle Catenae." *Journal of Biblical Literature* 91 (1972): 198–221.
————. "Toward the Isolation of Pre-Markan Miracle Catenae." *Journal of Biblical Literature* 89 (1970): 265–91.
Albertz, Martin. *Die synoptische Streitgespräche.* Berlin: Trowitzsch, 1921.
Alciphron. *The Letters.* Eng. trans. A. R. Benner and F. H. Fobes. The Loeb Classical Library. Cambridge: Harvard University Press; London: William Heinemann, 1949.
Alter, Robert. *The Art of Biblical Narrative.* New York: Basic Books, 1981.
Attridge, Harold W. *First-Century Cynicism in the Epistles of Heraclitus.* Harvard Theological Studies 29. Missoula, MT: Scholars Press, 1976.
Aune, David E. *Prophecy in Early Christianity and the Ancient Mediterranean World.* Grand Rapids: Wm. B. Eerdmans, 1983.
————. "Septem Sapientium Convivium (Moralia 146B–164D)." In *Plutarch's Ethical Writings and Early Christian Literature,* edited by H. D. Betz, 51–105. Studia ad Corpus Hellenisticum Novi Testamenti 4. Leiden: E. J. Brill, 1978.
Avi-Yonah, Michael, ed. *The Herodian Period.* The World History of the Jewish People, Series 1, vol. 8. Jerusalem: Massada, 1977.
Baird, William. "What is the Kerygma?: A Study of 1 Cor. 15,3–8 and Gal. 1,11–17." *Journal of Biblical Literature* 76 (1957): 181–91.
Baron, Salo W. *A Social and Religious History of the Jews.* 3 vols. (Rev. ed. [1952/58], 8 vols.) New York: Columbia University Press, 1937.
Barthes, Roland. *Writing Degree Zero and Elements of Semiology.* Boston: Beacon Press, 1970.
Beardslee, William A. *Literary Criticism of the New Testament.* Guides to Biblical Scholarship. Philadelphia: Fortress Press, 1970.
————. "Saving One's Life By Losing It." *Journal of the American Academy of Religion* 47 (1979): 57–72.
Betz, Hans Dieter. *Galatians: A Commentary on Paul's Letter to the Churches in Galatia.* Hermeneia. Philadelphia: Fortress Press, 1979.

—————. *Nachfolge und Nachahmung Jesu Christi im Neuen Testament*. Beiträge zur historischen Theologie 37. Tübingen: J. C. B. Mohr (Paul Siebeck), 1967.

Bickermann, Elias. *From Ezra to the Last of the Maccabees: Foundations of Post-Biblical Judaism*. New York: Schocken Books, 1962.

Billerbeck, Margarethe. *Epiktet: Vom Kynismus [Diatr. III,22]*. Ed. and trans. with commentary by M. Billerbeck. Philosophia antiqua 34. Leiden: E. J. Brill, 1978.

Blenkinsopp, Joseph. *Wisdom and Law in the Old Testament: The Ordering of Life in Israel and Early Judaism*. London and New York: Oxford University Press, 1983.

Booth, Wayne C. *Modern Dogma and the Rhetoric of Assent*. Ward Phillips Lecture Series, vol. 5. Notre Dame, IN: University of Notre Dame Press, 1974.

—————. *The Rhetoric of Fiction*. Chicago: University of Chicago Press, 1961.

Borges, Jorge Luis. *Doctor Brodie's Report*. New York: E. P. Dutton, 1972.

Boring, M. Eugene. *Sayings of the Risen Jesus: Christian Prophecy in the Synoptic Tradition*. Society for New Testament Studies Monograph Series 46. Cambridge and New York: Cambridge University Press, 1982.

Boucher, Madeleine. *The Mysterious Parable: A Literary Study*. The Catholic Biblical Quarterly Monograph Series 6. Washington: Catholic Biblical Association of America, 1977.

Bourdieu, Pierre. *Outline of a Theory of Practice*. Trans. Richard Nice. Cambridge Studies in Social Anthropology 16. Cambridge: Cambridge University Press, 1982.

Brandon, Samuel G. F. *Jesus and the Zealots*. Manchester: Manchester University Press, 1967.

Breech, James. *The Silence of Jesus: The Authentic Voice of the Historical Man*. Philadelphia: Fortress Press, 1983.

Bright, John. *The Kingdom of God: The Biblical Concept and Its Meaning for the Church*. Nashville: Abingdon-Cokesbury Press, 1953.

Brown, Peter. *The World of Late Antiquity A.D. 150–750*. New York: Harcourt Brace Jovanovich, 1971.

Brown, Raymond E. *The Community of the Beloved Disciple*. New York: Paulist Press, 1979.

—————. *The Gospel According to John*. 2 vols. (I–XII; XIII–XXI) Anchor Bible 29. Garden City, NY: Doubleday & Co., 1979.

Brown, Scott K. "James: A Religio-Historical Study of the Relations between Jewish, Gnostic, and Catholic Christianity in the Early Period through an Investigation of the Tradition about James the Lord's Brother." Ph. D. diss., Brown University, 1972.

Bultmann, Rudolf. *The Gospel of John: A Commentary*. Eng. trans. G. R. Beasley-Murray et al. Philadelphia: Westminster Press; Oxford: Basil Blackwell & Mott, 1971.

—————. *The History of the Synoptic Tradition*. Eng. trans. John Marsh, from *Die Geschichte der synoptischen Tradition*, 2d ed., 1931; 1st ed., 1921. New York and Evanston: Harper & Row, 1963.

—————. *Jesus and the Word*. Eng. trans. L. P. Smith and E. H. Lantero, from the German *Jesus*, 1926. New York: Charles Scribner's Sons, 1934.

_____. *Theology of the New Testament.* 2 vols. Eng. trans. Kendrick Grobel, from *Theologie des Neuen Testaments,* 1948/53. New York: Charles Scribner's Sons, 1951/55.

Burke, Kenneth. *A Grammar of Motives.* Englewood Cliffs, NJ: Prentice-Hall, 1945.

_____. *Language as Symbolic Action: Essays on Life, Literature and Method.* Berkeley and Los Angeles: University of California Press, 1966.

_____. *A Rhetoric of Motives.* Englewood Cliffs, NJ: Prentice-Hall, 1950.

_____. *The Rhetoric of Religion: Studies in Logology.* Boston: Beacon Press, 1961.

Burkert, Walter. *Homo Necans: Interpretationen altgriechischer Opferriten und Mythen.* Religionsgeschichtliche Versuche und Vorarbeiten 32. Berlin and New York: Walter de Gruyter, 1972.

_____. *Structure and History in Greek Mythology and Ritual.* Sather Classical Lectures 47. Berkeley and Los Angeles: University of California Press, 1979.

Butts, James R. "The Progymnasmata of Theon: A New Text with Translation and Commentary." Ph.D. diss., Claremont Graduate School, 1986.

Case, Shirley Jackson. *The Evolution of Early Christianity.* Chicago: University of Chicago Press, 1914.

Castelli, Elizabeth. "Mimesis as a Discourse of Power in Paul's Letters." Ph.D. diss., Claremont Graduate School, 1987.

Charlesworth, James H., ed. *The Old Testament Pseudepigrapha.* 2 vols. Garden City, NY: Doubleday & Co., 1983/85.

Collins, Adela Yarbro. *Crisis and Catharsis: The Power of the Apocalypse.* Philadelphia: Westminster Press, 1984.

Collins, John J. *The Apocalyptic Imagination: An Introduction to the Jewish Matrix of Christianity.* New York: Crossroad, 1984.

_____. *Between Athens and Jerusalem: Jewish Identity in the Hellenistic Diaspora.* New York: Crossroad, 1983.

Conzelmann, Hans. "On the Analysis of the Confessional Formula in I Corinthians 15:3–5." *Interpretation* 20 (1966): 15–25.

_____. "The Mother of Wisdom." In *The Future of Our Religious Past: Essays in Honor of Rudolf Bultmann,* edited by J. M. Robinson, 230–43. New York: Harper & Row, 1971.

_____. *An Outline of the Theology of the New Testament.* Eng. trans. John Bowden. New York and Evanston: Harper & Row, 1969.

Cornelius Nepos. *Great Generals of Foreign Nations.* Eng. trans. John C. Rolfe. The Loeb Classical Library. Cambridge: Harvard University Press; London: William Heinemann, 1947.

Cross, Frank Moore. *The Ancient Library of Qumran and Modern Biblical Studies.* Haskell Lectures, 1956–57. Garden City, NY: Doubleday & Co., 1958.

Crossan, John Dominic. "A Basic Bibliography for Parables Research." *Semeia* 1 (1974): 236–74.

_____. *Cliffs of Fall: Paradox and Polyvalence in the Parables of Jesus.* New York: Seabury Press, 1980.

_____. *The Dark Interval: Towards a Theology of Story.* Niles, IL: Argus Communications, 1975.

————. "Divine Immediacy and Human Immediacy, Towards a First Principle in Historical Jesus Research." Unpublished paper for the Jesus Seminar, St. Meinrads, IN, October, 1985.

————. "Empty Tomb and Absent Lord (Mark 16:1–8)." In *The Passion in Mark: Studies on Mark 14–16,* edited by W. Kelber, 135–52. Philadelphia: Fortress Press, 1976.

————. *Finding Is the First Act: Trove Folktales and Jesus' Treasure Parable.* Semeia Studies 9. Missoula, MT: Scholars Press; Philadelphia: Fortress Press, 1979.

————. *In Fragments: The Aphorisms of Jesus.* San Francisco: Harper & Row, 1983.

————. "Parable and Example in the Teaching of Jesus." *New Testament Studies* 18 (1971–72): 285–307.

————. *In Parables: The Challenge of the Historical Jesus.* New York: Harper & Row, 1973.

————. *Raid on the Articulate: Comic Eschatology in Jesus and Borges.* New York: Harper & Row, 1976.

————. "The Seed Parables of Jesus." *Journal of Biblical Literature* 92 (1973): 244–66.

Culler, Jonathan. *Structural Poetics: Structuralism, Linguistics, and the Study of Literature.* Ithaca, NY: Cornell University Press, 1975.

Culpepper, R. Alan. *Anatomy of the Fourth Gospel: A Study in Literary Design.* Foundations and Facets. Philadelphia: Fortress Press, 1983.

Davies, W. D. *Paul and Rabbinic Judaism: Some Rabbinic Elements in Pauline Theology.* London: SPCK, 1948.

Delobel, J., et al., eds. *Logia: Les Paroles de Jésus.* Louvain: Uitgeverij Peeters, 1982.

Derrett, J. D. M. "The Anointing at Bethany and the Story of Zacchaeus." In *Law in the New Testament,* 266–78 . London: Darton, Longman & Todd, 1970.

————. *Law in the New Testament.* London: Darton, Longman & Todd, 1970.

Derrida, Jacques. *Dissemination.* Eng. trans. Barbara Johnson. Chicago: University of Chicago Press, 1981.

————. *Of Grammatology.* Eng. trans. Gayatri Chakravorty Spivak. Baltimore: Johns Hopkins Press, 1976.

Detienne, Marcel, and Jean-Pierre Vernant. *Cunning Intelligence in Greek Culture and Society.* Eng. trans. Janet Lloyd. Atlantic Highlands, NJ: Humanities Press, 1978.

Dewey, Joanna. *Markan Public Debate: Literary Technique, Concentric Structure, and Theology in Mark 2:1–3:6.* Society of Biblical Literature Dissertation Series 48. Missoula, MT: Scholars Press, 1980.

Dibelius, Martin. *From Tradition to Gospel.* Eng. trans. Bertram Lee Woolf from *Die Formgeschichte des Evangeliums,* 1919. New York: Charles Scribner's Sons, 1934.

Diels, Herman, ed. *Die Fragmente der Vorsokratiker.* 3 vols. 9th ed. Berlin: Weidmann, 1959.

Dio Chrysostom. *Discourses.* Eng. trans. J. W. Cohoon. The Loeb Classical Library. Cambridge: Harvard University Press; London: William Heinemann, 1971.

Diogenes Laertius. *Lives of Eminent Philosophers*. 2 vols. Eng. trans. R. D. Hicks. The Loeb Classical Library. Cambridge: Harvard University Press; London: William Heinemann, 1931/38.

Dodd, C. H. *According to the Scriptures: The Sub-Structure of New Testament Theology*. New York: Charles Scribner's Sons, 1953.

_____. *The Interpretation of the Fourth Gospel*. Cambridge: Cambridge University Press, 1953.

_____. *The Parables of the Kingdom*. Shaffer Lectures, Yale, 1935. Garden City, NY: James Nisbet & Co., 1935.

Donahue, John R. *Are You the Christ?: The Trial Narrative in the Gospel of Mark*. Society of Biblical Literature Dissertation Series 10. Missoula, MT: Scholars Press, 1973.

_____. "From Passion Traditions to Passion Narrative." In *The Passion in Mark: Studies on Mark 14-16*, edited by W. Kelber, 1-20. Philadelphia: Fortress Press, 1976.

_____. "Temple, Trial, and Royal Christology." In *The Passion in Mark: Studies on Mark 14-16*, edited by W. Kelber, 61-79. Philadelphia: Fortress Press, 1976.

Döring, Klaus. *Exemplum Socratis: Studien zur Sokratisnachwirkung in der kynisch-stoischen Popularphilosophie der frühen Kaiserzeit und im frühen Christentum*. Wiesbaden: Steiner, 1979.

Dormeyer, Detlev. *Die Passion Jesu als Verhaltensmodell: Literarische und theologische Analyse der Traditions- und Redaktionsgeschichte der Markuspassion*. Neutestamentliche Abhandlungen 11. Münster: Aschendorff, 1974.

Douglas, Mary T. "Deciphering a Meal." In *Myth, Symbol, and Culture*, edited by C. Geertz, 61-81. New York: W. W. Norton & Co., 1971.

_____. *Natural Symbols: Explorations in Cosmology*. New York: Pantheon Books, 1970.

_____. *Purity and Danger: An Analysis of Concepts of Pollution and Taboo*. London: Routledge & Kegan Paul, 1966.

Dudley, D. R. *A History of Cynicism from Diogenes to the 6th Century A.D*. London: Methuen, 1937.

Duke, Paul D. *Irony in the Fourth Gospel*. Atlanta: John Knox Press, 1985.

Duling, Dennis C. *Jesus Christ through History*. New York: Harcourt Brace Jovanovich, 1979.

Dumont, Louis. *Homo Hierarchicus: The Caste System and Its Implications*. Eng. trans. M. Sainsbury, L. Dumont, and B. Gulati. Chicago: University of Chicago Press, 1980.

Durkheim, Émile. *The Elementary Forms of the Religious Life: A Study in Religious Sociology*. Eng. trans. Joseph Ward Swain. London: George Allen & Unwin; New York: Macmillan Co., 1915.

Edwards, Richard A. *A Theology of Q: Eschatology, Prophecy, and Wisdom*. Philadelphia: Fortress Press, 1976.

Efroymson, David P. "The Patristic Connection." In *Anti-Semitism and the Foundations of Christianity*, edited by Alan T. Davies, 98-117. New York: Paulist Press, 1979.

Elliott, John H. *A Home for the Homeless: A Sociological Exegesis of I Peter, Its Situation and Strategy*. Philadelphia: Fortress Press, 1981.

Epictetus. *The Discourses as Reported by Arrian.* 2 vols. Eng. trans. W. A. Oldfather. The Loeb Classical Library. Cambridge: Harvard University Press; London: William Heinemann, 1941.

Evans, Craig A. "Isaiah 6:9–10 in Early Jewish and Christian Interpretation." Ph.D. diss., Claremont Graduate School, 1983.

Feeley-Harnik, Gillian. *The Lord's Table: Eucharist and Passover in Early Christianity.* Philadelphia: University of Pennsylvania Press, 1981.

Fischel, Henry A. "Studies in Cynicism and the Ancient Near East: The Transformation of a Chria." In *Religions in Antiquity: Essays in Memory of Erwin Ramsdell Goodenough,* edited by J. Neusner, 372–411. Studies in the History of Religions 14. Leiden: E. J. Brill, 1968.

Fitzmyer, Joseph A. *The Dead Sea Scrolls: Major Publications and Tools for Study.* Sources for Biblical Study 8. Missoula, MT: Scholars Press, 1975.

————. *Pauline Theology: A Brief Sketch.* Englewood Cliffs, NJ: Prentice-Hall, 1967.

Fletcher, Angus. *Allegory: The Theory of a Symbolic Mode.* Ithaca, NY: Cornell University Press, 1964.

Flusser, David. *Die rabbinischen Gleichnisse und der Gleichniserzähler Jesus.* Judaica et Christiana 4. Frankfurt: Peter Lang, 1981.

Fortna, Robert T. *The Gospel of Signs: A Reconstruction of the Narrative Source Underlying the Fourth Gospel.* Studiorum Novi Testamenti Societas Monograph Series 11. Cambridge: Cambridge University Press, 1970.

Foucault, Michel. *The Archaeology of Knowledge.* Eng. trans. A. M. Sheridan Smith. New York: Pantheon Books, 1972.

————. *Madness and Civilization: A History of Insanity in the Age of Reason.* Eng. trans. Richard Howard. New York: Pantheon Books, 1965.

————. *The Order of Things: An Archaeology of the Human Sciences.* New York: Pantheon Books, 1971.

Fowler, Robert M. *Loaves and Fishes: The Function of the Feeding Stories in the Gospel of Mark.* Society of Biblical Literature Dissertation Series 54. Chico, CA: Scholars Press, 1981.

Freyne, Seán. *Galilee, From Alexander the Great to Hadrian 323 B.C.E. to 135 C.E.: A Study of Second Temple Judaism.* Wilmington, DE: Michael Glazier; Notre Dame, IN: University of Notre Dame Press, 1980.

————. *The Twelve, Disciples and Apostles: An Introduction to the Theology of the First Three Gospels.* London: Sheed & Ward, 1968.

Fuchs, Ernst. *Studies of the Historical Jesus.* Studies in Biblical Theology 42. Eng. trans. Andrew Scobie. Naperville, IL: Alec R. Allenson, 1964.

Fuller, Reginald H. *The Foundations of New Testament Christology.* New York: Charles Scribner's Sons, 1965.

Funk, Robert W. *Jesus as Precursor.* Semeia Supplements 2. Missoula, MT: Scholars Press; Philadelphia: Fortress Press, 1975.

————. *Language, Hermeneutic and Word of God.* New York: Harper & Row, 1966.

————, ed. *New Gospel Parallels,* vols. 1–2. Foundations and Facets. Philadelphia: Fortress Press, 1985.

————. "The Parable as Metaphor." In *Language, Hermeneutic and Word of God,* 133–62. New York: Harper & Row, 1966.

―――――. *Parables and Presence: Forms of the New Testament Tradition.* Philadelphia: Fortress Press, 1982.

―――――. "Poll on the Parables." *Foundations & Facets Forum* 2,1 (1986): 54–80.

―――――. "The Real Jesus. What did he really say?" Unpublished paper: University of Redlands, CA, May, 1981.

―――――. "Saying and Seeing: Phenomenology of Language and the New Testament." *Journal of Bible and Religion* 34 (1966): 197–213.

―――――. "Structure in the Narrative Parables of Jesus." *Semeia* 2 (1974): 51–81.

Gager, John G. *Kingdom and Community: The Social World of Early Christianity.* Englewood Cliffs, NJ: Prentice-Hall, 1975.

Georgi, Dieter. "Weisheit Salomos," In *Jüdische Schriften aus Hellenistisch-Römischer Zeit,* band III/4:390–478. Gütersloh: Gerd Mohn, 1980.

Girard, René. *Le bouc émissaire.* Paris: Grasset, 1982.

Golzio, K. H. *Der Tempel im alten Mesopotamian und seine Parallelen in Indien.* Leiden: E. J. Brill, 1983.

Goodenough, E. R. "The Political Philosophy of Hellenistic Kingship." In *Yale Classical Studies I,* 55–102. New Haven: Yale University Press, 1928.

Grant, Frederick C. *The Economic Background of the Gospels.* Oxford: Oxford University Press; London: Humphrey Milford, 1926.

Grant, Robert M. *The Bible in the Church: A Short History of Interpretation.* New York: Macmillan Co., 1948.

Greenspoon, Leonard. "The Pronouncement Story in Philo and Josephus." *Semeia* 20 (1981): 73–80.

Greimas, A. J. *Sémantique structurale. Recherche de méthode.* Paris: Larousse, 1966.

Gutmann, Joseph, comp. *The Synagogue: Studies in Origins, Archaeology and Architecture.* The Library of Biblical Studies. New York: Ktav, 1975.

Hahn, Ferdinand. *The Titles of Jesus in Christology.* Eng. trans. Harold Knight and George Ogg, from *Christologische Hoheitstitel: Ihre Geschichte im frühen Christentum,* 1963. London: Lutterworth Press, 1969.

Hamerton-Kelly, Robert G., ed. *Violent Origins: Ritual Killing and Cultural Formation.* Palo Alto, CA: Stanford University Press, 1987.

Hanson, R. P. C. *Allegory and Event: A Study of the Sources and Significance of Origen's Interpretation of Scripture.* Richmond: John Knox Press; London: SCM Press, 1959.

Haran, Menahem. *Temples and Temple-Service in Ancient Israel: An Inquiry into the Character of Cult Phenomena and the Historical Setting of the Priestly School.* Oxford: Clarendon Press, 1978.

Harrisville, Roy A. *The Concept of Newness in the New Testament.* Minneapolis: Augsburg Publishing House, 1960.

Hellholm, David, ed. *Apocalypticism in the Mediterranean World and the Near East: Proceedings of the International Colloquium on Apocalypticism, Uppsala, August 12–17, 1979.* Tübingen: J. C. B. Mohr (Paul Siebeck), 1983.

Hengel, Martin. *Judaism and Hellenism: Studies in Their Encounter in Palestine during the Early Hellenistic Period.* 2 vols. Eng. trans. J. Bowden. Philadelphia: Fortress Press; London: SCM Press, 1974.

―――――. *Nachfolge und Charisma: Eine exegetischreligionsgeschichtliche Studie zu Mt 8,21f. und Jesu Ruf in die Nachfolge.* Zeitschrift für die neutestamentliche Wissenschaft Beihefte 34. Berlin: Alfred Töpelmann, 1968.

————. "Proseuche und Synagogue, Jüdische Gemeinde, Gotteshaus und Gottesdienst in der Diaspora und in Palästina." In *Tradition und Glaube: Das frühe Christentum in seiner Umwelt*, Festschrift Karl G. Kuhn, edited by Gert Jeremias, H.-W. Kuhn, and H. Stegemann, 157–84. Göttingen: Vandenhoeck & Ruprecht, 1971.

————. *Victory over Violence: Jesus and the Revolutionists.* Eng. trans. David E. Green. Philadelphia: Fortress Press, 1973.

————. *Was Jesus a Revolutionist?* Facet Books 28. Eng. trans. William Klassen. Philadelphia: Fortress Press, 1971.

Hilgert, Earle. "Bibliographia Philoniana 1935–1981." In *Aufstieg und Niedergang der römischen Welt: Geschichte und Kultur Roms im Spiegel der neueren Forschung*, vol.2.21.1, edited by Wolfgang Haase, 47–97. Berlin and New York: Walter de Gruyter, 1984.

Hippocrates. *Works.* 4 vols. Eng. trans. W. H. S. Jones. The Loeb Classical Library. Cambridge: Harvard University Press; London: William Heinemann, 1967.

Hock, Ronald F. "Another Look at Jeremias' *Parables of Jesus:* Prolegomena to a New Study of the Parables." Unpublished paper for the Society of Biblical Literature, Stanford, CA, March, 1982.

————, and Edward N. O'Neil. *The Chreia in Ancient Rhetoric*, vol. 1: *The Progymnasmata.* Atlanta: Scholars Press, 1986.

Hoehner, Harold W. *Herod Antipas.* Society for New Testament Studies Monograph Series 17. Cambridge: Cambridge University Press, 1972.

Hoffman, Lawrence A. *The Canonization of the Synagogue Service.* Notre Dame, IN, and London: University of Notre Dame Press, 1979.

Hoffmann, Paul. *Studien zur Theologie der Logienquelle.* Münster: Aschendorff, 1972.

Hoïstad, Ragnar. *Cynic Hero and Cynic King.* Uppsala: Bloms, 1948.

Holmberg, Bengt. *Paul and Power: The Structure of Authority in the Primitive Church as Reflected in the Pauline Epistles.* Lund: C. W. K. Gleerup, 1978.

Hommel, Hildebrecht. "Herrenworte im Lichte sokratischer Überlieferung." *Zeitschrift für die neutestamentliche Wissenschaft* 57 (1966): 1–23.

Hönig, Sidney B. "The Ancient City Square: The Forerunner of the Synagogue." In *Aufstieg und Niedergang der römischen Welt: Geschichte und Kultur Roms im Spiegel der neueren Forschung*, vol.2.19.1, edited by Wolfgang Haase, 448–76. Berlin and New York: Walter de Gruyter, 1979.

Horsley, Richard A. "'Like One of the Prophets of Old': Two Types of Popular Prophets at the Time of Jesus." *Catholic Biblical Quarterly* 47 (1985): 435–63.

————. "Menahem in Jerusalem: A Brief Messianic Episode among the Sicarii— Not 'Zealot Messianism.'" *Novum Testamentum* 27 (1985): 334–48.

————. "Popular Messianic Movements around the Time of Jesus." *Catholic Biblical Quarterly* 46 (1984): 471–95.

Horsley, Richard A., and John S. Hanson. *Bandits, Prophets, and Messiahs: Popular Movements at the Time of Jesus.* New Voices in Biblical Studies. New York and Chicago: Winston-Seabury Press, 1985.

Hultgren, Arland J. *Jesus and His Adversaries: The Form and Function of the Conflict Stories in the Synoptic Tradition.* Minneapolis: Augsburg Publishing House, 1979.

————. "The Pistis Christou Formulation in Paul." *Novum Testamentum* 22 (1980): 248–63.

Hultkrantz, Åke. "Ecology of Religion: Its Scope and Methodology." In *Science of Religion: Studies in Methodology,* edited by Lauri Honko, 221–36. Proceedings of the Study Conference of the International Association for the History of Religions, Turku, Finland, August 27–31, 1973. The Hague: Mouton Press, 1979.

————. "The Indians and the Wonders of Yellowstone: A Study of the Interrelations of Religion, Nature and Culture." *Ethnos* 19 (1954): 34–68.

Humphrey, Hugh M. *A Bibliography for the Gospel of Mark, 1954–1980.* Studies in the Bible and Early Christianity 1. New York and Toronto: Edwin Mellen, 1981.

Jackson, Howard. "The Death of Jesus in Mark and the Miracle of the Cross." *New Testament Studies* 33 (1987): 16–37.

Jacobson, Arland D. "Wisdom Christology in Q." Ph.D. diss., Claremont Graduate School, 1978.

Jeremias, Joachim. *The Eucharistic Words of Jesus.* Eng. trans. Norman Perrin. New York: Charles Scribner's Sons; London: SCM Press, 1966.

————. *Jerusalem in the Time of Jesus: An Investigation into Economic and Social Conditions during the New Testament Period.* Eng. trans. F. H. Cave and C. H. Cave. Philadelphia: Fortress Press, 1969.

————. "παῖς θεοῦ." In *Theological Dictionary of the New Testament* 5, edited by G. Kittel and G. Friedrich, 654–717. Eng. trans. G. W. Bromiley. German ed., 1954. Grand Rapids: Wm. B. Eerdmans, 1967.

————. *The Parables of Jesus.* Eng. trans. S. H. Hooke, from *Die Gleichnisse Jesus,* 6th ed., 1962, 1st ed., 1947. New York: Charles Scribner's Sons, 1955.

————. "Die Salbungsgeschichte Mk 14.3–9." In *Abba: Studien zur neutestamentlichen Theologie und Zeitgeschichte,* 107–15. Göttingen: Vandenhoeck & Ruprecht, 1966.

Jewett, Robert. *The Captain America Complex: The Dilemma of Zealous Nationalism.* Philadelphia: Westminster Press, 1973.

————. "Romans as an Ambassadorial Letter." *Interpretation* 36 (1982): 5–20.

Jewett, Robert, and John Shelton Lawrence. *The American Monomyth.* Garden City, NY: Doubleday, Anchor Books, 1977.

Johnson, Luke Timothy. "Rom. 3:21–26 and the Faith of Jesus." *Catholic Biblical Quarterly* 44 (1982): 77–90.

Johnson, Scott. "'Star Wars' Trusts in Our Innocence, Not Our Nightmares." *Los Angeles Times,* Opinion, May 7, 1985.

Josephus. *Jewish Antiquities,* Books 18–20. Eng. trans. Louis Feldman. The Loeb Classical Library. Cambridge: Harvard University Press; London: William Heinemann, 1949.

————. *The Jewish War,* vols. 2–3. Eng. trans. H. St. J. Thackeray. The Loeb Classical Library. Cambridge: Harvard University Press; London: William Heinemann, 1956/57.

————. *The Life.* Eng. trans. H. J. Thackeray. The Loeb Classical Library. Cambridge: Harvard University Press; London: William Heinemann, 1946.

Judge, E. A. *The Social Pattern of the Christian Groups in the First Century.* London: Tyndale Press, 1960.

Juel, Donald. *Messiah and Temple: The Trial of Jesus in the Gospel of Mark.* Society of Biblical Literature Dissertation Series 31. Missoula, MT: Scholars Press, 1977.

Jülicher, Adolf. *Die Gleichnisreden Jesu.* 2 vols. Tübingen: J. C. B. Mohr (Paul Siebeck), 1888/99.

Jüngel, Eberhard. *Paulus und Jesus: Eine Untersuchung zur Präzisierung der Frage nach dem Ursprung der Christologie.* Tübingen: J. C. B. Mohr (Paul Siebeck), 1962.

Käsemann, Ernst. *The Testament of Jesus: A Study of the Gospel of John in the Light of Chapter 17.* Eng. trans. G. Krodel. London: SCM Press; Philadelphia: Fortress Press, 1968.

Kautsky, Carl. *Der Ursprung des Christentums: Eine historische Untersuchung.* Stuttgart: Dietz, 1908.

Kealy, Seán P. *Mark's Gospel: A History of Its Interpretation from the Beginning until 1979.* New York and Ramsey, NJ: Paulist Press, 1982.

Kee, Howard C. "Aretalogy and Gospel." *Journal of Biblical Literature* 92 (1973): 402–22.

_____. *Community of the New Age: Studies in Mark's Gospel.* Philadelphia: Westminster Press, 1977.

_____. *Jesus in History: An Approach to the Study of the Gospels.* New York: Harcourt Brace Jovanovich, 1970.

Kelber, Werner H. "Apostolic Tradition and the Genre of the Gospel." Unpublished paper for the Symposium on Discipleship, Marquette University, April 15–17, 1983.

_____. *The Kingdom in Mark: A New Place and a New Time.* Philadelphia: Fortress Press, 1974.

_____. *The Oral and the Written Gospel: The Hermeneutics of Speaking and Writing in the Synoptic Tradition, Mark, Paul, and Q.* Philadelphia: Fortress Press, 1983.

_____, ed. *The Passion in Mark: Studies on Mark 14–16.* Philadelphia: Fortress Press, 1976.

Kennedy, George A. *New Testament Interpretation through Rhetorical Criticism.* Chapel Hill and London: University of North Carolina Press, 1984.

Kermode, Frank. *The Genesis of Secrecy: On the Interpretation of Narrative.* The Charles Eliot Norton Lectures, 1977–78. Cambridge and London: Harvard University Press, 1979.

Kingsbury, Jack Dean. *The Christology of Mark's Gospel.* Philadelphia: Fortress Press, 1983.

Klauck, Hans-Josef. *Herrenmahl und hellenistischer Kult: Eine religionsgeschichtliche Untersuchung zum ersten Korintherbrief.* Neutestamentliche Abhandlungen, n.F. Band 15. Münster: Aschendorff, 1982.

Kloppenborg, John S. *The Formation of Q: Trajectories in Ancient Wisdom Collections.* Studies in Antiquity and Christianity. Philadelphia: Fortress Press, 1987.

_____. *Q Parallels: Synopsis, Critical Notes, and Concordance.* Sonoma, CA: Polebridge Press, 1988.

Knox, Wilfred L. *The Sources of the Synoptic Gospels.* 2 vols. Edited by H. Chadwick. Cambridge: Cambridge University Press, 1953/57.

Koester, Helmut. "History and Development of Mark's Gospel (From Mark to *Secret Mark* and 'Canonical' Mark)." In *Colloquy on New Testament Studies: A Time for Reappraisal and Fresh Approaches*, edited by Bruce Corley, 35–57. Proceedings of the Colloquy sponsored and held at Southwestern Baptist Theological Seminary, Fort Worth, Texas, 5–6 November 1980. Macon, GA: Mercer University Press, 1983.

_____. *Introduction to the New Testament*. Vol. 1, *History, Culture, and Religion of the Hellenistic Age*. Vol. 2, *History and Literature of Early Christianity*. Philadelphia: Fortress Press; Berlin and New York: Walter de Gruyter, 1982.

_____. "One Jesus and Four Primitive Gospels." In *Trajectories through Early Christianity*, edited by J. M. Robinson and H. Koester, 158–204. Philadelphia: Fortress Press, 1971.

Kraabel, A. Thomas. *Judaism in Western Asia Minor under the Roman Empire*. Studia Post-Biblica. Leiden: E. J. Brill, 1971.

Kraeling, Carl H. *The Synagogue*. The Excavations at Dura-Europos. New Haven: Yale University Press, 1956.

Kramer, Werner R. *Christ, Lord, Son of God*. Eng. trans. Brian Hardy from *Christos Kyrios Gottessohn*, 1963. Studies in Biblical Theology 50. London: SCM Press; Naperville, IL: Alec R. Allenson, 1966.

Krentz, Edgar. *The Historical-Critical Method*. Guides to Biblical Scholarship. Philadelphia: Fortress Press, 1975.

Kuhn, Heinz-Wolfgang. *Ältere Sammlungen im Markusevangelium*. Studien zur Umwelt des Neuen Testaments 8. Göttingen: Vandenhoeck & Ruprecht, 1971.

Kümmel, Werner Georg. *The New Testament: The History of the Investigation of Its Problems*. Eng. trans. S. McLean Gilmour and Howard C. Kee. Nashville and New York: Abingdon Press, 1972.

Landman, Leo. *Jewish Law in the Diaspora: Confrontation and Accommodation*. New York: Ktav, 1968.

Lee, Thomas Robert. *Studies in the Form of Sirach 44–50*. Society of Biblical Literature Dissertations 75. Atlanta: Scholars Press, 1986.

Lentricchia, Frank. *After the New Criticism*. Chicago: University of Chicago Press, 1980.

Lévi-Strauss, Claude. *Introduction to a Science of Mythology*. 4 vols. Eng. trans. J. Weightman and D. Weightman. New York: Harper & Row, 1964/68.

_____. *The Savage Mind*. Eng. trans. G. Weidenfeld. Chicago: University of Chicago Press, 1966.

_____. *Structural Anthropology*. Eng. trans. C. Jacobson and B. G. Schoepf. New York: Basic Books, 1963.

Limbeck, Meinrad. *Die Ordnung des Heils: Untersuchungen zum Gesetzesverständnis des Frühjudentums*. Kommentare und Beiträge zum Alten und Neuen Testament. Düsseldorf: Patmos-Verlag, 1971.

Lindars, Barnabas. *New Testament Apologetic: The Doctrinal Significance of the Old Testament Quotations*. Philadelphia: Westminster Press, 1961.

Linnemann, Eta. *Jesus of the Parables: Introduction and Exposition*. Eng. trans. John Sturdy, from *Gleichnisse Jesu: Einführung und Auslegung*, 3d ed., 1964, 1st ed. 1961. New York: Harper & Row, 1966.

————. *Studien zur Passionsgeschichte.* Forschungen zur Religion und Literatur des Alten und Neuen Testaments 102. Göttingen: Vandenhoeck & Ruprecht, 1970.

Longenecker, Richard N. *Biblical Exegesis in the Apostolic Period.* Grand Rapids: Wm. B. Eerdmans, 1975.

Lucian. *Works.* 8 vols. Eng. trans. A. M. Harmon et al. The Loeb Classical Library. Cambridge: Harvard University Press; London: William Heinemann, 1961/67.

Lührmann, Dieter. *Die Redaktion der Logienquelle.* Wissenschaftliche Monographien zum Alten und Neuen Testament 33. Neukirchen-Vluyn: Neukirchener, 1969.

McCall, Marsh H. *Ancient Rhetorical Theories of Simile and Comparison.* Cambridge: Harvard University Press, 1969.

Mack, Burton L. "Gilgamesh and the Wizard of Oz: The Scholar as Hero." *Foundations and Facets Forum* 1,2 (1985): 3–29.

————. "Imitatio Mosis: Patterns of Cosmology and Soteriology in the Hellenistic Synagogue." *Studia Philonica* 1 (1972): 27–55.

————. "The Innocent Transgressor: Jesus in Early Christian Myth and History." *René Girard and Biblical Studies. Semeia* 33 (1985): 135–65.

————. "The Kingdom Sayings in Mark." *Foundations and Facets Forum* 3,1 (1987): 3–47.

————. *Logos und Sophia: Untersuchungen zur Weisheitstheologie im hellenistischen Judentum.* Studien zur Umwelt des Neuen Testaments 10. Göttingen: Vandenhoeck & Ruprecht, 1973.

————. "Philo Judaeus and Exegetical Traditions in Alexandria." In *Aufstieg und Niedergang der römischen Welt: Geschichte und Kultur Roms im Spiegel der neueren Forschung.* Series 2, vol. 21/1. Edited by Wolfgang Haase, 227–71. Berlin and New York: Walter de Gruyter, 1984.

————. "Weisheit und Allegorie bei Philo von Alexandrien: Untersuchungen zum Traktat De Congressu eruditionis." *Studia Philonica* 5 (1978): 57–105.

————. *Wisdom and the Hebrew Epic: Ben Sira's Hymn in Praise of the Fathers.* Chicago Studies in the History of Judaism. Chicago: University of Chicago Press, 1985.

————. "Wisdom Makes a Difference: Alternatives to Messianic Configurations." In *Judaisms and Their Messiahs.* Edited by Jacob Neusner, 15–48. Cambridge: Cambridge University Press, 1987.

Mack, Burton L., and Edward N. O'Neil. "Hermogenes of Tarsus." In *The Chreia in Ancient Rhetoric: Vol. 1 The Progymnasmata,* 153–81. Ronald F. Hock and Edward N. O'Neil. Texts and Translations 27. Atlanta: Scholars Press, 1986.

Mack, Burton L., and Vernon K. Robbins. *Patterns of Persuasion in the Gospels.* Sonoma, CA: Polebridge Press, 1989.

McFague, Sallie. *Speaking in Parables: A Study in Metaphor and Theology.* Philadelphia: Fortress Press, 1975.

McKnight, Edgar V. *What Is Form Criticism?* Guides to Biblical Scholarship. Philadelphia: Fortress Press, 1969.

Macksey, Richard, and Eugenio Donato, eds. *The Structuralist Controversy: The Languages of Criticism and the Sciences of Man.* Baltimore: Johns Hopkins Press, 1970.

Malherbe, Abraham J. *The Cynic Epistles: A Study Edition.* Sources for Biblical Study 12. Missoula, MT: Scholars Press, 1977.

_____. *Social Aspects of Early Christianity*. Baton Rouge and London: Louisiana State University Press, 1977.

Malina, Bruce J. "Jewish Christianity: A Select Bibliography." *Australian Journal of Biblical Archaeology* 1 (1973): 60–65.

_____. *The New Testament World: Insights from Cultural Anthropology*. Atlanta: John Knox Press, 1981.

Marcus, Joel. "The Mystery of the Kingdom of God: The Markan Parable Chapter (Mark 4:1–34) and the Theology of the Gospel as a Whole." Ph.D. diss., Columbia University, 1985.

Martyn, J. Louis. *History and Theology in the Fourth Gospel*. New York and Evanston: Harper & Row, 1968.

Marxsen, Willi. *The Beginnings of Christology: A Study in Its Problems*. Facet Books 22. Eng. trans. Paul J. Achtemeier. Philadelphia: Fortress Press, 1969.

_____. *The Beginnings of Christology Together with the Lord's Supper as a Christological Problem*. Philadelphia: Fortress Press, 1979.

_____. *The Lord's Supper as a Christological Problem*. Eng. trans. Lorenz Nieting. Philadelphia: Fortress Press, 1970.

Mathews, Shailer. *The Social Teaching of Jesus: An Essay in Christian Sociology*. New York: Macmillan Co., 1897.

Maurer, Christian. "Knecht Gottes und Sohn Gottes im Passionsbericht des Markusevangeliums." *Zeitschrift für Theologie und Kirche* 50 (1953): 1–38.

Mauss, Marcel. *The Gift: Forms and Functions of Exchange in Archaic Societies*. Eng. trans. Ian Cunnison. New York: W. W. Norton & Co., 1967.

Meeks, Wayne A. *The First Urban Christians: The Social World of the Apostle Paul*. New Haven and London: Yale University Press, 1983.

_____. "The Man from Heaven in Johannine Sectarianism." *Journal of Biblical Literature* 91 (1972): 44–72.

_____. *The Prophet-King: Moses Traditions and the Johannine Christology*. Novum Testamentum Supplements 14. Leiden: E. J. Brill, 1967.

Meeks, Wayne A., and Robert L. Wilken. *Jews and Christians in Antioch in the First Four Centuries of the Common Era*. Sources for Biblical Study 13. Missoula, MT: Scholars Press, 1978.

Meyers, Eric M., and James F. Strange. *Archaeology, the Rabbis, and Early Christianity: The Social and Historical Setting of Palestinian Judaism and Christianity*. Nashville: Abingdon Press, 1981.

Miller, Merrill P. "Targum, Midrash and the Use of the Old Testament in the New Testament." *Journal for the Study of Judaism* (1971): 29–82.

Mohr, Till Arend. *Markus- und Johannespassion: Redaktions- und traditionsgeschichtliche Untersuchung der markinischen und johanneischen Passionstradition*. Abhandlungen zur Theologie des Alten und Neuen Testaments 70. Zürich: Theologischer Verlag, 1982.

Montgomery, James A. *The Samaritans; the Earliest Jewish Sect: Their History, Theology and Literature*. Philadelphia: Winston Press, 1907.

Neusner, Jacob. *Early Rabbinic Judaism*. Leiden: E. J. Brill, 1975.

_____, ed. *Judaisms and their Messiahs at the Turn of the Christian Era*. Cambridge: Cambridge University Press, 1987.

————. *A Life of Rabban Yohanan ben Zakkai Ca. 1–80 C.E.* Studia Post-Biblica 6. Leiden: E. J. Brill, 1962.

————. *Das pharisäische und talmudische Judentum.* Texte und Studien zum antiken Judentum 4. Tübingen: J. C. B. Mohr (Paul Siebeck),1984.

————. *From Politics to Piety: The Emergence of Pharisaic Judaism.* Englewood Cliffs, NJ: Prentice-Hall, 1973.

Newton, Michael. *The Concept of Purity at Qumran and in the Letters of Paul.* Society for New Testament Studies Monograph Series 53. New York and Cambridge: Cambridge University Press, 1985.

Nickelsburg, George W. E. "The Genre and Function of the Markan Passion Narrative." *Harvard Theological Review* 73 (1980): 153–84.

————. *Jewish Literature between the Bible and the Mishnah: A Historical and Literary Introduction.* Philadelphia: Fortress Press, 1981.

————. *Resurrection, Immortality and Eternal Life in Intertestamental Judaism.* Harvard Theological Studies 26. Cambridge: Harvard University Press; London: Oxford University Press, 1972.

Nilsson, Martin P. "Die Götter des Symposions." In *Opuscula Selecta: Linguis Anglica, Francogallica, Germanica Conscripta,* 1:428–42. Lund: C. W. K. Gleerup, 1951/60.

O'Neil, Edward N., ed. and trans. *Teles (The Cynic Teacher).* Missoula, MT: Scholars Press, 1977.

Oppenheimer, A'haron. *The 'Am Ha'aretz: A Study in the Social History of the Jewish People in the Hellenistic-Roman Period.* Arbeiten zur Literatur und Geschichte des Hellenistischen Judentums 8. Leiden: E. J. Brill, 1977.

Osiek, Carolyn A. *What Are They Saying about the Social Setting of the New Testament?* Ramsey, NJ: Paulist Press, 1984.

Ovid. *Ex ponto.* Eng. trans. Arthur L. Wheeler. The Loeb Classical Library. Cambridge: Harvard University Press; London: William Heinemann, 1953.

Pagels, Elaine. *The Gnostic Gospels.* New York: Random House, 1979.

Paquet, Leonce. *Les Cyniques Grecs: Fragments et Termoignages.* Ottawa: Editions de l'Université d'Ottawa, 1975.

Patte, Daniel. *Early Jewish Hermeneutic in Palestine.* Society of Biblical Literature Dissertation Series 22. Missoula, MT: Scholars Press, 1975.

————. *What Is Structural Exegesis?* Guides to Biblical Scholarship. Philadelphia: Fortress Press, 1976.

Pépin, Jean. *Mythe et Allegorie: Les origines Grecques et les contestations Judeó-Chrétiennes.* Aubier: Editions Montaigne, 1958.

Perelman, Chaim. *Realm of Rhetoric.* Eng. trans. William Kluback. Notre Dame: University of Notre Dame Press, 1982.

Perelman, Chaim, and Lucie Olbrechts-Tyteca. *The New Rhetoric: A Treatise on Argumentation.* Eng. trans. John Wilkinson and Purcell Weaver. Notre Dame, IN: University of Notre Dame Press, 1969.

Perkins, Pheme. *Hearing the Parables of Jesus.* New York: Paulist Press, 1981.

Perrin, Norman. *Jesus and the Language of the Kingdom: Symbol and Metaphor in New Testament Interpretation.* Philadelphia: Fortress Press, 1976.

————. *The Kingdom of God in the Teaching of Jesus.* Philadelphia: Westminster Press, 1963.

_____. "The Use of (Para)didonai in Connection with the Passion of Jesus in the New Testament." In *Der Ruf Jesu und die Antwort der Gemeinde: Festschrift für Joachim Jeremias,* edited by Eduard Lohse, 204–12. Göttingen: Vandenhoeck & Ruprecht, 1970.

_____. *What Is Redaction Criticism?* Guides to Biblical Scholarship. Philadelphia: Fortress Press, 1969.

Perrin, Norman, and Dennis C. Duling. *The New Testament: An Introduction. Proclamation and Parenesis, Myth and History.* New York: Harcourt Brace Jovanovich, 1974.

Petersen, Norman R. *Literary Criticism for New Testament Critics.* Guides to Biblical Scholarship. Philadelphia: Fortress Press, 1978.

_____. "The Reader in the Gospel." *Neotestamentica* 18 (1984): 38–51.

_____. *Rediscovering Paul: Philemon and the Sociology of Paul's Narrative World.* Philadelphia: Fortress Press, 1985.

_____. "Story Time and Plotted Time in Mark's Narrative." In *Literary Criticism for New Testament Critics,* 49–80. Guides to Biblical Scholarship. Philadelphia: Fortress Press, 1978.

Polag, Athanasius. *Fragmenta Q: Textheft zur Logienquelle.* Neukirchen-Vluyn: Neukirchener, 1979.

Poland, Franz. *Geschichte des griechischen Vereinswesens.* Leipzig: B. G. Teubner, 1909.

Poliakov, Léon. *The Aryan Myth.* New York: New American Library, 1977.

Polzin, Robert M. *Biblical Structuralism: Method and Subjectivity in the Study of Ancient Texts.* Semeia Supplements. Missoula, MT: Scholars Press; Philadelphia: Fortress Press, 1977.

Porton, Gary G. "The Pronouncement Story in Tannaitic Literature: A Review of Bultmann's Theory." *Semeia* 20 (1981): 81–100.

Plato. *The Republic.* Eng. trans. Paul Shorey. The Loeb Classical Library. Cambridge: Harvard University Press; London: William Heinemann, 1969.

Plutarch. *Moralia.* 16 vols. Eng. trans. Frank Cole Babbitt, et al. The Loeb Classical Library. Cambridge: Harvard University Press; London: William Heinemann, 1927–69.

_____. *Parallel Lives.* 11 vols. Eng. trans. Bernadotte Perrin. The Loeb Classical Library. Cambridge: Harvard University Press; London: William Heinemann, 1928/1943.

Propp, Vladimir. *Morphology of the Folktale.* Austin: University of Texas Press, 1968.

Quintilian. *The Institutio Oratoria.* 4 vols. Eng. trans. H. E. Butler. The Loeb Classical Library. New York: G. P. Putnam's Sons; London: William Heinemann, 1920/22.

Rappaport, Roy. *Ecology, Meaning and Religion.* Richmond, CA: North Atlantic Books, 1979.

Reese, James M. *Hellenistic Influences on the Book of Wisdom and Its Consequences.* Analecta Biblica 41. Rome: Biblical Institute Press, 1970.

Reumann, John. *"Righteousness" in the New Testament: Justification in the United States Lutheran-Roman Catholic Dialogue.* With Responses by Joseph A. Fitzmyer and Jerome D. Quinn. Philadelphia: Fortress Press; New York: Paulist Press, 1982.

Riches, John Kenneth. *Jesus and the Transformation of Judaism.* London: Darton, Longman & Todd, 1980.

Riesner, Rainer. *Jesus als Lehrer: Eine Untersuchung zum Ursprung der Evangelien-Überlieferung.* Wissenschaftliche Untersuchungen zum Neuen Testament, Reihe 2; 7. Tübingen: J. C. B. Mohr (Paul Siebeck), 1981.

Robbins, Vernon K. "Classifying Pronouncement Stories in Plutarch's Parallel Lives." *Semeia* 20 (1981): 29–52.

————. *Jesus the Teacher: A Socio-Rhetorical Interpretation of Mark.* Philadelphia: Fortress Press, 1984.

————. "Last Meal: Preparation, Betrayal, and Absence (Mark 14:12–25)." In *The Passion in Mark: Studies on Mark 14–16,* edited by Werner H. Kelber, 21–40. Philadelphia: Fortress Press, 1976.

Robinson, James M. "Die Hodajot-Formel in Gebet und Hymnus des Frühchristentums." In *Apophoreta: Festschrift für Ernst Haenchen zu seinem 70. Geburtstag am 10. Dezember 1964,* edited by W. Eltester, 194–235. Zeitschrift für die neutestamentliche Wissenschaft und die Kunde der älteren Kirche 30. Berlin: Alfred Töpelmann, 1964.

————. "The Johannine Trajectory." In *Trajectories through Early Christianity,* edited by J. M. Robinson and H. Koester, 232–68. Philadelphia: Fortress Press, 1971.

————. *A New Quest of the Historical Jesus.* Studies in Biblical Theology 5. Naperville, IL: Alec R. Allenson, 1959.

Safrai, Shemuel. "Jewish Self-Government." In *The Jewish People in the First Century: Historical Geography, Political History, Social, Cultural, and Religious Life and Institutions,* edited by S. Safrai and M. Stern, 1: 377–449. Compendia Rerum Iudaicarum ad Novum Testamentum, Section I. Assen, Netherlands: Van Gorcum; Philadelphia: Fortress Press, 1974.

Safrai, S., and M. Stern, eds. *The Jewish People in the First Century: Historical Geography, Political History, Social, Cultural, and Religious Life and Institutions.* Compendia Rerum Iudaicarum ad Novum Testamentum, Section I. 2 vols. Assen, Netherlands: Van Gorcum; Philadelphia: Fortress Press, 1974/76.

San Nicolò, Mariano. *Aegyptisches Vereinswesen zur Zeit der Ptolemäer und Römer.* 2 vols. Münchner Beiträge zur Papyrusforschung und antiken Rechtsgeschichte 2/1. 2d ed. München: C. H. Beck, 1972.

Sanders, E. P. *Jesus and Judaism.* London: SCM Press, 1985.

Sanders, James A. *Torah and Canon.* Philadelphia: Fortress Press, 1972.

Sandmel, Samuel. *Philo of Alexandria: An Introduction.* New York: Oxford University Press, 1979.

Schalit, Abraham. *König Herodes: Der Mann und sein Werk.* Studia Judaica 4. Berlin: Walter de Gruyter, 1969.

Schenk, Wolfgang. *Der Passionsbericht nach Markus: Untersuchungen zur Überlieferungsgeschichte der Passionstraditionen.* Leiden: E. J. Brill; Gütersloh: Gerd Mohn, 1974.

————. *Synopse zur Redenquelle der Evangelien: Q-Synopse und Rekonstruktion in deutscher Übersetzung mit kurzen Erläuterungen.* Düsseldorf: Patmos-Verlag, 1981.

Schenke, Ludger. *Der gekreuzigte Christus: Versuch einer literarkritischen und traditionsgeschichtlichen Bestimmung der vormarkinischen Passionsgeschichte.* Stuttgarter Bibelstudien 69. Stuttgart: Katholisches Bibelwerk, 1974.

_____. *Studien zur Passionsgeschichte des Markus: Tradition und Redaktion in Markus 14,1–42.* Forschung zur Bibel 4. Würzburg: Echter Verlag; Stuttgart: Katholisches Bibelwerk, 1971.

Schmidt, Karl Ludwig. *Der Rahmen der Geschichte Jesu: Literarkritische Untersuchungen zur ältesten Jesusüberlieferung.* Berlin: Trowitzsch & Sohn, 1919.

Schmithals, Walter, and Antonius H. J. Gunneweg. *Authority.* Eng. trans. John E. Steely. Biblical Encounter Series. Nashville: Abingdon Press, 1982.

Schneider, Carl. *Geistesgeschichte des antiken Christentums.* 2 vols. München: C. H. Beck, 1954.

Schneider, Gerhard. *Die Passion Jesu nach den drei älteren Evangelien.* Biblische Handbibliothek 11. München: Kösel Verlag, 1973.

Schoeps, Hans Joachim. *Jewish Christianity.* Eng. trans. Douglas R. A. Hare. Philadelphia: Fortress Press, 1969.

_____. *Paul: The Theology of the Apostle in the Light of Jewish Religious History.* Eng. trans. Harold Knight. Philadelphia: Westminster Press; London: Lutterworth Press, 1961.

Schottroff, Luise, and Wolfgang Stegemann. *Jesus von Nazareth: Hoffnung der Armen.* Urban Taschenbücher 639. Stuttgart: Kohlhammer, 1978.

Schreiber, Johannes. *Die Markus-passion: Wege zur Erforschung der Leidensgeschichte Jesu.* Hamburg: Furche, 1969.

_____. *Die Theologie des Vertrauens.* Hamburg: Furche, 1967.

Schürer, Emil, Géza Vermès, and F. Miller. *The History of the Jewish People in the Age of Jesus Christ.* Edinburgh: T. & T. Clark, 1973.

Schürmann, Heinz. "Beobachtungen zum Menschensohn-Titel in der Redequelle." In *Jesus und der Menschensohn: Für Anton Vogtle,* edited by R. Pesch, R. Schnackenburg, and O. Kaiser, 124–47. Freiburg: Herder, 1975.

Schütz, John Howard. *Paul and the Anatomy of Apostolic Authority.* Society for New Testament Studies Monograph Series 26. New York and Cambridge: Cambridge University Press, 1975.

Schweitzer, Albert. *The Quest of the Historical Jesus: A Critical Study of Its Progress from Reimarus to Wrede.* Eng. trans. W. Montgomery from *Von Reimarus zu Wrede: Eine Geschichte der Leben-Jesu-Überlieferung,* 1906. London: A. & C. Black, 1910.

Schweizer, Eduard. *The Lord's Supper According to the New Testament.* Facet Books 18. Philadelphia: Fortress Press, 1967.

Scott, Bernard Brandon. *Jesus, Symbol-Maker for the Kingdom.* Philadelphia: Fortress Press, 1981.

Seeley, David. "The Concept of the Noble Death in Paul." Ph.D. diss., Claremont Graduate School, 1987.

Semeia 20: Pronouncement Stories, edited by Robert C. Tannehill. Chico, CA: Scholars Press, 1981.

Seneca. *Epistles.* 3 vols. Eng. trans. Richard M. Gummere. The Loeb Classical Library. Cambridge: Harvard University Press; London: William Heinemann, 1925–43.

Shaw, Graham. *The Cost of Authority: Manipulation and Freedom in the New Testament*. London: SCM Press, 1983.

Smith, Dennis Edwin. "Social Obligation in the Context of Communal Meals: A Study of the Christian Meal in I Corinthians in Comparison with Graeco-Roman Communal Meals." Ph.D. diss., Harvard University, 1980.

Smith, Dwight Moody. *The Composition and Order of the Fourth Gospel: Bultmann's Literary Theory*. Yale Publications in Religion 10. New Haven: Yale University Press, 1965.

Smith, Jonathan Z. "The Bare Facts of Ritual." *History of Religions* 20 (1980): 112–27. Reprinted in his *Imagining Religion*, 53–65.

————. "Good News Is No News: Aretalogy and the Gospel." In *Christianity, Judaism and Other Greco-Roman Cults: Studies for Morton Smith at Sixty*, Part 1, edited by Jacob Neusner, 21–38. Studies in Judaism in Late Antiquity 12. Leiden: E. J. Brill, 1975. Reprinted in his *Map Is Not Territory*, 190–207.

————. *Imagining Religion: From Babylon to Jonestown*. Chicago Studies in the History of Judaism. Chicago: University of Chicago Press, 1982.

————. *Map Is Not Territory: Studies in the History of Religions*. Studies in Judaism in Late Antiquity 23. Leiden: E. J. Brill, 1978.

————. "A Pearl of Great Price and a Cargo of Yams: A Study in Situational Incongruity." *History of Religions* 16 (1976): 1–19. Reprinted in his *Imagining Religion*, 90–101.

————. "Social Description of Early Christianity." *Religious Studies Review* 1 (1975): 19–25.

————. "The Influence of Symbols upon Social Change: A Place on Which to Stand." *Worship* 44 (1970): 457–74. Reprinted in his *Map Is Not Territory*, 129–46.

————. *To Take Place: Toward Theory in Ritual*. Chicago Studies in the History of Judaism. Chicago: University of Chicago Press, 1987.

————. "The Temple and the Magician." In *God's Christ and His People: Studies in Honor of Nils Alstrup Dahl*, edited by J. Jervell and W. Meeks, 233–47. Oslo: Universitetsforlaget; Sandvika: Nye Intertrykk, 1977. Reprinted in his *Map Is Not Territory*, 172–89.

————. "Wisdom and Apocalyptic." In *Religious Syncretism in Antiquity: Essays in Conversation with Geo Widengren*, edited by Birger A. Pearson, 131–56. Symposium Series for the American Academy of Religion and Institute of Religious Studies, University of California, Santa Barbara, no. 1. Missoula, MT: Scholars Press, 1975. Reprinted in his *Map Is Not Territory*, 67–87.

Smith, Morton. *Clement of Alexandria and a Secret Gospel of Mark*. Cambridge: Harvard University Press, 1973.

————. *Jesus the Magician*. San Francisco: Harper & Row, 1978.

————. "Palestinian Judaism in the First Century." In *Israel: Its Role in Civilization*, edited by Moshe Davis, 67–81. New York: Jewish Theological Seminary of America; Harper & Brothers, 1956.

————. *Palestinian Parties and Politics that Shaped the Old Testament*. Lectures on the History of Religions, New Series 9. New York: Columbia University Press, 1971.

————. "Prolegomena to a Discussion of Aretalogies, Divine Men, the Gospels and Jesus." *Journal of Biblical Literature* 90 (1971): 174–99.

Spengel, Leonard. *Rhetores Graeci*. 4 vols. Leipzig: B. G. Teubner, 1853/56.

Steck, Odil Hannes. *Israel und das gewaltsame Geschick der Propheten*. Wissenschaftliche Monographien zum Alten und Neuen Testament 23. Neukirchen-Vluyn: Neukirchener, 1967.

Stendahl, Krister. *Paul Among Jews and Gentiles: And Other Essays*. Philadelphia: Fortress Press, 1976.

Stern, M. "The Hasmonean Revolt and Its Place in the History of Jewish Society and Religion." *Journal of World History* 2 (1968): 92–106.

—————. "The Jewish Diaspora." In *The Jewish People in the First Century: Historical Geography, Political History, Social, Cultural and Religious Life and Institutions*, edited by S. Safrai and M. Stern, 1:117–83. Compendia Rerum Iudaicarum ad Novum Testamentum, Section I. Philadelphia: Fortress Press; Assen, Netherlands: Van Gorcum, 1974.

—————. "The Reign of Herod and the Herodian Dynasty." In *The Jewish People in the First Century: Historical Geography, Political History, Social, Cultural, and Religious Life and Institutions*, edited by S. Safrai and M. Stern, 1:216–307. Compendia Rerum Iudaicarum ad Novum Testamentum, Section I. Philadelphia: Fortress Press; Assen, Netherlands: Van Gorcum, 1974.

Stone, Michael E. "The Book of Enoch and Judaism in the Third Century B.C.E.." *Catholic Biblical Quarterly* 40 (1978): 479–92.

—————, ed. *Jewish Writings of the Second Temple Period: Apocrypha, Pseudepigrapha, Qumran Sectarian Writings, Philo, Josephus*. Compendia Rerum Iudaicarum ad Novum Testamentum, Section II, vol. 2. Philadelphia: Fortress Press; Assen, Netherlands: Van Gorcum, 1984.

—————. *Scriptures, Sects, and Visions: A Profile of Judaism from Ezra to the Jewish Revolts*. Cleveland: William Collins & Co.; Philadelphia: Fortress Press, 1980.

Sweet, J. P. M. "The Theory of Miracles in the Wisdom of Solomon." In *Miracles: Cambridge Studies in Their Philosophy and History*, edited by C. F. D. Moule, 113–26. London: A. R. Mowbray, 1965.

Tannehill, Robert C. "Introduction: The Pronouncement Story and Its Types." *Semeia* 20 (1981): 1–14.

—————. *The Sword of His Mouth*. Semeia Supplements 1. Philadelphia: Fortress Press; Missoula, MT: Scholars Press, 1975.

—————. "Varieties of Synoptic Pronouncement Stories." *Semeia* 20 (1981): 101–20.

Taylor, Vincent. *The Formation of the Gospel Tradition: Eight Lectures*. 2d ed. London: Macmillan & Co., 1933.

—————. *The Gospel According to Mark*. London: Macmillan & Co., 1952.

Tcherikover, Victor A. *Hellenistic Civilization and the Jews*. Eng. trans. S. Applebaum. Philadelphia: Jewish Publication Society of America, 1959.

Theissen, Gerd. *The Miracle Stories of the Early Christian Tradition*. Eng. trans. Francis McDonagh from *Urchristliche Wundergeschichten*, 1974. Philadelphia: Fortress Press, 1983.

—————. *Sociology of Early Palestinian Christianity*. Eng. trans. John Bowden. Philadelphia: Fortress Press, 1978.

—————. "Wanderradikalismus: Literatur soziologische Aspekte der Überlieferung von Worten Jesu im Urchristentum." *Zeitschrift für Theologie und Kirche* 70 (1973): 245–71.

Theological Dictionary of the New Testament. 10 vols. Edited by G. Kittel and G. Friedrich. Eng. trans. G. W. Bromiley. Grand Rapids: Wm. B. Eerdmans, 1964/76.

Tiede, David Lenz. *The Charismatic Figure as Miracle Worker.* Society of Biblical Literature Dissertation Series 1. Missoula, MT: Scholars Press, 1972.

Timothy, Hamilton B. *The Early Christian Apologists and Greek Philosophy: Exemplified by Irenaeus, Tertullian and Clement of Alexandria.* Philosophical Texts and Studies 21. Assen, Netherlands: Van Gorcum, 1973.

Tolbert, Mary Ann. *Perspectives on the Parables: An Approach to Multiple Interpretations.* Philadelphia: Fortress Press, 1979.

Turner, Victor. *The Forest of Symbols: Aspects of Ndembu Ritual.* Ithaca, NY: Cornell University Press, 1967.

―――――. *The Ritual Process: Structure and Anti-Structure.* Lewis Morgan Lectures, 1966. Chicago: Aldine Publishing Co., 1969.

Turner, Victor, and Edith Turner. *Image and Pilgrimage in Christian Culture: Anthropological Perspectives.* Lectures on the History of Religions, New Series 11. New York: Columbia University Press, 1978.

Vaage, Leif. "The Community of Q: The Ethics of an Itinerant Intelligence." Ph.D. diss., Claremont Graduate School, 1986.

―――――. "'To Wear Soft Raiment (Matt. 11:8) . . . To Live in Luxury (Luke 7:25)': Clarifying a Characterization." Unpublished paper for the Society of Biblical Literature, Anaheim, CA, 1985.

Vanderkam, James C. "Intertestamental Pronouncement Stories." *Semeia* 20 (1981): 65–72.

Vermès, Géza. *The Dead Sea Scrolls in English.* Baltimore: Penguin Books, 1962.

―――――. *Jesus the Jew: A Historian's Reading of the Gospel.* London: William Collins Sons, 1973.

Via, Dan Otto, Jr. *Kerygma and Comedy in the New Testament: A Structuralist Approach to Hermeneutic.* Philadelphia: Fortress Press, 1975.

―――――. *The Parables: Their Literary and Existential Dimension.* Philadelphia: Fortress Press, 1967.

Vielhauer, Philipp. "Erwägungen zur Christologie des Markusevangeliums." In *Zeit und Geschichte: Dankesgabe an Rudolf Bultmann zum 80. Geburtstag,* edited by Erich Dinkler, 155–69. Tübingen: J. C. B. Mohr (Paul Siebeck), 1964.

―――――. "Gottesreich und Menschensohn in der Verkündigung Jesu." In *Festschrift für Günther Dehn zum 75. Geburtstag am 18. April 1957 dargebracht von der Evangelisch-Theologischen Fakultät zu Bonn,* edited by Wilhelm Schneemelcher, 51–79. Neukirchen: Erziehungsvereins, 1957.

Walz, Christianus. *Rhetores Graeci.* 9 vols. Stuttgart: Cottage, 1832/36.

Wechsler, Eduard. *Hellas im Evangelium.* Berlin: Metzner, 1936.

Weeden, Theodore J. *Mark: Traditions in Conflict.* Philadelphia: Fortress Press, 1971.

―――――. "Recovering the Parabolic Intent in the Parable of the Sower." *Journal of the American Academy of Religion* 47 (1979): 97–120.

Weiss, Johannes. *Jesus' Proclamation of the Kingdom of God,* edited and Eng. trans. R. H. Hiers and D. L. Holland from *Die Predigt Jesu vom Reiche Gottes,* 1892. Philadelphia: Fortress Press, 1971.

Wells, G. A. *The Historical Evidence for Jesus*. Buffalo: Prometheus Books, 1982.

Wettstein, Johannes Jacob. ʽΗ Καινὴ Διαθήκη. 2 vols. Amsterdam: Ex officina Dommeriana, 1751.

Wifstrand, Albert. *Die alte Kirche und die griechische Bildung*. Dalp-Taschenbücher 388D. Bern: A. Francke, 1967.

Wilder, Amos N. *Early Christian Rhetoric: The Language of the Gospel*. New York: Harper & Row, 1964.

————. *Jesus' Parables and the War of Myths: Essays on Imagination in the Scriptures*. Philadelphia: Fortress Press, 1982.

Williams, Sam K. *Jesus' Death as Saving Event: The Background and Origin of a Concept*. Harvard Dissertations in Religion 2. Missoula, MT: Scholars Press, 1975.

Windisch, Hans. "Die Notiz über Tracht und Speise des Täufers Johannes und ihre Entsprechungen in der Jesusüberlieferung." *Zeitschrift für die neutestamentliche Wissenschaft* 32 (1933): 67–79.

Wire, Antoinette C. "The Structure of the Gospel Miracle Stories and Their Tellers." *Semeia* 11 (1978): 83–113.

Wrede, William. *The Messianic Secret*. Eng. trans. J. C. G. Greig from *Das Messiasgeheimnis in den Evangelien*, 1901. Cambridge: J. Clarke, 1971.

Zeitlin, Solomon. *The Rise and Fall of the Judaean State: A Political, Social and Religious History of the Second Commonwealth*. 2 vols. Philadelphia: Jewish Publication Society of America, 1962/67.

Ziebarth, Erich G. L. *Das griechische Vereinswesen*. Leipzig: Hirzel, 1896.

INDICES

SUBJECTS

ANCIENT AUTHORS AND WRITINGS

HELLENISTIC LITERATURE

HEBREW SCRIPTURES

JEWISH LITERATURE

NEW TESTAMENT

EARLY CHRISTIAN LITERATURE

INDEX III

MODERN AUTHORS